THE ROUGH GUIDE TO

GUATEMALA

This eighth edition updated by

Robert Savage

Contents

TEMPLE OF THE GREAT JAGUAR AT TIKAL

Introduction to Guatemala

Spanning a mountainous slice of Central America immediately south of Mexico, Guatemala is loaded with incredible natural, historical and cultural appeal. As the birthplace and heartland of the ancient Maya, the country is in many ways defined by the legacy of this early civilization. Their rainforest cities were abandoned centuries ago, but Maya people continue to thrive in the Guatemalan highlands, where traditions and religious rituals, mingled with Catholic practices, endure to form the richest and most distinctive Indigenous identity in the hemisphere.

Guatemala today is very much a synthesis of Maya and colonial traditions, fused with the omnipresent influences of twenty-first-century Latin and North American culture. Baroque churches dating back to the Spanish Conquest coexist with pagan temples that have been sites of worship for millennia. Highland street markets prosper alongside glitzy shopping malls, and pre-Columbian festival dances are performed by teenage hip-hop fans.

Guatemala is still a developing nation, a young democracy with a turbulent and **bloody history** that's beset by deep-rooted inequalities. And yet, despite alarming levels of poverty and unemployment, most Guatemalans are extraordinarily courteous and helpful to travellers, and only too eager to help you catch the right bus or practise your Spanish.

It's this genuine and profound hospitality, combined with the country's **outstanding cultural legacy** and **astonishing natural beauty,** that makes Guatemala such a compelling place for travellers.

Where to go

Guatemala offers a startling range of landscapes, defined by extremes. Most travellers first head for **Antigua**, the delightful former colonial capital, its refined atmosphere and

WOMEN MAKING CORN TORTILLAS FOR A FESTIVAL

VOLCANOES

Overshadowing the southern half of the country, a chain of **volcanoes** extends in an ominous arc from 4220m-high Tajumulco on the Mexican border to the frontier with Honduras. Depending on how you define a volcano – some vulcanologists do not classify lateral cones in the folds of a larger peak to be volcanoes, for example – Guatemala has somewhere between 33 and 40. Three of these – **Pacaya, Santiaguito and Fuego –** are highly active, regularly belching soaring plumes of smoke and ash. An ascent up Pacaya (see page 70) rarely fails to disappoint as it's usually possible to view spectacular orange lava flows, but occasionally access is not possible due to volcanic activity. The 2018 Fuego eruption killed at least 159 people, and thousands were left homeless.

Lago de Atitlán is actually the former caldera of a giant volcano that cataclysmically blew its top some 85,000 years ago. So much magma was expelled that most of the vast cone collapsed, and centuries of rainwater filled the depression, creating today's lake. At present, the three volcanoes that line its shores can all be climbed. The most accessible is **Volcán San Pedro** (see page 130) which entails a return trek of around eight to nine hours. Licensed guides accompany all hikers.

café society contrasting with the chaotic fume-filled streets of Guatemala City. Next on your list should be the Maya-dominated **western highlands**, a region of mesmerizing beauty, with volcanic cones soaring above pine-clad hills, traditional villages and shimmering lakes. The strength of Maya culture here is overwhelming with each village having its own textile weaving tradition and unique fiesta celebrations.

Lago de Atitlán, a beautiful lake ringed by sentinel-like volcanoes, is unmissable. The shores of the lake are dotted with charming Indigenous settlements such as **San Juan La Laguna**, which has a good textile cooperative and several artists' galleries, and **San Pedro La Laguna**, with its bohemian travellers' scene and rock-bottom prices. High up above the lake, the traditional Maya town of **Sololá** has one of the country's best

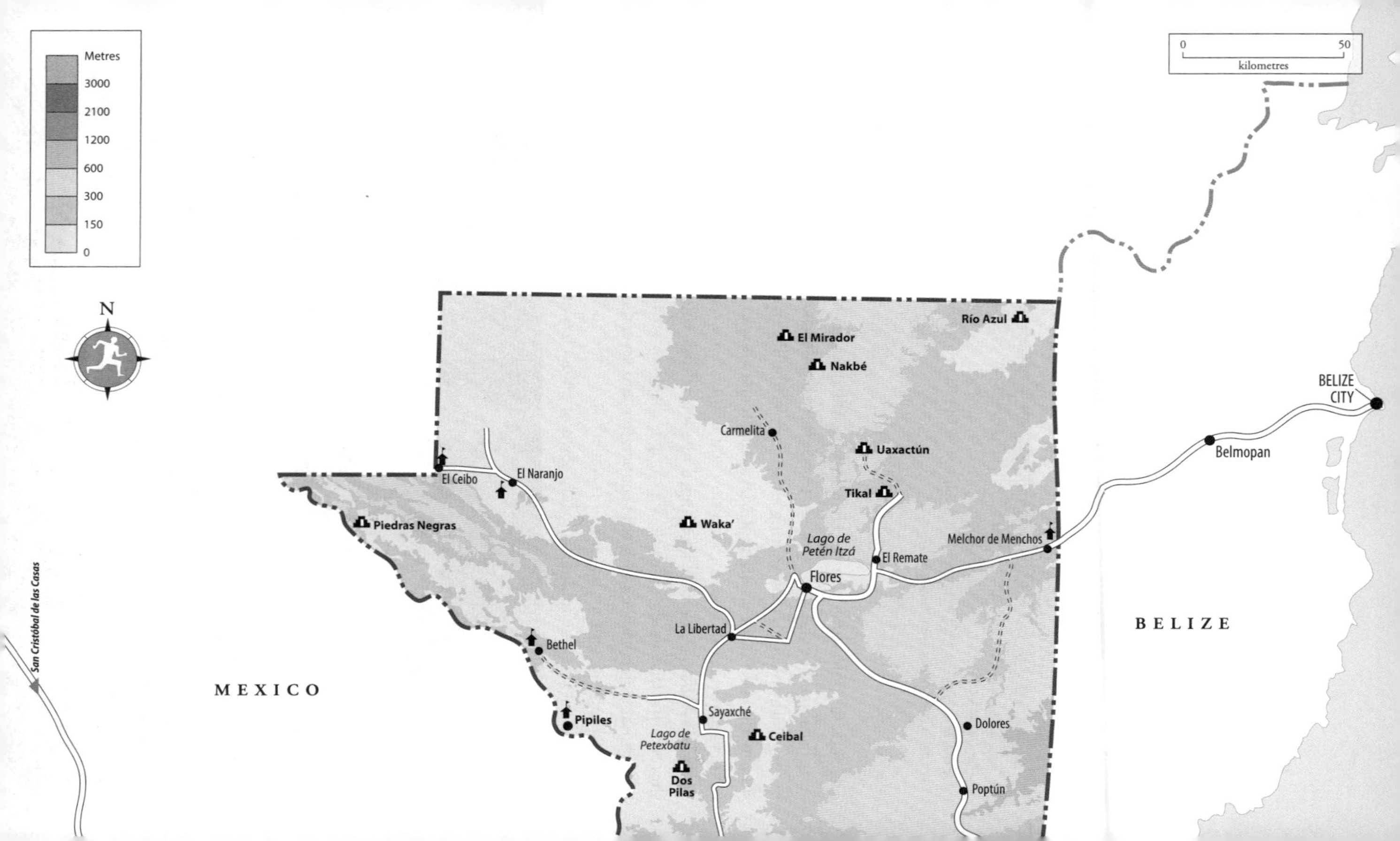

Metres
3000
2100
1200
600
300
150
0
N
0
50
kilometres
Río Azul
El Mirador
Nakbé
Carmelita
Uaxactún
Tikal
Waka'
El Ceibo
El Naranjo
Piedras Negras
Lago de
Petén Itzá
El Remate
Flores
Melchor de Menchos
BELIZE
CITY
Belmopan
BELIZE
La Libertad
Bethel
MEXICO
Sayaxché
Pipiles
Lago de
Petexbatu
Ceibal
Dos
Pilas
Dolores
Poptún
San Cristóbal de las Casas

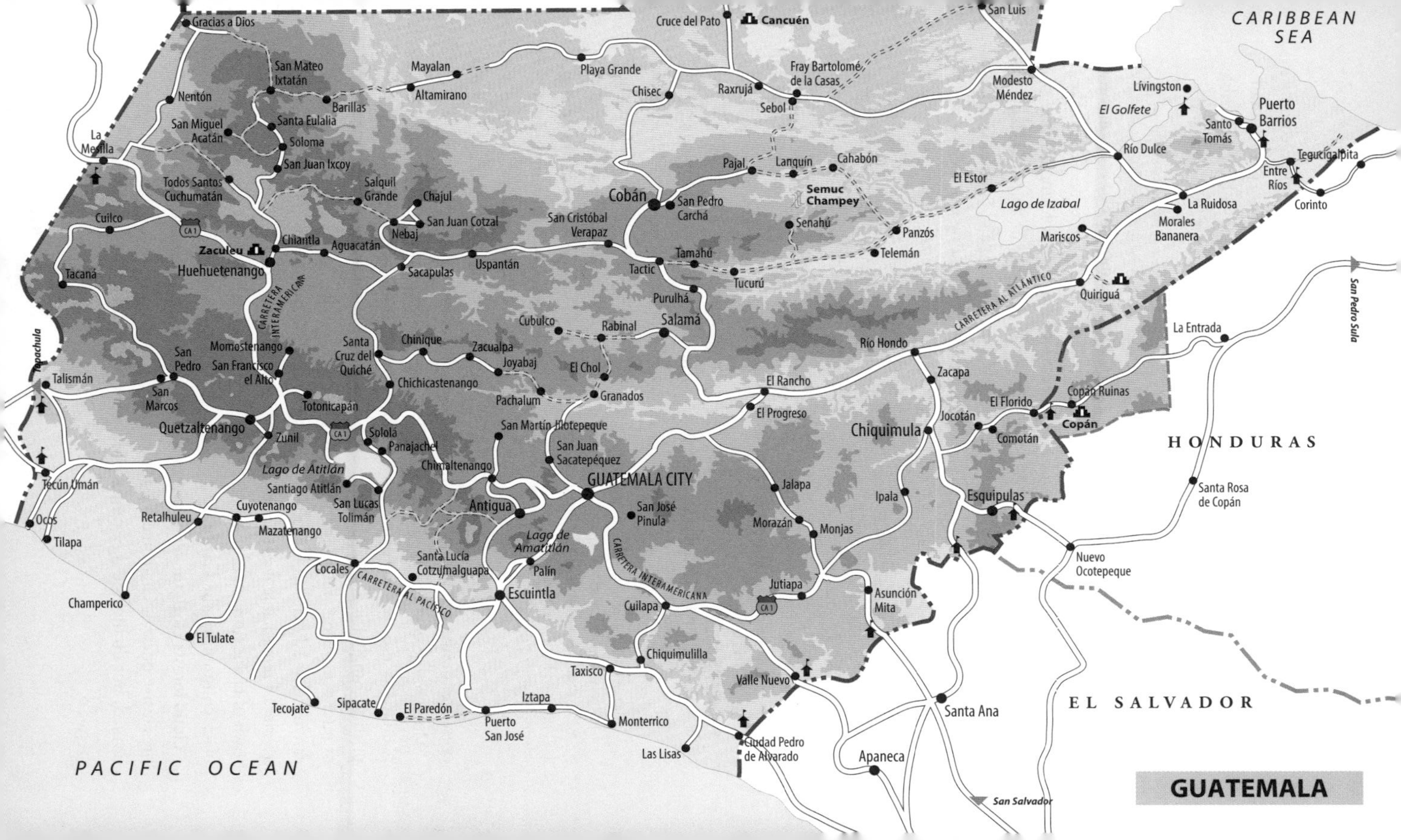
GUATEMALA
CARIBBEAN SEA
PACIFIC OCEAN
HONDURAS
EL SALVADOR
San Pedro Sula
San Salvador
Tapachula
GUATEMALA CITY
Antigua
Cobán
Quetzaltenango
Huehuetenango
Zaculeu
Cancuén
Copán
Semuc Champey
Quiriguá
Lago de Izabal
Lago de Atitlán
Lago de Amatitlán
El Golfete
Carretera Interamericana
Carretera al Atlántico
Carretera al Pacífico
CA 1
Gracias a Dios
San Mateo Ixtatán
Nentón
Barillas
Mayalan
Altamirano
Playa Grande
Cruce del Pato
San Luis
Chisec
Raxrujá
Fray Bartolomé de la Casas
Sebol
Modesto Méndez
Livingston
Puerto Barrios
Santo Tomás
Río Dulce
Tegucigalpita
Entre Ríos
Corinto
La Ruidosa
Morales
Bananera
Mariscos
El Estor
Panzós
Telemán
Cahabón
Lanquín
Pajal
Senahú
San Pedro Carchá
Tamahú
Tucurú
Tactic
Purulhá
Salamá
Rabinal
Cubulco
El Chol
Granados
San Cristóbal Verapaz
Uspantán
Sacapulas
Chajul
San Juan Cotzal
Nebaj
Salquil Grande
Aguacatán
Chiantla
San Juan Ixcoy
Soloma
Santa Eulalia
San Miguel Acatán
Todos Santos Cuchumatán
La Mesilla
Cuilco
Tacaná
San Pedro
San Marcos
Momostenango
San Francisco el Alto
Totonicapán
Santa Cruz del Quiché
Chinique
Zacualpa
Joyabaj
Pachalum
Chichicastenango
Sololá
Panajachel
Zunil
Talismán
Tecún Umán
Ocós
Tilapa
Retalhuleu
Cuyotenango
Mazatenango
Champerico
El Tulate
Santiago Atitlán
San Lucas Tolimán
Chimaltenango
San Martín Jilotepeque
San Juan Sacatepéquez
Santa Lucía Cotzumalguapa
Cocales
Palín
Escuintla
Tecojate
Sipacate
El Paredón
Puerto San José
Iztapa
Taxisco
Monterrico
Las Lisas
Chiquimulilla
Cuilapa
San José Pinula
El Rancho
El Progreso
Río Hondo
Zacapa
Chiquimula
Jocotán
Comotán
El Florido
Copán Ruinas
La Entrada
Santa Rosa de Copán
Nuevo Ocotepeque
Esquipulas
Ipala
Jalapa
Morazán
Monjas
Jutiapa
Asunción Mita
Valle Nuevo
Ciudad Pedro de Alvarado
Santa Ana
Apaneca

FACT FILE

- The republic of Guatemala's 108,890 square kilometres include dozens of **volcanoes** (four are active), 328km of **Pacific** coastline and 74km of **Caribbean** coast.
- Guatemala's **population** was estimated at 18.3 million in 2024, with a growth rate of 1.47 percent per annum (one of the highest in the western hemisphere).
- Ethnically, the population is almost equally divided between Indigenous **Maya** and **ladinos** (who are mainly of mixed race), although there are tiny numbers of black Garífuna (about eight thousand in all), Chinese and non-Maya Xinca.
- Remittances from Guatemala's large expatriate community in the US are the country's main source of foreign income, equivalent to over ten percent of its GDP.
- **Tourism** is the nation's main income earner, followed by coffee, sugar, clothing exports and bananas.
- About 46 percent of Guatemalans are nominally **Roman Catholic** – the lowest figure in Latin America – though many highland Maya practise a unique mix of religions that's heavily dependent on ancient religious ritual.
- The nation is a **democratic republic**, headed by a president who is head of both state and government.

(and least-touristy) markets, a complete contrast to the vast twice-weekly affair at **Chichicastenango**, with its incredible selection of souvenirs, weavings and handicrafts.

To the west, the proud provincial city of **Quetzaltenango** (Xela) is an important language school centre, and also makes an excellent base for exploring the forest-fringed crater lake of **Volcán Chicabal**, the sublime natural spa of **Fuentes Georginas** and some fascinating market towns. Guatemala's greatest mountain range, the **Cuchumatanes**, is a little further distant. In these granite peaks you'll find superb scenery and some of the most isolated and traditional villages in the Maya World, with **Nebaj** and **Todos Santos Cuchumatán** both making good bases for some serious hiking and adventure.

The Pacific coast is generally hot, dull and disappointing to visit, with scrubby, desolate beaches backed by a smattering of mangrove swamps. One exception is the relaxed seaside village of **Monterrico**, which has some good accommodation and is part of a wildlife reserve where you can watch sea turtles come ashore to lay their eggs. There's also a small but growing surf scene at **Paredón.**

Much of the **east** of the country is **tropical**, replete with banana and cardamom plantations and coconut palms. This region has some stunning lakes, including pristine, jungle-fringed **Laguna Lachúa** and **Lago de Izabal**, whose shores boast plenty of interesting spots, including an amazing hot-spring waterfall and the Boquerón canyon. The lake drains into the Caribbean via the **Río Dulce**, which flows through a series of remarkable jungle-clad gorges. At the mouth of the river is the fascinating town of **Lívingston**, an outpost of Caribbean culture and home to Guatemala's only black community, the Garífuna.

Cloud forests cloak the fecund Verapaz hills of central Guatemala, harbouring the elusive quetzal, Guatemala's national symbol. Cultural sites in the east are quite limited, but do include the compact Maya site of **Quiriguá** and the first-class ruins of

THE CHURCH OF SAN ANDRÉS XECUL

Copán. For history buffs, both sites offer a fascinating glimpse into the ancient Maya civilisation.

The vast **rainforests** of Petén occupy most of the country's north. This unique lowland area, which makes up about a third of the country, is covered with dense tropical forest and savannah. Though loggers and ranchers have laid waste to large chunks of the terrain, nature reserves alive with wildlife remain, many dotted with outstanding Maya ruins.

From the delightful town of **Flores**, superbly situated on an islet on Lago de Petén Itzá, or the low-key village of **El Remate**, it's easy to reach **Tikal**, the most impressive of all Maya sites, rivalling any ruin in Latin America. The region's forest also envelops numerous smaller sites, including the striking **Yaxhá**, Aguateca and Uaxactún. For the ultimate adventure in Guatemala the ancient, remote Preclassic sites of the extreme north require days of tough hiking to reach. Giant **El Mirador**, in its day a Mesoamerican metropolis, is the main draw, but there are dozens of other unrestored sites to explore, situated in the densest rainforest in the country – if you have the time and energy.

When to go

Guatemala has one of the most pleasant climates on earth – the tourist board refers to it as the "land of the eternal spring" – with much of the country enjoying warm days and mild evenings year-round. The climate is largely determined by **altitude**. In those areas between 1300 and 1600m, which includes Guatemala City, Antigua, Lago de Atitlán and Cobán, the air is almost always fresh and the nights mild and, despite the heat of the midday sun, humidity is never a problem. Parts of the departments of Quetzaltenango, Huehuetenango and El Quiché are above this height, and so have a cooler, damper climate with distinctly chilly nights between early December and late February. Low-lying Petén suffers from sticky, steamy conditions most of the year, as do the Pacific and Caribbean coasts, though here at least you can usually rely on the welcome relief of a sea breeze.

The **rainy season** runs roughly from May to October, with the worst of the rain falling in September and October. In Petén, however, the season can extend into December. Even at the height of the wet season, though, the rain is usually confined to late afternoon downpours, with most of the rest of the day being warm and pleasant. Visiting Petén's more remote ruins is best attempted between February and May, as the mud can be thigh-deep during the height of the rains.

The **busiest times** for tourism are between December and March, and again in July and August. Language schools and hotels are fullest during these periods, and many of them hike their prices correspondingly.

Author picks

For the eighth edition of *The Rough Guide to Guatemala*, our author travelled to every corner of this beautiful country; these are some of their own, personal highlights that they discovered along the way:

Epic ruin The original American superpower, the giant Preclassic site of El Mirador (see page 269) remains buried in the Petén jungle; its epic scale and grandeur is steadily being revealed.

Ultimate lake view Lago de Atitlán is outrageously picturesque at any time of day, but at dawn the volcano views from the slopes of the Indian Nose peak (see page 130) have an ethereal majesty.

Easiest volcano hike The cone of Volcán Chicabal (see page 148) is a fairly gentle ascent and contains a magical crater lake encircled by cloud forest.

Sonic boom Howler monkeys are nature's loudest creature; hear them in full force at Yaxhá (see page 280), Lago de Petexbatún (see page 275) or Tikal (see page 257).

Best kayaking Explore the incomparable Río Dulce gorge (see page 203) at your leisure, and watch out for manatees.

Tranquil Town The tiny island settlement of Flores (see page 248) is absurdly picturesque, with stunning views from its lakeside promenade.

Fantastic nature A 200m cylindrical hole in the limestone crust, El Cimarrón (see page 166) is a breathtaking vision close to the Mexican border.

Best surf spot The emerging surf scene at Paredón (see page 181) is gaining popularity with its reliable waves and laid-back vibe, making it a must-visit for surfers.

Ultimate cave experience Lanquín Caves (see page 230) offer a thrilling underground adventure where visitors can admire the impressive stalagmites and stalactites while bats dart around overhead.

Our author recommendations don't end here. We've flagged up our favourite places – a perfectly sited hotel, an atmospheric café, a special restaurant – throughout the Guide, highlighted with the ★ symbol.

HOWLER MONKEY

LAGO DE ATITLÁN

25 things not to miss

It's not possible to see everything that Guatemala has to offer in one visit, and we don't suggest you try. What follows is a selective taste of the country's highlights, from wildlife-rich nature reserves to colonial cities and Indigenous markets. All highlights have a page reference to take you straight into the Guide, where you can find out more.

1 LAGO DE ATITLÁN

See page 115

Encircled by three volcanoes, the awesome crater lake of Lago de Atitlán was famously described by Aldous Huxley as "the most beautiful lake in the world".

2 MAYA TEXTILES

See page 109

Every Maya village has its own unique weaving heritage, its women wearing *huipiles* of breathtaking designs and colours.

3 CENTRO HISTÓRICO

See page 55

Yes it's gritty, but the capital's historic centre boasts a wealth of colonial sights and big city delights.

4 RÍO DULCE

See page 203

Cruise up the jungle-cloaked gorges and estuaries of Guatemala's "sweet river" by boat, and marvel at the scenery and birdlife.

5 QUETZAL

See page 222

Rare and elusive, Guatemala's national bird inhabits the cloud forests of the Verapaces.

6
C828BPK
7
8

6 VOLCÁN DE PACAYA

See page 70

Trek up this volcano for an unforgettable encounter with the lava-oozing cone of Pacaya, one of Central America's most active.

7 CHICKEN BUSES

See page 28

Garishly painted and outrageously uncomfortable, there's never a dull journey aboard Guatemala's iconic fume-belching *camionetas*.

8 HIGHLAND HIKING

See pages 137 and 109

Explore the beguiling, lofty trails of Guatemala's western highlands: the town of Quetzaltenango and Nebaj are good bases.

9 SEMANA SANTA

See page 78

During Easter Week, head to either Antigua for its epic Catholic processions, or Santiago Atitlán to witness the symbolic confrontation between the pagan saint Maximón and Christ.

10 STUDYING SPANISH

See page 42

Guatemala has dozens of excellent language schools that offer one-on-one tuition and homestay packages at rock-bottom rates.

11 THE IXIL REGION

See page 108

The Guatemalan highlands at their most bewitching: the costume and scenery of this Maya region are astonishing.

12 ANTIGUA

See page 72

The graceful former capital, with an incredible legacy of colonial architecture, is one of the most elegant cities in the Americas.

13 TIKAL

See page 257

This unmatched Maya site has it all: monumental temples and palaces set in a tropical forest alive with spider monkeys and chattering parakeets.

14 RON ZACAPA CENTENARIO

See page 34

Indulge in a glass or two of the world's best rum.

15 RAINFOREST WILDLIFE

See page 347

Guatemala's jungle reserves are ideal places to seek out wildlife including keel-billed toucans, monkeys and, perhaps, a big cat.

13

14

15

16

16 LÍVINGSTON

See page 199

Strut your funky stuff to the drum-driven punta beat in the Garífuna town of Lívingston.

17 SEMUC CHAMPEY

See page 231

Explore the exquisite turquoise pools and river system around Semuc Champey, a natural limestone bridge.

18 MIRADOR BASIN

See page 269

Tramp through the jungles of the Reserva de la Biósfera Maya past 2000-year-old cities to the vast site of El Mirador.

19 CHICHICASTENANGO

See page 101

For souvenir hunters, this twice-weekly highland market is unsurpassed.

20 YAXHÁ

See page 280

This massive Maya site, superbly positioned on the banks of Lago de Yaxhá, has dozens of large temples and impressive monuments.

17

18
19
20

21
22
23

21 MAXIMÓN

See page 126

Visit the pagan temple of this liquor-swilling, cigar-smoking evil saint.

22 MONTERRICO

See page 183

A rich nature reserve and village on the Pacific coast, with a sweeping dark-sand beach where three species of sea turtle nest.

23 TODOS SANTOS CUCHUMATÁN

See page 158

A fascinating highland Maya town, home to one of the finest textile traditions in Latin America, which hosts a legendary fiesta, with a rip-roaring horse race.

24 COPÁN RUINS

See page 294

There's a plethora of exquisitely carved stelae and altars, a towering hieroglyphic stairway and an outstanding museum at the magnificent ruins of Copán.

25 COFFEE

See page 226

Sample some of the world's finest single estate roasts in Cobán, the easy-going capital of Alta Verapaz.

Itineraries

Our grand tour covers Guatemala's highlights, while the other two routes focus on ancient Maya ruins (and their rainforest setting) and the spectacular western highlands. The trips below give a flavour of what Guatemala has to offer and what we can plan and book for you at www.roughguides.com/trips.

GRAND TOUR

❶ **Antigua** Guatemala's former capital – a mandatory stop – is a heady vision of cobbled streets, colonial mansions, Baroque churches and the nation's best dining scene. See page 72

❷ **Chichicastenango** A short hop by bus from Antigua, this highland town renowned for its unique blend of Maya and Catholic religion and a huge twice-weekly market. See page 101

❸ **Lago de Atitlán** An idyllic lake, surrounded by volcanoes and dotted with Maya villages, with all kinds of activities on offer – from scuba diving to studying Spanish. See page 115

❹ **Flores** A short flight from Guatemala City, this relaxed, pocket-sized colonial gem juts into the azure Lago de Petén Itzá. See page 248

❺ **Tikal** An hour from Flores, this is the Maya World's number one archeological site. See page 257

❻ **Semuc Champey** Gorgeous kingfisher-blue series of limestone pools in the tropical forests of Alta Verapaz; close by you'll find some impressive cave systems. See page 231

❼ **Río Dulce** An amazing sight, this impressive gorge system (around four hours by bus from Semuc Champey) is the highlight of Guatemala's Caribbean region. See page 203

❽ **Guatemala City** An untamed capital that gets a bad press, but contains the nation's best museums and a lively cultural life. See page 52

ANCIENT MAYA

❶ **Lago de Petexbatún** Organize a boat trip in nearby Sayaxché around this jungle-fringed lake, taking in the highly impressive sites of Aguateca and Dos Pilas. See page 275

❷ **Flores** Just 90 minutes by bus from Sayaxché, the town of Flores is a good place to eat out and set up trips to the best of Peten's ruins. See page 248

❸ **Yaxhá-Nakúm-Naranjo National Park** This protected reserve can be visited as a day trip from Flores. It contains the huge Maya site of Yaxhá in a jaw-dropping location on the banks of an emerald lake, and Nakúm, with well-restored ceremonial buildings. See page 280

4 Tikal Lording it above the surrounding rainforest, Tikal's giant temples, palaces, plazas and monuments make it a superstar Maya attraction. See page 257

5 El Mirador Two thousand years ago this Preclassic city was approaching its peak. Today it's the most enigmatic and remote of all Petén's major ruins. See page 269

6 Nakbé The first substantial Maya settlement, this Preclassic site is graced with soaring temples and is surrounded by wildlife-rich jungle. See page 272

7 Quiriguá A modest site in the south of the country, with a collection of giant, carved stelae out of all proportion to its size. See page 192

8 Copán Just over the border in Honduras, Copán boasts an astounding hieroglyphic stairway, some exquisite carving and, close by, the lovely town of Copán Ruinas. See page 294

WESTERN HIGHLANDS

1 Chichicastenango If you've an eye for a souvenir, this market (Thurs & Sun) is bursting with colourful clothing, eye-dazzling textiles, ceramics and leather. See page 101

2 Ixil An isolated region of evergreen hills and forested mountains, bowl-shaped valleys and some of the most traditional Maya villages in the nation. See page 108

3 Todos Santos Cuchumatán At the end of a vertiginous journey from Huehuetenango, this Mam village is famous for its textiles, walking trails and breathtaking scenery. See page 158

4 Quetzaltenango (Xela) Guatemala's second city is coming into its own with an expanding cultural scene. See page 137

5 Volcán Tajumulco Hike Central America's highest peak, a 4220m cone close to the Mexican border. See page 152

6 Laguna Chicabal A short ride from Xela, this near-circular volcanic lake makes a perfect day-trip. See page 148

7 Fuentes Georginas A high-altitude natural hot-spring spa, halfway up a volcano – the ideal place to soak away an afternoon. See page 147

8 Lago de Atitlán Surrounded by dramatic volcanoes, the lake is the ideal place to paddle a kayak, learn some Spanish or party hard with other travellers. See page 115

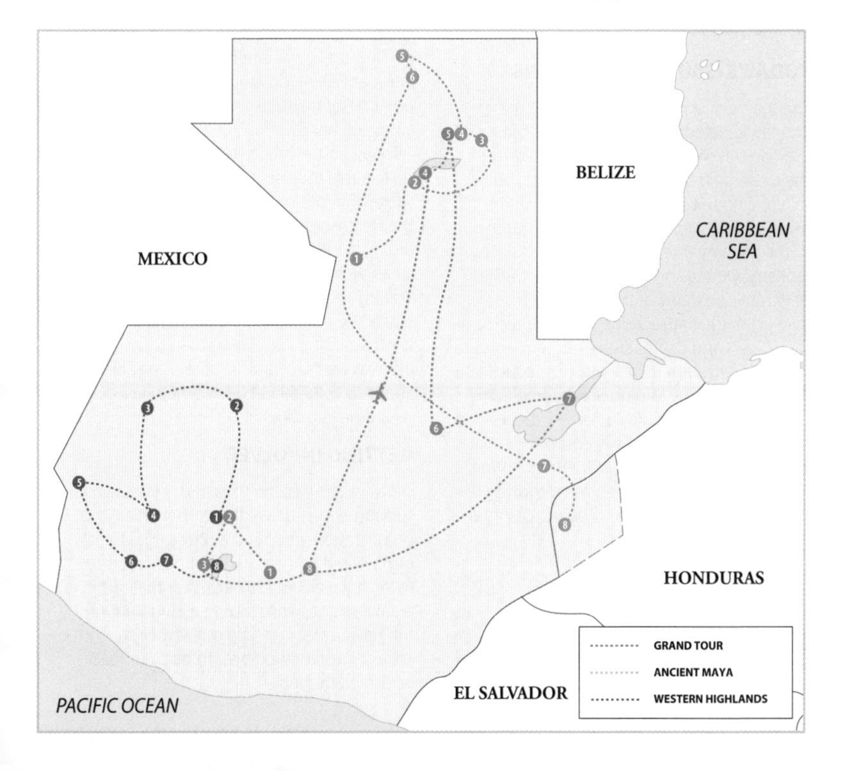

Sustainable travel

Getting an accurate read on what is and what isn't a sustainable travel option in Guatemala can be trying, but not impossible.

Guatemala once boasted one of the richest biospheres in the world, but after successive corrupt governments, slash-and-burn agriculture, massive deforestation and over-exploited water resources, a tipping point has been reached. Visitors to Guatemala can, however, do their part to help slow down the trend, minimize their footprint and begin to reverse the tide.

TODAY'S ISSUES AND OPTIONS

The majority of international airlines that connect Guatemala with the rest of the world provide travellers with the option to offset their carbon footprint when booking, but minimizing the impact after arrival can be more of a tall order. This is thanks, in large part, to the primary threads in the nation's economic tapestry. One example of this is the forests of Petén. Like many of the country's most revered natural attractions, it's also a cash cow for loggers and cattle raisers, not to mention the drug cartels that clear airstrips to facilitate the cocaine trade. Mining and hydroelectric power projects also play a part – especially so when you factor in that the cost of electricity is among the highest in Latin America. Worse still, Indigenous rights are often forgotten or outright ignored when new power plants and mining sites are planned.

COMMUNITY ACTION

Thanks, however, to an increasingly well-organized network of community groups, many of the projects that would have done the most harm have been halted or abandoned. Ixcán villagers, for example, successfully blocked the completion of the Franja Transversal del Norte highway, given that it would then facilitate plans for mining and power plants in the region. A trend of nationwide protests has also emerged when new projects are announced – making local TV and news networks a good starting point for travellers to keep abreast of current issues. These groups, in partnership with the newly installed (and refreshingly uncorrupt) President Bernardo Arévalo, help make it possible for travellers to play their part and lend a helping hand.

Today, conservation partnered with sustainable tourism is becoming big (and successful) business. Leading that charge is the Defensores de la Naturaleza (Ⓦ defensores.org.gt), an ecological group that operates in areas such as the Bocas del Polochic reserve. Visiting and staying within their national parks, biosphere reserves and wildlife refuges is one way that visitors can target their tourism money in a way that's helpful. Another is planning ahead to volunteer at one of their sites during your time in Guatemala.

GETTING INVOLVED

For travellers wishing to focus their sustainable support efforts on wildlife conservation, the conservation group Arcas (Ⓦ arcasguatemala.org) will put you on solid footing. Visitors to Petén are welcome to pitch in at their wild animal refuge, while those passing through the Hawaii area can help out at their sea turtle project – established here to help combat wildlife trafficking.

BABY TURTLES WALKING TOWARDS THE OCEAN

CHICHICASTENANGO MARKET, WESTERN HIGHLANDS

Basics

Getting there

Most people get to Guatemala by plane, arriving in the capital, Guatemala City. Flores airport, near Tikal, also has a few flights from Belize City. Guatemalan land and sea entry points are relatively hassle-free, unless you're bringing your own transport, in which case you can expect red tape and delays.

Airfares always depend on the season, with the highest being from Christmas to February, around Easter and in July and August. Booking your tickets **online** cuts out the costs of agents and middlemen. Check out Momondo (Ⓦmomondo.com), an excellent flight search engine for great deals. Discount or auction sites are other possibilities, as are airlines' own websites.

Flights from the US and Canada

Most flights to Guatemala are routed through a few US **hub cities**: Atlanta, Chicago, Dallas, Fort Lauderdale, Houston, Los Angeles, Miami and New York. You'll also find several non-direct options via San Salvador (with Avianca) and Mexico City (Aeroméxico). **Prices** vary wildly, depending on the season and promotional fares; return flights start at around US$350 from Fort Lauderdale or Orlando with Spirit Airlines, while return fares from either Houston or New York are typically US$440–700.

From Canada, as there are no direct connections to Guatemala, your best bet is to fly via one of the US gateway cities. Return flights from Toronto typically cost Can$500–850, from Vancouver Can$600–850.

Flights from the UK and Ireland

There are no **direct flights** from the UK to Guatemala; most itineraries travel via the US cities of Atlanta, Houston, New York or Miami. Other options include flying via Madrid on Iberia or via Mexico with a number of airlines and then on to Guatemala. Prices for return flights to Guatemala City are around £530 low season/£900 high season, whichever airline and route you take.

From Ireland, there are good deals via Amsterdam and Panama City with KLM/Copa and many options via US gateway cities. Expect to pay around €600 low season/€900 high season.

Flights from Australia, New Zealand and South Africa

There are no **direct flights** from Australasia to Guatemala, so most travellers fly via the US. Tickets cost Aus$2000–3000 (depending on the season) from Sydney (via LA or San Francisco) or NZ$2500–3500 from Auckland. Delta and United usually have the best fares. If you want to visit Guatemala as part of a longer Latin American trip it often costs only a little more to book an open-jaw ticket flying into Guatemala City and returning from Panama.

From South Africa return flights start at about R20,000; South African Airways (via New York) and United (via Houston) often have the best rates.

Buses

From **southern Mexico**, very regular daily buses leave Tapachula for Guatemala City (see page 64). A daily minibus connects San Cristóbal de Las Casas with Antigua (see page 80), passing drop-off points for Huehuetenango, Quetzaltenango and Panajachel. There's also a daily bus linking Cancún with Flores, with one minibus taking you to the Belize–Mexico border and another connection travelling via Belize City and the Guatemalan border to Flores (see page 249). Shuttle bus connections between Palenque and Flores are another option (see page 249).

Very regular buses connect **San Salvador** with Guatemala City (see page 64) and there are also shuttle buses between El Tunco beach and Antigua. From **Honduras** there are direct daily links between Copán and Guatemala City/Antigua, and daily buses from both San Pedro Sula and Tegucigalpa to Guatemala City. These routes make cross-border travel convenient and relatively straightforward.

A BETTER KIND OF TRAVEL

At Rough Guides we are passionately committed to travel. We believe it helps us understand the world we live in and the people we share it with – and of course tourism is vital to many developing economies. But the scale of modern tourism has also damaged some places irreparably, and climate change is accelerated by most forms of transport, especially flying. We encourage all our authors to consider the carbon footprint of the journeys they make in the course of researching our guides.

Several companies operate buses between **Panama City** and Guatemala City via Costa Rica, Nicaragua, Honduras and El Salvador. These involve nights in hotels on the way and several days of travel (see page 64).

Boats

From Punta Gorda, **Belize**, there's a daily boat to Puerto Barrios (see page 198) and twice-weekly connections to Lívingston (see page 198).

You can also arrive in Guatemala from **Mexico**, crossing the Usumacinta River at Frontera Corozal (see page 278).

Tours

Particularly if you have specialist interests, or prefer to have someone else take care of the nitty-gritty for you, it can be well worth taking an **organized tour**. The operators listed below offer both bespoke and group tours; prices do not include airfares to the region, unless stated.

TOUR OPERATORS

Adventure Life US Ⓦ adventure-life.com. Small-group specialists with a choice of excellent tours in Guatemala, using experienced guides and visiting community-run projects.

Adventures Abroad US Ⓦ adventures-abroad.com Comfortable small-group tours; their twelve-day Guatemala tour includes Copán.

Cayaya Birding Guatemala Ⓦ cayaya-birding.com. Resident specialists with unmatched knowledge of birding hot spots. Great tours include a fifteen-day Birding Loop trip and customized itineraries.

Cox & Kings UK Ⓦ coxandkings.co.uk. Offers a variety of tours to multiple ruin sites, flying into and out of Guatemala City.

eXito US Ⓦ exitotravel.com. North America's top specialist for travel to Latin America.

Far Horizons US Ⓦ farhorizons.com. Superb small-group archeological trips, guided by Mayanists, including a "Capital Cities of the Ancient Maya" tour that takes in Tikal and Quiriguá.

Intrepid Travel UK Ⓦ intrepidtravel.com. Small-group trips with an emphasis on cross-cultural contact and low-impact tourism. Tours have different comfort-level options.

Journey Latin America UK Ⓦ journeylatinamerica.co.uk. UK-based experts for airfares and all-round travel advice to Guatemala and the region.

Lost World Adventures US Ⓦ lostworld.com. A selection of tempting tours (nine include Guatemala). Their "Guatemalan Multi-sport" takes in cycling, hiking and kayaking.

Maya Expeditions Guatemala City Ⓦ mayaexpeditions.com. Adventure tour specialists offering everything from whitewater rafting day-trips and paragliding, to expeditions to remote Maya sites like Piedras Negras.

Terra Guatemala Ⓦ terra-guatemala.com. Very well guided and thought-out trips, arranged by locals.

Trailfinders UK Ⓦ trailfinders.com. One of the best-informed and most efficient flight agencies for independent travellers. Also offers some Central American tours, including eleven-day "Classic Guatemala".

Tucan Travel US & UK Ⓦ tucantravel.com. Latin America specialists with over a dozen inexpensive, sociable tours through the Maya region and Central America.

Viaventure Ⓦ viaventure.com. Specialized operator offering top-class tailor-made tours with expert guides. Offers very flexible, innovative travel experiences.

Wilderness Travel Ⓦ wildernesstravel.com. Well-organized cultural and wildlife adventure trips. The "Guatemala Private Journey" tour takes in all the main sites.

Getting around

Local buses are the main form of transport. These buses may be decrepit, uncomfortable, fume-filled and overcrowded, but they give you a unique opportunity to mix with ordinary Guatemalans. If you opt only for tourist shuttles, you'll be missing out on one of the country's most essential experiences. More comfortable buses – some of them quite fast and luxurious – ply the main highways, but once you leave the central routes and head off on the byways, there's usually no alternative to a bumpy ride inside a chicken bus or a microbus (minibus). No trains operate in Guatemala.

The country's road system has been substantially upgraded in the last few years, but **dirt roads** are the norm in some rural areas, where the going can be painfully pedestrian. Fortunately, whatever the pace of your journey, you'll always have the spectacular Guatemalan countryside to wonder at.

By bus

Buses are cheap and convenient, and can be wildly entertaining. For the most part the service is extremely comprehensive, reaching even the smallest of villages. Guatemala has three main classes of public bus, plus private shuttle bus services.

Chicken buses (second-class buses)

"Chicken buses", known as **camionetas**, are the most common and easily distinguished by their trademark clouds of thick, black, noxious fumes and rasping exhausts. *Camionetas* are old North American school buses, with limited legroom, and the seats and aisles are usually crammed with passengers. You may find that the driver tends to have a fixation on speed and overtaking on blind corners, while his helper (*ayudante*) always seems to be overworked and under-age. It's the *ayudante*'s job to scramble up to the roof to retrieve your rucksack, collect the fares and bellow out the destination to all. While travel by second-class bus may be uncomfortable, it is never dull, with chickens clucking, music assaulting your eardrums and snack vendors touting for business.

Almost all chicken buses operate out of **public bus terminals**, often adjacent to the market; between towns you can hail buses and they'll almost always stop for you – regardless of how many people are already on board.

Tickets are (nearly always) bought on the bus, and while fares are very cheap (around US$1–1.50 an hour), gringos do sometimes get charged more – try to keep an eye out for what the locals are paying.

Pullmans (first-class buses)

The so-called **pullman**, usually a Greyhound-style bus, is rated as first-class, and tickets can be bought in advance. These "express" services are more expensive than the regular buses – around US$2–2.50 an hour, with some even more luxurious, more pricey options. Services vary tremendously: some companies' buses are double-deckers, with reclining seats and ice-cold air conditioning, while other operators use decrepit vehicles. Each passenger is allocated a seat and all pullmans are pretty punctual.

Pullmans usually leave from the **private offices** of the bus company and they only run the main routes, connecting the capital with Río Dulce and Flores/Santa Elena, Quetzaltenango, Huehuetenango, the Mexican border, Chiquimula and Esquipulas, Puerto Barrios, Cobán, Copán and the rest of Central America. Note that **tickets** are often collected by conductors at the end of the journey, so make sure you don't lose yours.

Minibuses

Non-tourist **minibuses** (*microbuses*) are very common in Guatemala, particularly on paved roads (where they are more numerous and frequent than chicken buses). They usually operate from the **main bus station**, or use a separate terminal close by. Microbus **fares** work out at about US$1.75 per hour.

Shuttle buses

Providing fast, nonstop links between the main tourist centres, **shuttle buses** are very popular. Conveniently, passengers are picked up from their **hotels**, so you won't have to lug any heavy bags around. Services are expanding rapidly and now cover virtually everywhere that tourists travel in any number, and it's usually easy to organize an *especial* service (for a price) if your destination is not on a regular route. At around US$5–10 an hour, shuttles are **expensive**, but drivers are almost always more cautious than regular bus drivers.

PICK-UPS

In remote parts of the country **pick-ups** (*picops*) supplement bus services, and for sheer joy of travel, you can't beat the open-air views (unless it's raining!). Passengers are charged about US$1.50 an hour.

By plane

The only scheduled **internal flight** currently operating in Guatemala is from the capital to Flores. Flights take fifty minutes (as opposed to eight hours or more on the bus). Two airlines, Avianca (Ⓦavianca.com) and TAG (Ⓦtag.com.gt), offer daily return flights (see page 249). Tickets can be bought from travel agents or online; the former often charge less.

By car

Very few visitors rent cars in Guatemala. That said, driving through the country certainly offers unrivalled freedom, though traffic is incessantly heavy in the capital and always busy along the Interamericana and the highway to Puerto Barrios. **Local driving** practices can be alarming, too, including overtaking on blind corners. All the main routes are paved, but beyond this many roads are often extremely rough. Filling stations (*gasolineras*) are common.

Parking and **security** are an issue, particularly in towns. Always leave your car in a guarded car park or choose a hotel with secure parking. Speed bumps (*túmulos*) are everywhere, even on main highways.

Derrumbes means landslides, and *frene con motor* (brake with motor) indicates a steep descent. **Local warning signs** are also worth getting to know. The most common is the presence of a branch on the road, which indicates that there is a broken-down car or a hazard ahead.

Renting a car costs from US$40 a day for a tiny hatchback or around US$95 for a 4WD by the time you've added the extras. Always take full-cover insurance and be aware that many companies will make you sign a clause so you are responsible for the

ADDRESSES

Almost all towns in Guatemala are based on the **grid system**, with avenidas (Av) running in one direction (north to south) and calles (C) east to west, often numbered. All **addresses** specify the street first, then the block, and end with the zone. For example, the address "Av la Reforma 3–55, Zona 10" means that the building is on Avenida la Reforma, between 3 and 4 calles, at no. 55, in Zona 10 (if it was on Av la Reforma 9–55, it would be between 9 and 10 calles). In Antigua, calles and avenidas are also divided according to their direction from the central plaza – north, south, east or west (norte, sur, oriente and poniente). Diagonales (diagonals) are what you'd expect – a street that runs in an oblique direction.

first US$1000 in the event of an accident, damage or theft. Local rental companies are listed throughout this guide for main towns.

Taking **your own car** into Guatemala entails a good deal of bureaucracy. You'll be issued a car permit (usually valid for thirty days) at the border, and there are hefty penalties if you overstay. An insurance policy for Central America is necessary. If you plan to continue further south into Central America, expect to pay for more entry permits.

US, Canadian, EU, Australian and New Zealand driving licences are valid in Mexico and throughout Central America.

By taxi and tuk-tuk

Taxis are available in all the main towns. The app-based taxi service Uber is present in Antigua and the capital and usually works out around half the price of a regular taxi. Local taxi drivers will almost always be prepared to negotiate a price for an excursion to nearby villages or sites. If you can organize a group, this need not be an expensive option.

Three-wheeled Thai **tuk-tuks** have proliferated throughout Guatemala in the last few years, operating as taxis, buzzing around the streets, Bangkok-style. They are common in most towns, except in Guatemala City and Quetzaltenango. It's best to fix the fare in advance.

By bike and motorbike

Bicycles are quite common in Guatemala, and cycling has to be one of the most popular sports. You'll be well received almost anywhere if you travel by bike, and most towns will have a repair shop. Be warned, though, that the main roads include plenty of formidable potholes, and it's a rare ride that doesn't involve at least one steep climb – chicken buses (see page 28) will carry bikes on the roof if you can't face the hills. Make sure you bring a bike lock in case you need to leave it outside.

You can **rent bikes** in towns including Antigua, Panajachel and Quetzaltenango; mountain bikes can be rented by the day or week. For real two-wheel enthusiasts, Guatemala Venture and Old Town Outfitters, both in Antigua (see page 81), offer a range of challenging bike trips, with half and full day rental options. In Guatemala City, *Quetzalroo* (see page 143) has excellent escorted bike trips of the capital.

Motorbikes are increasingly popular in Guatemala, though very few travellers get around this way and locating parts can be tricky. For guided rides, CA Tours (see page 121) based in Antigua, are the experts, with day trips available.

By ferry and boat

In **Petén**, there are a number of possible boat routes, including tours around Lago de Petén Itzá from Flores. Several terrific boat trips start in the town of Sayaxché, including the trip to Lago de Petexbatún and Aguateca and along the Río de la Pasión to Ceibal. Along the **Pacific coast**, you can explore the mangroves of the Chiquimulilla canal from Monterrico and Paredón.

Guatemala's most spectacular boat journey, however, is through the **Río Dulce gorge**, either starting in Lívingston or Río Dulce Town. The public boats that cover this route will give you a quick glance at the scenery but you can't beat a slow cruise. Volcano-framed **Lago de Atitlán** is another idyllic place to experience by boat: public *lanchas* connect all the main villages, or you can charter a boat in Panajachel by the hour.

Accommodation

Guatemalan hotels come in all shapes and sizes, and unless you're really off the beaten track there's usually a good range of accommodation to choose from. There are bargains and bad deals at every level.

ACCOMMODATION PRICE CODES

The hotel prices quoted in this book are for the least expensive room for two people in high season, not including breakfast – but do allow for the fluctuations outlined above. Other options are usually available, including rooms with two beds, single rooms, dormitory accommodation in hostels and so on. The following key has been outlined based on these criteria. It has been applied throughout the guide to all accommodation listings and all prices are in US dollars.

$ = $20 or lower
$$ = $20–$40
$$$ = $40–$75
$$$$ = $75 and over

Guatemala really is a budget travellers' dream, and you should be able to find a clean double room for US$25–30 (or less) in any town in the country, except the capital and Antigua. At the top end of the scale, you can stay in some magnificent colonial hotels decorated with real taste. In the mid-price bracket, you'll also find some brilliant places – you can still expect character and comfort, but perhaps without the service and facilities.

Accommodation options have a bewildering assortment of **names**: *hoteles, hosteles, pensiones, posadas, hospedajes* and *casas de huespedes*. The names don't always mean a great deal, but budget places are usually called *hospedajes* and anything called a *hotel* is usually a bit more upmarket. Virtually all the main travellers' centres have backpacker-style hostels with dormitories and a sociable vibe.

Prices are highest in Guatemala City and Antigua but extremely cheap in the western highlands. At fiesta and **holiday times**, particularly Holy Week and Christmas, rooms are more expensive and much harder to find, and the July–August tourist season can be busy – book ahead.

Hostels

Most Guatemalan **hostels** tend to be owned and often run by expats, and are geared up to budget travellers' needs, with excellent travel information, grub and perhaps a bar. Facilities in many hostels are improving all the time, and some now feature pools and lounge areas for guests. Dorm rooms tend to be the best budget-friendly option but try to avoid huge dormitories; the best places tend to have a maximum of eight beds. Some hostels offer single-sex dorms and also private rooms for couples, though these are generally poor value. You can expect to pay US$10–15 for a bed in a dorm, or US$20–30 for a room.

Hotels

The cheapest **hotels** (below US$25) are simple and sparse, often with a shared bathroom at the end of the corridor. In most towns, upwards of US$30 will give you a private bathroom with hot water. In the mid-range (around US$50–75) your room should be comfortable and attractive, while for US$100 and up you can expect high standards of comfort and luxury, with facilities such as swimming pools, gyms and a restaurant.

It's only in Petén, the Oriente and on the coasts that you'll need a fan or **air conditioning**. In the highlands, some hotels have logwood fires to keep out the winter chill. **Mosquito nets** are not that common in hotels, so if you plan to spend some time in Petén or by the coast you should bring your own from home, though they are usually available locally.

Camping

Campsites are extremely few and far between. It's really not worth bringing a tent as there are only a handful of places in the entire country that offer a designated, secure place to camp. If you're planning to do a jungle hike or volcano climb, tour agencies will sort out tents (or hammocks and mosquito nets). For renting camping gear contact Old Town Outfitters in Antigua (see page 81), or Quetzaltrekkers inside the *Casa Argentina* hotel in Quetzaltenango (see page 143).

Food and drink

Guatemalan food is filling, good value and can be very flavoursome. The cuisine has evolved from Maya, Latin American and Western traditions – though they usually overlap now to form what Guatemalans call *comida típica*. Popular tourist centres

EATING OUT PRICE CODES

The restaurant prices quoted in this book are for a two-course meal for one including a glass of wine or similar. The following key has been applied throughout the guide based on these criteria and all prices are in US dollars.

$ = $5 or lower
$$ = $5–$10
$$$ = $10–$20
$$$$ = $20 and over

tend to have more varied menus and plenty of choice for vegetarians, and in Antigua and Lago de Atitlán you can feast on a wide selection of global dishes.

In places orientated more to a **Guatemalan clientele**, you're likely to be offered a lot of simply prepared grilled or fried meat dishes and have much less choice. Off the beaten path the diet can get pretty monotonous, with things revolving around the "three-card trick" of eggs, beans and tortillas for breakfast, lunch and dinner. The concept of healthy eating has yet to really penetrate Central America, and a lot of local food tends to be full fat by definition.

Where to eat

Unless you're in a tourist-orientated place, your choice is usually between a restaurant and a **comedor**. The latter are simple, often scruffy-looking local places serving big portions of food at low prices. In a comedor there is often no menu, and you simply ask what's on offer, or look into the bubbling pots. **Restaurants** are slightly more formal and expensive and only found in large towns.

Many locals prefer to eat from **street food stalls**, which sell meals at rock-bottom prices. They're usually clustered around marketplaces. The food tends to be fresh, flavourful, and offers an authentic taste of local cuisine. You'll find **fast-food joints** in towns and on highways. *Pollo Campero* is a *KFC*-style Guatemalan-owned fried-chicken chain. While on the road, you'll also come across the local version of fast food: **vendors** offering a huge selection of drinks, sweets, local specialities and even complete meals. Treat this kind of food with a degree of caution, bearing in mind the potential lack of hygiene.

In every main tourist centre you'll also find gringo-geared café-restaurants, often foreign-owned places with **cosmopolitan** menus featuring sandwiches, salads and curries, stir-fries and the like, and plenty of **vegetarian** options. There's usually wine by the glass, cappuccinos and lattes, and fresh fruit shakes. Such indulgence does come at a price.

Breakfast

Traditionally, Guatemalans eat a substantial **breakfast** of tortillas, eggs and beans, sometimes with sour cream or fried plantains. Eggs can be served a myriad different ways, using some superb, often spicy sauces. Pancakes (*panqueques*) are also common, but can be disappointing as they're often made from a mix out of a packet. Up in the highlands, breakfast often includes a plate of **mosh**, a porridge made with milk and oats – it's the ideal antidote to the early morning chill.

In touristy towns things get a lot more eclectic, with all sorts of granola and muesli options available, plus fresh fruit, honey and yoghurt. The bread in these places is often freshly baked.

Lunch

Lunch is the main meal of the day, and this is the best time to fill up as restaurants and comedores offer a *comida corrida*, or *menú ejecútivo*: a set two- or three-course meal (usually soup and grilled meat) and includes a drink. In touristy towns you should also be able to get anything from paninis and wraps with imported cheese to sushi and noodles.

Dinner

For Guatemalans, dinner (taken 7–9pm) is a light meal. Mexican-style dishes, including tacos and enchiladas are popular. In the tourist hot spots, particularly Antigua, there's a tremendous choice of restaurants, serving cuisine from around the world, with Italian, Japanese, Indian, Thai, North American and of course Guatemalan and Mexican food available.

Snacks

Guatemalans are fond of their **street food** *refracciones* (snacks) – these include *tostadas* and *tamales*, steamed cornmeal stuffed with chicken or another bit of meat. For a quick bite, many locals opt for a *shuco* (literally a "dirty", a food cart that sells Guatemalan-style hot dogs), which is a bread bun filled with a

TOP 5 RESTAURANTS

El Artesano See page 131
Bistro Cinq See page 84
Café Sabor Cruceño See page 135
Gracia Cocina de Autor See page 68
Izakaya See page 84

sausage (or *chorizo*) and guacamole. Taco stands are also very widespread.

Cakes and **pastries** are widely available, but tend to be pretty dull and dry.

Guatemalan cuisine

Guatemalan **cuisine** does not vary that much regionally (except on the Caribbean coast) though some areas have famous local dishes (see page 34). **Vegetarians** are rarely catered for specifically, except in tourist-oriented restaurants. It is, however, fairly easy to get by eating plenty of beans and eggs (which are always on the menu), guacamole, and *chiles rellenos* (baked peppers) filled with delicious veg.

Most meals in Guatemala traditionally revolve around the basic staples of beans and maize, though diets are changing due to increased exposure to international cuisine. **Beans** (*frijoles*) are usually served in two ways: *volteados* (boiled, mashed, and then refried) or *parados* (served whole with a little onion and garlic). For the Maya, **maize** is almost as nourishing spiritually as it is physically – in Maya legend, humankind was originally formed from maize. In Guatemala the grain appears most commonly in the form of a corn tortilla, which is similar to a small, thick wrap. Maize is traditionally ground by hand and shaped by clapping it between the palms, a method still in widespread use; the tortilla is then cooked on a *comal*, a flat pan of clay placed over the fire. Guatemalan tortillas should be eaten while warm, and are usually brought to the table wrapped in cloth. Fresh tortillas have a lovely pliable texture, with a delicate, slightly smoky taste. Maize is also used to make a number of traditional snacks. **Chillies** are an essential ingredient of the Guatemalan diet (especially for the Q'ek'chi Maya), usually served as a spicy sauce (*salsa picante*), or sometimes placed raw or pickled in the middle of the table.

Squash (*güisquil*) is the main Maya vegetable, often used in dishes along with meat, tomato and onion; **pacaya**, a rather stodgy local vegetable, is another.

Dishes and specialities

Nomenclature is confusing – a dish of **cornmeal** wrapped inside banana leaves or corn husks and steamed could take any number of names depending upon flavourings, which change from region to region. Plain steamed cornmeal is a *tamal blanco*; stuff it with meat and tomato salsa, however, and it becomes either a *chuchito* or a *tamale*. If blended with potato, it's a *pache* – these are common in the Xela area. Up in the Ixil, and around Rabinal, look out for *boxboles*, cornmeal flavoured with spices, almond and a pinch of chilli, and cooked inside a pumpkin leaf. Mixed with *frijoles*, a *tamal* is a *bollo*, *tayuyo* or *tamalito de frijol*. When sweet, it's a *camallito de cambray* (with anise) or an *elote*. Keep an eye out for a red lantern outside a house – this indicates the family has fresh *tamales* for sale.

The corn **tortilla** can also be prepared in a myriad ways. Fried and topped (typically with guacamole and salty cheese), it's a *tostada*, while rolled or folded around a filling – meat and cheese is always popular – it may be a taco, enchilada or *doblada*. Usually a salsa, based on a blend of ripe tomato and *miltomates* (green tomatoes), is served with these dishes. A *pupusa* (called a *baleada* in Honduras) is a fresh tortilla stuffed with anything, but usually including refried beans, *repollo* (pickled shredded cabbage leaves) and cheese.

Encasing food in an egg **batter** and frying it either *envueltos* ("wrapped") or *frituras* ("fritter style") is another popular cooking style. *Chiles rellenos*, peppers stuffed with vegetables and meat, are especially delicious. Simpler, often vegetarian variations abound, using green bean or cauliflower, but look out for those made with *güisquil* (squash), *flor de izote* (the slightly bitter petals of a palm) or *bledo*, a leaf similar in flavour to spinach.

Salads are often simple, though several variations are well worth trying, including *piloyada*, a hearty

CARIB COOKING

The eastern coast of Guatemala has a different culinary tradition. Here **Creole** and **Garífuna** cooking, which incorporates the influences of the Caribbean and Africa, is easy to find in Puerto Barrios and Lívingston. Seafood dominates the scene, along with coconut and plantain. *Tapado* is probably the region's signature dish, a seafood soup that's a superb mix of fish (typically snapper), prawns, coconut milk, peppers, plantain and spices, though you'll also find plenty of grilled fish, lobster, conch fritters and *pan de coco* (coconut bread).

affair based on plump red beans with eggs, tomatoes and meat; *iguaxte*, cooked potato or vegetables flavoured with a paste of pumpkin seeds, dried chillies and sometimes tomato; and *chojín*, which is radish-based and often made with cheese and either pork or pork crackling (*chicharrón*). **Fiambre**, a vast salad of pickled vegetables with cured sausage (mixed with beetroot in central Guatemala and often barley in the Quetzaltenango area) is perhaps the country's most celebrated dish; it's eaten on All Saints' Day around a family grave in the cemetery.

Many traditional dishes are variations on chunky **soups** or subtly spiced tomato-based stews (*caldos*, *cocidos* or *sopas*), while most large towns have a place that specializes in **ceviche** (raw fish marinated in lime juice), and on the coast it's customary to order fried fish or *camarones* (shrimps), and wash it down with Gallo beer.

Sweets, snacks and desserts tend to be very sweet. *Rellenitos* – cooked, mashed plantain, stuffed with sweetened beans and fried – are widely available, as is *mole de plátano*, which is plantain served in a sweet, spiced cocoa-flavoured sauce. Vegetables – for example, sweet potato, pumpkin or *chayote* – may be simmered in sugar syrups until they are caramelized or stuffed with a sweet mixture. Among the cake selection, *pastel borracho* is soaked in rum syrup before being iced, while *pastel de elote* is made with corn.

Drink

To start off the day most Guatemalans drink a cup of hot **coffee** or **tea** (both are usually taken with plenty of sugar). Espresso machines are becoming much more widespread and you'll be able to get a cappuccino in most towns. Out in the sticks it's usually instant coffee with powdered milk. **Atol**, a warm, sweet drink made with maize, rice or even plantain and sugar is also very popular, especially in the highlands. It's the perfect beverage for chilly evenings.

At other times of day, **soft drinks** are usually drunk with meals. Coca-Cola, Pepsi, Sprite and Fanta (all called *aguas*) are common, as are *refrescos*, thirst-quenching water-based drinks with a little fruit flavour added; *rosa de jamaica* and *tamarindo* are two of the more unusual variants. In many places, you can also get a *licuado*, a delicious, thick, fruit-based drink with either milk or water added (milk is safer).

Tap water in the main towns is purified, and you can usually taste the chlorine. However, this doesn't mean that it won't give you stomach trouble – stick to bottled water, *agua pura* (see page 40).

Alcohol

Gallo, a medium-strength lager, is the most popular **beer** in Guatemala; indeed many Guatemalan men consider it the national drink, and the brewer promotes it as "Nuestra Cerveza" (our beer). Unfortunately it's a pretty bland brew. The main competitor, Brahma, a Brazilian beer, is a little more interesting with a slightly spicy finish. Moza, a dark brew with a somewhat caramel flavour, is worth trying but a little sweet. Other hard-to-come-by brands (all lagers) include the premium beer Montecarlo, Dorada Draft and Cabro. Imported brands are scarce. The 33cl bottles of beer are the cheapest in a bar, but watch out for litre bottles, which work out to be very good value. There's a small but growing craft beer scene in Guatemala City and Antigua; both places now have microbreweries.

As for **spirits**, rum (*ron*) and *aguardiente*, a clear and lethal sugar-cane spirit, are very popular and cheap. Ron Botran Añejo is a half-decent rum, while the fabulously smooth and aromatic Ron Zacapa Centenario is one of the world's best; indeed, it regularly wins international prizes.

Hard drinkers will soon get to know Quetzalteca and Venado, two readily available **aguardientes** that fire up many a fiesta. If you're after a real bargain, then try locally brewed alcohol (*chicha*), which is practically given away. Its main ingredient can be anything:

TOP 5 LOCAL DISHES

You'll find some terrific, almost curry-style dishes, in Guatemala – particularly in Maya areas. Look out for the following, which can come with a variety of different meats or ingredients:

Jocón Memorable, richly spiced sauce that combines ground sesame and pumpkin seeds, tomatillos and coriander.

Kak-ik A speciality of Cobán: a turkey broth with coriander and mint.

Pepián Spicy sauce made throughout the country: a mole-style mix that includes toasted seeds, dried chilli and cinnamon (and occasionally chocolate).

Pulique Lightly spiced sauce flavoured with coriander and capsicum.

Suban-ik Tasty, spicy meat dish that hails from Chimaltenango, with lots of chilli and peppers.

apple, cherry, sugar cane, peach, apricot and quince are just some of the more common varieties.

Chilean and Argentinean **wines** are usually available anywhere where tourists gather. A glass of house wine is usually US$5–6 in cafés and restaurants; bottles start at US$15 (or much less if bought in a supermarket).

Note that there's a **national curfew** on the sale of alcohol after 1am, which is strictly enforced.

The media

There are some decent English-language publications available in Guatemala, mainly geared towards the tourist market. It's easy to keep up to date with current affairs online.

Newspapers and magazines

Guatemala has a number of daily **newspapers**. The best of the dailies is the forthright *El Periódico* (Ⓦ www.elperiodico.com/es), which has some excellent columnists and investigative journalism. Guatemala's most popular paper is the *Prensa Libre* (Ⓦ prensalibre.com), which features comprehensive national and quite reasonable international coverage. *Siglo 21* (Ⓦ s21.com.gt) is also a good read. In the Quetzaltenango area, check out the local paper *El Quetzalteco*. As for the periodicals, *La Crónica* (Ⓦ cronica.gt) concentrates on current Guatemalan political affairs and business news with a smattering of foreign coverage.

In theory, the nation's newspapers are not subject to restrictions, though significant pressures and threats are still exerted by criminal gangs and those in authority. Being a campaigning or investigative journalist in Guatemala remains an incredibly dangerous profession, and every year there are several contract killings.

English-language publications

There are a number of free **English-language** publications, which can be picked up in hotels and restaurants where tourists congregate. *Revue* (Ⓦ revuemag.com) is a glossy, ad-heavy colour magazine with articles about Guatemalan culture and history. *Qué Pasa* (Ⓦ quepasa.gt) is another Antigua-based cultural magazine. In the Quetzaltenango area, *Xela Who?* (Ⓦ facebook.com/xelawhomag) concentrates on cultural life in the second city. For coverage of development issues and Guatemalan society *Entremundos* (Ⓦ entremundos.org) excels; it's widely available in Quetzaltenango, and at occasional spots around the nation.

Radio and television

Guatemala has an abundance of **radio** stations, though variety is not their strong point. Most transmit a turgid stream of Latin pop and cheesy merengue. Try Atmósfera (96.5FM) for rock, Radio Infinita (100.1FM) for everything from indie and electronica to hip hop and jazz, or internet-only Radio Marimba (Ⓦ radiomarimba.com) for (you've guessed it) marimba. Radio Punto (90.5FM) has news and discussions (in Spanish).

Television stations are also in plentiful supply. Most of them broadcast Mexican and US shows (which are subtitled or dubbed into Spanish) and there are lots of religious channels. Many hotel rooms have cable TV, which often includes (English-language) news channels.

Festivals

Traditional fiestas are one of the great excitements of a trip to Guatemala, and every town and village, however small, devotes at least one day a year to celebration. The main day is normally prescribed by the local saint's day, though the celebrations often extend a week or two

LADINO MUSIC

Mainstream **ladino music** in Guatemala, much of it originating in Miami, Panama, the Dominican Republic and Puerto Rico, reflects modern Latin American sounds. The sound on the street is **reggaetón**, which uses a dancehall reggae beat, fused with rapping and electronic beats. **Merengue** – fast moving, easy-going and very rhythmic – is also very popular, as is salsa.

Guatemala's best-known singer is popstar **Ricardo Arjona**, born in Jocotenango near Antigua, who has sold over 20 million albums and won a Grammy. The video of his song *Fuiste Tú* features spectacular Guatemala landscapes and has more than 1.2 billion YouTube views.

GARÍFUNA FIESTAS

Fiestas in **Lívingston**, on Guatemala's Caribbean coast, have different traditions and swing to their own rhythms. Some of the best dancing you'll ever see is to the hypnotic drum patterns of Garífuna punta, which betrays a distinctive West African heritage.

The Garífuna really know how to party, and if you get the chance to attend a fiesta, be prepared for some explosively athletic shimmying and provocative hip movements – nineteenth-century Methodists were so outraged they called it "devil dancing". **Garífuna day** (Nov 26) is the ideal time to see Lívingston really celebrate, though there seems to be a punta party going on most weekends.

around that date. With a bit of planning you should be able to witness at least one fiesta – most of them are well worth going out of your way for. A list of some of the best regional fiestas appears at the end of each chapter in this guide.

Until recently, **fiestas** came in two basic models – except Garífuna events (see box) – and were broadly ladino (Latin) or Maya in style. Ladino towns' fiestas involved fairgrounds and processions, beauty contests and perhaps the odd marching band and nights dancing to Latin music. In the Maya highlands, traditional dances with costumes and musicians dominated the celebrations. But today there's a certain blurring of the boundaries between the two and some fiestas in Indigenous villages have Latin music and dancing. What they all share is an astonishing energy and an unbounded enthusiasm for drink, dance and fireworks.

Fiestas in Guatemala are above all chaotic, and the measured rhythms of traditional dance and music are usually obscured by the crush of the crowd and the huge volumes of alcohol consumed by participants. If you can join in the mood, there's no doubt that fiestas are wonderfully entertaining and that they offer a real insight into Guatemalan culture, ladino or Indigenous. Despite the chaos, the sense of community and tradition shines through.

Fiesta dances

In Guatemala's Maya villages traditional **dances** – heavily imbued with history and symbolism – form a pivotal part in the fiesta celebrations. The most common dance is the **Baile de la Conquista**, which re-enacts the victory of the Spanish over the Maya, while at the same time managing to ridicule the conquistadors. Most are rooted in pre-Columbian traditions (see page 340).

Fiesta music

Guatemalan **music** combines many different influences, but yet again it can be broadly divided between ladino (see page 35) and Maya. For fiestas, bands are always shipped in, complete with a crackling PA system and a strutting lead singer. Traditional Guatemalan music is dominated by the marimba, a type of wooden xylophone that originated in Africa. The oldest versions use gourds beneath the sounding board and can be played by a single musician, while modern models, using hollow tubes to generate the sound, can need as many as seven players. Marimba orchestras play at every occasion, for both ladino and Indigenous communities. In the remotest of villages you sometimes hear them practising well into the night. Other important instruments, especially in Maya bands, are the *tun*, a drum made from a hollow

GUATEMALA'S BEST FIESTAS

Easter Week Semana Santa processions, Antigua. See page 78
Easter Week Maximón confronts Christ in Santiago Atitlán. See page 127
July 31–August 6 National Fiesta of Folklore, Cobán. See page 237
August 12–15 Marimba-playing marathon, Nebaj, in the Ixil region. See page 109
September 15 Independence Day nationwide, particularly impressive in Guatemala City.
October 31 Pagan skull-bearing procession, San José, Petén. See page 254
November 1 Kite-flying festival, Santiago, Sacatepéquez and Sumpango. See page 71
November 1 Drunken horse race, Todos Santos Cuchumatán. See page 158
November 26 Garífuna day, Lívingston. See page 199
December 21 Maya-style bungee jump in Chichicastenango. See page 101

log; the *tambor*, another drum traditionally covered with the skin of a deer; *los chichines*, a type of maracas made from hollow gourds; the *tzijolaj*, a kind of piccolo; and the *chirimia*, a flute.

Sports and outdoor pursuits

Guatemalans have a furious appetite for spectator sports and the daily papers always devote four or five pages to the subject. Fútbol (soccer) tops the bill, and if you get the chance to see a major game it's a thrilling experience, if only to watch the crowd. There's a great website, Ⓦguatefutbol.com (Spanish only), dedicated to the national sport – the two big local teams, both from Guatemala City, are Municipal and Communications. Otherwise, cycling, boxing and basketball are all popular.

Hiking

Guatemala has great **hiking**, particularly volcano climbing, which is certainly hard work but almost always worth the effort – unless you end up wrapped in cloud, that is. There are 37 **volcanic peaks**; the tallest is Tajumulco in the far west, which at 4220m is a serious undertaking, and should only be tackled when you've been acclimatized to an altitude of over 2000m for a few days. Among the active peaks, Pacaya is a fairly easy climb and a dramatic sight (although not always actively spewing lava, as the tour companies' photographs would have you believe). **Trekking trips** up volcanoes and along highland trails are organized by a number of tour operators in Antigua, Nebaj, Quetzaltenango and San Pedro La Laguna.

Sadly, there have been some occasional **attacks** (often armed, but usually nonviolent) on hikers climbing volcanoes, and around the shores of Lago de Atitlán. Incidents happen randomly, so take some precautions: it's much safer to walk in a group, and check the security situation before setting out.

TOP 5 HIKES

Acatenango summit Seriously challenging assault on a high volcanic peak. See page 87

El Mirador Jungle trek to a ruined city. See page 269

Indian Nose Great views of Lago de Atitlán and its volcanoes. See page 130

Volcán Chicabal Hike through pine forests before descending to a sacred crater lake. See page 148

Volcán Santa María Scale the cone of this immense volcano. See page 147

Sportfishing

There's excellent ocean and freshwater **fishing** in Guatemala. The **Pacific** coast offers exceptional sportfishing, with some of the best waters in the world for sailfish, as well as dorado, mahi mahi and some blue marlin, jack crevalle, yellow and black tuna, snapper and bonito. Most companies operate out of Puerto Quetzal or Iztapa (see page 183). The **Caribbean** side, including Lago de Izabal, also offers excellent opportunities for snook and tarpon. In **Petén** the rivers and lakes are packed with sport fish, including snook, tarpon and peacock bass, and lakes Petexbatún, Izabal and Yaxhá all offer superb fishing.

A four-night **fishing package** including an 8m boat, captain, meals, transport connections and accommodation on the Pacific coast costs from US$3000 (based on four anglers). If this is beyond your budget and you're looking for a more casual arrangement, talk to the local fishermen in Iztapa, Sayaxché or El Estor.

Whitewater rafting

Guatemala's dramatic highland landscape and tumbling rivers also provide some excellent opportunities for **whitewater rafting**. Trips down the Río Cahabón and seven other rivers are organized by Maya Expeditions, 13 Av 14–70, Zona 10, Guatemala City (Ⓦmayaexpeditions.com), giving you the chance to see some very remote areas and also visit some of the country's most inaccessible Maya sites. Customized itineraries are also possible.

Caving and tubing

Caving is another popular activity, especially in the area north of Cobán where you can explore great caverns and tube down underground rivers. The northern Alta Verapaz region (see page 232), particularly Lanquín, Chisec and Candelaria and Finca Ixobel (see page 247) are the places to head for. Guided tours are available in these areas for both beginners and experienced cavers.

Mountain biking

There are terrific **mountain-bike trails** throughout the highlands and several professional operators organize trips. Guatemala Ventures, Old Town Outfitters and Backshop Tours all in Antigua (see page 81), have excellent bikes and tour options, for a half-day escorted ride. Further west, Atitlán Adventure Tour (see page 135) organizes excellent mountain-bike excursions around the crater of Lago de Atitlán.

Kayaking & SUP

Two of the best areas for **kayakers** are the Río Dulce region with its stunning gorge and myriad jungle tributaries, and the sublime shoreline around Lago de Atitlán. The backwater lagoons of Monterrico are another good option. Hotels in all these places offer kayaks for rent. Little Santa Cruz la Laguna is something of a kayaking and SUP hotspot on Lago de Atitlán. Contact kayaking specialists Los Elementos for expert advice and guided paddles or SUP Atitlán for stand-up tours around the lakeshore.

Scuba diving

The seas off Guatemala have little to offer compared with the splendours of the neighbouring Belizean or Honduran coastal waters. Nevertheless, there are some **diving** possibilities, including Lago de Atitlán, where the professional ATI Divers (see page 135) offer instruction, training and fun dives.

Surfing

There is some **surfing** in Guatemala, but with a strong undertow along much of the Pacific coast, conditions are not ideal. Nevertheless there's a growing surf scene at Paredón, near Sipacate, where you'll find a surf lodge (see page 182), boards for rent and instructors (US$15–20/lesson). You'll also find reliable breaks at Iztapa. Heli Life (Ⓦ heli.life/surf) run regular surf trips around Guatemala.

Culture and etiquette

Guatemalans have a deserved reputation as some of the most civil, polite people in Latin America. They're nowhere near as upfront as many Latinos and quite formal in social situations. Understanding of local social etiquette will greatly enhance your trip.

Greetings

Whether you're clambering aboard a packed public minibus in the country or attending a high-society dinner party in the capital, it's normal to introduce yourself with a polite **greeting** of "buenos días/tardes" (good morning/afternoon or evening). Up in the highlands, if you're walking a trail or passing through a small village, it's usual to say hello to everyone you meet. It's actually very common for locals, even senior officials, to say *a sus órdenes* (literally "at your orders") as they help you out. If you're introduced to someone, a gentle handshake and a *con mucho gusto* ("pleased to meet you") is appropriate.

Clothing

There's no special **dress code** for women to consider when visiting Guatemala, though you might want to avoid very short skirts or tight tops to avert potential hassle. Generally in Indigenous areas, most local women wear a calf-length skirt, but it's fine for foreigners to wear trousers or knee-length short pants. By the coast or around a hotel pool, sunbathing in a swimsuit is perfectly acceptable, though keep your bikini top on.

Guatemalan men very rarely wear shorts, except on the beach, but foreigners can do as they please without offence – except perhaps to a formal engagement.

You should bear in mind that while most **Maya** are proud that foreigners find their textiles attractive, clothing has a profound significance, related to their identity and history – it's not wise for women travellers to wear men's shirts or trousers, or for men to wear *huipiles*. No matter what your gender identity, it's best to dress fairly conservatively when entering a church; knee-length shorts and T-shirts are suitable.

Women travellers

Guatemala is, on the whole, a safe country for **female travellers**, and it's an extremely popular destination for thousands of solo travellers, most of whom have an amazing experience. It's best to dress fairly modestly (see above) and avoid getting yourself into situations where trouble might arise. In towns, particularly the capital, take a taxi home after dark. Trust your instincts. Most Guatemalan men do not adopt especially macho mannerisms; indeed most are softly spoken and quite deferential to foreign women. That said, if you do encounter hassle it's best to remain firm, assertive and uninterested. As most local men are short in stature, it's possible to adopt an authoritative stance if you're tall. Some hustlers do hang around dance clubs and bars looking to pick up gringas, but most of these guys have a wife and kids at home.

Religion

Guatemala is the least Catholic Latin American country. It's estimated that around forty percent of the population now belong to one of several dozen US-based **Protestant** churches (see page 339). Many of Guatemala's Catholics also continue to practise ancient Maya religious customs in the Indigenous villages of the highlands. There has been a resurgence of interest in **Maya spiritualism** among young, educated Guatemalans since the end of the civil war in 1996, and attending "shamanic colleges" has become fashionable. Guatemala City also has tiny Jewish and Muslim communities.

Tipping

In smart restaurants a ten percent **tip** is appropriate, but in most places, especially the cheaper ones, tipping is the exception rather than the rule. Taxi drivers are not normally tipped.

Toilets

The most common names are *baños* or *servicios*, and the signs are usually *damas* (women) and *caballeros* (men). **Toilets** are nearly always Western-style (the squat bog is very rare), with a bucket for your used paper. Standards vary greatly. Public toilets are rare; some are quite well looked after by an attendant who charges a fee to enter and sells toilet paper, while others are filthy. It may be worth carrying your own toilet paper in case of emergencies.

Shopping

Guatemalan crafts, locally known as artesanías, are very much a part of Maya culture, stemming from practices that in most cases predate the arrival of the Spanish. Many of these traditions are highly localized, with different villages specializing in particular crafts. It makes sense to visit as many markets as possible, particularly in the highland villages, where the colour and spectacular settings are like nowhere else in Central America.

Artesanías

The best place to buy Guatemalan **crafts** is in their place of origin, where prices are reasonable and the craftsmen and -women get a greater share of the profit. If you haven't the time to travel to remote highland villages, the best places to head for are Chichicastenango on market days (Thursday and Sunday) and the shops and street hawkers in Antigua and Panajachel.

The greatest craft in Guatemala has to be **textile weaving**. Each Maya village has its own traditional designs, woven in fantastic patterns and with superbly vivid colours. All the finest weaving is done on the backstrap loom, using complex weft float and wrapping techniques. Chemical dyes have been dominant in Guatemala for over a century now, but a few weavers are returning to the use of natural dyes in some areas, including Lago de Atitlán where San Juan La Laguna is something of a hot spot.

One of the best places to start looking at textiles is in Antigua's Nim Po't (see page 86), a huge store with an excellent collection of styles and designs, and myriad other crafts too. Guatemala City's Museo Ixchel is another essential visit.

Next to Guatemalan weaving most other crafts suffer by comparison. However, if you hunt around, you'll find good ceramics, masks, basketry, blankets, mats, silver and jade. Antigua has the most comprehensive collection of shops, followed by Panajachel.

Markets

For shopping – or simply sightseeing – the **markets** of Guatemala are some of the finest anywhere in the world. The large markets of Chichicastenango, Sololá and San Francisco el Alto are all well worth a visit, but equally fascinating are the tiny weekly gatherings in remote villages like San Juan Atitán and Chajul, where the atmosphere is hushed and unhurried. In these isolated settlements market day is as much a social event as a commercial affair, providing the chance for villagers to catch up on local news, and perhaps enjoy a tipple or two, as well as sell some vegetables and buy a few provisions. Most towns and villages have at least one weekly event, particularly in the western highlands (see page 166) and also the Verapaces. **Haggling** is common but do so politely and with a smile. Remember that for many sellers, this is their livelihood so remain respectful and try not to over-negotiate, especially if you can afford to pay more.

Health

Most visitors enjoy Guatemala without experiencing any health problems. However, it's always easier to become ill in a country with a different climate, food and germs – still more so in a poor country

with lower standards of sanitation than you might be used to.

It's vital to get the best **health advice** you can before you set off, and there are a number of websites offering health precautions and disease prevention advice (see page 42). Pay a visit to your doctor or a travel clinic as far in advance of travel as possible, and if you're pregnant or likely to become so, mention this at the outset. Many clinics also sell the latest travel health products, including water filters and medical kits. Finally you'll definitely need health **insurance**.

Once you're in Guatemala, what you eat and drink is crucial. In addition to the hazards mentioned under "Intestinal troubles" (see below), contaminated food and water can transmit the hepatitis A virus, which can lay a victim low for several months with exhaustion, fever and diarrhoea, and can even cause liver damage.

Vaccinations, inoculations and malaria precautions

There are no obligatory **inoculations** for Guatemala (unless you're arriving from a "high-risk" area of yellow fever – northern South America and equatorial Africa). Nevertheless, there are several you should have anyway. Make sure you're up to date with tetanus and typhoid vaccinations and consider having hepatitis A and tuberculosis (TB) jabs. Long-term travellers or anyone spending time in rural areas should think about having hepatitis A and B and the rabies vaccines – though there are caveats for the latter (see page 41).

The risk of catching **malaria** is low, though it is a danger in some parts of the country (particularly in the rural lowlands). It's not a problem in the big cities, or anywhere above 1500m – which includes Antigua, Guatemala City, Chichicastenango, Lago de Atitlán, Quetzaltenango and virtually all of the western highlands. However, if you plan to visit any lowland areas, including Petén, Alta Verapaz and the Pacific or Caribbean coasts, you could consider taking a course of tablets.

Recommended prophylactics include doxycycline (though not for pregnant women), which you need to start taking a day before arrival and for a month after you leave the region. Chloroquine (inexpensive, available without prescription and safe in pregnancy) is another option, but you'll need to begin taking the pills a week before you enter an area where there's a risk of malaria and continue for four weeks after you return. Malarone is another alternative drug, though it's not suitable for pregnant women or babies.

Whichever anti-malarial you choose, you should still take precautions to avoid getting bitten by insects: always sleep in screened rooms or under nets in lowland areas; burn mosquito coils; cover up arms and legs, especially around dawn and dusk when mosquitoes are most active; and apply insect repellent (with 25–50 percent DEET; but not to children under 2).

Prevalent in some areas (usually occurring in epidemic outbreaks in lowland urban areas), **dengue fever** is a viral infection transmitted by mosquitoes, which are active during the day. Above 1800m it's not a concern, but there have been (a few) cases in Antigua (1533m) and Lago de Atitlán (1562m) during the rainy season (May–October). Fever, aches and joint pain (its old name was "break-bone fever") are often followed by a rash. Though most people make a full recovery after a few days, children are particularly at risk. There is no vaccine or specific treatment, so you need to pay great attention to avoiding bites.

The zika virus (also carried by mosquitos) is also present in Guatemala. Symptoms include fever, rashes and headaches. It's particularly dangerous for unborn children. There's no medical treatment but analgesics and antipyretics can be used to alleviate symptoms.

Intestinal troubles

Despite all the dire warnings given here, a bout of **diarrhoea** is the medical problem you're most likely to encounter. Its main cause is simply the change of diet: the food in the region contains a whole new set of bacteria, and perhaps rather more of them than you're used to. If you're struck down, take it easy for a day or two, drink lots of bottled water and eat only the blandest of foods – papaya is good for soothing the stomach and is crammed with vitamins. Only if the symptoms last more than four or five days do you need to worry. Finally, if you're taking oral contraception or any other orally administered drugs, bear in mind that severe diarrhoea can reduce their efficacy.

Cholera is an acute bacterial infection, identifiable by watery diarrhoea and vomiting. However, risk of infection is extremely low in Guatemala (and symptoms are rapidly relieved by prompt medical

WHAT ABOUT THE WATER?

Contaminated **water** is a major cause of sickness in Guatemala and you should never even brush your teeth with tap water. Always use bottled water (*agua pura*), which is available everywhere, often from large water dispensers, so you can top up your own bottle. Bottles and small plastic bags are also available from stores.

attention and clean water). If you're spending any time in rural areas you also run the risk of picking up various **parasitic infections**: protozoa – amoeba and giardia – and intestinal worms; these are quite common around Lago de Atitlán. These sound hideous, but once detected they're easily treated with antibiotics. If you suspect you may have an infestation, take a stool sample to a good pathology lab and go to a doctor or pharmacist with the test results (see below).

More serious is **amoebic dysentery**, which is endemic in many parts of the region. The symptoms are similar to a bad dose of diarrhoea but include bleeding too. On the whole, a course of flagyl (metronidazole) will cure it.

Bites and stings

Taking steps to avoid getting bitten by **insects**, particularly mosquitoes, is always good practice. Ticks, which you're likely to pick up if you're walking or riding in areas with domestic livestock (and sometimes in forests), need careful removal with tweezers. Head or body lice can be picked up from people or bedding, and are best treated with medicated shampoo; very occasionally, they may spread typhus, characterized by fever, muscle aches, headaches and eventually a measles-like rash. If you think you have it, seek treatment from a doctor.

Scorpions are common; mostly nocturnal, they hide during the heat of the day – often in thatched roofs. If you're camping, or sleeping under a thatched roof, shake your shoes out before putting them on and try not to wander round barefoot. Their sting is painful (rarely fatal) and can become infected, so you should seek medical treatment if the pain seems significantly worse than a bee sting. You're less likely to be bitten by a **spider**, but seek medical treatment if the pain persists or increases.

You're unlikely to see a **snake**, and most are harmless in any case. Wearing boots and long trousers will go a long way towards preventing a bite – tread heavily and they will usually slither away. If you do get bitten, remember what the snake looked like, immobilize the bitten limb and seek medical help immediately; antivenins are available in most main hospitals.

Swimming and snorkelling might bring you into contact with potentially dangerous or venomous sea creatures. If you are stung by a **jellyfish**, clean the wound with vinegar or iodine.

Rabies is rare, but does exist. You should avoid touching animals, give dogs a wide berth, and treat any bite as suspect: wash any wound immediately with soap or detergent and apply alcohol or iodine if possible. Act immediately to get treatment – rabies can be fatal once symptoms appear. There is a vaccine, but it is expensive and three shots are necessary (over a period of three weeks) before travel.

Heat and altitude problems

Two other common causes of illness are **altitude** and the **sun**. The best advice in both cases is to take it easy; allow yourself time to acclimatize before you race up a volcano, and build up exposure to the sun gradually. If going to altitudes above 2700m, you may develop symptoms of Acute Mountain Sickness (AMS), such as breathlessness, headaches, dizziness, nausea and appetite loss. More extreme cases might cause vomiting, disorientation, loss of balance and coughing up of pink frothy phlegm. The simple cure – a slow descent – almost always brings immediate recovery.

Tolerance to the sun takes a while to build up. Use a strong sunscreen and, if you're walking during the day, wear a hat and try to keep in the shade. Avoid dehydration by drinking plenty of water or fruit juice. The most serious result of overheating is heatstroke, which can be potentially fatal. Lowering the body temperature (by taking a tepid shower, for example) is the first step in treatment.

Medical help

For minor medical problems, head for a **farmacia** – there's one in every town and most villages (look for the green cross). Pharmacists are knowledgeable and helpful, and many speak some English. They can also sell drugs over the counter that are only available on prescription at home. Every capital city has **doctors** and **dentists**, many trained in the US, who speak good English. Your embassy will always have a list of recommended doctors, and we've included some throughout this guide in our "Directory" sections for the main towns.

Health **insurance** is essential and for anything serious you should go to the best private hospital you can reach. If you suspect something is amiss with your insides, it might be worth heading straight for the local pathology lab before seeing a doctor. Many rural communities have a **health centre** (*centro de salud* or *puesto de salud*), where health care is free, although there may only be a nurse or health worker available and you can't rely on finding anyone who speaks English. Should you need an injection or transfusion, make sure that the equipment is sterile (it might be worth bringing a sterile kit from home) and ensure any blood you receive is screened.

MEDICAL RESOURCES

Canadian Society for International Health T 613 241 5785, W csih.org. Extensive list of travel health centres.

CDC US T 1 800 232 4636, W cdc.gov. Official US government travel health site.

International Society for Travel Medicine US T 1 404 373 8282, W istm.org. Full list of travel health clinics.

MASTA (Medical Advisory Service for Travellers Abroad) W masta-travel-health.com.

South African Society of Travel Medicine W sastm.org.za. Lists travel medicine providers.

Travellers' Medical and Vaccination Centre Australia T 1300 658 844, W traveldoctor.com.au. Travel clinics in Australia and New Zealand.

Tropical Medical Bureau Ireland T 1850 487 674, W tmb.ie.

Living in Guatemala

Plenty of travellers get seduced by Guatemala's natural beauty, the low cost of living and the hospitality of its citizens. Many choose to put down roots for a while to study Spanish. Similarly there are myriad opportunities for voluntary workers, and dozens of excellent projects, though little in the way of paid work.

Studying Spanish

The **language school** industry is big business, with around sixty well-established schools and many less reliable setups. Most schools offer a weekly deal that includes four or five hours one-on-one tuition a day, plus full board with a local family. This kind of all-inclusive package works out at between US$200 and US$400 a week (most are in the US$200–300 bracket) depending on the school and location.

It's important to bear in mind that the success of the exercise is dependent both on your personal commitment to study and on the enthusiasm and aptitude of your teacher – if you are not happy with the teacher you've been allocated, ask for another. Insist on knowing the number of other students that will be sharing your family house; some schools (mainly in Antigua) pack as many as ten foreigners in with one family. Virtually all schools have a student liaison officer, usually an English-speaking foreigner who acts as a go-between for students and teachers.

Where to study

The first decision to make is to choose where you want to study. The three most popular choices are Antigua, Quetzaltenango and Lago de Atitlán. Beautiful **Antigua** (see page 85) is undoubtedly an excellent place to study Spanish, though the major drawback is that there are so many other students and tourists here that you'll probably end up spending your evenings speaking English. **Quetzaltenango** (see page 142) has a different atmosphere, with a stronger "Guatemalan" character and far fewer tourists; here students tend to mix more with locals away from school. **Lago de Atitlán** is popular with young travellers and has very cheap rates. Though standards are not generally as high as the other two places there are decent schools in San Pedro La Laguna (see page 129), Panajachel (see page 121) and San Marcos La Laguna (see page 133). Other towns with schools include Cobán (see page 228), Flores (see page 250), Monterrico (see page 154), Nebaj (see page 110), San Andrés and San José in Petén (see page 250) and, in Honduras, Copán (see page 293).

Many schools lay on after-school activities like salsa lessons, cooking classes, visits to villages, films and cultural lectures, and even hiking trips. In Quetzaltenango most schools have a social ethos and fund development projects in the region. You'll find some schools have academic accreditation agreements with North American and European universities.

The **website** W guatemala365.com is a good place to begin a search for a Spanish school, with a list of professional schools, feedback from students and some good tips about the relative advantages of different study centres.

Volunteering and paid work

There are dozens of excellent organizations offering **voluntary work** placements in Guatemala. Medical and health specialists are desperately needed, though there are always openings in other areas, from work helping to improve the lives of street children to environmental projects and wildlife conservation. Generally, the longer the length of time you can commit to, and the higher your level of Spanish, the more in demand you'll be.

Two organizations provide links between volunteers and projects in Guatemala. Quetzaltenango-based **Entremundos**, 6 C 7–31, Zona 1 (W entremundos.org), has contacts with over one hundred development projects in the Xela area and a few further afield; check out their online database.

As for paid work, **teaching English** is your best bet, particularly if you have a recognized qualification like TEFL (Teaching English as a Foreign Language). There are always a few vacancies for staff in the gringo bars of Antigua, and in backpackers' hostels. The *Revue* (see page 35) and notice boards in Antigua, San Pedro La Laguna and Quetzaltenango also occasionally advertise vacancies.

VOLUNTEERING PROJECTS

Ak'Tenamit Ⓦ thegtfund.org. Health, education, business training and agriculture volunteer positions in a large, established project, working with Q'eqchi' Maya in the Río Dulce region.
Animal Aware Ⓦ animalaware.org. Help out in an animal welfare centre for abandoned pets near Sumpango.
Arcas Ⓦ facebook.com/pg/ArcasGuatemala. Volunteers needed in Petén to help rehabilitate wild animals including monkeys for release back into forests, and opportunities to help out in a sea turtle reserve on the Pacific coast. You have to pay to volunteer on these programmes.
Casa Alianza Ⓦ covenanthouse.org. Charity helping street children in Central America. The work is extremely demanding.
Casa Guatemala Ⓦ casa-guatemala.org. Skilled workers (particularly teachers) and helpers needed to work with street children and orphans in the Río Dulce region.
Escuela de la Calle Ⓦ escueladelacalle.org. Help educate and mentor street kids in Quetzaltenango. Linked to hiking group Quetzaltrekkers (see page 143).
Habitat for Humanity Ⓦ habitatguate.org. House-building projects in all 22 departments across the nation.
Idealist Ⓦ idealist.org. A massive database of links to a wide range of projects in the region – from ecotourism to human-rights work, with both voluntary and paid work opportunities.
Ix-Canaan Ⓦ ixcanaan.com. Health professionals needed to help out in a Petén-based project.
NISGUA Ⓦ nisgua.org. Coordinates the Guatemalan Accompaniment Project, which monitors and supports human-rights workers and campaigners in Guatemala.
Safe Passage Ⓦ safepassage.org. Teachers, tutors, helpers and support staff needed to help children who work on the Guatemala City rubbish dump. A five-week commitment is needed.
Upavim Ⓦ upavim.org. Community development on the outskirts of Guatemala City, with opportunities for nursery workers and teachers using the Montessori method. A four-month minimum term is required.

TRAVEL ADVICE WEBSITES

Australian Department of Foreign Affairs Ⓦ dfat.gov.au. Travel advice and reports on countries including Guatemala.
British Foreign and Commonwealth Office Ⓦ fco.gov.uk. Constantly updated advice for travellers on circumstances affecting safety.
US State Department Ⓦ travel.state.gov. Details the dangers of travelling in most countries of the world. The information can be a little alarmist.

Travel essentials

Accessible travel

Guatemalans are extremely helpful and eager to help travellers who have additional needs. Nevertheless, visitors with **disabilities** are faced with many obstacles. Wheelchair users will have to negotiate their way over cobbled streets, cracked (or nonexistent) pavements and potholed roads in cities, towns and villages. Getting around Guatemala by public transport can be exhausting for anyone, but trying to clamber aboard a packed chicken bus with a wheelchair or walking sticks presents a whole set of other challenges. Plenty of disabled travellers do successfully make their way around the country, though. Most of the main sites are connected by tourist shuttle minibuses, which pick you up from your hotel, and have a driver whose job it is to assist passengers with their luggage. Many Guatemalan hotels are low rise (and larger, upmarket places often have lifts and ramps), so it shouldn't be too difficult to find an accessible room. You'll only find disabled toilets in the most expensive hotels.

Climate

Much of the country maintains a warm **climate** year-round (see box), though it is largely determined by altitude, and there are regional variations (see page 10). The rainy season runs roughly from May to October, with the worst of the rain usually falling in September.

Costs

Guatemala is one of the **cheapest** countries in the Americas for travellers, though there are plenty of opportunities for a modest (or serious) splurge if you feel like it. If you are extremely frugal you may be able to get by on around US$175 a week in most parts of the country, or below US$150 in a budget travellers' hub like San Pedro La Laguna. However, if you're after a little more comfort (travelling by shuttle bus and staying in rooms with an en-suite bathroom) you can expect to spend around US$250 per head per week, if you're travelling as a couple, while solo travellers should reckon on perhaps US$300 a week. For around US$100 per day you can expect to live quite well. Things are more expensive in regions where the local economy is tourist driven (Antigua in particular). A sales tax (IVA) of twelve percent is usually included in the price you're quoted in most places, except smart hotels. Similarly,

AVERAGE MONTHLY TEMPERATURES AND RAINFALL

	Jan	Feb	Mar	Apr	May	Jun	Jul	Aug	Sep	Oct	Nov	Dec
GUATEMALA CITY												
(ºC)	24	25	26	27	26	25	25	25	24	24	23	23
(ºF)	75	77	78	81	78	77	77	77	75	75	73	73
Rain (mm)	4	4	6	28	160	275	240	209	328	155	29	6
HUEHUETENANGO												
(ºC)	23	24	25	26	25	25	25	25	24	24	23	22
(ºF)	73	75	77	78	77	77	77	77	75	75	73	72
Rain (mm)	4	9	21	36	113	203	114	125	218	137	31	5
PUERTO BARRIOS												
(ºC)	27	28	29	31	32	31	30	30	30	30	29	28
(ºF)	81	82	84	88	90	88	86	86	86	86	84	82
Rain (mm)	221	113	113	132	193	272	489	322	295	351	318	245
TIKAL												
(ºC)	27	28	30	31	31	31	30	30	30	29	28	27
(ºF)	81	82	86	88	88	88	86	86	86	84	82	81
Rain (mm)	64	30	62	53	117	222	169	117	183	186	122	41

the ten percent INGUAT accommodation tax is often excluded in luxury places, but rarely elsewhere.

Crime and personal safety

Personal safety is a serious issue in Guatemala. While the vast majority of the two million tourists who come every year experience no problems at all, general crime levels are high, and it's not unknown for criminals to target visitors, including tourist shuttle buses. There is little pattern to these attacks, but some areas can be considered much safer than others. Warnings have been posted throughout this guide where incidents have occurred. It's wise to register with your embassy on arrival, try to keep informed of events, and avoid travelling at night. Officially, you should carry your passport (or a photocopy) at all times.

It's important to try to minimize the chance of becoming a victim. Petty theft and pickpocketing are likely to be your biggest worry. **Theft** is most common in Guatemala City's Zona 1 and its bus stations, but you should also take extra care when visiting markets popular with tourists (like Chichicastenango) and during fiestas. Avoid wearing flashy jewellery and keep your money (and smartphones) well hidden. It's worth taking care when using ATMs, too, as there have been some scams reported that involved cloned cards (see page 47). When travelling, there is actually little or no danger to your pack when it's on top of a bus, as it's the conductor's responsibility alone to go up on the roof and collect luggage. Be sensitive to your surroundings: watching a film on the latest tablet or waving around an iPhone on a chicken bus is not a good idea.

Muggings and violent crime are of particular concern in Guatemala City. There's little danger in the daylight hours but don't amble around at night; use a taxi. There have also been a few cases of armed robbery in Antigua, Quetzaltenango and on the trails around Lago de Atitlán. The Pacaya and San Pedro volcanoes are now well guarded and considered safe.

Your first course of action if you're the victim of any crime (or dispute) is to contact the excellent people at **PROATUR** (see box) who are the experts in dealing with any issues that affect tourists. They'll also liaise with the police and organize police statements (for insurance purposes).

Drugs including marijuana and cocaine are readily available in Guatemala. Be aware that drug offences can be dealt with severely and even the possession

USEFUL NUMBERS

Police ☎ 120
PROATUR/INGUAT ☎ 1500 (24hr)
Red Cross ambulance ☎ 125

of some weed could land you in jail. If you do get into a problem with drugs, it may be worth enquiring with the first policeman if there is a "fine" (*multa*) to pay, to save expensive arbitration later. At the first possible opportunity, get in touch with your embassy in Guatemala City (see page 69) and negotiate through them; they will understand the situation better than you.

Guatemala's **police** force has a poor reputation. Corruption is rampant and inefficiency the norm, so don't expect much help if you experience any trouble. That said, they don't have a reputation for intimidating tourists. If for any reason you do find yourself in trouble with the law, be as polite as possible. Tourist police forces have been set up in Antigua, Panajachel and Tikal, and English-speaking officers should be available to help you out in these places.

The sheer number of armed security guards on the streets and posted outside restaurants and stores is somewhat alarming at first, but after a few days you get used to their presence, even if it is disconcerting to see an 18-year-old with a gun outside *McDonald's*.

Electricity

Power (110–120 volts) and plug connections (two flat prongs) are the same as North America. Anything from Britain or Europe will need an **adaptor**. Cuts in the supply and fluctuations in the current are fairly common.

Entry requirements

Citizens from most Western countries (including the US, UK, Canada, Australia, New Zealand, South Africa, Norway and most, but not all, EU states) need only a valid **passport** to enter Guatemala for up to ninety days. Passport holders from other countries (including some Eastern European nations) qualify for a Guatemalan **visa**, but have to get one from a Guatemalan embassy or consulate. Citizens from most developing world nations, including much of Asia and Africa, need to apply for a visa well in advance. If you're wondering whether you'll need a visa, phone an embassy for the latest entry requirements; Guatemala has embassies in all the region's capitals.

Although there's no charge to enter or leave the country, **border officials** at land crossings commonly ask for a small fee, which is destined straight for their back pockets. You might try avoiding such payments by asking for *un recibo* (a receipt); but prepare yourself for a delay at the border.

It's possible to **extend your visit** for a further ninety days, up to a maximum of 180 days. To do this, go to the immigration office (*migración*) in Guatemala City at 6 Av 3–11, Zona 4 (Mon–Fri 8.30am–4.30pm; Ⓣ 2411 2411). You'll need to present your passport, a photocopy of both the biodata page (with your picture and personal details) and your Guatemala entry stamp. You'll also need a photocopy of a valid credit card (front and back), a completed visa extension document and two black-and-white passport-sized photos (there's a photo booth next door to the office). You'll then need to pay the extension fee; your extension is usually issued about eight days later. After 180 days you have to (officially) leave Guatemala for 24 hours to a country outside the so-called **CA-4** Central American region: the nearest two nations are Belize and Mexico.

GUATEMALAN EMBASSIES AND CONSULATES

For a full list of Guatemalan embassies consult Ⓦ minex.gob.gt (Spanish only), and click on "directorios", following the link to "embajadas".

Australia Unit 9–11 National Circuit Engineering House, Barton, ACT 2600, Canberra Ⓣ 02 6489 1311 Ⓦ minex.gob.gt.

Belize 8 A St, King's Park, Belize City Ⓣ 223 3150, Ⓦ minex.gob.gt

Canada 130 Albert St, Suite 1010, Ottawa ON K1P 5G4 Ⓣ 613 233 7188, Ⓦ minex.gob.gt.

PROATUR

If you're a victim of crime, or need travel assistance, your first port of call should be **INGUAT** (Ⓣ 1500, Ⓔ proatur@INGUAT.gob.gt, Ⓦ INGUAT.gob.gt), an excellent organization specifically set up to help tourists in Guatemala. There's a PROATUR representative on the ground in every department in the country (see their website for contact information, including mobile phone numbers); staff can even liaise with local police and embassy staff on your behalf, and occasionally they may organize a police escort to accompany travellers along highways known for banditry. In addition, there's a 24-hour call centre, staffed by English speakers who can assist with anything from updates on road conditions and bus timetables to security issues, and their Facebook and Twitter feeds give live updates about travel, traffic and security in Guatemala.

Germany Joachim-Karnatz-Allee 47, Ecke Paulstrasse, 10557 Berlin Ⓣ 030 206 4363, Ⓦ botschaft-guatemala.de.
Honduras Colonia Lomas del Guijaro, c/Londres, Bloque B, casa 0440 Tegucigalpa Ⓣ 2232 5018, Ⓦ honduras.minex.gob.gt. Consulate: 23 Av & 11 C, S.O., Colonia Trejo, San Pedro Sula Ⓣ 2556 9550, Ⓔ conssanpedsula@minex.gob.gt.
Japan 38 Kowa Building, 9th floor, Room 905, 4-12-24, Nishi-Azabu, Tokyo 106–0031 Ⓣ 380 01830, Ⓔ embjapon@minex.gob.gt.
Mexico Embassy: Av Explanada 1025, Lomas de Chapultepec 11000, Mexico D.F. Ⓣ 55 5540 7520, Ⓔ embaguatemx@minex.gob.gt; Consulate: 1 C Sur Poniente 26, Comitán, Chiapas Ⓣ 963 100 6816, Ⓔ conscomitan@minex.gob.gt
Netherlands Java Straat 44, 2585 AP The Hague Ⓣ 302 0253, Ⓦ minex.gob.gt.
New Zealand Contact Australia.
UK 105A Westbourne Grove, London W2 4UP Ⓣ 020 7221 7448, Ⓦ minex.gob.gt.
US 2220 R St NW, Washington DC 20008 Ⓣ 202 745 4953, Ⓦ gt.usembassy.gov. Consulates located in many cities, including Chicago, Houston, LA, Miami, New York, San Diego and San Francisco.

Insurance

A comprehensive **travel insurance** policy is essential for visitors to Guatemala. Medical insurance (you want coverage of US$2,000,000) should include provision for repatriation by air ambulance, and your policy should also cover you for illness or injury, and against theft.

Contact a specialist travel insurance company, or consider the travel insurance deal offered by Rough Guides (see box). A typical travel insurance policy usually provides cover for the loss of baggage, tickets and – up to a certain limit – cash or cheques, as well as cancellation or curtailment of your journey. Many of them exclude so-called dangerous sports (this can mean scuba diving, whitewater rafting, windsurfing and kayaking) unless an extra premium is paid.

When securing baggage cover, make sure that the per-article limit – typically under US$1000/£750 – will cover your most valuable possession. If you need to make a claim, you should keep receipts for medicines and medical treatment, and in the event you have anything stolen, you must obtain an official statement (*una afirmación*) from the police.

Internet

Web services are very well established in Guatemala. **Wi-fi** is very common in all the main tourist centres, where most hotels, hostels and cafés provide access. Internet access via 4G and 3G is also widely available. You'll find cybercafés everywhere too. Connection speeds are generally fairly swift in the main urban centres but can be painfully pedestrian in more remote areas. Rates vary, starting at US$0.50 per hour.

Laundry

Almost every town has at least one **laundry**; most will wash and dry a load for you for US$3–5. Self-service laundries are rare. Many hotels and pensiones also offer laundry facilities.

LGBTQ+ travellers

Homosexuality is legal for consenting adults aged 18 or over. However, though Guatemalan society is not as overtly macho as many Latin American countries, it's wise to be discreet and avoid too much affection in public. There's a small, almost entirely male scene in Guatemala City (see page 68), where there's an annual Pride march in June. The Spanish-only website Ⓦ gayguatemala.org is a useful LGBTQ+ resource.

Mail

Postal services are quite reliable, though many locals use courier companies to send important packages and documents overseas. Generally, an airmail letter to the US or Canada takes about a week, to Europe from ten days to two weeks. Receiving mail is not generally a worry as long as you have a reliable address – many language schools will hold mail for you. The Poste Restante (*Lista de Correos*) system is no longer operational.

Bear in mind it's very expensive to send anything heavy home. You may want to use a specialized shipping agency instead: there are agencies in Antigua and Panajachel.

Maps

International Travel Maps and Books (ITMB) publishes a reasonable Guatemala map (1:500,000). Locally produced alternatives include an offering by INGUAT using a scale of 1:1,000,000.

The Instituto Geográfico Militar produces the only large-scale maps of the country. At a scale of 1:50,000, these maps are accurately contoured, although many other aspects are now very out of date. You can consult and purchase them at the institute's offices, Av de las Américas 5–76, Zona 13, Guatemala City (ⓦ ign.gob.gt).

Money

Guatemala's **currency**, the quetzal (Q), has been very stable for more than a decade. But because fluctuations can and do take place, we have quoted all prices throughout this guide in US dollars. The **US dollar** is by far the most widely accepted foreign currency in Guatemala; that said, it is not a semi-official one, and you can't get by with a fistful of greenbacks and no quetzals. Euros and other foreign currencies are tricky to cash; try foreign-owned hotels.

Debit and **credit cards** are very useful for withdrawing currency from bank ATMs but are not widely accepted elsewhere, so don't count on paying with them except in upmarket hotels and restaurants. Beware of expensive surcharges (ten percent is sometimes added) if you do want to pay by a card in many stores.

Cashpoints (**ATMs**) are very widespread, even in small towns. Charges of US$3–5 per withdrawal are widespread. It's important to note that most Central American ATMs do not accept five-digit PIN numbers; contact your bank at home in advance if you have one. Travellers' cheques are now virtually impossible to cash anywhere in Guatemala. US dollar bills are always a handy backup.

Note that all the official **currency exchange** counters at Guatemala City airport offer appalling rates (see page 64). At the main land-border crossings there are usually banks and a swarm of money changers who generally give fair rates for cash.

Opening hours and public holidays

Guatemalan **opening hours** are subject to considerable variation, but in general most offices, shops, post offices and museums are open between 8/9am and 5/6pm, though some take an hour or so break for lunch. Banking hours are extremely convenient, with many staying open until 7pm from Monday to Friday, but closing at 1pm on Saturdays.

Archeological sites are open every day, usually from 8am to 5pm, though Tikal is open longer hours. Almost all businesses close down during the principal **public holidays** (see box).

Phones

There are no **area codes** in Guatemala. To call a number from abroad simply dial the international access code, followed by the country code (ⓣ 502) and the number (all are eight digit).

Use applications like Skype and Viber for free **international calls**. Otherwise international calls can be made via the internet from cybercafés for around US$0.25 per minute. Local calls are cheap, and can be made from communications offices or phone booths.

Mobile (cell) phones

Most North American and European **mobile phones**, if unlocked, will work in Guatemala. To avoid roaming charges all you'll need is a local SIM card (Tigo and Claro are the most popular networks and have excellent coverage). All new SIMs have to be officially registered (for security purposes), and you'll have to

ATM SCAM

A number of travellers have reported an **ATM scam** operating in Guatemala, particularly in Antigua. Cardholders are finding their bank accounts drained of cash, days or even months after they've used a cash machine. It's probable that scammers are "skimming" or using cloned cards. Check your balance regularly – and it's worth changing your pin code when you return to your home country.

PUBLIC HOLIDAYS

January 1 New Year's Day
Semana Santa The four days of Holy Week leading up to Easter
May 1 Labour Day
June 30 Army Day, anniversary of the 1871 revolution
August 15 Guatemala City fiesta (Guatemala City only)
September 15 Independence Day
October 12 Discovery of America (only banks close)
October 20 Revolution Day
November 1 All Saints' Day
December 24 Christmas Eve (from noon)
December 25 Christmas
December 31 New Year's Eve (from noon)

show your passport to get one. Phones can also be bought locally from as little as US$25 (including a calling credit). Keep an eye out for "*doble*", "*triple*" and even "*cuádruple*" offer days, when you get several times the top-up credit you pay for.

Photography

In Indigenous areas and the countryside you should avoid taking pictures of **children** unless you get permission from their parents. Sadly children are stolen from their families every year in Guatemala, and rumours persist that Westerners steal babies for adoption. Indigenous people are also extremely superstitious and believe that adult strangers can give their children *mal de ojo* (the "evil eye") if they give them too much attention, which makes kids sick. There's less of an issue in urban areas, where the population is better educated, but even here be sensitive.

Otherwise Guatemala is an exceptionally rewarding destination for photographers, with outstanding scenic and human interest. It's polite to ask before taking portraits, but if you're in a marketplace using a zoom it's easy to get shots of people without being too intrusive.

Memory cards for digital cameras are widely available; print film should be brought from home.

Time

Guatemala is on the equivalent of **Central Standard Time** in North America, six hours behind GMT. Daylight saving is not used. There is little seasonal change – it gets light around 6am, with sunset at around 5.30pm in December, or 6.30pm in June.

Tourist information

Information about Guatemala is easy to come by inside the country, but less available in Europe or North America. In the US, you can call **INGUAT**, Guatemala's tourist information authority, on the toll-free number ⓣ1 888 464 8281, while Guatemalan embassy staff in Europe and Canada can often help out too. The material produced by INGUAT is colourful, though much of it is of limited practical use. Often specialist travel agents are excellent sources of information.

INGUAT staff in Guatemala City, at 7 Av 1–17, Zona 4 (ⓣ2421 2800, ⓦvisitguatemala.gt), are helpful and English-speakers are available. The organization has smaller branches in Antigua, Flores, Panajachel and Quetzaltenango, and at the airports in Flores and Guatemala City. All branches should have hotel listings and dozens of brochures and leaflets. INGUAT also helps maintain a travel and security assistance phone line for tourists in Guatemala (ⓣ1500).

In the UK, the **Guatemalan Maya Centre**, 94b Wandsworth Bridge Rd, London SW6 2TF (ⓣ020 7371 5291, ⓦmaya.org.uk), is a fine Guatemalan resource centre. It's open by appointment only, with over 2500 books on Guatemala, videos, periodicals and an incredible textile collection.

USEFUL WEBSITES

ⓦ**atitlan.com** Concentrates on the Atitlán region, with interesting features plus some hotel and restaurant listings.
ⓦ**ccb.turismocopan.com/en** Informative site dedicated to the Copán region in Honduras.
ⓦ**famsi.org** Academic reports from Mayanists.
ⓦ**ghrc-usa.org** The Guatemala Human Rights Commission publishes news, analysis and in-depth reports on the nation.
ⓦ**lanic.utexas.edu** The Guatemala page on the Latin American Network Information Center's website is a fine portal; here you'll find a comprehensive set of links: nonprofits, language schools, magazines and museums, as well as various academic and tourism resources.
ⓦ**mayaparaiso.com** Dedicated to the Río Dulce and Lago de Izabal area, with a busy message board.
ⓦ**mesoweb.com** All the latest reports about the ancient Maya.
ⓦ**mimundo.org** Superb photojournalism from an independent reporter.
ⓦ**revuemag.com** Content from the popular Antigua-based tourism and travel magazine.
ⓦ**xelapages.com** Concentrates on the Quetzaltenango area, with comprehensive language-school and business listings, plus popular discussion boards.

facebook.com/xelawhomag Dedicated to Guatemala's second city, with good cultural information and practical content.

Travel with children

It can be exceptionally rewarding to travel with **children** in Guatemala. Most locals, particularly in Indigenous areas, have large families so your kids will always have some company. By bringing your children along to Guatemala, you'll take a big step towards dismantling the culture barrier and families can expect an extra warm welcome. Hotels, well used to putting up big Guatemalan families, are usually extremely accommodating.

Obviously, you'll have to take a few extra precautions with your children's health, paying particular care to hygiene and religiously applying sunscreen. Dealing with the sticky tropical heat of Petén or the Pacific coast is likely to be one of the biggest difficulties, but elsewhere humidity is much less of a problem.

As young children are rarely enthralled by either modern highland or ancient Maya culture, you may want to plan some excursions: the giant Xocomíl water park and Parque Xetulul theme park (see page 178) and Auto Safari Chapín (see page 189) make great days out for kids. In Guatemala City, the Museo de los Niños, Aurora Zoo and Mundo Petapa Irtra are a lot of fun too.

The sheer diversity of animals (including howler and spider monkeys and coatis) make Tikal very popular. And the thrill of riding a chicken bus or buzzing around Lago de Atitlán or the Río Dulce in a *lancha* is quite something. Take extra care if you head for the Pacific beaches, as every year several children (and adults) drown in the strong undertow.

For **babies**, you'll find baby milk and disposable nappies (diapers) are widely available in super-markets and pharmacies; take an extra stock if you're visiting really remote areas. Every town in the country has at least a couple of pharmacies, and medication for children is available. Breast-feeding in public is fine.

Guatemala City, Antigua and around

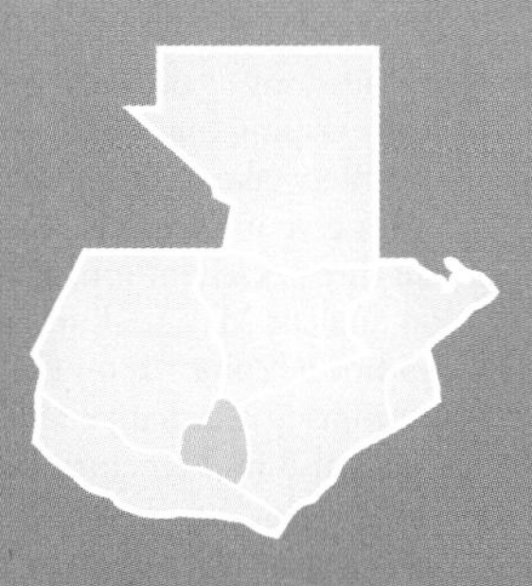

SANTA CATALINA ARCH, ANTIGUA

Guatemala City, Antigua and around

Situated just 40km apart, the two cities of Guatemala City and Antigua could hardly be more different. The capital, Guatemala City, is a fume-filled maelstrom of industry and commerce with few attractions to detain the traveller, though a day or two spent visiting its museums and soaking up the (limited) cultural scene won't be wasted. Antigua is everything the capital is not: tranquil, urbane and resplendent with evocative colonial buildings and myriad cosmopolitan cafés and restaurants. Not surprisingly, this is where most travellers choose to base themselves.

Guatemala City sprawls across a huge upland basin, surrounded by craggy hills and volcanic cones. Its shapeless and swelling mass ranks as the largest city in Central America, home to more than four million people, and it's Guatemala's undisputed centre of politics, power and wealth. The capital has an intensity and vibrancy that are both its fascination and its horror, and for many visitors dealing with the city is an exercise in damage limitation as they struggle through bus fumes and crowds. For years urban decay has tainted the heart of the city, the **centro histórico**, but initiatives in more recent years have revitalized the district as streets have been pedestrianized, buildings restored and new cafés and bars have opened.

Antigua, on the other hand, is the most impressive colonial city in Central America, with a tremendous wealth of architectural riches. With around forty-six thousand inhabitants, the city's graceful cobbled streets, elegant squares, churches and grand houses are ideal to explore on foot. The town's renowned **language schools** also attract students from all over the world, and education and tourism are the city's prime sources of wealth.

The countryside around Antigua and Guatemala City – a delightful landscape of volcanoes, pine forests, *milpas* (cornfields) and coffee farms – also begs to be explored. Looming over the capital is **Volcán de Pacaya**, one of the most active peaks in Latin America, while the volcanoes of **Agua** and **Acatenango** are also well worth climbing.

You'll also find countless interesting villages to visit in this area, including **San Andrés Itzapa**, where there is a pagan shrine to the "evil saint" San Simón, and **Jocotenango** which boasts museums dedicated to coffee production and Maya music. The one Maya ruin in the area that can compete with the lowland sites further north is **Mixco Viejo**, which enjoys a breathtaking, remote setting.

Guatemala City

GUATEMALA CITY is not a place to visit for its beauty or architectural charm. First impressions of the centre are pretty grim, with potholed streets choked by pollution from rasping buses and grinding levels of poverty all too evident. Understandably, few travellers take to *la capital*, and many avoid it completely.

But give it a chance, and you'll find it does offer some metropolitan pleasures. There are three excellent **museums**: the archeological and Popol Vuh (which both concentrate on ancient Maya culture) and the Ixchel, dedicated to the country's stellar textile tradition. **Zona 1** is on the up as landmark buildings are renovated and new venues promoting alternative rock bands and electronic DJs emerge. Dotted around the city you'll also find cinemas and North American-style shopping malls.

That said, the disparities of life in the city are extreme, with glass skyscrapers towering over sprawling slums and shoeless widows peddling cigarettes to designer-clad clubbers. Take a little extra care here as **street crime** is a problem, mainly involving bag snatching

GUATEMALA CITY CATHEDRAL

Highlights

❶ **Museo Ixchel** A terrific museum dedicated to Guatemalan textiles and weaving traditions. See page 61

❷ **Museo Nacional de Arqueología y Etnología** One of the world's most important collections of Maya sculptures and artefacts with a particularly fine selection from Piedras Negras. See page 62

❸ **Volcán de Pacaya** Trek up an active volcano and get up close and personal with lava flows. See page 70

❹ **Centro Histórico** Explore the capital's historic centre on foot, taking in the huge Parque Central and some impressive architecture. See page 55

❺ **Antigua's colonial architecture** A stunning legacy of Baroque churches, colonial mansions and graceful plazas that form a World Heritage Site. See page 72

❻ **Semana Santa, Antigua** Witnessing the sombre ceremony and processions of the continent's most fervent Easter celebrations is an unforgettable experience. See page 78

❼ **Antigua dining** Antigua's restaurant scene is vibrant and eclectic, with everything from gourmet French to authentic Guatemalan. See page 83

HIGHLIGHTS ARE MARKED ON THE MAP ON PAGE 54

– be particularly careful at transport terminals – and use taxis to get around after 8pm. Gang violence is a serious issue in the poor outer suburbs, though this is highly unlikely to concern travellers.

Brief history

The pre-conquest Maya city of **Kaminaljuyú**, its ruins still scattered among the western suburbs, emerged as an important settlement as far back as 800 BC. By the time of Christ it was a thriving Maya city. During Early Classic times (250–600 AD) it was allied with the great northern power of Teotihuacán (near present-day Mexico City) and controlled key trade routes.

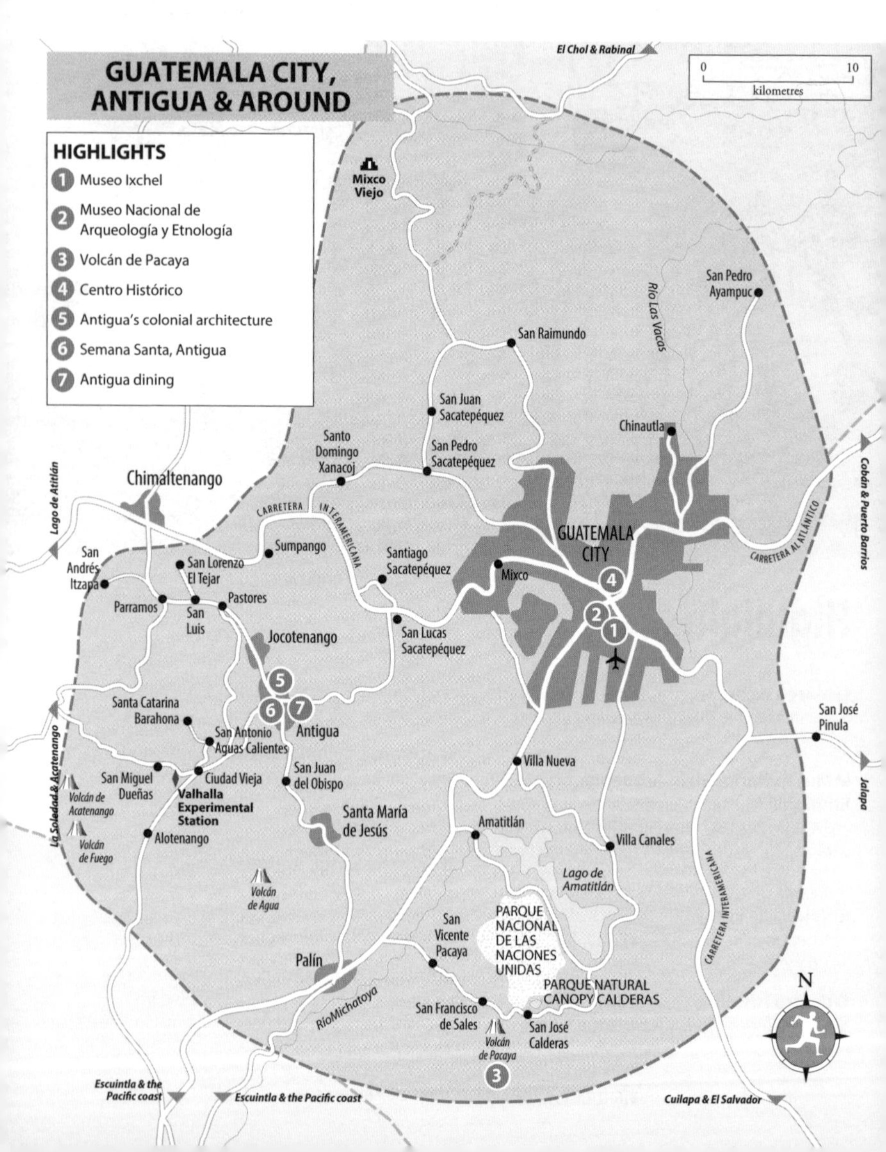

At the height of its prosperity, Kaminaljuyú was home to a population of some fifty thousand and dominated the surrounding highlands. But, following the decline of Teotihuacán around 600 AD, it was surpassed by the great lowland centres, and by around 700 AD it was abandoned.

Colonial era

Eight centuries later, following months of devastating earthquakes, the Spanish were forced to flee Antigua and established a new capital at Guatemala City's present site. Early development was slow: the 1863 census listed just 1206 residences. One of the factors affecting the city's growth was the existence of a major rival, Quetzaltenango, which competed with the capital in both size and importance. But in 1902 Quetzaltenango was razed to the ground by a massive earthquake, and subsequently Guatemala City became unquestionably the country's primary city.

The twentieth century to today

After recovering from more devastating seismic activity in 1917, Guatemala City has grown at an incredible rate, the flight from the fields escalating in the 1970s and 1980s as waves of internal refugees sought an escape from the civil war in the countryside. **Economic migrants** high on hope continue to flock to the capital, the resultant population explosion filling once-uninhabited deep ravines with precariously situated new barrios.

The last few years have seen a concerted effort to boost civic pride, improve transport, add greenery and address pollution. Though the overriding issue of security remains a key concern, a more appealing vision of the future is emerging, with successful initiatives like the Transmetro bus system and Paseo Cayala (an open-air mall) a sign of progress.

Zona 1

The hub of the old city is **Zona 1**, which is also the busiest part of town. This is the **centro histórico**, a world of low-slung, crumbling nineteenth-century townhouses and faceless concrete blocks, car parks, noise and dirt. Regeneration is steadily improving the district, particularly along recently pedestrianized Sexta Avenida where once-grand edifices have been renovated and new cafés have opened. In the **far south** of the zone the streets broaden and the architecture changes; this part of town contains a mix of buildings (including the impressive Teatro Nacional) from different eras.

Parque Central

An imposing plaza that forms the country's political and religious centre, the **Parque Central** is the point from which all distances in Guatemala are measured. This square, flanked by the grand **Palacio Nacional** and **cathedral**, was originally the scene of a huge central market. Today it's a good place to absorb city life as ladino and Indigenous *capitaleños* stroll, chat and snack and pigeons, shoe-shiners and raving Evangelicals jostle for space.

On the west side of the square is a concrete bandstand, the **Concha Acústica**, where marimba and classical music performances are staged twice weekly (Wed 4–6pm & Sat 3.30–5pm; free).

Palacio Nacional

Parque Central • Charge; includes 30min tour (roughly hourly) in English or Spanish • Ⓦ mcd.gob.gt/palacio-nacional-de-la-cultura • Transmetro Mercado Central

Presiding over the entire northern end of the main plaza is the gargantuan **Palacio Nacional**, built from green-hued stone in a mixture of Spanish colonial and Neoclassical styles. The palace was commissioned in 1939 under the auspices of President Ubico – a characteristically grand gesture from the man who believed that he was a reincarnation of Napoleon. For decades it housed the executive branch of the

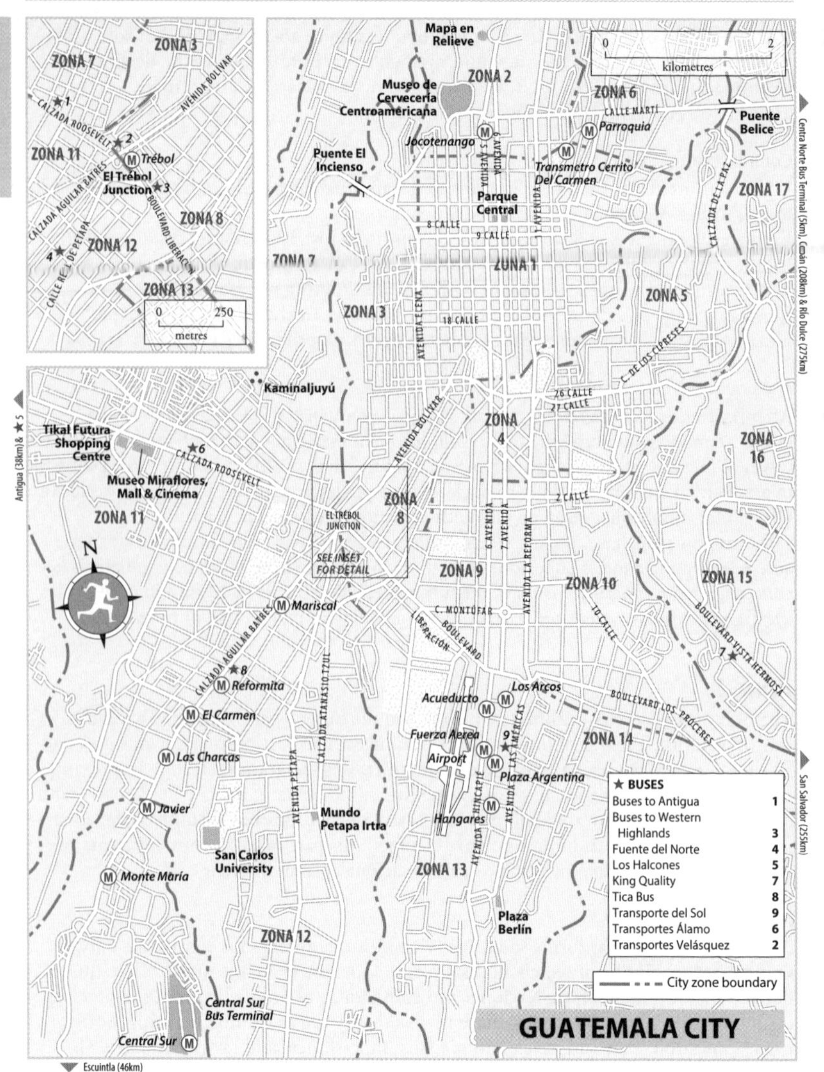

government, and periodically its steps have been fought over during assorted coups, but now it hosts cultural exhibitions.

The tour includes a look at the palace's two graceful Moorish-style courtyards and the grandiose **Salas de Recepción**, complete with stained-glass windows representing key aspects of Guatemalan history.

Guatemala City Catedral

Parque Central • Free • catedralbicentenaria.org • Transmetro Mercado Central

Completed in 1868, its grand facade merging the Baroque and the Neoclassical, Guatemala City's **Catedral** has a solid, squat form designed to resist the force of earthquakes and, for the most part, it has succeeded. In 1917 the bell towers were

GUATEMALA CITY: ZONAS 1 & 4
ACCOMMODATION
La Coperacha 1
Hotel Ajau 7
Hotel PanAmerican 2
Hotel Spring 4
El Poeta BnB 3
Posada Belén 5
Theatre International Hostel 6
EATING
Altuna 8
Café León 5
Chikach 1
La Discoteca Cafe y Musica 3
Flor de Lis 9
Long Wah 2
Rey Sol 6
Rocque Rosito 4
Saúl 7
DRINKING & NIGHTLIFE
Black Club 6
Las Cien Puertes 1
Genetic Majestic 7
El Gran Hotel 4
La Luna 3
El Portal 2
El Príncipe Gris 8
Soma 5
Trovajazz 9
BUSES
ADN 3
Fuente del Norte and other 1st/2nd class buses to Petén 4
Línea Dorada 2
Litegua 1
Rutas Orientales 6
Transportes Galgos 5
Museo Del Holocausto Guatemala (250 m), Parque Minerva & Mapa en Relieve (1.75km)
Trébol junction (1.25km) & Kaminaljuyú (3km)
Palacio Nacional
Mercado Central
Parque Centenario
PARQUE CENTRAL
National Library
La Catedral
Parque del Centenario
Cyber
Museo Nacional de Historia
Colón
Museo Nacional de Artes y Industrias Populares
Capuchinas
San Miguel de Capuchinas
Centro Cultural de España
San Agustín
Palacio de Correos
Correos
Iglesia de San Francisco
Police Headquarters
Casa Mima
Gómez Carrillo
Parque Concordia
Belén
ZONA 1
Tipografía
El Amate Plaza
Plaza Barrios
Museo del Ferrocarril
El Calvario
Mercado Sur Dos
San José Fortress
Municipal
Estadio Nacional Mario Flores
Teatro Nacional
Banco de Guatemala
Bolívar
Gran Centro Comercial
Santa Expiatorio
4 Grados Sur
IGA
CUATRO GRADOS NORTE
4 Grados Norte
Cultura Hispánica
Migración
Santa Cecilia
Exposición
Plaza de la República
ZONA 4
Iglesia Yurrita
Botanical Gardens
Torre del Reformador
Terminal
Ministerio de la Defensa Nacional

GUATEMALA CITY: ORIENTATION, ZONES AND ADDRESSES

Broadly speaking, the city divides into two distinct halves. The northern section mainly comprises **Zona 1**, the historic, if run-down part of town containing the main plaza, the Parque Central, some museums and many of the first-class bus company terminals. **Zona 2** even further north also has a couple of sights.

The modern half of the city is to the south, comprising **zonas 9 and 10**, which are separated by the main artery of Avenida La Reforma. Further south still, **zonas 13 and 14** hold wealthy, leafy suburbs and are home to the airport, a cluster of guesthouses and more museums and cinemas.

Zona 4 serves as a buffer between the two parts of town; here you'll find many civic buildings, the tourist office and the National Theatre.

ADDRESSES

When it comes to finding an address in the city, always check the **zone** first and then the street. For example "4 Av 9–14, Zona 1" is in Zona 1, on 4 Avenida between 9 and 10 calles ("4 Av 3–14" would be between 3 and 4 calles), house number 14. You may see street numbers written as 1a, 7a etc, rather than simply 1, 7. This is technically more correct, since the names of the streets are not One Avenue and Seven Street, but First (*primera*), Seventh (*séptima*) and so on. A capital "A" used as a suffix indicates a smaller street between two large ones: 1 C A is a short street between 1 and 2 calles.

brought down and the cupola fell, destroying the altar, but the central structure, though cracked and patched up over the years, has remained intact. Inside there are three main aisles, all lined with arching pillars, austere colonial paintings and intricate altars supporting an array of saints.

The cathedral's most poignant aspect is found outside: etched into the pillars that support the entrance railings are the names of thousands of the "**disappeared**", victims of the civil war, including an astounding number from the department of El Quiché.

Mercado Central

8 C & 8 Av • Free • Transmetro Mercado Central

At the rear of the cathedral is the hulking **Mercado Central**, which replaced a building destroyed in the 1976 earthquake. Taking no chances, the architect apparently modelled the structure on a nuclear bunker, sacrificing any aesthetic concerns to the need for strength. Inside you'll find a good selection of handicrafts from across the country: textiles, leatherware, ceramics and basketry as well as fruit, vegetables and flowers. In the basement there's a fine selection of cheap and authentic **food stalls**, snack stands and juice bars.

Museo Nacional de Historia

9 C 9–70 • Charge • mcd.gob.gt/museo-nacional-de-historia • Transmetro Mercado Central

Southeast of the market, the **Museo Nacional de Historia** features a selection of artefacts relating to Guatemalan history, including documents, clothes, paintings and even a conquistador's sword or two, though there's no information in English. Probably the most interesting displays are the photographs by Eadweard Muybridge, famed for his studies of human and animal motion, who, in 1875, was one of the first people to undertake a study of the country.

Museo del Holocausto Guatemala

6 Av 1–88 • Free • mdh.org.gt • Transmetro San Sebastián

Dedicated to the Nazi Holocaust, this museum opened in 2016 and has excellent if harrowing displays, in English and Spanish, about the genocide of Jewish and Roma people in Europe.

Sexta Avenida

6 Av between Parque Central & 18 C

The city's main commercial artery for decades, **Sexta Avenida** was lined with glamorous department stores, cinemas and cafés during its heyday in the late nineteenth century. People from all over the city would promenade the Sexta to see and be seen. But the character of the street took a downturn in the 1980s, as stalls choked the pavements and the grand stores and cinemas closed.

In 2009, the city authorities implemented a renovation programme, clearing the street traders, planting trees and pedestrianizing the entire avenida (bicycles are permitted) between the Parque Central and 18 Calle, making Sexta a delight to stroll once again. Be sure to stop by the well-kept **Parque Concordia**, take in the elaborate facade of the **Iglesia de San Francisco** and admire the Art Deco **Teatro Lux** building as you explore the street.

Palacio de Correos

7 Av 11–67 • Free • Ⓦ correosytelegrafos.civ.gob.gt • Transmetro Correos

The Baroque post office, the **Palacio de Correos**, is one of the city's most arresting structures, with an elaborate terracotta-and-cream facade and decorative bridge that spans 12 Calle. It also doubles as a cultural centre, home to theatre groups and dance academies.

Casa Mima

8 Av 14–12 • Charge • Ⓣ 5620 3907 • Transmetro Belén

Casa Mima is an immaculately restored late nineteenth-century townhouse with original furnishings from various design movements, including Art Nouveau. The decor offers a fascinating glimpse into a wealthy household, with lavish rooms kitted out with gilded mirrors, chandeliers, oriental rugs, hand-painted wallpaper and curios including a gloriously detailed dolls' house and a ninety-year-old "talking machine" (a gramophone). The house even has a private chapel complete with a fabulous wooden altar.

Museo del Ferrocarril

9 Av 18–03 • Charge • Ⓣ 2208 4747 • Transmetro Plaza Barrios

Occupying a splendidly renovated old train station – Guatemala City's main station until it mysteriously burned down in 1996 – the excellent **Museo del Ferrocarril** is dedicated to the history of Guatemalan railways. Passenger trains may no longer run in Guatemala, but you can get a great perspective on how the old network functioned here. You'll find several old steam engines and carriages to clamber over and examine, plus rooms stuffed with railway curiosities including staff uniforms and tickets. Also on show are several lovingly polished classic cars.

Teatro National

24 C 3–81 • Charge for guided tours of building in Spanish, book ahead • Ⓦ mcd.gob.gt/centro-cultural-miguel-angel-asturias • Transmetro Centro Cívico

Perched on a hill in the far south of Zona 1, the landmark **Teatro Nacional**, also known as the Miguel Ángel Asturias Cultural Centre, is one of the city's most prominent and unusual structures. Completed in 1978 and designed by the late Guatemalan architect (and artist) Efraín Recinos, its form evokes a huge ship, painted blue and white, with portholes for windows. The interior is equally impressive: its stunning main theatre complete with balconies finished in gold lacquer is breathtaking. Don't miss the modernist chandelier, which evokes a model of a molecular structure, in the lobby.

The complex, which also includes an open-air theatre and gardens with quirky concrete seating, was built over the ruins of the **San José Fortress**, a nineteenth-century castle that was all but destroyed during the 1944 revolution.

Zona 2

North of the old city centre is **Zona 2**, bounded by a deep-cut ravine. There are a couple of attractions in this (mainly residential) district.

Mapa en Relieve

Av Simeón Cañas Final • Charge • T 3377 9999 • Transmetro Hipódromo del Norte

About 2km north of the Parque Central, the slightly kitsch **Mapa en Relieve**, a relief map of Guatemala, covers 2500 square metres and has a couple of viewing towers.

Its vertical scale is out of proportion to the horizontal, making the mountains look incredibly steep. It does nevertheless give you a good idea of the general layout of the country, from the ruggedness of the highlands to the sheer size of Petén.

Museo de Cervecería Centroamericana

3 Av Norte Final, Finca El Zapote • Free • W cerveceriacentroamericana.com

Cervecería Centroamericana, Guatemala's largest brewery, has been producing Gallo beer at this factory in the north of the city for 125 years. Today, around a dozen inoffensive beers are brewed here, including the lagers Dorada, Victoria, Montecarlo and Gallo. The **Museo de Cervecería Centroamericana**, containing some interesting antique curios and photographs related to the history of beer-making in Guatemala is diverting enough, but the highly informative tour is even better, allowing you access to the plant so you can gaze into the vast stainless steel vats and view the bottling process. The tour finishes, appropriately, with a glass or two of complimentary amber nectar.

Zona 4

To the south, Zona 1 merges into **Zona 4** around the **Centro Cívico**. This collection of concrete multistorey administrative buildings, mainly dating from the 1960s, includes the **Banco de Guatemala** on 7 Avenida, which is bedecked with bold modern murals and stylized glyphs recounting Guatemala's history. The zone also contains the main **tourist office**, Inguat, on 7 Avenida (see page 66).

Iglesia Yurrita

Ruta 6 8–52 • Free • T 2360 7920 • Transmetro Torre del Reformador

An outlandish building designed in an exotic neo-Gothic style, the **Iglesia Yurrita** seems to belong more to a horror movie set than the streets of Guatemala City. The interior contains a fabulous carved wooden altar – just as wild as the exterior. Iglesia Yurrita was finally completed in 1944, forty years after it was originally commissioned as a private chapel by the rich philanthropist Felipe Yurrite Casteñeda. His house, in the same style, stands alongside and is now a restaurant: Casa Yurrita.

Zonas 9 and 10

Directly south of Zona 4, these neighbouring zones are split down the middle by Avenida La Reforma: Zona 9 is to the west and Zona 10 on the east. **Zona 9** is a mixed suburb of middle-class housing, a hotel or two and an eclectic assortment of businesses and few sights. **Zona 10** forms one of the smartest parts of town, taking in a couple of excellent museums and **Zona Viva**, an upmarket enclave of hotels, restaurants and bars.

Torre del Reformador

7 Av & 2 C, Zona 9 • Free • Transmetro Torre del Reformador

The **Torre del Reformador**, Guatemala's answer to the Eiffel Tower, is a steel structure built along the lines of the Parisian model. It was constructed in honour of President Barrios, who transformed the country between 1871 and 1885; a bell at the top is rung every year on June 30 to commemorate the Liberal victory in the 1871 revolution.

Botanical Gardens

C Mariscal Cruz 1–56, Zona 10 • Charge • jardinbotanico.usac.edu.gt • Transmetro Torre del Reformador

The city's small but pretty **Botanical Gardens** contain a selection of species, many neatly labelled in Spanish and Latin. In the grounds, there's also an anachronistic **natural history museum**, with a collection of mouldy stuffed birds, which include a quetzal, and curios such as swordfish swords and some horrific pickled rodents.

Museo Ixchel

6 C Final, Zona 10 • Charge; includes entrance to Museo Popol Vuh • museoixchel.org

The capital's best-organized museum, the **Museo Ixchel** is dedicated to Maya culture, with particular emphasis on traditional weaving. It contains a stunning array of hand-woven fabrics, including some very impressive examples of ceremonial costumes. There's also information (in Spanish and English) about the techniques, dyes, fibres and the way in which costumes have changed over the years. Weavers

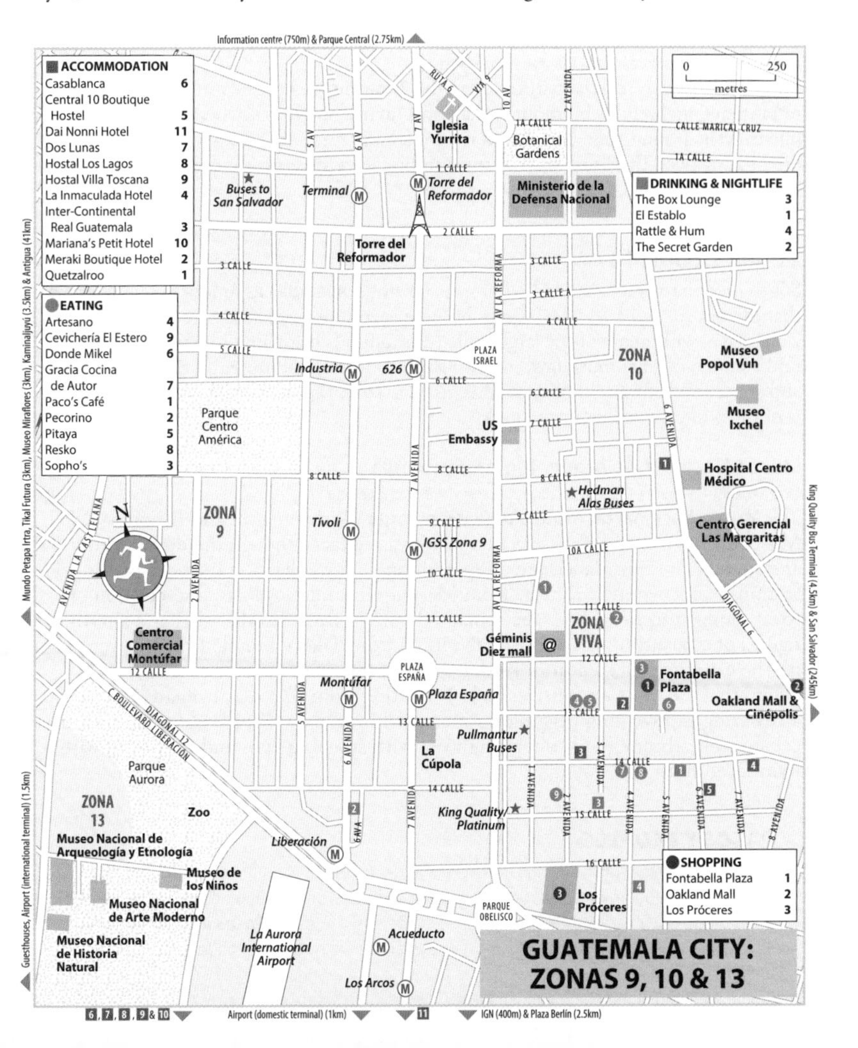

can usually be seen in action and there's a permanent exhibition of paintings by Guatemalan artists Andrés Curruchich (1891–1969), who painted scenes of rural life around San Juan Comalapa, and Carmen Pettersen (born 1900), who depicted traditional costumes on canvas.

Museo Popol Vuh

6 C Final, Zona 10 • Charge; includes entrance to Museo Ixchel • Ⓦ popolvuh.ufm.edu

Next to the Museo Ixchel, the **Museo Popol Vuh** has a small but outstanding collection of artefacts from archeological sites all over the country. The Preclassic room contains some Olmec ceramics and sculptures from Kaminaljuyú, while highlights of the Classic section include an altar from Naranjo and some demonic-looking incense burners. In the Postclassic room is a replica of the Dresden Codex, one of only three extant pre-conquest Maya books, while the colonial era is represented by assorted ecclesiastical relics and processional crosses.

Zona Viva

Zona 10, centred around 10 C and 3 Av • Transmetro Plaza España

The swankiest commercial part of town, the **Zona Viva** is a prosperous area of restaurants, nightclubs, boutiques, malls and luxury hotels. It's generally considered safe to walk around here at night, so it's not a bad option if you want to get a meal and hit a bar or two. This area, and the surrounding leafy streets is the natural playground for the nation's elite.

Zonas 12 and 13

South of Zona Viva, Avenida La Reforma becomes **Avenida Las Américas**, a boulevard that divides zonas 13 and 14. Things become even more exclusive here than in the Zona Viva, with many of the large walled compounds belonging to embassies. You'll find a clutch of state **museums**, including the archeological museum, the airport, zoo and some excellent guesthouses in this district; **Zona 12**, meanwhile, to the northwest, is of most interest for its theme park.

Museo Nacional de Arqueología y Etnología

6 C & 7 Av, Zona 13 • Charge • Ⓦ artemaya.culturaguate.com • Transmetro Acueducto

The **Museo Nacional de Arqueología y Etnología** (Archeological and Ethnological Museum) has a world-class selection of Maya artefacts, though the displays are antiquated, and most labels are in Spanish only. The collection includes prehistoric sections, some wonderful stelae from Machaquilá and Dos Pilas, a re-creation of a royal tomb from Río Azul, spectacular jade masks from Takalik Abaj and a terrific replica of a beautifully carved wooden lintel from Tikal's Temple IV. However, it's the exhibits collected from Piedras Negras, one of the most remote sites in Petén, that are most impressive: Stela 12, dating from 672 AD, brilliantly depicts a cowering captive king begging for mercy, while also on display is a monumental carved stone throne (J-6), richly engraved with superb glyphs and decorated with a twin-faced head.

PASOS Y PEDALES

On Sundays (8am–2pm), Avenida La Reforma and Avenida Las Américas, its extension to the south, are closed to motorized traffic as joggers, cyclists, skateboarders and street performers flood the streets in a fiesta-esque atmosphere. The scheme, called **Pasos y Pedales** ("Steps and Pedals") attracts 15,000 people most weeks, and has also been extended to five other areas in the capital's suburbs.

Museo Nacional de Arte Moderno

6 C & 7 Av, Zona 13 • Charge • mcd.gob.gt/museo-de-arte-moderno-carlos-merida • Transmetro Acueducto

Opposite the archeological museum, the **Museo Nacional de Arte Moderno**, which also suffers from poor presentation, boasts some imaginative geometric paintings by Dagoberto Vásquez and a collection of startling exhibits by Efraín Recinos (1928–2011), including a colossal marimba-tank sculpture. The permanent collection also holds a selection of bold Cubist art and massive murals by **Carlos Mérida**, Guatemala's most celebrated artist, which draw strongly on ancient Maya tradition.

Museo Nacional de Historia Natural

6 C & 7 Av, Zona 13 • Charge • mcd.gob.gt/museo-nacional-de-historia-natural • Transmetro Acueducto

The **Museo Nacional de Historia Natural** has a neglected air about it. It features a range of scraggy-looking stuffed animals from Guatemala and elsewhere as well as a few mineral samples.

Parque Aurora zoo

5 C, Zona 13 • Charge • aurorazoo.org.gt • Transmetro Acueducto

The city's **zoo** is quite impressive, with animals divided into three main geographical zones. You'll find lions, hippos and giraffes in the African section; Bengal tigers, Indian elephants and the reticulated python (the world's longest snake) in the Asian area; tapirs, monkeys, and virtually all the continent's big cats, including some well-fed jaguars, in the Americas region. The zoo is also open on full moon nights, which is an excellent time to see nocturnal animals.

Museo de los Niños

5 C 10–00, Zona 13 • Charge • museodelosninos.com.gt • Transmetro Acueducto

The **Museo de los Niños** (Children's Museum) is slightly more recreational than educational, with a huge ball-game room and trampolines as well as an operating theatre display and a hands-on music room.

Mundo Petapa Irtra

Av Petapa 42–36, Zona 12 • Charge • irtra.org.gt

Mundo Petapa Irtra, an excellent theme park in the southwest suburbs of Zona 12, scores highly for thrills and spills with some excellent rides, a ferris wheel, mini-zoo and large swimming pool as well as picnic areas and snack bars. Thursday is by far the least busy time to visit.

Zonas 7 and 11: Kaminaljuyú

23 Av, Zona 7 • Charge • mcd.gob.gt/kaminal-juyu

Way out on the western edge of the capital, the modest ruins of **Kaminaljuyú** are all that's left of a Maya city that once housed around fifty thousand people and thirteen ball courts. Unlike the massive temples of the lowlands, these structures were built of adobe, and most have been lost to erosion and urban sprawl. Today the archeological site is little more than a series of earth-covered mounds and a favourite spot for footballers and romantic couples. A couple of sections have been cut into by archeologists, but it's virtually impossible to get any impression of Kaminaljuyú's former scale and splendour – for that you'll have to visit the Miraflores museum.

Museo Miraflores

Calzada Roosevelt, Zona 11 • Charge • museomiraflores.org.gt

A ten-minute walk south of the ruins, the excellent modern **Museo Miraflores** details the history of Kaminaljuyú (in English and Spanish) and its importance as a trading centre. Exhibits include striking stone sculptures and stelae pieces, ceramics,

1

A BRIEF HISTORY OF KAMINALJUYÚ

First settled as far back as 1000 BC, **Kaminaljuyú** had grown to huge proportions by 100 AD, featuring some two hundred flat-topped **pyramids**. Beneath each of these structures lay entombed a member of the nobility; a few have been unearthed to reveal the wealth and sophistication of the culture. The power of the city faded throughout the second and third centuries, but there was a renaissance after 400 AD when the Guatemalan highlands fell under the domination of Teotihuacán in central Mexico. The invaders prized Kaminaljuyú for its access to nearby obsidian mines and trade routes, but the fall of Teotihuacán around 600 AD weakened the city, resulting in its eventual demise.

impressive jade jewellery, obsidian flints and a scale model of Kaminaljuyú. The grounds encompass several temple mounds, one of which has been penetrated by a tunnel that leads to a chamber boasting a noble's tomb and some spectacular artefacts.

ARRIVAL AND DEPARTURE GUATEMALA CITY

Arriving in Guatemala City is always a bit disconcerting. Wherever you arrive, you should take a taxi to your destination in the city (unless it's a block or two away), or use the Transmetro bus.

BY PLANE

Aurora airport (dgac.gob.gt) is in Zona 13, some way south of the centre, but close to Zona 10. It's a slick, modern airport with good facilities including numerous cafés and duty-free stores.

Transport into the city The easiest way to get to and from the airport is by taxi: you can pre-pay your fare from a taxi desk; to Zona 10 costs about US$15, Zona 1 around US$20. Uber cabs work out at roughly half regular taxi rates. Virtually all Guatemala City's four- and five-star hotels, as well as the guesthouses in Zona 13, offer free pick-ups from the airport, if you let them know when you're arriving. Don't risk the city buses that leave from outside the airport because of security concerns. There's no Transmetro stop within walking distance of the airport.

Getting to Antigua Regular shuttle buses run to Antigua from the airport (roughly US$12/person, three minimum) until about 10pm. A taxi to Antigua from the airport is about US$40, Uber cab around $25.

Currency exchange Note that all the official-looking Global Exchange currency exchange booths offer derisory rates (25 percent lower than the banks') and represent a total scam. Seek out the Banrural bank in Arrivals instead, where you can change US dollars (or euros) at fair rates. There's also an ATM.

Airport taxes Taxes are always included in the price of your ticket.

BY BUS

First-class buses Travelling by first-class (pullman) bus, you'll arrive at the private depot of the company you're using (most are in Zona 1 or 10) or the huge Centra Norte terminal in the northeast of the city. Note that many Zona 1 depots are located in an unsavoury part of the city; be on your guard for petty thieves.

Second-class buses "Chicken buses" use two main transport hubs. Buses for the western highlands use bus stops (there's no terminal) at 41 C between 7 Av and 11 Av, Zona 8, which is very close to Trébol Transmetro stop. All buses for southern Guatemala (including the border with El Salvador, Monterrico, Retalhuleu and the Mexican border) plus Santiago Atitlán use the Centra Sur terminal (also known as Centro de Mayorio) in Zona 12. This has a Transmetro stop directly above it and security guards. Note that from Antigua it's far easier, quicker and safer to take a shuttle bus; but it is possible to connect with second-class services at Trébol Transmetro stop.

Domestic destinations Antigua (second-class from 21 C & 2 Av, Zona 3, via Trébol junction, every 10min until 6.30pm; 1hr–1hr 30min); Chichicastenango (second-class from 41 C, Zona 8, every 30min; 3hr); Chiquimula (RO every 30min until 7pm; L 4 daily; 3hr 30min); Cobán (MB hourly; 5hr); El Florido border (L 1 daily at 6pm; 4hr 45min); Esquipulas (RO every 30min until 8pm); Flores (FN 17 daily, LD 3 daily, ADN 2 daily; 8–9hr); Huehuetenango (LD 1 daily, LH 6 daily, TV 5 daily; 5hr 30min); La Mesilla (LD 1 daily, LH 2 daily; 7hr 30min); Monterrico (second-class from Centra Sur, 2 daily; 3hr 30min; or travel via Iztapa which has hourly onward connections); Nebaj (second-class from 41 C, Zona 8, 6 daily; 5hr 15min); Panajachel (second-class from 21 C & 1 Av Zona 1 via 41 C, Zona 8, 8 daily until 4.30pm; 3hr 30min); Puerto Barrios (L 17 daily, 5hr 30min–6hr 30min); Poptún (take a Flores bus; 7hr); Quetzaltenango (TA 6 daily, FN 2 daily, LD -2 daily, TG 3 daily; 4hr); Río Dulce Town (L 5 daily; 5hr – or catch a Flores bus); San Pedro La Laguna (second-class from 41 C, Zona 8, 8 daily; 3hr 45min); Santiago Atitlán (second-class from Centra Sur, 10 daily; 3hr); Tecún Umán (FN 6 daily; 6hr).

International destinations Copán, Honduras (HA 1 daily at 4.30pm; 6hr 30min); La Ceiba, Honduras (HA 1 daily at 4.30am; 12hr); Managua, Nicaragua (TS 1 daily at 2am, TB 2 daily; 18–28hr); San Pedro Sula, Honduras (FD 1 daily, HA 1 daily, RO 2 daily; 9–11hr); San Salvador, El Salvador (TS 2 daily, TB 1 daily, P 3–4 daily, KQ 2 daily, TG 1 daily; 5hr), Tapachula, Mexico (TB 1 daily, TG 2 daily; 6hr), Tegucigalpa, Honduras (HA 1 daily 4.30pm; 13hr; or travel via a stopover in San Salvador, around 36hr in total with P (1 daily) or TB (1 daily).

BY CAR

Car rental Two good local companies are Tabarini, 2 C A 7–30, Zona 10 (T 2444 2400, W tabarini.com) and Adaesa, 4 C A 16–57, Zona 1 (T 2220 2180, W adaesa.com).

GETTING AROUND

It's best to avoid all city buses other than the **Transmetro** and Transurbano due to **security** concerns, and always take **taxis** after dark.

BY BUS

Guatemala City has an excellent rapid transit bus network, the Transmetro, which operates on dedicated bus lanes that are closed to all other traffic making it by far the fastest way around the city. There are currently five routes; more are planned. Transmetro articulated buses are modern, a/c, wheelchair-friendly and only stop every kilometre or so. Transport police provide security. No food or drinks are permitted on board.

Tickets Transmetro tickets are cheap and payable in cash at the station before boarding.

Orange line (Line 12) Connects Plaza Barrios and the Centro Cívico with points to the southwest, along Av Bolívar via the Trébol junction and down to the Centra Sur bus terminal. It's useful for passengers on second-class buses to and from the highlands who want to connect with Zona 1, and operates from 4.30am till 10pm (Sat & Sun 4.30am–9pm).

Green line (Line 13) Runs north–south from Plaza Barrios, 18 C in Zona 1, along 6 Av through zonas 4 and 9 to Zona 13, returning along 7 Av; buses run between 5am until 9pm (weekends 5am–8pm).

Purple line (Lines 1 & 2) This does a loop through Zona 1 north of Tipografía station to the Hipódromo del North (for the Mapa en Relieve).

Blue line (Line 18) connects the distant Centra Norte bus terminal with Plaza Barrios in Zona 1.

The **Yellow Line** is not really of use for travellers.

Transurbano Transurbano buses are slower and not as modern as Transmetro, and do not run on designated lanes, but are considered safe by locals. The huge drawback with these services is that to use them you have to obtain a SIGA travel card (free; available at stations including Plaza Barrios and Centra Norte), for which you'll have to present your passport. One of the most useful is Ruta 311V, which connects the Centra Norte bus terminal with Zona 1.

BY TAXI

Metered taxis Metered taxis include Amarillo (T 2470 1515).

Non-metered taxis Widely available but not properly regulated and therefore there are some security risks using them.

Ride-hailing apps Uber operates across the city. Rates are very reasonable: about half of those charged by metered taxis.

BUS COMPANIES IN GUATEMALA CITY

Fuente del Norte (FN) has two terminals: 17 C 8–46, Zona 1 (for Petén and Honduras) and Calzada Aguilar Batres 7–55, Zona 12 (for Tecún Uman border) (W transportesfuentedelnorte.com/en).

Hedman Alas (HA) 2 Av 8–73, Zona 10 (W hedmanalas.com).

Comfort Premium (KQ) 4 Av 13–60, Zona 10 (W comfortpremium.com).

Línea Dorada (LD) 16 C 10–03, Zona 1 (T 2415 8900).

Litegua (L) 15 C 10–40, Zona 1 & Centra Norte (T 2326 9400).

Los Halcones (LH) Calzada Roosevelt 37–47, Zona 11 (T 2433 9180).

Monja Blanca (MB) Centra Norte (W monjablanca.com).

Pullmantur (P) Based at *Holiday Inn*, 1 Av 13–22, Zona 10 (W pullmantur.com).

Rutas Orientales (RO) 21 C 11–60, Zona 1 & Centra Norte (W rutasorientales.com).

Tica Bus (TB) Calzada Aguilar Batres 18–35, Zona 12 (W ticabus.com).

Transportes Álamo (TA) 12 Av A 0–65, Zona 7 (W transportesalamo.com).

Transportes Galgos (TG) 7 Av 19–44, Zona 1 (T 2220 6018).

Transporte del Sol (TS) *Hotel Crowne Plaza*, Av Las Américas 9–08, Zona 13 (W transportedelsol.com).

Transportes Velásquez (TV) 0 C 31–70, Zona 7 (T 4053 9687).

1

INFORMATION AND TOURS

Tourist information The main Inguat tourist office (inguat.gob.gt) is at 7 Av 1–17, Zona 4, and has English-speaking staff and plenty of brochures.

Tours *Quetzalroo* (see page 66) offers an excellent bike tour of the city (charge). Non-guests are welcome to join; book ahead. Clark Tours, 7 Av 14–76, Zona 9 (clarktours.com.gt) offer half- and full-day bus tours.

Travel agents Viajes Tivoli, 6 Av 8–41, Zona 9 (viajestivoli.com), is a good all-round agent offering tours across Guatemala and selling airline tickets.

ACCOMMODATION

You'll pay more for a bed in the capital than in the rest of Guatemala. **Zona 1** is not a great area to be hunting for a room late at night, but it's safe enough in the day and early evening. Many travellers stay close to the airport, in **Zona 13**, where there are some good options – virtually all offer free airport pick-ups and drop-offs, though be sure to book ahead and note there are no restaurants or cafés close by. Upmarket hotels (and the odd hostel) are clustered together in a relatively safe part of town, in **Zona 10**, within reach of the **Zona Viva**, where there's a glut of restaurants and bars.

ZONAS 1 & 2

La Coperacha 4 Av 2–03 5855 2950; map page 57. Sociable hostel run by welcoming Guatemalans. It has a boho feel, bikes for rent, good travel information and a filling complimentary breakfast. It's a 15min walk from the Parque Central. Dorms $, doubles $$

Hotel Ajau 8 Av 15–62 hotelajau.net; map page 57. Right in the heart of the city, this Art Nouveau hotel has a traditional ambience and very helpful staff. The 45 rooms, all with TVs, are well scrubbed, if a little bare; many are en suite. There's a comedor for breakfast and evening meals. $$

Hotel PanAmerican 9 C 5–63 2244 0850.gt; map page 57. Historic hotel a block from the Parque Central, with a strong Guatemalan identity. The sixty spacious rooms are a little dated, but spacious, and rates include a filling breakfast in the stately *Restaurante Salón Real*. $$$$

Hotel Spring 8 Av 12–65 hotelspring.com; map page 57. Large, dependable budget lodge with over forty clean, functional rooms. There's a pretty courtyard and café for socializing, laundry service and drinking water. $$

El Poeta BnB 10 Av 9–49 5579 7451; map page 57. Well set-up, this spot has six decent and clean rooms. A very generous cooked breakfast is included. There's free filtered water and it's close to all Zona 1's attractions. $$

Posada Belén 13 C A 10–30 5702 6737; map page 57. This peaceful refuge is run by the hospitable Sanchinelli family and occupies a beautiful old building, with a gorgeous garden patio and plenty of quiet areas for reading. Excellent home-cooked meals are served in the stately dining room. No children under 5. $$$

Theatre International Hostel 8 Av 14–17 4202 5112; map page 57. Party hostel where guests score access to a hot tub, ample lounging areas, a kitchen and a courtyard. However, old timers should heed its ageist rules (over-45s are barred!). Dorms $, doubles $$

ZONA 10

★ **Central 10 Boutique Hostel** 6 Av 14–49, Zona 10 2293 4124; map page 61. This excellent travellers' hangout sets new standards in the capital with its contemporary decor and pool. Bunk beds have private lockers, curtains and power sockets and staff are switched on and welcoming. Dorms $, doubles $$

★ **La Inmaculada Hotel** 14 C 7–88 inmaculadahotel.com; map page 61. This boutique place offers modernist decor, an enviable location on the edge of the Zona Viva and high service standards. The thirteen rooms are kitted out in real style with luxury bedding, LCD TVs, L'Occitane toiletries and impressive attention to detail. There's a restaurant, peaceful garden to enjoy and rates include airport transfers. $$$$

Inter-Continental Real Guatemala 14 C 2–51 ihg.com; map page 61. Luxury hotel in the heart of the Zona Viva, where the palatial rooms, many with sweeping city views, boast great beds and Egyptian cotton sheets. You'll find French, Japanese and international restaurants, plus a (small) heated outdoor pool. $$$$

Meraki Boutique Hotel 13 C 3–57 2331 4320, booking.com; map page 61. Stylish, modern boutique hotel where the rooms boast fine-quality furnishings and bedding. It's a short walk from everything in Zona 10 and staff are super-helpful. $$$$

★ **Quetzalroo** 6 Av 7–84 quetzalroo.com; map page 61. Deservedly one of the most popular hostels in the city, with a fine location close to the Zona Viva. There's a fun, communal vibe, good accommodation, three shower rooms, a guests' kitchen, TV lounge and laundry. Rides to the airport (or bus terminal) transportation are included. Excellent bike tours (see page 66) of the city are offered too. Dorms $, doubles $$

ZONA 13

Casablanca 15 C 7–35 hotelcasablancainn.com; map page 61. Tasteful guesthouse in a tranquil location with comfortable accommodation. All rooms are light, airy and spacious, with bathrooms (most en suite). There's a well-stocked bar and an attractive sitting room. Breakfast and airport transfers included in rates. $$$

Dai Nonni Hotel 5 Av A 5–30 dainonnihotel.com; map page 61. In a peaceful residential area, this attractive B&B offers comfort and cleanliness with well-presented, modern rooms. Staff are welcoming and helpful and there's a choice of four set (complimentary) breakfasts. $$$

★ **Dos Lunas** 21 C 10–92 hoteldoslunas.com; map page 61. A home from home for travellers, this very efficiently run and welcoming guesthouse is owned and managed by Guatemalteca Lorena and her Dutch husband Henk. Rooms are spotless and attractively presented and rates include free airport transfers, and a great breakfast. Tourist and transportation advice is second to none. Book well ahead. Dorms $, doubles $$

Hostal Los Lagos 8 Av 15–85 loslagoshostal.com; map page 61. Just 400m from the airport, this guesthouse has good-quality rooms and dorms. Staff are friendly and informative; free airport transfers are offered. Dorms $, doubles $$$

★ **Hostal Villa Toscana** 16 C 8–20 hostalvillatoscana.com; map page 61. A classy B&B with stylish, very well-presented rooms, all with cable TV; no. 9 has a balcony, and the suite has a private terrace. Wi-fi is efficient, as are the staff and there's a pleasant garden to enjoy. $$$

Mariana's Petit Hotel 20 C 10–17 marianaspetithotel.com; map page 61. A welcoming guesthouse very close to the airport with inexpensive rates, clean rooms, a quiet location and free airport transfers. There are books to browse and a terrace for drinks and dining. $$

EATING

In **Zona 1** you'll find a great selection of inexpensive places to eat, with lunchtime a particularly good time for a filling feed. Excellent set-price, three-course menus are available; try the streets west of the Parque Central. For really cheap, tasty eats head to the stalls inside the **Mercado Central** (see page 58). International options – including steak houses, and Asian and European places – are grouped together in the **Zona Viva** (Zone 10). Cafés serving espresso-style coffee and snacks are found all over the city.

ZONA 1

★ **Altuna** 5 Av 12–31 restaurantealtuna.com; map page 57. Elegant, formal and expensive Spanish restaurant rich in ambience serving terrific fish and seafood such as *bacalao con pimientos a la Vasca* (Basque-style salt cod with pepper sauce), as well as succulent meat cuts and imported Iberian hams and cheeses. There's also a good tapas menu (Tues–Sat evenings only). You'll find a second branch in Zona 10 at 10 C 0–45. $$$$

★ **Café León** 8 Av 9–15 tclgt.com; map page 57. Atmospheric old-school café with gleaming espresso machines and vintage photographs that's a downtown headquarters for Guatemalan intellectuals and characters. Most are here to linger over a treacle-thick espresso, milky *café con leche* or one of the regional coffees (from across Guatemala) though there are also good breakfasts, cakes (*cubiletes*, empanadas), sandwiches and refreshing *raspado* (iced lime juice). There's a second Zona 1 branch at 12 C 6–23. $$

Chikach 3 C 4–24 chikach.com; map page 57. For healthy vegetarian food, including salads and veggie burgers, burritos and dishes made from amaranth grain look no further than this inviting little café. Also home to a store, for all your natural product needs (soaps, lotions and even black salt from Quiché). $

La Discoteca Cafe y Musica, 9 C 4–69 cafediscoteca.com; map page 57. A welcoming café that (as the name suggests) marries coffee and disco. Also boasts an outstanding selection of teas and desserts. $

Long Wah 6 C 3–75 longwah.com; map page 57. Affordable Chinese restaurant, consistently recommended by locals with a menu that includes *wontons* and *chow mein*. They also offer food to go. $$

Rey Sol 11 C 5–51 2232 3516, facebook.com/restaurantereysol; map page 57. Vegetarian café-restaurant serving pasta, Mexican-style dishes and dishes like *pinchos veganos* (vegan kebabs) in slightly uninspiring surrounds. Also acts as a health food store, selling good bread, granola, soya milk, herbal teas and veggie snacks. $$

Rocque Rosito 8 Av & 9 C 2232 7343; map page 57. Set in historic premises, this spacious café has banquette seating and sofas. It's ideal for a coffee or juice and a quick bite, and you'll find tasty crêpes and sandwiches on the food menu. $

Saúl Bistro Lux, 6 Av & 11 C gt.saulemendez.com; map page 57. Hip café in an old cinema foyer complete with movie-theatre-style seats, classic film posters and vintage projection equipment. On the menu are includes delicious crêpes, inventive salads and tasty "toasts" (artisan bread with generous toppings). $$

ZONA 4

Flor de Lis Ruta 3 & Via 5 fdlxibalba.com; map page 57. Flying the flag for contemporary Central America cuisine, this acclaimed restaurant offers (seasonal) a la carte and ten-course tasting menus. Dining here is quite an occasion, mingling with the city's creative classes, in an industrial-style space with an open kitchen. $$$$

ZONA 10

Artesano 13 C 2–33 artesano-inc.com; map page 61. This upmarket restaurant is a great spot for good value vegan fare. The menu is refined and there's a decent wine list to boot. $$

1

LGBTQ+ GUATEMALA CITY

Guatemala City's small **LGBTQ+ scene** is quite underground and concentrated around a few (almost entirely male) venues: consult guatemalacity.gaycities.com for the latest info. After parties are frequent after the nationwide 1am curfew.

Black Club 11 C 2–54, Zona 1 facebook.com/blackandwhitebargt; map page 57. Previously the Black & White, this well-established bar-club is an intimate space and attracts a lively crowd with themed nights, go-go dancers and events.

Genetic Majestic Vía 3 & Ruta 3, Zona 4 facebook.com/GeneticMajesticClub; map page 57. The city's largest (mainly) gay club is a classy place with has three floors (including a roof terrace), and plays pumping house music. There are themed nights and go-go dancers.

Trovajazz Via 6 3–55, Zona 4 trovajazz.com; map page 57. Intimate venue with a good reputation that showcases quality jazz, blues, acoustic and *trova* (Latin American folk). There's usually an entry fee, but some nights there's no charge.

Cevichería El Estero 2 Av 14–32 5833 7146; map page 61. A casual place serving some of the best ceviche in the city. The price of most dishes includes a beer. $$

Donde Mikel 13 C 5–19 dondemikel.com; map page 61. Spanish restaurant whose authentic food draws a very loyal clientele. The short menu features delicious starters like *sardinillas*, and fish and meat mains including *puyazo* (rump steak). Always busy, so reserve a table. $$

★ **Gracia Cocina de Autor** 14 Av & 4 C 2366 8699, facebook.com/pg/graciacocinadeautor; map page 61. This intimate, stylish place offers contemporary global cuisine with lots of fish and seafood and the best cuts of meat (like *entraña a la parrilla*), all presented immaculately. Don't miss Sunday brunch. $$$$

Paco's Café 1 Av 10–43; map page 61. Try this bustling little comedor for a traditional breakfast, snack (tacos are steal) or a filling set lunch: less than $5 buys you a bowl of soup, grilled meat with rice, vegetables and tortillas, a drink and a dessert. $

Pecorino 11 C 3–36, facebook.com/pecorinoguatemala; map page 61. An authentic, well-regarded Italian restaurant: its elegant interior and delightful, sensitively lit garden make a fine setting for a memorable meal. Feast on fresh pasta, pizza from a wood-fired oven or delicious fish, seafood and grilled meats. $$$

Pitaya 13 C 2–75 2334 3884; map page 61. Terrific juice bar with an amazing selection of healthy blends (including wheatgrass shots, lots of smoothies and supplement options including Omega 3 and ginseng) as well as salads, wraps (try a "Mr Avocado") and breakfasts. $$

Resko 14 C 4–12 2363 4150; map page 61. Inexpensive, welcoming comedor, popular with office staff, which offers fine-value meals for the location and a menu that changes daily. Breakfasts are cheap and filling, and the lunch deal includes soup, tortillas and a drink. $

Sopho's Fontabella Plaza, 12 C 12–59 sophosenlinea.com; map page 61. This charming bookstore café is a delightfully civilized (if pricey) place to browse for a book or magazine, sip a *café con leche* and snack on a sandwich or slice of cake. The perfect spot to meet a friend or relax on your own with a book. The set lunch changes daily. $$

DRINKING AND NIGHTLIFE

Nightlife in the capital essentially it comes down to two choices: gritty **Zona 1**, which has some highly atmospheric old bars and raucous student places, or Zona 10's **Zona Viva**, largely the domain of wealthy *Guatemaltecos*, and replete with upmarket bars and clubs. It's best not to stroll around Zona 1 late at night, but Zona 10 is considered safe enough. For information on Guatemala's **clubbing** and DJ scene, consult facebook.com/electronik.net.

ZONA 1

With a grungy appeal, and popular with students, Zona 1 can be a good night out: try the bars on Pasaje Aycinena for a few drinks. Note that personal safety can be a concern here, so it's best to get around by taxi late at night.

Las Cien Puertes Pasaje Aycinena, 9 C 6–47 2232 8502; map page 57. The city's definitive bohemian bar is popular with artists, students and political activists and located in a beautiful run-down arcade. Graffiti-splattered walls, good sounds (with live music some nights) and moderate prices.

El Gran Hotel 9 C 7–64, facebook.com/ElGranhotel; map page 57. This bar-cum-cultural centre draws a young crowd with alt rock bands and trance DJs, film and poetry evenings and stand-up comedy. On weekend nights, or when a popular band is playing, the atmosphere is raucous. Expect a cover charge, with two or three live bands a week.

La Luna Pasaje Aycinena, 9 C 8–59, facebook.com/lalunaguatemala; map page 57. Small, sociable little bar in a lovely historic building that has live music (Tues–Sat), mainly *trova* (Latin American folk) and acoustic; there's sometimes a cover charge. Doubles as a little café during the day.

★ **El Portal** Pasaje Rubio, 9 C between 6 & 7 Av ⓣ 2232 3617; map page 57. One of Che Guevara's old drinking haunts, and the decor has little changed since those days. It's a fantastic place to share a *chibola* of *cerveza mixta*, munch on a few (complimentary) *boquitas* and soak up the scene: hard drinkers glued to bar stools and wandering *trios* of musicians prowling the tables, mariachi-style.

Soma 11 C 4–27 ⓣ 2253 0406; map page 57. Gregarious bar that's a magnet for the city's young artistic crew. Regularly features live acts (mainly indie and alternative rock). Also operates as a cultural centre and café.

ZONA 4

El Príncipe Gris Cervecería, Casa del Águila Cultural Center, Vía 5 ⓦ elprincipegris.com; map page 57. One of Guatemala's few brewpubs, this hip craft beer mecca offers satisfying stouts, IPAs and ales. Hearty grub (sausages, burgers) is available too.

ZONA 9

The Secret Garden 6 Av A, ⓦ instagram.com/thesecretgardengt; map page 61. The capital's premier club for non-commercial electronic house, techno, dubstep and drum 'n' bass music, with excellent resident DJs (and guests from across the globe).

ZONA 10

The Zona Viva in Zona 10 is an upmarket area with American-style bars and clubs playing Latino and European dance music and pop hits.

The Box Lounge 15 C 2–23; ⓦ facebook.com/TheBoxLoungeGroove; map page 61. One of the capital's electronic hubs, with an underground vibe and sociable atmosphere. Features live house, electro, funk and techno DJs; check their Facebook page for a schedule.

El Establo 14 C 5–08 ⓣ 4206 9554, ⓦ instagram.com/establoz10; map page 61. Large, classy bar-restaurant that attracts a wealthy middle-aged crowd. Sounds range from jazz to classic rock, with live bands on Thurs and Sat.

Rattle & Hum 4 Av & 16 C, ⓦ facebook.com/Rattleandhumbar; map page 61. Stylish little Australian-owned bar, popular with expats and locals alike. The lively atmosphere is a major draw. While they do serve food, it's quite pricey and the quality of dishes doesn't always match the cost.

ENTERTAINMENT

Centro Cultural de España 6 Av 11–02, Zona 1, ⓦ cceguatemala.org. In a spectacular location inside an Art Deco cinema, showcasing an innovative selection of arthouse, European and independent Latin American movies, plus occasional classics. Also hosts plays and concerts.

Cinépolis Oakland Mall, Diagonal 6 13–01, Zona 10 ⓦ cinepolis.com.gt. This multiplex has the best-quality audiovisuals in the city, and even offers "butler service" tickets, which get you a leather seat and drinks brought to your seat.

Teatro Nacional Off 6 Av, Zona 1. The national complex has several theatres, including an amphitheatre, and stages some prestigious events including symphony orchestras and ballet. You can find out what's on via ⓦ mcd.gob.gt.

SHOPPING

For souvenirs, foodstuffs and everyday items check out Zona 1's **Mercado Central** (see page 58).

★ **Fontabella Plaza** 12 C 12–59, Zona 10 ⓦ fontabella.com; map page 61. Classy shopping centre, with boutiques and restaurants scattered around little courtyards. Check out Sopho's bookstore for English titles, Saúl for fashion and Flights de Vinoteca for a glass of wine.

Oakland Mall Diagonal 6 13–01, Zona 10 ⓦ oaklandplace.com.gt; map page 61. Upmarket mall with stores including Diesel, Apple and Zara, a good food court and cinema.

Paseo Cayalá Blvd. Rafael Landivar, ⓦ cayala.com. This huge village-like monument to consumerism caters to the city's elite, with its faux-classical architecture and upmarket shopping and entertainment options. Located 4km east of the centre.

Los Próceres 16 C 2–00, Zona 10 ⓦ proceres.com; map page 61. A mid-range mall, with more than two hundred stores, including many budget clothes, electrical and phone shops, some food stalls, a multi-screen cinema, a café or two and a good spa.

DIRECTORY

Banks ATMs and banks are very widespread, and there are several inside Los Próceres mall. You can exchange euros at Banco Internacional, Av Las Américas 12–54, Zona 13.

Embassies Most are in the southeastern quarter of the city, along Av La Reforma and Av Las Américas: Australia, contact the embassy in Mexico; Belize, 5 Av 5–55, Zona 14 (ⓣ 2367 3883, ⓦ embajadadebelize.org); Canada, 13 C 8–44, Edificio Edyma Plaza, Zona 10 (ⓣ 2363 4348, ⓦ canadainternational.gc.ca); Germany, Edificio Reforma 10, Av La Reforma 9–55, Zona 10 (ⓣ 2364 6700, ⓦ guatemala.diplo.de); Honduras, Edificio Plaza Coorporativa, Torre 2, Av La Reforma 6–64, Zona 9 (ⓣ 2332 6281); Mexico, 2 Av 7–57, Zona 10 (ⓣ 2420 3400, ⓦ https://embamex.sre.gob.mx/Guatemala); New

Zealand contact the embassy in Mexico; South Africa (honorary), Universidad Francisco Marroquín, 6 C Zona 10 (T 2338 7905); Sweden, Edificio Reforma 10, Av La Reforma 9–55, Zona 10 (T 2384 7300, W swedenabroad.com); United Kingdom, Torre Internacional, 16 C 0–55, Zona 10 (T 2380 7300, W www.gov.uk/foreign-travel-advice/guatemala); United States, Av La Reforma 7–01, Zona 10 (T 2326 4000, W usembassy.gov/guatemala).

Immigration The main immigration office (*migración*) is 6 Av & Ruta 4, Zona 4 (T 2411 2411). Visas can be extended here (see page 45).

Internet Wi-fi is very widespread. Cyber, 7 Av & 9 C, Zona 1, has quick connections.

Laundry Lavandería el Siglo, 2 C 3–42, Zona 1, offers a wash and dry.

Libraries The Guatemalan American Institute, or IGA, at Ruta 1 and Vía 4, Zona 4, has the best library for English books (W iga.edu). There's also the National Library, Parque del Centenario, and specialist collections at the Ixchel and Popol Vuh museums (see page 61).

Medical care Centro Médico, 6 Av 3–47, Zona 10 (T 2332 3555, W centromedico.com.gt) is a private hospital with 24hr emergency care and has English-speaking staff. Your embassy should also have a list of bilingual doctors.

Police The main police station is on the corner of 6 Av and 14 C, Zona 1. In an emergency, dial T 120.

Post office The main post office is at 7 Av and 12 C, Zona 1.

Around Guatemala City

The one sight that really warrants a day-trip from the capital is **Volcán de Pacaya**, a highly active cone, though this is actually easier to visit from nearby Antigua, from where most tours leave. From Guatemala City, the highway to the Pacific passes through endless suburbs, a swathe of new housing projects and giant *maquila* (clothing assembly) factories until you glimpse the (polluted) waters of Lago de Amatitlán nestling at the base of the Pacaya volcano.

To the northwest of the capital lies a hilly, forested area that, despite its proximity, is little tainted by the influence of the city. The one sight out this way, the **Mixco Viejo ruins**, the ancient capital of the Poqomam Maya, enjoy the most dramatic setting of any archeological site in Guatemala.

Volcán de Pacaya

Rising to a height of 2250m, **Volcán de Pacaya** regularly spits out clouds of rock and ash in the country's most dramatic sound-and-light extravaganza. The current period of eruption began in 1965, and colonial records show that it was also active between 1565 and 1775. Today it certainly ranks as one of the most accessible and exciting volcanoes in Central America, and a trip to the cone is an unforgettable experience (although sulphurous fumes and very high winds can make an ascent impossible some days). The best time to watch the eruptions is at night, when the volcano can spout plumes of brilliant orange lava.

It's a steep but steady hour's **climb** up a good path through *milpas* and thickish forest until you suddenly emerge on the lip of an exposed ridge from where you can see the cone in all its brutal beauty. In front of you is a massive bowl of cooled lava, its fossilized currents flowing away to the right; opposite is the cone itself, a jet-black triangular peak that occasionally spews rock and ash. It's usually possible to **descend**, and pick your way carefully across the lava fields until you reach a section that's oozing molten lava. If you've brought a marshmallow along, toast yourself a snack.

Many standard tours don't allow enough time, but it's a further 45 minutes to the **summit** of the cone itself. The route passes between charred stumps of trees, and then up the slippery ashen sides of the cone itself, a terrifying but thrilling ascent, eventually bringing you face to face with bubbling patches of molten magma and minor eruptions (if conditions permit). A noxious, choking brew of sulphurous fumes swirls around the lip of the crater and you'll feel the heat of the ash and lava beneath your feet. The climb certainly shouldn't be attempted when Pacaya is highly active – check with your tour agency about the state of the eruptions before setting out.

ESSENTIALS **VOLCÁN DE PACAYA**

Though it is possible to climb the cone independently, virtually everyone chooses to join a group as part of a **tour**, escorted by a guide. Antigua is the best place to organize things; in addition to budget tours, there are adventure sports specialists (see page 81) that run more comfortable and expensive trips that include food and drink.

Gran Jaguar Tours 4 C Poniente 30, Antigua 7832 2712. Handles virtually all budget trips from Antigua, no matter where you book your ticket. Daily tours leave Antigua at 6am and 2pm, returning six to seven hours later. Expect a no-frills excursion: drivers are not safety-conscious and you're likely to be packed inside an ancient minibus. Entrance fees to the Pacaya National Park are not included.

Geo Travel Guatemala 3168 8625, geotravelguatemala.com. Hike Pacaya with an expert British geologist.

Safety Safety on Pacaya (once the site of regular attacks by bandits) is no longer a concern, as park guards accompany groups.

Equipment People do ascend the peak in all kinds of footwear but wear hiking boots if you have them. Tour minibuses drop you off in the village of San Francisco de Sales, where you'll be surrounded by dozens of young boys urging you to buy a walking "steek", rent a torch (flashlight) or a horse.

Guides Once you've paid your entrance fee to the Pacaya National Park in San Francisco de Sales you'll be assigned a local guide to accompany your group up the trail.

Parque Natural Canopy Calderas

Free • facebook.com/parquenaturalcalderas

Nestling in the northern slopes of Pacaya is **Parque Natural Canopy Calderas**, a protected zone that encompasses a delightful highland lake and a dense patch of rainforest, close to the *aldea* of San José Calderas. The park is a privately owned nature reserve where you can go horse-riding (charge per hour) or swing through the jungle from professionally built platforms along a 700m network of cable that slices through the forest. It's essential to call ahead and book activities.

Mixco Viejo

Charge • Buses (5 daily) to Pachalum from 41 C & 8 Av, Zona 7, in Guatemala City, pass Mixco Viejo

Mixco Viejo was the capital of the Poqomam Maya, one of the main pre-conquest tribes. The site itself is thought to date from the thirteenth century, and its construction, designed to withstand siege, bears all the hallmarks of the troubled times before the arrival of the Spanish. Protected on all sides by deep ravines, it can be entered only along a single-file causeway. At the time the Spanish arrived, in 1525, this was one of the largest highland centres, with nine temples, two ball courts and a population of around nine thousand. Though the Spanish cavalry and their Mexican

SANTIAGO'S DAY OF THE DEAD

Santiago's local fiesta to honour the **Day of the Dead** on November 1 is one of the nation's most spectacular, with massive **kites** flown from the cemetery to release the souls of the dead from their agony. The festival is immensely popular, and thousands of Guatemalans (and tourists) come every year to watch the spectacle. The colourful kites, made from paper and bamboo, are huge circular creations, measuring up to about 3m in diameter. Teams of young men struggle to get them aloft while the crowd looks on with bated breath, rushing for cover if a kite comes crashing to the ground. All in all it's quite a scene, the cemetery lined with even larger kites of up to 10m across that are too heavy to get off the ground but which form an impressive backdrop. Early mornings are often calm, with the wind usually picking up around lunchtime, so you may want to time your arrival accordingly.

1

FINDING YOUR FEET IN ANTIGUA

As in most Guatemalan towns, Antigua is laid out on a grid system, with **avenidas** running north–south, and **calles** east–west. Each street is numbered and has two halves, either a north and south (*norte/sur*) or an east and west (*oriente/poniente*), with the **Parque Central** as the centre. But poor street lighting and the use of old street names ensure that most people get lost at some stage. If you get confused, remember that the Agua volcano, the one that hangs most immediately over the town, is to the south.

allies defeated Poqomam forces, the city remained impenetrable until a secret entrance was revealed, allowing the Spanish to enter virtually unopposed and to unleash a massacre of its inhabitants.

Mixco Viejo's **plazas** and **temples** are laid out across several flat-topped ridges. Like all the highland sites the structures are fairly low – the largest temple reaches only about 10m in height – and are devoid of decoration. It is, however, an interesting site in a spectacular setting, and during the week you'll probably have the ruins to yourself, which gives the place all the more atmosphere.

Santiago Sacatepéquez and around

Heading west of Guatemala City along the Carretera Interamericana, the serpentine three-lane highway climbs steadily until it reaches **San Lucas Sacatepéquez**, where there's a junction for Antigua and the festival town of **SANTIAGO SACATEPÉQUEZ**. A somewhat scruffy, sprawling highland settlement some 4km north of the highway, it's only really worth dropping by for the annual **kite festival** (see box) though it also hosts a large **market** (Tues & Sun). The neighbouring village of **SUMPANGO**, 6km west along the Interamericana, has an identical Day of the Dead tradition.

ARRIVAL AND DEPARTURE — SANTIAGO SACATEPÉQUEZ AND AROUND

By bus All buses between Antigua and Guatemala City pass through San Lucas Sacatepéquez.

Organized tours You'll have no problem reaching either Santiago Sacatepéquez or Sumpango on fiesta day, when travel agencies send fleets of minibuses up to the villages from Antigua.

Antigua

Superbly situated in a sweeping highland valley, **ANTIGUA** is one of the Americas' most enchanting colonial cities. In its day this was one of the great cities of the Spanish empire, serving as the administrative centre for all of Central America and Mexican Chiapas.

Antigua has become Guatemala's foremost tourist destination, a favoured hangout for travellers. The beauty of the city itself is the main attraction, particularly its remarkable wealth of **colonial buildings** – churches, monasteries and grand family homes – that provide an idea of the city's former status. You'll find the ambience unhurried and enjoyable, with a sociable bar scene and superb choice of restaurants adding to the appeal. Antigua's **language schools** are another big draw, pulling in students from around the globe.

Expats contribute to the town's cosmopolitan air, mingling with local villagers selling their wares in the streets, and the Guatemalans from the capital who come here at weekends to eat, drink and enjoy themselves. The downside is that perhaps this uniquely civilized and privileged city, with its café culture and boutiques, can feel at times a little too bourgeois and isolated from the rest of Guatemala for some travellers' tastes.

You could spend days exploring Antigua's incredible collection of colonial buildings. If you'd rather just visit the gems, make **Las Capuchinas**, **San Francisco**, **Santo Domingo** and **Casa Popenoe** your targets.

Brief history

In 1541, after a mudslide from Agua volcano buried the Spanish capital at **Ciudad Vieja**, Antigua was selected as a safer base. Here the new capital grew to achieve astounding prosperity. Religious orders competed in the construction of schools, churches, monasteries and hospitals, while bishops, merchants and landowners built grand townhouses and palaces.

The city reached its peak in the middle of the eighteenth century, after the 1717 earthquake prompted an unprecedented building boom, and the population rose to around fifty thousand. By this stage Antigua was a genuinely impressive place, with a university, printing press and a newspaper. But in 1773 two devastating shocks reduced much of the city to rubble and a decision was made to abandon ship in favour of the modern capital. Fortunately, there were many who refused to leave and Antigua was never completely deserted.

Since then the city has been gradually repopulated, particularly in the last hundred years or so, with middle-class Guatemalans fleeing the capital and a large number of foreigners attracted to Antigua's relaxed and sophisticated atmosphere. The fate of Antigua's ancient **architecture**, meanwhile, has become a growing concern. Efforts are being made to preserve this unique legacy, especially after Antigua was listed as a UNESCO World Heritage Site in 1979. Local **conservation** laws are very strict (extensions to houses are virtually impossible) and traffic reduction initiatives have eased noise and environmental pollution.

Parque Central

Antigua's focal point has always been its commanding central plaza, the **Parque Central**. In colonial times the plaza held a bustling market, which was cleared periodically for bullfights, military parades, floggings and public hangings. The calm of today's shady plaza, largely isolated from the city's traffic and replete with benches and well-tended flowering shrubs is relatively recent. Don't miss the risqué central fountain, its water jets gushing from the nipples of breast-squeezing mermaids.

Antigua Catedral

Parque Central • T 7832 0909 • Charge

Of the structures surrounding the plaza, Antigua's **Catedral** is the most arresting, particularly at night when its intricate facade is evocatively illuminated. Built in 1670, the cathedral replaced a poorly built earlier edifice. The new construction was the most spectacular colonial building in Central America – it boasted an immense dome, five aisles, eighteen chapels and an altar inlaid with mother-of-pearl, ivory and silver – but the 1773 earthquake all but destroyed the building. Today only two of the original interior chapels remain; take a peek inside and you'll find several colonial sculptures.

To get some idea of the vast scale of the original building, check out the **ruins** to the rear, where there's a mass of fallen masonry and rotting beams, broken arches and hefty pillars, all cracked and moss-covered, the great original cupola now just a window to the sky. Buried beneath the floor are some of the great names of the Conquest, including Pedro de Alvarado, his wife, Beatriz de la Cueva, Bishop Marroquín and the historian Bernal Díaz del Castillo. At the very rear of what was once the nave, steps lead down to a burial vault that's regularly used for Maya religious ceremonies – an example of the coexistence of pagan and Catholic beliefs that's so characteristic of Guatemala.

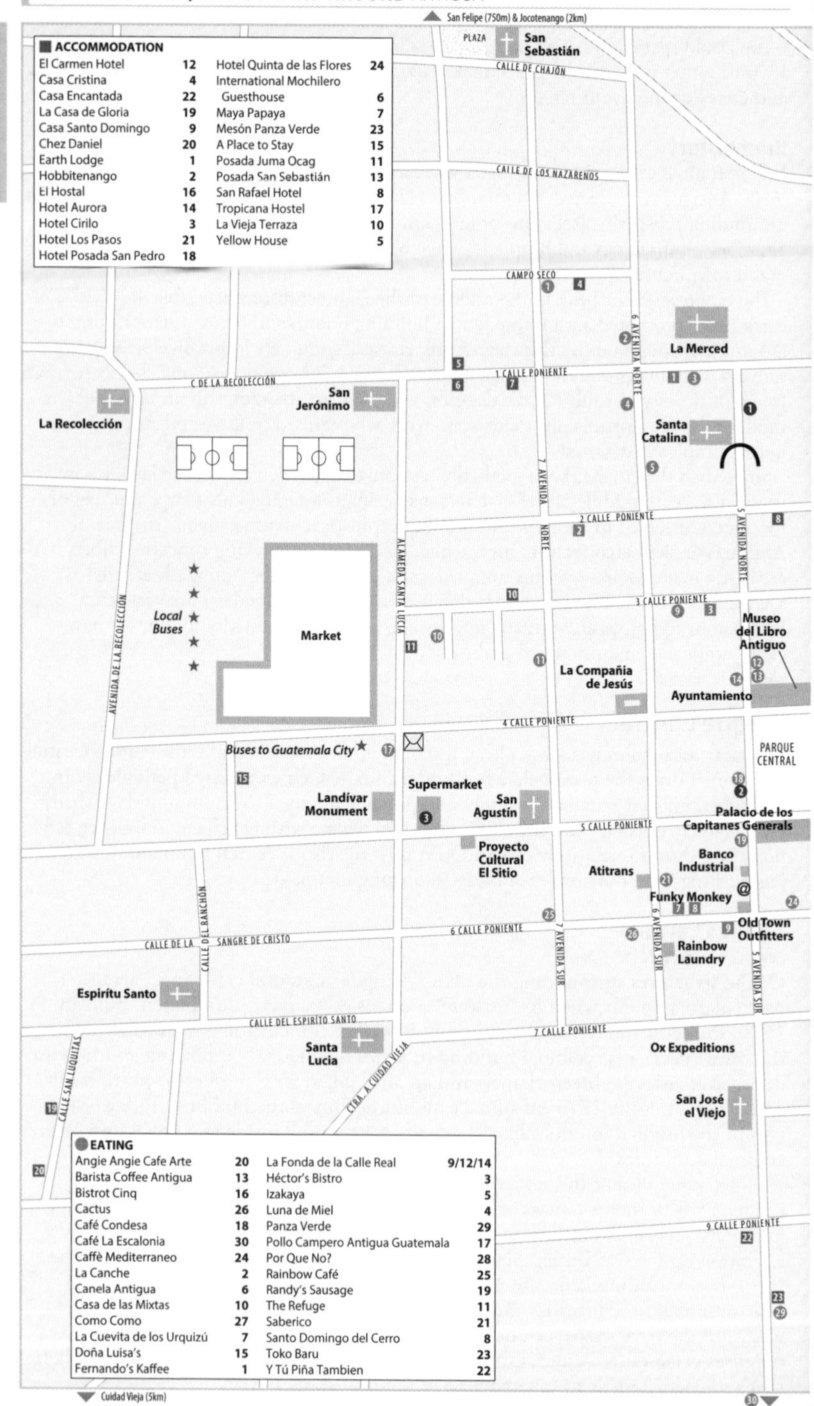
San Felipe (750m) & Jocotenango (2km)
ACCOMMODATION
El Carmen Hotel 12
Casa Cristina 4
Casa Encantada 22
La Casa de Gloria 19
Casa Santo Domingo 9
Chez Daniel 20
Earth Lodge 1
Hobbitenango 2
El Hostal 16
Hotel Aurora 14
Hotel Cirilo 3
Hotel Los Pasos 21
Hotel Posada San Pedro 18
Hotel Quinta de las Flores 24
International Mochilero Guesthouse 6
Maya Papaya 7
Mesón Panza Verde 23
A Place to Stay 15
Posada Juma Ocag 11
Posada San Sebastián 13
San Rafael Hotel 8
Tropicana Hostel 17
La Vieja Terraza 10
Yellow House 5
PLAZA
San Sebastián
CALLE DE CHAJÓN
CALLE DE LOS NAZARENOS
CAMPO SECO
6 AVENIDA NORTE
La Merced
1 CALLE PONIENTE
C DE LA RECOLECCIÓN
San Jerónimo
La Recolección
Santa Catalina
7 AVENIDA NORTE
2 CALLE PONIENTE
5 AVENIDA NORTE
ALAMEDA SANTA LUCIA
3 CALLE PONIENTE
Museo del Libro Antiguo
Local Buses
Market
AVENIDA DE LA RECOLECCIÓN
La Compañía de Jesús
Ayuntamiento
4 CALLE PONIENTE
Buses to Guatemala City
PARQUE CENTRAL
Supermarket
Landívar Monument
San Agustín
Palacio de los Capitanes Generals
5 CALLE PONIENTE
Proyecto Cultural El Sitio
Banco Industrial
Atitrans
Funky Monkey
Old Town Outfitters
6 CALLE PONIENTE
Rainbow Laundry
CALLE DE LA SANGRE DE CRISTO
CALLE DEL RANCHÓN
7 AVENIDA SUR
6 AVENIDA SUR
5 AVENIDA SUR
Espiritu Santo
CALLE DEL ESPIRITO SANTO
7 CALLE PONIENTE
Santa Lucia
Ox Expeditions
CTRA. A CUIDAD VIEJA
CALLE SAN LUQUITAS
San José el Viejo
9 CALLE PONIENTE
EATING
Angie Angie Cafe Arte 20
Barista Coffee Antigua 13
Bistrot Cinq 16
Cactus 26
Café Condesa 18
Café La Escalonia 30
Caffè Mediterraneo 24
La Canche 2
Canela Antigua 6
Casa de las Mixtas 10
Como Como 27
La Cuevita de los Urquizú 7
Doña Luisa's 15
Fernando's Kaffee 1
La Fonda de la Calle Real 9/12/14
Héctor's Bistro 3
Izakaya 5
Luna de Miel 4
Panza Verde 29
Pollo Campero Antigua Guatemala 17
Por Que No? 28
Rainbow Café 25
Randy's Sausage 19
The Refuge 11
Saberico 21
Santo Domingo del Cerro 8
Toko Baru 23
Y Tú Piña Tambien 22
Cuidad Vieja (5km)

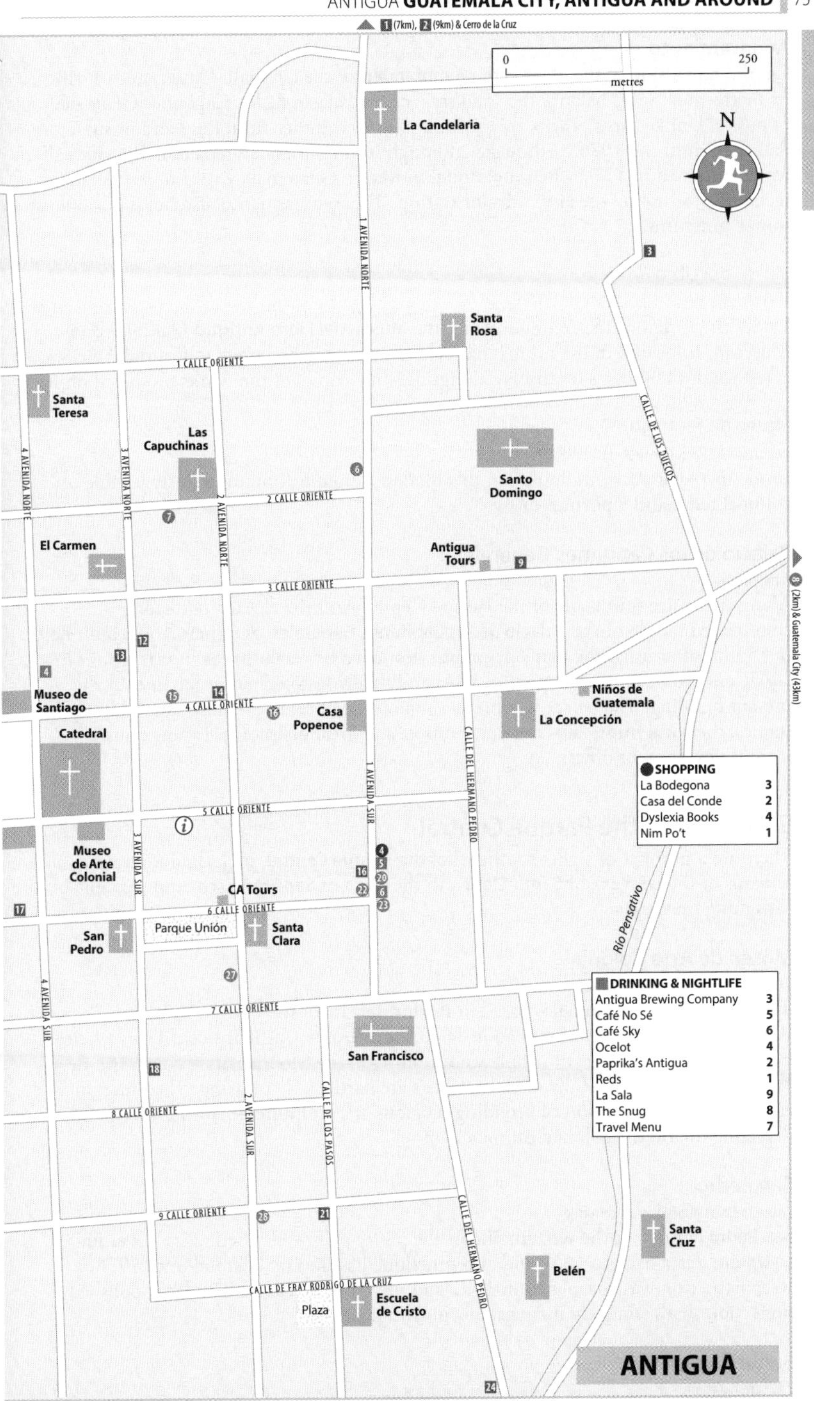
1 (7km), 2 (9km) & Cerro de la Cruz
0
250
metres
N
La Candelaria
1 AVENIDA NORTE
Santa Rosa
1 CALLE ORIENTE
Santa Teresa
Las Capuchinas
CALLE DE LOS DUCOS
Santo Domingo
4 AVENIDA NORTE
3 AVENIDA NORTE
2 AVENIDA NORTE
2 CALLE ORIENTE
El Carmen
Antigua Tours
3 CALLE ORIENTE
8 (2km) & Guatemala City (43km)
Museo de Santiago
4 CALLE ORIENTE
Casa Popenoe
Niños de Guatemala
La Concepción
Catedral
1 AVENIDA SUR
CALLE DEL HERMANO PEDRO
SHOPPING
La Bodegona 3
Casa del Conde 2
Dyslexia Books 4
Nim Po't 1
5 CALLE ORIENTE
Museo de Arte Colonial
3 AVENIDA SUR
CA Tours
6 CALLE ORIENTE
San Pedro
Parque Unión
Santa Clara
Río Pensativo
DRINKING & NIGHTLIFE
Antigua Brewing Company 3
Café No Sé 5
Café Sky 6
Ocelot 4
Paprika's Antigua 2
Reds 1
La Sala 9
The Snug 8
Travel Menu 7
4 AVENIDA SUR
7 CALLE ORIENTE
San Francisco
8 CALLE ORIENTE
2 AVENIDA SUR
CALLE DE LOS PASOS
9 CALLE ORIENTE
Santa Cruz
Belén
CALLE DE FRAY RODRIGO DE LA CRUZ
Plaza
Escuela de Cristo
ANTIGUA
San Juan del Obispo (5km) & Santa María de Jesús (11km)

Ayuntamiento

On the north side of the plaza is the **Ayuntamiento**, the city hall. Dating from 1740, its metre-thick walls balance the solid style of the Palacio de los Capitanes Generales opposite. Unlike most others, this building survived earlier rumblings and wasn't damaged until the 1976 earthquake, although it has since been repaired. The city hall was abandoned in 1779 when the capital moved to Guatemala City, but it was later reclaimed for use by the city's administration. The Ayuntamiento also holds a couple of minor museums.

Museo del Libro Antiguo

Ayuntamiento, Parque Central • T 7832 5511 • Charge

Under the arches of the Ayuntamiento, the **Museo del Libro Antiguo** (Antique Book Museum) is located in the rooms that held the first printing press in Central America. A replica of the press is on display alongside some copies of the works produced on it.

Museo de Santiago

Ayuntamiento, Parque Central • T 2239 5000 • Charge

Inside the Ayuntamiento building, this modest museum contains a dusty jumble of colonial relics and a portrait or two.

Palacio de los Capitanes Generales

Parque Central

Along the entire south side of the Parque Central runs the elegant two-storey colonnaded facade of the **Palacio de los Capitanes Generales**. A structure was built here in 1558, but as usual the first version was destroyed by earthquakes. It was rebuilt in 1761, only to be damaged again in 1773 and finally restored along the lines of the present building. The palace was home to the colonial rulers and also housed barracks, stables, the royal mint, law courts, tax offices and great ballrooms. It now houses various government offices.

Southeast of the Parque Central

There are a number of sights **southeast of the Parque Central**, including the vast remains of the convent of **Santa Clara** and the ruins of **San Francisco**, and a couple of intriguing **museums**.

Museo de Arte Colonial

5 C Oriente 5 • T 7832 0429 • Charge

The **Museo de Arte Colonial** is based in the former site of the University of San Carlos Borromeo, an institution founded in 1676. At first only Castilians could study here, but later a broader range of people were admitted. The Moorish-style courtyard, deep-set windows and beautifully ornate cloisters are particularly pleasing. The museum contains a good collection of brooding religious art, sculpture, furniture and murals depicting life on the colonial campus.

San Pedro

Parque La Unión • Open for services • Free

San Pedro church, at the western end of the pretty palm-tree-lined plaza of **Parque La Unión**, dates back to 1662 and also functioned as the city hospital until 1976. Reconstruction was completed in 1991 and the Baroque facade now has a polished perfection that's strangely incongruous in Antigua.

Santa Clara

2 Av Sur 27 • Charge

At the eastern end of Parque La Union is the convent and church of **Santa Clara**, founded in 1699. This became a popular place for well-to-do young ladies to take the veil, as the hardships were none too hard, and the nuns had earned a reputation for their cooking by selling bread to the aristocracy. The original convent was destroyed in 1717, as was the second in 1773, and little remains of the church except its ornate facade, which is floodlit at night. Today you can amble about the ruins of the convent, which cover an entire city block, and pick out the original bread oven, cloisters and huge central courtyard. There's no information on site, but guides are available at the entrance.

In front of Santa Clara are the elegant arches of an impressive open-air stone *pila*, washing pools where local women gather to scrub, rinse and chat.

Casa Popenoe

1 Av Sur • entrance by guided tour only, book in advance • Charge • Ⓦ casapopenoe.ufm.edu

The grand colonial **Casa Popenoe**, a mansion built in 1634, is now maintained by the Universidad Francisco Marroquín as a historical monument. The structure was in ruins when, in 1932, Dr Wilson Popenoe, a United Fruit-company scientist, began its comprehensive restoration. Inside there's an incredible collection of furniture and art, including portraits of Bishop Marroquín and a menacing-looking Alvarado himself. The kitchen and servants' quarters have also been carefully renovated, and you can see the bread ovens and pigeon loft (which would have provided the original occupants with their mail service). Dr Popenoe died in 1972, but his family continued to live in the house until 2007. Entrance is by a (highly informative) guided tour only (minimum five people, book ahead), in English or Spanish.

San Francisco

1 Av Sur • **Ruins and museum** free • **Church** charge

One of the oldest in Antigua, the church of **San Francisco** dates from 1579 and grew into a vast religious and cultural centre that included a school, a hospital, music rooms, a printing press and a monastery. The church originally boasted highly decorative mouldings and sculpture along its nave, but these were ruined by earthquakes. Inside the church is the tomb of **Hermano Pedro de Betancourt**, a Franciscan from the Canary Islands who is credited with powers of miraculous intervention by the faithful – Pope John Paul II made him Central America's first saint in 2002.

The **ruins** of the monastery are among the most impressive in Antigua, with colossal fallen arches and pillars lying strewn over extensive gardens and grassy verges. Don't miss the superb museum here and its astounding "hall of miracles" which contains dozens of crutches and walking sticks left behind by grateful pilgrims, who credit Hermano Pedro with divine healing, and the hundreds of plaques giving thanks for his services.

North and east of the Parque Central

The essential sights **north and east of the Parque Central** include the terrific ruins of **Las Capuchinas** and **Santo Domingo**, which both have excellent museums, **La Merced** and the emblematic arch of **Santa Catalina**. Further out to the northeast along 1 Avenida Norte, the badly damaged ruins of the churches of **Santa Rosa**, **Candelaria** and **Nuestra Señora de los Dolores del Cerro** are of interest to ruined-church buffs only.

El Carmen

3 Av Norte • No public access to ruins

The hermitage of **El Carmen** was originally one of the city's great churches, dating back to 1638, but the top half of the facade collapsed in 1976 and today the complex lies in ruins. There's a popular artesanías **market** next to the remains of the church.

1

Las Capuchinas

2 C Oriente & 2 Av Norte • cnpag.com • Charge (including ruins access and museum)

The largest of the city's convents, **Las Capuchinas** are some of the best preserved but least understood ruins in Antigua. The Capuchin order was the most rigorous in Antigua. Numbers were restricted to 25, with nuns sleeping on wooden beds with straw pillows. Once they had entered the convent it's thought the women were not allowed any visual contact with the outside world; food was passed to them by means of a turntable and they could only speak to visitors through a grille.

The ruins

The convent **ruins** are the most beautiful in Antigua, with fountains, courtyards and massive earthquake-proof pillars. The tower or "retreat" is the most unusual feature, with eighteen tiny cells set into the walls of its top floor, each having its own independent sewage system. Two of the cells have been returned to their original condition to demonstrate the extreme austerity of the nuns' lives. The lower floor, which functioned as a meat storage room, is dominated by a massive pillar that supports the structure above. The exterior of this architectural curiosity is also interesting, ringed with small stone recesses that represent the Stations of the Cross.

Museum

Occupying two upper wings of the main courtyard, the Las Capuchinas **museum** beautifully showcases some terrific religious art and ecclesiastical artefacts including colonial-era sculptures and portraits. There are information panels in Spanish, English and Chinese.

Santo Domingo

3 C Oriente • Charge (for entire complex) • casasantodomingo.com.gt/museums

Once forming the largest monastery in Antigua, the immense complex of **Santo Domingo** is today largely occupied by a luxury hotel, *Casa Santo Domingo* (see page 82). Substantial parts of the gorgeous grounds of the hotel have been

SEMANA SANTA IN ANTIGUA

Antigua's **Semana Santa** (Holy Week) celebrations are perhaps the most extravagant and impressive in all Latin America – a week of vigils, processions and pageants commemorating the most solemn week of the Christian year. The celebrations start with a procession on **Palm Sunday**, representing Christ's entry into Jerusalem, and continue through the week, climaxing on **Good Friday**. On Thursday night the streets are carpeted with meticulously drawn patterns of coloured sawdust, and on Friday morning a series of processions re-enacts the progress of Christ to the Cross. Setting out from the churches of **La Merced** and **Escuela de Cristo** and the village of **San Felipe** at around 8am, groups of penitents, clad in purple or white and wearing peaked hoods, carry images of Christ and the Cross on massive platforms, accompanied by solemn dirges played by local brass bands and clouds of incense. After 3pm, the hour of the Crucifixion, the penitents change into black.

It is a great honour to be involved in the procession but no easy task – the great cedar block carried from La Merced weighs some 3.5 tonnes and needs eighty men to lift it. Some of the images displayed date from the seventeenth century, and the procession itself is thought to have been introduced by Alvarado in the early years of the Conquest.

Check the exact details of events with the tourist office, which should be able to provide you with a map detailing the routes of the processions. During Holy Week virtually every hotel in Antigua is full, and the entire town is packed, but as enterprising locals rent out spare rooms there's always a bed to be had somewhere.

sensitively converted into a cultural zone, which includes several small **museums**, the monastery ruins, various subterranean crypts, artisans' workshops, exhibitions of local textiles and crafts, a re-creation of an early pharmacy and an art exhibition space. Together they form a rewarding, highly atmospheric sight well worth half a day of your time.

Museo Colonial and crypts

The **Museo Colonial** harbours an exquisite array of religious artefacts and treasures from the Spanish era, including a breathtaking collection of golden crowns, silver lecterns and chalices and sculptures of angels, saints and cherubs. You can tour the monastery's four **crypts**, including the Calvary crypt which has an impressive mural of Christ and the Crucifixion. The crypts are dotted around the ruined remains of Santo Domingo's 68m-long church.

Museo Arqueológico

Inside the **Museo Arqueológico** are some impressive Maya ceramics, including intricately painted drinking vessels, funerary urns and incense burners in an exhibition room that has walls painted with scenes from the famous murals of Bonampak.

Museo Arte de Precolombino y Vidrio Moderno

The **Museo Arte de Precolombino y Vidrio Moderno** (Museum of Precolumbian Art and Modern Glass) has exhibitions of Maya artefacts and ceramics together with contemporary glassworks that are supposed to have been influenced by them – a slightly bizarre concept.

La Merced

1 C Poniente • Charge

The church of **La Merced** boasts one of the most intricate and impressive facades in the city. It has been beautifully restored, painted mustard-yellow and white, and crammed with plaster moulding of interlaced patterns. The church is still in use, but the cloisters and **gardens** lie ruined, exposed to the sky. In the centre of one of the courtyards is a monumental tiered fountain with four pools, which were used by the Mercedarian brothers for breeding fish.

Santa Catalina arch

5 Av Norte

One of Antigua's most emblematic structures, the **Santa Catalina arch** is all that remains of the original convent founded here in 1609. By 1697 it had reached maximum capacity with 110 nuns and six novices, and the arch was built so that they could walk between the two halves of the establishment without being exposed to the outside world. Restored in the nineteenth century, it's now a favoured spot for photographers, as the view to the Volcán de Agua is unobstructed from here.

Cerro de la Cruz

Northeast of Antigua, the **Cerro de la Cruz**, a hilltop with a giant cross, has commanding views of the city and Volcán de Agua. It was a mugging hot spot for years but an ever-present police presence has meant it's now considered perfectly safe. Nevertheless it's probably best not to walk here – take a tuk-tuk for a small fee.

West of the Parque Central

The last of Antigua's major ruins lie **west of the Parque Central**, near the bus station. This is the busiest part of town, the streets humming with traffic and people during the day.

1

CRIME AGAINST TOURISTS IN ANTIGUA

Visitors to Antigua should be aware that crimes against **tourists** – mainly street robberies – do occur occasionally. Pickpockets frequent the market and muggers do sometimes target people (like tipsy foreigners) late at night. Police patrol the streets but it's still wise to follow the usual **precautions**: avoid quiet areas after dark and take a taxi home after 10pm. If you want to visit **viewing spots**, such as the Cerro de la Cruz, take a taxi or tuk-tuk, or join one of the trips organized by PROATUR.

La Compañia de Jesús

6 Av Norte • Free • Ⓦ aecid-cf.org.gt

Now a cultural centre, **La Compañia de Jesús** was an educational establishment and church operated by the Jesuits until King Carlos III of Spain, feeling threatened by their growing power, expelled them from the colonies in 1767. Its cloisters and premises have been beautifully renovated by the Spanish government and it now hosts art exhibitions, lectures and events and is home to an excellent library and courtyard café. The church remains in ruins.

San Jerónimo

C de La Recolección • Charge

The spectacular ruined remains of **San Jerónimo**, a school built in 1739 which later functioned as a customs house, boast well-kept gardens woven between huge blocks of fallen masonry and crumbling walls. Parts of the two-storey cloisters and kitchen have been restored, and classical music concerts are regularly performed here.

La Recolección

C de La Recolección • C harge

Behind San Jerónimo, a cobbled road leads to the even larger, and more chaotic ruin of **La Recolección**, where the shell of the colossal original church is piled high with the remains of its roof and walls. Friars started building a monastery and church here in 1701 but only months after its completion in 1717, the complex was brought to the ground by a huge earthquake. This second version was destroyed in 1773 and has been steadily decaying ever since.

ARRIVAL AND DEPARTURE — ANTIGUA

By local bus The main bus terminal is beside the market. Because of its position off the Interamericana, few bus routes originate in Antigua. Most travellers don't take local buses to Guatemala City as they use an inconvenient terminal in the capital located in Zona 3, 1.5km west of the centre (and also due to security concerns); shuttle minibuses drop you off at your destination, and represent a more expensive but safer option. If you're heading to the western highlands, catch the first bus to Chimaltenango and transfer there. The following buses all leave from the main terminal, except the Panajachel bus (operated by Transportes Rebuli, which leaves from 4 C Poniente, just east of the market) and Hedman Alas (Whedmanalas.com) buses to Copán, Honduras (2 daily) which leave from Hotel de Don Rodrigo, 5 Av Norte 17.

Destinations Chimaltenango (every 15min; 40min); Ciudad Vieja (every 20min; 15min); Escuintla (every 45min; 1hr 15min); Guatemala City (every 10–15min; 1hr–1hr 30min); Panajachel (7am daily; 2hr 45min); San Antonio Aguas Calientes (every 30min; 20min); San Juan del Obispo (hourly; 15min); Santa María de Jesús (every 30min; 30min).

By shuttle bus Minibuses can be booked through most travel agents, including Atitrans and Adrenalina Tours (see below). Shuttles cost typically triple the price of public buses, but they are much more comfortable and a bit quicker. For shuttles to El Tunco beach and León see Ⓦ gekkotrailsexplorer.com/services.

Destinations Chichicastenango (1–2 daily; 2hr 30min); Cobán (daily; 6hr); Copán, Honduras (daily; 6hr); El Tunco, El Salvador (3–4 weekly; 5hr); Guatemala City (8 daily; 1hr–1hr 30min); Lanquín (daily; 8hr 30min); León, Nicaragua (3–4 weekly, 16hr); Monterrico (8am daily; 2hr 30min); Panajachel (2–3 daily; 2hr 30min); Quetzaltenango (daily; 3hr 45min); San Cristóbal de las Casas, Mexico (daily; 12hr); San Marcos La Laguna (3 daily; 3hr 15min); San Pedro La Laguna (3 daily; 3hr).

GETTING AROUND

By taxi Uber cabs are available in Antigua. Regular taxis wait on the east side of the Parque Central, or call ⓣ7832 0479. For a female cab driver, call Chiqui on ⓣ5715 5720.
By tuk-tuk Rides cost roughly US$1.50.
Bike rental Guatemala Ventures, Old Town Outfitters and Ox Expeditions (see below) all rent quality mountain bikes.
Car and motorbike rental Tabarini, 6 Av Sur 22 (ⓣ7832 8107, ⓦtabarini.com), has cars from around and 4WD available. Simoon Rentals & Tours, 6a Av Nor (ⓣ5488 6550, ⓦsimoontours.com), rents scooters by the day.

INFORMATION

Tourist information Inguat, 5 C Oriente 11 (ⓣ2290 2810 ⓔinfo-antigua@inguat.gob.gt). Staff are pretty efficient, English is spoken and you can pick up a free city map. Consult The Antigua-based magazine *Revue* (ⓦrevuemag.com) for useful information, listings and articles.
Tourist assistance PROATUR (ⓣ1500 and ⓣ5578 9835, ⓦguiagt.com/item/proatur-programa-de-asistencia-al-turista) helps victims of crime (see page 45) and will also escort tourists around Antigua, including up to Cerro de la Cruz.
Guidebooks Two excellent guidebooks devoted to Antigua are *Antigua Guatemala: The City and Its Heritage* by Elizabeth Bell and *Antigua for You*, by Barbara Balchin De Koose. Both are available in town.
Notice boards Everything from salsa classes to private language tuition is advertised in popular hostels like *El Hostal* (see page 82), as well as the *Rainbow Café* (see page 83).

TRAVEL AGENTS

Adrenalina Tours 2 C Poniente 3 ⓣ7832 1108, ⓦadrenalinatours.com. Good for shuttle buses and bespoke tours across the country.
Antigua Tours by Elizabteh Bell 5a Av Nor 4 ⓦantiguatours.net. Offers tours across Guatemala.
Atitrans 6 Av Sur 8 ⓣ7832 3371, ⓦatitrans.net. Runs shuttle bus connections all over Guatemala.
Viajes Tivoli 4 C Oriente 10 ⓣ7832 4274, ⓦviajestivoli.com. A recommended all-rounder for flights and tours.

ACTIVITIES AND TOURS

ADVENTURE SPORTS AND ACTIVITIES

Guatemala Venture 1 Av Sur 15 ⓦguatemalaventure.wixsite.com/antigua. An excellent range of mountain biking trips plus bike rental. Horse-riding, caving, birdwatching and volcano climbs are also offered.
Moto Tours 9 A Calle Oriente 14 ⓣ3185 8939, ⓦmototours-guatemala.com. Motorbike tours around Antigua and beyond.
Old Town Outfitters 5 Av Sur 12 ⓦadventureguatemala.com. Volcano hikes including Acatenango, mountain-bike excursions (Sip 'n' Cycle takes in a coffee plantation) plus rock-climbing trips and sea kayaking. Also rents tents, sleeping bags, packs and bikes.
Ox Expeditions 7 C Poniente 17 ⓦoxexpeditions.com. Very well set up for volcano hiking, including Acatenango. Try their Hike-Zip-Bike which includes ziplining, biking and hiking.
Ravenscroft Stables 2 Av Sur 3 ⓦravenscroftstables.wixsite.com/home. Horse-riding around the nearby village of San Juan del Obispo.

TOURS

Antigua Tours Casa Santo Domingo, 3 C Oriente 28 ⓦantiguatours.net. Excellent walking tours of Antigua led by local historians.
Niños de Guatemala Casa Convento Concepción, 4 C Oriente 41 ⓣ7832 8033, ⓦninosdeguatemala.org. Superb tours of non-touristy villages in the Antigua area, taking in niche industries like a chicken bus workshop as well as the NGO's own school.

ACCOMMODATION

Whether you're after a room in a colonial mansion or a bed in a dorm, Antigua has a plentiful supply, except around **Holy**

VOLCANO TOURS FROM ANTIGUA

Volcán de Pacaya (see page 70) near Guatemala City is a spectacular and very active volcano that can spew towering plumes of smoke and brilliant orange lava – though such fire 'n' brimstone shows only happen sporadically. Gran Jaguar Tours (see page 71) offers basic, inexpensive trips, while adventure tour specialists (see above) charge more for a day-hike.

Other cones to climb include volcanoes **Agua** (see page 88) and **Acatenango** (see page 87), the toughest climb in this region, which gives a great view of the highly active neighbouring cone of **Fuego**.

1

Week when the place is packed and prices soar. If you're travelling as a family or a group, consider renting a house; Guatemala Vacation Rental (T 5502 5353, W guatemala-vacation-rentals.com) has a good selection. There are also two good guesthouses in the mountains above Antigua: *Earth Lodge* (see page 83) and *Hobbitenango* (see page 83).

ANTIGUA

El Carmen Hotel 3 Av Norte 9 W elcarmenhotel.com; map page 74. A very classy hotel close to the Parque Central, with gorgeous rooms and high standards of service. The roof terrace is the perfect spot to enjoy a cocktail. $$$$

Casa Cristina Callejón Camposeco 3A T 7832 0623; map page 74. Offers fine value, with fourteen very clean and attractive rooms, all with private hot-water bathrooms; those on the upper floors enjoy more natural light and privacy. There's a rooftop sun terrace, free coffee, drinking water and wi-fi. $$

Casa Encantada 9 C Poniente 1 W casaencantada-antigua.com; map page 74. Boutique hotel with ten immaculate rooms, most with four-poster beds, and all with delightful bathrooms. There's a small pool, a rooftop terrace and breakfast is included. $$$$

La Casa de Gloria C San Luquitas 3B T 4374 1391, E lacasadegloria@yahoo.com; map page 74. Sociable guesthouse run by a welcoming Guatemalan (a salsa and Spanish teacher) with five private rooms and a kitchen. It's about a ten-min walk southwest of the Parque Central. $

Casa Santo Domingo 3 C Oriente 28 W www.casasantodomingo.com.gt; map page 74. This historic hotel enjoys simply stunning grounds (with two pools and several museums) that are particularly evocative at night when hundreds of candles are lit. However at times it lacks intimacy due to its sheer size (there are 128 rooms) and popularity with tour groups and wedding parties. $$$$

Chez Daniel Calle de San Luquitas 20 W chezdanielantigua.blogspot.com; map page 74. Spacious, spotless rooms face a garden courtyard at this French-owned guesthouse, which has a quiet location a ten-minute walk from the centre. Rates include a great continental breakfast with home-made croissants. $$$

El Hostal 1 Av Sur 8 W hostelworld.com; map page 74. This well-managed hostel has inviting dorms that have space and style, all with lockers. The shower facilities are spotless, there's a great central courtyard for chilling. Rates include breakfast. Dorms $, doubles $$

★ **Hotel Aurora** 4 C Oriente 16 W hotelauroraantigua.com; map page 74. Very centrally located, Antigua's original hotel occupies a fine colonial building. The seventeen spacious rooms face a lovely grassy courtyard and fountain, though some do suffer a little street noise. Rates include breakfast. $$$$

★ **Hotel Cirilo** C de los Duelos 11 W hotelciriloantigua.com-hotel.com; map page 74. The *Cirilo* enjoys a serene setting, with rooms facing the evocative ruins of a colonial chapel and garden, and its luxurious rooms (with fireplaces) represent wonderful value. Staff are super-helpful and you'll love the solar-heated lap pool, lounge and food in the café-restaurant. $$$$

Hotel Los Pasos 9 C Oriente 19 W hotellospasos.com; map page 74. Classy hotel with very inviting accommodation, tastefully presented with exposed stone walls and Maya textiles and some with jacuzzi baths. The gardens and restaurant are equally attractive. $$$$

Hotel Posada San Pedro 3 Av Sur 15B W facebook.com/www.posadasanpedro.net; map page 74. A fine colonial residence on a quiet street, with spacious, excellent-value rooms, all with hand-carved wooden furniture and private bathrooms (most with tubs). Accommodation is grouped around two garden patios, and there's a guests' kitchen and roof terrace. $$$

Hotel Quinta de las Flores C del Hermano Pedro 6 W quintadelasflores.com; map page 74. This hotel's spectacular garden – with swimming pool and children's play area – is truly wonderful, an oasis bursting with rare plants, shrubs and trees. The rooms and *casitas* (each sleeping five, with two bedrooms and kitchen) are attractively decorated, and there's a restaurant. It's a 15min walk south of town. $$$$

International Mochilero Guesthouse 1 C Poniente 33 T 3592 3601; map page 74. A ten-minute walk north of the Parque Central, this hospitable place offers very cheap rates, especially for private doubles, which are bare but OK for a night or two. Staff are friendly, and there's a garden, storage room and guests' kitchen. Dorms $, doubles $$

Maya Papaya 1 Calle Poniente 20 T 5825 7586; map page 74. This spot has rooms finished to a very high standard, with fine-quality bedding and lovely bathrooms (and there's a female-only dorm). Service is friendly and the courtyard bar-restaurant is a great spot to hang out. Dorms $, doubles $$

Mesón Panza Verde 5 Av Sur 1 W panzaverde.com; map page 74. Now under new ownership, this Antigua institution has rooms and suites spread over two colonial-style buildings. It's also home to a top-drawer restaurant, art gallery and lap pool. $$$$

A Place to Stay 5 Calle Poniente Callejón Landivar 42 T 5610 8714, W booking.com; map page 74. A relaxed, sociable hostel with comfy beds and excellent complimentary breakfast. It's located on the west side of town near the bus station. There's a midnight curfew. Dorms $, doubles $$

★ **Posada Juma Ocag** Av Alameda Santa Lucía Norte 13 T 7832 3109; map page 74. Right opposite the market, this very tidy and hospitable guesthouse has immaculately presented, if smallish, rooms decorated with local fabrics; all have good beds, a wardrobe or clothes rack, private bathroom and reading lights. There's a small patio, free drinking water, kitchen and a laundry room. Book well ahead. $$

Posada San Sebastián 3 Av Norte 4 T 7832 2621, W booking.com; map page 74. A tasteful B&B with tastefully decorated rooms, each replete with antiques and artwork and cable TV. There's also a roof terrace, bar and breakfast is complimentary. $$$

San Rafael Hotel 2 C Poniente 7 W thesanrafaelhotel.com; map page 74. Exuding elegance, this very tasteful colonial hotel boasts immaculately presented rooms, most with stately fireplaces and oriental rugs, set around a delightful courtyard. A delicious breakfast is included. $$$$

★ **Tropicana Hostel** 6 C Poniente 2 W tropicanahostel.com; map page 74. This luxe hostel has it all: a pool, hot tub, ping-pong table, garden, terrace, bar, full menu and a welcoming vibe. The cheaper dorms (with triple-deck bunks) have fifteen beds, but the high ceilings and fine-quality mattresses help compensate. Dorms $, doubles $$

La Vieja Terraza 3 C Poniente 24B T 5092 6021; map page 74. This cheap party hostel has a fine roof terrace, which is the perfect spot to take advantage of the all-day happy hour and barbecues. However accommodation is basic and mattresses thin. Dorms $, doubles $$

Yellow House 1 C Poniente 24 T 7832 6646, W yellowhouseantigua.com; map page 74. A welcoming, locally-owned hostel that enjoys a lovely rustic-style roof terrace with hammocks, greenery and views. Accommodation tends to be on the small side but attractive; the cabin-like upstairs rooms are lovely (no. 10 has its own little private terrace). Rates include the use of a kitchen and a good buffet breakfast. Dorms $, doubles $$

AROUND ANTIGUA

★ **Earth Lodge** 7km northeast of Antigua W earthlodgeguatemala.com; map page 74. To really escape the crowds head to this rural retreat (and avocado farm) which enjoys sweeping views of the Panchoy valley and its volcanoes. Accommodation options include A-frame cabañas, a wood-cabin dorm, campsite and tree houses. Wholesome meals are served, and there's a Maya-style sauna and good walking trails. Consult their website for transport information (you can arrange a pick-up from Antigua). Dorm $, cabañas $$

Hobbitenango 9km northeast of Antigua W hobbitenango.com; map page 74. High, high up in the hills above Antigua, this is a quirky, artistically designed place with amazing volcano views (five can be seen on clear days from a lookout nearby), good grub and stellar cocktails. They also host an annual music festival here. Shuttles connect the lodge with Antigua four times a day, for a small fee. Dorms $, cabins $$$

EATING

Antigua has Guatemala's most varied and exciting dining scene, with most types of **global cuisine** represented. It's possible to snack well for a few bucks or dine in style for around US$25/head. The only thing hard to come by can be authentic Guatemalan **comida típica** – which will be a relief if you've been subsisting on eggs and beans in the mountains.

CAFÉS

Barista Coffee Antigua 5 Av Norte 4 T 7832 2211; map page 74. An intimate café right on the plaza serving all the best blends. There's also a decent breakfast menu. $$

★ **Café Condesa** West side of Parque Central – go through the Casa del Conde bookshop W cafecondesa.com.gt; map page 74. A classy café with a gorgeous cobbled patio, smart dining rooms and gurgling fountains. Great for breakfasts, and the salads are superb. There's always a daily special main dish and cake. $$

Café La Escalonia 5 Av Sur 36 C T 7832 7874; map page 74. This lovely café (located inside a plant nursery) is a really peaceful retreat and much of the food is organic. Tuck into healthy breakfasts, *pan de hierbas* sandwiches with salsa dips, pies and salads. They also sell beer and wine. Located 800m south of the Parque Central. $$

Canela Antigua 1 Av Norte 14 T 5992 4180; map page 74. Owned by a master baker from San Francisco, this fine new café is just the place to satisfy all your pastry needs, with artisan breads, cookies and wonderful cinnamon rolls. Offers good breakfast and lunch deals. $$

Doña Luisa's 4 C Oriente 12 W donaluisaxicotencatl.com; map page 74. One of Antigua's most renowned café-restaurants, set in a historic colonial mansion. Offers a straightforward menu of sandwiches, burgers, baked potatoes and salads. The adjoining bakery is one of the best in town. $$

Fernando's Kaffee 7 Av Norte 43 W fernandoskaffee.com; map page 74. Fernando, the very hospitable English-speaking Guatemalan owner, selects and roasts (on the premises) his own hard bean arabica coffee from high-altitude, small estates; he also makes delicious gourmet chocolate. Enjoy your breakfast, sandwich or lunch in the pretty courtyard at the back. $$$

Rainbow Café 7 Av Sur 8 W rainbowcafeantigua.com; map page 74. Courtyard café-restaurant that offers a tempting choice of imaginative salads, Mexican and vegetarian dishes and filling breakfasts, with a daily set lunch for a good deal. There's live music every night, regular political and social lectures and it's also home to a good secondhand bookshop. $$

The Refuge 7 Av Norte 18A W refugecoffeeroasters.com; map page 74. Run by serious baristas, this stylish little café that prides itself that "coffee is our main focus" – though they also sell cakes should you need a sweet treat. $$

Saberico 6 Av Sur 7 W saberico.com.gt; map page 74.

1

Deli-café-restaurant with a lovely shady walled garden at the rear. On the menu you'll find paninis, pancakes, pies, salads, omelettes, pasta and sandwiches. They also sell gourmet chocolate. $$

Y Tú Piña Tambien 1 Av Sur 10B ⓦfacebook.com/YTuPina; map page 74. This arty hangout has fine fruit juices and smoothies, excellent breakfasts and many gluten-free dishes. $$

RESTAURANTS

Angie Angie Cafe Arte 1 Av Sr 11A ⓦfacebook.com/angieangie.cafearte; map page 74. Argentinian-owned restaurant that scores for succulent grilled meats (try the *entraña*), flavoursome salads, fresh pasta, wood-fired pizza and *empanadas argentinas* (savoury pastries). Pass through the deli section and you'll find a lovely rear garden setting for your meal, with tables set around a log fire at night. There's live music (blues, jazz, Latin) some nights. $$

★ **Bistrot Cinq** 4 C Oriente 7 ⓦbistrotcinq.com; map page 74. This stellar restaurant remains one of the nation's very best, with highly proficient French cooking, decor that combines modern and colonial influences and professional, informed service. The menu is short and to the point, with classics like steak frites and onion soup, and always some excellent daily specials. $$$$

Cactus 6 C Poniente 21 ⓦfacebook.com/cactusantigua; map page 74. Mexican-owned, this casual specializes in tacos (try the shrimp and bacon) which are prepared to perfection, as well as filling burritos and mighty fine margaritas. There's live music some nights. $$

Caffè Mediterraneo 6 C Poniente 6A ⓦcaffemediterraneoantigua.com; map page 74. This Italian restaurant has a good reputation for its authentic fresh pasta, *antipasti* and grilled meats. The menu changes monthly, and there's always a daily special or two. $$$

La Canche 6 Av Norte 42; map page 74. For a very local experience, chow down at this humble store-cum-comedor. Filling Guatemalan *comida típica* is the order of the day – take your pick from the steaming pots. Tables are shared; if there's space someone will shout "*¡hay lugar!*". $

Casa de las Mixtas 1 Callejón, off 3 C Poniente; map page 74. A bright little comedor on a quiet lane with inexpensive set meals that really hit the spot, and filling breakfasts. There's a lovely roof terrace for al fresco dining. $

Como Como 2 Av Sur 12 ⓦfacebook.com/comocomoantigua; map page 74. Atmospheric restaurant where you can feast on beautifully-presented pasta, meat and vegetarian dishes in an attractive dining room or outside on the sheltered, candle-lit patio. $$$

La Cuevita de los Urquizú 2 C Oriente 9 ⓦfacebook.com/LaCuevitaDeLosUrquizu; map page 74. A good place to try some typical Guatemalan dishes – choose from the bubbling pots at the restaurant entrance. $$

La Fonda de la Calle Real 3 C Poniente 7 ⓦlafondadelacallereal.com; map page 74. An Antigua institution since 1975, you're guaranteed flavoursome, authentic Guatemalan food in this moderately priced restaurant. Meat dishes are excellent, try the *pepian* (chicken or vegetables in a rich spicy sauce of pumpkin seeds and chilli). $$$

Héctor's Bistro 1 C Poniente 9A ⓦfacebook.com/hbistro; map page 74. A cramped, atmospheric place by La Merced church that's packed every night with diners eating in every available nook and cranny (including on the bar) such is its popularity. It's easy to understand why, as the French-inspired menu is superb. No reservations, so arrive early (before 6pm), come for lunch, or be prepared to wait. $$$$

★ **Izakaya** 6 Av Norte 19A ⓦfacebook.com/izakayaantigua; map page 74. An exceptional restaurant owned by a *Nobu*-trained chef and her partner that has an understated feel: the menu (Japanese fusion) is short and premises are quite simply furnished. There's an open kitchen, so you can watch the tempura, roasted eggplant and miso, and delectable fillets of fish and meats being expertly prepared. $$$$

Luna de Miel 6 Av Nor 40 ⓦlunademielantigua.com; map page 74. Some of the best healthy eating in town, with a menu that also includes some truly calorific treats. Try the crepes if you're craving something sweet. $$

Panza Verde 5 Av Sur 19 ⓦpanzaverde.com; map page 74. Very classy and consistently good European-style restaurant with a well-chosen menu of fish and meat (try the sesame encrusted tuna) and desserts to die for. The setting is sublime, too, with tables grouped around a delightful courtyard garden. $$$$

Pollo Campero Antigua Guatemala Norte Centro Histórico ⓣ7832 1094; map page 74. For a no-frills fried chicken dinner, there's no better spot in town. The portion-to-price ratio is also pretty worthwhile, especially if you're sticking to a daily budget. $

Por Que No? 2 Av Sur & 9 C Oriente ⓣ5610 2274; map page 74. Quirky, cosy little place complete with wacky decor and graffiti-enriched walls run by a very friendly team. There's a short, afforable menu (try the shrimp with Cobanero sauce or a peppercorn steak). $$

Randy's Sausage 5a Calle Poniente, Casa 3 ⓦfacebook.com/randyssausage; map page 74. Simply the best sausages in town – try a spicy Italian, bratwurst or chorizo. $

Santo Domingo del Cerro On a hilltop directly above Antigua ⓦfacebook.com/pg/santodomingocerro; map page 74. This spectacularly situated restaurant and cultural space, operated by the hotel *Casa Santo Domingo* makes an extraordinary setting for a meal with Antigua rolled out below you. Dishes include pizza from a wood-fired oven and fine steaks. After your meal, explore the gardens and paths, contemporary sculptures and the Miguel Ángel Asturias "museum" – a room filled with a few of the Nobel Prize-winning author's possessions. Connected to Antigua by regular minibuses from the hotel. $$$$

Toko Baru 1 Av 17A ⓣ4166 5298; map page 74. This popular and budget-friendly spot is known for serving up a variety of pretty authentic Middle Eastern favourites (particularly falafel and shawarma kebabs) as well as offering Asian dishes including curries, satay and spring rolls. $$

DRINKING AND NIGHTLIFE

Antigua has a lively **drinking** scene with everything from dive bars and Irish pubs to spectacular places in colonial premises, so whether you're after a cold beer or a glass of absinthe, you'll find it here. There were no **clubs** operating at the time of research, though you can dance at *La Sala*. If you want to learn **salsa**, the teacher Gloria Villata is highly recommended; contact her on ⓣ4374 1391 or ⓔsalsacongoloria@yahoo.com.

Antigua Brewing Company 4 Calle Poniente 4 ⓦantiguabrewingco.com; map page 74. Superb microbrewery where you can sup on a quality IPA, ale or in the pub or enjoy the staggering volcano views from the terrace. Regularly hosts live bands.

★**Café No Sé** 1 Av Norte 11C ⓦfacebook.com/CafeNoSe; map page 74. Quirky and bohemian, this terrific candlelit bar is an Antiguan HQ for a crew of hard-drinking local artists and creative types, wasters and wannabes, travellers and expats – plus the odd stray dog. There's good acoustic music virtually nightly, comfort food and an adjoining *mescal* bar serving the house brand: Ilegal.

Café Sky 1 Av Sur ⓣ7832 7300; map page 74. Head up here for panoramic views of Antigua's volcanic surrounds. There's a full cocktail list, and it's the perfect place for a sundowner.

Ocelot 4 Av Norte 3 ⓣ2783 20268; map page 74. Probably Antigua's classiest bar, *Ocelot* is a great place for a relaxed drink, with elegant furnishings, gingham floor tiles, seductive cocktails and live music most nights. Tasty meals are also served, and there's an excellent quiz (trivia) on Sun evenings.

Paprika's Antigua 2 Calle Poniente 6 ⓣ7761 0679; map page 74. This long-running bar is a good bet for happy hour.

Reds 1 C Poniente 3; map page 74. Popular sports bar with pool tables, good beer selection and a pub grub menu that takes in local food, Mexican meals and curries. A good bet if you want to catch that English Premier League, La Liga or American football game.

La Sala 6 C Poniente 9 ⓦfacebook.com/pg/lasalabar; map page 74. Bar-club where DJs spin electronica and house music, Latin music on Sundays and party anthems on Saturday nights. Thursday is Ladies night.

The Snug 6 C Poniente 14 ⓦfacebook.com/thesnugantigua; map page 74. This pint-sized Irish bar is small but perfectly formed, an intimate spot to sip a beer or two. There's live music on weekend nights.

Travel Menu 6 C Poniente 14 ⓦfacebook.com/travelmenuantigua; map page 74. Sociable bar-grill with live music every night. The bar is well stocked and the menu features comfort grub like fish 'n' chips.

ENTERTAINMENT

A number of small video **cinemas, cafés and language schools** show a range of Western and Latin American films on a daily basis. Weekly listings are posted on notice boards all over town and in *Revue* magazine.

LANGUAGE SCHOOLS IN ANTIGUA

Antigua has over 20 established language schools, and many more quite decent establishments. Whether you're just stopping for a week or two to learn the basics, or settling in for several months in pursuit of total fluency, it's an excellent place to learn Spanish: it's a beautiful, relaxed town, lessons are inexpensive (though tend to cost more than in other areas of Guatemala) and there are several superb schools. The following schools employ experienced teachers and offer four or five hours of one-on-one sessions (Monday to Friday) and full family-based lodging and meals.

Antigüena Spanish Academy 1 C Poniente 10, ⓦspanishacademyantiguena.com

Centro Lingüístico Maya 5 C Poniente 20, ⓦcentrolinguisticomaya.com

Christian Spanish Academy 6 Av Norte 15, ⓦlearncsa.com

Francisco Marroquín Language School 6 Av Norte 43, ⓦspanishschoolplfm.com

Ixchel Spanish School 4 Av Norte 32, ⓦixchelschool.com

Ixquic 7 Av Norte 74, ⓦixquic.edu.gt

Probigua 6 Av Norte 41B, ⓦprobigua.com

San José El Viejo 5 Av Sur 34, ⓦsanjoseelviejo.com

Spanish Academy Sevilla 1 Av Sur 17 C, ⓣ7832 5101

Tecún Umán Spanish School 6 C Poniente 34A, ⓦtecunumanschool.edu.gt

1

Proyecto Cultural El Sitio 5 C Poniente 15, facebook.com/ProyectoCulturalElSitio. Latin American and arthouse movies, plus art exhibitions and cultural events including theatre, concerts and lectures. There's a library here too.

SHOPPING

La Bodegona 4 C Poniente and Alameda Santa Lucía 7962 2828; map page 74. One of the city's most useful supermarkets, selling all the essentials.

Casa del Conde West side of Parque Central 7832 3322; map page 74. Bookstore with a good selection of new English-language books about Guatemala as well as travel guides, novels and photography titles.

Dyslexia Books 1 Av Sur 11, 3103 5281, facebook.com/DyslexiaLibros; map page 74. The best secondhand bookstore in town, with lots of interesting fiction and non-fiction in English, Spanish and other European languages.

Nim Po't 5 Av Norte 29 nimpotexport.com; map page 74. Selling fine textiles at fair prices, this warehouse-like store is something of a museum of contemporary Maya weaving, with a stunning array of complete costumes, plus other artesanías including wooden masks and basketry.

DIRECTORY

Banks There are many ATMs in town, including at Banco Industrial, 5 Av Sur 4, just south of the plaza.

Crime If you're a victim of a crime in Antigua, contact English-speaking PROATUR rep José Ángel Quiñonez (5578 9835), who will help you deal with the police and file a report. The police headquarters is outside town.

Internet and phones Free wi-fi is very common in cafés and hotels. Funky Monkey, 5 Av Sur 6, has fast connections and modern terminals (daily 8am–10pm).

Laundry Rainbow Laundry, 6 Av Sur 15 (daily 7.30am–8pm).

Medical care Hospital Privado Hermano Pedro, Av Recolección (7832 1190), offers 24hr emergency service. Dr Marco Antonio Bocaleti has a surgery on 3 Av Norte 1 (7832 4835) and speaks English and German. Ivory Pharmacy is at 6 Av Sur 11 (daily 7am–10pm; 7832 5394).

Post office Av Alameda Santa Lucía (Mon–Fri 8am–5pm).

Around Antigua

The countryside surrounding Antigua is superbly fertile and breathtakingly beautiful, peppered with olive-green coffee bushes and overshadowed by three volcanic cones. The valley is dotted with small villages, ranging from the traditional Indigenous settlement of **Santa María de Jesús** to genteel **San Juan del Obispo**, which is dominated by a huge colonial palace. You'll also find two excellent museums in **Jocotenango**, just north of Antigua. No place is more than thirty minutes away.

GETTING AROUND — AROUND ANTIGUA

Buses southwest Very regular buses leave the Antigua terminal for Ciudad Vieja, San Antonio and San Miguel Dueñas (for Valhalla); the last ones return around 7pm.

Buses to San Juan del Obispo Hourly buses to San Juan leave from the market in Antigua (7am–6pm; 20min) or you can catch any bus heading for Santa María de Jesús, and it's a 5min walk from the main road.

Buses to Santa María de Jesús Buses run from Antigua to Santa María every 30min or so from 6am to 7pm; the trip takes 30min.

Buses north Buses run between San Andrés Itzapa and Antigua about every 45 min. Any bus heading to Chimaltenango also passes through Jocotenango and via the access roads for the hot springs and San Andrés Itzapa.

Southwest of Antigua

Heading out to the **southwest of Antigua** you pass between the flanks of the Agua volcano to the east and the soaring peaks of Acatenango and Fuego on your west side. Sights include a great **macadamia farm**, a **weaving village** and of course the **volcanoes** themselves; **hikes** are best organized in Antigua (see page 81).

Ciudad Vieja

The first settlement of interest southwest of Antigua is **CIUDAD VIEJA**, just east of the highway, a scruffy and unhurried place with a distinguished past: it was near here that the Spanish established their second capital in Guatemala, Santiago de los Caballeros, in 1527. Today, however, there's no trace of the original city, and all that remains from that time is a solitary tree, in a corner of the plaza, which bears a plaque commemorating the site of the first mass ever held in the country. The plaza also boasts an eighteenth-century colonial **church** that has been restored.

San Antonio Aguas Calientes

Three kilometres west of Ciudad Vieja, on the other side of the highway, is **SAN ANTONIO AGUAS CALIENTES**, an Indigenous village set on one side of a steep-sided bowl beneath the peak of Acatenango. San Antonio is famous for weaving, characterized by its complex floral and geometric patterns, and there's an indoor textile market next to the plaza where you can find a complete range of the local output.

Valhalla Experimental Station

1km before the village of San Miguel Dueñas • Ⓦ valhallamacfarm.com

Valhalla Experimental Station is an intriguing farm that grows thousands of **macadamia nut** trees using non-grafted stock (which bear bigger crops and are more disease resistant) as well as blueberry bushes. Visitors are very welcome, and a short tour will reveal all the secrets of nut harvesting and roasting; later there's a chance to sample delicious macadamia pancakes in the café or buy cosmetics and chocolates.

Volcán de Acatenango

Majestic **Acatenango** is the toughest volcano climb in the Antigua region, an exhausting but exhilarating six- to seven-hour hike. Its summit peaks at 3975m, making it the third largest cone in the country. An access fee is now payable at the start of the hike. The route is along a trail of slippery volcanic ash that rises with unrelenting steepness through thick forest. Only for the final 50m or so does it emerge above the tree line, before reaching the top of the lower cone. To the south, after another hour's gruelling ascent, is the summit, accessed via a great grey bowl from where there's a magnificent view out across the valley below. On the opposite side is the Agua volcano and, to the right, the fire-scarred cone of Fuego. Looking west you can see the three volcanic peaks that surround Lago de Atitlán and beyond them the Santa María volcano, high above Quetzaltenango.

THE UNLUCKY ONE

After abandoning their short-lived first settlement near the Kaqchikel capital of Iximché, the Spanish founded **Santiago de los Caballeros** on St Celia's Day in 1527. Set amid perfect pastures in the shadow of the Acatenango and Agua volcanoes, the new city quickly flourished, and within twenty years things had really started to take shape, with a school, a cathedral, monasteries and farms stocked with imported cattle. But while most Spaniards were still settling in, their leader, the rapacious **Alvarado**, was off in search of action, wealth and conquest. In 1541 he set out for the Spice Islands, travelling via Jalisco, where he met his end, crushed to death beneath a rolling horse.

When news of Alvarado's death reached his wife, **Doña Beatriz**, she plunged the capital into an extended period of mourning, staining the entire palace with black clay, inside and out. She appointed herself as her husband's replacement, and on September 9, 1541, became the first woman to govern in the Americas, signing the declaration as *La Sin Ventura* (the unlucky one) – a fateful premonition.

On the night of Beatriz's inauguration, an earthquake shook Volcán de Agua's crater, releasing a great wave of mud that swept away the capital, killing the new ruler and most of her courtiers. Today the exact site of the original city is still the subject of some debate, but the general consensus puts it about 2km to the east of Ciudad Vieja.

Several agencies in Antigua run **hiking trips** (see page 81), usually involving camping halfway up the cone and then an ascent in the early hours of the morning.

Southeast of Antigua

The road **southeast of Antigua** slaloms up the side of the Agua volcano, passing a fascinating colonial palace on its way up to the village of Santa María de Jesús, base camp for hiking the cone.

San Juan del Obispo

The small village of **SAN JUAN DEL OBISPO** is an attractive, quiet little place of cobbled streets with fine views of the great domes of Antigua. San Juan is renowned for its **chocolate** production, which is something of a local cottage industry.

Palacio de Francisco Marroquín

Beside the church • Free, donation requested

San Juan's one outstanding sight is the **Palacio de Francisco Marroquín**, named for the first bishop of Guatemala. The palace is currently home to a dozen or so nuns, and if you knock on the great wooden double doors one of them will give you a tour in Spanish. Marroquín, who arrived in Guatemala with Alvarado, is credited with having introduced Christianity to the Maya, as well as reminding the Spaniards about it from time to time. On the death of Alvarado's wife (see box), Marroquín assumed temporary responsibility for the government, and was instrumental in the construction of Antigua. He died in 1563, having spent his last days in the vast palace he'd built for himself here in San Juan.

The palace interior, arranged around two courtyards, is highly impressive. Several rooms still contain their original furniture, as well as a portrait of Marroquín himself. Excellent information panels (in Spanish and English) detail the life of the bishop, who many Guatemalans see as the first father of the nation and credit for introducing the concept of multiculturalism. Attached to the palace is a fantastic **church** and chapel with ornate woodcarvings, plaster mouldings and austere religious paintings.

Santa María de Jesús

Up above San Juan the road arrives in the scruffy Indigenous village of **SANTA MARÍA DE JESÚS**, starting point for the ascent of the Agua volcano. Perched high on the shoulder of the great peak, some 500m above Antigua, the village boasts magnificent views of the Panchoy valley and east towards the smoking cone of Pacaya. It was founded at the end of the sixteenth century for Maya transported from Quetzaltenango: they were given the task of providing firewood for Antigua and the village earned the name "Aserradero", lumber yard. Since then it has developed into a farming community where the women wear beautiful purple *huipiles*.

Volcán de Agua

Volcán de Agua is the easiest and by far the most popular of Guatemala's big cones to climb, and on Saturday nights dozens of people spend the night at the summit. It's an exciting ascent with a fantastic view to reward you at the top. The trail starts in Santa María de Jesús (see above): first visit the village municipalidad (opens at 6am) and buy a ticket, you'll be assigned a guide (this is an additional fee which you can share with others as part of a group). It's a fairly straightforward, though tough, climb on a clear (often rubbish-strewn) path, taking around five hours, and the peak, at 3766m, is always cold at night. There is shelter (though not always room) in a small chapel at the summit, and the views certainly make it worth the struggle. Reckon on three hours to return.

FIESTAS AROUND GUATEMALA CITY AND ANTIGUA

The region around Guatemala City and Antigua is not prime **fiesta** territory; however, a few villages, listed below, have some firmly established traditions and dramatic celebrations. The following are just a selection of the highlights.

JANUARY–MAY

January 1–5 Santa María de Jesús, main day Jan 1.
February First Friday in Lent, Antigua; San Felipe de Jesús has a huge pilgrimage.
Holy Week Celebrated with fervour in Antigua (see page 78).
May 1 Guatemala City; Labour Day is marked by marches and protests.

JUNE–AUGUST

June 24 San Juan del Obispo and Comalapa have large fiestas.
July 25 Antigua, in honour of Santiago.
August 15 Jocotenango and Guatemala City.

SEPTEMBER–NOVEMBER

September 29 San Miguel Dueñas; dances include Los Toritos.
October 18 San Lucas Sacatepéquez; dances include Moors and Christians.
October 28 San Andrés Itzapa; all-nighter with San Simón paraded through the town.
November 1 Sumpango and Santiago Sacatepéquez; massive kites flown.

As there have been (occasional) **robberies** reported on the outskirts of Santa María it's best to team up with an Antigua adventure sports company (see page 81) and not attempt the hike on your own.

North of Antigua

The route to Chimaltenango, **north of Antigua**, passes through a succession of sprawling villages, presenting a scruffy introduction to the western highlands. There are some interesting attractions along the way, however, including a fine **cultural centre**, some **hot springs** and the temple of a **pagan saint**.

Jocotenango

Long notorious for its seedy bars, the grimy suburb of **JOCOTENANGO**, "place of bitter fruit", is set around a huge, dusty plaza where there's a weathered, dusty-pink Baroque church. In colonial times, Jocotenango was the gateway to Antigua, where official visitors would be met to be escorted into the city. Today the main industries are coffee production and woodcarving; there's an excellent selection of bowls and fruits in the family-owned **Artesanías Cardenas Barrios** workshop on Calle San Felipe, where they have been working at the trade for five generations.

Centro Cultural La Azotea

Charge, including tour in English or Spanish • Ⓦ laazotea.gt • Special minibuses run hourly from Antigua's Parque Central to the Centro

Joco's principal attraction is 500m west of the plaza, in the shape of the **Centro Cultural La Azotea**. **Casa K'ojom**, which forms one half of the cultural centre compound, is a purpose-built museum dedicated to Maya culture, especially music. The history of Indigenous musical traditions is clearly presented from its pre-Columbian origins, through sixteenth-century Spanish and African influences – which brought the marimba, bugles and drums – to the present day, with audiovisual documentaries highlighting fiestas and ceremonies. Other rooms are dedicated to the village weavings of the Sacatepéquez department and the cult of Maximón (see 90).

THE WICKED SAINT OF SAN ANDRÉS ITZAPA

San Andrés shares with many western highland villages (including Zunil and Santiago Atitlán) the honour of revering **San Simón**, or Maximón, the wicked saint, whose image is housed in a pagan chapel in the village. His abode is home to drunken men, cigar-smoking women and hundreds of burning candles, each symbolizing a request. Curiously this San Simón attracts a largely ladino congregation and is particularly popular with sex workers. Inside the dimly lit shrine, the walls are adorned with hundreds of plaques from all over Guatemala and Central America, thanking San Simón for his help. For a small fee, you may be offered a *limpia*, or soul cleansing, which involves one of the resident women workers beating you with a bushel of herbs while you share a bottle of local firewater, *aguardiente*, with San Simón (it dribbles down his front); the attendant will periodically spray you with alcohol from her mouth. If you are in the region, try to get to San Andrés on **October 28** when San Simón is removed from his sanctuary and paraded through the town in a pagan celebration featuring much alcohol and dancing.

Next door, the **Museo de Café** offers the chance to look around a working organic coffee farm that dates back to 1883. All the technicalities of husking, sieving and roasting are clearly explained, and an interpretive trail leads through the bushes of the finca. If you're here in February or March when the coffee plants flower, you'll discern a wonderfully fragrant scent in the air, a little like jasmine.

San Lorenzo El Tejar hot springs

Four kilometres north of Jocotenango • charge

The village of **SAN LORENZO EL TEJAR** has some enjoyable hot (or at least warm) **springs**; they're a couple of kilometres from the main road. If you want to bathe in the sulphurous waters, you can either use the cheaper communal pool or, for a few bucks, rent one of your own – a little private room with a huge tiled tub. Sundays can get very busy with local families.

San Andrés Itzapa

About 10km north of Jocotenango, beyond Parramos, a side road branches to **SAN ANDRÉS ITZAPA**, famed as a base for the cult of San Simón, or **Maximón** (see page 90). The so-called wicked saint's abode is a short stroll from the central plaza, up a little hill – you should spot street vendors selling charms, incense and candles. If you get lost, ask for the Casa de San Simón. San Andrés' Tuesday **market** is also worth a visit.

The western highlands

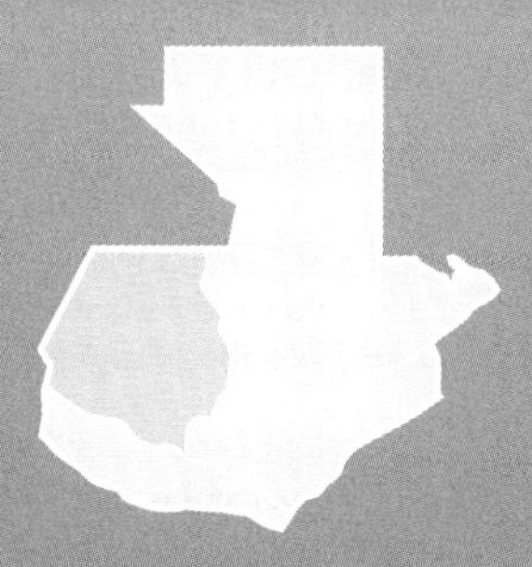

TODOS SANTOS CUCHUMATÁN

The western highlands

Guatemala's western highlands, stretching from the outskirts of Antigua to the Mexican border, are perhaps the most beautiful and captivating part of the entire country. Two main features dominate the area: a chain of awesome volcanoes on the southern side, and the high Cuchumatanes mountain range that looms over the north of the region. Strung between these two natural barriers is a series of spectacular forested ridges, lakes, gushing streams and plunging, verdant valleys. The highland landscape is defined by many factors, but above all altitude. At lower levels the vegetation is almost tropical, supporting dense forests and crops of coffee, bananas and vegetables. Higher up in the hills, pine, cedar and oak forests are interspersed with patchwork fields of maize and potatoes. In the highest terrain, known as the *altiplano*, the land is largely treeless and often wrapped in cloud, suited only to hardy herds of sheep and goats.

This region is predominantly peopled by the **Maya**, who have lived here continuously for two thousand years. Maya society, languages and traditions are markedly different from mainstream Latin American culture, and exploring their bewitchingly beautiful highland home is a highlight to any trip in Guatemala.

With stunning mountain scenery yielding colourful market towns and whitewashed colonial churches at every turn, you're spoilt for places to visit. **Lago de Atitlán**, surrounded by volcanoes and with its idyllic shores harbouring some fascinating villages, is absolutely unmissable. To the north is the fabled market town of **Chichicastenango** and the wildly beautiful peaks and remote, intensely traditional communities of the **Ixil**, a region that is excellent for hiking.

Heading west, you'll reach Guatemala's second city, **Quetzaltenango** (Xela), an ideal base for visiting Maya villages and the hot springs of **Fuentes Georginas** and for climbing the perfectly proportioned volcanic cone of **Santa María**. Beyond this, you start encountering the massive granite peaks of the Cuchumatanes; there are excellent walking trails around the spectacular Mam Maya village of **Todos Santos Cuchumatán**. The extreme northwest of this region, around **Gracias a Dios**, is opening up to tourism, with pine-fringed lakes and spectacular natural attractions.

Historical sites, such as the pre-conquest cities of **Iximché**, **K'umarkaaj** and **Zaculeu**, are also worthy of your attention – although they don't bear comparison to Tikal and the lowland ruins.

Brief history

A peripheral area during the Classic Maya civilization (250–900 AD), the western highlands were colonized towards the end of the twelfth century by **Toltecs** from central Mexico. With the Toltecs established as overlords, local tribes bitterly contested regional hegemony. The most powerful tribes were the **K'iche'**, based at their capital K'umarkaaj, the **Mam** at Zaculeu and **Kaqchikel** at Iximché. Smaller tribal groups such as the Ixil also occupied clearly defined areas.

The colonial era

The **arrival of the Spanish** in 1523 was a disaster for the Maya population. Leader **Pedro de Alvarado** and his conquistadors first defeated the K'iche', and by 1527 they had the entire western highlands under their control with a combination of military discipline,

VIEW OF SAN JUAN LA LAGUNA, LAGO DE ATITLÁN

Highlights

❶ **The Ixil region** Hike the hillside trails of this remote, intensely traditional Indigenous region. See page 108

❷ **Lago de Atitlán** An awesome steep-sided crater lake ringed by volcanoes and diminutive Indigenous villages. See page 115

❸ **San Pedro La Laguna** This town has a breathtaking lakeside location and its boho vibe makes it a draw for young travellers. See page 126

❹ **Quetzaltenango** Guatemala's refined second city has a great highland setting and is an excellent base for studying Spanish. See page 137

❺ **Fuentes Georginas** Offering the perfect place to linger over a long afternoon, these sublime hot-spring-fed pools are situated halfway up a volcano. See page 147

❻ **The Cuchumatanes** The Cuchumatanes mountain range offers a high-altitude plateau, the most dramatic road trip in the country and some deeply traditional villages, including Todos Santos Cuchumatán. See page 156

❼ **Around Gracias a Dios** This area yields some superb sights including a 200m-deep sinkhole, two beautiful cenotes and a collection of minor ruins. See page 165

HIGHLIGHTS ARE MARKED ON THE MAP ON PAGE 96

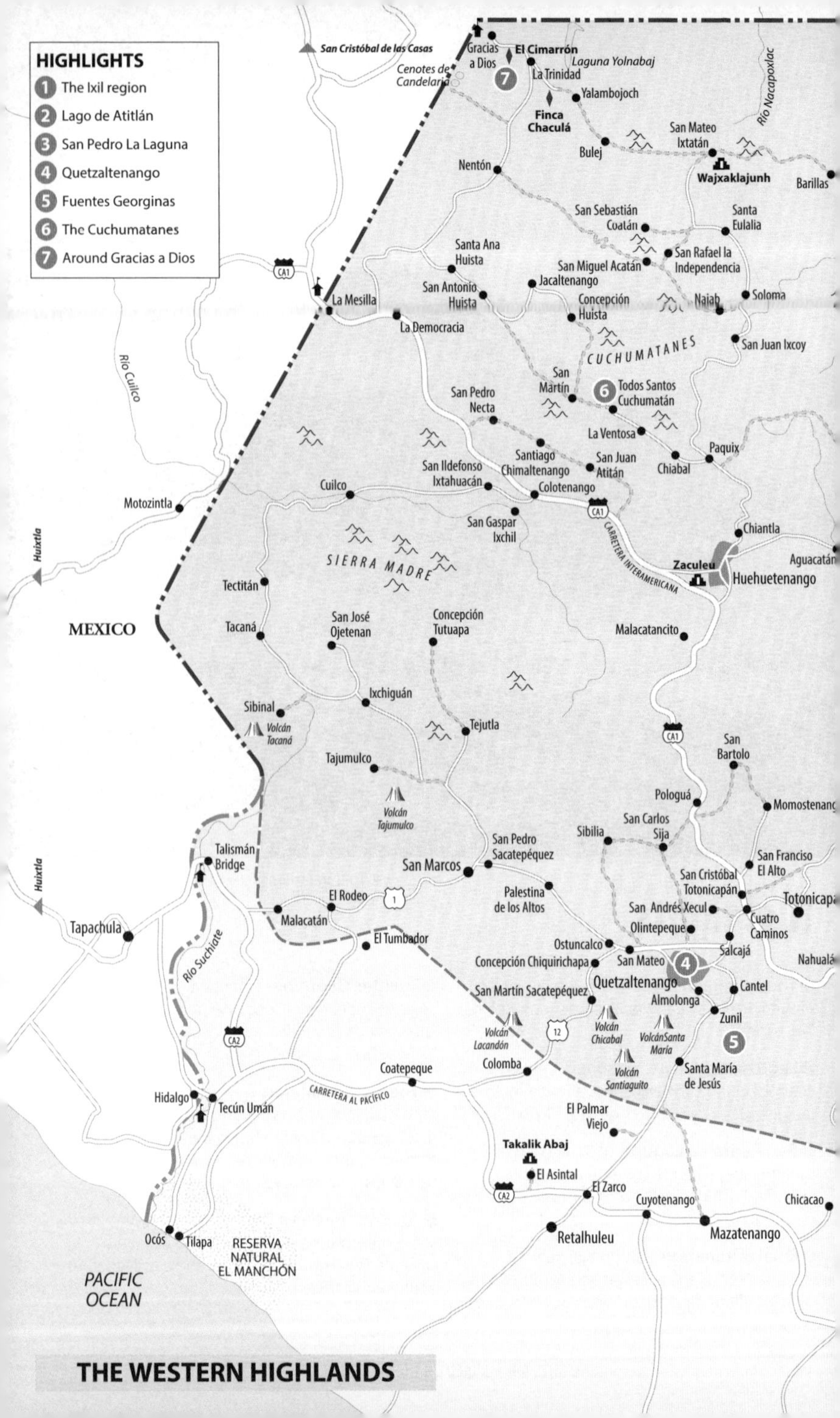
HIGHLIGHTS
1 The Ixil region
2 Lago de Atitlán
3 San Pedro La Laguna
4 Quetzaltenango
5 Fuentes Georginas
6 The Cuchumatanes
7 Around Gracias a Dios
THE WESTERN HIGHLANDS
MEXICO
PACIFIC OCEAN
San Cristóbal de las Casas
Gracias a Dios
El Cimarrón
Laguna Yolnabaj
Cenotes de Candelaria
La Trinidad
Yalambojoch
Finca Chaculá
Río Nacapoxlac
San Mateo Ixtatán
Bulej
Nentón
Wajxaklajunh
Barillas
San Sebastián Coatán
Santa Eulalia
Santa Ana Huista
San Rafael la Independencia
San Miguel Acatán
Jacaltenango
San Antonio Huista
Concepción Huista
Najab
Soloma
La Mesilla
La Democracia
San Juan Ixcoy
CUCHUMATANES
Río Cuilco
San Martín
Todos Santos Cuchumatán
San Pedro Necta
La Ventosa
Santiago Chimaltenango
San Juan Atitán
Chiabal
Paquix
San Ildefonso Ixtahuacán
Cuilco
Colotenango
Motozintla
San Gaspar Ixchil
CARRETERA INTERAMERICANA
Chiantla
Huixtla
SIERRA MADRE
Zaculeu
Aguacatán
Huehuetenango
Tectitán
Tacaná
San José Ojetenan
Concepción Tutuapa
Malacatancito
Ixchiguán
Sibinal
Volcán Tacaná
Tejutla
Tajumulco
Volcán Tajumulco
San Bartolo
Pologuá
Momostenango
San Carlos Sija
Sibilia
San Pedro Sacatepéquez
San Francisco El Alto
Talismán Bridge
San Marcos
Palestina de los Altos
San Cristóbal Totonicapán
Totonicapán
El Rodeo
San Andrés Xecul
Cuatro Caminos
Malacatán
Olintepeque
Tapachula
El Tumbador
Ostuncalco
Salcajá
Río Suchiate
San Mateo
Concepción Chiquirichapa
Nahualá
Quetzaltenango
San Martín Sacatepéquez
Cantel
Almolonga
Zunil
Volcán Lacandón
Volcán Chicabal
Volcán Santa María
Volcán Santiaguito
Colomba
Santa María de Jesús
Coatepeque
CARRETERA AL PACÍFICO
Hidalgo
Tecún Umán
El Palmar Viejo
Takalik Abaj
El Asintal
El Zarco
Cuyotenango
Chicacao
Mazatenango
Retalhuleu
Ocós
Tilapa
RESERVA NATURAL EL MANCHÓN
CA1
CA2
1
12

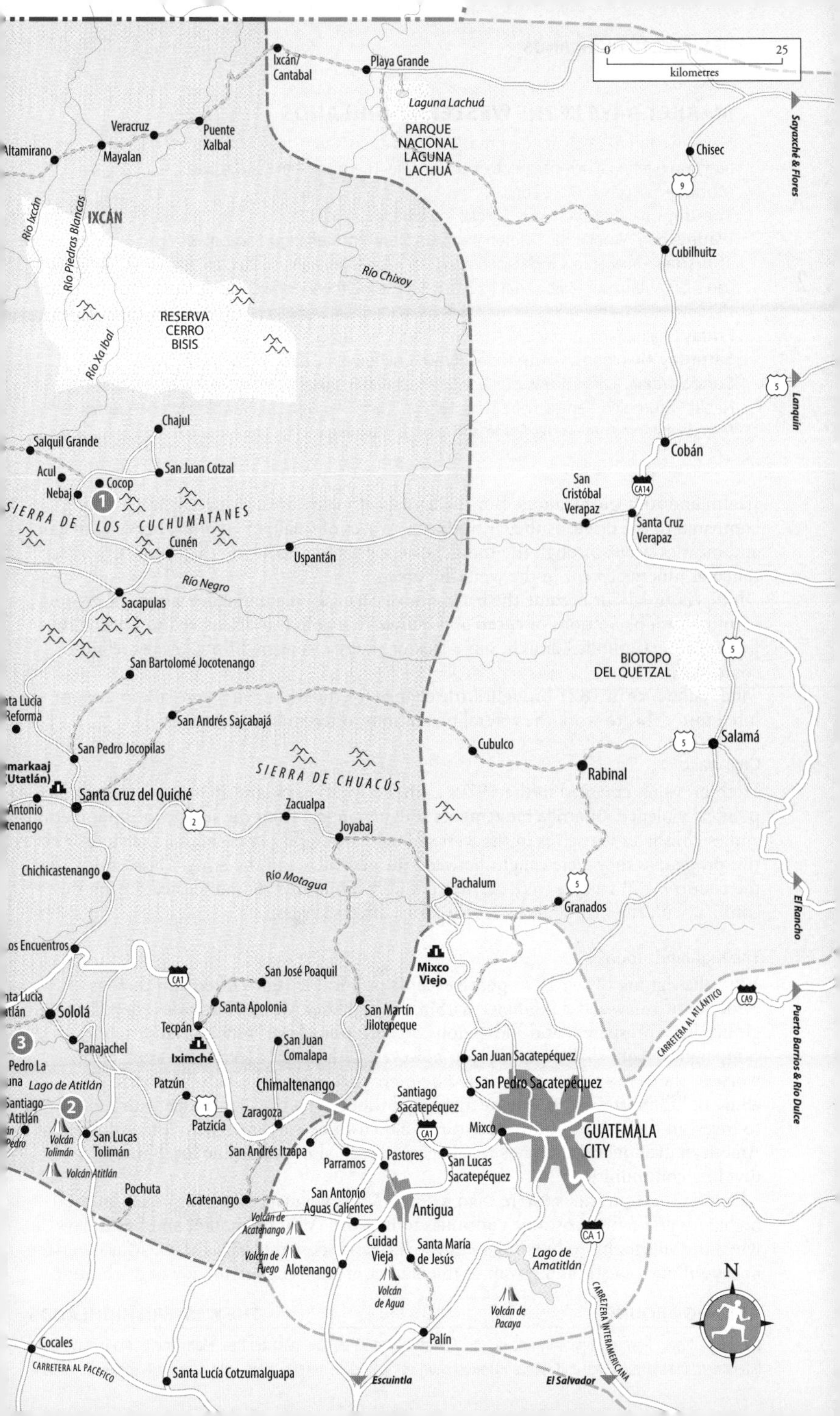
0
25
kilometres
Ixcán/
Cantabal
Playa Grande
Laguna Lachuá
PARQUE
NACIONAL
LAGUNA
LACHUÁ
Veracruz
Puente
Xalbal
Altamirano
Mayalan
IXCÁN
Río Ixcán
Río Piedras Blancas
Río Xa Ibal
RESERVA
CERRO
BISIS
Río Chixoy
Sayaxché & Flores
Chisec
Cubilhuitz
Lanquín
Chajul
Salquil Grande
San Juan Cotzal
Acul
Cocop
Nebaj
SIERRA DE LOS CUCHUMATANES
Cunén
Uspantán
Cobán
San
Cristóbal
Verapaz
Santa Cruz
Verapaz
Río Negro
Sacapulas
San Bartolomé Jocotenango
BIOTOPO
DEL QUETZAL
San Andrés Sajcabajá
Cubulco
Salamá
Rabinal
San Pedro Jocopilas
SIERRA DE CHUACÚS
Santa Cruz del Quiché
Zacualpa
Joyabaj
Chichicastenango
Río Motagua
Pachalum
Granados
El Rancho
Los Encuentros
Mixco
Viejo
San José Poaquil
Santa Apolonia
Sololá
Panajachel
San Martín
Jilotepeque
Tecpán
Iximché
San Juan
Comalapa
CARRETERA AL ATLÁNTICO
Puerto Barrios & Río Dulce
San Juan Sacatepéquez
San Pedro Sacatepéquez
Lago de Atitlán
Patzún
Chimaltenango
Santiago
Sacatepéquez
Zaragoza
Patzicía
Mixco
GUATEMALA
CITY
Volcán
Tolimán
San Lucas
Tolimán
Volcán Atitlán
San Andrés Itzapa
Parramos
Pastores
San Lucas
Sacatepéquez
Pochuta
Acatenango
San Antonio
Aguas Calientes
Antigua
Volcán de
Acatenango
Volcán de
Fuego
Alotenango
Cuidad
Vieja
Santa María
de Jesús
Lago de
Amatitlán
Volcán
de Agua
Volcán de
Pacaya
CARRETERA INTERAMERICANA
N
Palín
Cocales
CARRETERA AL PACÍFICO
Santa Lucía Cotzumalguapa
Escuintla
El Salvador

MARKET DAYS IN THE WESTERN HIGHLANDS

Make an effort to catch as many **market days** as possible – they're second only to local fiestas in offering a rich perspective of Maya life. These are some of the best:

Monday San Juan Atitán; Zunil.
Tuesday Chajul; Olintepeque; Sololá; Totonicapán.
Wednesday Almolonga; Colotenango; Cotzal; Momostenango; Sacapulas.
Thursday Aguacatán; Chichicastenango; Jacaltenango; Nahualá; Nebaj; Panajachel; Sacapulas; San Juan Atitán; San Mateo Ixtatán; San Rafael La Independencia; Soloma; Tajumulco; Uspantán; Zacualpa.
Friday Chajul; San Francisco el Alto; San Martín; Santiago Atitlán; Sololá.
Saturday Almolonga; Cotzal; Todos Santos Cuchumatán; Totonicapán.
Sunday Aguacatán; Chichicastenango; Jacaltenango; Joyabaj; Momostenango; Nahualá; Nebaj; Ostuncalco; Panajachel; Sacapulas; San Juan Comalapa; San Martín Jilotepeque; San Mateo Ixtatán; Santa Eulalia; Soloma; Uspantán; Zacualpa.

stealth and strategic alliances. But the damage done by Spanish swords was nothing compared to the **diseases** they introduced. Waves of smallpox, typhus, bubonic plague and measles swept through the Indigenous population, reducing their numbers by as much as ninety percent in the worst-hit areas.

Indigenous labour became the backbone of Spanish rule in Guatemala, with income coming from plantations of **cacao** and **indigo.** The colonists attempted to impose the power of the Catholic Church, but a lack of clergy meant traditional Maya religion could continue.

Independence in 1821 brought little change for the Maya who were still forced (or lured into debt) to work the coastal plantations, often in horrific conditions.

Civil war

Fresh pressures emerged in the 1970s as the Maya were caught up in waves of horrific political violence. **Guerrilla movements** sought support from the Indigenous population and established themselves in the western highlands. The Maya became the victims in this process, as they were caught between the guerrillas and the army. Thousands fled the country, 440 villages were destroyed and two hundred thousand died during the conflict, with the highlands by far the worst affected region.

The highlands today

With the signing of the 1996 **peace accords** political tensions lifted and there is evidence of a new self-confidence within the highland Maya. Grass-roots development groups have prospered, and Indigenous organizations have launched land rights campaigns. Many challenges remain, however, with poverty levels still some of the worst in the hemisphere, exacerbated by high birth rates and unemployment. The allure of "El Norte" entices many away, and though many exiles return with money to invest in their communities, centuries-old customs are threatened. The influence of American **evangelical churches** (see page 338) can also undermine local hierarchies, dividing communities.

Despite these pressures, more than a dozen Maya languages are still spoken in the highlands and native costume continues to be worn. Visit on **market** and **fiesta** days when the villages fill to bursting, and you'll clearly sense the values of the Maya world in the subdued bustle and gossip of the market or from the intense joy of celebration.

GETTING AROUND — THE WESTERN HIGHLANDS

By bus Buses flow continuously along the Carretera Interamericana between 6am and 7pm, and tourist shuttles serve all the main centres. Many minor roads have been paved in recent years, and transport connections have improved greatly. Often the most practical plan of action is to base yourself in one of the larger places and then make a series of day-trips to village markets and fiestas, although even the smallest settlements will usually offer some kind of accommodation.

The Carretera Interamericana

The serpentine **Carretera Interamericana** (Pan-American highway) forms the main artery of transport in the highlands, and this road and its junctions will inevitably become very familiar. Virtually the entire route between Guatemala City and the turn-off for Quetzaltenango is now a smooth four-lane highway, though traffic is always heavy. The first of three major junctions you'll get to know is the less than lovely **Chimaltenango**, from where you can make connections to Antigua. As you continue west, **Los Encuentros** is the next main junction, where one road heads off to the north for Chichicastenango and another branches south to Panajachel. Beyond this is **Cuatro Caminos**, from where side roads lead to Quetzaltenango, Totonicapán and San Francisco el Alto. The Carretera Interamericana continues on to Huehuetenango before it reaches the Mexican border at La Mesilla. Virtually every bus travelling along the highway will stop at all of these junctions.

Chimaltenango

Grimy **CHIMALTENANGO**'s main focal point is the Carretera Interamericana, which cuts through the southern side of the town. Frankly it's a traffic-plagued hell hole, the grossly polluted roadside littered with mechanics' workshops and sleazy bars. There's absolutely no reason to hang around here, and you should take care with your bags if you are changing buses as pickpockets are known to target disorientated travellers.

ARRIVAL AND DEPARTURE — CHIMALTENANGO

By bus Chicken buses to Antigua leave every 15min between 6am and 7pm from the turn-off on the highway. You can also pick up connections to all points west on the highway and Guatemala City (every 15min; 1hr) here.

San Martín Jilotepeque

To the north of Chimaltenango, it's a 19km ride past plunging ravines and pine forests to the village of **SAN MARTÍN JILOTEPEQUE**. San Martín had to be rebuilt following the 1976 earthquake, but its sprawling Sunday market is well worth a visit. The local weaving, women's *huipiles* especially, is some of the finest you'll see, with intricate and ornate patterning, predominantly in reds and purples.

ARRIVAL AND DEPARTURE — SAN MARTÍN JILOTEPEQUE

By bus Buses to San Martín leave the market in Chimaltenango every 30-40min from 5am to 6pm for the 30min trip, with many continuing on to Joyabaj.

San Juan Comalapa

Around 16km west of Chimaltenango, there's a turn-off for the village of **SAN JUAN COMALAPA** which has a collection of eroded pre-Columbian sculptures displayed in its plaza, and a monument to Rafael Alvarez Ovalle, who composed the Guatemalan national anthem. Looking out over the plaza is a fine Baroque church that dates from colonial times. As ever, the best time to visit is for the **market**, on Sunday, which brings people out in force.

The villagers of Comalapa have something of a reputation as **folk artists**. The tradition began with **Andrés Curuchich** (1891–1969), who painted simple scenes documenting village life; there's a permanent exhibition devoted to his paintings at the Museo Ixchel, Guatemala City (see page 61). Several dozen painters continue Curuchich's tradition, and their work can be bought in galleries in the town.

Two blocks from the plaza, **Museo de Arte Maya** (3 C 0–74; charge) has a good collection of folk art as well as Maya ceramics and artefacts and some fascinating old photographs.

ARRIVAL AND DEPARTURE — SAN JUAN COMALAPA

By bus Buses to San Juan Comalapa run about every 30min from Chimaltenango with the journey taking around 45min. In addition, you will also find a number of microbuses waiting at the highway turn-off.

Iximché

IXIMCHÉ, the pre-conquest capital of the Kaqchikel, is 5km south of the Interamericana on a beautiful exposed site, isolated on three sides by plunging ravines and surrounded by pine forests. The majority of the buildings, originally built of adobe, have disappeared, but the site – which had a population of about ten thousand – is very atmospheric.

Brief history

Iximché was first established around 1470. From the early days of the Conquest the Kaqchikel Maya allied themselves with the Spanish, in order to defeat their tribal enemies the K'iche'. Grateful for the assistance, the Spanish established their **first headquarters** near here on May 7, 1524. The Kaqchikel referred to Alvarado as *Tonatiuh*, the son of the sun, and as a mark of respect he was given the daughter of a Kaqchikel king as a gift. Within months, however, the Kaqchikel rebelled, outraged by Alvarado's demands for tribute. The conquistador retaliated by burning Iximché and then moved operations to the greater safety of Ciudad Vieja, a short distance from Antigua.

George W. Bush stopped by Iximché in 2007 and was treated to a marimba display and a demonstration of the Maya ball game. Not everyone was pleased with his presence, however, and Maya elders later held a ceremony to spiritually cleanse the site and the residual "bad energy".

The ruins

Charge

The **ruins of Iximché** are made up of four main plazas, a couple of ball courts and several small pyramids. In most cases only the foundations and lower parts of the original structures were built of stone, while the upper walls were of adobe, with thatched roofs supported by wooden beams. You can make out the ground plan of many of the buildings, but it's only the most important all-stone structures that still stand. The most significant buildings were those clustered around courts A and C, and on the sides of **Temple 2** you can make out some badly eroded murals.

It's thought that Iximché was a **ceremonial centre** used for religious rituals, and Maya worship still takes place here down a small trail through the pine trees behind the final plaza. Archeological digs have unearthed the decapitated heads of sacrifice victims, burial sites, grinding stones, obsidian knives, a flute made from a child's femur and large numbers of incense burners.

Iximché's shady setting is perfect for a **picnic**; you can buy drinks at the site.

ARRIVAL AND DEPARTURE — IXIMCHÉ

By bus To get here, hop off any bus travelling along the Carretera Interamericana at the turn-off for Tecpán. The centre of Tecpán town is about 500m from the road, from where microbuses leave for the ruins every 20min and the ride takes about 10min. Be sure to bring small change for the bus fare.

El Quiché

At the heart of the western highlands, the department of **El Quiché** encompasses the full range of Guatemalan scenery. The south is fertile and heavily populated while to the north the landscape becomes increasingly dramatic, rising to the massive, rain-soaked peaks of the **Cuchumatanes**. For the traveller, El Quiché has a lot to offer, including **Chichicastenango**, the scene of a vast, twice-weekly market and still a pivotal centre of Maya religion. Beyond here are the ruins of **K'umarkaaj**; further to the north, the sheer scale of the mountain scenery is exhilarating. Isolated villages set in superb highland bowls sustain a wealth of Indigenous culture and occupy a misty, mysterious world of their own – above all in the land of the **Ixil**.

Brief history

The region takes its name from the greatest of the pre-conquest tribal groups, the **K'iche'**, who overran much of the highlands by 1450 from their capital at K'umarkaaj. With little in the way of plunder, this remote, mountainous terrain remained an unimportant backwater for the Spanish. The region became a centre of intense guerrilla activity in the late 1970s and was the scene of unrivalled repression, as tens of thousands of villagers were wiped out by the military. Today these highlands remain a stronghold of Maya culture, and El Quiché, dotted with small villages and mountain towns, is the scene of some superb fiestas and markets.

Chichicastenango

North from **Los Encuentros** junction, the road drops down through dense pine forests into a deep ravine before beginning a tortuous ascent around a seemingly endless series of switchbacks until reaching **CHICHICASTENANGO**. Dubbed Guatemala's "Mecca del Turismo", Chichi is a compact and traditional town of cobbled streets, though the charming old adobe houses are now outnumbered by modern concrete structures. Twice a week the town's highland calm is shattered by the Sunday and Thursday **markets**, which attract many tourists, traders and Maya weavers from throughout the central highlands.

The market is by no means all that sets Chichicastenango apart, for it's also a major centre of culture and **religion** where over the years Maya traditions and folk Catholicism have been treated with a rare degree of respect. Today the town has an important collection of Maya artefacts, parallel Indigenous and ladino governments and two churches that make no effort to disguise their acceptance of unconventional pagan worship.

Locals adhere to the ways of **traditional weaving**, the women wearing superb *huipiles* with flower motifs. The men's costume of short trousers and jackets of black wool embroidered with silk is highly distinguished, although it's very expensive to make and these days almost all men opt for Western dress. For Sundays and fiestas, however, a handful of *cofrades* (elders of the religious hierarchy) still wear the *traje* clothing and

FIESTA TIME IN CHICHICASTENANGO

Chichicastenango's appetite for religious fervour is especially evident during the **fiesta** of Santo Tomás, from December 14 to 21. It's a spectacular occasion, with attractions including the *Palo Volador*, in which men dangle by ropes from a 20m pole (see page 340), a live band or two, a massive procession, traditional dances, clouds of incense, gallons of *chicha* and deafening fireworks. On the final day, all babies born in the previous year are brought to the church for christening. **Easter** is also celebrated with tremendous energy and piety.

parade through the streets bearing spectacular silver processional crosses and antique incense burners.

Santo Tomás

Main plaza • Free

At the main church of **Santo Tomás** in the southeast corner of the plaza, the local K'iche' Maya (called *Maxeños*) have been left to adopt their own style of worship, blending pre-Columbian and Catholic rituals. The church was built in 1540 on the site of a Maya altar and rebuilt in the eighteenth century; it's said that Indigenous locals became interested in worshipping here after Francisco Ximénez, the resident priest from 1701 to 1703, started reading their holy book, the **Popol Vuh** (see box). Seeing that he held considerable respect for their religion, they moved their altars from the

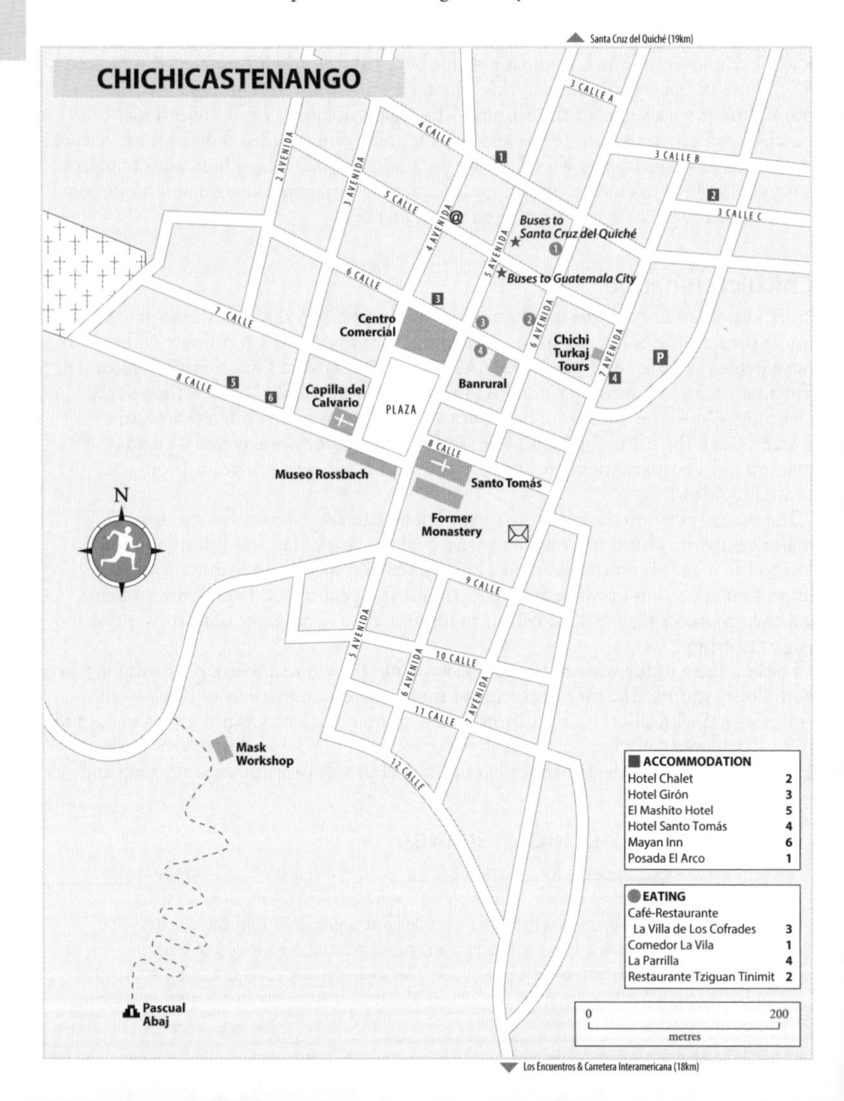

THE POPOL VUH

Written in K'umarkaaj shortly after the arrival of the Spanish, the more than nine thousand lines of the **Popol Vuh** detail the cosmology, mythology and traditional history of the K'iche'. The first of the two parts of this sacred poem is an account of the K'iche's **creation** by their god, who is known as **Heart of Sky**. According to the Popol Vuh, at first there was only water and sky; the creator then formed earth and mountains, plants and trees. Heart of Sky turned his attention to animals, and created creatures of the forest including deer, birds and jaguars. Unsatisfied with these animals, the creator fashioned humans from corn paste after twice failing to make man from mud and wood. The Popol Vuh then recounts the adventures of the ancestors of mankind, the **hero twins** (or wizard twins) Hunahpú and Xbalanqué, which culminate in an epic struggle with the death lords of **Xibalbá**, the Maya underworld. The twins ultimately triumph, and the cycle of creation is born.

The Popol Vuh's second half describes the wanderings of the K'iche' ancestors as they migrate south from the Toltec area of Mexico and settle in the highlands of Guatemala. Evidence gathered by archeologists and epigraphers strongly supports the accuracy of this part of the epic. The book concludes with a history of K'iche' royalty, and suggests a shared lineage with these kings and their gods. Dennis Tedlock's translation of the Popol Vuh (see page 351) is regarded as the definitive text.

hills and set them up inside the building, where this ancient, unique hybrid of Maya and Catholic worship continues today.

Before entering the church, it is customary to make offerings in a fire in front of the building and burn *copal* and *estoraque* incense in perforated cans, a practice that leaves a cloud of sweet smoke hanging over Santo Tomás's stone steps. It's highly offensive to take **photographs** inside the building – you shouldn't even contemplate it.

The front door is reserved for *cofrades* and senior church officials, so you must enter through the **side door**. Inside is an astonishing scene of avid worship. A soft hum of constant murmuring fills the air as the faithful kneel to place candles on low-level stone platforms for their ancestors and the saints. For these people, the entire building is alive with the **souls of the dead**, each located in a specific part of the church: the place of the "first-people", the ancient ancestors, is beneath the altar railing, ordinary folk are to the west in the nave. Equally important are the **Catholic saints**, who receive the same respect and are continuously appealed to with offerings of candles and alcohol. Last, but by no means least, certain areas within the church, and particular patterns of candles, rose petals and *chicha*, are used to invoke specific types of blessings, such as those for children, travel, marriage, harvest or illness.

Museo Rossbach

Main plaza • T 4228 5376 • Charge

On the south side of the plaza, **Museo Rossbach** houses a wide-ranging collection of pre-Columbian artefacts, mostly small pieces of ceramics (including some demonic-looking incense burners), jade necklaces and earrings, and stone carvings (some of which are two thousand years old). A few interesting old photographs of Chichi as well as local weavings and masks are also on display.

The mural on the museum's exterior depicts a familiar scene from the civil war years, with military helicopters flying over burning villages.

Capilla del Calvario

Main plaza • Free

On the west side of the plaza, the whitewashed **El Calvario** chapel is like a miniature version of Chichi's main church – its steps also the scene of incense-burning rituals. Inside, the atmosphere is equally reverential as prayers are recited around the smoke-blackened wooden altar, and women offer flowers and stoop to kiss a supine image of Christ, entombed inside a glass cabinet.

The shrine of Pascual Abaj

South downhill along 5 Av, then along 9 C; follow the track for 10min past a mask workshop up to the shrine • Free • 2421 2800

The hills around the town are replete with Maya shrines, the closest of which is **Pascual Abaj**, located about 1km from the centre of town. Although the site is regularly visited by tourists, it's important to remember that the **Maya ceremonies** held here are deeply religious and you should keep your distance and be sensitive about taking photographs.

The shrine is laid out with several small **altars** facing a stern-looking pre-Columbian sculpture. Ceremonies, usually overseen by a shaman, always incorporate clouds of incense, liquor swilling and incantations, along with offerings of flowers and maybe a sacrificed chicken. In 1957, Pascual Abaj's altars were smashed by reforming Catholics, but traditionalists gathered the scattered remains and patched them together.

ARRIVAL AND DEPARTURE — CHICHICASTENANGO

By bus There's no bus station in Chichi, although the corner of 5 C and 5 Av operates loosely as a terminal. Buses heading between Guatemala City and Santa Cruz del Quiché pass through Chichi; coming from Antigua, you can easily connect with these buses in Chimaltenango. Chicken buses also run from Pana (with extra services on market days) and Quetzaltenango. If you're heading north, it's usually quickest to take the first bus to Santa Cruz del Quiché (every 20min; 30min), from where buses go to Nebaj and Uspantán.

Destinations Guatemala City (every 20min; 3hr); Panajachel (4–6 daily; 1hr 15min); Quetzaltenango (7 daily; 2hr 30min); Santa Cruz del Quiché (every 20min; 30min).

Shuttle buses On market days shuttle services run the route from Antigua to Panajachel (or San Pedro La Laguna) via Chichi, allowing you to spend a few hours at the market before continuing on to Lago de Atitlán; the reverse journey is possible too. Contact Chichi Turkaj Tours, 7 Av 05–31 (5070 6580, facebook.com/pg/ChichiTurkajTours).

ACCOMMODATION

Hotels can be in short supply on Saturday nights before the Sunday market, but you shouldn't have a problem on other days.

Hotel Chalet 3 C 7–44 hotelchaletchichicastenango.com; map page 102. A good highland inn, with attractive doubles and twins decorated with Maya artesanías and beds with woollen blankets; all are en suite. It's solar-powered and you can eat your breakfast (extra) on the roof terrace overlooking the town. $$

Hotel Girón 6 C 4–52 5527 1101, facebook.com/hotelyrestaurantegiron; map page 102. This hotel, set just off the street, could not be more central. It offers functional, spacious, pine-trimmed rooms with clean bathrooms and safe parking. $$

CHICHICASTENANGO'S MARKET

There's been a **market** at Chichicastenango for hundreds, if not thousands, of years and despite the touristy side of the event, local people continue to come twice a week to trade their wares. On **Sundays** and **Thursdays**, Chichicastenango's streets are lined with stalls and packed with buyers, and the choice is overwhelming, ranging from superb-quality Ixil *huipiles* to wooden dance-masks and everything in between, including pottery, gourds, belts and blankets, plus a gaudy selection of fabrics. You can still pick up some authentic **weaving**, but you need to be prepared to wade through a lot of very average material – and haggle hard. Prices are pretty competitive, but for a real bargain you should head further into the highlands – or to Panajachel, which is a better bet for *típica* clothing.

For a brilliant vantage point over the **vegetable market**, head for the indoor balcony on the upper floor of the Centro Comercial building on the north side of the main plaza. You'll be able to gawk at the villagers below (as well as take photographs without fear of being intrusive) as they haggle and chat over bunches of carrots and onions. It's possible to pick out costumes from all over the highlands, including *huipiles* from the Atitlán villages, and even from as far away as Chajul; "space cowboy" shirts, tailored like cowboy shirts but in outlandish colours, are worn by men from the neighbouring Sololá area (see page 115).

El Mashito Hotel 8 C 1–7 ⓣ5168 7178, ⓦfacebook.com/hotelelmashito; map page 102. Lime-green structure with a selection of simple, clean, well-presented rooms, all with cable TV and some with private bathrooms. The owner is a friendly soul and there are excellent rates for solo travellers. No wi-fi. $$

Hotel Santo Tomás 7 Av 5–32, ⓦfacebook.com/HST.SantoTomas; map page 102. A large whitewashed colonial-style hotel built around two courtyards with (heated) swimming pool, restaurant and pleasant lounge-bar. Rooms are spacious, decorated with local artefacts and textiles and some have fireplaces (though avoid the streetside options which suffer from traffic noise). Very popular with tour groups on market days. $$$$

Mayan Inn 8 C & 3 Av ⓦmayaninn.com.gt; map page 102. A historic hotel where the classy rooms boast period furniture, fireplaces and real charm. There's a snug lounge-bar but the restaurant is overpriced. Guests are assigned a member of the staff, who all wear mock-traditional dress, to attend you. Rack rates are very high, so look at online booking sites for the best deals. $$$$

★ **Posada El Arco** 4 C 4–36 ⓣ4584 0061; map page 102. This fine guesthouse, run by a hospitable English-speaking Guatemalan who lived in the US for decades, has charm and character. Guests are looked after well (try the home-made jams and peanut butter) and the rooms are large and attractive with good wooden beds and reading lights; rooms 6 and 7 have access to a pleasant terrace. There's also a beautiful garden with stunning highland views and secure parking. $$$

2

EATING

Chichi is a good place to indulge in hearty, good-value Guatemalan food – though many restaurants are geared to tourist wallets. Food stalls on the plaza (**market days** only) serve up authentic highland stews and broths. Note that Chichi can be very quiet on non-market days, when many places keep irregular hours.

Café-Restaurant La Villa de Los Cofrades 6 C & 5 Av ⓣ5510 6657; map page 102. At street level this place operates as a café serving espresso and sweet or savoury crêpes; the restaurant upstairs is good for barbecued meats and set meals with a view of the market. $$

Comedor La Vila 6 Av & 5C; map page 102. A little north of the centre, this clean comedor scores for *comida típica* at low rates. $$

La Parrilla 6 C & 5 Av ⓣ7756 1321; map page 102. Set in a small courtyard, this is a good place to get away from the market crowds. It offers great breakfasts while meat lovers should try the *especial la parrilla*; all plates come with vegetables, rice and a soup starter. $$$

Restaurante Tziguan Tinimit 5 Av & 6 C ⓣ7756 1144, ⓦfacebook.com/tziguan.tinamit; map page 102. A large dining hall, painted with images of the Maya cosmos. Most of the grilled meat, pasta and pizza dishes are similarly priced but there's always a daily special (such as *longaniza* sausages, similar to *chorizo*) for less. $$$

DIRECTORY

Banks There are plenty of banks open on Sunday, including Banrural, 6 C (Tues–Sun 9am–5pm), which has an ATM.

Santa Cruz del Quiché

The capital of the department of El Quiché, **SANTA CRUZ DEL QUICHÉ**, lies half an hour north of Chichicastenango. Quiché, as it is usually called, is a large, featureless town, but it does serve as the jumping-off point for the nearby ruins of **K'umarkaaj** and is a transport hub for the Ixil region. **Market** days are the same as in Chichicastenango – Thursday and Sunday – with stalls sprawling south and east of the plaza down to the bus station.

Dominating the central **plaza** of Santa Cruz del Quiché is a large colonial church and clock tower built with stone from the ruins of K'umarkaaj. In the middle of the plaza, a defiant statue of the K'iche' hero Tecún Umán stands prepared for battle, but his position is undermined somewhat by the ugly urban tangle of shabby stores and streets that surround the square.

ARRIVAL AND INFORMATION — SANTA CRUZ DEL QUICHÉ

By bus The grubby bus terminal is about four blocks south and a couple east of the central plaza.

Destinations Guatemala City, via Chichicastenango (every 20min; 3hr 30min); Joyabaj (every 30min; 1hr 45min); Nebaj (5 daily; 2hr 30min); Quetzaltenango (8 daily; 3hr); Totonicapán (6 daily; 1hr 30min); Uspantán (6 daily; 2hr 30min).

By microbus Microbuses supplement the chicken bus services to Sacapulas (every 45min until 6pm), Totonicapán (hourly until 6pm) and Uspantán (hourly until 6pm).

Services Banrural, at the northwest corner of the plaza, has an ATM.

ACCOMMODATION AND EATING

Panaderia y Restaurante San Miguel Opposite the church ⊕7755 1488. This bakery-cum-café offers filling local food, including *empanadas* and sandwiches, though the pastries and cakes can be very dry. $

Hotel Rey Kiche 8 C 0–39 ⊕7755 0827, ⊕hotelreykiche@gmail.com. A brick-faced hotel that has spacious, plain rooms (singles, doubles and triples) with firm beds, TVs, desks and wardrobes. There's free tea, coffee and water available, and a comedor too (breakfast and dinner only). $$

K'umarkaaj (Utatlán)

4km west of Santa Cruz del Quiché • Charge

Early in the fifteenth century, riding on a wave of successful conquest, the K'iche' king Gucumatz (Feathered Serpent) founded a new capital, **K'umarkaaj**. A hundred years later the Spanish arrived, renamed the city Utatlán, and then destroyed it, leaving the **ruins** that can be visited today.

K'umarkaaj's dramatic setting, surrounded by deep ravines and pine forests, is impressive, and its historical significance intriguing. Little restoration has taken place and once-grand temples and palaces are today just grassy mounds. The small **museum** has a scale model of what the original city may once have looked like.

Brief history

The splendour of the city, which once contained 23 palace buildings, signified the strength of the **K'iche' empire**, which at its height boasted a population of around a million. By the time of the Conquest, however, the K'iche' empire was fractured. Their first encounter with the Spanish was a heavy defeat near Quetzaltenango, resulting in the loss of their leader Tecún Umán. The K'iche' then invited the Spanish to their capital, but on seeing the fortified city, the conquistador feared a trap and captured K'iche' leaders Oxib-Queh and Beleheb-Tzy. His next step was characteristically straightforward: "As I knew them to have such a bad disposition to service of his Majesty, and to ensure the good and peace of this land, I burnt them, and sent [soldiers] to burn the town and destroy it."

The plaza

You'll find three remaining **temple buildings** – the monuments of Tohil, Auilix and Hacauaitz – which were simple pyramids topped by thatched shelters on the central plaza. The Temple of the Sovereign Plumed Serpent once stood in the middle of the plaza, but these days just the foundations of this circular tower can be made out. The only other feature that's still vaguely recognizable is the **ball court**. Perhaps the most interesting thing about the site today is that *costumbristas* (Maya religious practitioners) still come here to perform sacred **rituals**. The entire area is covered in small burnt circles – the ashes of incense – and chickens are regularly sacrificed.

La cueva

Beneath the plaza is a 100m-long **tunnel** (follow the sign for **la cueva**). Inside are nine shrines, the same number as there are levels of the Maya underworld, Xibalbá. Devotees pray at each shrine, but it is the ninth one, housed inside a chamber, that is most actively used for sacrifice, incense and alcohol offerings. Why the tunnel was constructed remains uncertain, but local legends suggest that it was dug by the K'iche' to hide their women and children from the advancing Spanish. Others believe it represents the caves of Tula mentioned in the Popol Vuh (see page 103). Tread carefully inside the tunnel, as some of the side passages end abruptly with precarious drops. If a ceremony is taking place, you'll hear the mumbling of prayers and smell incense smoke as you enter, in which case it's wise not to disturb the proceedings by approaching too closely. It's also recommended to bring a torch as the tunnel can be quite dark in certain areas.

ARRIVAL AND DEPARTURE — K'UMARKAAJ (UTATLÁN)

By bus or taxi From Santa Cruz del Quiché buses and microbuses heading to Totonicapán pass the site; or take a taxi (return trip, with 1hr at the ruins).

On foot It's a pleasant 40min stroll from Santa Cruz del Quiché, heading south from the plaza along 2 Av, then turning right down 10 C, which takes you to the site.

East to Joyabaj

A paved road runs east from Santa Cruz del Quiché, beneath the impressive peaks of the **Sierra de Chuacús**, through a series of villages set in beautiful rolling farmland. The first of these, **Chiché**, is a sister village to Chichicastenango, with which it shares costumes and traditions, though the market here is on Wednesday. Next is **Chinique**, followed by larger **Zacualpa**, which has Thursday and Sunday markets in its imposing plaza. The latter village's name means "where they make fine walls", and in the hills to the north are the remains of a pre-conquest Maya settlement.

The small town of **JOYABAJ**, the last place out this way, also has a small archeological site to its north. The 1976 earthquake almost totally flattened Joyabaj, killing hundreds of people; the crumbling facade of the colonial church is one of the few physical remains. However, in recent years the town has bounced back, and the Sunday **market** is a huge affair well worth visiting. Regular buses (every 30min) connect the town with Santa Cruz del Quiché.

Sacapulas

The isolated town of **SACAPULAS**, an hour north from Quiché, is set in a spectacular position on the Río Negro beneath the dusty foothills of the Cuchumatanes. Sacapulas has a small colonial **church**, with some finely carved wooden images of saints, and a good **market** every Thursday and Sunday, held beneath the two huge ceiba trees in the plaza. Some of the women still wear impressive *huipiles* and tie their hair with elaborate pompoms, similar to those of Aguacatán.

Since long before the arrival of the Spanish, **salt** has been produced here in beds beside the Río Negro, a valuable commodity that earned the town a degree of importance. It's still collected upstream from the bridge and sold from roadside stalls on the north bank of the river.

ARRIVAL AND INFORMATION — SACAPULAS

By bus There are connections to/from Santa Cruz del Quiché (every 45min; 1hr), Uspantán (every 45min; 1hr 30min) and Nebaj (6 daily; 1hr 15min). Buses also run to Aguacatán (7 daily; 1hr 30min), from where there are excellent connections to Huehuetenango. The last transport to all destinations is between 6pm and 7pm.

Services You'll find a Banrural and an ATM on the plaza.

ACCOMMODATION AND EATING

Look out for stalls selling the (very) sweet local snack called **melcocha**, sold all over the country. You'll find cheap comedores and snack vendors dotted around the plaza.

Comedor y Hospedaje Tujaal ☎ 4383 7657. This friendly riverside place has 11 basic rooms with private bathrooms and TV. The food here includes the local *mojarra* river fish and dishes like *pollo dorado* or *bistek*. Food $, accommodation $$

THE FLYING ANGELS OF JOYABAJ

The town's **fiesta** in the second week of August comprises five days of unrelenting celebration. There are some fantastic traditional dances performed, as well as the spectacular *Palo Volador*, in which "flying" men (*ángeles*) spin to the ground from a huge wooden pole. Though the fiesta is in many ways a hybrid of Maya and Christian traditions, the *ángeles* symbolize none other than the wizard twins of the Popol Vuh, who descended into the underworld to do battle with the Lords of Death.

Uspantán

East of Sacapulas, a dirt road rises steeply, clinging to the mountainside and quickly leaving the Río Negro far below. As it climbs, the views are superb, with tiny Sacapulas dwarfed by the sheer size of the landscape. The road eventually reaches **USPANTÁN**, a small town lodged in a chilly gap in the mountains and often soaked in steady drizzle. Rigoberta Menchú (see page 341), the K'iche' Maya woman who won the 1992 Nobel Peace Prize, is from **Chimel**, a tiny village in this region. Few people hang around long here, but there are some decent hotels.

ARRIVAL AND DEPARTURE — USPANTÁN

By bus and microbus Microbuses leave for Cobán (every 45min until 5pm; 3hr) and Santa Cruz del Quiché (every 45min until 6pm; 2hr 30min); chicken buses also serve these routes. Note that the road east to Cobán is a hair-raising journey and connections may not be possible in heavy rains. Buses do cover this route all year round but the section just beyond the bridge over the Río Negro is prone to landslides and involves a nerve-racking zigzag up a mountainside.

ACCOMMODATION AND EATING

Cafeteria María Luisa 6 Av & 7 C, Zona 2. A clean, welcoming little café-comedor that serves breakfasts, snacks and set lunches. $

Hotel Posada Doña Leonor 6 C 4–09, Zona 1 T 7951 8041, W facebook.com/elhoteldeuspantan. Efficiently run hotel with 21 very clean and well-maintained rooms, all equipped with TVs, and bathrooms (some en suite) with reliable hot water, ensuring a comfortable stay. As it's priced per person, single travellers get a good deal and there's a good comedor and wi-fi. $$

The Ixil region

High up in the Cuchumatanes, in a landscape of steep hills, bowl-shaped valleys and gushing rivers, is the **Ixil region**. Here **Nebaj**, **Chajul** and **Cotzal**, three remote and extremely traditional towns, share a language spoken nowhere else in the country. These lush, rain-drenched highlands are hard to reach and have proved notoriously difficult to control, and today's relaxed atmosphere of highland Maya colour and customs conceals a bitter history of protracted conflict.

The beauty of the landscape and the strength of **Indigenous culture** in the Ixil are both overwhelming. When church leaders moved into the area in the 1970s, they found very strong communities in which the people were reluctant to accept new authority for fear that it would disrupt traditional structures, and where women were included in decision-making. Counterbalancing these strengths are the horrors of the **human rights abuses** that took place here during the civil war, which must rate as some of the worst anywhere in Central America. Despite this terrible legacy, however, the fresh green hills are some of the most beautiful in the country, and the friendly, accommodating towns offer a relaxed and distinctive atmosphere in a misty world of their own.

Brief history

Before the arrival of the Spanish, Nebaj was a sizeable centre, producing large quantities of **jade**. The Conquest was particularly brutal in these parts, however. After several setbacks, the Spaniards finally managed to take Nebaj in 1530, by which time they were so enraged that the settlement was burned to the ground and the survivors enslaved as punishment. Things didn't improve with the coming of independence: the Ixil people were regarded as a source of cheap labour and forced to work on the coastal plantations. Many never returned, and even today large numbers of local people still migrate to the coast, Guatemala City and the US in search of work.

In the late 1970s and 1980s, the area was hit by waves of horrific violence as it became the main theatre of operation for the **Guerrilla Army of the Poor** (see page 112). After the **1996 peace accords**, a degree of normality steadily returned to the area as villagers came back to their ancestral settlements to rebuild their homes. However, the region remains desperately poor and opportunities are so limited that in some villages the majority of men are living in "el Norte", their remittances forming a vital part of the local economy.

Nebaj

NEBAJ is the largest of the three settlements in the Ixil region. A bustling market town, it's scruffy around the edges, with potholed streets and a dwindling number of attractive old adobe houses that are being steadily replaced by undistinguished concrete structures. Aesthetic grumbles aside, Nebaj has undoubtedly managed to retain its highland charm and is becoming a popular base for adventure-minded travellers drawn by the opportunity to get off Guatemala's main gringo trail. With a temperate climate and gorgeous scenery all around, Nebaj makes a good base for **hiking** – Acul and Cocop are both within striking distance – though some places can also be reached by microbus if you're not feeling so energetic. If you're in town for the second week in August, you'll witness the **Nebaj fiesta**, which includes processions, fireworks, dances, epic drinking sessions and a marimba-playing marathon.

The plaza and market

There's not that much to do in Nebaj itself. The pretty, recently remodelled **plaza** is the focal point for the community, housing the main municipal buildings and the large whitewashed **Catholic church** – inside its door on the left are dozens of crosses, forming a memorial to those killed in the civil war. The small **market**, a block east of the church, is worth investigating. It's fairly quiet most days, but on Thursdays and Sundays, the numbers swell as traders sell secondhand clothing from the US, electrical goods from China and fruit and vegetables from all over the Guatemalan highlands.

Museo/Centro Cultural Kumool

5 Av & 2 C • Charge • T 7756 0273 W facebook.com/MuseoDeArqueologiaCCKNebaj

Nebaj's **museum**, which is also known as the **Centro Cultural Kumool**, has modern displays that chart the region's history and culture; particularly interesting highlights include Postclassic Maya ceramics and a basalt altar from Escuintla.

ARRIVAL AND DEPARTURE — NEBAJ

By bus The main bus terminal is two blocks southeast of the plaza, opposite the market. For Huehuetenango change in Sacapulas.

Destinations Chajul (regularly 5.30am–6pm; 45min); Cotzal (regularly 5.30am–6pm; 40min); Guatemala City (5 daily; 6hr); Santa Cruz del Quiché (6 daily; 2hr 30min).

By microbus Microbuses leave from various places around town. There are regular services to Acul (5.30am–6pm; 30min), two daily microbuses to Cobán (5am & 1pm; 6hr) and regular microbuses from 7 C for the Cunén junction (every 40min; 30min) for connections to Uspantán.

NEBAJEÑO TEXTILES

The **textiles** woven in Nebaj are unusual and intricate, especially the women's *huipiles*, which are a mass of complex geometrical designs. Until recently, greens, yellows, reds and oranges were omnipresent, worn with brilliant red *cortes* (skirts), though clothes of other hues are now worn. The most spectacular part of Nebaj *traje* is the dramatic women's headcloth, a length of hand-loomed fabric that's decorated with "pompom" tassles that they pile up above their heads. Very few men now wear traditional dress, preferring to buy secondhand North American clothes from the market. The scarlet male ceremonial jackets are dusted down for fiestas, however; formal looking and ornately decorated, they're said to have been modelled on those worn by Spanish officers.

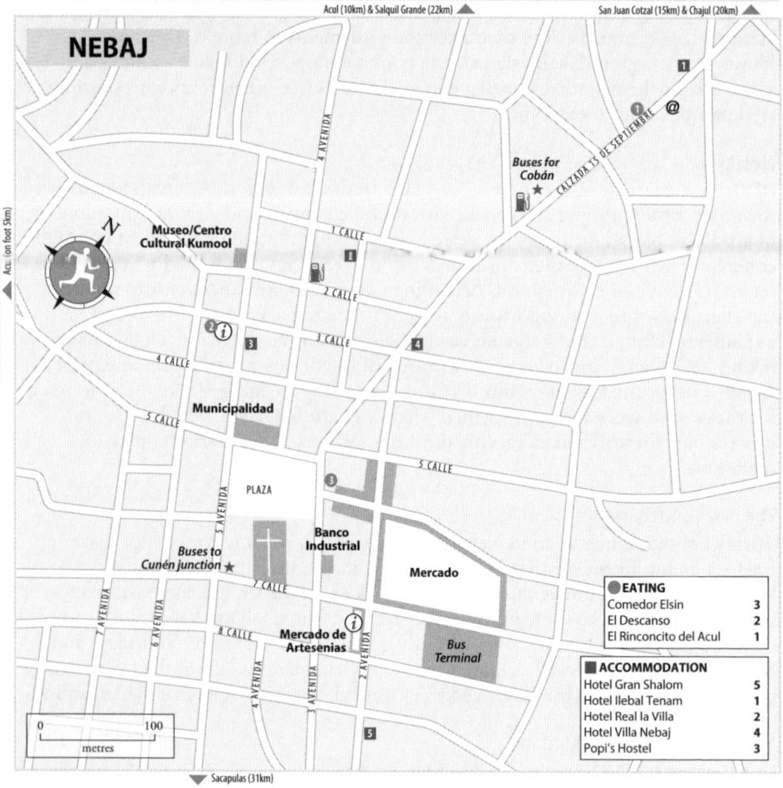

NEBAJ

EATING
Comedor Elsin 3
El Descanso 2
El Rinconcito del Acul 1

ACCOMMODATION
Hotel Gran Shalom 5
Hotel Ilebal Tenam 1
Hotel Real la Villa 2
Hotel Villa Nebaj 4
Popi's Hostel 3

INFORMATION AND ACTIVITIES

Tourist information *El Descanso*, the restaurant on 3 C (see page 111), is a one-stop shop for Nebaj visitors and easily the best place to go for information on local activities and to get online (☎ 5749 7450). Cooking classes, weaving lessons and other activities can be arranged here for an hourly fee; they can even prepare a Maya sauna for you. There's also an information office (in theory daily 8am–5pm) inside the Mercado de Artesanías, 2 Av, but it's frequently closed; they do, however, stock copies of *Guía de Senderismo*, a superb hiking guide (charge) to the Ixil region, with excellent maps.

Guías Ixiles, also inside *El Descanso*, 3 C (☎ 4516 2059). Guided walks (charge per head, with a minimum of two people); a range of walks, from day-hikes to Acul and Cocop to a spectacular three-day trek to Todos Santos, are offered. No guides speak English.

Language school Nebaj Language School, based at *El Descanso*, 3 C (☎ 7756 0207). A week of one-on-one tuition and a family homestay with meals will set you back approximately US$200.

ACCOMMODATION

Nebaj has some good budget places, many with inimitable highland charm, though nothing luxurious. There are also excellent rural lodges in nearby **Acul** (see page 112).

Hotel Gran Shalom 2 Av 9–15, Zona 5 ☎ 7756 0000; map page 110. It's not actually very grand, but the owners are hospitable and helpful and it's a comfortable, relaxed place to stay. All the rooms are spacious and well kept, with private bathroom and TV, and overlook a central garden. No wi-fi. $$

Hotel Ilebal Tenam Calzada 15 de Septiembre ☎ 7755 8039; map page 110. An efficiently run *hospedaje* with dozens of rooms, ranging from the small and functional to the attractive and comfortable – those in the rear block have TVs and private bathrooms. The hot water is reliable. $

★ **Hotel Real la Villa** Calzada 15 de Septiembre ☎ 7755 8060; map page 110. The smartest hotel in town is a colonial-style place with comfortable accommodation set around a small grassy courtyard. The spacious rooms all have attractive furniture, including wardrobes and hand-carved wooden headboards, as well as good mattresses, TVs and modern en-suite bathrooms. $$$

Hotel Villa Nebaj Calzada 15 de Septiembre 2–37 ☎7756 0005; map page 110. This garish four-storey construction is something of a blot on the landscape, but the accommodation is extremely comfortable – all the clean, attractive rooms have quality beds, bedside lights and cable TV, and the Ixil fabrics add a splash of colour. Those without private bathroom are a real bargain. $$

Popi's Hostel 5 Av 3–35 ☎4872 5299; map page 110. Founder Popi has moved on, but this hostel remains a good place to meet other travellers, and has pretty fast wi-fi (a rarity in these parts). Plus, you can have a slice of apple pie or yoghurt smoothie. However, the rooms are very basic, set around a yard. Dorms $, doubles $$

2

EATING

When in Nebaj, make sure to try **boxboles**, a delicious Ixil dish made of maize dough and a little meat that's wrapped and steamed in a *güisquil* leaf. For superb local **cheese**, made in the valley of Acul (see below) head either to the farm itself or *El Rinconcito del Acul*.

Comedor Elsin East side of the plaza; map page 110. Classic Guatemalan comedor, with humble surrounds and smoke from the kitchen, that has a loyal clientele. Expect hearty portions of *pollo dorado*, *chorizo* and *longaniza* (sausage) for bargain prices. No alcohol. $

★ **El Descanso** 3 C ☎5749 7450; map page 110. This is the only real gringo-geared spot in town, a well-run and popular hangout for backpackers and development workers (and many locals), with sofas, wi-fi and internet access. The menu includes local and Western breakfasts, pasta, Mexican dishes, sandwiches and grilled meats. It's also your best bet for a beer, glass of wine or even a cocktail. It's run by locals and service is snappy and attentive. $$

El Rinconcito del Acul Calzada 15 de Septiembre ☎4006 9678; map page 110. Something really different, this excellent little place only offers one thing – thick tortillas stuffed with Chancol cheese (made in Acul) or smoked *chorizo*. They'll also serve you a good coffee or glass of wine, or you can buy a whole cheese from the store next door. $$

DIRECTORY

Banks Banco Industrial, 3 Av, has an ATM.

Pharmacy Farmacia Tu Bienestar Nebaj, Canton jactzal.

Internet Most hotels, guesthouses and some cafés offer wi-fi but the speed is often limited and outages can occur.

Acul

One of the most interesting walks from Nebaj takes you to the village of **ACUL**, an hour and a half away via a steep track. Starting from the church in Nebaj, head east downhill along 5 Calle. At the bottom of the dip, as the road divides, take the right-hand fork and head out of town. Just after you pass the last houses, it's just possible to make out some **pre-Columbian burial mounds** in the corn fields on your right. These are still used for Maya religious ceremonies.

Beyond here the wide track switchbacks up a steep hillside, before dropping down into Acul, one of the original "model villages" into which people were herded after their homes were destroyed by the army. The municipality now has a population of around five hundred Ixil and K'iche' Maya families. Sights are few, but it's fascinating to see how well the place has come on in the past few years; every home has a little plot of land for growing maize and vegetables, and there's a lovely Baroque-style whitewashed **church**.

Finca San Antonio

On the road to Nebaj, 500m from Acul • ☎4022 2143

While you're in Acul you simply have to buy some cheese at the **Finca San Antonio** on the eastern side of the village, a dairy farm run by the Azzari family (who founded the finca in the 1930s). The farmhouse (and neighbouring hacienda) enjoy a breathtaking setting, with views over a paradisal valley of rich pastureland and pine trees to a mighty fold in the Cuchumatanes mountains. You can stay here, too (see below), which is a real treat.

ARRIVAL AND DEPARTURE — ACUL

A good number of **minibuses** (roughly every 30min until 5.30pm; 30min) connect Acul with Nebaj. The road to Acul can be a bit rough, especially during rainy season, but the views make it worthwhile. Be sure to bring cash to pay for the minbus as there are few ATMs in rural areas so it pays to come prepared.

ACCOMMODATION

★ **Finca San Antonio** On the road to Nebaj, 500m from Acul ⓣ 4022 2143. One of the best rural lodges in the country, this dairy farm – one of Guatemala's best cheeses is made here – has delightfully rustic but comfortable, simply furnished rooms with private bathrooms and piping-hot water. Outstanding home-cooked meals are prepared with fine-quality meat, with wine and beer available. Horse-riding (a three-hour trip, including a guide) and hiking guides can be arranged for an additional charge. $$$

Hacienda Mil Amores Next door to Finca San Antonio, on the road to Nebaj, 500m from Acul ⓣ 5704 4817. Very well built stone cottages, each with fireplaces and verandas with views, and hearty cooking is offered. Non-guests are welcome to drop by for lunch – order the tortillas with melted Chancol cheese. $$$

Hostal Y Comedor Doña Magdalena ⓣ 5782 0891. This excellent little *posada* in the village has rooms (one with a private bathroom) that front a pretty flowering garden. It's run by a friendly Ixil woman who also serves tasty meals. $

2

Cocop

A half-day circular walk climbs up the steep eastern edge of the natural bowl that surrounds Nebaj to the small village of **COCOP** and back to the main Nebaj–Cotzal road. Starting in the centre of Nebaj, walk south along 2 Avenida past *Gran Hotel Ixil* until the end of the road, bear right, and then take the first left downhill to the bridge. Cross the bridge and you'll quickly reach the *pueblo* of **Xemamatzé** on the edge of Nebaj. This village used to be home to a huge internment camp where Ixil villagers who had surrendered to the army were subject to lengthy "repatriation" treatment. In Xemamatzé, take the signposted gravel track uphill to Cocop – this climbs steadily for about an hour to 2300m. Back across the valley there are spectacular views towards Nebaj. The track continues round the mountain then gradually descends to Cocop below.

GUERRILLA WARFARE IN THE IXIL

The bitter **civil war** of the 1970s and 1980s ravaged the western highlands, and left the Ixil devastated by the conflict between the **Guatemalan army** and the insurgent **Ejército Guerrillero de los Pobres** (the EGP, or Guerrilla Army of the Poor). By 1996, when the guerrilla war officially ended, nearly all of the region's smaller villages had been destroyed and fifteen thousand to twenty thousand people had been killed, with thousands more displaced. Most of the victims were villagers, dying not because of their political beliefs but because they had been caught between the army and the EGP, who saw the creation of a liberated zone in the Ixil as the springboard to national revolution. Investigations later found the Guatemalan military responsible for more than ninety percent of civilian deaths in the Ixil.

THE 1970S: THE RISE OF THE EGP

The EGP first entered the area in 1972, when a small group of guerrilla fighters crossed the Mexican border and began building links with locals, impressing some villagers with plans for political and social revolution. The guerrillas opened their military campaign in 1975 with the **assassination of Luis Arenas**, a finca owner from near Chajul, who employed hundreds of labourers under a system of debt bondage. The EGP shot Arenas in front of hundreds of his employees as he was counting the payroll. According to the group, workers joined them with cries of "Long live the poor, death to the rich". But other accounts describe how people walked for days to pay their last respects to Arenas.

These actions prompted a huge response from the armed forces, who began killing, kidnapping and torturing suspected guerrillas and sympathizers. The EGP was already well entrenched, however, and by late 1978 was regularly occupying villages, holding open meetings and tearing down debtors' jails. In January 1979 they killed another local landowner, Enrique Brol, of Finca San Francisco near Cotzal. On the same day, the EGP also briefly took control of Nebaj itself, summoning the whole of the town's population, as well as Western travellers, to the central plaza, where they denounced the barbaric inequalities of life in the Ixil.

COMMUNITY TOURISM IN SAN JUAN COTZAL

Based just behind the plaza in San Juan Cotzal is an excellent **community tourism** project called Tejidos Cotzal (T 4621 9725). The project aids dozens of local weavers, who use natural dyes and backstrap looms; you can buy their work at the office. Guided tours (charge per person, minimum two people) are offered, taking in visits to the weavers' homes, and to see other craftspeople, such as candlemakers, at work; prices include a great lunch of local food like *boxboles* (see page 111). Hikes to a Maya hilltop altar to watch a religious ceremony and to local waterfalls are also offered.

The village has been rebuilt on old foundations; during the civil war it was razed to the ground and 98 villagers were massacred by the army. Today, however, it's a pretty little settlement in a delightful setting beside a gurgling river. A few stores sell fizzy drinks; for something stronger ask to see the village's *cusha* liquor distillery. To head back, walk straight ahead from the crossroads in the centre of the village, past the Emmanuel church for a lovely hour's stroll along the V-shaped valley through sheep-filled meadows. At the end of the trail is the village of **Río Azul** on the main Cotzal–Nebaj road, from where you can wait for a microbus or pick-up, or hike back to Nebaj in an hour and a half.

San Juan Cotzal

The small town of **SAN JUAN COTZAL** is beautifully set in a gentle dip in the valley, sheltered beneath the Cuchumatanes and often wrapped in a damp blanket of mist. In the

THE 1980S

The army responded with a wave of horrific attacks on the civilian population. Army units swept through the area, committing atrocities, burning villages and massacring thousands. Nevertheless, the strength of the guerrillas continued to grow, and in 1981 they again launched an **attack on Nebaj**, by then a garrison town. Shortly afterwards the army chief of staff, Benedicto Lucas García (the president's brother), flew into Nebaj to threaten locals that if they didn't "clean up their act" he'd bring five thousand men "and finish off the entire population".

The army changed its tactics under new president Ríos Montt, using anti-Communist propaganda and conscripted **civilian patrols** (PACs) to ensure the loyalty of the people. Villagers were given ancient rifles and told to protect their communities from guerrillas. The army swept through the Ixil, razed fifty villages to the ground and settled the displaced in new "model" communities. With the EGP retreating to more remote terrain, Ixil people began to adapt to the army's new-found dominance, many opting to reject contact with the guerrillas.

Hit hard, the EGP responded with desperate acts. On June 6, 1982, guerrillas stopped a bus near Cotzal and executed thirteen civil patrol leaders and their wives; eleven days later a guerrilla column entered the village of **Chacalté**, where the civil patrol had been particularly active, and killed a hundred people.

The army's offer of **amnesty** soon drew refugees out of the mountains: between 1982 and 1984 some 42,000 people turned themselves in, fleeing a harsh existence under guerrilla protection. Others returned after years spent living like nomads, hunting animals in the jungles of the Ixcán to the north. By 1985 the guerrillas had been driven back into a handful of mountain strongholds.

PEACE ACCORDS

Skirmishes continued until the mid-1990s, but ceased with the signing of **peace accords**. Since then, ex-guerrillas and former civil patrollers have resettled the old village sites and communities have been rebuilt.

CHAJUL COSTUME

The women of Chajul are terrific weavers, their *huipiles* richly embroidered with animals and symbols, filling the streets with colour. Until recently, all the textiles created here used to be woven in scarlet thread, though nowadays royal blue is almost as common. Look out, too, for the women's earrings, which are made of old coins strung up on lengths of wool. The traditional red jackets of the men are an extremely rare sight these days. Make sure you visit the shop run by the local **weaving cooperative**, Va'l Vaq Quyol, between the church and the market, where you'll find some of the best-quality handmade textiles in the country at very decent prices.

1920s and 1930s, this was the largest and busiest of the three Ixil towns, as it was from here that the fertile lands to the north were colonized. Today Cotzal is a quiet, friendly little place with a very attractive little plaza. Market days here are Wednesday and Saturday.

ACCOMMODATION AND EATING — SAN JUAN COTZAL

El Maguey Two blocks north of the plaza ⓣ 7765 6199. A simple yet convenient *hospedaje* where the rooms have TV; bathrooms are shared. The hotel's comedor offers large set meals. $$

Chajul

Last but by no means least of the Ixil settlements is **CHAJUL**, replete with a good stock of old adobe houses, their wooden beams and red-tiled roofs blackened by the smoke of cooking fires. It is also the most traditional and least bilingual of the Ixil towns. The streets are usually bustling with activity and local women gather to wash clothes at the stream that cuts through the middle of the village. Here boys still use blowpipes to hunt small birds, a skill that dates from the earliest of times. Time your arrival for **market days** (Tues & Fri) when the town is at its most lively.

Chajul church

The colonial **church** on the plaza is fascinating: you enter through a colossal wooden door carved with animal motifs, and the huge old structure is full of gold leaf and topped by a timber ceiling of massive beams. It's home to the **Christ of Golgotha** and the target of a large pilgrimage on the second Friday of Lent – a particularly exciting time to visit.

Museo Maya Ixil

150m northwest of the plaza • Free • ⓣ 4236 3149

The modest little **Museo Maya Ixil** has a small collection of dusty Postclassic Maya ceramics and craftwork from the Chajul region including basketry, carved slingshots, pottery and textiles. A guerrilla's uniform (from civil war years) and rifle is also displayed. They also sell handicrafts.

INFORMATION AND TOURS — CHAJUL

Limitless Horizons Ixil Next to the Salón Municipal ⓦ limitlesshorizonsixil.org. This excellent development project is immersed in the town, providing funding for schooling and a library. Contact them for local hiking guides, weaving classes and tours of Chajul and region.

ACCOMMODATION AND EATING

Most of Chajul's (few) *pensiones* are very run-down. Local families also rent out beds in their **houses** to travellers. You'll find a handful of **comedores** just off the plaza, of which *Sarai* is the best.

Posada Vetz K'aol 500m southwest of the plaza ⓣ 4604 6837. This *posada* is in a gorgeous old historic building with wood-panelled walls, and is kept tidy by the helpful manager. The big rooms, with good wooden bunk beds and blankets, are set up for groups but anyone is welcome. There's a lovely sitting room with a fireplace and inexpensive food and espresso coffee is available. Dorms $, doubles $$

DIRECTORY

Banks Banrural on the plaza has an ATM.
Internet Supernet, 200m southwest of the plaza, is one of several places in town where you can get online for a reasonable cost..

Lago de Atitlán

Lake Como, it seems to me, touches the limit of the permissibly picturesque; but Atitlán is Como with the additional embellishments of several immense volcanoes. It is really too much of a good thing. After a few days of this impossible landscape one finds oneself thinking nostalgically of the English Home Counties.

Aldous Huxley, Beyond the Mexique Bay (1934)

Whether or not you share Huxley's refined sensibilities, there's no doubt that **LAGO DE ATITLÁN** is astonishingly beautiful, and most people find themselves captivated by its scenic excesses. Indeed its appeal is so intoxicating that a handful of gringo devotees have been rooted to its shores since the 1960s, and today Atitlán rates as one of the country's prime tourist attractions.

Hemmed in on all sides by volcanoes and steep hills, the lake is at least 320m deep and measures 18km by 12km at its widest point. Depending on the time of day its waters shift through an astonishing range of blues, steely greys and greens as the sun moves across the sky. Mornings are usually calm, but by early afternoon the *xocomil* wind makes boat travel quite a rock'n'roll experience.

The strength of Maya culture evident here is profound. Many of the villages remain intensely traditional – **San Antonio Palopó**, **Santiago Atitlán** and **Sololá** are some of the very few places in the entire country where Maya men still wear *traje* – despite the tourist presence. Around the southwestern shores, from Santiago to San Pablo La Laguna, **Tz'utujil** is spoken, while from San Marcos La Laguna to Cerro de Oro the **Kaqchikel** language predominates.

Most travellers base themselves in one lakeside village and visit other *pueblos* from there. **Panajachel** is the main resort, an enjoyable if touristy town that has an abundance of hotels and restaurants. **San Pedro La Laguna**, with budget digs and a party vibe, is the main backpacker hangout, while those seeking tranquillity head for **Santa Cruz**, **San Marcos** or isolated spots on the north side of the lake. Other possibilities include San Juan, Santiago Atitlán and Santa Catarina Palopó, all of which have a hotel or two.

Sololá and around

Some 12km south of the Los Encuentros junction on the Carretera Interamericana is **SOLOLÁ**, the departmental capital and gateway to the lake. Perched on a natural

CRIME AGAINST TOURISTS AROUND LAGO DE ATITLÁN

It is rare but not unknown for hikers to be **robbed** in the Atitlán area. Statistically, the chance of you becoming a victim is extremely small, and hundreds of hikers enjoy trouble-free walks around the lakeshore every month. Nevertheless, if you plan to hike any of the volcanoes or the trails between San Pedro and Santa Cruz, check out the security situation first. The back road between Santiago and San Pedro should be avoided as robberies have been reported. Guesthouse and hotel staff are usually well informed.

balcony some 600m above the water, the town itself isn't much to look at, but its huge central plaza is certainly good for people-watching.

Sololá is one of the only places in the country that has parallel Indigenous and ladino governments, and is one of Guatemala's largest Maya towns with tradition dominating daily life. The town's symbol, still seen on the back of the men's jackets, is an abstraction of a bat, referring to the royal house of Xahil from pre-conquest times. Several other villages can be reached from Sololá, most of them within walking distance.

Friday market

Sololá's **Friday market** (there's also a smaller one on Tuesday) is one of Central America's finest, a mesmeric display of colour and commerce that Aldous Huxley described as "a walking museum of fancy dress". Traders are drawn from all over the highlands, as well as thousands of Sololá Maya, the women covered in striped red cloth and the men in their outlandish "space cowboy" shirts, woollen aprons and wildly embroidered trousers. It's a non-touristy affair, great for people-watching and photographic opportunities, but not for souvenir hunting.

Santa María Concepción

About 8km to the east of Sololá is tiny **Santa María Concepción**, an exceptionally quiet farming village with a spectacularly restored, whitewashed colonial church whose altar

PARADISE IN PERIL

Atitlán's beauty remains overwhelming, although recent pressures are decidedly threatening. Sediment analysis has shown that the **lake water has risen and fallen** in cycles for hundreds of years, but after the tropical storm Stan Atitlán rose 5m in eighteen months, an unprecedented event that caused businesses to flood and beaches to disappear and threatened livelihoods. The once-idyllic lakeside pathway in Santa Cruz (a village particularly badly affected) disappeared, and docks in San Pedro and San Juan had to be rebuilt. For visitors, the impact was at first pretty minimal, with only a handful of lakefront hotels losing land and Atitlán looking as beautiful as ever. But in 2018, with the lake continuing to rise, and more businesses being affected, owners are slowly migrating to higher levels. Theories rage as to why the lake is rising so quickly – some reckon landslides caused by Stan have blocked underwater drainage channels – but for Maya with centuries of local knowledge it was less of a surprise; their villages sit high above the shore, and many sold lakefront land to foreigners.

Cyanobacteria is another huge issue. This blue-green algae occurs in lakes worldwide, feeding on pollution from agricultural runoff and human waste. Periodically and following a period of warm, settled sunny weather, a smelly gooey green mass of algae will carpet the surface of Atitlán, at times affecting around thirty percent of the lake, and only fading as the temperature cools and high winds break it up. The threat remains for years as phosphorus- and nitrogen-rich nutrients remain in the lake. Meanwhile, the local **fishing industry**, which once thrived on the abundance of small fish and crabs, has been crippled by the introduction of **black bass** that eat the smaller fish and water birds. Much of the good fresh fish you eat nowadays is farmed.

has some wonderful gilded cherubs. The walk out here, along a dirt track skirting the hills above Panajachel, offers superb views across the lake.

San Jorge La Laguna

Clinging to a hillside below Sololá, **San Jorge La Laguna** is a small hamlet built of cinder block and adobe with sweeping lake vistas. Villagers have suffered a long history of disasters: the settlement was founded by refugees from the 1773 earthquake in Antigua, and its original lakeside incarnation was swept into the water by a landslide, persuading the people to move up the hill (though some land-hungry residents have recently returned to set up a new community there).

ARRIVAL AND DEPARTURE **SOLOLÁ AND AROUND**

By bus Buses run from Sololá to both Panajachel (20min) and Los Encuentros (20min) every 15min or so until 7.30pm; minibuses also run to the nearby *pueblos* of Santa María Concepción and San Jorge La Laguna.

Panajachel

Ten kilometres south of Sololá, separated by a precipitous descent, is **PANAJACHEL**, Atitlán's main tourism centre. Over the years what was once a small Maya village has become something of a resort, with a sizeable population of long-term foreign residents whose numbers are swollen by tourists. Panajachel is one of those inevitable destinations for travellers, and although no one ever owns up to actually liking it, most people seem to drop by for a day or two.

Not so long ago (although it seems an entirely different age) Panajachel was a quiet little **Kaqchikel Maya** settlement. The old village has been enveloped by a construction boom, and though most of the new buildings are pretty nondescript, its lakeside setting is superb. Maya people continue to farm in the river delta behind the town, and the Sunday market, bustling with people from all around the lake, remains oblivious to the tourist invasion.

The old village

The **old village** – a handful of narrow lanes grouped around a sombre, stone-faced Catholic church that dates from 1567 – is not particularly picturesque, though its narrow lanes are worth a little exploration. The **market** has recently been revamped, but is still resolutely geared to local needs rather than tourist tastes; it's a block to the north of the church.

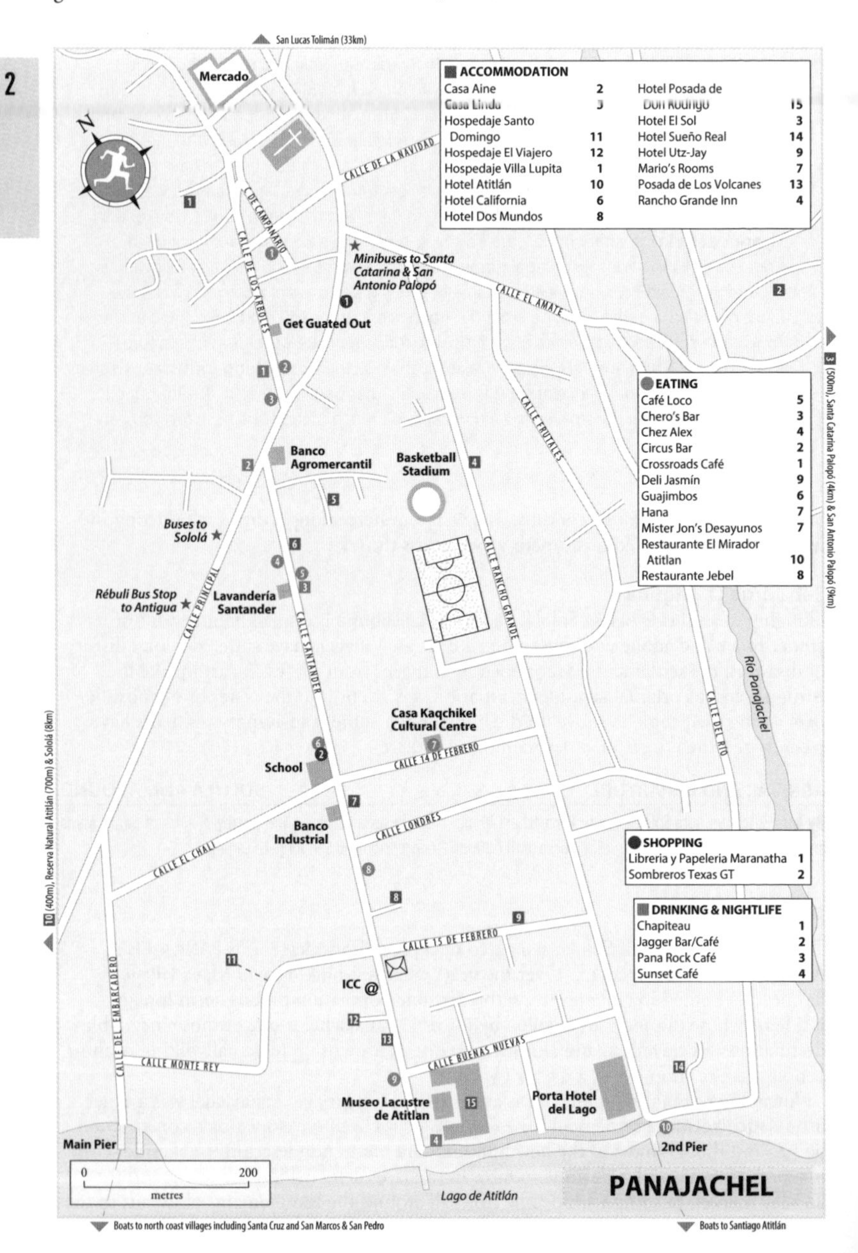

INTO THE VORTEX

Some of Atitlán's more mystically minded gringos love to talk about Atitlán being one of the world's few **vortex energy fields**, along with the Egyptian pyramids and Machu Picchu. Though you are unlikely to see fish swimming backwards or buses rolling uphill to Sololá, the lake does have an undeniable draw, and recent discoveries indicate it was probably a place of pilgrimage during Preclassic Maya times when the ceremonial site of Samabaj (see page 120) thrived. Back in the 1960s and 1970s, Panajachel was the premier Central American **hippie hangout**, though it's now fully integrated into the tourism mainstream and is as popular with Guatemalans (and Mexicans and Salvadoreans) as Westerners. The lotus eaters and crystal gazers have not all deserted the town, though – many remain, working as healers, therapists and masseurs – while others have simply reinvented themselves as capitalists, owning restaurants and exporting handicrafts. In many ways it's this **gringo crowd** that gives the town its modern character and identity – vortex energy centre or not.

Calle Santander

The main tourist drag of **Calle Santander** cuts a colourful path through the modern heart of Pana. This kilometre-long street boasts dozens of stores and stalls, loaded up with a kaleidoscopic collection of weaving and handicrafts from all over Guatemala, as well as an amazing selection of places to eat and drink. **Street hawkers**, weighed down with armfuls of *típica* textile shirts and gaudy trinkets, ply their goods with daunting persistence, and buzzing tuk-tuks weave their way along the lane touting for business.

Casa Kaqchikel Cultural Centre

C 14 de Febrero • Free • casacakchiquel.com

The handsome **Casa Kaqchikel Cultural Centre**, constructed in 1948, was originally built as a luxury hotel by a Swiss countess and is said to have hosted guests including Ché Guevara, Ingrid Bergman and Klaus Kinski. Today there's a fascinating collection of old photographs, postcards and documents relating to Pana and the lake. It's also home to two good restaurants (see page 122), and occasionally hosts musical events, readings and art exhibitions.

Museo Lacustre de Atitlan

In the grounds of Hotel Posada de Don Rodrigo, C Santander • Charge

The modern **Museo Lacustre de Atitlan** is dedicated to the turbulent geological history that led to the creation of the lake. There's also an interesting collection of Maya artefacts, including Preclassic- and Classic-era ceramics and some terrific ceremonial incense burners. Don't miss the adjacent space dedicated to the underwater Maya site of **Samabaj** (see page 120), which attempts to re-create what it's like to dive the site with the aid of high-tech gadgetry and dramatic lighting.

The beach and promenade

Due to rising lake water there's almost nothing left of Pana's **beach**, at the southern end of Calle Santander, and swimming is not recommended due to poor water quality. However, the promenade is an ideal place to stretch your legs, particularly around sunset.

Reserva Natural Atitlán

1km west of the centre • Charge • atitlanreserva.com • Pay for a tuk-tuk ride, or walk 15min from Panajachel

The **Reserva Natural Atitlán** is a privately run forest reserve on the steep slopes of the lake. There are several walking trails (20–75min) through dense foliage, and viewing platforms from where spider monkeys and small mammals, including possum and kinkajou, are often spotted. Inside the reserve there's a **butterfly park** with dozens of species, including golden orange monarch and blue morpho, plus a breeding laboratory; you can also see orchid gardens and aviaries. Eight **zip lines** (charge), ranging between 90m and 320m, offer an unparalleled perspective of the forest and lake.

ARRIVAL AND DEPARTURE — PANAJACHEL

By bus Buses to and from Sololá stop on C Principal and continue to the marketplace. The bus to and from Antigua departs from a separate stop on C Principal.
Destinations Antigua (Mon–Sat 10.45am; 2hr 45min); Chichicastenango (4–6 daily; 1hr 30min); Cocales (6 daily; 2hr); Guatemala City (8 daily; 3hr 15min); Quetzaltenango (7 daily; 2hr 30min).

GETTING AROUND

By tuk-tuk or taxi Tuk-tuks (charge per head) are everywhere in Pana. Taxis wait by the Santiago dock, or you can call one on ☎ 7762 1571.
By boat Most lakeside villages are served by *lanchas* – small, fast boats that depart when the owner has enough passengers to cover fuel costs. You usually won't have to wait long, but at quiet times of the day you may have to hang around for up to 30min. Panajachel has two piers. The main pier, at the end of C del Embarcadero, serves the villages on the northern side of the lake: Santa Cruz (about 15min), Jaibalito (20min), Tzununá (30min) and San Marcos (40min). This pier is also home to direct (15min) and non-direct (50min) boats to San Pedro, from where you can easily get to San Juan. The second pier, at the end of C Rancho Grande, is for Santiago Atitlán (25min by *lancha*) and lake tours. The last boats on all routes leave around 7.30pm. A semi-official fare system is in place, with different fees for shorter or longer journeys. Locals pay less. Keep in mind that some *lancheros* try to charge more for the last boat of the day.

SAMABAJ

For years scuba divers have come across ceramic fragments and artefacts from Maya times beneath Lago de Atitlán. But in December 2011 news emerged that the remains of an important ceremonial Maya settlement, dubbed **Samabaj**, had been discovered offshore from the tiny village of Cerro de Oro on the south side of the lake. (The site had actually been known about since 1997, but its location had been kept secret to deter thieves.)

Samabaj is highly unusual on many fronts. Most of the Maya remains found in the Atitlán region date back five hundred years or so, but Samabaj was a **Preclassic Maya** site that thrived more than two thousand years ago. Archeologists have established links with the Preclassic Maya superpower of El Mirador, way to the north in Petén, which controlled a huge network of trade links throughout Mesoamerica.

The **condition** of the pieces discovered, including a stela (found still standing upright on the lake bed) and a colossal 1.5m incense burner, were remarkable, some displaying their original paint. The number of altars and religious artefacts found indicates that Samabaj was a place of **pilgrimage**. Originally the site was located on an island (dock foundations have been discovered at Samabaj and on the mainland), and pilgrims would have travelled by boat to reach it, but in around 250 AD an abrupt rise in Atitlán's lake water flooded the site forever, preserving the monuments around 18m to 30m below the surface.

In 2012 an archeology team investigated the underwater site, resulting in a documentary film *Mayan Blue*, broadcast by the National Geographic Channel. Lead archaeologist on the project, Sonia Medrano, argues that after this flood a legend developed that Samabaj represented Xibalba (the underworld) for the Classic Maya.

Officially it's forbidden to dive the site, but Guatemala City-based scuba schools regularly ignore regulations and dive Samabaj most weekends, threatening its archeological integrity as divers pick over the ruins. ATI Divers based in Santa Cruz (see page 135) will know the latest situation.

You can view many of the discoveries for yourself in Panajachel's Museo Lacustre de Atitlan (see page 119).

INFORMATION AND ACTIVITIES

Tourist information The website atitlan.com has some good historical and cultural information and details upmarket accommodation options in the Atitlán area.

Tours Tours of the lake usually visit San Pedro, Santiago Atitlán and San Antonio Palopó and can be booked in most travel agencies and hotels; all leave around 9am and return by 4pm.

Travel agents Atitrans, *Anexo Hotel Regis*, C Santander (7762 0146, atitranspanajachel.com), is a professional nationwide agency that offers tours of the region and shuttle buses; Adrenalina Tours, C Santander (5308 1489, adrenalinatours.com) is another good option, offering excellent shuttle bus connections and lake and highland tours.

Bike and motorbike rental Motos Maco, C Navidad (5421 2001, macobajaj@yahoo.com), rents scooters (by the hour or the day) and 200cc trail bikes; Emanuel, C 14 de Febrero, has mountain bikes with decent daily rates.

Language schools Pana has two language schools where you can study Spanish, though rates are cheaper in San Pedro La Laguna. Escuela Jabel Tinamit, Callejon las Armonias (7762 6058, jabeltinamit.com), and Jardín de América, off C El Chalí (4581 7974, jardindeamerica.com) are both professional.

Watersports Canoes and kayaks can be rented by the hour from the promenade; note the lake is usually much calmer in the morning. Contact ATI divers for scuba diving or Los Elementos (see page 135) for guided kayak tours; both are based in nearby Santa Cruz La Laguna.

2

ACCOMMODATION

Panajachel has dozens of **hotels and guesthouses**. Most are in the budget and mid-range categories, but there are a couple of good pricier options too, if you fancy a splurge.

Casa Aine Callejón Chotzar 0–41 3509 9526; map page 118. Smart little B&B with rooms, studios and an apartment in a home that enjoys a leafy garden and pool. Located a 15min walk from the centre. $$$

Casa Linda Down an alley off the top of C Santander 7762 0386; map page 118. A traditional, family-managed place in a quiet location with a gorgeous fecund central garden to enjoy. There are 21 neat, simple rooms, with balcony or veranda, that are priced per person (so solo travellers get a great deal). $$

Hospedaje Santo Domingo Down a path off C Monterrey santodomingopana.com; map page 118. A travellers' stronghold with a very tranquil setting and a garden ideal for chilling. Rooms are simple but good value, some with en-suite bathrooms. $$

Hospedaje El Viajero Off C Santander 7762 0128, hospedajeelviajero.com; map page 118. Peaceful place with an excellent location close to the lakeshore. All rooms have en-suite bathrooms and cable TV, and there's a (basic) guests' kitchen and laundry facilities. It's priced per person, so singles are a steal. $$

★ **Hospedaje Villa Lupita** Callejón El Tino 4450 2944; map page 118. Superb *hospedaje* in an old town location where everything is beautifully set up. The pretty, very clean and good-value rooms (some with private bathroom) boast highland rugs and blankets and come with reading lights and good mattresses. Guests get free drinking water and coffee and can expect a warm welcome from the family owners. $$

Hotel Atitlán 1km west of the centre hotelatitlan.com; map page 118. Landmark hotel that enjoys a sublime lakeside location with idyllic gardens of flowering scrubs like heliconias, passion flowers and bougainvillea (but also caged birds). Rooms boast volcano views, though the decor is now somewhat dated. $$$$

Hotel California C Santander hotelcaliforniapana.com; map page 118. On the bustling main street, this modern hotel has smart, well-designed accommodation with magnolia walls, pale wood and terracotta tiles. Expect a little noise in the street-facing rooms. There's a very smart restaurant across the road, *Chez Alex*. $$$

Hotel Dos Mundos C Santander hoteldosmundos.com; map page 118. This hotel has spacious, comfortable *casitas* set to one side of a palm-filled garden with a swimming pool. Breakfast is included for most rooms, and discounts are often available. $$$$

Hotel Posada de Don Rodrigo C Santander posadadedonrodrigo.com; map page 118. Colonial-style hotel with a lakeside location and outdoor pool. The accommodation is comfortable but a little perfunctory for the price – most rooms don't have lake views and they currently charge for wi-fi. Those in the newer wing (301–311) offer better value and fine vistas. $$$

Hotel El Sol 1km from the centre, on the road to Santa Catarina Palopó 7762 6090, booking.com; map page 118. Japanese-owned hotel with super-clean accommodation including a spacious eight-person dorm, singles and doubles. The bathrooms have reliable hot showers. Dorms $, doubles $$

Hotel Sueño Real C Ramós 7762 0608, hotelsuenoreal@hotmail.com; map page 118. Excellent little family-run guesthouse with immaculate rooms, each with ikat curtains and highland blankets. It's located very close to the lakeshore and there's a free breakfast included. $$$

★ **Hotel Utz-Jay** C 15 de Febrero hotelutzjay.com; map page 118. This fine place has rustic, comfortable rooms and adobe-and-stone *casitas* dotted around extensive grounds that boast a hot tub and *tuj* (sauna). There's good home-cooked food available in the restaurant. $$$

Mario's Rooms C Santander 7762 1313; map page 118. A justifiably popular and efficiently run place, close to the lake and in the thick of things. The smallish rooms are well presented, some airy and light with private bath, others more basic, and the shared balconies overlook a slim courtyard. Free water and (light) breakfast. $$

Posada de los Volcanes C Santander 5–51 posadadelosvolcanes.com; map page 118. Well-presented, bright rooms, all with good beds, modern bathrooms and cable TV; some have lake views. Its location, close to the lakeshore, is excellent. $$$

Rancho Grande Inn C Rancho Grande ranchograndeinn.com; map page 118. One of Pana's original inns, this B&B has spacious chalets and rooms dotted around lovely grassy, shady grounds. Offers local character, in the form of local fabrics and period furnishings, but some rooms are a little dark. There's a small pool, and the breakfast pancakes are legendary. $$$$

EATING

Panajachel has an abundance of cafés and **restaurants**, with Italian, Mexican, American, Asian and some good local places. Cheap comedores can be found close to the market and good fish restaurants are located by the Santiago dock.

Café Loco C Santander 4704 3588, cafelococoffee.com; map page 118. Hip Korean-owned café, where every imaginable coffee combo is available from an assortment of high-tech coffee machinery, prepared by a couple of complete Java-istas. Their other branch is in Gangnam (!). Meals are also offered. $

Chero's Bar C de los Árboles; map page 118. Simple *pupusería* where the Salvador-style healthy snacks are made right in front of you, including veggie options. It doubles as a low-key bar with cheap drink specials, cocktails and wine by the glass available. $$

Chez Alex C Santander 7762 1602, facebook.com/chezalexpana; map page 118. High-end fine dining, with a European menu featuring dishes like *wiener schnitzel*, snails, fondue, lamb chops and a long wine list. It's expensive and quite formal, with starched tablecloths and fancy cutlery. $$$$

Circus Bar C de los Árboles circusbar.com.gt; map page 118. Offering the best pizza in Pana, this atmospheric restaurant is divided into little sections with walls covered in circus memorabilia. Also offers good salads, bruschettas, pasta and grilled meats. Full bar including cocktails (and mocktails) and live music (jazz, salsa, flamenco, *bolero*, *trova*) most evenings. $$

Crossroads Café C del Campanario 0–27 crossroadscafepana.com; map page 118. A real find, this simple yet very welcoming little place is tucked away on a small lane in the old town. It's run by an American perfectionist who selects, blends and roasts his own beans from the Guatemalan highlands and far beyond. Also offers herbal teas, rich hot chocolate and delicious fresh pastries and cakes. $$

★ **Deli Jasmín** C Santander 7762 2585; map page 118. A delightful garden setting for a bite to eat, the *Deli* has healthy breakfasts, sandwiches, salads, Mexican dishes and *tempeh* (Indonesian wholebean tofu). There's a second branch halfway up C Santander with the same menu. $$

Guajimbos Halfway down C Santander 7762 0063; map page 118. South American-style *churrasco* restaurant, serving up huge portions of prime cuts of beef and chicken as well as cheaper options like *choripan* (a *chorizo* sandwich). There's live music some evenings. $$$

Hana Casa Kaqchikel Cultural Centre, C 14 de Febrero restaurantehana.com; map page 118. Terrific new Japanese-owned restaurant in a historic courtyard setting, ideal for sushi, udon dishes, donburi and tempura. There's a good beer selection, and sake and green tea is available. Free delivery. $$$

Mister Jon's Desayunos Casa Kaqchikel Cultural Centre, C 14 de Febrero mister-jon.com; map page 118. Taking the morning shift inside Casa Kaqchikel, this is the place for an American-style breakfast in Pana, with excellent pancakes, omelettes, granola and all the hearty sides you could desire. $$

Restaurante El Mirador Atitlan Lakeside, by the Santiago Pier, atitlanrestaurantes.com/; map page 118. A huge *palapa*-roofed place with spectacular lake views and a reliable menu offering large portions of dependable Guatemalan favourites: try *camarones especial Atitlán*. $$$$

Restaurante Jebel C Santander 7762 2388; map page 118. Casual vegetarian place where the menu features a hit list of global classics: falafel, Indonesian gado-gado, pasta and Mexican dishes. $$

DRINKING AND NIGHTLIFE

Panajachel buzzes at weekends and during holidays; the town's mini **Zona Viva** is around the southern end of C de los Árboles. Many places have happy hours, and either live music or a DJ.

Chapiteau C de los Árboles 4503 7527, facebook.com/chapiteaupanajachel; map page 118. Disco with a lively dancefloor on weekend nights. Salsa instructors are often at hand early in the evening to sort out your steps. Cover charge.

Jagger Bar/Café C Santander 4198 3096; map page 118. Large open-sided bar-restaurant with live music several times a week.

Pana Rock Café C Santander 7762 2194; map page 118. A kind of *Hard Rock Café* theme bar. It's a decent place to watch sports games. Live rock music on weekend nights.

Sunset Café By the lake ⊕7762 0003; map page 118. For a sundowner this café and bar can't be beat, with fine volcano views; overpriced food is also served.

SHOPPING

For Guatemalan textiles, clothes and handicrafts there are dozens of stores along C Santander.

Libreria y Papeleria Maranatha Calle Principal 18 ⊕7762 2586; map page 118. Has a decent choice of books on Maya culture, Central American society and politics, maps and guidebooks.

Sombreros Texas GT C Santander ⊕7762 0869; map page 118. An amazing selection of Panamas, trilbies, Stetsons and Mexican hats.

DIRECTORY

Banks Banco Industrial, C Santander, has an ATM, and there's a 5B ATM at the northern end of the road too.

Emergencies Contact the local English-speaking PROATUR rep (⊕5874 9450) if you need assistance.

Internet ICC, C Santander.

Laundry Lavandería Santander, C Santander opposite *Pana Rock Café* (Mon–Sat 7am–8pm), charges per pound of washing, drying and folding.

Medical care Dr Edgar Barreno speaks good English; his office is down the first street that branches to the right off C de los Árboles (⊕7762 1008).

Pharmacy Farmacia La Unión, C Santander.

Post office C Santander and C 15 de Febrero, or try Get Guated Out on C de los Árboles (⊕7762 0595) for bigger shipments.

Telephone Get Guated Out, C de los Árboles, has very inexpensive rates to landlines and mobiles worldwide, should you need to make any calls during your visit.

The eastern shore

There are two roads around the lake's **eastern shore** from Panajachel. The shoreline road heads as far as **San Antonio Palopó** via **Santa Catarina Palopó** while the other route climbs up to the lip of the crater and heads towards Godínez.

Santa Catarina Palopó

Just 4km from Pana, **SANTA CATARINA PALOPÓ** is a small village with no sights (except a whitewashed colonial church) but an interesting **weaving** tradition; the *huipiles* worn here have dazzling zigzags in vibrant shades of turquoise or purple. The women of Santa Catarina have a reputation for being persistent vendors, so expect to be pressed for a purchase if you stop by.

San Antonio Palopó

Continuing along the lakeside road brings you to **SAN ANTONIO PALOPÓ**, a larger and more traditional village than Santa Catarina Palopó, squeezed in beneath a steep hillside. The hillsides above San Antonio are well irrigated and terraced, and older men still wear the village *traje* of red shirts with vertical stripes and short woollen kilts. The central **church** is worth a look; just to the left of the entrance are two ancient bells. Two **weaving stores** on the main road sell local textiles.

ARRIVAL AND DEPARTURE — THE EASTERN SHORE

By minibus and pick-up Minibuses and pick-ups run along the lakeshore to Santa Catarina Palopó and San Antonio Palopó from C El Amate, Panajachel (every 15min 6am–7pm).

ACCOMMODATION

Much of the lake's eastern shore has been developed, and great villas and **luxury hotels** have come to dominate the environment.

SANTA CATARINA PALOPÓ

Casa Palopó 2km south of Santa Catarina ⊕casapalopo.com. The sumptuous and very tasteful *Casa Palopó* offers lovely rooms kitted out with grand furniture and oil paintings, each with million-quetzal lake views. The restaurant, on an elevated terrace is good (if pricey) and you'll find gorgeous grounds, with a pool area also facing the lake. $$$$

Hotel Villa Santa Catarina Between the village and lakeshore ⊕villasdeguatemala.com/es. Colonial-style place with smallish and comfortable, if not exceptional, rooms that face the hotel's large pool. $$$$

SAN ANTONIO PALOPÓ

Hotel Terrazas del Lago By the water ⊕4496 3565. A relaxing base, this simple hotel occupies a point at the southern end of the village and has comfortable rooms with stone walls and beautiful lake views. Excellent meals of local dishes (including *empanadas)* are served, and the family owners are welcoming and attentive. $$$

San Lucas Tolimán

Taking the high road from Pana, you pass through the tiny village of **San Andrés Semetabaj** and ramshackle **Godínez** before descending abruptly to **SAN LUCAS TOLIMÁN**. Set apart from the other lakeside settlements in many ways, this largely ladino town, surrounded by coffee fincas, is probably the least attractive of the lot. Both the Tolimán and Atitlán **volcanoes** can be climbed from here, though trips are easier to organize in Pana or San Pedro. The main **market** days are Thursday and Sunday.

ARRIVAL AND DEPARTURE — SAN LUCAS TOLIMÁN

By bus Very regular buses run from San Lucas to Santiago Atitlán and there are hourly buses to Guatemala City via Cocales. There are also six daily buses to Panajachel (1hr) plus occasional boat connections.

ACCOMMODATION

Hotel Tolimán Just above the lakeshore ⓦhoteltoliman.com. Classy, tranquil hotel with lovely grounds overlooking the lake. There's a pool and comfortable rooms that have a colonial feel. Dining here is a real treat, with meals featuring veggies from their organic garden. $$$

Los Tarrales South of San Lucas at Km164 on the road to Cocales ⓦtarralesreserve.com. A birders' paradise, this coffee finca and rural lodge borders a nature reserve and offers specialist birdwatching tours (charge per person for a half-day guided hike) with expert guides. Transport up to the cloud forest can be arranged, and guests regularly report seeing more than one hundred species on their visits. Common bird sightings include the Horned Guan, Blue Seedeater and more. The lodge's rooms are functional, certainly not fancy. Filling meals are also available. $$$

Santiago Atitlán

In the southwest corner of the lake, set to one side of a sheltered horseshoe inlet, **SANTIAGO ATITLÁN** is overshadowed by the cones of the San Pedro, Atitlán and Tolimán volcanoes. It's the largest and most important of the lakeside towns, and also one of the most traditional, being the main centre of the Tz'utujil-speaking Maya. The modest remains of the ancient Tz'utujil fortified capital, **Chuitinamit-Atitlán** are close by, and are easily visited.

Today Santiago is an industrious sort of place in a superb setting, though ugly new concrete and cinder block constructions besmirch its aesthetic appeal. During the day the town becomes fairly commercial, its **main street** (which runs up from the dock) lined with souvenir shops and art galleries. Expect to be hustled by hawkers, particularly if you visit during the huge Friday-morning **market**.

Santiago Atitlán church

The fabulous old colonial Catholic **church** is worth a look for its fascinating Maya religious detail. Its huge central altarpiece, carved when the church was under *cofradía* control, culminates in the shape of a mountain peak and a cross, symbolizing the Maya world tree. Dozens of statues of saints (all bedecked in Indigenous attire) line the walls. On the right as you enter, a stone memorial commemorates **Father Stanley Rother**, an American priest who served in the parish from 1968 to 1981. Father Rother was a committed defender of his parishioners in an era when, in his own words, "Shaking hands with an Indian has become a political act". Branded a communist by President García, he was assassinated by a paramilitary death squad like hundreds of his countrymen before and after him.

SANTIAGO STYLE

The **traditional costume** of Santiago, still worn a fair amount by the older men, is both striking and unusual. The men wear long shorts, which, like the women's *huipiles*, are white- and purple-striped and intricately embroidered with birds and flowers. Traditionally women might also have worn a **xk'ap**, a band of red cloth approximately 10m long, wrapped around their heads, which has the honour of being depicted on the 25 centavo coin. Sadly, this headcloth has almost disappeared, though you may still see it at fiestas and on market days, when it's worn by canny girls eager to attract the eye of tourists (and charge for a photo).

Chuitinamit

Open access to ruins • Free • Boat from the dock in Santiago; charge 1hr return trip

Opposite Santiago Atitlán on the lower flanks of the San Pedro volcano, a steep ten-minute hike up from the lake, are the Postclassic Maya ruins of **Chuitinamit**. This small site, originally called **Chiya**, was the fortified capital of the Tz'utujil before the conquistador Alvarado and his Kaqchikel allies laid waste to the place in 1524 – arriving in a flotilla of three hundred canoes. Sadly, the site is in pretty poor shape today as locals have re-carved the stone monuments (and even added a Virgin Mary), creating Disneyesque figures. That said, Chuitinamit is still actively used by shamen for **ceremonies** and its position high above the lake affords panoramic views. The paths around the site are littered with Maya ceramic fragments and obsidian arrowheads.

Maximón's abode

Santiago is one of the main places where Maya pay homage to **Maximón** (see page 126), the "evil" saint who can usually be found drinking liquor and smoking a cigarette. It costs a few quetzals to enter his abode, and you'll have to pay extra to take his picture. Local children will lead you to his residence (Maximón moves every year or so) for a small tip.

Museo Cojolya

300m up from the dock, on the right • Free • Ⓦ cojolya.org.gt

The small **Museo Cojolya** is a museum of **weaving**, with excellent displays (in English and Spanish) on the tradition of backstrap weaving in Santiago, natural dyes and types of cotton and methods of spinning and weaving. You can see local women in action here, weaving classes can be arranged (contact them two days in advance) and a range of very good-quality shirts, bags and souvenirs are sold. Guided tours of weavers' homes and workshops can also be arranged for a fee.

Activities around Santiago

You can rent a **canoe** and paddle out into the lake – just ask around at the dock. North of Santiago is a small island, surrounded by reeds, which has been designated a **nature reserve**, originally for the protection of the *poc*, or Atitlán grebe, a flightless water bird. Sadly, predatory black bass (a species introduced in the 1950s for sportfishing) ate all the young birds and the *poc* is now extinct.

The Tolimán and Atitlán **volcanoes** can both be climbed from Santiago, but it's always best to take a guide to smooth the way, as there have been robberies. Contact Asotur (Ⓣ 5160 9805, Ⓔ asotur@hotmail.com), a group of licensed guides with an office in a hut just up from the dock, who can lead you to the volcanoes and many other sights around Santiago.

ARRIVAL AND INFORMATION — SANTIAGO ATITLÁN

By boat *Lanchas* connect Santiago with both San Pedro (15min) and Panajachel (20min); they leave when full. Larger boats also make the odd crossing; there are timetables at the dock.

MAXIMÓN, THE EVIL SAINT

The **precise origin** of Maximón, the evil saint, is unknown, but he's also referred to as San Simón, Judas Iscariot and Pedro de Alvarado in Santiago Atitlán, and always seen as an enemy of the Church. Some say that he represents a Franciscan friar who chased after young Indigenous girls, and that his legs are removed to prevent any further indulgence. **"Max"** in the Mam dialect means tobacco, and Maximón is associated with ladino vices such as smoking and drinking; more locally he's known as *Rij Laj* or *Rilej Mam*, the powerful man with a white beard.

Throughout the year he's looked after by a *cofradía*. Such is Maximón's fame these days, and the number of tour groups visiting Santiago, that locals actually use one tourist-geared Maximón house (which outsiders are directed to) and a second location where they can pay their respects to the powerful folk sinner-saint in peace. You'll only likely be invited to the latter – a crepuscular pagan shrine where stuffed animals hang from the ceiling and incense and tobacco fill the air – if you have good local connections. Make a contribution to fiesta funds if you do get an invite.

By bus The town is well connected by bus to Cocales and Guatemala City (8 daily 3am–4pm), and microbuses leave for San Lucas Tolimán.

Information The website santiagoatitlan.com is an excellent resource.

Services There's an ATM on the north side of the plaza.

ACCOMMODATION

Hotel Bambú A 10min walk north of the dock ecobambu.com. Beautiful thatched-roofed stone bungalows and rooms set around a large grassy lakefront plot, plus an excellent restaurant with Spanish specialities. $$$$

Hotel Chi-Nim-Ya On the left uphill from the dock 7721 7131. A simple place with basic rooms (some with private bathrooms) set around a courtyard. $$

Mystical Yoga Farm On the shore opposite Santiago mysticalyogafarm.com. Eco-yoga retreat on the lower flanks of the San Pedro volcano, with a lakefront plot. The ethos is very strict: it's alcohol-, drug- and electricity-free and guests are asked to only bring organic toiletries and "spiritual" books to share. Rates include all meals, yoga and meditation. Dorms $$$, shared bungalow $$$$

★ **Posada de Santiago** 1km south of town posadadesantiagoatitlan.com. An excellent lakeside B&B with delightful rooms, suites and cottages built from volcanic stone. Guests have free access to mountain bikes, canoes, a hot tub, sauna and pool and there's a fine restaurant with very flavoursome cooking (try the blue corn *taquitos* or smoked chicken breast Pibil) and an excellent wine list. $$$

EATING

The **hotels** *Bambú* and *Posada de Santiago* both have excellent restaurants.

Café Rafa 400m up from the dock 7721 7896, facebook.com/CafeRafa. A casual café with street tables ideal for people-watching, fast wi-fi and a fine line-up of coffee creations (beans are sourced from the owner's farm), smoothies and snacks. $$

Wach'alal 400m up from the dock. A clean, good-value comedor, with an unpronounceable name but satisfying *comida típica* and lake fish. $$

San Pedro La Laguna

Around the other side of the San Pedro volcano from Santiago is the town of **SAN PEDRO LA LAGUNA**, one of Central America's prime places for young travellers to hang out and **party**. San Pedro has a distinctively bohemian feel, and there's plenty of bongo-bashing and bong-smoking counterculture in evidence. Bars pump out reggae and trance till the early hours of the morning, which upsets some locals (most of whom are evangelical Christians). Periodically, crackdowns curtail the party action.

If you've no interest in the high life, you'll still find plenty to do in San Pedro, with **yoga** classes, good **language schools** and plenty of **hiking** trails. It's the kind of place people love or hate – come and make your own mind up.

The setting is simply spectacular. The town sits on the lower slopes of the San Pedro volcano, while to the northwest the steep ridged edge of the Atitlán caldera rises to an

HOLY SMOKE

Easter celebrations are particularly special in Santiago, and as Holy Week draws closer the town comes alive with expectation and excitement. **Maximón** maintains an important role in the proceedings. On Monday of Holy Week his effigy is taken to the lakeshore where it is washed, on Tuesday he's dressed, and on Wednesday the idol is housed in a small chapel close to the plaza. Here he waits until **Good Friday**, when the town is the scene of a huge and austere religious procession, the plaza packed with everyone dressed in their finest traditional costume. Christ's statue is paraded solemnly through the streets, arriving at the church around noon, where it's tied to a cross and raised above the altar. At around 3pm the *cofrades* arrive to cut him down from the cross, and Christ is lowered into a coffin. Then pandemonium erupts as dozens of the faithful spray his image with perfume, and the air becomes thick with fragrance and aerosol fumes. Penitents bear Christ out of the church on a vast cedar platform, inching forward and back, taking around two hours to exit the church, before there's a **symbolic confrontation** in the plaza with Maximón, who is carried out of an adjoining chapel by his bearers.

The presence of Maximón, decked out in a felt hat and Western clothes, with a cigar in his mouth, is scorned by reforming Catholics and revered by the traditionalists.

irregular peak known as Indian Nose. San Pedro is a town of two halves. The Maya village sits above the lake, while the gringo zone, replete with bars and cafés, occupies the lower part of town.

Museo Tz'unun Ya'

Between the docks • Charge • ⓣ 5869 6646

Not far from the Panajachel dock, the **Museo Tz'unun Ya'** community museum focuses on the geology of the lake and the history and culture of the Tz'utujil people. You can also arrange guided tours of San Pedro here.

Museo Maya Tz'utujil

Between the docks • Charge

Dedicated to Atitlán's Maya culture, the modest **Museo Maya Tz'utujil**, around 100m southeast of Museo Tz'unun Ya', has examples of traditional weaving from local villages, some interesting old photographs and a small library.

Samajib'al Achib'al

North side of Parque Central • Free • ⓣ 7721 8283

Samajib'al Achib'al is a (small) cultural centre featuring exhibitions of work by San Pedro artists. Pex, the American founder, is a videographer who is documenting the oral culture of the local Maya.

ARRIVAL AND DEPARTURE — SAN PEDRO LA LAGUNA

By boat There are two docks in San Pedro. All boats from Panajachel and villages on the north side of the lake, including Santa Cruz and San Marcos, arrive and depart from the Panajachel dock on the north side of town. Boats from Santiago Atitlán use a separate dock to the southeast, a 10min walk away.

By bus Buses connect San Pedro with Quetzaltenango (7 daily; 2hr 15min) and Guatemala City (9 daily; 3hr 30min); all leave from the Parque Central. Minibuses (about every 15min) connect the town with San Juan, San Pablo and San Marcos. Shuttles run to Chichicastenango, Quetzaltenango, Antigua, Cobán and Lanquín, Guatemala City, Huehuetenango and San Cristóbal de las Casas in Mexico.

INFORMATION, TOURS AND ACTIVITIES

There's no official **tourist information** office in San Pedro but the website ⓦ tzununya.com offers plenty of online guidance.

ACTIVITIES

Kayaks can be rented from the lakeshore west of the Pana dock.

Pools To unwind head to the thermal pools between the two docks for some serious relaxation, or just hang out by one of the three swimming pools: The Deep End is perhaps the best, just uphill from the Santiago dock (charge).

TOUR OPERATORS

Casa Verde Tours Up from the Panajachel dock ⓣ3659 9231. Offers horse-riding, hikes to Indian Nose and community walks; precise prices depend on numbers but rates are reasonable.

Maya Travel San Pedro Left of the Panajachel dock ⓦmayatravelsanpedro.com. Organizes treks up San Pedro volcano and to Indian Nose, horse-riding and bicycle rental by the day.

ACCOMMODATION

San Pedro has some of the cheapest, best-value accommodation in the country, but few mid-range options.

Casa Elena Left from the Pana dock ⓣ3302 6884; map page 128. No frills, just spartan, cheap rooms; you pay more for a private bath. There's a dock at the rear for swimming and a guests' kitchen. $

Casa Lobo Lakeshore, 1.5km south of Santiago dock ⓦfacebook.com/casalobobungalows; map page 128. Very tasteful place with stone bungalows and apartments, each equipped with huge beds, artwork, kitchenette and verandas set in a lovely garden. The hospitable German owners whip up a mean, healthy breakfast. It's about a 20min walk from town, situated right on the lakeshore. $$$$

Hotel Gran Sueño Left from the Pana dock ⓣ7721 8110; map page 128. Run by a welcoming family, this likeable place has clean, smallish rooms all with private bathrooms and TV. Some have nice touches like wall maps, and those on the upper level have lake views. $$

Hotel Mansión del Lago Up from Pana dock ⓣ7721 8124; map page 128. A well-built hotel with light, clean rooms all with pine beds, private bath and balcony areas with lake views. $$$

Hotel Maria Elena Left from Pana dock ⓣ5020 9866; map page 128. Two-storey block with spacious rooms, all with private bathrooms. The communal balconies have hammocks at the front for quality swinging time. $$

LANGUAGE SCHOOLS IN SAN PEDRO

San Pedro has established itself as a **language school** centre in recent years – the beautiful location and inexpensive schools drawing increasing numbers of students. Prices are still extremely cheap for one-on-one tuition and full board with a local family. These schools are recommended:

Casa Rosario South of Santiago Atitlán dock T 5945 9537, W casarosariospanishschool.com

Cooperativa Spanish School 400m south of Pana dock T 5858 2463, W cooperativeschoolsanpedro.edu.gt

Corazón Maya South of Santiago Atitlán dock T 5914 8575, W corazonmayaspanishschool.com

Lake Atitlan Spanish School Between the piers T 5466 7177, W lakeatitlanspanishschool.com

2

Hotel Mikaso Close to Santiago dock W hotelmikaso.com; map page 128. A Spanish-style place with quite elegant rooms; there's a comfy dorm (with en-suite bathroom) and a roof-terrace restaurant. Dorm $, doubles $$

Hotel Nahual Maya Left from the Pana dock T 7721 8158; map page 128. A smart, whitewashed colonial-style place set off the road with two floors of well-kept, attractive rooms; all have plenty of natural light and private bathrooms. Popular, so book ahead. $$$

Hotel Pinocchio Between the docks T 7721 8380; map page 128. Yes, it's a large concrete block, but the rooms are kept tidy, the huge garden is lovely, staff are welcoming and there's a guests' kitchen. Prices are flexible according to demand, so you should be able bargain at quiet times. $$

★ **Hotel Sak'cari El Amanecer** 7 Av 2–12, Zona 2 W sakcari.com; map page 128. By far the swankiest hotel in town, with a small pool and attractive grassy grounds that enjoy fine lake views. Rooms and apartments are well kept. There are free kayaks for guests, too. $$$$

Hotel San Antonio Left of the Pana dock T 7721 8196; map page 128. A good mustard-coloured place where all the inviting rooms have TVs and bathrooms, and there's a streetside café. $$

Mandala's Hostal Right from the Pana dock W mandalashostal.com; map page 128. This hostel is no-frills, but it is clean and offers decent value for money. You can expect basic digs and a bar-resto by the lake, with lots of drinking games and organized entertainment to rev up the young gap-year punters. Rates include breakfast. Dorms $, doubles $$

Mr Mullet's Left of Pana dock W mrmulletshostel.com; map page 128. A popular party hostel with simple, clean rooms with good mattresses and four-bed dorms with huge lockers; bathrooms (with hot water) are shared. There's a garden at the rear for chilling, and a bar area. Dorms $, doubles $$

Zoola Between the docks T 5578 8313; map page 128. Love-it-or-hate-it Israeli-owned lakeside hostel popular with young travellers. There's a great chill-out space shaded by canvas and a (tiny) lakeside pool, dorms are pleasant enough and there's tasty Middle Eastern food; however, the stoner vibe won't appeal to all. Minimum two-night stay; no advance reservations. Dorms $, doubles $$

EATING

San Pedro's **cafés** and **restaurants** have a decidedly international flavour, and most are also excellent value for money. Vegetarians are well catered for, and there are also a few typical Guatemalan comedores in the centre of the village.

★ **The Fifth Dimension** Pana dock T 3610 4981; map page 128. This casual restaurant serves a robust and varied selection of vegetarian dishes – and sometimes free smoothies too, depending on how the chef fairs with his daily health drink experiments. $$

Home Between the docks T 4255 2314; map page 128. Vegetarian restaurant that enjoys a leafy garden setting with tables under trees and a wide choice of curries, burritos, tofu stir-fries, wraps, lentil dishes and great set lunches. They also have a "delicate tummy" menu for those in need and very reasonably priced *licuados*. $$

Idea Connection Between the docks T 7721 8356; map page 128. Superb, very welcoming Italian-owned garden café with delicious breakfasts, pasta and pizza. It also operates as a bakery; check out their delicious bread and croissants. Fast wi-fi, and live music some evenings. $$

Nick's Place By the Pana dock W gonzjacky.wixsite.com/misitio; map page 128. Popular, locally owned restaurant with a superb-value menu of international and Guatemalan food and a fine lakefront location. $$

Zoola Between the docks T 5578 8313; map page 128. This relaxed hotel-restaurant has low tables set under a tent and serves commendable Israeli and Middle Eastern food. Service is very slow, so take a good book or enjoy a leisurely game of backgammon while you wait for your meal. The ambiance and unique setting make it a popular spot. $$$

DRINKING AND NIGHTLIFE

San Pedro's **bar action** is concentrated on the trail between the docks, and around the Pana dock. Most places have happy hours. *D'Noz*, *Buddha Bar* and other spots around town show movies.

HIKES FROM SAN PEDRO

The **San Pedro volcano**, which towers above the village of San Pedro La Laguna to a height of some 3020m, is largely covered with tropical forest; to hike up it get an early start (ideally before 5am) to maximize your chances of a clear view and to avoid the worst of the heat. It's a very steep path; the ascent takes around 3hr 30min to 4hr for most people, the descent 2hr to 2hr 30min. The hike is well organized and secure, with all walkers directed via a **base camp** (T 5593 8302) with information 2km south of town. Official **guides** (charge per person) then escort hikers up the volcano along a well-maintained trail with a stop at a *mirador* deck, which has superb lake views. Wildlife you may encounter includes wild boar and many species of bird, including turkeys. The peak itself is ringed by forest, which blocks the view over San Pedro, although an opening on the south side gives excellent views of Santiago.

An alternative hike that's possible to arrange with an agency (see page 128) is to the peak **Indian Nose**, which arguably provides the best view of the lake, its three volcanoes and, if it's clear, to four other distant cones on the horizon. Hikers are usually asked for an "access fee". But note there are several different paths to the summit, and rights of way are contested by three villages: periodically this causes disputes and hikers have been asked to stump up extra cash from time to time. Most tours leave around 4am and involve a 30min hike, but there are longer routes. This summit is regularly used for Maya religious ceremonies – if you do come across a ritual, it's best not to take photographs.

Alegre Pub Above Pana dock T 7721 8100; map page 128. Pub showing European football, NFL and NBA games, and serving comfort grub such as Sunday roasts, shepherd's pie and burgers. They have regular pool tournaments and games nights.

El Barrio Between the docks W facebook.com/ElBarrioSP; map page 128. An intimate little bar with a garden that has something on most nights of the week: Tuesdays are LGBTQ+ friendly, there's a quiz (trivia) on Wednesdays. Also serves reasonable grub including a good weekend "champagne" brunch.

Buddha Bar Between the docks T 4178 7979; map page 128. This scruffy multistorey American-owned bar is popular for its live music (everything from country to reggae; open mic night is Monday), DJ and comedy events, pool tables, dartboard, films and general craic.

DIRECTORY

Banks Banrural (Mon–Fri 8am–5pm, Sat 9am–12.30pm) has an ATM, and there's a second ATM by the Pana dock.

Internet Wi-fi is very widespread in San Pedro. Many hotels and restaurants offer wi-fi for guests, or alternatively you may choose to use your own data, but make sure you check the rates with your provider first.

The northern shore

The **northern shore** of the lake harbours a string of isolated, traditional villages. From San Pedro, a rough road runs as far as Tzununá and from there a spectacular path continues all the way to Sololá. Non-direct *lanchas* to Panajachel will call in at any village en route, but the best way to see this string of isolated settlements is **on foot**: it makes a fantastic day's walk, though check the security situation first (see page 115). A narrow strip of level land is wedged between the water and the steep hills most of the way, and where this disappears the path is cut into the slope, yielding dizzying views of the lake below. It takes between five and six hours to walk from San Pedro to Santa Cruz. You can get drinks, snacks and meals at all the villages along the way, which also all have accommodation.

San Juan La Laguna

From San Pedro it's just 2km to the tidy, tranquil little town of **SAN JUAN LA LAGUNA**, at the back of a sweeping bay. The beaches that surrounded the town can be periodically swamped by rising lake water but San Juan remains a pretty place to visit and something of a model for highland Guatemala. Citizens here take a real pride in the appearance of their town; streets are swept and you won't encounter any litter.

You'll find several good artist **galleries** and **weaving co-ops** just up from the dock, including Las Artesanías de San Juan and Asociación de Mujeres de Color – all have plenty of goods for sale.

Maximón shrine

In the centre of the village, next door to *Restaurant Chi'nimaya*, is a shrine to **Maximón** (see page 126). Inside you'll find the saintly sinner dressed in local garb – as this shrine attracts fewer visitors than those elsewhere, you may want to bring him some liquor or a cigar.

Rupalaj K'istalin

Tours • Charge per person • T 4772 2527 E rupalajkistalin@gmail.com

San Juan has developed an excellent **community guide** association, **Rupalaj K'istalin**, which allows travellers to visit natural dye-weaving co-ops, local forests for bird-watching, a medicinal plant nursery and coffee plantations, and to learn about local crafts (mats called *petates* are made from lake reeds), Maya ceremonies, local culture and folklore. Guides can also lead you to some extraordinary **archeological remains** that lie around the fringes of the town, including a huge Olmec head that's buried in coffee bushes and a carved stone monument that depicts a birth.

ARRIVAL AND INFORMATION — SAN JUAN LA LAGUNA

By pick-up/minibus Pick-ups and minibuses run between San Pedro and San Juan about every 15min.

Information Sites such as W atitlanliving.com and W guatemala.com are useful resources for travellers.

ACCOMMODATION AND EATING

★ **Café El Artesano** Centre of the village T 5763 6815. One of the best dining experiences in the country, this delightful garden café-restaurant was established by Ditres, a chef from the capital who tired of city life. His platters of cheese and cured meats are simply sublime, featuring a dozen or more artisan products that he's sourced from across Guatemala, which he serves with olives, nuts, home-made bread and a pickle or two. After you order, allow an hour for the cheese and meats to reach air temperature, uncork a bottle of wine and you're set. The rest of the menu takes in smoked fish, delicious salads and grilled meats. $$

Pa Muelle 200m up from the dock T 4141 0820. A fine choice, with a row of five immaculately presented rooms that share a lake-facing terrace with beautiful views. Staff are kind and helpful and there's a guests' kitchen, but no wi-fi. $$

San Pablo La Laguna

From San Juan, the lakeside road passes below the Tz'utujil settlement of **SAN PABLO LA LAGUNA**. This village's traditional speciality is the manufacture of rope from the fibres of the *maguey* plant; you can sometimes see great lengths being stretched and twisted in the streets.

Santa Clara La Laguna

A precipitous but paved road continues from San Pablo up to **SANTA CLARA LA LAGUNA**, a sprawling town situated in a plateau high above the western shore of the lake, renowned for its basketry. Women use *cañvera*, which is similar to bamboo, to make fine fruit bowls and other household goods here.

Parque Chuiraxamoló

9km north of Santa Clara La Laguna • Charge for admission and zip lines • T 5749 2886 • All buses running between San Pedro and the Carretera Interamericana pass the entrance

The spectacular **Parque Chuiraxamoló** is a forest reserve and adventure centre with two zip lines (including a 400m run), hiking and bike trails, kids' playground and picnic and camping areas. Perfect for families, nature lovers and adventure seekers. Visitors will also enjoy panoramic views of Lake Atitlán at various points throughout the park. It's professionally managed and offers a great day out.

San Marcos La Laguna

SAN MARCOS LA LAGUNA is famous for its holistic and healing centres, veggie cafés, yoga and rebirthing classes and all things esoteric. It's home to a merry bunch of foreigners of an artistic and spiritual persuasion, so if you're searching for a therapist or masseur this is the place.

The settlement has a decidedly tranquil feel – there's no real bar scene – so it's a perfect place to relax and read a book in your hammock and enjoy the natural beauty of the lake. **Hotels and restaurants** are clustered close to the water under thick forest cover, while the **Maya village** is inland on higher ground; relationships between the two communities remain a little distant. Apart from a huge stone **church**, built to replace a colonial original destroyed in the 1976 earthquake, there are no real sights in the Maya village.

San Marcos offers several **retreats**, including specialist yoga and meditation centres, and a spectacular new Tai Chi temple above the village. **Cambalacha** (W lacambalacha.org) is an arts project that teaches dance, music and theatre to local children; volunteers are always welcome and shows are also performed.

Cerro Tzankujil

500m west of the dock • Charge

The wooded peninsula of **Cerro Tzankujil**, which juts into the lake, has been developed for visitors – there are paths, a lookout point and kayaks for rent. There's a famous **cliff jump** here where you can plunge 6m or so into the lake (though it's not obligatory!). Tzankujil is also a sacred spot used for Maya ceremonies.

SAN MARCOS LA LAGUNA

ARRIVAL AND DEPARTURE

By boat There are connections to both San Pedro and Panajachel every 20min or so; the last boats are at 5pm.
By minibus From San Pedro it's a 20min ride in one of the regular minibuses.
On foot San Marcos is a 2hr walk from San Pedro.

ACTIVITIES

Kayaking Kayaks can be rented at Cerro Tzankujil (see above).
Language school San Marcos Spanish School, inside *La Fé* (W sanmarcosspanishschool.com), charges a flat fee per week for four hours of classes, excluding accommodation.
Meditation Set in leafy grounds uphill from the dock, Las Pirámides (T 5202 4168, W laspiramidesdelka.com) has retreats and courses (from seven days to three months). The Moon course lasts a month and includes hatha yoga, metaphysics, meditation techniques and an esoteric learning week, followed by a final week of fasting and complete silence. All accommodation is in comfortable, if smallish pyramid cabañas; there's also delicious vegetarian food. Drop-in yoga classes are also held here.
Swimming Swimming from wooden jetties by the lakeshore has become more troublesome as the lake water has risen in the last few years, but there are still docks for lake access.
Tai chi Based in a classically styled Chinese temple above the village, Seven Stars Taiji Tao Temple (T 4822 7171, E info@taotemple.org) only admits serious practitioners for select walk in classes, in exchange for a donation. However if you want to join their regular sessions, a minimum commitment of four weeks is required. It's an ideal place for those seeking a deeper, more focused practice.
Yoga Kaivalya, on the road to San Juan (T 3319 0450) is an impressive hatha yoya centre with drop-in sessions, courses and teacher training that gets good feedback; there are also tantra and meditation sessions. Yoga Forest (T 3301 1835, W kawoqforest.com), a 20min walk above the village, has a stunning location for its classes (daily rates include meals and shared accommodation) and courses.

ACCOMMODATION

Most of San Marcos' hotels and guesthouses are best reached from the **main dock** by *Posada Schumann*.
Centro Sonrisa Uphill from the dock T 5723 5426; map page 132. Very well-built thatched bungalows, some sleeping up to four and many with private bathrooms, dotted around a shady garden. There's a good bar-restaurant, too. $$
Circles Uphill from the dock T 3327 8961; map page 132. Above a pretty café, the accommodation here is clean and well presented, and there's a little terrace and garden for relaxing. Dorms $, doubles $$
Eco-Hotel La Paz Uphill from the dock W facebook.com/EcoHotelLaPaz; map page 132. Very spacious, rustic cottages, a superior six-bed, two-storey dorm, good home-cooking and yoga classes. Guests get the run of a lovely leafy garden with hammocks, there's a sauna/massage room and your host Benjamin is amiable. Dorms $, doubles $$
Hospedaje Panabaj In the village T 5678 0181; map page 132. Two-storey block in a quiet location, with basic rooms that face a garden. The shared bathrooms are kept tidy. $$
★ **Hotel Alegria** 300m west of the dock T 5893 7776; map page 132. Also known as Alegria Casa, this warm and welcoming spot is owned and operated by Santos – a host who pulls out all the stops for his guests. Ideal for the ferry with spacious rooms to boot. $$
Pachamama Hostel East of the dock T 3241 7330; map page 132. Just steps from the shore, this backpackers' stronghold has decent dorms and rooms, and an in-house café-restaurant. Dorms $, doubles $$
★ **Posada del Bosque Encantado** Uphill from dock W hotelposadaencantado.com; map page 132. This wonderful place has four huge, gorgeous adobe cottages with a shared terrace; they face a lovely garden. You'll find a *temascal* (sauna), hammocks to lounge in and a little café-restaurant serving tasty Guatemalan grub. $$$
Posada Schumann By the dock T 5202 2216; map page 132. A selection of attractive, good-value stone-and-timber rooms and bungalows (though due to rising lake waters some of the pretty lakeside garden has been lost). There's a Maya-style sauna, free use of kayaks and a nice, though slightly pricey, restaurant. $$$
Tul y Sol Short walk west of the dock T 5293 7997, W facebook.com/tulysolatitlan; map page 132. Very spacious, superb-value rooms at the rear of a lakeside restaurant (see below). You get a huge bed, nice wooden furniture, private bathrooms, lake views from a shared balcony and even a free breakfast for very little here. It's a total bargain for single travellers. $$

EATING

Perhaps unsurprisingly, given its demographic, San Marcos caters particularly well for **vegetarians**.
Blind Lemon's On the road to San Juan W blindlemons.com; map page 132. This colonial-style bar-restaurant showcases blues artists, films and a familiar US-style menu including burgers, Cajun grub and nachos. $$

Centro Sonrisa Uphill from the dock 5723 5426; map page 132. The restaurant at this popular guesthouse (see above) offers great pizza, and it's also a good spot for gourmet burgers and cocktails. $$

Comedor Mi Marquensita Susi In the village; map page 132. Simple local place just off the Parque Central, ideal for your fill of *comida típica* at very reasonable prices. $$

La Fé Inland from the dock 4005 2667; map page 132. Well-regarded restaurant with an eclectic menu of home-made soups, burritos, burgers and kebabs. It's renowned for its authentic Indian curries, and the nan breads are stupendously good. $$$

Il Giardino Inland from the dock facebook.com/ilgiardinoatitlan; map page 132. This vegetarian garden restaurant has a lovely setting and serves fresh pasta, great crêpes and breakfasts, and bakes its bread in house. They play classical music until noon here, offer fine juices and also have a full bar. $$

Moonfish Cafe On the road to San Juan 5382 6312; map page 132. The owners of this enjoyable café grow their own leaves for the delicious salads and much of the menu (burritos, falafel) is organically sourced. The house coffee is also organic, and fabulously smooth. $$

Restaurante Japonés Allala By the football field 5873 7529; map page 132. Authentic Japanese-owned garden restaurant ideal for delicious noodle dishes, veggie tempura, sushi, *onigiri*, miso soup and sake. $$

Tul y Sol Short walk west of the dock facebook.com/tulysolatitlan; map page 132. French-owned lakeside restaurant with fairly expensive mains (fish, shrimps and grilled *lomito*). Snacks are also served. $$$$

DIRECTORY

Banks The nearest banks and ATMs are in San Pedro La Laguna.

Internet Wi-fi is very common in hotels and restaurants. Internet quality varies depending on where you are and outages may occur.

Tzununá

Beyond San Marcos, the villages feel more isolated. The first one you come to is **TZUNUNÁ**, a scruffy-looking, very traditional place strung up a steep hillside. Originally it sat at the lakeside, but after it was badly damaged by a flood in 1950, the people rebuilt their homes on higher ground. As ever the local costume is striking, the women wearing vivid red *huipiles* striped with blue and yellow on the back.

ACCOMMODATION — TZUNUNÁ

Lomas de Tzununá 800m east of the dock lomasdetzununa.com. Perched high above the lake, this is a magnificently sited and well-managed hotel. The lovely cottages all come with huge, sliding glass doors that make the most of the unsurpassed lake vistas. There's a small pool, kayaks and bikes for rent and a good restaurant with a healthy menu. Rates include breakfast. $$$$

Jaibalito

The lakeside road indisputably ends at *Lomas de Tzununá*, giving way to a narrow path cut out of the steep hillside. The next village, **JAIBALITO**, nestling between soaring *milpa*-clad slopes, is another place that was extremely isolated until recent years. For now it remains resolutely Kaqchikel – little Spanish is spoken – though the opening of several tourist-geared businesses means that outside influence is growing.

ACCOMMODATION AND EATING — JAIBALITO

Art & Coffee Hotel In the centre of the village facebook.com/ArtAndCoffeeGT. Upmarket café, gallery and hotel with a robust menu and an excellent variety of baked goodies. $$$

La Casa del Mundo A steep 5min walk from the village lacasadelmundo.com. Clinging to a cliffside, this is not the place for anyone who suffers from vertigo, with accommodation (budget rooms, doubles, stone cabins and a suite) that takes full advantage of the dramatic location. There's a fantastic on-site restaurant offering a variety of dishes that complement the beautiful surroundings but some of the facilities involve extra charges including kayaks and the lakeside tub. $$$

★ **Posada Jaibalito** In the centre of the village 5192 4334. A superb guesthouse, the heart of the community, owned by an ethically minded German. One of the best-value places in Guatemala, it has a fine six-bed dorm (with lockers and en-suite bathroom), great private rooms, tasty and inexpensive Guatemalan and European food (available for non-guests also) and very cheap drinks – treat yourself to a shot of 23-year-old Ron Zacapa or a bottle of wine. Dorms $, doubles $$

Santa Cruz La Laguna

Gorgeous **SANTA CRUZ LA LAGUNA**, stretching for about 2km in a verdant ribbon along the lakeshore, is a supremely tranquil and beautiful village. With some terrific accommodation, yoga classes, kayaking and hiking, it's not surprising its star is on the rise. Above all, it's the (almost) complete lack of roads that really makes this place – just one little lane snakes up to the Maya village high above the lakeshore, and the only access is by boat. With no traffic to contend with, the lake really comes into its own, and it's very easy to be seduced by the mellow pace of life, watching hummingbirds buzz between exotic flowers or Maya boatmen fish for crabs.

Most of the **lakeshore** has been bought up by foreigners and wealthy Guatemalans, while the Maya village is high above the water. The two communities coexist well, with many villagers employed in foreign businesses. Unfortunately the rise in Atitlán's lake water sometimes swamps the shoreline paths, but it's still possible to explore the Santa Cruz bay using a system of gangplanks and trails.

Maya village

Perched on a shelf 150m above the lake, you'll immediately notice the contrast between the affluent shore and the Indigenous community in the **Maya village**, who live in rudimentary conditions. There are no real sights in the village itself, though lake views are truly spectacular and there's a sixteenth-century church on the plaza. The charity **Amigos de Santa Cruz** (Ⓦamigosdesantacruz.org) does sterling work improving opportunities for the local Maya by funding environmental, educational and health programmes. Visitors are welcome to drop by the highly impressive **Cecap** centre, just below the plaza, which Amigos helped establish, where you can take a look at the library and workshops and have a drink or meal in the **café**, which is staffed by catering students.

ARRIVAL AND DEPARTURE — SANTA CRUZ LA LAGUNA

By boat There's no road access to Santa Cruz. Boats (every 20min or so 6am–7.30pm) connect the community with Panajachel (15min) and all villages to the west including San Marcos (20min) and San Pedro (25min).

By tuk-tuk Tuk-tuks buzz between the lakeshore and Maya village, or you can hike it in 15min.

TOURS AND ACTIVITIES

Swimming is great in Santa Cruz (the lake water is cleaner away from the centre), **kayaking** is also very popular and you can **scuba dive** with ATI Divers. There's some excellent **hiking**, too, including a walk to a waterfall above the village football pitch, and another to Sololá along a spectacular path. Staff at the *Iguana Perdida* (see page 136) will be able to get you on the right track for these walks.

Adventure Tours Atitlán Ⓣ5355 8849, Ⓦtours-atitlan.com. Owned and operated by Maya guide and Santa Cruz resident Pedro Juan Solis and his brothers, who all speak fluent English, this company offers lots of tours: excellent mountain-bike trips in the hills behind Santa Cruz, birdwatching walks, and extended trips around the highlands.

ATI Divers At the Iguana Perdida, on the lakefront Ⓦatidivers.com. Dive the lake with this professional scuba school. Fun dives and PADI Open Water courses are available.

Los Elementos 400m west of the dock Ⓦkayakguatemala.com. Owner Lee Beal offers fine kayak tours (or you can just rent one and explore yourself) plus hiking on the high trail above the village, up Cerro de Oro and beyond. Recuperate with a massage or spa service here afterwards.

ACCOMMODATION AND EATING

Santa Cruz has some wonderful accommodation. The main village **dock** beside the *Iguana Perdida* is at the centre of things but boatmen will drop you off at any of the places reviewed here; all have private docks (except *Villa Eggedal*). All the hotels have good **restaurants**, and these are the best places to eat in town.

★**Café Sabor Cruceño** Maya village Ⓦfacebook.com/CafeSaborCruceno. With truly spectacular views and memorable food, this café-restaurant is an excellent reason to make the hike (or tuk-tuk ride) up to the village. Feast on local specialties like *jocón* (meat cooked with sesame and pumpkin seeds, peppers and *tomatillos*) and *suban-ik*, which are prepared with love and flair. The café really benefits the community, providing training for the residents of Santa Cruz. $$

Casa Rosa Just east of the dock ⓣ5803 2531. This lakefront place offers beautiful, peaceful gardens, spacious bungalows and smallish but neat rooms. There's excellent home-style cooking served in the farmhouse-style kitchen or the stylish lakefront lounge-café. Doubles $$, bungalows $$$

La Fortuna at Atitlán 1km east of Santa Cruz ⓦlafortunaatitlan.com. Located on the tiny, virtually private bay of Pachisotz, an isolated but wonderful setting, this place has two gorgeous Indonesian-style wooden bungalows and two smaller cabañas, each with outdoor bathrooms and very fine attention to detail. There's also a landmark lakeside restaurant serving exceptional, creative global cuisine and offering a fine wine selection. Cabañas and bungalows available. $$$$

Hotel Arca de Noé Lakeside ⓦhotelarcadenoeatitlan.com. Managed by local Maya tour guide Pedro Solis, this place offers rustic but comfortable enough stone cottages and rooms, with or without private bathrooms, spread around an expansive, very beautiful, terraced lakeside garden. There's good home cooking, including a communal set dinner. $$$

★ **Iguana Perdida** Lakeside ⓦlaiguanaperdida.com. The hub of the lakeside community, the *Iguana* has one of the most convivial atmospheres in Lago de Atitlán. There are basic dorms and budget rooms, as well as more luxurious options, but it's the lakefront location and social vibe that really makes this place. Dinner is a three-course communal affair. The hotel also offers yoga classes, an open mic night, massages, a TV lounge, book exchange, kayak rental, scuba diving and great travel advice. Dorms $, doubles $$

★ **Isla Verde** 10min walk west of the dock ⓦislaverdeatitlan.com. Nestled in a tranquil spot in the western corner of the Santa Cruz bay, with lovely little A-frame bungalows, each with fine lake views. The sublimely situated decked restaurant juts over the lake and offers healthy, nutritious meals ($$$). There is also a large yoga space and lovely gardens to enjoy. $$$

Villa Eggedal East side of the bay, above the shore ⓦvillaeggedal.com. Lovely studio apartments and *casitas* (one of which has four bedrooms) in a gorgeous garden; they all enjoy stunning lake views and come with kitchens and luxury bathrooms. Managed by the *Iguana Perdida*. Per week: studios $$$, *casitas* $$$$

Villa Sumaya Paxanax bay, a 15min walk east of the dock ⓦbooking.com. A sublime retreat centre-cum-hotel with a prime lakefront location and stunning rooms – those in the *torre* are larger – each with a stupendous lake view, plush beds and stylish decor. Also boasts a great restaurant, library, hot tub, computer room and sauna. Spa treatments and massages are available and there are daily yoga/meditation/Pilates sessions to really get you in holiday mode. $$$$

Los Encuentros to Cuatro Caminos

Heading west from the Los Encuentros junction to Cuatro Caminos, the **Carretera Interamericana** runs through some fantastic high-mountain scenery. The views alone are superb, and if you have time to spare it's well worth dropping into **Nahualá** for the market.

NAHUALÁ RESISTANCE

At the end of the nineteenth century the government confiscated much of Nahualá's **land**, as they did throughout the country, and sold it to **coffee** planters. In protest, the entire male population of Nahualá walked the 150km to Guatemala City and demanded to see **President Barrios** in person, refusing his offers to admit a spokesman and insisting that they all stood as one. Eventually, they were allowed into the huge reception room where they knelt with their foreheads pressed to the floor, refusing to leave until they were either given assurances of their land rights or allowed to buy the land back, which they had done twice before. They saved their land this time, but since then much of it has gradually been consumed by coffee bushes all the same.

On another occasion, during the 1930s under President Ubico, **ladinos** were sent to the town as nurses, telegraph operators and soldiers. Once again the Nahualáns appealed directly to the president, insisting that their own people should be trained to do these jobs, and once again their request was granted. Ubico also wanted to set up a government-run drink store, but the villagers chose instead to ban **alcohol**, and Nahualeños who got drunk elsewhere were expected to confess their guilt and face twenty lashes in the town's plaza.

NAHUALÁ CRAFTS

Nahualá is a major artisan centre, with a fine **weaving** tradition. Men wear outlandish-looking day-glo bright yellow and pink shirts with beautifully embroidered collars, kilt-like woollen "skirts" (called *rodilleras* or *ponchitos*) and huge hats and leather sandals similar to those of the ancient Maya. Woollen garments, including *capixay* cloaks and jackets, are also woven locally. The town is also famous for its **woodwork** – Nahualá carpenters churn out a good proportion of the country's hand-carved wardrobes and bedsteads.

Nahualá

NAHUALÁ ("place of sorcerers") is a small, deeply traditional town 1km or so north of the highway, at the base of a huge, steep-sided intensely farmed bowl. The unique atmosphere of isolation from and indifference to the outside world makes Nahualá one of the most impressive and unusual K'iche' communities.

The town itself is not much to look at, a sprawl of old cobbled streets and adobe houses mixed with many more concrete structures, but the inhabitants have a reputation for fiercely preserving their independence and have held out against ladino incursions with exceptional tenacity (see box). There are a few basic *pensiones*, but it's best to visit the town as a **day-trip** from the lake or Quetzaltenango.

The self-imposed alcohol ban of the 1930s has long been lifted, and if you're here for the fiesta on November 25 you'll see that the people are keen to make up for all those dry years. The **Sunday market** always finds the town full to bursting; there's also a smaller market on Thursdays.

ARRIVAL AND DEPARTURE — NAHUALÁ

By bus Take any bus along the Carretera Interamericana between Los Encuentros and Cuatro Caminos, and alight at the Puente Nahualá, from where minibuses run the 1km or so uphill to the town centre.

Quetzaltenango (Xela)

Guatemala's second city, **QUETZALTENANGO (XELA)**, is the natural hub of the western highlands. It can't claim to be a tourist attraction in its own right, but the city's ordinariness is in many ways its strength – it's a resolutely Guatemalan place. Off the main gringo trail, it has a hospitality and friendliness that belies its size and slightly subdued provincial atmosphere. Bizarre though it may seem, Quetzaltenango's character and appearance is vaguely reminiscent of an industrial town in northern England – grey and cool with friendly, down-to-earth inhabitants, who have a reputation for formality and politeness. Locally, the city is usually referred to as **Xela** (pronounced "shey-la"). Meaning "under the ten", the name is probably a reference to the surrounding peaks. At an elevation of 2330m, Quetzaltenango is always cold in the early mornings; the city wakes up slowly, getting going only once the warmth of the sun has made its mark.

The city is an important **educational centre**, its universities and colleges attracting students from all over the country, while its Spanish schools (see page 142) are internationally renowned. More and more **development** projects are also basing themselves here, and this growing outside influence is steadily injecting a cosmopolitan feel into the city's bars, restaurants and cultural life. Many overseas visitors settle easily into the relatively easy-going pace of the city; it also makes an excellent base for exploring this part of the country, making **day-trips** to villages, basking in hot springs like **Fuentes Georginas**, or hiking in the mountains.

Quetzaltenango is divided into **zones**, although for the most part you'll only be interested in **zonas 1 and 3**, which contain the city centre and the area around the Minerva bus terminal respectively. The centre, heavily indebted to Neoclassicism, is a monument to stability, with great slabs of grey stone belying a history of turbulence and struggle. Things deteriorate as you head away from the main plaza, **Parque Centro América**, with thick traffic and fumes blighting the highland air, particularly around the main bus terminal.

Brief history

Originally there was a walled city here called **Xelajú**, but it was destroyed during the conquest – Pedro de Alvarado is said to have killed the K'iche' king, Tecún Umán, in hand-to-hand combat. The victorious Spanish founded a new town, Quetzaltenango, "the place of the quetzals", the name probably chosen because of the brilliant green quetzal feathers worn by the K'iche' nobles and warriors.

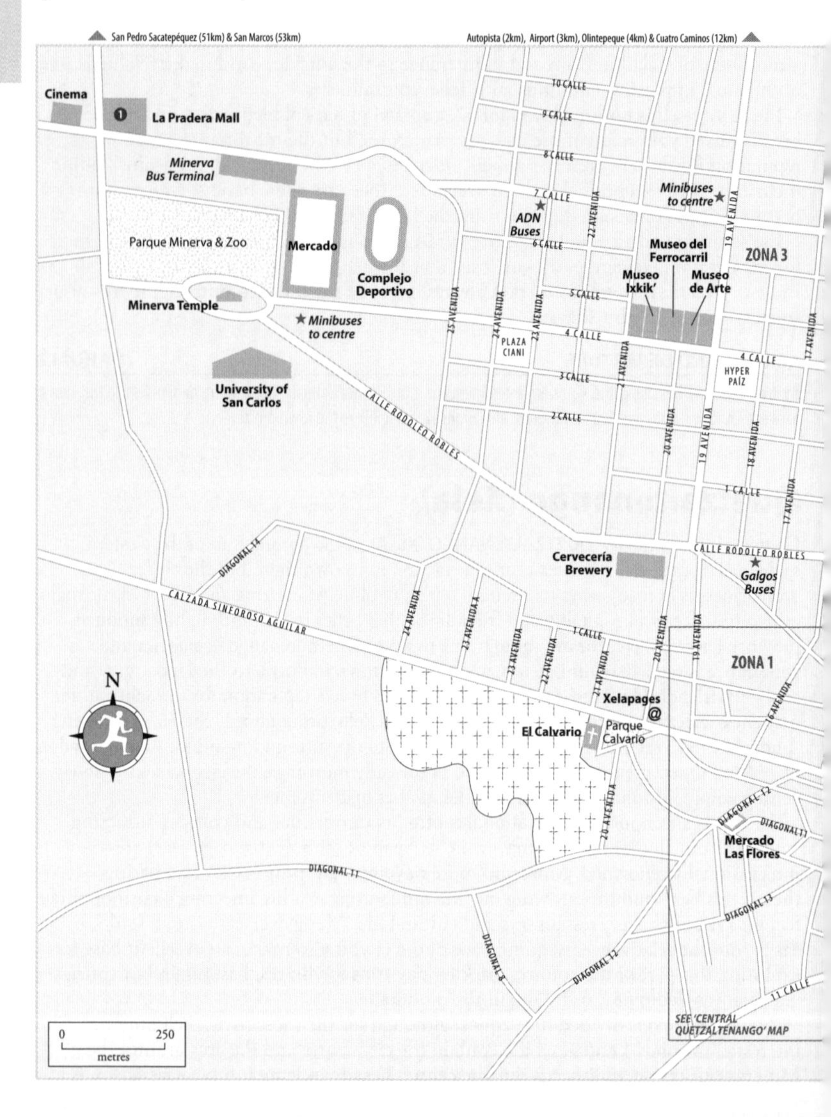

Under **colonial** rule Quetzaltenango flourished as a commercial centre, benefiting from the fertility of the surrounding farmland and good connections to the port at Champerico. When the prospect of independence eventually arose, the city was set on deciding its own destiny. After the Central American Federation broke with Mexico in 1820, Quetzaltenango declared itself the capital of the independent state of **Los Altos**, which incorporated most of the western highlands. But the separatist movement was put down by force and the city had to accept provincial status. Quetzaltenango remained an important centre of commerce and culture, however, its wealth and population continued to grow, and it remained a potent rival to the capital.

All this, however, came to an abrupt end when the city was almost totally destroyed by the massive **1902 earthquake**. Rebuilding took place in a mood of high hopes; all

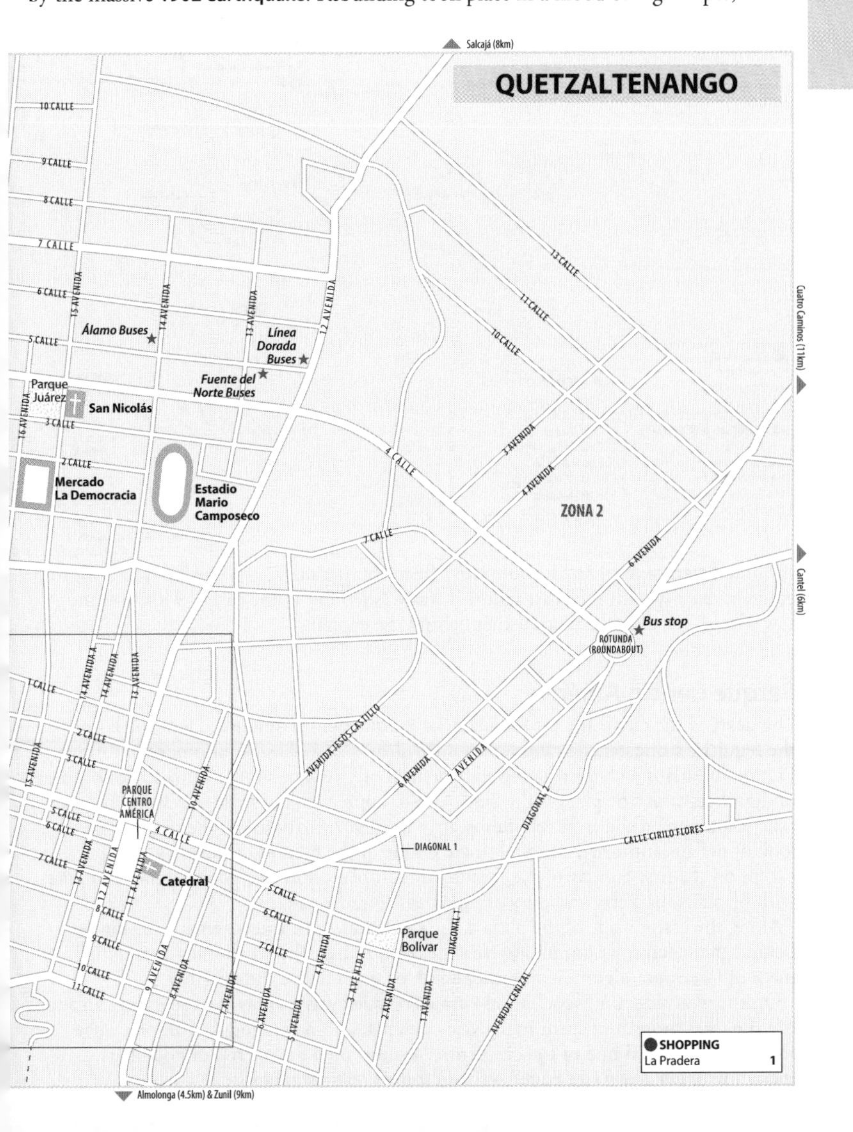

the grand **Neoclassical** architecture dates from this period. A new **rail line** was built to connect the city with the coast, but this was washed out in the early 1930s, and the town steadily fell further and further behind the capital.

Parque Centro América

The heart of the city is the central plaza, or **Parque Centro América**. Here you'll find the requisite stone benches and well-tended shrubs as well as a monument to former President Barrios – all overshadowed by a mass of Greek columns. With an atmosphere of dignified calm, the plaza is the best place to appreciate the sense of self-importance that accompanied the city's rebuilding after the 1902 earthquake. The buildings have a look of defiant authority, although there's none of the buzz of business you'd expect – except on the first Sunday of the month when it plays host to a good artesanías **market**, with blankets, basketry and piles of *típica* weavings for sale.

Along the eastern side of the plaza is the **cathedral**, with a new cement version set behind the spectacular crumbling front of the original. There's another unashamed piece of Greek grandeur, the **municipalidad**, or town hall, a little further up.

On the west side, the Neoclassical **Pasaje Enríquez** was planned as a sparkling arcade of upmarket shops, but spent many years derelict, and now, though still somewhat shabby, is the social hub of the city centre. Inside you'll find a crop of good bars, including *Salón Tecún* (see page 144) and some great restaurants.

Casa de la Cultura

Parque Centro América • Charge

At the bottom end of the plaza, the **Casa de la Cultura** is Quetzaltenango's most blatant impersonation of a Greek temple. On the **ground floor** you'll find a display of assorted documents, photographs and pistols from the liberal revolution and the state of Los Altos (see above), sports trophies, and a room dedicated to the marimba. **Upstairs** there are some modest Maya artefacts, historic photographs and a bizarre natural-history room where, among the dusty displays of stuffed bats and pickled snakes, you can see the macabre remains of assorted freaks of nature, including a four-horned goat.

Beyond Parque Centro América

Away from the plaza the city spreads out, a mixture of the old and new. Out in Zona 3 is the **Mercado La Democracia**, a vast, covered market complex with stalls spilling out onto the streets. A couple of blocks north of the market, next to the **Parque Juárez**, stands the modern **Iglesia de San Nicolás**, a bizarre and ill-proportioned neo-Gothic building, sprouting sharp arches. In the northwest of the city you'll find three small **museums**, all in the shell of the former train station building.

Teatro Municipal

14 Av & 1 C

Lording it over a little plaza replete with busts of celebrated local artists and writers, **Teatro Municipal** is one of the city's spectacular Neoclassical edifices, heavy with grey stone and columns. On clear days, there's a spectacular perspective of Volcán Santa María from here.

Museo del Ferrocarril

4 C & 19 Av, Zona 3 • Charge

Dedicated to the long-gone **railway** that once connected Xela to the Pacific coast, the **Museo del Ferrocarril** is located in the city's former **train station**. Exhibits are not particularly well presented, but you'll find curiosities including original train seats and tickets and you can watch a short documentary (in Spanish) about the line.

Museo Ixkik'

4 C & 19 Av, Zona 3 • Charge • T 5653 5585

The **Museo Ixkik'** concentrates on Maya *traje*, with examples of village **costumes** from across the highlands and one room devoted to Xela itself. Ceremonial *huipiles* are displayed that are only worn on fiesta days. Guides are often here to explain each weaving's meaning.

Museo de Arte

4 C & 19 Av, Zona 3 • Charge

The **Museo de Arte** boasts an important collection of more than two hundred paintings from artists including the architect/murallist Efraín Recinos (1928–2011), whose hand can be seen in many of Guatemala's major buildings. Local painter Rodrigo Díaz has a studio here and is often at hand to show you around.

Zoo and around

4 C, Zona 3 • Free

On the western edge of town, the **Minerva temple** is another of the city's Greek-style monuments. Just behind the temple is a little **zoo**, doubling as a kids' playground. The cages are small but all the animals – including birds, monkeys and pizotes – are well cared for.

LANGUAGE SCHOOLS IN QUETZALTENANGO

Quetzaltenango boasts dozens of **language schools**, many of a very high standard, and makes an excellent place to really immerse yourself in Guatemalan culture. Its relatively large population means that you shouldn't have to share a family home with other gringos. Few local people speak much English, so many students find the city is a good place to progress quickly in their language studies. An added benefit of choosing to study in Quetzaltenango is that most schools fund **community development** and environmental projects. All of the schools listed here are well established and employ professional teachers, however this is not an exhaustive list:

Casa de Español Xelajú Callejón 15, Diagonal 13–02, Zona 1 ⓣ 7761 5954, ⓦ casaxelaju.com
Celas Maya 6 C 14–55, Zona 1 ⓦ celasmaya.com
La Democracia 9 C 15–05, Zona 3 ⓣ 5515 5517
Inepas 15 Av 4–59, Zona 1 ⓦ inepas.org
Juan Sisay 15 Av 8–38, Zona 1 ⓦ juansisay.com
Kie Balam Diagonal 12 4–46, Zona 1 ⓦ kiebalam.com
Madre Tierra 13 Av 8–34, Zona 1 ⓦ madre-tierra.org
Miguel de Cevanates 12 Av 8–31, Zona 1 ⓦ learn2speakspanish.com
El Nahual 28 Av 9–54, Zona 1 ⓣ 5606 1704
La Paz 2 C Callejón 16 2–47, Zona 1 ⓣ 4018 2180
Pop Wuj 1 C 17–72, Zona 1 ⓦ pop-wuj.org
Proyecto Lingüístico Quetzalteco de Español 5 C 2–40, Zona 1 ⓦ plqe.org

Minerva bus terminal and market

Below the Minerva temple are the sprawling, dusty **Minerva bus terminal and market**. It's here that you can really sense the city's role as the centre of the western highlands, with Indigenous traders from all over the area doing business, and buses heading to or from every imaginable village and town.

ARRIVAL AND DEPARTURE — QUETZALTENANGO (XELA)

Unfortunately, all bus arrival and departure points are nowhere near the centre. Note that for travel to Guatemala City and beyond it's more comfortable and always cheaper to use first-class buses rather than shuttles.

SECOND-CLASS BUSES

Second-class buses arrive and depart from the chaotic Minerva Bus Terminal on the city's northwestern edge; to get to the city centre, walk 300m through the market stalls to 4 C and catch a microbus marked "Parque". To get to the bus terminal from the centre of town, microbuses leave from the corner of 4 C and 14 Av, a block west of Parque Centro América.

Destinations Chichicastenango (7 daily; 2hr 30min); Coatepeque (every 30min; 1hr 45min); Guatemala City (every 20min; 4hr); Huehuetenango (every 30min; 2hr); La Mesilla (6 daily; 3hr 45min); Momostenango (every 30min; 1hr 15min); Panajachel (6 daily; 2hr 30min); Retalhuleu (every 30min; 1hr 15min); San Francisco el Alto (every 30min; 45min); San Pedro La Laguna (7 daily; 2hr 15min); Santa Cruz del Quiché (7 daily; 3hr); Tecún Umán (hourly; 3hr); Totonicapán (every 20min; 1hr); Zunil (from Minerva via 10 C and 9 Av, Zona 1, every 30min; 30min).

FIRST-CLASS BUSES

Five companies operate first-class buses to and from the capital (15 daily in total; 4hr), each with their own private terminal; for the latest schedules check out ⓦ xelawho.com.

Álamo 14 Av 5–15, Zona 3 (ⓣ 7767 4582).
Fuente del Norte 5 C & 13 Av, Zona 3 (ⓦ transportesfuentedelnorte.com).
Galgos C Rodolfo Robles 17–43, Zona 1 (ⓣ 7761 2248).

SHUTTLE BUSES

Shuttle buses are offered by travel agents (see below); destinations include Chichicastenago (market days only), Panajachel, Antigua, Cobán, Guatemala City, San Pedro La Laguna and San Cristóbal de las Casas in Mexico.

INFORMATION AND TOURS

Tourist information Inguat, Parque Centro América (Mon–Fri 9am–5pm, Sat 9am–1pm; ⓣ 7761 4931) is not very helpful; you'll find travel agencies much better informed.

Listings and websites The English-language magazine *Xela Who* (ⓦ xelawho.com) has good listings and features about the city. Check out the website ⓦ xelapages.com for hotel and cultural information and discussion forums.

TOUR OPERATORS

AeroBike 2 Diagonal 29-3 ⓣ 7767 7298. Bike specialists who run excellent guided mountain-bike rides around the Xela area and offer bike rental (see page 144).

Adrenalina Tours Pasaje Enríquez, Parque Centro América ⓣ 5308 1489, ⓦ adrenalinatours.com. Recommended for shuttle buses, tours of the Xela region, hikes and volcano climbs.

Altiplano's 6 C & 7 Av 4748 6952, altiplanos.com.gt. Reliable locally owned operator with trekking and tour programmes to villages around Xela and beyond.

Diversity Tours 15 Av 3–86 7761 2545. Contact them for shuttle buses, and tours of sights including the Santiaguito viewpoint and Tajumulco.

Quetzaltrekkers Inside Casa Argentina, 12 Diagonal 8–37 7765 5895, quetzaltrekkers.com. Offers some outstanding hikes, including a three-day trek from Xela to Atitlán (minimum donation required) and a day hike to Fuentes Georginas, plus rock climbing. All profits go to a charity for street children.

2

ACCOMMODATION

Quetzaltenango cannot boast a huge choice of hotels, but does have some decent **budget places**. All the places we have reviews here are within a 10min walk of **Parque Centro América**.

Black Cat Hostel 13 Av 3–33, Zona 1 5550 5614; map page 140. Offering a quiet but very central location, this is a deservedly popular hostel, with a sociable vibe and a hip bar area with retro sofas. The dorms are fine, shared bathrooms are clean, but the private rooms are overpriced. Rates include a massive breakfast (choose from ten options). Dorms $, doubles $$

Casa Argentina 12 Diagonal 8–37, Zona 1 7761 2470, casargentina.xela@gmail.com; map page 140. Long-standing backpackers' hangout that has seen better days. Dozens of small rooms (most with TVs and a few with bathrooms), a "dorm city" (with more than twenty beds!) and guests' kitchen. Also home to Quetzaltrekkers (see above). Dorms $, doubles $$

Casa Mañen 9 Av 4–11, Zona 1 7765 0786; map page 140. Attractive B&B with a good selection of spacious rooms, which have plenty of local charm thanks to the use of highland textiles and furnishings. Rooms 8 and 9 have fireplaces, and the two suites offer sofas and fridges. There's also a rooftop terrace and the breakfast (included) is a veritable banquet. Rooms and suites available. $$$$

★ **Casa Renaissance** 9 C 11–26, Zona 1 3121 6315; map page 140. Welcoming Dutch-owned place in a fine old townhouse with five huge rooms, gorgeous original floor files, free tea, coffee and water, sunny patios, a guests' kitchen, fast wi-fi, good bathrooms and a TV lounge. There are discounted weekly rates. $$$

Hostal Miguel 12 Av 8–31, Zona 1 cervantesspanishschool.com; map page 140. Nine very simple rooms in a slightly ramshackle old house that are basic but inexpensive. There's a living room with TV and cooking facilities, and it is also home to a language school. $$

Hostal Siete Orejas 2 C 16–92, Zona 1 3070 6470; map page 140. Flashpacker place with very high-quality, spacious rooms, each with hand-carved beds, good mattresses and a wooden chest of drawers. Dorms $, doubles $$$

Hotel Modelo 14 Av A 2–31, Zona 1 7761 2529, hotel-modelo.com; map page 140. Classy, historic hotel with elegant dining and reception areas and plenty of character. The rooms are spacious though the decor is old-fashioned, all have tiny private bathrooms (note that streetside rooms can be noisy on weekend nights). The annexe is a slightly cheaper, similar alternative. Rates include breakfast. $$$$

Pensión Bonifaz 4 C 10–50, Zona 1 hotelpensionbonifaz.com; map page 140. Landmark hotel, founded in 1935, with a beautiful facade and prime location on the north side of the Parque Centro América. It retains an air of faded upper-class pomposity, and has a smart restaurant and small pool. However, rooms vary greatly; all are spacious, but some are a little dated. $$$$

EATING

As Quetzaltenango steadily becomes more international, the choice of **restaurants** and cuisines improves every year. The centre boasts more than a dozen good cafés, many of which offer free **wi-fi**.

Cardinali's 14 Av 3–41, Zona 1 7761 7400; map page 140. Long-running Italian restaurant of the gingham tablecloths and hanging Chianti flask school. Good for pizza or pasta with huge portions at (fairly) moderate prices. $$

El Cuartito 13 Av 7–09, Zona 1 facebook.com/elcuartitocafeyjardin; map page 140. Xela's hippest little café-bar has a Mediterranean-influenced menu with options for breakfast including Spanish toast with tomato, garlic and olive oil. Good smoothies and cocktails, too. The decor is quirky and clientele bohemian.

★ **La Esquina Asiatica** 9 Av 6–79, Zona 1 3385 9702; map page 140. Owned by a woman from Singapore, this enjoyable restaurant has authentic East Asian classics like pad thai, satay, Vietnamese spring rolls and noodle dishes. Prices are very reasonable and the surroundings (on the upper floor of a historic building) are atmospheric. $$

La Luna 8 Av 4–11, Zona 1 4253 1809; map page 140. Crammed with curios and antiques, *La Luna* is famous for its seven different varieties of authentic drinking chocolate, though note that they are (outrageously) pre-sweetened to local tastes. Snacks are also served. $

El Pasaje Mediterraneo Pasaje Enríquez, Zona 1 4839 7385; map page 140. A classy tapas restaurant with two attractive dining rooms and an appealing menu of dishes from Spain, Greece, Turkey and Italy; there's a decent wine list, too. Reckon on three or four tapas for two people. $$

Sabor de la India 15 Av 3–64, Zona 1 7761 2785;

map page 140. Indian-owned place serving filling and pretty authentic curries and lots of vegetarian options – including a decent *thali*. $$

Sagrado Corazón 1 14 Av 3–08, Zona 1 ☎7767 3684; map page 140. This small, informal place is a great spot to try Guatemalan specialities including *jocón* (meat cooked with a sauce of sesame and pumpkin seeds, peppers and *tomatillos*). $$

Sagrado Corazón 2 9 C 9–00, Zona 1 ☎5619 6626; map page 140. Large, popular comedor that scores highly for its honest Guatemalan grub, and in particular its dirt-cheap breakfasts. The set lunch is a winner too, and there's always a veggie version available. $

Dos Tejanos Pasaje Enríquez, Zona 1 ☎7765 4360; map page 140. The "two Texans" serves toothsome dishes like barbecued ribs, chicken-fried chicken and fajitas. $$

Ut'z Hua 12 Av & 3 C, Zona 1 ☎7768 3469; map page 140. Specializes in Guatemalan (including Maya) cuisine including local sausages, fried fish and seven kinds of highland soup. $$

Xela Green 14 Av & 5 C, Zona 1 ☎5370 1023; map page 140. A short walk from the Parque Centro América, this casual vegetarian café serves imaginative and surprisingly filling vegan appetisers. The mock-meat burger is particularly convincing. $$$

DRINKING AND NIGHTLIFE

Bars are clustered around Pasaje Enríquez and along 14 Av A; clubs are spread throughout the city. To find **what's on**, pick up a copy of *Xela Who?* (Ⓦfacebook.com/xelawhomag). Salsa Latina Academy (Diagonal 12 6–58; Ⓦsalsalatina.shop) is a professional **dance school**.

Anclas Xela 14 Av A 1–37, Zona 1 Ⓦteatromunicipalquetzaltenango.org; map page 140. This lively and sophisticated bar is located within the Municipal Theatre. It's well known for high-end cocktails.

Bajo La Luna 8 Av 3–72, Zona 1 ☎5440 5450; map page 140. In an atmospheric cellar, this wine bar is perfect for a relaxed drink (though they do have occasional parties). You can nibble on a cheese platter or munch a burger and fries while you imbibe.

Billares Victoria 3 C 12–57, Zona 1 Ⓦfacebook.com/BillaresVictoria; map page 140. Pool tables and table football are available in this spacious bar with friendly staff. On weekends the place gets rammed with young quetzaltecos.

El Cuartito 13 Av 7–09, Zona 1 Ⓦfacebook.com/elcuartitocafeyjardin; map page 140. Popular with Xela's artistic community, this small, happening bar with shabby-chic decor (including lighting made from old beer bottles) has live music and DJs some nights. Doubles as a café in the day.

★ **Salón Tecún** Pasaje Enríquez, Zona 1 ☎5960 6210; map page 140. Xela's most dependable and popular bar, this atmospheric pub-like drinking institution has long been a favourite with both locals and travellers, and for good reason. There's a sociable interior and bench seating outside in the arcade. They also serve good bar food, making it the ideal place to grab a bite to eat.

ENTERTAINMENT

Quetzaltenango is a good place to catch a movie or a play and there's a pretty good **cultural programme** of events. You'll find a multi-screen cinema by La Pradera mall, near the Minerva bus terminal. Check *Xela Who?* (Ⓦfacebook.com/xelawhomag) for the latest schedules.

Blue Angel 7 C 15–79, Zona 1. Offers a daily video programme with a large selection of movies (mainly Hollywood blockbusters and cult films). You can also select a film at most times of day and watch it in a private room. Doubles as a café, with a good Sunday brunch.

Casa N'oj 7 C 12–12, Zona 1 ☎7761 4400. Art exhibitions, film screenings, lectures and cultural events housed in a wonderful restored building just off the Parque Centro América.

Teatro Municipal 14 Av A & 1 C, Zona 1 Ⓦteatromunicipalquetzaltenango.org. A Neoclassical theatre that hosts contemporary and traditional dance, plays, concerts and exhibitions.

SHOPPING

Despensa Familiar 3 Av & 7 C, Zona 1 Ⓦmaxidespensa.com.gt; map page 140. Supermarket in the centre of town.

Leyendas (Libros&Café-Xela) 14 Av 2–42, Zona 1 ☎7761 0832; map page 140. This charming bookshop is known for its excellent range of cultural and political books and guidebooks, and has a café (for espresso coffee and a bagel).

La Pradera Just behind the Minerva market, Zona 3 Ⓦcentroscomercialespradera.com; map page 138. The shopping mall La Pradera boasts more than a hundred stores.

DIRECTORY

Banks There are several banks on the Plaza Centro América, including Banrural which has an ATM.

Bike rental AeroBike 2 Diagonal 29-3 (☎7767 7298) rents mountain bikes (by the day and the week) – and offers bike tours (see page 143).

Car rental Tabarini, 9 C 9–21 (2444 4200, tabarini.com), has cars with competitive daily rates.

Internet and phones Xelapages, 4 C 19–48, is very professional and has quick connections, and cheap rates for phones. Wi-fi is very common in Quetzaltenango's cafés.

Laundry Lavandería Emanuel, 7 C 13–29. Good value for a full wash and dry.

Medical care Hospital San Rafael, 9 C 10–41 (4149 1104).

Police If you're in trouble or have been the victim of crime, first contact the PROATUR rep (4149 1104) for the Xela area.

Post office 15 Av and 4 C.

Around Quetzaltenango

The area **around Quetzaltenango** offers some of the country's most evocative highland scenery, with volcanic cones soaring above forested ridges, and a number of fascinating Indigenous villages to explore. Straddling the coast road south of the city are **Almolonga** and **Zunil**, where you'll find superb hot springs, including **Fuentes Georginas**, a stunning natural spa. Just west of here the **Santa María volcano**, towering above Quetzaltenango, is a terrific, if exhausting, excursion. The most accessible climb in the area lies southwest of the city, up **Volcán Chicabal** to an exquisite crater lake set in the extinct volcano's cone.

North of the city, the traditional Maya town of **Olintepeque** is renowned for its shrine devoted to the pagan saint of San Pascual. A little further distant are **Totonicapán**, a departmental capital, and the famous market town of **San Francisco el Alto**, perched on a rocky outcrop. Beyond here, in the midst of a pine forest, lies **Momostenango**, the country's principal wool-producing centre.

Almolonga

The most direct route from Quetzaltenango to the coast takes you through a narrow gash in the mountains to the village of **ALMOLONGA**, just 5km from Quetzaltenango. Almolonga is K'iche' for "the place where water springs", and streams gush from the hillside, channelled to the waiting crops. This is the region's market garden: the flat land, far too valuable for houses, is parcelled up into neat, irrigated fields.

In markets throughout the western highlands, the women of Almolonga corner the vegetable trade; it's easy to recognize them, dressed in their bold, orange zigzag *huipiles* and wearing beautifully woven headbands. The village itself has **markets** on Wednesday and Saturday mornings – the latter being the larger – when the town is crammed with people, while piles of scrubbed radishes and gleaming carrots are swiftly traded.

The village **church** is an arresting banana-yellow-and-white affair that backs onto the plaza. Inside there's a wonderfully gaudy gilded **altar** with a silver statue of a crusading San Pedro, complete with bible, set behind protective bars. Pay the caretaker a quetzal and the whole altar lights up in a riot of technicolour fluorescent tubes, including a halo for the saint.

Los Baños

A couple of kilometres south of Almolonga • charge

At **Los Baños** about ten different operations offer a soak in hot-spring water; Fuentes Saludable and El Recreo are good options. For two or three bucks you get a private room, a sunken concrete tub, and enough hot water to drown an elephant. In a country of lukewarm showers, it's paradise.

ARRIVAL AND DEPARTURE ALMOLONGA

By bus Buses from Quetzaltenango leave the Minerva terminal every 15min, via a stop at 9 Av and 10 C in Zona 1, to Almolonga and Los Baños on their way to Zunil.

Copavic glass factory

1km south of Cantel village • Buses every 20min from Quetazltenango's Minerva terminal

Around 6km southeast of Xela, the **Copavic glass factory** is one of Guatemala's most successful cooperatives. Copavic uses one hundred percent recycled glass and exports the finished product all over the world. Visitors are welcome to see the glass-blowers in action, or visit the factory shop, which sells a fine selection of glasses, vases, jugs and other assorted goods.

Zunil

Some 5km down the valley from Almolonga is **ZUNIL**, another centre for vegetable growing. The plaza is dominated by a beautiful white **colonial church** with twin belfries and a magnificent Baroque facade – complete with a quetzal and vines. Inside an intricate silver altar is protected behind bars. The women of Zunil wear vivid purple *huipiles* and carry incredibly bright shawls; during the Monday **market** the streets are awash with colour. Just below the plaza is a **textile cooperative**, where hundreds of women market their beautiful weavings.

Zunil is also renowned for its adherence to the cult of **San Simón** (or Maximón), the evil saint. You can meet the man himself in his pagan temple (see page 126); children will take you to his abode for a small tip.

ARRIVAL AND DEPARTURE ZUNIL

By bus Buses to Copavic and Zunil (30min) run from Quetzaltenango's Minerva bus terminal every 20min or so; you can also catch a bus from the centre of town beside the Shell petrol station at 10 C and 9 Av in Zona 1. Buses bound for Retalhuleu also pass by Zunil.

VISITING SAN SIMÓN IN ZUNIL

Zunil's reputation for the worship of **San Simón** is well founded. Every year on November 1, at the end of the annual fiesta, San Simón – also known elsewhere as Maximón (see page 126) – is moved to a new house. His effigy sits in a darkened room, dressed in Western clothes, and guarded by several attendants, including one whose job it is to remove the ash from his lighted cigarettes – this is later sold off and used to cure insomnia, while the butts are thought to provide protection from thieves. San Simón is visited by a steady stream of villagers, who come to ask his assistance, using candles to indicate their **requests**: white for the health of a child, yellow for a good harvest, red for love and black to wish ill on an enemy. The petitioners touch and embrace the saint, and just to make sure that he has heard their pleas they also offer cigarettes, money and *aguardiente* liquor. Meanwhile, outside the house, a bonfire burns continuously and more offerings are given over the flames, including whole eggs – if they crack it signifies that San Simón will grant a wish.

If you visit San Simón, you will be expected to **contribute** to his upkeep (US$1 or so), and pay to take photographs. While the entire process may seem chaotic and entertaining, it is in fact deeply serious – proceed with respect.

ACCOMMODATION

Las Cumbres 1km south of Zunil ⓦlascumbres.com.gt; map page 145. This spa hotel has attractive rooms, all with chunky wooden beds and fireplaces, and most with huge bathtubs fed by hot-spring water and private saunas (rooms 6–9 enjoy the best views). There's a gym, squash court and restaurant and the spa is open to visitors. Unfortunately it's beside a busy highway. $$$$

Fuentes Georginas

8km south of Zunil • Charge • ⓣ5704 2959

In the hills above Zunil, reached via a steep road which switchbacks through magnificent volcanic scenery, **Fuentes Georginas** is a spectacular natural spring spa situated on the evergreen slopes of Volcán Pico Zunil. The pools here are surrounded by fresh green ferns, thick moss and lush forest, and to top it all there's a **restaurant** with a well-stocked bar. It's a blissful place to spend a few hours soaking away the chicken bus blues or recovering from a volcano climb in the heavenly steaming pools. Unfortunately the eco-vibe is spoiled by cheesy piped music. Fuentes Georginas has barbecue and picnic areas.

ARRIVAL AND DEPARTURE — FUENTES GEORGINAS

By bus There's a dedicated shuttle bus service from Xela: buses (daily 9am & 2pm; 30min) leave from the Fuentes office, 14 Av and 5 C. Otherwise, minibuses head up from Zunil on demand.

ACCOMMODATION

Fuentes Georginas ⓣ5704 2959. Just below the pools, these stone bungalows are a little dank and musty but have a certain rustic charm, each with bathtub, two double beds and fireplaces (wood is provided). $$$

Volcán Santa María

Around 15km due south of Quetzaltenango, the perfect cone of **Volcán Santa María** rises to a height of 3772m, with the volcano towering over most of the Xela valley. It's possible to climb Santa María as a day-trip, but to really see it at its best you need to be on top at dawn, either sleeping on the freezing summit or camping at a site part of the way up and climbing the final section in the dark by torchlight. Full moon trips are also an option. The volcano's highest point is marked by an altar where the Maya burn *copal* and sacrifice animals, and on a clear day the **view** will take your breath away – as will the cold if you get here in time to watch the sun rise. In the early mornings the Quetzaltenango valley is blanketed in a layer of cloud, and while it's still dark the lights of the city create a patch of orange glow; as the sun rises, its first rays eat into the cloud, revealing the land beneath.

Below, to the south, is the angry, lava-scarred cone of **Santiaguito**, which has been in constant eruption since 1902. Every now and then it spouts a great grey cloud of rock and dust hundreds of metres into the air. To the **west**, across a chaos of twisting hills, are the cones of Tajumulco and Tacaná, marking the Mexican border. But most impressive is the view to the **east**. Wrapped in the early morning haze, four more volcanic cones can be seen, two above Lago de Atitlán and two more above Antigua – one of which, highly active Fuego, often emits a puff of smoke.

It's highly advisable to climb Santa María with one of the Quetzaltenango **tour operators** (see page 142) who will organize transport, food and water for the trip. You should also be acclimatized to the altitude before attempting the hike.

San Martín Sacatepéquez

Southwest from Xela, the road to the coast winds down 21km to the farming centre of **SAN MARTÍN SACATEPÉQUEZ**, also known as San Martín Chile Verde. This isolated Mam-speaking village is set in the base of a natural bowl and hemmed in by steep, wooded hills. The men here wear a particularly unusual costume made up of a long white tunic with thin red stripes, ornately embroidered around the cuffs and tied around the middle with a red sash; the women wear beautiful red *huipiles* and blue *cortes*.

ARRIVAL AND DEPARTURE — SAN MARTÍN SACATEPÉQUEZ

By bus Buses and minibuses between the Minerva terminal in Quetzaltenango and Coatepeque pass through San Martín (every 30min; 40min). Make sure you board a bus for the right San Martín as there are several in the Xela area.

Laguna Chicabal

A two-hour hike from San Martín brings you to **Laguna Chicabal**, a spectacular lake set in the cone of the Chicabal volcano that is the site of Maya religious rituals. To reach the start of the hike, get the bus to drop you off at the stop for "la laguna" and head uphill through the outskirts of the village. Follow the steep track for forty minutes until it levels out near the entrance to the Chicabal reserve (entry fee) where there's a football field and some rustic **cabins** ($ per person).

A good signposted trail then ascends again through forest to the rim of the cone, before descending to the **lake**. At the water's edge, you enter a different world, eerily still, disturbed only by the soft buzz of a hummingbird's wings or the screech of parakeets. Quetzals and horned guan are also (rarely) seen in the surrounding cloud forest.

Small **sandy bays** bear charred crosses and bunches of fresh-cut flowers mark the site of ritual sacrifice. On May 3 every year *costumbristas* gather here for ceremonies to mark the fiesta of the Holy Cross; at any time, but around this date especially, you should take care not to disturb any **rituals** that might be taking place. You are welcome to camp at the shore, though you'll have to bring all your own supplies. Swimming is prohibited.

On your return route you can climb some vertiginous steps to a *mirador* from where there are breathtaking, panoramic views of the emerald lagoon, and, if the cloud gods permit, you'll be treated to stunning views of the nearby volcanoes including Santa María and Santiaguito, Tajamulco and Tacaná.

Olintepeque

Just 6km north of Quetzaltenango, perched on the edge of the Xela plain, is the small textile-weaving town of **OLINTEPEQUE**. According to some accounts this was the site of the huge and decisive battle between the Spanish and K'iche' warriors, but these days it's better known as a peaceful little place with an intriguing **pagan shrine** and a great Tuesday **animal market**. The latter gets going soon after daylight, winding down by noon, by which time hundreds of pigs on leads, chickens, goats and cattle have been prodded and poked over, bought and sold.

Capilla de Rey San Pascual

The pagan temple **Capilla de Rey San Pascual**, in the centre of town behind the huge Catholic church, is dedicated to an idol believed by devotees to have supernatural powers. San Pascual is certainly a curious sight: a 0.3m-high effigy with an exposed skull bedecked in gaudy robes, surrounded by hundreds of candles and offerings of flowers. Numerous plaques give thanks for his ability to heal the sick (and bring misfortune to enemies). A flight of steps leads up to an exposed platform known as the *quemadero* ("bonfire") where the faithful whisper incantations through clouds of pungent *copal* (incense) smoke.

ARRIVAL AND DEPARTURE — OLINTEPEQUE

All **buses** for Olintepeque leave from the Minerva terminal in Quetzaltenango (every 30min; 20min).

Salcajá

Between the Cuatro Caminos junction and Quetzaltenango, the unappealing ladino town of **SALCAJÁ** is one of Guatemala's main commercial **weaving** centres.

Salcajá's other claim to fame is that (according to most sources) its modest-looking **Ermita de San Jacinto**, with a simple facade embellished with plasterwork pineapples and bananas, was the first church built in Guatemala. If you drop by the small **museum** (5 Av & 2 C; free; ☎7768 8750) behind the church they'll unlock the great doors of the church – inside there's an ornate original altarpiece.

While you're in town it would be silly not to sample the *caldo de fruitas* (fruit-based) or *rompopo* (egg and *aguardiente*) **liquors**, which are both made in Salcajá. Many places can sell you a shot or a bottle, including the museum.

ARRIVAL AND DEPARTURE — SALCAJÁ

Regular **buses** from the Minerva terminal run to Salcajá (every 20min; 20min).

San Andrés Xecul

A few kilometres northwest of Salcajá, the village of **SAN ANDRÉS XECUL** boasts an astonishing canary-yellow Catholic **church**, with a facade that's a riot of vines dripping with plump, purple fruit and podgy little angels scrambling across the surface. The twin jaguars at the top are said to represent the hero twins of the Maya holy book, the Popol Vuh (see page 103). Inside are some fabulously chintzy chandeliers made of glass stones, coins and rosary beads.

The village's other religious activities are less orthodox. It's a centre for Maya worship, and in the 1970s the artist Carmen Petterson claimed that a "university" for shamen was operating in the village; there's also an actively used shrine to **Maximón**, Guatemala's pagan saint (see page 126) – locals will direct you there.

ARRIVAL AND DEPARTURE — SAN ANDRÉS XECUL

By bus Buses (every 40min; 25min) leave the Minerva terminal in Quetzaltenango for San Andrés; the last service is scheduled to return at around 6pm.

San Cristóbal Totonicapán

One kilometre west of the Cuatro Caminos junction, the ladino town of **SAN CRISTÓBAL TOTONICAPÁN** is generally a quiet place that holds a position of importance as a source of **fiesta costumes**. (It's not to be confused with neighbouring Totonicapán, 12km away, which is in a separate region.) San Cristóbal's colossal Baroque **colonial church** is its main landmark, with a magnificent wood-beamed roof and some fantastic frescoes. Look out too for the extravagant side-altars with images of saints made from ornate silverwork. **Easter week** is an impressive time to visit, when there are huge processions to the church, or you could drop by for the Sunday market.

ARRIVAL AND DEPARTURE — SAN CRISTÓBAL TOTONICAPÁN

A good number of **buses** from the Minerva terminal run to San Cristóbal (every 30min; 30min).

San Francisco el Alto

From a magnificent hillside setting, the small town of **SAN FRANCISCO EL ALTO** hosts the largest weekly **market** in the country. Each Friday traders from every corner of Guatemala make the trip, many arriving the night before, and some starting to sell by candlelight from as early as 4am. Throughout the morning a steady stream of buses and trucks fills the town to bursting; by noon the market is at its height, buzzing with activity.

The upper section of the market is an open field used as an **animal market**, where everything from pigs to parrots changes hands. Prospective buyers inspect the animals' teeth and tongues, and at times the scene degenerates into a chaotic wrestling match, with pigs and men rolling in the dirt. Below is the town's plaza, dominated by **textiles** and clothing, mainly *ropa americana*. Here the streets are filled with vegetables, fruit, pottery and cheap comedores.

For a really good perspective of the market action and surrounding countryside, pay the caretaker a quetzal and climb up to the **church roof**, from where you can take some fantastic photos from a great vantage point.

ARRIVAL AND DEPARTURE — SAN FRANCISCO EL ALTO

By bus Buses run to San Francisco from the Minerva terminal in Quetzaltenango (every 20min; 45min). Many also stop at the rotunda on the east side of town.

Momostenango

Less than an hour from San Francisco, **MOMOSTENANGO** is a small, isolated highland town renowned for its **wool** production. Momostecos travel throughout

THE TZOLKIN YEAR

Momostenango's religious **calendar** is still based on the 260-day *Tzolkin* year – made up of thirteen twenty-day months – which has been in use since ancient times. The most celebrated ceremony is *Guaxaquib Batz*, "Eight Monkey", which marks the beginning of a new year. Originally, this was a purely **pagan ceremony**, starting at dawn on the first day of the year, but the Church has muscled in on the action and it now begins with a Catholic service the night before. The next morning the people make for Chuitmesabal (Little Broom), a small hill about 2km west of town. Here offerings of broken pottery are made before age-old altars. (Momostenango means "the place of the altars".) The entire process is overseen by shamen responsible for communicating with the gods. At dusk the ceremony moves to Nim Mesabal (Big Broom), another hilltop, where the *costumbristas* pray and burn incense throughout the night.

THE FISCAL KING

The Toto valley has always held out against outside influence, isolated in a world of its own, and in 1820 was the scene of one of the most famous **Maya rebellions**, sparked by demands for tax. The Indigenous people expelled all of the town's ladinos and crowned their leader, Atanasio Tzul, the "king and fiscal king". His reign lasted only 29 days, ending when state troops from the capital violently quashed the rebellion – a stone memorial commemorates the event in the town's southern plaza.

the country peddling their blankets, scarves and rugs, and years of experience have made them experts in the hard sell. The wool is also used in a range of traditional costumes, including the short skirts worn by the men of Nahualá and San Antonio Palopó as well as the jackets of Sololá. The ideal place to buy Momostenango blankets is in the **Sunday market**, which fills the town's two plazas, or the smaller Wednesday occasion.

A visit at this time will also give you a glimpse of Momostenango's other feature: its rigid adherence to **Maya tradition**. Opposite the entrance to the church, you may see people making offerings of incense and alcohol on a small fire, muttering their appeals to the gods. While here, you can also take a walk to **los riscos**, a set of bizarre sandstone pillars on the northern edge of town.

ARRIVAL AND DEPARTURE — MOMOSTENANGO

By bus Buses run to Momostenango from the Minerva terminal in Quetzaltenango, passing through Cuatro Caminos and San Francisco el Alto on the way (every 30min from 7am; 1hr 15min). The last bus returns around 5pm.

ACCOMMODATION AND EATING

You'll find **comedores** on the main plaza, but otherwise there are very few options.

Hotel Otoño 3Av A 1–48 ⓣ7736 5013. This hotel is a perfectly adequate option, with modern rooms, priced per person. All have generous en-suite bathrooms and some have balconies. $$

Totonicapán

TOTONICAPÁN, capital of one of the smaller departments, is a pleasant if unremarkable provincial town reached down a direct road leading east from Cuatro Caminos. As you enter Toto you pass one of the country's finest *pilas* (communal washing places), ringed with Gothic columns. Surrounded by rolling hills and pine forests, the town stands at the heart of a heavily populated and intensely farmed region.

Toto's Tuesday and Saturday **morning markets** fill its two plazas to bursting. The town is an important centre of **commercial weaving**, producing much of the *jasped* cloth worn as skirts by Indigenous women throughout the country.

Casa de la Cultura

8 Av 2–17 • ⓣ7766 1575

To take a closer look at the work of local artisans, head for the visitor centre, the **Casa de la Cultura**. It organizes guided walks around the fringes of town (charge, for two to six people) that take in sacred Maya sites, mask- and fiesta costume-making workshops and weavers' houses. Lunch is included and funds raised help benefit the community.

El Abrisco

7km north of Toto • Charge includes guide

The forest reserve of **El Abrisco** is 7km north of town on the road to Santa Cruz del Quiché. Trails lead around the protected area and your guide will explain (in Spanish only) the trees and their significance to the local Maya culture. Large owls, which the locals call *buho*, are common here, and you'll find rustic, basic cabañas ($), a campsite and a kids' play area.

ARRIVAL AND DEPARTURE — TOTONICAPÁN

By bus Buses and minibuses for Totonicapán leave from Quetzaltenango's Minerva terminal (every 30min; 1hr) passing through Cuatros Caminos; the last minibus returns from Toto at 7.30pm.

ACCOMMODATION AND EATING

In addition to the options reviewed here, for inexpensive **eats** you could try one of the comedores scattered around the town's two plazas.

Dino's Upstairs at 6 C 7–45, Zona 4 ☎ 7766 2671. Large, modern restaurant serving grilled meats, pizza, pasta, steak, sandwiches, seafood and salads. $$

Hotel Milan 5 C & 4 Av ☎ 5909 6696. The best hotel in town, with modern, comfortable rooms and a restaurant. $$$

The department of San Marcos

Leaving Quetzaltenango you can head west to the little-visited department of **San Marcos** – home of the country's highest volcano, **Tajumulco**, and some magnificent highland scenery. The route passes through Ostuncalco and then the **twin towns** of San Marcos and San Pedro Sacatepéquez (these form the main population centre in these parts but hold little interest for visitors).

Northwest of here there's some magnificent high country, and a paved road that fringes the **Tajumulco** and **Tacaná volcanoes**. Continuing along this remote route you pass through the isolated villages of Tectitán and Cuilco, and can eventually loop up to the Carretera Interamericana.

Volcán Tajumulco

North of San Pedro, the road climbs steeply through thick pine forests and emerges onto a high, grassy plateau. Here it crosses a great boggy expanse to skirt around the edge of **Volcán Tajumulco**, whose 4220m peak is the highest in Central America. It's best climbed from the roadside hamlet of **Tuichán** (the exact drop-off point is called Llana de la Guardia) from where it's about five hours to the summit. It's not a particularly hard climb as long as you're **acclimatized** – the risk of altitude sickness is a serious concern at this height. As there have been land disputes around the volcano it's best to hike with a guide who knows the terrain: Quetzaltrekkers (see page 143) and other tour operators in Quetzaltenango organize trips up Tajumulco.

North to the Carretera Interamericana: Tacaná

Up here the land is sparsely inhabited, with barren rocky ridges soaring over adobe houses and flocks of sheep and goats. After Tuichán you approach the village of **Ixchiguán**, set on an exposed hillside at 3050m, surrounded by bleak rounded hills and in the shadow of the two towering volcanic cones. The road climbs to the **Cumbre de Cotzil**, a spectacular 3400m pass, before descending to the scruffy town of **TACANÁ** – less than 10km from the Mexican border. Looming above the village is the active cone of **Volcán Tacaná** (4064m). The volcano is regularly climbed (the last small eruption was in 1986), but do check on its status if you plan a trek.

ARRIVAL AND DEPARTURE — TACANÁ

By bus First catch a bus from Quetzaltenango to San Pedro (every 20min; 1hr 30min). Buses from San Pedro run via Tuichán (1hr 15min) for Tacaná (3hr) hourly until 3pm. Heading on from Tacaná, minibuses leave roughly hourly for Cuilco (2hr) from where there are regular buses to Huehuetenango.

Huehuetenango and around

At the foot of the mighty Cuchumatanes, **HUEHUETENANGO** is a departmental capital and the focus of trade and transport for a vast area of northwestern Guatemala. Its atmosphere is provincial and pretty relaxed, though heavy traffic, much of which thunders through the town centre, reduces this appeal somewhat.

Before the arrival of the Spanish it was the site of one of the residential suburbs that surrounded the Mam capital of **Zaculeu** (the ruins of this site, just a few kilometres from town, are worth a visit). Under colonial rule it was a small regional centre with little to offer beyond a steady trickle of silver and a stretch or two of grazing land. Today the department is famous for its rich, complex, high-quality **coffee** – which you'll have ample opportunity to sample in the town's cafés.

Parque Central

Huehuetenango is a likeable if unremarkable place, its character best expressed in the unhurried atmosphere of the attractive **Parque Central**, where shaded walkways are surrounded by grand administrative offices. Overlooking this square are a shell-shaped bandstand, clock tower and a grand Neoclassical **cathedral**, a solid whitewashed structure with a facade crammed with Doric pillars and Grecian urns. In the middle of the plaza, there's a **relief map** of the department that gives you an idea of the mass of rock that dominates the region, and its deep river valleys, even if the scale is warped.

ARRIVAL AND DEPARTURE — HUEHUETENANGO

Most **buses** use the chaotic bus terminal, halfway between the Carretera Interamericana and town. Here each bus company has its own office, at which you should ask for the latest schedule (the timetables painted on the walls are often out of date). Note that it is standard practice, even for second-class buses, to buy your ticket in advance.

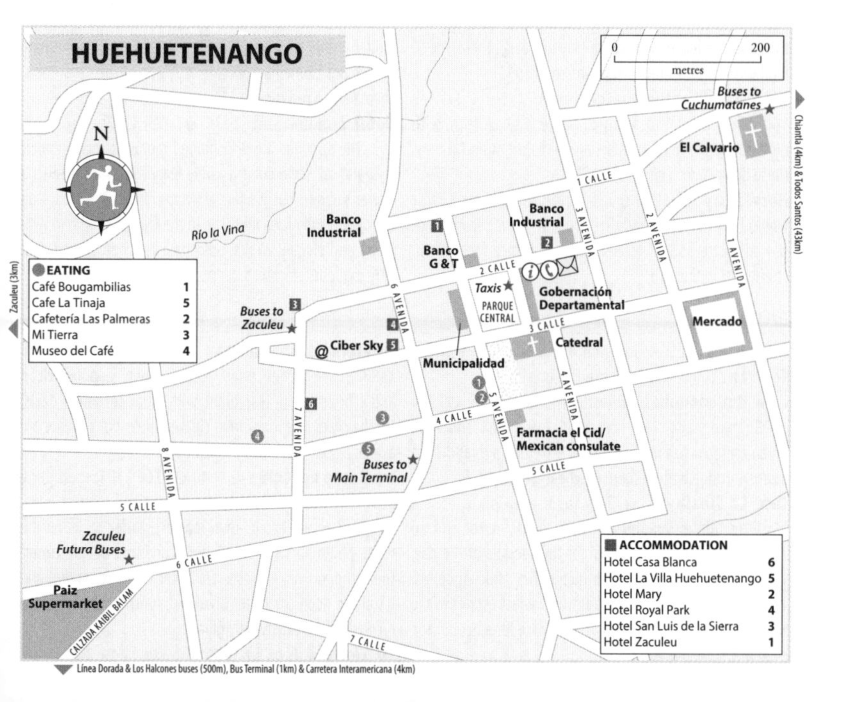

Microbuses connect the town centre with the terminal, leaving from 6 Av, between 4 and 5 calles. There's also a microbus stand by El Calvario church, 1 Av and 1 C for services to Cobán, Todos Santos and all towns along the road to Barillas. Buses to Zaculeu leave from the corner of 2 C and 7 Av. If you want to go to Antigua, take a capital-bound bus and change at Chimaltenango; for Lago de Atitlán or Chichicastenango change at Los Encuentros.

FIRST-CLASS BUS COMPANIES

Los Halcones 10 Av 9–12 loshalcones.com.gt. Five daily to Guatemala City, two daily to La Mesilla.

Transportes Velásquez Main terminal 7764 7594. Five daily to Guatemala City.

SECOND-CLASS BUSES AND MICROBUSES

Destinations Aguacatán (every 30min; 40min); Barillas (hourly; 6hr 30min); Cobán (daily 1.30pm; 5hr 30min) Cuilco (hourly; 2hr); Gracias a Dios (3 daily; 4hr 30min); Guatemala City (every 30min; 5hr 30min); La Mesilla, Mexican border (every 30min; 2hr); Nebaj – travel via Aguacatán and Sacapulas; Nentón (8 daily; 3hr 15min); Quetzaltenango (every 30min; 2hr); Sacapulas (2 daily, 11.30am & 12.30pm; 2hr); San Juan Atitán (6 daily; 1hr 15min); San Mateo Ixtatán (hourly; 5hr); San Miguel Acatán (4 daily; 4hr 30min); San Rafael La Independencia (4 daily; 4hr 15min); Soloma (every 45min; 3hr); Todos Santos (hourly; 2hr 15min); Yalambojoch (2 daily; 5hr).

INFORMATION, TOURS AND ACTIVITIES

Information There's no Inguat office in Huehue.

Adrenalina Tours This operator is based in Quetzaltenango (see page 142) but offers the best tours of the Huehue region, including a great two-day trip to El Cimarrón , Finca Chaculá and Laguna Brava.

Language schools Huehuetenango is a good place to learn Spanish as you don't rub shoulders with many other gringos. Academia de Español Xinabajul, 4 Av 14–14, Zona 5 (7764 6631, guatemala365.com) receives positive reports from students.

ACCOMMODATION

Huehuetenango has a pretty good range of **hotels**, all a short walk from the Parque Central, but no luxury options.

Hotel Casa Blanca 7 Av 3–41 7769 0775; map page 153. Classy hotel, centred on a colonial-style house and its twin patios, though there is some modern accommodation. The spacious rooms have very attractive furnishings, but those on the lower floor can be a little dark. There's good food served in the gorgeous dining room. $$$

Hotel La Villa Huehuetenango 3 C 6–34 7769 1600; map page 153. This mid-range hotel is clean, with modern rooms. Those upstairs are fairly bright and cheery, those downstairs a bit gloomy. $$

Hotel Mary 2 C 3–52 7764 1618; map page 153. It would benefit from a little TLC, but this basic secure place has adequate budget rooms that will suffice for a night. There's a comedor too. $$

Hotel Royal Park 6 Av 2–34 7762 7775; map page 153. Flashy place with a gaudy colour scheme, but the tiled rooms, most with two double beds, are all spacious and well equipped. Rates include breakfast and there's parking. $$$

Hotel San Luis de la Sierra 2 C 7–00 7764 9217, hsanluis@gmail.com; map page 153. A well-run, modern hotel with attractive if small rooms, all with pine furnishings; some have wonderful views of the mountains. There's also a restaurant. $$$

Hotel Zaculeu 5 Av 1–14 3073 1377; map page 153. The spacious if old-fashioned rooms at this colonial-style inn are set around a lovely leafy courtyard (there's a newer section, but it's far less appealing). Don't pass up the opportunity for a nightcap in the fantastic old bar, with piano and elegant chairs. Solo travellers get a good deal here as rooms are priced per person. $$

EATING

Many budget places are grouped around the **Parque Central**; a couple of them are good for a beer too.

Café Bougambilias Opposite the cathedral 7764 0105; map page 153. This four-storey pink and lurid green comedor has fine breakfasts – try the highland-style *mosh*: porridge with cinnamon, wheat and sugar. $

Café La Tinaja 4 C 7764 1513; map page 153. A hip little café/restaurant/store with quirky decor and an arty vibe. Check out the board for the specials of the day, which might include Mexican quesadillas and baguettes. They serve coffee (and sell beans from) select estates in the Huehue department. It's also a good place for a beer in the evenings. $$

Cafetería Las Palmeras Opposite the cathedral 5783 2967; map page 153. A highly popular, clean and efficiently run restaurant with great set-lunch deals; try the *chiles rellenos* or fried chicken. Delicious *tamales* are available (Sat only) for a bargain. $$

★ **Museo del Café** 4 C 7–40 7764 1101; map page 153. A veritable temple to the arabica and robusta bean, this garden café has its own roastery, coffee sacks on the walls, photographs of coffee fincas and tons of café curios. Great cappuccino, espresso and filter coffee is served, and it's also a good choice for breakfast, lunch or dinner – the *menu del día* is satisfyingly filling. $$

Mi Tierra 4 C 6–46 4618 5538; map page 153.

Intimate little restaurant, set in a covered patio that's popular with office workers at lunchtime. Guatemalan dishes like *bistek* and Mexican classics too feature strongly. $$

DIRECTORY

Banks Banco G&T Continental, on the Parque Central, and Banco Industrial on 6 Av both have ATMs.
Internet Ciber Sky, 3 C & 7 Av.
Mexican consulate Inside the Farmacia el Cid on the south side of the Parque Central (T 7764 1366).
Post office 2 C 3–54 (Mon–Fri 8am–5pm).
Supermarket Palz, 6 C & 10 Av, is a well-stocked supermarket southwest of the town centre.

Zaculeu

Charge • Buses to the "ruinas" every 30min from 7 Av, between 2 and 3 calles in Huehuetenango

A few kilometres to the west of Huehuetenango are the ruins of **ZACULEU**, capital of the **Mam**, who were one of the principal pre-conquest highland tribes. The site includes several large temples, plazas and a ball court, but unfortunately it was restored pretty unsubtly by a latter-day colonial power, the United Fruit Company, in 1946 and 1947. The walls and surfaces were levelled off with a layer of thick white plaster, leaving them stark and undecorated. There are no roof-combs, carvings or stucco mouldings, and only in a few places does the original stonework show through. Even so, the site has a peculiar atmosphere of its own and is worth a look; surrounded by trees and neatly mown grass, with fantastic views of the mountains, it's also an excellent spot for a picnic.

There's a small **museum** on site with examples of some of the burial techniques used – bodies were crammed into great urns, interred in vaults and also cremated – and some interesting ceramics.

Brief history

The site of Zaculeu, first occupied in the fifth century, is thought to have been a religious and administrative centre for the **Mam**, and the home to its elite; the bulk of the population most likely lived in small surrounding settlements. After a period of subjugation under the rival K'iche' tribe in the fifteenth century, the Mam reasserted their independence, only for another expansionist empire, the **Spanish** – a yet more brutal alternative – to arrive. Following a massacre by the Spanish of five thousand Mam warriors to the south, Mam chief Kaibal Balam withdrew to the safety of Zaculeu, which was protected by ravines and walls. The Spanish army prepared for a lengthy siege, giving the Maya a choice: become Christians "peacefully" or face "death and destruction".

Attracted by neither option, the Mam struggled to hold out against the invading force, but after about six weeks under siege, his army starving to death, Kaibal Balam surrendered. With the bitterest of ironies a bastardized version of his name has been adopted by one of Guatemala's crack army regiments – the "Kaibiles", who were responsible for numerous massacres during the 1970s and early 1980s.

Chiantla

The village of **CHIANTLA** is backed right up against the mountains, 5km north of Huehuetenango. The main point of interest is the colonial **church**. Built by Dominican friars, it is now the object of one of the country's largest pilgrimages, held annually on February 2 in honour of its image of the **Virgen del Rosario**. She is thought to be capable of healing the sick, and at any time of the year you'll see people who've travelled from all over Guatemala asking for her assistance. A mural inside the church depicts a rather ill-proportioned Spaniard watching over the Maya toiling in his mines, while on the wall opposite the Maya are shown discovering God. The precise connection between the two is left somewhat vague, but presumably the gap is bridged by the Virgin.

ARRIVAL AND DEPARTURE **CHIANTLA**

By bus Buses from Huehuetenango to Chiantla run frequently from the main terminal (every 15min until 8pm; 15min). There are a couple of options for boarding: you can catch one as it passes the Parque Central in the town centre, or wait for a bus at the Calvario (by the junction of 1 Av and 1 C).

Aguacatán

Some 25km east of Huehuetenango, **AGUACATÁN** is a small agricultural town strung out along a very long main street, and the only place in the country where the Akateko and Chalchitek languages are spoken. It's best visited for the huge **Sunday market**, which actually gets under way on Saturday afternoon, when traders arrive early to claim the best sites. On Sunday mornings people pour into town, cramming into the market and plaza, and soon spilling out into the surrounding area. Around noon the tide turns as the crowds start to drift back to their villages, with donkeys leading their drunken drivers home.

The **traditional costume** worn by the women of Aguacatán is unusually simple: their skirts are made of dark blue cotton and the *huipiles*, which hang loose, are decorated with bands of coloured ribbon on a plain white background. This plainness, though, is set off by the local speciality – the *cinta*, or headdress, an intricately embroidered piece of cloth combining blues, reds, yellows and greens, in which the women wrap their hair.

ARRIVAL AND DEPARTURE **AGUACATÁN**

By bus or minibus Minibuses and buses run from Huehuetenango to Aguacatán every 30min until about 7pm (45min). Beyond Aguacatán a paved road runs east out along a ridge, eventually dropping down to the riverside town of Sacapulas 1hr 30min away; minibuses cover this route every 30min until about 5pm. For Nebaj take a Sacapulas bus and catch a connection there.

The Cuchumatanes

The **Cuchumatanes**, rising to a frosty 3837m just to the north of Huehuetenango, are the largest non-volcanic peaks in Central America, stretching from the Mexican border to the highlands of Alta Verapaz.

The mountain **scenery** is magnificent, ranging from wild, exposed craggy outcrops to lush, tranquil river valleys. The upper parts of the slopes are barren, scattered with boulders and shrivelled cypress trees, while the lower levels are richly fertile, cultivated with corn, coffee and some sugar. Between the peaks, in the deep-cut valleys, are hundreds of tiny villages, isolated by the enormous landscape.

It's an immensely rewarding area, offering a rare glimpse of Maya life and some of the country's finest **fiestas** and **markets**. The mountains are also ideal for **hiking**, particularly if you've had enough of struggling up volcanoes.

The most accessible of the villages is **Todos Santos Cuchumatán**, which is also one of the most fascinating – its horse-race fiesta on November 1 has to be the most outrageous in Guatemala. North of here a remote road leads to Barillas through some of the most compelling Maya settlements in Guatemala, including deeply traditional **San Mateo Ixtatán**. A trip into this mountainous area reveals an exceptional wealth of Maya culture. In this world of jagged peaks and deep-cut valleys Spanish is definitely the second language, and women rigidly adhere to traditional costume, offering an ideal opportunity to witness Maya life at close quarters.

Brief history

This area had little to entice the **Spanish**, and they only exercised vague control, occasionally disrupting things with bouts of religious persecution. The people were, for the most part, left to maintain their old ways, and their traditions are still very much evident in the fiestas, costumes and **folk Catholicism**.

In the 1970s and 1980s, the violence and terror of the **civil war** sent thousands fleeing across the border to Mexico. Most families returned from exile in the 1990s, settling back to life in their old communities, but the cycle of **emigration** has repeated itself again in recent years, as thousands of young villagers have sought work in the US.

From Huehuetenango to Paquix

Heading north out of Huehuetenango, the road to the Cuchumatanes – paved until San Mateo Ixtatán – passes through Chiantla before beginning the long climb up the vertiginous south face of the mountain chain. Buses sway around endless switchbacks, but the views back across the valley are superb. If you're driving, you can stop at a *mirador* almost at the top of the 1000m ascent for a spectacular vista of the chain of volcanoes away to the south, including the near-flawless coned profile of the **Volcán Santa María**. There's a little café at the *mirador*, from where you can savour the views.

Paquix and around

Eventually the road to the Cuchumatanes levels out in a *región andina*, a desolate, grassy 3000m-high plateau suspended between the peaks that's usually wrapped in cloud in the late afternoon. At the three-way **Paquix junction** you'll find a couple of comedores, a petrol station and the turn-off for Todos Santos.

Directly behind Paquix's *Comedor Amparito* a wonderful **hiking trail** climbs for an hour and a half up the side of Chikox mountain, then descends for 45 minutes to a lookout. From here there's a sublime vista over Huehuetenango to a volcano-studded horizon.

ARRIVAL AND DEPARTURE PAQUIX

All **buses** for both Barillas and Todos Santos to/from Huehuetenango pass through Paquix (about 1hr 15min).

ACCOMMODATION AND EATING

Unicórnio Azul 6km southeast of Paquix unicornioazul.com. An exceptional French-/Guatemalan-owned ranch at an altitude of 3000m that organizes superb horse-riding excursions (an hour's ride is included in the room rate during high season). Guides for hikes, birdwatching and mountain biking can be arranged. Accommodation is in very attractive adobe-walled rooms (though they have no heating, a hot-water bottle is provided). The food ($$$) is farm-fresh and delicious; rates include breakfast. $$$$

Chiabal

At a lung-challenging 3300m, the lonely livestock-raising settlement of **CHIABAL** is one of the highest villages in all Central America. A good **community tourism** initiative (5381 0540) has been established with guided **hikes,** including one trail up to the 3666m Piedra Cuache *mirador*, homestay accommodation and the chance to herd llama and sheep. The village is 4km west of Paquix and served by all transport between Huehuetenango and Todos Santos.

La Torre

Six kilometres west of Chiabal, **La Ventosa** is another high-altitude village perched between peaks. From here a trail leads north to **La Torre** (at 3837m the highest non-volcanic mountain in Guatemala). It's around an hour and a half to the top, a stunning hike that passes one-room adobe farmsteads and then weaves through a pine- and cedar-tree forest before arriving at the summit, which is topped with antennae. On clear days (mornings are best) a jagged profile of distant volcanoes, from Tacaná to Tolimán, pierces the horizon to the south.

Todos Santos Cuchumatán

West of La Ventosa, the road steadily descends and you'll soon start to see the explosively coloured traditional costume of the Todosanteros. Spectacularly sited in its own deep-cut river valley, the small town of **TODOS SANTOS CUCHUMATÁN** is strung out along an elongated main street plotted with some venerable old wooden houses. It's a pretty settlement, with a small plaza and a colonial-style whitewashed church, but the village is totally overwhelmed by the looming presence of the Cuchumatanes mountains that insulate Todos Santos from the rest of the world.

The depth of **tradition** evident here is startling. Men fill the streets with colour in their red-and-white-striped trousers, black woollen breeches, brilliantly embroidered shirt collars and natty straw hats; women wear dark blue *cortes* and superbly intricate purple *huipiles*. This is one of the few places where people still use the 260-day *Tzolkin* **calendar** (see page 150), which dates back to ancient times. Highland traditions and the epic surroundings have long captivated visitors, and photographers in particular, though you should be wary of taking pictures of people – particularly children. In this isolated community rumours persist that some foreigners steal babies.

Todos Santos is a great place to simply hang out but it would be a shame not to try a traditional **sauna** (*chuc;* a small stone sauna, shaped like a beehive) while you're here – most guesthouses will prepare one for you.

Tucumanchum

Above the village – follow the track that goes up behind the *Comedor Katy* – is the small Maya site of **Tucumanchum**, where you'll find a couple of grass-covered mounds sprouting pine trees and two large crosses. The site is regularly used by *costumbristas* for the burning of incense and the ritual sacrifice of animals.

The market

If you can't make it for the fiesta (see box), the Saturday **market** is another good time to see the village come to life. Textile shoppers will also find two excellent co-ops selling quality **weavings**: one is located next to the *Casa Familiar* and the other (Cooperativa Estrella de Occidente) is just east of the plaza on the main street.

The museum

Around 300m east of the plaza • charge

The town's little community **museum** has some fine festival costumes, a marimba or two, a collection of masks, assorted Maya ceramics and archeological finds and some

ALL SAINTS FIESTA IN TODOS SANTOS

One spectacular annual event, which brings emigrants home to Todos Santos from as far away as Canada, is the famous November 1 **fiesta** for All Saints (*todos santos*). For three days the village is taken over by unrestrained drinking, dance and marimba music. The festival starts with an all-day **horse race**, which begins as a massive stampede, as riders tear up the course, thrashing their horses, capes flowing behind them. At either end of the run they take a drink before burning back again. As the day wears on some riders retire, collapse, or tie themselves on their mounts, leaving only the toughest to continue.

On the second day, **The Day of the Dead**, the action moves to the cemetery, with marimba bands and drink stalls setting up among the graves for a day of intense ritual that combines grief and celebration. By the end of the fiesta, the streets are littered with collapsed villagers and the jail packed with brawlers.

Organized trips to the Todos Santos fiesta (one or two days) are offered by tour agencies in Quetzaltenango and Lago de Atitlán. If you're travelling independently bear in mind that it's very difficult to find **accommodation** during the fiesta; book well in advance.

wonderful old photos. Fortunato Mendoza, the owner, is an expert on local customs and he (or his daughter) are usually around to put things in context – ask them to show you the Mam wet weather "raincoat" made from leaves.

ARRIVAL AND INFORMATION — TODOS SANTOS CUCHUMATÁN

By bus Hourly buses and microbuses run to/from Huehuetenango (2hr 15min).

Information The community website Ⓦ todossantoscuchumatanes.weebly.com is dedicated to the Todos Santos region.

2

ACCOMMODATION

★ **Casa Familiar** 100m uphill from the plaza Ⓣ 5737 0112, Ⓔ wovent@gmail.com. A hospitable and comfortable highland hotel with renovated rooms that have TVs, woven bedspreads and private hot-water bathrooms. They'll prepare a *chuj* sauna here and offer excellent cooking in the restaurant (meals are great, though a little pricier than other places in town). There's an on-site store selling local weavings, too. $$$

Hotelito Todos Santos Up a lane on the left before you reach the Casa Familiar Ⓣ 3030 8950. A good cheap choice with basic but bargain-priced singles and clean doubles with private bathrooms and TV. $$

EATING

Comedor Evelin 150m east of the plaza, then just up a steep lane Ⓣ 5721 2121. Run by an industrious ladina, this place offers inexpensive grub, including filling breakfasts. $$

Comedor Katy Just up from the plaza Ⓣ 4593 9831. Cheap-and-cheerful place serving filling *comida típica,* perfect for travellers on a budget. $

DIRECTORY

Bank The Banrural bank on the plaza has an ATM.

Internet Internet access is available from a couple of places on the main drag.

Tours Rigoberto Pablo Cruz (Ⓣ 5206 0916, Ⓔ rigoguiadeturismo@yahoo.com) is a good local tour guide who offers trips and leads hikes around Todos Santos; he speaks Mam, Spanish and English. The guide Roberto Bautista (Ⓣ 4384 4379, Ⓔ roberbautista@yahoo.es) is also recommended.

Around Todos Santos

The scenery **around Todos Santos** is some of the most spectacular in all Guatemala, and there's no better place to leave the roads and set off on foot. In a day you can walk across to **San Juan Atitán**, and from there loop back to Huehuetenango. Alternatively, you can travel (on foot or by bus) down the valley from Todos Santos to **San Martín**, a route that offers superb views.

Hiking to San Juan Atitán

The village of **SAN JUAN ATITÁN** is around a five-hour walk from Todos Santos, across a beautiful, isolated valley. Mondays and Thursdays are the best days to do this hike – if you set out early in the morning (around 6.30am) you can arrive in San Juan before the market there has finished.

The walk follows the track up past the *Casa Familar*, and climbs steeply above the village through endless muddy switchbacks. You reach the top of the ridge after about an hour and, if the skies are clear, you'll be rewarded by an awesome view of the Tajumulco and Tacaná volcanoes. Here the track divides: to the right are the scattered remains of an ancient **cloud forest** and a lovely grassy valley, while straight

LEARNING SPANISH AND MAM IN TODOS SANTOS

Hispano Maya (Ⓣ 5163 9293, Ⓦ hispanomaya.weebly.com), opposite the *Hotelito Todos Santos*, offers four to five hours' instruction a day – plus accommodation and meals with a local family. Excursions and activities are run too. As Spanish is the second language here (after Mam), it's as much about the cultural experience as the studying.

ahead is the track to San Juan, dropping down past some huts, through beautiful forest. The route takes you up and down endless exhausting ridges, and over a total of five gushing streams.

Between the fourth and fifth streams – about three hours on from Todos Santos – you'll find an ideal place for a **picnic** overlooking the valley. Soon after here the track swings up to the left, over another pass, and the village of San Juan, strung out along the steep hillside, comes into view in the distance (though it is still more than an hour's walk away).

San Juan is an intensely traditional place: most men still wear dark brown woollen *capixayes* (a kind of knee-length poncho) over a scarlet shirt, held in place by a sash, and plain white trousers. The high-backed sandals worn here are a style depicted in ancient Maya carvings.

Like most of these mountain villages, San Juan is pretty quiet, active only on **market days**, Monday and Thursday. The central square has a giant palm tree and a pretty garden, and there are spectacular views across the valley.

ARRIVAL AND DEPARTURE — SAN JUAN ATITÁN

Microbuses and **pick-ups** to Huehuetenango leave (roughly) every hour or so from 6am (1hr).

Hiking to San Martín

As you head down the valley from Todos Santos, **SAN MARTÍN**, a three-hour walk away, is the next place of any size. This village is inhabited almost entirely by ladinos but its Friday **market** attracts Indigenous people from communities far and wide. A little beyond the village the road down the valley divides, with a right fork that leads around the steep western edge of the Cuchumatanes. On a clear day there are spectacular views, reaching well into Mexico. The route continues through the poor and ragged village of **Concepción Huista** from where a road plunges to Jacaltenango.

Jacaltenango

Perched on a plateau overlooking the limestone plain that stretches out across the Mexican border, **JACALTENANGO** is the heart of an area that was once very traditional, inhabited by a small tribe of Akateko-speakers. Several notable **books** about Maya customs were researched here in the early twentieth century, including the classic *The Year Bearer's People* by Douglas Byers. More recently, the village's most famous resident, Víctor Montejo, documented his experiences during the dark days of the civil war in his book *Testimony: Death of a Guatemalan Village.*

Today **coffee** cultivation (mostly Fair Trade-certified) dominates the local economy and the town has a calm and fairly prosperous feel. **Market day** is Sunday.

ARRIVAL AND INFORMATION — JACALTENANGO

By bus and microbus Microbuses and buses connect Todos Santos with Jacaltenango (roughly every 90min until 4pm; 1hr 40min). Regular buses also run between the town and the Carretera Interamerica highway just south of the La Mesilla border post.

Bank Banrural on 2 C 2–11 has an ATM.

The high road to Barillas

North of the Paquix junction (see page 157), a lonely paved road runs across the mass of the Cuchumatanes, crossing the exposed central plateau before finally dropping into the more temperate coffee country around Barillas. This magnificent, isolated highland area encompasses a network of deeply traditional Indigenous villages and three separate **linguistic zones**. Between **San Juan Ixcoy** and **Santa Eulalia**, Q'anjob'al is spoken; around **San Miguel Acatán**, it's Akateko; and in the **San Mateo Ixtatán** region the language is Chuj.

THE MAYA PRIESTS OF THE CUCHUMATANES

Ethnographer **Krystyna Deuss**, founder of the Guatemalan Maya Centre, London (W maya.org.uk), is the author of *Shamans, Witches and Maya Priests: Native Religion and Ritual in Highland Guatemala*. She has been studying traditions in remote Cuchumatanes communities for decades, focusing her attention on the prayersayers, who occupy a position parallel to that of local priests. Here she explains their role and the key rituals.

THE CALENDAR

Some of the purest **Maya rituals** remaining are found among the Q'anjob'al Maya of northwestern Cuchumatanes. The office of *alcalde resador* (chief prayersayer) still exists here and the 365-day *Haab* calendar is used in conjunction with the 260-day *Tzolkin*. The former ends with the five days of *Oyeb' ku'*, when adult souls leave the body; the return of the souls on the fifth day brings in the new year. As this always falls on a day of *Watan*, *Lambat*, *Ben* or *Chinax*, these four-day lords are known as the "Year Bearers" or "Chiefs". The *Haab* year begins either at the end of February or the beginning of March, coinciding with the corn-planting season.

PRAYERSAYER DUTIES AND TRADITIONS

The **duty of the prayersayer** is to protect his village from evil and ensure a good harvest by praying for rain at planting time and for protection against wind, pests and disease while the corn is maturing. He's usually a man in his 60s or 70s, and his year of office – during which he and his wife must remain celibate – begins on January 1.

In Santa Eulalia, Soloma and San Miguel Acatán, where traditions are particularly strong, he lives in a purpose-built prayersayer's house. Here he's visited by traditionalists and left gifts of corn, beans, candles and money.

On the altar of the house stands the **ordenanza**, a chest that contains religious icons and ancient village documents. This chest serves as a symbol of authority and as a sacred object, and can only be opened by the *alcalde resador*, in private, once a year.

The *resador*'s whole day is spent in prayer: at his home altar before the *ordenanza*, in church and at sacred sites marked by crosses. Prayers for rain are often accompanied by the ritual sacrifice of turkeys, whose blood is poured over candles and incense, which is then burned at the sacred places the following day. These ceremonies are not open to the public.

NEW YEAR RITUALS

Festivals more in the public domain happen on **January 1** when the incumbent *alcalde resador* hands over his responsibilities to his successor. In **Soloma**, after an all-night vigil, the *ordenanza* is carried in procession to the middle of the market square and put on a makeshift altar under a pine arch. When the incoming group arrives there are prayers and ritual drinking, and they receive their wooden staffs of office; after this, the outgoing *alcalde resador* is free to leave for his own home. The new prayersayer's group stays in the marketplace, collecting alms and drinking until 3pm, when they carry the *ordenanza* back to the official residence in a somewhat erratic procession. Notwithstanding a further night of vigil and ceremonial drinking, at 7am the following morning the *alcalde resador* sets out on his first prayer-round to the sacred mountains overlooking the town.

In **San Juan Ixcoy** the year-end ceremonies differ in that the new *resador* is not appointed in advance. Here the outgoing group carries the *ordenanza* to a small chapel on the night of the 31st and leaves it in the care of a committee of traditionalists. The usual all-night vigil with prayers, ritual drinking and collecting alms continues throughout the following day while everyone waits anxiously for a candidate to turn up. As the office of *resador* is not only arduous but also expensive, the post is not always filled. The *ordenanza* sometimes stays locked in the chapel for several days before a volunteer takes on the office again rather than let the *ordenanza* and the tradition be abandoned.

The **road to Barillas** was something of a dead end until recent years but new bridges across the mighty rivers of the Ixcán and road improvements have now opened up a slow, if challenging route east of Barillas to Playa Grande (in neighbouring Alta Verapaz).

Paquix to San Juan Ixcoy

Beyond **Paquix** (see page 157) the road runs through a couple of magical valleys, where great grey boulders lie scattered among ancient-looking oak and cypress trees, their trunks gnarled by the bitter winds. A few families manage to survive the rigours of the altitude, collecting firewood and tending flocks of **sheep**.

Continuing north the road gradually winds down off the plateau, clinging to a hillside, the highway cut out of the sheer rock-face and often wrapped in clouds. On your right are two huge incisor-shaped rocky outcrops, known locally as the **Piedras de Captzín**, which are sacred to the Q'anjob'al Maya of these parts.

The first village you come to is **SAN JUAN IXCOY**, an apple-growing centre drawn out along the valley floor. In season, around the end of August, passing buses are besieged by an army of fruit sellers but there's no particular reason to stop at other times. This innocent-looking village has a past marked by violence. In 1898, following a dispute about pay, the Maya of San Juan murdered the local labour contractor, and in a desperate bid to keep the crime secret they slaughtered all but one of the village's ladino population. The authorities responded mercilessly, killing about ten Maya for the life of every ladino. In local mythology the revolt is known as *la degollación*, the beheading.

Soloma

Around 13km from San Juan Ixcoy, over another range of hills, the unattractive town of **SOLOMA** is the largest, busiest and richest of the settlements in the northern Cuchumatanes. Its flat valley floor was once the bed of a lake, and the steep hillsides still come sliding down at every earthquake or sustained cloudburst. The long white *huipiles* worn by the women of Soloma are similar to those of San Mateo Ixtatán and the Lacandones, and are probably as close as any in the country to the style worn before the Conquest. These days only a few elderly women don them for **market** days (Thursday and Sunday).

ARRIVAL AND DEPARTURE — SOLOMA

There are regular **buses** connecting Soloma with Huehuetenango (every 45min; 3hr) and Barillas (hourly; 4hr).

ACCOMMODATION AND EATING

Comedor Rosy 4 Av & 4 C. It's a little dark inside but this large comedor serves up hearty highland meals, including flavoursome *pepián* and steaming broths. $$

Hotel Don Chico 4 Av 3–65 ☎ 7780 6087. This concrete block north of the plaza has adequate, if uninspiring rooms. It's cheap for solo travellers, and there's a restaurant, wi-fi (unusual in the remote highlands) and underground parking. $$

La Villa On the road to Huehue, southern entrance of town ☎ 4983 8751. A three-storey mock-colonial hotel with decent rooms, all with cable TV and en-suite bathrooms. There's wi-fi and a large restaurant. $$

DIRECTORY

Bank Banrural at 6 C 7–03 has an ATM and will change dollars.

Internet Several places offer internet connections in the streets around the plaza. Mobile data may be more reliable.

Santa Eulalia

Leaving Soloma the paved road soon ends, and you continue over another range of hills to the large village of **SANTA EULALIA**, where highland religious ritual is adhered to very strongly. The historic but crumbling **church** which graced the plaza for more than a century has been demolished, but a concrete replacement is nearing completion, in an intricate colonial baroque style that's similar to the original – except that the words "Txajul Ewul" (the town's name in the Q'anjob'al language) have been added to the facade. A traditional **Maya altar**, wreathed in incense smoke, remains in front of the church.

Beyond Santa Eulalia is the **Cruce Pett** junction, beyond which the Barillas road pushes on north through pastureland, skirting patches of pine forest, with exhilarating views west towards Mexico. The sense of isolation is immense up on this beautiful 3000m-high plateau, and you'll barely see a soul except for shepherd boys and their goats.

San Rafael La Independencia

At the **Cruce Pett** junction, 5km north of Santa Eulalia, there are comedores and a branch road that cuts off to the west, curving around the peaks of the Cuchumatanes to the village of **SAN RAFAEL LA INDEPENDENCIA**, 11km away. Perched on an outcrop with magnificent views down towards the Mexican border, this peaceful Akateko-speaking settlement amounts to not much more than a scattering of old timber houses and utilitarian concrete structures. Nevertheless, it makes an enjoyable place to spend a day or two, at the heart of a very traditional region where Maya customs remain very strongly observed.

Centro Cultural Maya Akateko

Above the *municipalidad* • Free • ⓣ 7779 7239

The **Centro Cultural Maya Akateko** is a **cultural centre** with a fascinating collection of old artefacts, including polychrome ceramics, obsidian flints, a 2m-long blowpipe and some interesting photographs. The staff can put you in touch with guides (Pedro Juan Méndez Martinez is recommended) who can lead you to the Maya ruins of **Tenam**, the Chimbam chapel, Xeyatak ceremonial centre and the numerous sacred caves and altars that dot the hills around.

ACCOMMODATION — SAN RAFAEL LA INDEPENDENCIA

Tienda San Andrés One block downhill from the plaza. You can stay in the basic rooms above this shop, though you should be prepared for the fact that there is no hot water here. $

San Miguel Acatán

From San Rafael it's just 4km to the larger, much less attractive village of **SAN MIGUEL ACATÁN**. It's less traditional than San Rafael, but has better transport connections and you'll find a couple of *hospedajes*, plenty of comedores, a lively Sunday **market** and a branch of Banrural.

ARRIVAL AND DEPARTURE — SAN MIGUEL ACATÁN

There are a number of **buses** from Huehuetenango to San Miguel, which travel via San Rafael (5 daily; 4hr 30min).

San Mateo Ixtatán

Back on the road to Barillas, it's 24km from Cruce Pett to **SAN MATEO IXTATÁN**, the most traditional of the string of settlements along the highway. Its name derives from the Nahuatl for "abundance of salt", which is still a major industry in the communally owned mines around the village. The town tumbles down a steep east-facing hillside, occupying the ground between two plunging river valleys. The people here speak **Chuj** and form part of a Maya group who occupy the extreme northwest corner of the highlands and some of the forest beyond; their territory borders that of the Lacandón, a jungle tribe from Mexico.

San Mateo certainly enjoys a spectacular setting, but it's a poor and isolated town: 70 percent of adults are illiterate, and alcoholism is a huge problem. The best time to visit, other than for the fiesta (Sept 17–21), is on a **market day**, Thursday or Sunday.

Traditional dress is becoming less common, but the older women here still wear unusual and striking *huipiles*, long white gowns embroidered in brilliant reds, yellows and blues, radiating out from a star-like centre. You may also see men wearing short woollen poncho-like tunics called *capixayes*, often embroidered with flowers around the collar and quetzals on the back.

The church

San Mateo's cream-coloured **church**, its wonky facade embellished with niches and the images of saints, has a pagan character that barely offers a passing reference to conventional Catholicism. Smoke from a Maya altar attended by *costumbristas* drifts across the courtyard in front of the church, while inside devotees kneel on the nave floor clutching candles, the stone walls reverberating with the constant murmur of solemn incantations.

Wajxaklajunh

Just below the village are the quite substantial unrestored Maya ruins of **Wajxaklajunh**, which enjoy a magical position overlooking the San Mateo valley and down to ridge after ridge of hills on the horizon to the east. Here you'll find several temples, including the pyramid-shaped structure known as **Yolk'u**, a ball court and a couple of weathered stelae shaded by cypress trees.

ARRIVAL AND INFORMATION — SAN MATEO IXTATÁN

By bus San Mateo has bus connections with Huehuetenango (roughly hourly; 5hr), Barillas (hourly; 1hr 30min) and to the village of Yalambojoch, to the northwest (one daily bus and infrequent pick-ups; 2hr 30min).

Information The website ixtatan.org, run by development project the Ixtatán Foundation, is a good source of information. There are several places in town to get online.

ACCOMMODATION AND EATING

Hotel Magdalena Uphill from the parque 4515 1515. The best place in town; its tiled rooms are in good shape, with private bathrooms that have hot water. $$

Los Picones 200m uphill from the church 4035 8354. On the upper floor of a concrete building, this clean, welcoming comedor offers filling meals including *milanesas*, grilled beef and chicken, all served with soup and vegetables. $

Barillas and around

Beyond San Mateo the road drops steadily east to **BARILLAS**, a ladino frontier town 28km away in the relative warmth of the tierra templada at 1450m and devoted to coffee production. If you're heading to or from Laguna Lachúa (see page 236) it's an obvious place to break the journey, with well-swept streets and a prosperous air (but few attractions).

About 18km north of Barillas (take the dirt road towards the village of Yolhuitz) is the beautiful hourglass-shaped **Laguna Maxbal**, which is ringed by forest – locals say it's possible to see a quetzal bird here some mornings. You'll need your own transport to get here.

ARRIVAL AND INFORMATION — BARILLAS

By bus Buses (9 daily; 6hr 30min) connect Barillas and Huehuetenango. Buses to Playa Grande (roughly hourly until 3pm; 5–6hr depending on road conditions) leave from opposite the *Hotel Arizona*. Microbuses connect the bus terminal with the centre of town.

Services Banrural, 3 Av 2–28, Zona 1, has an ATM.

ACCOMMODATION AND EATING

Hotel Arizona 3 C 7–19, Zona 6 7780 2758. Close to the bus terminal, this pink-and-green hotel has simple tiled rooms and is handy if you have an early start to Playa Grande. $$

Hotel Villa Virginia On the plaza, Zona 1 7780 2236. Set in the very heart of town, this dependable hotel offers decent en-suite rooms, perfect for a good night's rest after a day of exploring. $$

West to the Mexican border

The extreme **northwest corner** of the western highlands receives very few visitors (except travellers crossing its two border posts) yet contains some remarkable natural attractions. Places to stay are thin on the ground, but from the superb community lodge of **Finca Chaculá** you can make day-trips to the astonishing sinkhole of El Cimarrón, lovely lake Laguna Yolnabaj and the exquisite Candelaria cenotes. This border region sits at a lower altitude than the neighbouring, far chillier, Cuchumatanes, with most sights located between 700m and 1300m.

The main **roads** into the region are paved and in good condition: from Huehuetenango the Carretera Interamericana runs for 79km through the spectacular, gorge-like Selegua valley to the Mexican border at **La Mesilla**. Just before La Mesilla, from the roadside village of **Camoja Grande**, a paved road leads off to the north, paralleling the frontier. This road crosses a dusty white limestone plateau to the town of **Nentón**, then continues towards Gracias a Dios, a second, more remote border post.

It's possible to continue east from Finca Chaculá towards Laguna Lachuá and Alta Verapaz using a remote, rough road via the towns of San Mateo Ixtatán and Barillas. Or, you could alternatively make a loop south from San Mateo Ixtatán back to Huehuetenango via the spectacular high road across the Cuchumatanes via Soloma.

Finca Chaculá and around

The string of **farming communities** along the border strip between **Gracias a Dios** and Finca San Francisco have a fascinating history. Thirty years ago this region was thickly forested and very sparsely populated, but it's been steadily settled after the civil war by refugees, most of whom are originally from Maya villages in the Cuchumatanes mountains. These people fled the conflict to live in Mexico, some of them spending more than a decade in exile. Many fought with the guerrillas, others for the Guatemalan army. An excellent community **lodge** established in Finca Chaculá now provides visitors with a superb base to explore the region's many lakes, trails and sights.

Additionally, the lodge is a great example of sustainable tourism, offering insights into the local culture and history while supporting the community.

THE MEXICAN BORDER: LA MESILLA AND GRACIAS A DIOS

AT LA MESILLA

The two sets of **immigration** checkpoints are 3km apart and connected by collective taxis. On the **Mexican side** very regular buses run to Comitán (1hr 15min), where you change for San Cristóbal de las Casas. Heading **into Guatemala**, second-class buses to Huehuetenango leave the border every thirty minutes (2hr) until 7pm and there are occasional services to Quetzaltenango (4hr) too. Most travellers use **shuttle bus** connections between San Cristóbal de las Casas and towns in Guatemala including Quetzaltenango, Panajachel and Antigua; consult Adrenalina Tours (W adrenalinatours.com) for the latest schedule. There's a Banrural bank (with ATM), plenty of moneychangers and some cheap hotels if you're stuck.

AT GRACIAS A DIOS

This remote border crossing is 8km northwest of **La Trinidad** junction and has both Guatemalan and Mexican immigration posts. The Banrural bank here will change pesos and dollars but there's no ATM. Just over the border, the village of Carmixán has transport for Comitán where you can get your Mexican entry stamp.

FIESTAS IN THE WESTERN HIGHLANDS

The western highlands are the home of the traditional Guatemalan fiesta. These are some highlights.

JANUARY

22–26 San Pablo La Laguna, main day Jan 25.
23–27 San Pablo, department of San Marcos.
28–Feb 2 Jacaltenango.

FEBRUARY

Jan 28–Feb 2 Chiantla, main day Feb 2.
8 Ostuncalco.
8–13 Santa Eulalia, main day Feb 8.

MARCH

Varies Chajul, the second Friday in Lent marked by huge pilgrimages.
Holy Week Santiago Atitlán, Maximón paraded through the streets, usually on the Wednesday; San Cristóbal Tonicapán, the biggest processions in the Xela area.

APRIL

22–28 San Marcos, main day April 25.
24 San Jorge La Laguna.
25 San Marcos La Laguna.
29–May 4 Barillas.
Varies Zacualpa and Aguacatán, fiestas to mark forty days from Holy Week.

MAY

6–10 Uspantán, main day May 8.
8–10 Santa Cruz La Laguna.

JUNE

12–14 San Antonio Palopó, Lago de Atitlán, main day June 13.
21–25 San Juan Ixcoy, north of Huehuetenango.
21–25 Olintepeque, just north of Quetzaltenango.
22–25 Cotzal, main day June 24.
22–26 San Juan Atitán, main day June 24.
23–26 San Juan La Laguna, main day June 24.
24 Comalapa.
24–30 San Pedro Sacatepéquez.
26–30 Soloma, main day June 29.
27–30 San Pedro La Laguna, main day June 29.
28–30 Almolonga, main day June 29.

El Cimarrón

The prime attraction in the area, the astonishing sinkhole of **El Cimarrón** is a near-perfect cylindrical depression in the limestone crust measuring about 200m across and around 210m deep. At the bottom is dense forest, though there's no route down as the walls are near vertical. It's a breathtaking sight, and you'll no doubt have your heart in your mouth as you inch your way around the edge of the drop-off, your sense of vertigo intensified by the presence of a vulture or two keeping an eye on your progress. The silence at this special place is palpable, the sense of isolation broken only by the omnipresent buzz of cicadas.

JULY

12–17 Huehuetenango.
21–Aug 4 Momostenango, July 25 is a very important day in the Maya religious calendar, and Aug 1 is the main fiesta day.
22–27 Chimaltenango, main day July 26.
23–27 Santiago Atitlán, main day July 25.

AUGUST

1–4 Sacapulas, main day Aug 4.
9–15 Joyabaj, main day Aug 15. Superb fiesta; traditional dances here include the *Palo Volador.*
10–13 Santa Clara La Laguna, main day Aug 12.
11–17 Sololá, main day Aug 15.
12–15 Nebaj, main day Aug 15.
14–19 Santa Cruz del Quiché, main day Aug 18.

SEPTEMBER

12–18 Quetzaltenango, main day Sept 15.
17–21 San Mateo Ixtatán, main day Sept 21.
24–30 Totonicapán, main day Sept 29.
25–30 San Miguel Acatán, main day Sept 29.
26–Oct 5 Tecpán.

OCTOBER

1–6 San Francisco el Alto, main day Oct 4.
2–6 Panajachel, main day Oct 4.
15–20 San Lucas Tolimán, Lago de Atitlán, main day Oct 18.

NOVEMBER

1–2 Todos Santos Cuchumatán, a wild, alcohol-infused horse race on Nov 1, with everyone heading to the cemetery on Nov 2 for All Souls' Day.
7–12 San Martín Jilotepeque, main day Nov 11.
22–26 Zunil, main day Nov 25.
23–26 Nahualá, main day Nov 25.
25 Santa Catarina Palopó, Lago de Atitlán.
27–Dec 1 San Andrés Xecul, main day Nov 30.

DECEMBER

5–8 Huehuetenango, main day Dec 8.
7 The Burning of the Devil is celebrated in most highland towns with bonfires and men running around dressed as devils.
14–21 Chichicastenango, very impressive fiesta, main day Dec 21.

The (unmarked) trailhead to El Cimarrón is at Km 399 on the road between La Trinidad junction and Gracias a Dios, from where it's a 45-minute walk. You can park a vehicle by some low stone walls (actually remnants of a small Maya site), but as the path to the sinkhole is not easy to make out you'll need a guide (contact Finca Chaculá).

Cenotes del Candelaria

42km south of La Trinidad junction • Charge per car • Driving, head for Km 374 on the La Trinidad junction–Nentón road, from where it's a 17km drive along a dirt road (high-clearance vehicles only) to Río Jordan village, where you pay the admission charge

The **Cenotes del Candelaria**, glorious azure lakes ringed by tropical dry forest, lie on private land some 2km from the border with Mexico. They're utterly pristine, untouched by tourism, with crystal-clear waters. You can swim in the first cenote, and as it's at an altitude of 700m, the water temperature is a pretty balmy 24°C year-round. The second cenote, which is larger, has some cave art that you can just glimpse from its eastern bank.

Driving to the cenotes you'll crisscross the beautiful turquoise Río Lagarte several times.

Yalambojoch

Around 22km east of the border post **Gracias a Dios** (see box), the village of **YALAMBOJOCH** is something of a transport hub for these parts. It's also the jumping-off point for the spectacular cobalt-blue waters of **Laguna Yolnabaj**, a large lake 5km to the north that's also known as Laguna Brava. Locals, many of whom are *repatriados* (returned refugees from Mexico), have launched a reforestation programme around the lake and act as guides. *Finca Chaculá* and Adrenalina Tours (see page 142) run trips here.

Finca San Francisco

The recent history of Yalambojoch is bound up with that of **FINCA SAN FRANCISCO**, a smaller village just to the east. In 1982 the army massacred around three hundred people here and the entire population of the surrounding area fled for their lives, crossing the border into Mexico. Finca San Francisco has some small Maya temples, and also a plaque commemorating those who died in the massacre.

ARRIVAL AND DEPARTURE — WEST TO THE MEXICAN BORDER

By bus Two daily buses leave Gracias a Dios for Huehuetenango (4am & 9am; 4hr 30min) via Nentón. In addition, a 5am bus leaves for Huehuetenango (10hr) via San Mateo Ixtatán and Soloma; pick-ups also run the Yalambojoch–San Mateo Ixtatán route (2hr 30min). At other times of day regular microbuses connect Gracias a Dios with Finca San Francisco and also run between Gracias a Dios and Nentón (every 30min; 45min), from where there's plenty of transport to the Carretera Interamericana and Huehuetenango.

Tours *Finca Chaculá* runs superb tours (half or full day) to El Cimarrón, Laguna Yolnabaj, the Candelaria cenotes and minor Maya ruins; guides only speak Spanish.

ACCOMMODATION AND EATING

★ **Finca Chaculá** 8km east of La Trinidad junction, 1.5km south of the main Gracias a Dios–Yalambojoch road; the turn-off is at the village of Chaculá ⓦ unicornioazul.com. One of the most enjoyable rural lodges in the country, with huge, beautifully presented rooms in a nineteenth-century farmhouse building. Staff (no English is spoken) look after guests incredibly well, and delicious home-cooked food is served in a stately dining room, with wine and beers available. Electricity is very limited, so it's candles at night (but you can recharge mobiles). There's a little lake a 5min walk away for swimming, and some minor archeological ruins close by too. $$$

The Pacific coast

MONTERRICO BEACH

The Pacific coast

A sweltering strip of low-lying, tropical land, some 300km long and 50km wide, Guatemala's Pacific coast is also known, among locals, as La Costa Sur. Featureless yet fertile, the coastal plain is a land of vast fincas, dull commerce-driven towns and ramshackle seaside resorts. The main draw should be the coastline, though as the sand is black and the ocean has a dangerous underlow this region is not that popular with travellers. But if you're yearning for some ocean air and can pick your spot carefully, the coast does have some appeal, with a couple of attractive beaches and some intriguing attractions dotted along the Pacific highway.

It's certainly not a resort, but the little seaside settlement of **Monterrico** has an unspoiled charm and is well worth a visit. Here you'll find a superb beach (a magnet for sea turtles) and a rich network of mangrove wetlands to explore. Tiny **Paredón** also has a fine oceanic beach, good surf and a travellers' vibe, while in the far west the twin villages of **Tilapa** and **Tilapita** offer sweeping sands, no crowds and relatively safe swimming.

Several ancient Mesoamerican cultures once flourished in the region, leaving some important archeological remains. The one site in the area that comes close to ranking with those elsewhere in the country is **Takalik Abaj**, outside Retalhuleu, which displays both Maya and Olmec heritage.

With offshore waters filled with stupendous numbers of sailfish, tarpon, tuna and marlin, the Pacific coast is steadily gaining a reputation as a world-class **sportfishing** location – **Iztapa** and **Puerto Quetzal** are the main bases for excursions. The region also has a couple of world-class **theme parks** on the Pacific slope that represent a huge draw for families.

Brief history

It's generally held that sophisticated **Olmec** influence – emerging first in Mexico and spreading along the coast – shaped both **Ocós** and **Iztapa** cultures, which thrived here after 1500 BC. These were small, village-based societies that developed considerable skills in the working of stone and pottery.

Between 400 and 900 AD, parts of the coastal plain were overrun by the **Pipil**, who migrated south from Mexico, bringing new architectural styles and artistic skills. They established settlements with compact ceremonial centres and rubble-filled pyramids and traded cacao. The first **Spaniards** to set foot in Guatemala did so on the Pacific coast. In **colonial times** indigo and cacao were cultivated and cattle ranches established, but the inhospitable climate and accompanying diseases took their toll, and for the most part the region remained a miserable backwater. It was only after **independence** that commercial agriculture began to dominate. By the early twentieth century, the area was important enough to justify the construction of two **railways** to the coast and a line to the Mexican border.

Today the coastal strip is the country's most **intensely farmed** region, with entire villages effectively owned by vast fincas. There's a little domestic tourism but in general it's **agribusiness** – palm oil, bananas and sugar on the coast and coffee on the Pacific slope – that dominates the local economy.

GETTING AROUND — THE PACIFIC COAST

By bus The Pacific highway is served by a near-constant flow of pullmans and second-class buses. Buses travelling from Guatemala City to the Mexican border (5hr) stop at most of the main towns en route. If you plan to leave the

TAKALIK ABAJ RUINS

Highlights

❶ **Tilapa and Tilapita** Palm trees line the fine, dark sand beaches where the gently sloping shores create some of the coast's best spots for a swim. See pages 174 and 175

❷ **Takalik Abaj** This small but rewarding archeological site features well-executed Olmec and Maya carvings. See page 177

❸ **Xocomil and Xetulul leisure parks** The country's largest water park and its neighbouring amusement complex offer a glut of slides, pools and chutes, plus some thrilling rides – great fun for all the family. See page 178

❹ **Surfing** Guatemala's best surfing point, Paredón, is a rustic, mellow place where it's easy to indulge in some serious beach time and enjoy great wave action. See page 181

❺ **Sportfishing** The country's Pacific coast offers world-class conditions for sportfishing. The two major centres are Puerto Quetzal and Iztapa, Guatemala's oldest port. See page 183

❻ **Monterrico** Oceanside village boasting Guatemala's most enjoyable beach, famous for its nesting sea turtles, plus an extensive network of mangrove swamps to explore. See page 183

HIGHLIGHTS ARE MARKED ON THE MAP ON PAGE 174

highway, connections are less frequent but still regular to most coastal towns.

By shuttle bus Shuttle buses run to Monterrico and Paredón from Antigua.

Tilapa and around

Most travellers arriving in Guatemala's extreme west forgo the beaches in these parts and head straight from the border to Quetzaltenango or Guatemala City. But for total relaxation, a day or two in tranquil **Tilapita**, dipping your toes in the warm ocean and visiting the neighbouring **nature reserve**, will be time well spent.

Tilapa

South of Tecún Umán (see page 176), a paved road paralleling the border passes endless palm-oil and banana plantations to the humble little village of **TILAPA**. The dark-sand beach here has a relatively gently shelving profile compared with many places on this coast, so the undertow is less fierce and it's easier for children to paddle in safety. Lifeguards are only posted on weekends though.

Reserva Natural El Manchón-Guamuchal

The coastline forms part of the **Reserva Natural El Manchón-Guamuchal**, which covers some 30km of prime turtle-nesting beach and extends around 10km inland to embrace a belt of swamp and mangrove, which is home to crocodiles, iguanas, kingfishers, storks, white herons, egrets and an abundance of fish.

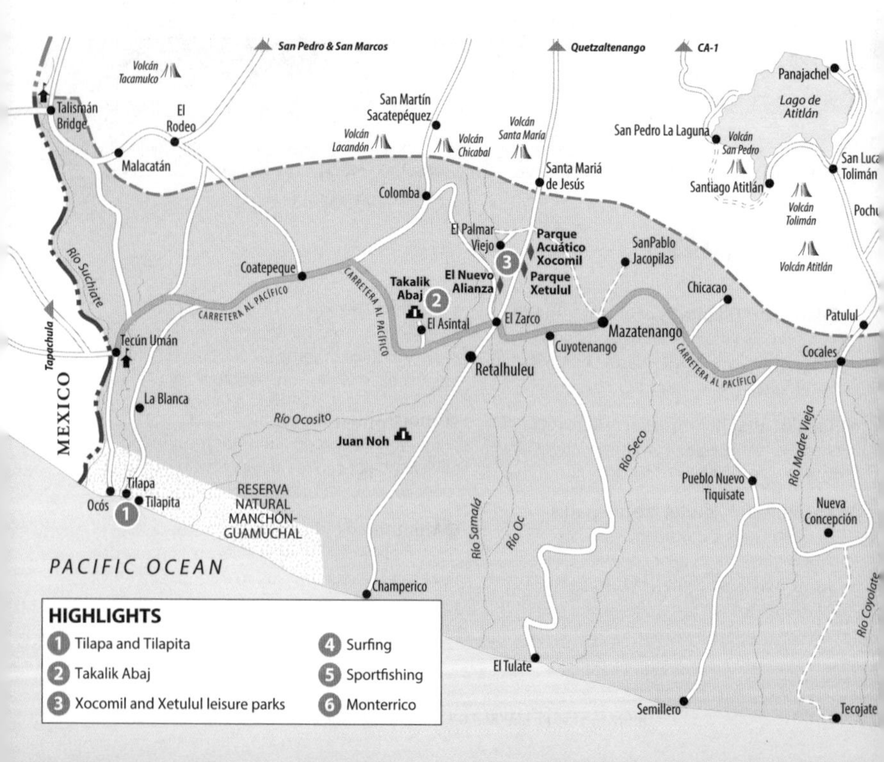

If you're interested in exploring the area's **wetlands**, speak to one of the local boatmen in Tilapa or Tilapita about taking a tour (charge per hour) of the canals and lagoons.

Tilapita

On the other side of an estuary from Tilapa is the even tinier, and more agreeable, beach settlement of **TILAPITA**. Here there's a real opportunity to get away from it all and enjoy a superb stretch of clean, dark sand and the ocean (with not too much undertow).

Just next to the *El Pacífico* hotel is a small **turtle hatchery**, with protected enclosures where eggs are buried until they hatch, and some information boards (the olive ridley turtle is the main visitor here).

ARRIVAL AND INFORMATION — TILAPA AND AROUND

By bus Regular buses connect Coatepeque and Tilapa (every 30min, last bus returns at 6pm; 2hr). If you're travelling along the Carretera al Pacífico, just wait at the Tilapa junction on the highway for a connection.

By boat Boatmen buzz you up the canal that connects Tilapa and Tilapita. There's a small charge per person for the 10min ride; it's possible to wade over at low tide.

Information Consult the website playatilapa.com for more information about the village.

ACCOMMODATION AND EATING

In Tilapa you'll find a row of beach **comedores** dispensing good, fresh prawns and fried fish, plus cold Gallo beer.

El Pacífico Tilapita playatilapa.com. Popular with travellers, this place, run by a welcoming couple, offers rooms with decent mattresses, fans and showers – though you might want to bring your own mosquito net. There's a pool, which is (usually) filled at the weekend, and good food is served, including fresh fish ($$). Ice-cold beer, too. No advance reservations. $$

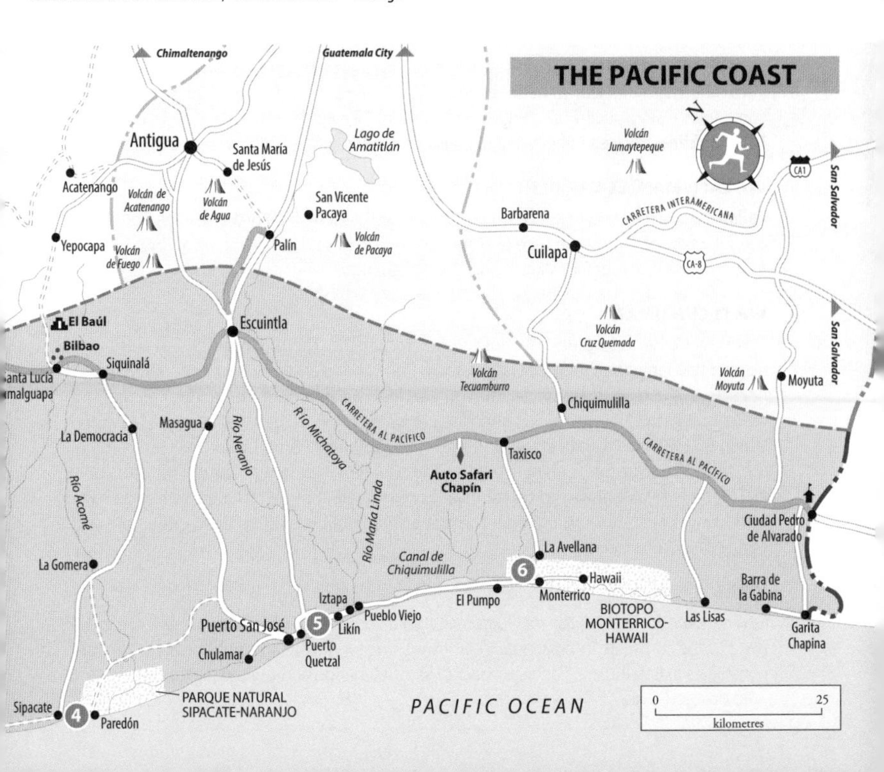

Along the coastal highway

Heading east from the border you pass a succession of dull, incessantly hot, purely commercial towns. **Retalhuleu** is slightly more attractive than most, close to which are the intriguing Maya-Olmec ruins of **Takalik Abaj**. North of Retalhuleu you're within easy reach of the terrific theme parks of **Parque Acuático Xocomil** and **Parque Xetulul**.

Coatepeque

The first place of any importance along the highway, **COATEPEQUE** is a shabby, furiously busy town where coffee is processed. As it's infamous for its street gangs, and the climate is oven hot and perpetually sticky, it's best to avoid hanging around, though you may have to change buses here.

ARRIVAL AND DEPARTURE — COATEPEQUE

By bus From the bus terminal, buses run regularly until about 7pm to the two Mexican border crossings, Quetzaltenango (via both Colomba and Zunil) and the capital.

Destinations Guatemala City (every 30min; 4hr); Quetzaltenango (every 30min; 1hr 30min); Retalhuleu (every 20min; 50min); Talismán (every 20min; 1hr 30min); Tecún Umán (every 20min; 40min).

ACCOMMODATION

Villa Real 6 C 6–57 ⓣ 7775 6134. If you do get stuck in Coatepeque, this hotel is a good option, with comfortable, if smallish, modern singles and doubles, a restaurant and secure parking. $$

THE MEXICAN BORDER: TALISMÁN/TECÚN UMÁN

The two **border posts**, Talismán and Tecún Umán are both open 24 hours. Minibuses run from Tapachula in Mexico to Talismán and Tecún Umán until 9pm (every 20min; 30min). Three companies – King Quality (also known as Platinum), Tica Bus and Línea Dorada (see page 65) – run **direct buses** between Tapachula and Guatemala City (5 daily in total; 6hr).

VIA TALISMÁN (EL CARMEN)

Talismán, also referred to as El Carmen, is the more relaxed of the two crossings. There's a regular flow of buses from here to Malacatán, where buses head along on a slow, mountainous route for San Marcos and Quetzaltenango.

VIA TECÚN UMÁN

This busy border is favoured by most commercial traffic. **Tecún Umán** has an authentic frontier flavour with all-night bars, lost souls, contraband and moneychangers. Cycle rickshaws (charging an unofficial immigration fee) snake through the traffic. Pullmans run by Galgos, King Quality, Tica Bus and Línea Dorada connect Guatemala City with Tecún Umán on their way to Tapachula, and there are additional second-class services from the capital's Centra Sur terminal. Heading into Guatemala, a steady stream of buses runs along the coastal highway to Guatemala City while direct buses to Quetzaltenango run until about 4pm; after this time get the first bus to Retalhuleu ("Reu") and get an onward connection from there.

VISAS

Few nationalities need a visa for Guatemala, but if you don't qualify for a waiver you can head to the consulate in Tapachula. The same is true for Mexico, through there are Mexican consulates in Retalhuleu, Quetzaltenango, Huehuetenango and Guatemala City for those who do need a visa.

Retalhuleu

Set 6km south of the Carretera al Pacífico, **RETALHULEU** – usually shortened to **Reu** ("Ray-oo") – is a relatively civilized place compared with the chaos elsewhere on the coast. Palm trees line the entrance road to the town, while the **plaza** retains a degree of faded authority: towering Greek columns grace the elegant *municipalidad* and there's an imposing colonial church.

Museo de Arqueología y Etnología

Parque Central • Charge

The small **Museo de Arqueología y Etnología**, inside the *municipalidad* on the plaza, has a collection of Maya anthropomorphic figurines that show a strong Mexican influence and some evocative old photographs of the region.

ARRIVAL AND INFORMATION — RETALHULEU

By bus Most buses running along the coastal highway pull into the bustling Retalhuleu terminal on 7 Av and 10 C, a 10min walk from the plaza.

Destinations Champerico (every 15min; 1hr); Guatemala City (every 30min; 3hr); Quetzaltenango (every 30min; 1hr 15min); Tecún Umán (every 20min; 1hr 30min); El Tulate (roughly hourly; 1hr 45min).

Banks There are several banks around the plaza, including the Banco Agromercantil, which has an ATM.

ACCOMMODATION AND EATING

Cafeteria La Luna 5 C & 8 Av ⊙4203 1890. Two blocks south of the plaza, this dependable place has satisfying *comida típica*, including tasty breakfasts.

Hotel América 8 Av 9–32 ⊙7771 1154. An inexpensive place to stay, with well-kept rooms with fan and private bathrooms. $$

Judy's Home 10 C 5-40 Av ⊙3573 0494. A cosy B&B, with inviting rooms that have a contemporary look. Breakfast with a view is served on the terrace. $$$

Takalik Abaj

19km west of Retalhuleu • Charge, guide extra

The archeological site of **Takalik Abaj** has cast fresh light on the development of early Maya civilization, particularly the influence of **Olmec** culture. First settled around 1800 BC, the city came to preside over trade routes along the Pacific littoral, controlling the movement of jade, cacao and obsidian. Early ceremonial buildings and monuments were executed in Olmec style between 800 and 400 BC, including the characteristic pot-bellied humans with swollen eyelids, but by the late Preclassic period, Maya-style carvings of standing rulers were beginning to replace Olmec art. Later in the Classic era some of the Maya World's most exquisite jade masks were created here – they now reside in Guatemala City's Museo Nacional de Arqueología y Etnología (see page 62).

The ruins

You can only access the Olmec's urban centre, while the city's outskirts are spread over five coffee plantations. The first substantial structure you encounter is **Terraza 3**, a low, rectangular stepped temple with three stone Olmec-head statues facing a ceremonial Maya altar. Some of the finest carved stelae are in front of **Temple 12**, which is the site's largest, with a 56m-wide base; Monument 67 depicts a jaguar head; Monument 68 is toad-like; Monument 9, a rare representation of an owl; and, most impressive of all, the grouping of **Altar 8** and **Monument 5**, which has a date of 126 AD and shows twin kings presiding over bound captives. Facing Temple 12 is **Temple 11**, resembling a grassy mound, which is mid- to Late Classic Maya and has seven more stelae in front of it. More good carvings lie round the back of Temple 12 including Olmec-style Monument 99, which shows a baboon-like creature with a protruding jaw.

Behind Temple 12 is a small building that serves as a **museum**, containing a model of Takalik Abaj along with assorted carvings and ceramics. There are also several fairly miserable animal enclosures that contain pizotes, spider monkeys and porcupines, among other creatures.

ARRIVAL AND DEPARTURE — TAKALIK ABAJ

By bus To get to Takalik Abaj, take a local bus or shared taxi from Reu to El Asintal, a small village 15km to the west, from where you can either catch a pick-up or walk the 4km to the site through coffee and cacao plantations.

By car If you're driving, take the Asintal turn-off from the coastal highway.

North of Retalhuleu

The **El Zarco** junction above Reu marks the start of one of the country's most **scenic** roads, which heads up into the highlands passing two impressive **leisure parks** and the abandoned village of El Palmar Viejo. It then skirts the plunging lower slopes of the Santa María and Zunil **volcanoes** before emerging in the valley of Quetzaltenango.

El Nueva Alianza

15km north of the El Zarco junction • Charge • T 5348 5290

Reached by a minor (dirt) road north of El Zarco, **El Nueva Alianza** is an organic, fairtrade coffee and macadamia farm run as a cooperative. You can tour the finca's handsome colonial-style mansion and its extensive grounds, which lead to a waterfall, and learn about coffee cultivation and processing (as well as their micro-hydro-electricity and biodiesel production). Volunteers are welcome, and accommodation (see below) and meals are available. Many Spanish schools and tour operators in Quetzaltenango run trips here.

Parque Museo Xulik

3km north of the El Zarco junction • Charge • T 5510 7144

Parque Museo Xulik is an impressive privately owned museum dedicated to superheroes, where you can pose with the Incredible Hulk, view all the Batman characters and browse thousands of toys and memorabilia covering everything from Ben 10 to Harry Potter. There's a café and mini-golf too.

Parque Acuático Xocomil

6km north of the El Zarco junction • Charge • W irtra.org.gt • Buses between Retalhuleu and Quetzaltenango pass the water park every 30min

A superb water park landscaped into the foothills of the highlands, **Parque Acuático Xocomil** is a vast complex with 1.2km of water slides, wave pools, swimming pools and artificial rivers amid grounds replete with replica Maya temples and copious greenery.

Parque Xetulul

6km north of the El Zarco junction • Charge, ride packages extra • W irtra.org.gt

Next to Parque Acuático Xocomil and run by the same group, **Parque Xetulul** is divided into different zones. The Plaza Chapina features re-creations of famous Guatemalan buildings, the Plaza España showcases a galleon, and Plaza Francia boasts replicas of Parisian structures. The park has some terrific rides, including the thrilling La Avalancha roller coaster and, like its sister complex, is clean, well run and extremely popular with Guatemalan families.

El Palmar Viejo

Buses between Retalhuleu and Quetzaltenango stop at the El Palmar Viejo turn-off, from where you can walk or wait for transport to cover the 3.5km route; there are also tours from Quetzaltenango (see page 142)

North of parks Xocomil and Xetulul, it's about 14km to a turn-off (on the west side of the road) that leads to the absorbing remains of the village of **El Palmar Viejo**. After torrential rains during Hurricane Mitch in 1998, mud flows swept through the centre of this farming community, cutting the church in two and leaving its western facade hanging over a ravine. Villagers were evacuated to the other side of the highway – leaving an overgrown ghost town that represents a haunting reminder of the destructive powers of the hurricane, which killed thousands.

ACCOMMODATION AND EATING — NORTH OF RETALHULEU

Irtra hotels Parque Acuático Xocomil irtra.org.gt. A family-friendly hotel complex with colonial-, Asian- and ranch-style places in the grounds of the water park. These are pricey for foreigners, but the superb facilities (including pools and sports) help compensate. $$$$

El Nueva Alianza 15km north of the El Zarco junction 4590 4283. This coffee finca and macadamia farm (see page 178) offers simple accommodation and a gregarious atmosphere, particularly on weekends. Meals ($$) are also available, to visitors and guests alike. Dorms $, doubles $$

3

Champerico

South from Retalhuleu, a good paved road heads 61km to the run-down beach resort of **CHAMPERICO**. Founded in 1872, it was originally connected to Quetzaltenango by rail and enjoyed a brief period of prosperity based on the export of coffee. In 1934 Aldous Huxley passed through but was distinctly unimpressed, pleased to escape "the unspeakable boredom of life at Champerico". Little has improved here except that the rusty old pier has been fixed up a little. Champerico spends most of its time waiting for the weekend, when hordes of weary city-dwellers descend on the coast to gorge on greasy fried fish and cratefuls of cold Gallo. Watch out for the dangerous **undertow** if you do want a dip; and stick to the main part of the beach – there have been muggings reported in isolated spots.

ARRIVAL AND DEPARTURE — CHAMPERICO

By bus Buses run between Champerico and Retalhuleu very regularly; the last bus leaves Champerico around 8pm.

Destinations Quetzaltenango (every 30min; 2hr 15min); Retalhuleu (every 15min; 1hr 20min).

El Tulate

Beyond Retalhuleu the highway runs east through **Cuyotenango**, a featureless town blighted by the thunder of the highway. Another branch road turns off from here to the isolated, palm-lined black sand beach **EL TULATE**. Here the village and the ocean are separated by a narrow expanse of mangrove swamp; boats ferry passengers across for a small charge. As it's a small place, you're virtually guaranteed a quiet place to chill once you're away from the strip of shore-side seafood comedores. The beach has a gentle shelving profile, so it's much better for paddling and swimming than most places along the Pacific coast.

UNDERTOW

Most of Guatemala's Pacific coastline is affected by a strong **undertow**, which occurs when big waves break on a shore with a steep profile. Because there's nowhere for the water to escape, it retreats backwards under the next breaking wave, creating a **downward force** close to the shore. Unless you're very confident in the ocean, it's best not to mess around if the surf is big. By not getting out of your depth, you can use your feet to jump up into the oncoming waves and let their force push you toward the shore. If you do get caught in an undertow, don't panic, as the downward force only lasts a second or two and you'll soon surface. Catch a breath, duck under the next breaker, and then work your way steadily back to shore.

ARRIVAL AND DEPARTURE

EL TULATE

By bus A number of buses (every 30min; 1hr 45min) struggle down here every hour or so from both Retalhuleu and Mazatenango.

ACCOMMODATION AND EATING

Beach shacks offer fried fish and shrimps; these are the best places to **eat** in town.

Playa Paraíso 1km east of the centre ⓣ5952 8394. Ageing but reasonable beachside place offering comfortable-enough bungalows with verandas. There are two pools and a restaurant. $$$

Santa Lucía Cotzumalguapa and around

If you head east along the speedy Carretera al Pacífico past Mazatenango you'll soon approach **SANTA LUCÍA COTZUMALGUAPA**, an uninspiring Pacific town a short distance north of the highway. The only reason to visit the area is to take a quick peek at some (minor) nearby Pipil and Maya **archeological** sites, the colossal Olmec carved figures at nearby **La Democracia** or the **surf at Sipacate** to the south.

3

Bilbao

Uphill from Santa Lucía plaza, along 4 Av • Free • Best to visit by taxi (see below)

In 1880 more than thirty Late Classic stone monuments were removed from the Pipil site of **Bilbao**, and nine of the very best were shipped to Germany. Four sets of stones are still visible *in situ*, however, and two of them perfectly illustrate the magnificent precision of the carving, beautifully preserved in slabs of black volcanic rock. Two large stones are carved with bird-like patterns, with strange circular glyphs arranged in groups of three. In the same cane field, further along the same path, is another badly eroded stone, and a final set with a superbly preserved set of figures and interwoven motifs.

El Baúl

5km northeast of Santa Lucía • Free • Best to visit by taxi (see below)

This hilltop site has two **stone monuments**, one a standing figure wearing a skirt and a spectacular headdress, the other a massive half-buried stone head (known as Dios Mundo) with a wrinkled brow and patterned headdress – this is possibly Huhuetéotl, the fire god of the Mexicans. In front of the stones is a set of small altars on which local people make animal sacrifices, burn incense and leave offerings of flowers.

Finca El Baul

7km north of Santa Lucía • Free • Best to visit by taxi (see below)

In the grounds of **Finca El Baul**, kept under a shelter, are a series of interesting carvings including some superb heads, a stone skull, a massive jaguar and an extremely well-preserved stela of a ball-court player (Monument 27) dating from the Late Classic period. Alongside all this antiquity is the finca's old steam engine, a miniature machine that used to haul sugar cane.

Finca Las Ilusiones

1.5km east of Santa Lucía; 1km east of town and then 400m up a signposted side road on the left • Charge • Best to visit by taxi (see below)

At **Finca Las Ilusiones** a collection of artefacts and stone carvings has been assembled in the **Museo Cultura Cotzumalguapa**. Two of the most striking figures are an

Olmec-style pot-bellied statue (Monument 58), probably from the middle Preclassic era, and a copy of Monument 21, which bears three figures, the central one depicting a ball player. There are several other carved pieces, including a fantastic stela, plus some more replicas and thousands of small stone carvings and pottery fragments.

ARRIVAL AND GETTING AROUND — SANTA LUCÍA COTZUMALGUAPA

By bus Pullmans now use a new bypass that avoids the centre of town. Most second-class buses running along the highway will drop you at the entrance road to Santa Lucía. From Centra Sur terminal in Guatemala City, second-class buses (every 30min; 1hr 45min) run to Santa Lucia's terminal, which is a few blocks from the plaza.

By taxi It's best not to tour of the sites around Santa Lucía Cotzumalguapa on foot as it's easy to get lost and there have been muggings. Take round-trip by taxi – you'll find plenty in the plaza in varying degrees of decrepitude – to tour them all.

ACCOMMODATION

Hotel Internacional Just south of the Carretera al Pacífico ☎ 7882 5496. About 500m south of the centre of Santa Lucía Cotzumalguapa, this hotel has spacious rooms with either fan or a/c. $$

3

La Democracia

Just east of Santa Lucía Cotzumalguapa is the run-down settlement of Siquinalá, from where a there's a road south to the coastal resort of Sipacate. Taking this branch road you'll soon arrive in **LA DEMOCRACIA**, an orderly little town 17km from Santa Lucía that's of particular interest as the home of a collection of archeological relics. To the east of town lies the site of **Monte Alto**; many of the best pieces found there are now spread around La Democracia's renovated plaza, under a vast ceiba tree. These "fat boys" are massive Olmec-style **stone heads** with simple, almost childlike faces, grinning with Buddha-like contentment. Some are attached to smaller rounded bodies and rolled over on their backs, clutching their swollen stomachs. They probably date from the mid-Preclassic period, around 500 BC.

On the plaza, the town museum, **Museum Regional de Arqueología** (charge), houses carvings, ceremonial yokes worn by ball-game players, pottery, grinding stones, a wonderful jade mask and a few more carved heads.

ARRIVAL AND DEPARTURE — LA DEMOCRACIA

Regular **buses** to La Democracia (every 30min; 15min) leave Siquinalá on the highway.

Sipacate and Paredón

Some 58 km from Santa Lucía Cotzumalguapa, the low-key village of **SIPACATE** is located inside the Parque Natural Sipacate-Naranjo, a mangrove coastal reserve. The black sand beach here is separated from the village by the opaque waters of the **Canal de Chiquimulilla**; boats ferry a steady stream of passengers to the waves. The best surf here is about 5km to the east on the near-virgin sands of neighbouring **Paredón beach**, where a growing **surf scene** is drawing more and more travellers. Waves average 2m and are most consistent between December and April, though conditions are usually tough for beginners. There are surf reports posted on the **Paredón Surf House** website (see page 182).

Many travellers end up spending more time in Paredón than they'd anticipated, investing in quality hammock time during the day and combing the beach for nesting turtles. Do be very careful **swimming** in the always-powerful ocean: riptides are common and there are no lifeguards. There are no banks or ATMs nearby, so stock up beforehand, and bring suncream and insect repellent as the Paredón mosquitoes are notoriously hungry.

ARRIVAL AND DEPARTURE — SIPACATE AND PAREDÓN

By bus Regular buses to Sipacate (8 daily; 2hr) leave Siquinalá on the highway. There are also two daily buses from the Centra Sur terminal in Guatemala City to Sipacate (4hr). Once you're in Sipacate village you need to catch a public boat to reach the beach. (It's a little complicated to reach Paredón from Sipacate, but the *Paredón Surf House* website has clear instructions.)

By shuttle bus From Antigua direct shuttles are operated by both *Paredón Surf House* and *Driftwood Surfer* (2hr).

By car If you've got your own wheels, you can reach Paredón via Puerto San José (see page 182). Take the coast road past Juan Gaviota and El Carrizal; the last section is a dirt/sandy track.

ACCOMMODATION AND EATING

Cocori Lodge Beachside in Paredón ☎5580 5325. This simple setup has dorms (with mosquito nets and lockers) and basic accommodation. The team here are at hand for surf lessons; boards and kayaks can be rented. Dorms $, doubles $$

Driftwood Surfer Beachside in Paredón Ⓦthedriftwoodsurfer.net. This exciting English-/American-owned travellers' favourite has dorms and rooms (all accommodation has a/c and en-suite bathrooms), a pool and a great elevated bar that catches the sea breeze. There's a social vibe, roast dinners on Sundays and surfboards for rent. Dorms $, doubles $$

★ **Hotel Paredón Surf House** Beachside in Paredón Ⓦparedonsurf.com. This beautifully constructed place has lovely thatched bungalows with Bali-style outdoor bathrooms, a loft dorm with quality mattresses and some very pretty seafront *casitas*. There's a small oceanside pool, tasty grub ($$), a full bar and a relaxed ambience. Surf lessons are available for an hourly fee and there are boards for rent. Horse-riding and canoe tours of the mangroves are offered (charge) and there's beach volleyball, massage and occasional yoga classes. Cash only. Dorms $$, suites and *casitas* $$$$

Escuintla and around

Southeast of the capital, bustling **ESCUINTLA** ranks as Guatemala's third largest city with a population of around 140,000. Despite its size there's nothing to see here, but you do get a good sense of life on the coast – its heat, pace and energy, as well as the frenetic industrial and agricultural commerce that drives it. The city dominates this stretch of Pacific coast, along with **Puerto San José**, formerly its most important port – though neither place is at all attractive.

ARRIVAL AND DEPARTURE — ESCUINTLA

By bus Buses to Escuintla leave Centra Sur terminal in Guatemala City until about 8pm. There are two terminals in Escuintla: for places en route to the Mexican border, buses run through the north of town and stop by the Esso station opposite the Banco Uno; buses east towards El Salvador leave from the main terminal on the south side of town, at the bottom of 4 Av.

Destinations Antigua (every 40min; 1hr); Guatemala City (every 20min; 1hr 15min); Puerto San José (every 20min; 1hr).

ACCOMMODATION AND EATING

To **eat** fresh seafood in a casual atmosphere, head to the row of *cevicherias* on 1 C near the Plaza Palmeras mall.

A Blanqui 1 C 3–55, Zona 2 ☎7889 6811. A huge bustling place that specializes in fresh seafood, *ceviche* and fried fish – a mixed plate includes conch, shrimp, fish, sea snails and squid. Mariachis prowl the tables, and there's a great atmosphere at lunchtime and during the early afternoon. $$

Hotel Costa Sur 12 C 4–13 ☎7884 1456. If you get stuck here this fair-value hotel is a good option, with rooms with a/c and secure parking. $$

Puerto San José

South from Escuintla the coast road heads through acres of cattle pasture to **PUERTO SAN JOSÉ**, the capital's nearest and most popular, if run-down, resort. Everything is geared to extracting as many quetzales as possible from the rowdy day-trippers who fill the beach at weekends, while the poor-value hotels cater to a largely drunken clientele. If you want to spend time on the coast, head to Monterrico or Paredón instead.

ARRIVAL AND DEPARTURE — PUERTO SAN JOSÉ

By bus Buses run between San José and Guatemala City's Centra Sur terminal. For Monterrico get the first microbus to Iztapa (also known as Pueblo Viejo) and change there.
Destinations Escuintla (every 20min; 1hr); Guatemala City (every 20min; 2hr 15min); Iztapa (every 30min; 30min); Monterrico (3 daily; 1hr 30min).

Puerto Quetzal

Leaving San José and following the coast in either direction brings you to the beach resorts of Guatemala's wealthy elite, who have established their own enclaves with holiday homes built in a pale imitation of Miami. Just east of San José, there's a container port and a **marina** at **PUERTO QUETZAL** with good facilities for yachts. It's also one of the main bases for sportfishing excursions (see page 37) in Guatemala, though there are no hotels, just a restaurant and dozens of berths.

Iztapa and around

East of Puerto San José, it's 13km to **IZTAPA**, a venerable little place that's an important base for **sportfishing**. Iztapa is Guatemala's oldest port – Spanish leader Pedro de Alvarado built boats here that took him to Peru and back. There's little sense of this historical past in Iztapa today but the sleepy little town does have a vague, faded charm and a nice setting on the bank of the Canal de Chiquimulilla. The sweeping black sand beach is on the eastern side at a separate village called **Pueblo Viejo** – a bridge (charge) spans the canal. There's pretty reliable **surf** here with right-handers and an occasional hollow, and no crowds, with only a couple of local surfers.

Beyond Iztapa a paved road traces the 25km coastline from Pueblo Viejo to Monterrico through a littoral landscape punctuated with **loofah** farms. Patches of this coastline are being developed but there are still vast empty stretches of clean, dark sand to enjoy if you pull down one of the side tracks.

ARRIVAL AND DEPARTURE — IZTAPA

A number of **buses** run from Iztapa to Guatemala City (6 daily; 2hr 30min) and Monterrico (every 30min; 1hr).

ACCOMMODATION

Hotels in Iztapa are either basic, salt-bitten places that attract domestic tourists or luxury lodges offering all-inclusive packages for **sportfishermen**.

Buena Vista ⓦ buenavistasportfishing.com. Boasts a canalside plot, a pool and good facilities, though rooms are pretty average. There's plenty of fresh seafood served. Per-person packages normally include four anglers and four fishing days. $$$$

Pacific Fins Resort ⓦ pacificfinsresort.com. Very attractive, modern two-bedroom villas, a couple of private rooms and a pool in palm-tree-shaded grounds. All-inclusive per-person packages are based on four anglers and four fishing days. $$$$

The same location also owns and operates the nearby **Sailfish Bay Lodge** With eight high-quality beachfront rooms, a waveside pool, restaurant and hot tub. $$$$

EATING

El Capitán Facing the canal in Iztapa ⓣ 5769 1320. This substantial restaurant is famous for its seafood, including good *ceviche* and plates of tasty fried shrimp. $$$

Monterrico and around

The setting of **MONTERRICO** is one of the finest on the Pacific coast, with the scenery reduced to its basic elements: a strip of dead-straight sand, a line of powerful surf, a huge empty ocean and an enormous curving horizon. It's a friendly, if slightly scruffy place, fringed by the waters of the Canal de Chiquimulilla which weaves through a

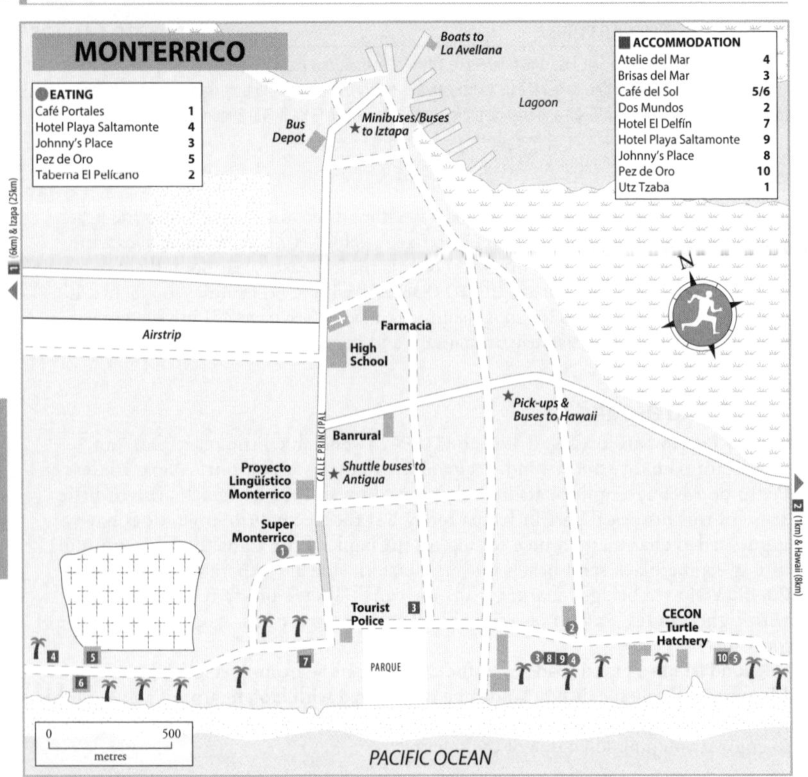

fantastic network of **mangrove swamps**. The atmosphere changes a little on weekends when party-geared visitors from the capital fill up the hotels.

Monterrico sits at the heart of the **Biotopo Monterrico–Hawaii**, a nature reserve that embraces a 20km-long beach-blessed slice of the Pacific coast and includes a vital turtle-nesting ground, abundant wetlands and the small villages of Monterrico and Hawaii. Sadly, however, the reserve's officially protected status does not prevent the widespread poaching of turtle eggs.

Monterrico beach

Monterrico's impressive **beach**, a prime turtle-nesting ground (see below), is a wide strip of dark grey sand that's continuously pummelled by the Pacific – with a power that sounds like rolling thunder. The beach's steep profile means there's usually a strong **undertow**. Lifeguards are posted here on weekends, but swimmers regularly get into trouble and drownings occur, so take great care. Squadrons of pelicans – flying in formation and nicknamed the "Monterrico air force" by locals – skim over the ocean, angling their wings to clip the crest of the wave as they glide along the coastline.

Turtle hatchery

Beachside, west of centre • Charge

Be sure to drop by the headquarters of CECON, which also runs the renowned local **turtle hatchery**. The visitor centre here occupies a large beachside area with a shaded section of sand where **turtle eggs** are reburied after they have been laid. A short trail runs from the headquarters along the edge of the reserve, past enclosures of freshwater turtles, alligators and green iguanas, which are also bred for release into the wild. There are information boards, some in English.

During nesting season, visitors can donate to the project by backing a turtle hatchling in the Saturday "**turtle race**" on the beach. Though CECON is otherwise responsible, and does some very good work, most experts are now uneasy about encouraging such races (as well as close contact or "petting" of turtles), as they involve grouping baby hatchlings together for days, a practice that exhausts and disorients the turtles and could interfere with the natal homing instinct by which they return to their beach of birth.

Mangrove swamp

Behind the beach and village, the extensive **mangrove swamp** is an unusually rich environment. These dark, nutrient-rich waters are superbly fertile, and four distinct types of mangrove form a dense mat of branches, interspersed with narrow canals, open lagoons, bulrushes and water lilies. The tangle of roots acts as a kind of **marine nursery**, offering small fish protection from their natural predators, while above the surface the dense vegetation and ready food supply provide an ideal home for hundreds of species of bird and a handful of reptiles and mammals, including racoon, iguana, alligator and opossum.

You should see a good range of **bird life**, including kingfisher, white heron and several species of duck. The Palmilla lagoon is a particularly good spot. Note, however, that if you **tour** the mangrove in a motorized boat you won't see much because the engine noise tends to frighten wildlife.

3

ARRIVAL, INFORMATION AND TOURS — MONTERRICO

By shuttle Shuttle buses link Monterrico with Antigua daily (2hr 15min), leaving Antigua at 8am and Monterrico at 4pm. Tickets can be bought at most hotels in Monterrico or from travel agents in Antigua.

By bus/minibus By public transport, there are two routes to Monterrico. The quickest way is via Puerto San José and Iztapa (but usually involves a bus change or two on the way). From Guatemala City's Centra Sur terminal buses leave for Monterrico (2 daily; 3hr 30min), Iztapa (6 daily; 2hr 30min) and Puerto San José (every 20min; 2hr 15min). There are very regular microbus links between Puerto San José and Iztapa (every 30min; 30min) and Iztapa and Monterrico (every 30min; 1hr) until 6pm. The other route is complicated and longer, perhaps taking four hours or so. Start by jumping aboard a bus bound for the El Salvador border at Ciudad Pedro de Alvarado (leaving every 30min from Centra Sur), alight at Taxisco, from where buses trundle down to La Avellana, and then get a boat to Monterrico.

By boat Boats (8 daily; 40min) charge per shuttle passenger or car between Monterrico and La Avellana.

Information Check out the community website, ⓦmonterrico-guatemala.com, for hotel and transport information.

Tours Local guides (look for them by the turtle hatchery; they have ID badges) can arrange tours of the mangroves. Or you can rent a *cayuco* (charge per hour) and paddle around yourself from the dock.

ACCOMMODATION

All Monterrico's accommodation is right on or just off the **beach**. Many places up their prices by 20–30 percent at weekends, when it's also best to book ahead.

Atelie del Mar Turn right before the beach and walk for 300m ⓦhotelateliedelmar.com; map page 184. Owned by a Finnish-Guatemalan couple, this couple- and family-friendly hotel is across the street from the beach and has lush gardens that surround two pools. All rooms have a/c, TVs, and reliable wi-fi, and breakfast at the (otherwise somewhat pricey) restaurant is included. **$$$$**

Brisas del Mar Turn left just before the beach; it's on the left ⓣ5500 0811, map page 184. This motel-like place has forty keenly priced bungalows (with fan or a/c) that are in decent shape, with private bathrooms, mosquito nets and good beds. All face a garden and large remodelled pool. There's a restaurant. Rooms with a/c are extra. **$$**

Café del Sol Turn right at the beach, 250m to the west ⓦfacebook.com/HotelCafedelSol; map page 184. Boasts a lovely beach-facing frontage, with sunbeds facing the ocean. It's a well-run place with a wide choice of accommodation divided between inland and beachside blocks. There's a restaurant, hot tub and three pools. **$$$**

THE TURTLES OF MONTERRICO

The huge, sparsely populated expanses of beach around Monterrico are prime nesting sites for three types of **sea turtle**, including the largest of them all, the giant leatherback. The **reserve** was originally established to protect the turtles from the soup pot and curb the collection of their **eggs**, which are considered an aphrodisiac in Guatemala. Further dangers to the turtles include being hunted for their shells, drowned inside fishing nets and poisoned by pollution, especially plastic bags that resemble jellyfish, a favourite food. Turtles almost always **nest** in the dark, and on a moonless night during egg-laying season, you have a good chance of seeing one in Monterrico.

LEATHERBACK

The gargantuan **leatherback** is by far the largest of the world's turtles, growing up to 3m in length and weighing up to 900kg. Called *baule* in Spanish, the leatherback gives the beach at Monterrico its name. They feed almost exclusively on jellyfish, diving as deep as 1200m below the surface in search of prey. It's the only turtle not to have a hard exterior shell; instead it has a layer of black, soft, rubbery skin. The leatherback frequents tropical and temperate waters from Malaysia to Scotland and makes one of the longest **migrations** of any creature on earth – one turtle was tracked journeying 20,000km from Indonesia to the US. The species, which has been around for one hundred million years, is in severe danger of **extinction** as a result of long-line fishing and gill netting. It nests at Monterrico between mid-October and late December. Nestings have plummeted in the Monterrico region in recent years, with only a handful recorded now each season.

3

OLIVE RIDLEY

Spread throughout the tropical waters of the Pacific, Atlantic and Indian oceans, the **olive ridley** is the most numerous of the world's eight species of marine turtle and also one of the smallest, typically around 80cm long and weighing around 35kg. Olive ridleys gather in huge numbers off favoured beaches to mate, after which the females return en masse to nest. They are **omnivores**, feeding on fish and shrimp as well as sea grass and algae. They are common visitors at Monterrico (where they are known as *parlamas*) during their nesting season between July and December.

GREEN TURTLE

Green turtles reach more than 1m in length, typically weigh 200kg and have a characteristic dark heart-shaped shell. They are found throughout the tropics and are mainly herbivores, eating sea grasses. Historically, green turtles have been killed for their fat in many parts of the world. It's this fat, which is green in colour – their shells are usually muddy brown or grey – that gives the turtle its name. The green turtle nesting season in Monterrico is also from July to December.

NESTING

All the species of turtle use similar **nesting techniques**, hauling themselves up the beach, laboriously digging a hole about 50cm deep with their flippers, and then with great effort depositing a clutch of a hundred or so soft, golfball-sized eggs. The turtles then bury the eggs and head back into the ocean. The eggs of the two smaller turtles take about fifty days to hatch, those of the leatherback require 72. When their time comes, the tiny turtles, no larger than the palm of your hand, use their flippers to dig their way out and make a mad dash for the water, desperately trying to avoid the waiting sea birds. Once they are in the water, their existence is still very hazardous for the first few years of life; only one in a hundred makes it to maturity.

Hotel El Delfín On the right at the beachfront ☎ 5702 6701; map page 184. This rambling place is owned by an enthusiastic, welcoming British-Guatemalan couple. All rooms have fans and mosquito nets, and a few have a/c (extra); the best bets are those that face the central patio. You'll find an international vibe, pool, bar, cheap food, semi-reliable wi-fi, and complimentary coffee in the mornings, plus iced water throughout the day. Your fourth night is free.

Dorms $, doubles $$

Hotel Playa Saltamonte Just off the beach 5456 9854, hotel.playa.saltamonte@gmail.com; map page 184. The Swiss-German owners of this hotel offer four clean, stylish rooms; rates include breakfast. There are two (small) pools and a restaurant, plus *Bar Bambas* on the upper level (see below). $$$

Johnny's Place Turn left at the beach and walk for 150m johnnysplacehotel.com map page 184. A backpacking favourite, with an enticing beachside location and nice chill-out zone (a *palapa* with hammocks). It offers a well-designed new beachside block (with simple rooms and beach-facing suites), bungalows (some ancient, some renovated), plus a/c rooms and a family-sized apartment. There's a main pool, and several bungalows have their own small pools as well. The party vibe has been turned down a notch recently but the bar still rocks on weekends (and serves good food). Dorms $, doubles $$

Dos Mundos 1.5km east of the centre hotelsdosmundos.com; map page 184. Luxurious option, with fourteen stunning, minimalist, *palapa*-roofed, detached a/c bungalows, each with a huge terrace and swanky bathroom, set in beachfront gardens. There's a fine pool overlooking the rollers, a kids' pool and a good, if pricey, restaurant. Rates include breakfast. $$$$

★ **Pez de Oro** Turn left at the beach and walk for 350m 5232 9534; map page 184. An attractive place to stay, with lovely, spotless, thatched cottages, all with mosquito nets, wooden furniture, and bedcovers made from Guatemalan textiles (nos. 1 and 13 have sea views). There are two palm-shaded pool areas and the beach-facing restaurant serves fine Italian and international food. $$$

Utz Tzaba About 6km before Monterrico in the pueblo of El Pumpo utz-tzaba.com; map page 184. A smart Dutch-owned place with immaculate a/c rooms and bungalows (each with living room and two bedrooms, some with kitchens) on a spacious seafront plot; there's a large pool, hot tub and a bar area. $$$$

EATING AND DRINKING

The **comedores** on C Principal all have near-identical menus (large portions of fried fish and shrimp) while on the beach itself the cuisine is more international.

Café Portales C Principal; map page 184. In the courtyard behind the Super Monterrico, this local favourite offers premium beer, wine and cocktails along with iced or hot coffee and pastries. There's wi-fi and plenty of shaded seating. $$

Hotel Playa Saltamonte Just off the beach 5456 9854, hotel.playa.saltamonte@gmail.com; map page 184. This hotel's bar-restaurant serves good breakfasts, fresh fish, shrimp and pasta dishes. On the upper level *Bar Bambas* has great ocean views and a good vibe. $$$

Johnny's Place Turn left at the beach and walk for 150m johnnysplacehotel.com; map page 184. Waveside café/bar that's renowned for its *ceviche*, which is available in four different styles, and also offers an extensive menu. There's some DJ and dance action most Saturdays. $$

Pez de Oro Turn left at the beach and walk for 350m 5232 9534; map page 184. This hotel restaurant has a pretty beachfront dining area with checked tablecloths and Italian food including fresh fish, salads, pasta and sandwiches.

★ **Taberna El Pelícano** Behind Johnny's Place 4001 5885; map page 184. Briga, the Swiss chef, serves fine European food, including fresh pasta, prime cuts of meat and grilled fish. The attractive thatched premises have atmosphere and make up for the lack of sea views. Well worth dropping by for lunch, when there's a daily special. Book ahead on weekends. $$$

DIRECTORY

Banks There are two banks; Banrural has an ATM.

Emergencies Contact PROATUR first on 5460 7045 or 1500.

Internet There are a couple of places on C Principal. Most hotels have wi-fi.

Language lessons Proyecto Lingüístico Monterrico (facebook.com/monterricoespanol) on the main drag, offers inexpensive one-on-one Spanish instruction and the option of full board with a family.

Hawaii

About 7km east along the beach from Monterrico, isolated **HAWAII** is a tiny, relaxed little fishing village. Other than the **turtle sanctuary**, the magnificent empty beach is the only sight in town.

Turtle sanctuary

Beachside, entrance to village • Donation appreciated • 5849 8988

Hawaii's large **turtle sanctuary**, run by the environmental group ARCAS, releases thousands of turtles each year. There's plenty to see, with a couple of trails, egg-count charts and lots of information about turtles and the myths and beliefs associated with them throughout the world. **Volunteers** are always needed (at any time of year, though June to November is the main nesting season). The work is primarily nocturnal, involving walking the beach collecting sea-turtle eggs and assisting in the management of the hatcheries. You can also help with environmental education, mangrove reforestation, construction and caiman and iguana captive-breeding.

ARRIVAL AND INFORMATION — HAWAII

By bus Buses connect Hawaii with Monterrico (every 1hr 30min; 30min).

ACCOMMODATION

Hotel Honolulu Beachside in the village hotelhonolulu.com.gt. Well-constructed, detached, screened wooden bungalows in neat beachside gardens plus two pools and restaurant. It's a little overpriced, but very peaceful (during the week). $$$$

From Escuintla to El Salvador

Heading east from Escuintla, after skirting a Guatemalan safari park the coastal highway passes **TAXISCO**, from where you can access La Avellana (which has boats to

FIESTAS ALONG THE PACIFIC COAST

Ladino culture dominates on the Pacific coast, so fiestas here tend to be more along the lines of fairs, with parades, amusement rides, fireworks, sporting events and heavy drinking.

JANUARY

12–15 Taxisco, events include bullfighting.
12–16 Colomba, events include bullfighting.

MARCH

11–19 Coatepeque, main day March 15.
16–22 Puerto San José, main day March 19.
Varies Ocós.

APRIL AND MAY

30–May 4 Chiquimulilla, main day May 3.

JULY

25 Coatepeque, in honour of Santiago Apóstol.

AUGUST

4–8 Champerico, main day Aug 6.

OCTOBER

20–26 Iztapa, main day Oct 24.

NOVEMBER

23–26 Siquinalá.

DECEMBER

6–12 Retalhuleu, main day Dec 8.
6–15 Escuintla, main day Dec 8.

Monterrico). Beyond here, lonely side roads lead to isolated beaches, including Las Lisas.

Auto Safari Chapín

Charge • autosafarichapin.com

The **Auto Safari Chapín** is Central America's only safari-style park. Here you'll find giraffes, hippos, water buffalo, tapir and big cats including African lions, pumas and jaguar. There's a superbly comprehensive collection of Central American animals, snakes and birds. The park is clean and well organized with viewing platforms and wildlife trails, and the animals are well cared for. The entrance fee entitles you to a trip through the park in a minibus, although you can drive yourself if you have a car, and there are swimming pools, a restaurant and picnic areas.

Las Lisas

A short distance before the border with El Salvador a side road runs off to the seashore village of **LAS LISAS**, which has no attractions of any sort but makes a nice place to kick back for a while spending time by the sea.

ARRIVAL AND DEPARTURE — LAS LISAS

There are regular **buses** between Las Lisas and the turn-off on the Carretera al Pacífico (hourly 7am–5pm; 30min).

ACCOMMODATION

Eco Hotel Playa Quilombo de Cucurumbé playaquilombo.net. Run by a welcoming couple from Belgium and Mexico, this simple hotel has a barefoot vibe, with charming rustic cabañas, a pool and a broad black sand beach to explore. The restaurant menu ($$) features seafood, salads and good veggie options. It's a 20min boat ride from the Las Lisas dock. Doubles $$, cabañas $$$$

Isleta de Gaia On a sandy offshore islet 7885 0044. This remote hotel has twelve bamboo-and-thatch bungalows with either ocean or lagoon views. There's a big pool, food prepared by a French chef and a lovely clean beach – though as ever you should watch out for the undertow (see page 179). You'll have to rent a boat to get to the hotel from the village of Las Lisas. $$$$

Ciudad Pedro de Alvarado

The coastal highway finally reaches the border with El Salvador at the small settlement of **CIUDAD PEDRO DE ALVARADO**. Most of the commercial traffic and all of the pullman buses use the highland route to El Salvador, and consequently things are fairly quiet and easy-going here.

ARRIVAL AND DEPARTURE — CIUDAD PEDRO DE ALVARADO

By bus Second-class buses run to and from Guatemala City every 30min or so until about 7pm, though minibuses run later to Chiquimulilla.

Crossing the El Salvadorean border The border at Ciudad Pedro de Alvarado is open 24 hours. The few places to stay on the Guatemalan side are run-down.

PENSION
9 CALLE

The Oriente and Izabal

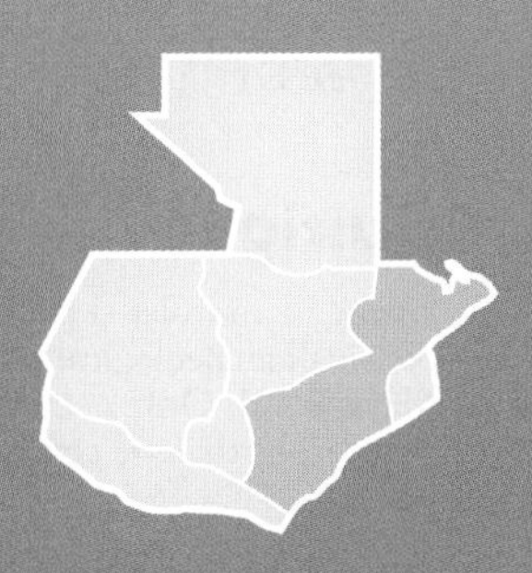

BASÍLICA DE ESQUIPULAS

The Oriente and Izabal

The region east of Guatemala City is the most disparate part of the country – a mix of near-desert, rainforest, mountains and lakes peopled by ladinos, creoles and isolated pockets of Maya. Close to the capital is a seldom-visited region of dry, sun-scorched hills known as the Oriente, centred on the towns of Chiquimula and Esquipulas. The eastern section of Guatemala, the department of Izabal, could not be more different. Here the climate is always thick with humidity and the land has a decidedly sultry, tropical feel, with rainforest reserves, a Caribbean coastline, a vast lake and a dramatic gorge system to explore.

Densely populated in Maya times, this region served as an important trade route and also was one of the main sources of **jade**. Connecting the capital with the Caribbean, the Motagua valley is a broad corridor of low-lying land between two high mountain ranges. Following the decline of Maya civilization, the area lay virtually abandoned until the end of the nineteenth century when the **United Fruit Company** established huge banana plantations and reaped massive profits. Today bananas are still the main crop, though cattle ranching is becoming increasingly important.

For the traveller, the main draw is exploring idyllic **Río Dulce** and the **Lago de Izabal** area – a vast expanse of fresh water ringed by isolated villages, rich wetlands and hot springs. The most spectacular section is undoubtedly the **Río Dulce gorge**, which is close to the coastal town of **Lívingston**, a laidback place that's home to Afro-Carib Garífuna people. You could also drop by the fascinating Maya ruins and giant stelae of **Quiriguá**, just off the main highway, the Carretera al Atlántico. South of here, the **Oriente** offers some magnificent scenery, with the **Ipala volcano** and its crater lake a particular highlight. **Esquipulas**, home of the famous black Christ and the scene of Central America's largest annual pilgrimage, is another curiosity.

The Motagua valley

Leaving Guatemala City, the main highway descends through the dry **Motagua valley**, a distinctly inhospitable landscape with cacti spiking the barren hillsides. The first place of any note is the **Río Hondo junction** where the road divides: one arm heads south to the Oriente and town of Esquipulas, while the main branch continues on to the coast.

Further down the valley the landscape starts to undergo a radical transformation; the flood plain opens out and there's a profusion of tropical growth. It was this supremely rich flood plain that was chosen by both the Maya and the United Fruit Company, to the great benefit of both.

Quiriguá

Sitting in an isolated pocket of rainforest, surrounded by an ocean of banana trees, the small archeological site of **Quiriguá** has some of the finest carvings in the entire Maya world. Only nearby Copán can match the magnificent **stelae**, altars and zoomorphs that are covered in well-preserved and superbly intricate glyphs and portraits.

The **ruins** are situated 69km beyond the junction at Río Hondo, and 4km from the main road, reached down a side road that serves the banana industry. Weather

STELA AT QUIRIGUÁ

Highlights

❶ **Quiriguá's carvings** This miniature Maya site in the midst of the rainforest yields astonishing riches, with colossal stelae and some of the finest carved altars in the entire Maya world. See page 195

❷ **Lívingston nightlife** Party punta-style with the Garífuna in the laidback beach bars of this captivating Caribbean town. See page 203

❸ **Río Dulce** Cruising through this soaring, jungle-clad gorge and exploring its magical tributaries is an exhilarating experience. See page 203

❹ **Hot-spring waterfall** Soak away an afternoon or two at the exquisite and highly unusual hot-spring-fed waterfall at the *Finca el Paraíso*. See page 206

❺ **Volcán de Ipala** At the summit of this remote, forest-fringed volcano is a stunning crater lake that is perfect for swimming. See page 210

❻ **Esquipulas** A vast basilica that's home to an ancient carving of a black Christ – the focus for the largest pilgrimage in Central America. See page 211

HIGHLIGHTS ARE MARKED ON THE MAP ON PAGE 194

conditions are decidedly **tropical**. Indeed, cloudbursts are the rule and the buzz of mosquitoes is almost uninterrupted – bring repellent.

Brief history

Quiriguá's early history is still relatively unknown, but during the Late Preclassic period (250 BC–300 AD) migrants from the north established themselves as rulers here. In the Early Classic period (250–600 AD), the area was dominated by **Copán**, just 50km away, with Quiriguá no doubt valued for its position on the banks of the Río Motagua, an important trade route and as a source of jade. It was during the rule of the great leader **Cauac Sky** that Quiriguá challenged Copán, capturing its leader, Eighteen Rabbit, in 738 AD and beheading him, probably with the backing of the "superpower" city of Calakmul. Quiriguá was then able to assert its independence and embark on a building boom: most of the great stelae date from this period. For a century Quiriguá dominated the lower Motagua valley. Under **Jade Sky**, who took the throne in 790, Quiriguá reached its peak, with fifty years of extensive building work, including a radical reconstruction of the acropolis. Towards the end of Jade

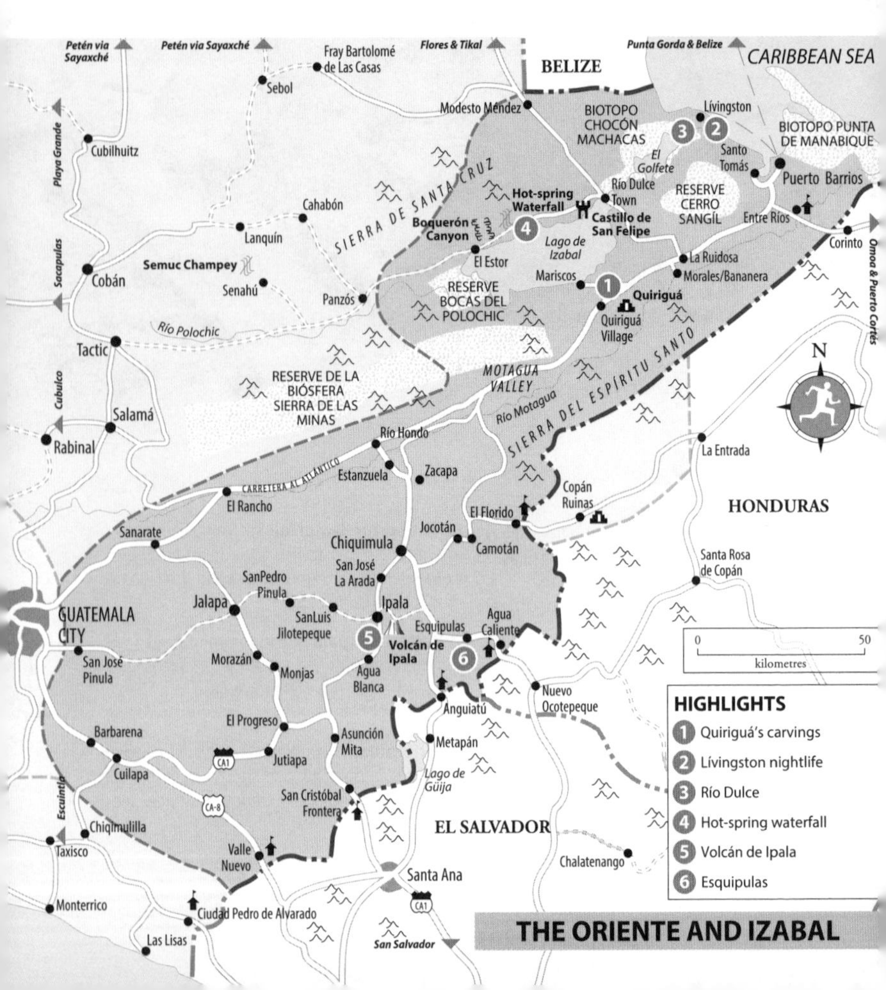

Sky's rule, in the middle of the ninth century, the historical record fades out, as does the period of prosperity and power.

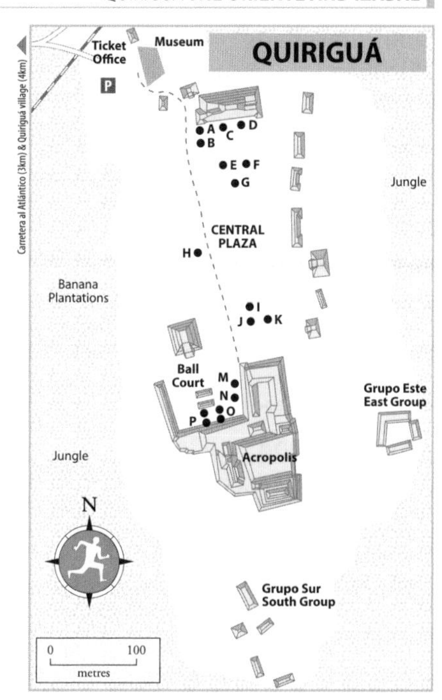

Quiriguá ruins

Charge

Entering the site you emerge at the northern end of the **Great Plaza**. On the left is a badly ruined pyramid, while directly ahead are the **stelae** for which Quiriguá is justly famous.

Stelae

The nine **stelae** in the plaza are the tallest in the Maya world and the quality of carving is remarkable. Similar in style in many ways to that of Copán, they feature portraits on the principal faces of the standing monuments and glyphs covering the sides. As for the figures, they represent the city's rulers, with Cauac Sky depicted on no fewer than seven (A, C, D, E, F, H and J). Two unusual features are particularly clear: the vast headdresses, which dwarf the faces, and the beards. Many of the figures are shown clutching a ceremonial bar, the symbol of office. The **glyphs**, crammed into the remaining space, record dates and events during the reign of the relevant ruler.

Largest of the stelae is E, which towers impressively at a height of 8m and weighs a massive 65 tonnes. All the stelae are carved from a fine-grained sandstone. Fortunately for the sculptors the stone was soft once it had been cut, and fortunately for us it hardened with age.

Zoomorphs

Another feature that has helped Quiriguá earn its fame is the series of bizarre, altar-like **zoomorphs**: six blocks of stone carved with interlacing animal and human figures. Some, like the turtle, frog and jaguar, can be recognized with relative ease, while others are either too faded or too elaborate to be easily made out. The best of the lot is P, which shows a figure seated in a Buddha-like pose.

Ball court and acropolis

At the southern end of the plaza, near the main zoomorphs, you can just make out the shape of a **ball court** hemmed in on three sides by viewing stands. The **acropolis** itself, the only structure of any real size that still stands, is bare of decoration. Trenches dug beneath it have shown that it was built on top of several previous versions, the earliest ones constructed out of rough river stones.

Museum

A small site **museum** has informative displays about the site's historical significance and its geo-political role in Maya times as well as a diorama showing the extent of the ruins that remain unexcavated.

Quiriguá village

The **village** – also known as Quiriguá – is just off the highway, about 2km back towards Guatemala City. It's a run-down sort of place, strung out along the railway track, but in the past it was famous for its hospital specializing in the treatment of tropical diseases, run by the United Fruit Company. This imposing building, which still stands on the hill above the track, is now a state-run workers' medical centre; there's a statue of Scottish doctor Neil Macphail (who ran the hospital here for forty years) in front of the structure.

ARRIVAL AND DEPARTURE — QUIRIGUÁ

By bus All buses running between Puerto Barrios and Guatemala City pass the turn-off for the ruins. From the turn-off tuk-tuks and motorbikes shuttle passengers back and forth to the archeological site.

On foot to the village If you want to walk back to Quiriguá village, you can take a short cut by heading towards the highway for 2km along the access road, then turning left (west) and following the (disused) train track – it's a further 1km to the village.

ACCOMMODATION

Hotel y Restaurante Royal Quiriguá village 5715 2810. Basic place with simple rooms, some with private bathrooms, that will do for a night. You can also get a meal of cheap *comida típica* here. $$$

Posada de Quiriguá Hillside above Quiriguá village 5349 5817. Japanese-owned guesthouse with immaculately clean rooms in a fertile garden setting. The doubles are very spacious. You'll find the food a real highlight, with fine Guatemalan and Japanese meals, good vegetarian choices and wonderful home-made drinking chocolate. It's not signposted, but tuk-tuk drivers know the place. $$

4

Puerto Barrios and around

Heading on towards the Caribbean from Quiriguá, the road traverses an evergreen landscape of cattle ranches and fruit trees, passing a junction for the ramshackle twin towns of **Morales** and **Bananera** (where non-express buses make a stop). A short distance beyond here you pass another junction, this one known as **La Ruidosa**, where the road splits: the highway to Petén heads north via Río Dulce Town, while if you continue east it's a further 49km to Puerto Barrios. Beyond Barrios, and only accessible by boat, is the **Punta de Manabique** peninsula, home to fine white sand beaches and wildlife-rich wetlands.

Puerto Barrios

Though in recent years hot and sprawling **PUERTO BARRIOS** has seen something of an upturn in its fortunes, with key infrastructure – including the container port – being modernized, it remains a pretty forlorn place. Barrios' once-fine legacy of old wooden Caribbean-style buildings has virtually disappeared, only to be replaced by faceless concrete blocks and an excess of hard-drinking bars. The only reason most travellers come here is to get somewhere else: to Lívingston or Belize by boat, or east to Honduras.

The town was founded in the 1880s by President Rufino Barrios, but its port facilities soon fell into the hands of the **United Fruit Company**, who used their control of the railways to ensure that the bulk of trade passed this way.

The mercado

The **mercado**, sprawling around disused railway lines at the corner of 9 Calle and 6 Avenida, is the town's main focus and the best place to start to get a feel for Barrios' modern identity. Lines of ladino vendors furiously whisk up lush fruit *licuado* drinks from a battery of blenders, while Garífuna women swat flies from piles of *pan de coco.*

Hotel del Norte

7 C & 1 Av

If you walk west along 7 Calle from the market, it's about 800m to the last surviving landmark of Barrios' Caribbean architectural heritage, the elegant **Hotel del Norte** (see below), its timber corridors warped by a century of storms and salty

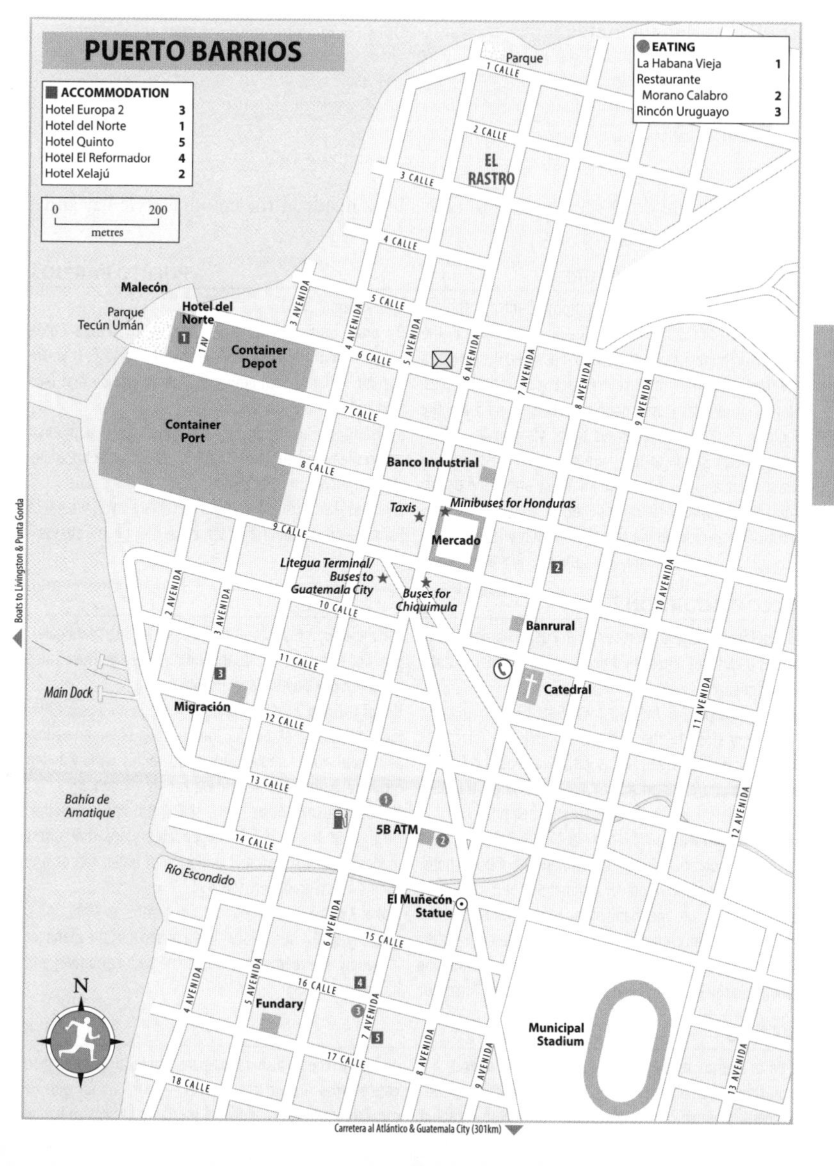

THE HONDURAS BORDER: PUERTO BARRIOS

Puerto Barrios is the jumping-off point to the **north coast of Honduras**, a fairly straightforward, if slow, journey. Minibuses depart from the *mercado* (every 30min; 1hr) and pass through the town of **Entre Ríos** (for *migración*) before continuing on to the border. You may be asked for unofficial border taxes of a dollar or two as you pass through, despite Honduras and Guatemala creating a customs union in 2018 (see page 209). Note that travellers with their own vehicles have reported lengthy delays and some less than official red tape entering Honduras here. The El Florido border further south is much less hassle if you are travelling with your own vehicle.

On the **Honduran side**, buses leave the border post at Corinto for Puerto Cortés (hourly; 2hr) via Omoa. If you set out early from Puerto Barrios, you should get to San Pedro Sula well before noon, from where it's certainly possible to catch an afternoon flight to one of the Bay Islands (or even make it to La Ceiba for the late afternoon boats to the Bay Islands).

air. Even if you don't stay, be sure to take a look inside at the colonial-style bar and dining room.

ARRIVAL AND DEPARTURE — PUERTO BARRIOS

By bus Puerto Barrios lacks a purpose-built bus station. Litegua buses (T 2326 9595, W litegua.com), some of the best in Guatemala, serve all destinations along the Carretera al Atlántico from a terminal at 6 Av, between 9 and 10 calles. Note that *directos* (some double-deckers) don't leave the highway, but non-direct buses travel via Morales, which adds at least 30min to the journey. Second-class buses to Chiquimula and microbuses to Río Dulce arrive and depart from a stop opposite Litegua's depot.

Destinations Chiquimula (hourly; 4hr 30min); Guatemala City (21 daily; 5hr 30min–6hr 30min); Río Dulce Town (every 40min; 2hr).

By boat *Lanchas* leave for Lívingston and Punta Gorda in Belize from the main dock at the end of 12 C. If you're heading to Belize, remember to clear *migración* first (see box) and pay your exit tax.

Destinations Lívingston (5 scheduled daily, additional services leave when full; 30min); Punta Gorda, Belize (daily 10am, 1pm & 2pm; 1hr 15min).

By taxi Taxis (called *carreras* here) are everywhere in Barrios – drivers tout for customers as they ply the streets.

ACCOMMODATION

Budget **hotels** are in short supply in Puerto Barrios, and as this is a very hot and humid town, you'll definitely want a fan, if not a/c.

Hotel Europa 2 3 Av &12 C T 7948 1292; map page 197. Very close to the dock, this motel-style place has decent (if ageing) clean rooms with two beds and TV with either fan or a/c. It's priced per person, so single travellers get a good deal and the owners are very helpful. $$

★ **Hotel del Norte** 7 C & 1 Av T 7948 0087; map page 197. A landmark, highly atmospheric Caribbean hotel, built entirely from wood. Unfortunately the facilities are pretty historic too, and many of the rooms lack bathrooms, but with this much faded style and heritage on offer the comfort levels are adequate enough. There's a swimming pool, and the location, overlooking the Bahía de Amatique and *malecón*, is magnificent. Meals, served in a mahogany-panelled restaurant are disappointing, however. There's also a modern block with bland a/c rooms. $$$

Hotel Quinto 7 Av & 16 C T 7948 8553; map page 197. Modern hotel (look out for the arresting blue-and-yellow paint job) with simple, very clean rooms with wooden furniture; bathrooms are cold water only, though. $$

Hotel El Reformador 7 Av & 16 C W hotelelreformador.com; map page 197. A dependable place that offers modern rooms set around patios, with either fan or a/c. There's a restaurant here too. $$$

Hotel Xelajú 8 Av, between 8 & 9 calles T 7948 0482; map page 197. Yes, it looks like a prison, but the manager is friendly, the rooms are clean (some with bathroom) and it's very secure. $$

EATING

Puerto Barrios really excels at **fish and seafood**, and you should certainly try some *tapado* (seafood soup with coconut, plantain and spices) while you're here – though it's not a cheap dish to prepare. There are some good **comedores** around the market – look out for *pan de coco* (coconut bread) and local speciality *tortillas de harina* (wheat tortillas stuffed with meat and beans).

La Habana Vieja 13 C, between 6 & 7 avs ⓣ 5617 8193; map page 197. Run by very welcoming Cuban exiles, and offering excellent meat dishes, a set lunch, good mojitos and coffee. There's an a/c interior and small street terrace. They sell Cuban rum, beer and cigars. $$$

Restaurante Morano Calabro 13 C, between 7 & 8 avs ⓣ 7948 1444; map page 197. A real find in Barrios, this authentic Italian restaurant has *antipasti* with imported meats and olives, excellent pasta and pizza, fish and meat dishes, a good wine selection and attentive, welcoming owners. $$

Rincón Uruguayo 7 Av & 16 C ⓣ 7948 6803; map page 197. Meat-eaters won't do better than this excellent place, which excels at *parrilladas* (South American-style meat barbecues) and has outside seating. $$$

DIRECTORY

Banks Banrural at 8 Av & 9 C, and Banco Industrial at 7 Av & 7 C; both have ATMs.

Immigration office The *migración* office is on 12 C, a block inland from the dock (ⓣ 5294 3628).

Post office 6 C & 6 Av.

Punta de Manabique

North of Puerto Barrios is **Punta de Manabique**, a hooked peninsula that juts into the Bahía de Amatique and contains many of Guatemala's best **beaches**. Most of the area has been designated a **nature reserve**. It's one of the richest wetland habitats in Central America, and the swamps, mangroves and patches of flooded rainforest are home to caiman, iguana, spider and howler monkeys, peccary, plus a few manatee, some jaguar, tapir and bountiful birdlife, including the extremely rare yellow-headed parrot (*Amazona oratrix*). The reserve also includes the adjacent coastal water and the only coral-reef outcrops in Guatemalan waters.

More than one thousand people eke out a living in Manabique, surviving by subsistence fishing (mainly for sardines, which are then salted), hunting (particularly iguana) and cultivating small rice paddies, though their livelihood is increasingly under threat from cattle ranchers. Efforts have been made to promote **ecotourism** in the area, but the main drawback is the cost of fuel needed to get here (access is only by boat).

4

INFORMATION AND TOURS — PUNTA DE MANABIQUE

Organized trips Speak to Lívingston tour operators including Exotic Travel (see page 202), about trips to Manabique. Prices very much depend on numbers.

Lívingston

Enjoying a superb setting overlooking the Bahía de Amatique, **LÍVINGSTON** offers a unique fusion of Guatemalan and Caribbean culture where marimba mixes with Marley. The town acts as a hub for both the displaced **Garífuna**, or Black Caribs (see page 200) and also for the Q'eqchi' Maya of the Río Dulce region.

Lívingston is undoubtedly one of the most fascinating places in Guatemala, but travellers' opinions about it tend to be sharply divided: many enjoy the languid rhythm of life and Lívingston's slightly ramshackle appeal while others just find the town shabby. Whichever your take, Lívingston certainly offers a welcome break from mainstream ladino culture: **Carib food** is generally excellent and varied, and Garífuna punta rock and reggae make a pleasant change from merengue and salsa. Another excellent reason to come to Lívingston is to take the spectacular trip through the **Río Dulce gorge** (see page 203).

The general atmosphere is pretty chilled, but not unaffected by the pressures of daily life in Central America. While Lívingston is not a threatening place, and there are no particular security concerns, the town does have its share of small-time **hustlers** eager to sell weed to travellers or scrounge a beer.

GARÍFUNA HISTORY AND CULTURE

The Garífuna people trace their history back to the island of **St Vincent** in the eastern Caribbean. In 1635 two Spanish ships carrying slaves from Nigeria were wrecked off the island, and in the following decades the survivors mixed with resident Native Americans, forming an **Afro-Carib** race. In their own language, they are *Garinagu*, or **Garífuna** – "cassava-eating people".

For years attempts by the British to gain control of St Vincent were repelled by the Garífuna, who were aided by the French. In 1783 the British imposed a treaty on the Garífuna, but they continued to defy British rule until 1796, when, after a year of bitter fighting, the French and the Garífuna surrendered.

The colonial authorities could not allow a free black society to survive, and a decision was made to deport the Garífuna, who were mercilessly hunted down. Hundreds died of starvation and disease. In March 1797, the remaining 2200 or so were loaded aboard ships and sent to **Roatán**, one of the Honduran Bay Islands, where they were abandoned.

SETTLEMENT IN CENTRAL AMERICA

Most Garífuna migrated from Roatán to the mainland where they worked as labourers, farmers and soldiers. In 1802, 150 Garífuna were taken as wood-cutters to southern Belize, from where they moved to **Lívingston** in 1806.

By the start of the twentieth century, the Garífuna were well established in the Lívingston area, with the women employed in bagging and stacking *cohune* nuts and the men working as fishermen. The Garífuna continued to travel widely in search of work, particularly in the **merchant navy**. Since the 1970s, many have left Central America for the US, where there's now a fifty thousand-strong population in New York. Today most Garífuna live in villages along the Caribbean coast of Honduras (a population of more than one hundred thousand) with smaller populations in Belize (around twenty thousand) and Nicaragua.

4

GARÍFUNA IN GUATEMALA

For many Guatemalans, the Garífuna remain something of a national curiosity. They are not only subjected to **discrimination**, but also viewed with a strange awe that gives rise to a range of fanciful myths, including accusations of voodoo. Such prejudices, and the isolated nature of the community – numbering only around eight thousand in Guatemala – mean many young Garífuna are more drawn to African-American (hip-hop) and Jamaican (rastafari) influences than to Latin culture.

LANGUAGE AND RELIGION

Most Garífuna speak Spanish (and some English) plus the unique Garífuna **language** that blends Arawak, Carib, French, English, Spanish and a few African words. Though virtually all worship at church, their Afro-Carib **dugu** (religion) – centred on ancestor worship – continues to be actively practised. *Dugu* is immersed in ritual, and death is seen as the freeing of a spirit, a celebration that involves dancing, drinking and music.

PUNTA MUSIC

Garífuna music, or **punta**, is furiously rhythmic, characterized by mesmeric drum patterns and ritual chanting, and it's very easy to hear its West African origins. The late **Andy Palacio** is the most renowned Garífuna musician; his 2007 album *Wátina* is considered his masterpiece. Critically acclaimed *Umalali: The Garífuna Women's Project* is another superb compilation of Garífuna music.

Lívingston beaches

The local palm-fringed **beaches** are slim and, though not of the Caribbean dream variety, do offer decent swimming once you're away from the centre; you'll find that the sand slopes into the sea very gradually here. On the east side of town, below some cliffs, is **Playa Capitania**, which is usually pretty quiet, though there's not much sand. **Playa Barrique**, on the northeast side of Lívingston, is the town's main beach – if you follow the coconut-studded shoreline north from here there are some nice stretches of sand.

Siete Altares waterfalls

5km northwest of town • Head along the shoreline from Playa Barrique and, just before the sands eventually peter out, take a path to the left

The most popular side-trip is to the **Siete Altares**, an imposing series of waterfalls, much more impressive in the rainy season. Robberies have occurred here occasionally, and though no incidents have been reported for some time, it's best to hire a local guide – ask at your hotel – or visit as part of a **tour**. Boardwalks have been constructed so you can access the most impressive upper section easily.

ARRIVAL AND DEPARTURE — LÍVINGSTON

The only way you can get to Lívingston is **by boat**, either from Puerto Barrios, the Río Dulce or Belize.

For the Río Dulce Boats for Río Dulce Town leave daily at 9am and 2pm. Tickets for the river trip up the *río* can be booked by any travel agent or hotel in Lívingston. The journey takes around 2hr 30min – all boats stop at some hot springs, Isla de los Pájaros (a bird sanctuary) and cruise past the Castillo de San Felipe – but are otherwise eager to get to Río Dulce Town quickly. To really get the most out of the stunning gorge scenery you need to do a more leisurely cruise (see page 203).

For Puerto Barrios *Lanchas* leave for Puerto Barrios (5 daily; additional services leave when full; 30min).

For Belize Boats run to Punta Gorda in Belize (Tues & Fri 7am; 1hr). Get your exit stamp at the *migración* (see page 198) the day before you leave; there's a fee.

For Honduras Combined boat/shuttle bus tickets are sold by Exotic Travel and other agencies to Copán, San Pedro Sula and La Ceiba.

4

INFORMATION AND TOURS

The most popular **tours** from Lívingston are the trip to Siete Altares, Playa Blanca and the slow cruise up the Río Dulce. If you want an educative, highly informed **walking tour** of the Garífuna barrio, contact Philip Flores (also known as Polo) on 4806 0643.

Happy Fish Travel C Principal 7947 0661, happyfishtravel.com. The best travel agent in town. The helpful owners can arrange trips (usually a minimum six people) around the area, including visits to the fine white sand beach of Playa Blanca and the Sapodilla Cayes off Belize for snorkelling.

ACCOMMODATION

Lívingston has a pretty good selection of places to stay, though those right on the **beach** are quite a hike from town. Book ahead on holidays.

Casa de la Iguana C Marcos Sánchez Díaz hotelcasadelaiguana.com map page 201. This hostel remains a party hot spot with drinking games, hedonism and all-round merriment. All accommodation – dorms and cabañas with shared (or private) bathrooms – is set around a large grassy plot. There's local and Western grub and excellent travel information. Dorms $, cabañas $$

Casa Nostra C Marcos Sánchez Díaz 7947 0842 map page 201. A small welcoming guesthouse ably run by gringo Stuart. His rooms are simple, kept clean and include free drinking water and coffee. The larger rooms can sleep up to four and there's a fine river frontage. The food is excellent, too (see below). $$$

★ **Hotel Casa Rosada** C Marcos Sánchez Díaz hotelcasarosada.com; map page 201. A lovely waterfront hotel run by a very hospitable couple from Guatemala and Belgium. The small, cheery wooden cabins are kept immaculately clean and have twin beds, nets and nice hand-painted detailing. Bathrooms are all shared but kept very clean. There's a huge, lush garden to enjoy and a private dock for sunbathing. Excellent, wholesome meals are served (see below). $$$

Hotel Doña Alida 150m northeast of C Principal 7947 0027 map page 201. The cliffside location is excellent, so even though this place is a little dated it's still worth considering. Rooms are spacious and clean many have fine sea (and sunset) views. $$

Hotel Ecológico Salvador Gaviota Playa Quehueche 7947 0874; map page 201. Right on a slim beach, with good rooms (with or without private bathrooms) and large thatched bungalows set in grassy grounds. Inexpensive local food including fresh fish (try their *tapado*) is also available. It's about a 40min walk west of the town centre; take a taxi from the main dock. Doubles $$, bungalows $$$

Hotel Garífuna Off C de la Iglesia 7947 0183; map page 201. A secure Garífuna-owned guesthouse with neat, clean and good-value rooms, all with fans and private showers. $$

Hotel Gíl Resort 150m east of C Principal 5206 8124; map page 201. A modern, comfortable hotel with attractive pine-trimmed rooms that are a little overpriced but comfortable and attractive nonetheless. There's a sea-view terrace and breakfast is included. $$$$

Hotel Ríos Tropicales C Principal 7947 0158; map page 201. Prices have risen here, but these well-presented rooms – some very spacious and with tasteful furniture and art, others much simpler – are still a good deal. There's a sunny patio at the rear with sofas and a little espresso bar at the front. $$$

Villa Caribe Just off C Principal villasdeguatemala.com; map page 201. This large resort hotel gets the tour group action, with a/c bungalows and spacious modern fan-cooled rooms boasting balconies with views to the bay. There's a pleasant bar, a swimming pool and gardens stretching to the shore. $$$$

EATING

For local food, you must try **tapado** (a coconut-based fish soup with plantain and spices). In general, restaurant **prices** are quite high for Guatemala.

Antojitos Gaby C Marcos Sánchez Díaz 7947 0663; map page 201. Busy, cheap little comedor with streetside tables serving local grub and good seafood (including *sopa caracol* and *tapado*). $

Buga Mama Just left of the jetty 1747-9790; map page 201. This restaurant occupies a fine old Caribbean building, and also has a huge rear deck – take your pick from either sea or street views. Good shrimp, pasta and salads and vegetarian dishes are on offer and there's a full bar (including wine by the glass). Staff are trained as part of the Ak'Tenamit project (see below), a good cause, but service can be spotty. Wi-fi. $$

★ **Casa Nostra** C Marcos Sánchez Díaz 7947 0842; map page 201. For food with a home-cooked flavour, look no further than this guesthouse restaurant. Breakfast options include granola, hot cakes and vegan pancakes; there's lots of seafood (try the garlic shrimp) and fish, and the pizzas are definitely the best in town. $$$

Hotel Casa Rosada C Marcos Sánchez Díaz hotelcasarosada.com; map page 201. Overlooking La Buga (the mouth of the Río Dulce) this hotel restaurant is a wonderfully relaxed place for healthy breakfasts, lunches and superb dinners and there are always good vegetarian options. Book ahead. $$$

Margoth C de la Iglesia 7947 0019; map page 201.

Perhaps the best place to try the traditional dish, *tapado*, this large Garífuna-owned restaurant also serves very tasty seafood and an extensive selection of delicious Garífuna dishes. $$

Las Tres Garifunas C Principal ⓣ 7947 0195; map page 201. A very popular café-restaurant, with an inexpensive menu and an excellent terrace for watching the world go by. $$

DRINKING AND NIGHTLIFE

For late night grooving, the **beach bars** at the end of C Principal have dancefloors and play reggae, punta, r'n'b and Latin music.

Casa de la Iguana C Marcos Sánchez Díaz ⓦ hotelcasadelaiguana.com; map page 201. The bar scene here is nearly always lively, and it's really popular with young travellers.

Ubafu C de la Iglesia ⓣ 4237 2218; map page 201. This intimate bar is a key place for live music, especially Garífuna punta. Bands play at weekends and the odd weekday too.

DIRECTORY

Banks You'll find two branches of Banrural on C Principal.

Immigration office The *migración* is on C Principal (daily 6am–6pm; ⓣ 7947 0081).

Internet Many places, including the hotels we've reviewed, have wi-fi. Rapidnet is 400m north of the dock.

Post office Just off C Principal.

The Río Dulce gorge

Reason enough to come to Lívingston is the spectacular trip through the **Río Dulce gorge**, a roughly 30km journey that eventually brings you to Río Dulce Town. From Lívingston, the river passes through a system of **gorges** with sheer, 100m-high rock faces draped in tropical vegetation and cascading vines. The **birdlife** is exceptional with white herons, sea eagles and squawking parakeets among the stunning tropical scenery. If you're very lucky you may even see a **manatee** – dawn is the best time.

4

Ak'Tenamit

Barra Lampara • Free • ⓣ 5908 3392, ⓦ aktenamit.org

Some 8km west along the Río Dulce from Lívingston, then up the Río Tatín, is **Ak'Tenamit**, a health and development centre that caters to the needs of more than a hundred Q'eqchi' Maya villages. Until the project was started in 1992 the people had neither schools, medical care, nor much else. Now there is a 24-hour clinic, schools and a floating dental clinic. Self-help programmes, a women's craft-making cooperative, an ecotourism centre and Maya cultural initiatives have also been launched. Volunteer doctors, nurses and dentists who can commit themselves for at least three months are needed. Visitors are invited to take a look around – there's also a short **interpretive trail** through the rainforest, and some handicrafts for sale.

CRUISING THE RÍO DULCE

Most people experience the **Río Dulce** as a fleeting glimpse from one of the public boats that zip between Río Dulce Town and Lívingston, but to experience the *río* properly you should invest some time and take it slow. As the most spectacular section is near Lívingston it makes sense to begin a cruise there. Day-trips typically take in several attractions – including some hot springs, swimming spots, jungle tributaries and Ak'Tenamit – but the real pleasure is simply enjoying the spectacular **gorge** itself, with all the time in the world to soak up the idyllic scenery, which can be arranged through tour operators or boatmen in Lívingston. Kayaking the gorge area and its jungle rivers from one of the hotels nearby (see page 204) is perhaps the perfect option.

Biotopo Chocón Machacas

Charge • ⓣ 7331 0904

Travel 1km or so upriver from Ak'Tenamit and you'll find a spot where warm sulphurous waters emerge from the base of a cliff – a good place for a dip. Just beyond, the gorge opens into a small lake, **El Golfete**, on whose northern shore is the **Biotopo Chocón Machacas**, a nature reserve designed to protect the habitat of the **manatee**, or sea cow, a threatened species that's seen around here from time to time. The manatee is a massive seal-shaped mammal that lives in both sea- and fresh water and, according to some, gave rise to the myth of the mermaid. Female manatees breastfeed their young, clutching them in their flippers, though – tipping the scales at as much as a ton – they're hardly as dainty as fairy-tale mermaids. The reserve was also set up to protect the area's rich wetlands and lowland rainforests (home to jaguar and tapir and wonderful birdlife) but recent encroachment by campesinos has led to a bitter battle over land use.

ACCOMMODATION — RÍO DULCE GORGE

There are a couple of fine **ecolodges** around 7km inland from Lívingston, just west of the gorge. Boats travelling between Río Dulce and Lívingston will drop you off at either of them, and both have kayaks available to explore this uniquely beautiful region.

Finca Tatín 400m up the Río Tatín from Río Dulce ⓦ fincatatin.com; map page 206. On a tributary of the Río Dulce, this jungle lodge is well set up for travellers, offering healthy food, table tennis, tubes, hammocks, walking trails, a gym and yoga space. There's a wide choice of accommodation: a dorm (above the bar), private rooms and two-storey cabins. Dorms $, doubles $$, cabins $$$

★ **The Round House Hostel** 1km west of Río Dulce gorge ⓦ roundhousehostel.com; map page 206. Right on the *río*, this sociable place is owned by a welcoming English-Dutch couple with well-presented dorms and rooms (all beds have mossie nets) and excellent cooking. There's a small pool (ideal for volleyball) and it's a great base to explore the area. Manatees are often seen directly offshore in the early morning. Dorms $, doubles $$

4

Río Dulce Town

As it heads upstream across the Golfete, the river closes in and passes several marinas and a monstrous concrete bridge at the squalid settlement of **RÍO DULCE TOWN** (sometimes also known as Fronteras), on the northern side of the river. The waterfront away from Río Dulce Town is a favourite playground for wealthy Guatemalans, with boats and hotels that would look very at home in Monte Carlo or the Hamptons.

Most Petén-bound traffic pauses here for a few minutes, and the town itself is little more than a truck stop. Though initial impressions are terrible it's very easy to escape all this, and the best hotels are in much more tranquil, attractive locations a short boat-ride away.

ARRIVAL AND INFORMATION — RÍO DULCE TOWN

By bus Buses to Petén, Guatemala City and Puerto Barrios leave and depart from bus stops on the highway, just north of the bridge. First-class services are run by Línea Dorada, Litegua, ADN and Fuente del Norte, all of which have offices on the highway. Minibuses to El Estor (every 45min; 1hr 30min) leave from a side road, just north of the Río Dulce bridge.

Destinations El Estor (every 45min; 1hr 30min); Flores (every 30min; 3hr 30min–4hr); Guatemala City (every 30min; 5–6hr); Lanquín (1 daily, 1.30pm from *Sundog Café*; 5hr); Poptún (every 30min; 1hr 45min); Puerto Barrios (hourly; 2hr); San Pedro Sula (daily 10am; 8hr); San Salvador (Fuente del Norte only, daily 10am; 7hr).

By boat For Lívingston via the Río Dulce gorge, *colectivo* boats (9.30am & 1.30pm, 2hr 30min; additional services until 4pm; 2hr) arrive and depart from a designated dock under the north side of the bridge. If you book through your hotel on either the 9.30am or 1.30pm departures a pick-up can usually be arranged. Downstream, the trip takes around 2hr, depending on how many stops are made. The boatmen usually cruise up to the Castillo de San Felipe for photographs (but do not stop there), slow down at an islet to see nesting cormorants and pelicans then stop for 15min at a place where hot springs bubble into the river and at another spot where water lilies are profuse. To explore the lake and river at a more leisurely pace, consider a slow cruise (see page 203), rent a kayak or try asking around in *Bruno's* or at your hotel.

Services Banrural and Banco Industrial, both with ATMs, are on the main drag in Río Dulce Town.

ACCOMMODATION

All the following hotels, except *Hostal del Río*, are a short boat-ride away from the main dock. Most offer a free **pick-up** service.

Casa Perico 3km northeast of the bridge casa-perico.com. Rustic Swiss-owned jungle hideaway with a relaxed atmosphere that's popular with budget travellers. All the buildings are wooden, built on stilts and connected by walkways. Trips are offered around the *río* and there are kayaks for rent. Dorms $, doubles $$, bungalows $$$

Hacienda Tijax Just across from the dock tijax.com. This riverside lodge has a pool and a range of accommodation from small, A-frame cabins to large bungalows (though none are great value for money); the restaurant's food is tasty, if a little overpriced. Also offers a canopy jungle walk, hiking trails and horse-riding. Cabins $$$, bungalows $$$$

Hostal del Río North of the bridge, by Sundog Café 5527 0767. There are no frills here, but the clean, functional rooms on offer all have bathrooms, and some have a/c. $$

Hotel Backpackers Underneath the south side of the bridge 5825 2070. This huge, rickety wooden structure has large dorms and some ramshackle doubles. Unfortunately it's looking pretty shabby these days (which is a shame as it's owned by the nearby Casa Guatemala children's home, and many of the young staff are former residents). Dorms $, doubles $$

Hotel Kangaroo On a creek opposite the Castillo hotel-kangaroo.com. Owned by an Australian-Mexican couple, this timber-and-thatch lodge has a six-person dorm and attractive rooms, some with private bathrooms. There's a jacuzzi, a fully stocked bar and filling tucker (though meals might be a little pricey for backpackers). Dorms $, doubles $$

★ **Tortugal** 4min by water taxi from the bridge tortugal.com. Offering fine value, the accommodation here is all very well presented: the two dorms are flashpacker-friendly, with quality mattresses, mosquito nets and lockers. There are also lovely spacious rooms, wood-and-thatch bungalows and a stunning luxury *casita*. Above the river-facing restaurant there's a chill-out area with pool table and library. Free kayaks for guests. Dorms $$, doubles & *casita* $$$

4

EATING AND DRINKING

Benedición a Dios Down a little side road off the main drag 5722 6842. This place is famous for its huge wheat tortillas, a local speciality topped with cabbage and marinated beef (there are veggie options, too). $$

Bruno's Under north side of the bridge 7930 5721. Popular yachtie hangout, with a wide menu of local and international grub including sandwiches, seafood and pasta. Wi-fi and a pool. $$

★ **Sundog Café** Down a lane on north side of the bridge 3136 7218. A social hub for travellers, this Swiss-run place offers great thin-crust pizza (from a wood-fired brick oven), baguettes and sandwiches (on delicious home-made bread), specials including *ceviche*, and espresso coffee. Also offers wine, and all spirits are double shots. $$

Lago de Izabal

The beautiful tropical area along the lush banks of the **Lago de Izabal** has a genuinely relaxed atmosphere and plenty to keep you occupied for a few days. A road around the northern shore of the lake provides a route up to the Verapaces, passing the idyllic **hot-spring waterfall** close to the *Finca el Paraíso* and the impressive **Boquerón canyon**. On the western side of the lake, the small town of **El Estor** is a good alternative base to explore these sights and the biodiverse wetlands of the **Reserva Bocas del Polochic**.

Castillo de San Felipe

San Felipe, 3km west of Río Dulce Town • Charge • Take a water taxi or minibus from Río Dulce bridge

Looking like a miniature medieval castle and marking the entrance to Lago de Izabal, the **Castillo de San Felipe** is a tribute to the audacity of British pirates, who used to sail up the Río Dulce to raid supplies and harass mule trains. The Spanish were so infuriated by this that they built the pocket-sized fortress here in 1652 to seal off the entrance to the lake, and a chain was strung across the river. Inside there are a maze of tiny rooms and staircases, plus plenty of cannons and panoramic views of the lake.

Hot-spring waterfall

Charge • Buses between Río Dulce and El Estor pass the hot spring hourly till 6pm

Beyond the Castillo de San Felipe the broad sweep of Lago de Izabal opens before you, with great views of the fertile highlands beyond the distant shores. A **hot-spring waterfall**, one of Guatemala's most remarkable natural phenomena, lies some 25km from Río Dulce, 300m north of the road in land owned by the *Finca el Paraíso* (see below). Here bathtub-temperature spring water cascades into pools cooled by a separate chilly flow of fresh river water, creating a sublime, steamy spa-like environment where it's easy to soak away an afternoon. Above the waterfall is a series of caves whose interiors are crowded both with bats and extraordinary shapes and colours – made even more memorable by the fact that you have to swim by torchlight to see them (bring your own flashlight).

ACCOMMODATION **HOT-SPRING WATERFALL**

Finca el Paraíso 2km south of the hot-spring waterfall ⓣ5575 9158; map page 206. This place enjoys a delightfully peaceful waterfront location, though the large cabañas are a little worn (and pricey for what you get). $$$

Boquerón Canyon

Seven kilometres west along the lakeshore from the hot-spring waterfall is the **Boquerón Canyon**, completely hidden yet just 500m from the road. Near-vertical cliffs soar to more than 250m above the Río Sauce, which flows through the bottom of the startling jungle-clad gorge, the riverbed dotted with colossal boulders. To see the canyon, employ one of the local **boatmen** who wait at the end of the signposted track from the main road. They'll paddle you upstream in logwood canoes for a small fee. The round trip takes thirty minutes or so, though it's possible to get your boatman to drop you off and return to pick you up later in the day. The canyon

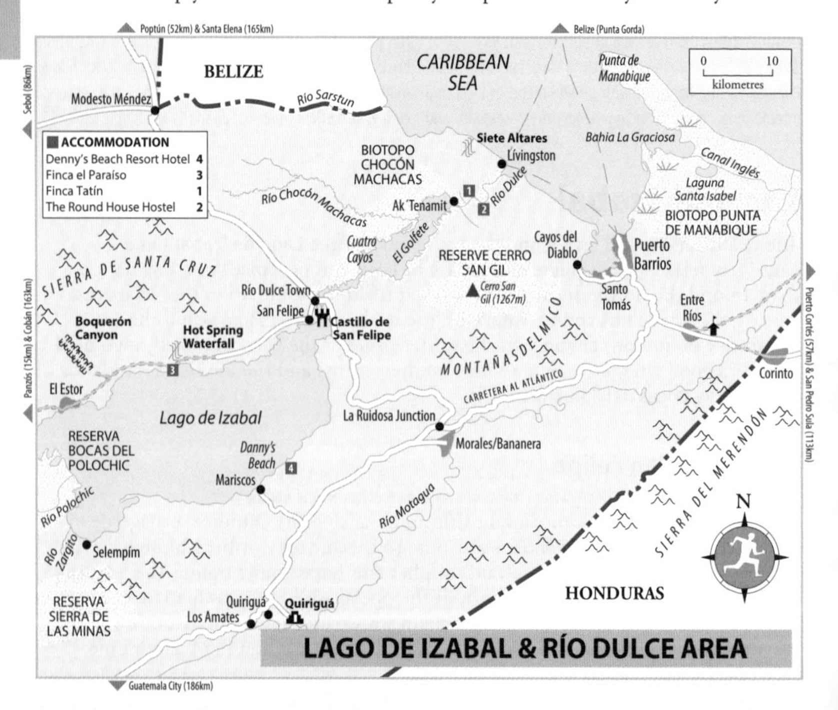

extends for 5km; if you want to explore Boquerón further make sure you have sturdy footwear as it's quite a scramble.

El Estor

As you head west beyond Boquerón, it's just 6km to the sleepy lakeside town of **EL ESTOR**, allegedly named by English pirates who came up the Río Dulce to buy supplies at "The Store". There are no sights in easy-going El Estor itself, though you could easily spend a few days exploring the surrounding area. Keep an eye out for huge green iguanas in the trees around town; locals hunt them with slingshots.

The town is located close to high-grade nickel deposits, the presence of which has provoked bitter disputes between mining companies and locals over the years. **Strip mining** has resumed, impacting the vast ecotourism potential of the region.

ARRIVAL AND INFORMATION — EL ESTOR

By bus Microbuses (every 45min; 1hr 30min) connect Río Dulce Town with El Estor until 6pm.

Information For local information the best contacts are Hugo at *Hugo's* restaurant on the plaza or Óscar Paz, who runs the *Hotel Vista del Lago* (see below). Both can arrange boats and guides to explore any of the region's attractions.

Services Banrural, 3 C & 6 Av, has an ATM.

ACCOMMODATION

El Estor has a decent choice of good-quality budget **accommodation**, though nothing much in other price categories.

Chaabil 3 C, lakeshore 7949 7272. The cabaña-style rooms here have fans, chunky wooden beds and private bathrooms, and some have fine lake views. Their restaurant offers a fine setting for meals of grilled meats and lots of seafood. $$

Hotel Ecológico Cabañas del Lago 1.5km east of the centre facebook.com/ecohotelcabanasdelago. Set in a tranquil shady lakeside plot, these wooden bungalows have seen better days and could be better presented and maintained. However, the location and fine food help compensate. Hugo, the genial owner, will give you a ride here if you drop by his restaurant (*Hugo's*) on the plaza. $$$

Hotel Vista del Lago Lakeside 7949 7658. This beautiful old wooden building by the lakeshore is claimed to be the original "store" that gave the town its name. Small, clean rooms with private bathrooms; those on the second floor boast superb views of the lake. $$$

Reserva Bocas del Polochic

Encompassing a substantial slice of lowland jungle on the west side of the lake, the **Bocas del Polochic** nature reserve is one of the richest wetland habitats in Guatemala. The green maze of swamp, marsh and forest harbours at least 224 species of bird, including golden-fronted woodpecker, Aztec parakeet and keel-billed toucan. It's also rich in mammals, including howler monkeys, which you're virtually guaranteed to see (and hear), plus rarely encountered manatees and tapirs, and alligators, iguanas and turtles. You can explore the reserve from the tiny Q'eqchi' village of **SELEMPÍM** just outside the reserve.

ARRIVAL AND INFORMATION — BOCAS DEL POLOCHIC

By boat To get to Selempím catch a public *lancha* from El Estor (Mon, Wed & Sat noon; 1hr 15min) or rent a private *lancha*. *Lanchas* should return to El Estor at 7am the same days, but check schedules at Defensores' office. Ask Hugo or Óscar in El Estor (see page 207) to recommend a local boatman.

Information Defensores de la Naturaleza, 5 Av & 2 C in El Estor (2310 2929, defensores.org.gt), manages the reserve and can help with information.

ACCOMMODATION

Selempím Lodge Bookings via Defensores (see above). This large mosquito-screened wooden house has bunk beds with mosquito nets. Guides are available to lead you on walks up into the foothills of the Sierra de las Minas and conduct kayak tours of the river delta. Rates include three substantial meals. $$

4

Mariscos and Denny's Beach

MARISCOS, the main town on the south side of Lago de Izabal, sees very few visitors now that the road around the northern shore of the lake is complete. Travellers only pass through to access **Denny's Beach**.

ARRIVAL AND DEPARTURE — MARISCOS AND DENNY'S BEACH

By bus and boat There's no road access to Denny's Beach. All buses along the Carretera al Atlántico will stop at La Trinchera junction, the turn-off for Mariscos, from where minibuses (every 30min; 30min) head into the town centre.

ACCOMMODATION

Denny's Beach Resort Hotel On the lake 6km east of Mariscos ⓦdennysbeach.com; map page 206. This beautiful Canadian-run resort enjoys a blissfully quiet and serene location right on what is considered Lago de Izabal's best beach. It's an ideal place to get away from it all, with detached cabañas, a dorm and an open-air restaurant. Kayak use is gratis, while wakeboarding, horseriding, hikes and trips around the lake can be arranged for a fee. They'll pick up and drop off guests for free from Mariscos; call ahead. Dorms $, bungalows $$$

El Oriente

The eastern highlands, often just called **El Oriente**, connect Guatemala City with El Salvador and Honduras and must rank as the least-visited part of the country. Virtually the entire population is ladino, and only a very few elderly people, in a couple of isolated areas, still speak Poqomam Maya, the region's Indigenous language.

The landscape lacks the immediate appeal of the western highlands – the peaks are lower and volcanoes here are heavily eroded. Close to the border with El

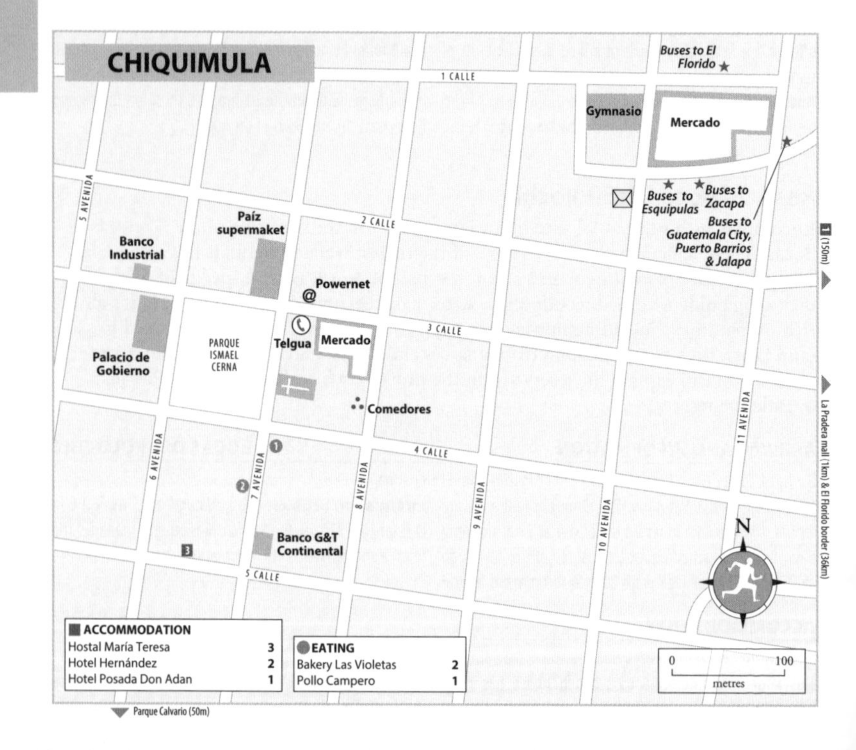

THE HONDURAS BORDER: EL FLORIDO

The Honduran border post at **El Florido** is open 24hr, and the two sets of **immigration** are a short walk apart. Since Guatemala and Honduras enacted the 2018 customs union, travellers no longer need to pay an exit tax; however, this seems to slip the mind of local officials on a rather frequent basis. There are banks and moneychangers at the border. Buses wait on the Honduran side to transport you to Copán Ruinas Town (every 20min; 20min).

Salvador the hills are incredibly fertile and the broad valleys lush with vegetation, but in the north of the area, around the key town of **Chiquimula**, things look very different, with dry rounded hills and dusty fields. From this region it's a short hop to the ruins of Copán in Honduras, while **Esquipulas**, with its famous basilica, and the lovely volcanic crater lake of **Ipala** are also close by. To get to the Oriente you branch off the **Carretera al Atlántico** at the Río Hondo junction, skirt Estanzuela, and head past Chiquimula and Esquipulas to the three-way border with Honduras and El Salvador.

Estanzuela

Three kilometres south of the Río Hondo junction, the remote small town of **ESTANZUELA** is completely forgettable except one curious sight, a small museum of paleontology. If you're passing in a car, it might be worth a quick diversion; the town centre is just 1km off the highway. **Museo de Paleontologia de Estanzuela** (free, ⓣ7933 6108) has curious exhibits including the fossil of a blue whale, manatee bones and the entire skeleton of a mastodon said to be some fifty thousand years old. More recent pieces include a small Maya tomb and some stelae.

4

Chiquimula

Set on the western side of the Highway 10, the large town of **CHIQUIMULA** is an ugly, hot, bustling place with a population of around 50,000. If you've just arrived in Guatemala, things only get better from here. Chiquimula's downtown streets and its huge plaza area – Parque Ismael Cerna – shaded by ceiba trees, are permanently congested by traffic. You could take a wander around the central **Mercado** near the plaza, which has a kitsch selection of cowboy gear alongside inexpensive comedores, but for most travellers Chiquimula is just a place to catch a bus to or from the **border** at **El Florido** (see box) and the ruins of Copán.

ARRIVAL AND DEPARTURE — CHIQUIMULA

By bus The bus terminal is a 10min walk northeast of the Parque Ismael Cerna on 1 C between 10 & 11 Av.
Destinations Anguiatú (every 30min; 1hr); Esquipulas (every 20min; 1hr); El Florido (every 30min; 1hr 30min); Guatemala City (hourly; 3hr 30min); Ipala (every 45min; 1hr); Puerto Barrios (hourly; 4hr 30min); Santa Elena, for Flores (5 daily; 7hr 30min).

ACCOMMODATION

Chiquimula is a very hot place, so shell out for a/c or make sure you have a good fan in your room.

Hostal María Teresa 5 C 6–21 ⓣ7942 0177; map page 208. Located a block south of the Parque Ismael Cerna, this hotel has a lovely garden courtyard and well-presented rooms with a/c and TV. $$

Hotel Hernández 3 C 7–41 ⓣ7942 0708, ⓔchapin54@yahoo.com; map page 208. A warren of a place run by a friendly family, with dozens of basic rooms in several different price categories – you pay a lot more for a/c and TV. There's safe parking and a small concrete pool for cooling off. $$

Hotel Posada Don Adan 2 C & 12 Av ⓣ7942 0014; map page 208. This place has tropical gardens, a large pool and restaurant, and the rooms (with or without a/c) are spacious and clean, if a bit garish. Fan-only singles are well priced. $$

EATING

Bakery Las Violetas 4 C & 7 Av facebook.com/Lasvioletaschiquimula; map page 208. For the best baked bread in town and the heartiest of sandwiches, you can't go wrong at this local bakery. The scent from the oven as it spills out into the street is reason enough to head inside for a quick breakfast or a more leisurely lunch. $$

Pollo Campero 4 C & 7 Av 7942 0916; map page 208. There's not a great deal of choice in town when it comes to restaurants, however Pollo Campero is a decent and reliable option, serving up inexpensive fried chicken dishes. It's borderline fast food, but good value. $$

DIRECTORY

Banks Banco G&T Continental, 7 Av 4–75, has an ATM.

Internet Powernet, on 3 C near the plaza, is a centrally located place to pick up internet connections.

Volcán de Ipala

About 20km south of Chiquimula • Charge, pay at the visitor centre • Buses between Chiquimula and Agua Blanca (every 45min) pass the trailhead at El Sauce, where there's an Inguat sign

The **Volcán de Ipala** (1650m) may at first seem a little disappointing – it looks more like a hill than a grand volcano. However, the cone is filled by a beautiful little crater lake and ringed by dense subtropical forest. You can walk round the lake in an hour and it's great for swimming, camping or a picnic (there are tables under shelters and barbecue grills).

From the trailhead it's a straightforward hour-and-a-half walk to the top, via a visitors' centre. Or, if you've got a (high clearance) vehicle, the lake can be accessed via a steep, rough track from the nearby town of **Agua Blanca**.

THE ESQUIPULAS PILGRIMAGE

The history of the **Esquipulas pilgrimage** probably dates back to pre-conquest times, when the valley was controlled by Chief Esquipulas. Even then the area was the site of an important religious shrine, perhaps connected with the nearby Maya site of Copán.

When the Spanish arrived, the chief was keen to avoid the usual bloodshed and chose to surrender without a fight; the grateful Spaniards named the city they founded at the site in his honour. The famed colonial sculptor **Quirio Cataño** was then commissioned to carve an image of Christ for the church constructed in the town, and in order to make it more likely to appeal to the local people he chose to carve it from **balsam**, a dark wood. (Another version has it that Cataño was hired by the Maya after one of them had seen a vision of a dark Christ on this spot.) In any event, the image was installed in the church in 1595 and soon was credited with miraculous powers. After the bishop of Guatemala, Pardo de Figueroa, was cured of a chronic ailment on a trip to Esquipulas in 1737, things really took off. The bishop ordered the construction of a new church, which was completed in 1758, and had his body buried beneath the altar.

Although this might seem straightforward, it doesn't explain why this figure has become the most revered in a country full of miracle-working saints. One explanation is that for the **Maya**, who until recently dominated the pilgrimage, it blends pre-Columbian and Catholic worship. The Maya pantheon included several black deities such as Ek Ahau, the black lord, who was served by seven retainers, and Ek'Chuach, the tall black god, who protected travellers.

The principal day of pilgrimage is **January 15**. Even the country's smallest villages will send a representative, their send-off and return marked by religious services. These, plus the thousands who come in their own right, ensure that Esquipulas fills to bursting. Buses choke the streets, while the most devoted pilgrims arrive on foot (some dropping to their knees for the last few kilometres). There's a smaller pilgrimage on **March 9**, and the faithful visit year-round.

THE EL SALVADOR AND HONDURAS BORDERS: ESQUIPULAS

El Salvador border The border at **Anguiatú** (24hr) is 39km from Esquipulas; most nationalities don't need a visa for stays of up to 90 days (also applies to the border below).
Honduras border The 24hr border crossing at **Agua Caliente** is 10km from Esquipulas. There's a Honduran consulate in *Hotel Payaquí*, 2 Av, Esquipulas; most nationalities don't need a visa.

Esquipulas

The final town on this eastern highway is **ESQUIPULAS**, which has a single point of interest: it is the most important Catholic shrine in Central America, its dark-hued **statue of Christ** the focus of a famous annual pilgrimage. The settlement, and valley, is dominated by the four perfectly white domes of the church, brilliantly floodlit at night. Below, the town is a messy sprawl of cheap hotels, souvenir stalls and overpriced restaurants. The **pilgrimage**, which continues all year, has created a booming religious resort where people come to worship, eat, drink and relax, in a bizarre combination of holy devotion and indulgence. The town also played an important role in modern politics: the first **peace accord** initiatives to end the civil wars in El Salvador, Nicaragua and Guatemala were signed here in 1987.

The Basilica

Inside the **Basilica** there's a constant scurry of hushed devotion amid clouds of smoke and incense. In the nave pilgrims approach the image on their knees, while others light candles, mouth supplications or simply stand in silent crowds. The **image** itself

FIESTAS IN THE ORIENTE AND IZABAL

JANUARY–MARCH

Jan 12–15 El Progreso (near Jutiapa), main day Jan 15.
Jan 15 Esquipulas, the biggest pilgrimage in Central America.
Jan 20–26 Ipala, main day Jan 23 (includes bullfighting).
March 9 Esquipulas, a smaller day of pilgrimage to the Black Christ.
March 12–15 Moyuta (near Jutiapa) and Olapa (near Chiquimula).
March (varies) Jocotán.

MAY–AUGUST

May 2–5 Jalapa, main day May 3.
May 5–9 Gualán (near Zacapa).
July 16–22 Puerto Barrios, main day July 19.
July 22–26 Jocotán (near Chiquimula).
July 23–27 Esquipulas, a fiesta in honour of Santiago Apóstol, main day July 25.
Aug 11–18 Chiquimula, main day Aug 15 (includes bullfighting).
Aug 25 San Luís Jilotepéque.

NOVEMBER–DECEMBER

Nov 7–14 Sanarate.
Nov 10–16 Jutiapa, main day Nov 13.
Nov 26 Lívingston, Garífuna day, a huge celebration.
Dec 4–9 Zacapa, main day Dec 8.
Dec 13–16 San Luís Jilotepéque.
Dec 22–27 Cuilapa.
Dec 24–31 Lívingston, carnival.

is most closely approached by a separate side entrance, where you can join the queue to shuffle past beneath it and pause briefly in front before being shoved on by the crowds behind. Back outside you'll find yourself among swarms of souvenir- and relic-hawkers.

ARRIVAL AND DEPARTURE — ESQUIPULAS

By bus and microbus Rutas Orientales runs a reliable bus service between Guatemala City and Esquipulas; its office is at the junction of 11 C (the main street) and 1 Av. Transportes María Elena (also on 11 C) runs buses to Santa Elena (near Flores, Petén) via Río Dulce Town and Poptún. There are microbuses from 11 C to the borders with El Salvador and Honduras at Agua Caliente. For Copán, catch a microbus towards Chiquimula and change buses at the junction on the highway that leads to El Florido (see page 209).

Destinations Agua Caliente (every 30min; 30min); Anguiatú (every 30min; 1hr); Chiquimula (every 20min; 1hr); Guatemala City (every 30min; 4hr 15min); Santa Elena (3 daily; 8hr 15min).

Services There are plenty of banks with ATMs in town, including Banco Industrial at 9 C & 3 Av.

ACCOMMODATION

Hotels fill up quickly on **weekends** in Esquipulas, when prices (always negotiable) rise. Cheap places lie north of the main road, 11 C.

Hotel Portal de la Fe 11 C ⓣ7943 4124. A well-presented colonial-style place offering clean, attractive rooms with wrought-iron bed frames and nice decorative touches. $$$

Hotel Posada Mamá Chilita 2 Av 11–58 ⓣ7943 4770. This hotel offers great value for money; rooms come with private bathrooms and guests can enjoy the on-site restaurant. $$

Hotel Villa Edelmira 3 Av 8–58 ⓣ7943 1431. A reliable family-run option with excellent rates for single travellers. $$

EATING AND DRINKING

Esquipulas offers particularly good value at **breakfast** time. As with the hotels, cheap places to eat are clustered on 11 C and in the streets to the north.

Restaurante La Frontera 11 C, opposite the park. There's usually a bustle about this large place which has a good selection of local dishes including *carne a la plancha*. $$

La Rotonda 1 Av 10–30 ⓦlarotondaesquipulas.com. This eye-catching red-and-green restaurant located just off the main drag has gained popularity for its Western and Mexican grub (tacos, burritos, burgers). It's also a great spot for coffee (including cappuccino), and they sell beers and spirits too. $$

Cobán and the Verapaces

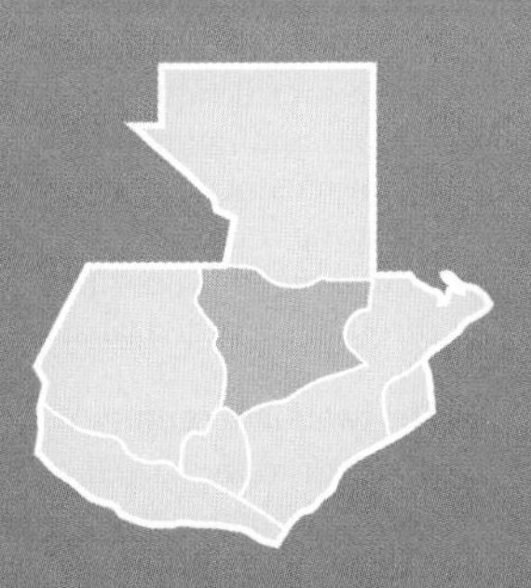

SEMUC CHAMPEY

Cobán and the Verapaces

The twin departments of the Verapaces harbour some of the most spectacular mountain scenery in the country, yet attract only a trickle of tourists. Alta Verapaz, in particular, is astonishingly beautiful, with fertile limestone landscapes and craggy, mist-wrapped hills. The highlands here are the wettest and greenest in Guatemala – ideal for the production of the cash crops of coffee, cardamom, flowers and ferns. Locals say it rains for thirteen months a year, alternating between straightforward downpours and drizzle they call the *chipi-chipi*. To the south, Baja Verapaz could hardly be more different: a sparsely populated area of deep valleys dotted with fiesta towns and parched hills that see very little rainfall.

In Baja Verapaz, the towns of **Salamá**, **Rabinal** and **Cubulco** are rightly renowned for their traditional fiestas, while **San Jerónimo** has some interesting historic sights. Guatemala's national bird, the quetzal can occasionally be seen in the cloud forests of this department: the **quetzal sanctuary** is one possible and accessible place to seek out these beautiful birds.

However, the hub of the region is **Cobán** in Alta Verapaz, a fairly attractive mid-sized mountain town with good accommodation and some very civilized coffeehouses and restaurants. Northeast of here, the exquisite natural bathing pools of **Semuc Champey** near **Lanquín** are surrounded by lush tropical forest and are a key travellers' hangout.

North of Cobán, a couple of natural attractions lie near the town of **Chisec**: the emerald lakes of **Lagunas de Sepalau** and the sinkhole of **Bombil Pek**. From Chisec it's a short hop to the remarkable **Candelaria caves** and the nearby ruins of **Cancuén**. In the extreme northwest of the region, the beautiful lake **Laguna Lachúa**, fringed by rainforest, is well worth the detour it takes to get there.

Brief history

Long before the Conquest, local Achi Maya had earned themselves a reputation as the most bloodthirsty of all the tribes, said to sacrifice every prisoner they took. Alvarado's Spanish army was unable to make any headway against them, and eventually he gave up trying to control the area, naming it *tierra de guerra*, the "land of war".

The Catholic Church, however, couldn't allow so many heathen souls to go to waste. Under the leadership of **Fray Bartolomé de Las Casas**, the Church made a deal with the conquistadors: if Alvarado would agree to keep all armed men out of the area for five years, the priests would bring it under control. In 1537 Las Casas set out into the highlands, befriended the Achi chiefs and learned the local dialects. By 1538 they had made considerable progress and converted large numbers of Maya. After five years the famous and invincible Achi were transformed into Spanish subjects, and the king of Spain renamed the province *Verapaz*, "True Peace".

During the colonial era the Verapaces remained isolated, their trade bypassing the capital by taking a direct route to the Caribbean along the Río Polochic and out through Lago de Izabal.

The twentieth century

The area really started to develop with the **coffee boom** at the turn of the twentieth century, when German immigrants flooded into the country to buy and run fincas. Around **Cobán** the new immigrants established an island of European sophistication, the German population reaching around two thousand by the 1930s, with its own

QUEZTAL, THE NATIONAL BIRD OF GUATEMALA

Highlights

❶ **Quetzal** Search for Guatemala's spectacularly plumed national bird in the cloud forests of the Verapaces. See page 222

❷ **Coffee in Cobán** Experience the uniquely smooth, medium-bodied and fragrant coffee for which Cobán is famous *in situ*. See page 226

❸ **Semuc Champey** These sublime turquoise pools, at the foot of a plunging river valley, are beautiful places to bathe. See page 231

❹ **Chisec** Peaceful little town that makes a good base for exploring the magical lakes of Lagunas de Sepalau and the sacred Maya cave of Bombil Pek. See page 233

❺ **Candelaria caves** An extraordinary limestone cave system, extending for more than 20km, with some immense chambers to investigate. See page 234

❻ **Laguna Lachúa** This little-visited national park is home to a stunning, near-circular lake rimmed by lowland jungle. The lush greenery provides the perfect habitat for jaguar and tapir. See page 236

HIGHLIGHTS ARE MARKED ON THE MAP ON PAGE 218

schools and clubs (and active Nazi party). A railway was built along the Polochic valley and Alta Verapaz became even more independent. This situation came to an end with World War II, when the US insisted the Guatemalan government expel the German landowners.

Today the Verapaz economy remains dominated by huge coffee fincas, along with cardamom production for the Middle Eastern market and the cultivation of flowers and vegetables for export. Campesinos have been forced to farm more and more marginal plots, and deforestation is a huge issue.

Baja Verapaz

A dramatic mix of dry hills and fertile valleys, **BAJA VERAPAZ** is crossed by a skeletal road network. The small towns of **Salamá** and **San Jerónimo**, situated on a flat-bottomed valley, have some intriguing historic sights, while to the west **Rabinal** and

MAYA IN THE VERAPACES

Taken as a whole, the Verapaces are very much **Indigenous** country: Baja Verapaz retains a small **Achi** Maya outpost around Rabinal, and in Alta Verapaz the Maya population are **Poqomchi'** and **Q'eqchi'**. The production of **coffee**, and more recently **cardamom** for the Middle Eastern market, has cut deep into their land and their way of life, the fincas driving many people off prime territory to marginal plots. **Traditional costume** is worn less here than in the western highlands, and in its place many Indigenous women have adopted a more universal Q'eqchi' costume, wearing the loose-hanging white *huipil* and machine-made *corte*. Maya men do not wear *traje* in the Verapaces.

Cubulco boast interesting markets and host deeply traditional fiestas. The other big attractions are the **quetzal sanctuary**, on the western side of the Cobán highway, and the forested mountains, waterfalls and wildlife inside the **Reserva Sierra de las Minas** just to the east.

San Jerónimo

At the eastern end of a fertile valley, 18km from the Cumbre junction, lies the tranquil small town of **SAN JERÓNIMO**. In the Conquest's early days, Dominican priests built a **church** and convent here and planted vineyards, eventually producing a wine lauded as the finest in Central America. In 1845, after the religious orders were abolished, an Englishman replaced the vines with sugar cane and began distilling an *aguardiente* that became equally famous. These days the area still produces sugar, though the cultivation of flowers for export and fish farming are more important.

San Jerónimo church

Parque Central • Free

Presiding over the central plaza, the village's seventeenth-century Baroque **church** contains a monumental gilded altar, brought from France, which was crafted from sheets of eighteen-carat gold.

Museo Regional del Trapiche

Hacienda de San Jerónimo • Donation requested • T 7940 2908

Downhill from the church, in a wonderful rural setting, are the remains of the convent complex: the Hacienda de San Jerónimo. Its sugar mill buildings now form the **Museo Regional del Trapiche** with displays that explain the history of the hacienda (which once employed more than one thousand workers) and refining process, while the extensive grassy grounds make an ideal place for a picnic.

Aqueduct

Southern outskirts of town • About a 10min walk from the plaza

The remains of a colonial **aqueduct**, built in 1679 and which originally supplied the sugar mill's waterwheels, is worth investigating. Many of its 124 original stone arches are still standing on the southern edge of town – just ask the way to the *acueducto antiguo*.

ARRIVAL AND DEPARTURE — SAN JERÓNIMO

Regular **minibuses** connect Salamá and San Jerónimo (every 30min 6am–7.30pm; 20min).

ACCOMMODATION AND EATING

Hotel Hacienda Real el Trapiche Western entrance to town T 7741 0200. Colonial-style hotel offering very attractive, well-priced rooms. Its restaurant offers home-cooked food. $$

MARKET DAYS IN THE VERAPACES

Monday Senahú; Tucurú.
Tuesday Chisec; El Chol; Cubulco; Lanquín; Purulhá; Rabinal; San Cristóbal Verapaz; San Jerónimo.
Saturday Senahú.
Sunday Chisec; Cubulco; Lanquín; Purulhá; Rabinal; Salamá; San Jerónimo; Santa Cruz Verapaz; Tactic.

Hotel Posada de Los Frayles 60m from El Calvario church ⓣ4520 5357. This place has a dash of colonial style, comfortable accommodation and the added benefit of a tree-fringed swimming pool. $$$

Salamá

Eight kilometres west of San Jerónimo is **SALAMÁ**, capital of the department of Baja Verapaz. The town has a relaxed and prosperous air; its population is largely ladino. Sights are slim on the ground, apart from its **museum** of the marimba – that said, it's also worth checking out the imposing colonial **bridge** on the edge of town, and the old **church**, the gilt of its huge altars darkened by age.

Casa del Quetzal y La Marimba

8 Av 3–20 • ⓣ5417 7622

Around 500m north of the Parque Central, the **Casa del Quetzal y La Marimba** is a little museum dedicated to Guatemala's national instrument, the magnificent marimba. There's a permanent exhibition of marimbas, some local crafts and historic photos.

ARRIVAL AND TOURS — SALAMÁ

By bus From Cobán or Guatemala City, you can take any bus between the two and get off at the junction known as La Cumbre de Santa Elena; from here microbuses run to Salamá. There are also microbuses from Cobán. Buses between Guatemala City's Centra Norte terminal run to Salamá (every 30min; 3hr); many continue on to Rabinal (3hr 45min) and Cubulco (4hr 15min). There's a steady stream of minibuses from Salamá to San Jerónimo, Rabinal and Cobán.

Destinations Cobán (every 45min; 1hr 30min); Cubulco (hourly; 1hr 30min); Guatemala City (every 30min; 3hr); Rabinal (every 30min; 45min); San Jerónimo (every 20min; 15min).

Eco-Verapaz 8 Av 7–12, Zona 1 ⓣ5722 9095, ⓔecoverapaz@hotmail.com. Offers good mountain biking, caving, hiking, horse-riding and cultural trips throughout the department.

ACCOMMODATION AND EATING

Deli-Donas 5 C 6–61 ⓣ7940 1121. Attractive café-restaurant just west of the Parque Central that's ideal for breakfasts, snacks, sandwiches coffee and home-made cakes. $$

Hotel Verapaz 8 Av 3–57 ⓣ7940 1126. An efficiently run hotel with comfortable beds, private hot-water bathrooms and cable TV. $$

Rabinal and around

Less than an hour from Salamá via a gap in the hills, **RABINAL** is a dusty, isolated farming town where the one-storey adobe and cinderblock houses are dominated by a large colonial church. Founded in 1537 by Bartolomé de Las Casas, Rabinal was the first of the settlements he established in his peaceful conversion of the Achi nation. The proportion of Indigenous inhabitants is high here and the fine **fiesta** (see box) has a uniquely Achi character. **Market days** (Tuesday and Sunday) are fascinating in Rabinal – look for some high-quality local artesanías, including carvings made from the *árbol del morro* (calabash tree) and traditional pottery.

Museo Comunitario Rabinal Achi

4 Av & 2 C, Zona 3 • Charge • museo.rabinal.info

The town's small **Museo Comunitario Rabinal Achi** is worth a visit, with exhibits on traditional medicinal practices, cultural history, local crafts including ceramics and weaving, and a moving room devoted to the impact of the civil war in the region (see page 221) including portraits of the dead.

Cerro Cayup

About 3km northwest of Rabinal, a steep ninety-minute hike away, are the ruins of one of the Achi nation's fortified cities, known locally as **Cerro Cayup**. The hilltop contains the remains of a temple and some fortifications and is actively used by Maya shamen for religious ceremonies. You can organize a guide at the museum to lead you here.

ARRIVAL AND INFORMATION — RABINAL

By bus Very regular services connect Rabinal with Salamá (every 30min; 45min). For Guatemala City, there are buses via La Cumbre (8 daily; 4hr) and via El Chol (3 daily; 6hr).

Services Banrural at 2 C & 2 Av, Zona 2, has an ATM.

ACCOMMODATION AND EATING

Cafetería Mishell del Rosario 1 C, behind the church. A reliable, casual comedor, with filling meals. $

Posada San Pablo 3 Av 1–50 7938 8025. This decent, well-run budget place is the best of Rabinal's several fairly basic hotels. $$

Cubulco

Leaving Rabinal, a paved road heads west, climbing a high ridge with fantastic views to the left into the uninhabited mountain ranges. The road then descends into the next valley to **CUBULCO**, an isolated town of Achi Maya and ladinos, surrounded on all sides by steep, forested peaks. There are few things to see here, but the town is renowned for its summer **fiesta**.

ACCOMMODATION AND EATING — CUBULCO

La Fonda del Viajero Mercado 7954 5451. There are several comedores in the market, but this scores highest marks, serving tasty, cheap *comida típica*. $$

Posada Paíz Next to the large farmacia in the centre of town (no phone). Nothing fancy here, but it's clean enough and some of the rooms come with private bathrooms. $

Reserva Sierra de las Minas

Forming one of Guatemala's largest expanses of **cloud forest**, the **RESERVA SIERRA DE LAS MINAS** is a misty, thinly populated region that harbours abundant wildlife such as

RABINAL AND THE CIVIL WAR

The Rabinal region suffered terribly during Guatemala's civil war – there were four **massacres** in 1982 alone. Local people have exhumed several of the mass graves that pepper the hillsides and reburied some of the 4400 victims from the municipality, in an effort to give those killed a more dignified resting place. In recent years, the Guatemalan state has addressed its role in *la violencia*, paying out US$8 million in compensation to surviving families and in 2011 President Colom apologized to relatives of the victims of the 1982 Dos Erres massacre near Rabinal, calling it "a stain on Guatemala's history".

The legal battle continues on several fronts with cases ongoing in the Inter-American Court. While some army generals who directed the campaign of terror have escaped justice, progress has been made. Five PUC (paramilitary conscripts) and at least five Kaibiles (special forces) have been jailed for their roles in the massacres – two sentences exceeding 6,000 years.

RABINAL'S UNESCO FIESTA

Rabinal's **fiesta**, which runs from January 19 to 24, is renowned for its dances, many of them precolonial in origin. The most famous is an extended dance drama known as the **Rabinal Achi** which re-enacts a battle between the Achi and K'iche' tribes and is unique to the town, performed annually on January 23 – it's been bestowed UNESCO World Heritage recognition. Others include the *patzca*, a ceremony to call for good harvests, using masks that portray a swelling below the jaw, and wooden sticks engraved with serpents, birds and human heads.

howler monkeys, white-tailed deer and coyotes. Birds found here include the emerald toucan, hummingbirds and fairly plentiful numbers of quetzals (see page 222).

This mighty mountain range is a tricky place to get to, with few access roads and incredibly steep terrain. For travellers, the main attraction is the spectacular **Salto de Chilascó** waterfall, which plunges 200m in two drops. It's accessed via a hike from the village of **Chilascó**, 12km east of the highway. The visitor centre in Chilascó, ⓣ5301 8928, is a good resource when planning a trip here.

Biotopo del Quetzal

Km 161, near Purulhá • ⓣ 3322 8596 • Charge

On the highway north to Cobán, just before the village of Purulhá, the **Biotopo del Quetzal** was established to protect the habitat of the endangered quetzal, Guatemala's

THE RESPLENDENT QUETZAL

The **quetzal**, Guatemala's national symbol (after which the country's currency and second city are named), has a distinguished past but an uncertain future. The bird's feathers have been sacred from the earliest of times, and in the strange cult of Quetzalcoatl, whose influence once spread throughout Mesoamerica, the bird was incorporated into the plumed serpent, a supremely powerful deity. To the Maya the quetzal was so sacred that killing one was a capital offence; it is also thought to have been the *nahual*, or spiritual protector, of the Maya chiefs. When Tecún Umán faced Pedro de Alvarado in hand-to-hand combat, his headdress sprouted the long green feathers of the quetzal, and when the conquistadors founded a city adjacent to the battleground they named it Quetzaltenango, "the place of the quetzals".

In modern Guatemala the quetzal's image saturates the country: it features on the national flag, and citizens honoured by the president are awarded the Order of the Quetzal. The bird is also considered a symbol of freedom, since caged quetzals die from the rigours of confinement. Despite all this, deforestation threatens the very existence of the bird, and the **Biotopo del Quetzal** is about the only serious step that has been taken to save it.

There are six species of the bird, but the male **resplendent quetzal** (found between southern Mexico and Panama) is the most exotically coloured. Its head is crowned with a plume of brilliant green, and chest and lower belly are a rich crimson; the unmistakeable iridescent green tail feathers (reaching some 60cm in length) are particularly evident in the mating season. The females, on the other hand, are an unremarkable brownish colour. The birds nest in holes found in dead trees, laying one or two eggs, usually in April or May.

MARIO DARY

The Biotopo del Quetzal is also known as the **Mario Dary Reserve**, in honour of an environmental campaigner who spent years campaigning for a cloud forest sanctuary to protect the quetzal, causing great problems for powerful timber companies in the process. He was murdered in 1988. An ecological foundation, Fundary, has been set up in his name to manage protected areas, including Punta de Manabique on the Caribbean coast.

FIESTA TIME IN CUBULCO

Cubulco is best visited for its annual fiesta. This is one of the few places where you can see the **Palo Volador**, a pre-conquest ritual in which men throw themselves from a 30m pole with a rope tied around their legs, spinning down towards the ground as the rope unravels, and hopefully landing on their feet. It's as dangerous as it looks, particularly when you bear in mind that most of the dancers are blind drunk; every few years an inebriated dancer falls from the top of the pole to his death. The fiesta still goes on, though, as riotous as ever, with the main action taking place on July 25. If you're in town at fiesta time be sure to taste the local **chilate** drink, made from corn and spices and served in fruit husks.

national bird (see page 222). The reserve covers a steep area of dense cloud forest, through which the Río Colorado cascades towards the valley floor, forming waterfalls and natural swimming pools. Two paths through the undergrowth from the road complete a circuit that takes you up into the woods above the reserve headquarters.

Quetzals are occasionally seen here but they're extremely elusive. The **best time of year** to visit is just before and just after the nesting season (between March and June), and the best time of day is sunrise. In general, the birds tend to spend the nights up in the high forest and float across the road as dawn breaks, to spend the days in the trees below. They can be easily identified by their jerky, undulating flight. A good place to look out for them is at one of their favoured feeding trees, the broad-leaved *aguacatillo*, which produces a small avocado-like fruit. Whether or not you see a quetzal, the forest itself (usually damp with *chipi-chipi*, a perpetual mist) is worth a visit: a profusion of lichens, ferns, mosses, bromeliads and orchids spread out beneath a towering canopy of cypress, oak, walnut and pepper trees.

ARRIVAL AND INFORMATION — BIOTOPO DEL QUETZAL

By bus Regular buses from Cobán (every 30min; 1hr) and Guatemala City (every 30min; 4hr) pass the entrance (at Km 161).

Information At the entrance to the reserve, just off the highway, there's a ticket office where you can get a map (for a fee) but very little other information.

ACCOMMODATION AND EATING

Hacienda Rio Escondido Km 144 ⓦ haciendarioescondido.com. This upmarket rural lodge has lovely wooden cabañas, some with two bedrooms, and a restaurant with excellent grilled meats. There's good birding in the forest around here. $$$

Hotel Posada Montaña del Quetzal Km 156.5 ⓣ 5800 0454. Offers attractive stone-and-timber bungalows with fireplaces and spacious doubles with private bathrooms; many have great forest views. There's also a restaurant, bar, swimming pool, walking trails and an orchid garden. Doubles $$$, bungalows $$$$

Ramtzul Resort Km 158.5 ⓦ facebook.com/ramtzul. The bizarre glass-fronted roadside restaurant is a blot on the landscape but at the rear are attractive, tasteful rooms built from bamboo, timber and stone – many with great views of the Verapaz hills. *Ram Tzul* sits on the edge of a large privately owned forest reserve, whose trails you are welcome to explore. $$$

Ranchitos del Quetzal Km 160.5 ⓦ ranchitosdelquetzal.com. Very close to the biotopo entrance, this rural lodge has well-furnished rooms on the fringe of a patch of cloud forest and a good café-restaurant. The owners are a delight, and will help you spot quetzals in the trees around the hotel. $$

Southern Alta Verapaz

Heading north of the quetzal sanctuary, the highway crosses into the department of **Alta Verapaz**, and another 13km takes you beyond the forests and into a luxuriant alpine valley of cattle pastures hemmed in by steep, perpetually green hillsides. Most people speed through this region on their way to Cobán, but there are a few interesting attractions to detain you if you have the time to explore these evergreen hills and their towns' curiosities. There's also a possible route east from here to the Caribbean along the **Polochic valley**.

Tactic and around

The first place of any size in southern Alta Verapaz is **TACTIC**, a small, mainly Poqomchi'-speaking town, which most buses bypass. The colonial **church** in the plaza is worth noting; it boasts an elaborate facade decorated with mermaids and jaguars.

High above the town up a long flight of steps, the pagan **Chi-ixim** chapel contains a dark-skinned Christ figure that attracts pilgrims from all over the country, but especially on January 15. Dozens of plaques of thanksgiving for miracles ascribed to the black saint of Chi-ixim, who also goes by the name Dios del Maíz ("Lord of Maiz"), adorn the walls.

ACCOMMODATION AND EATING — TACTIC AND AROUND

Café La Granja Km 187 on the highway cafelagranja.com. Just past the turn-off for Tactic, this ranch-style place has a menu of Guatemalan favourites plus sandwiches, pasta and salads in a great log-cabin-style setting. There's a kids' play area too. $$

Chí'ixím Eco Hotel Km 182.5, just off the highway 7953 9198. Rustic hotel which has comfortable bungalows with fireplaces and a spotless little dining room that serves some local dishes (meals $$). $$

San Cristóbal Verapaz and around

At the featureless settlement of **Santa Cruz Verapaz** there's a turn-off for **SAN CRISTÓBAL VERAPAZ**, an attractive town surrounded by fields of sugar cane and coffee set on the banks of the **Lago de Cristóbal**. The Poqomchi'-speaking Maya of San Cristóbal are among the last vestiges of one of the smallest highland tribes.

There's an excellent **community tourism** project here that allows visitors to explore the region with expert local guides and really get to grips with Poqomchi' culture. As all the hotels in town are pretty grim, you might want to drop by on a day-trip from Cobán.

Museo Katinamit

C del Calvario 0–03 • Charge, guide extra • 7950 4039

The **Museo Katinamit** hosts exhibits on the maguey plant, which is woven into bags, hammocks and rope; Verapaz flora and fauna; and music. Handicrafts are for sale too. The museum also acts as a base for the Centro Comunitario Educativo Poqomchi' (see below).

ARRIVAL, INFORMATION AND TOURS — SAN CRISTÓBAL VERAPAZ

By bus Microbuses and buses connect Cobán with San Cristóbal (about every 30min; 30min) until 7pm. They also run west to Uspantán (hourly; 2hr 15min) though the road is prone to landslides (see box).

Centro Comunitario Educativo Poqomchi' CECEP, at the Katinamit museum (7950 4896, cecep.cosmosmaya.info), organizes ethnotourism trips of Indigenous communities and sights around San Cristóbal including a hilltop Maya shrine, marimba factory and maguey-weaving villages. Spanish classes are also offered.

SEMANA SANTA IN SAN CRISTÓBAL

San Cristóbal knows how to throw a good **fiesta** – the town's biggest celebration runs from July 21 to July 26 (the main day is July 25) – and is also an excellent, almost tourist-free place to head for **Semana Santa**, when a 1km-long coloured sawdust carpet is created between the main church in the plaza and the Calvario chapel to the west.

HIGHWAY TO HELL

Heading west of San Cristóbal towards Uspantán (see page 108) the road passes through an unstable chunk of mountainous terrain that's prone to **landslides**. Hourly Cobán–Uspantán microbuses ply the route, but a hair-raising section involves inching along a precipitous slope; services may not run during heavy rains. West of the Río Negro bridge the highway is paved and in good shape. If you're driving, consider the long detour via Guatemala City.

The Polochic valley

If you're planning to head towards the Caribbean from Alta Verapaz the route east along the **Polochic valley** is the one to take – head east from the San Julián junction, shortly after Tactic on the Cobán–El Rancho highway. The scruffy towns along the length of this V-shaped valley hold little interest, but you'll witness an immense transformation in scenery as you drop down through the coffee-coated mountains and emerge into lush, tropical lowlands.

The first place at the upper end of the valley is **Tamahú**, 15km below which the town of **Tucurú** marks the point where the valley starts to open out and the river loses its frantic energy. In the hills above Tucurú is the spectacular **Chelemhá forest reserve**, where quetzals are common and there's a fine ecolodge (see below).

Continuing down the highway beyond Tucurú the road plunges abruptly, with cattle pastures starting to take the place of the coffee bushes. After 28km you reach **LA TINTA**, a sprawling town with at least one **place to stay**. Continuing east, it's just 13km to **TELEMÁN**, the largest of the squalid trading centres in this lower section of the valley.

Senahú and the Cuevas de Seamay

From Telemán a side road branches off to the north and climbs high into the fecund hills to the town of **SENAHÚ**, an important coffee centre that sits in a steep-sided bowl. Hikes run from here to the nearby **Cuevas de Seamay**, used by Maya shamen for ceremonies, and a track heads north to Semuc Champey and Lanquín, which is passable in the dry season by 4WD.

Panzós

Heading on down the Polochic valley from Telemán you soon reach the large town of **PANZÓS**, which was where the old Verapaz railway ended. In 1978 Panzós made international headlines when 53 protesting campesinos (including women and children) were killed by the army and police, one of the earliest massacres of General Lucas García's regime.

ARRIVAL AND DEPARTURE — THE POLOCHIC VALLEY

By bus Buses from Cobán for all towns on the Polochic valley leave at least hourly. From the highway, pick-ups and trucks head up side roads to settlements including Senahú and Cahabón. From Panzós buses run to Cobán (hourly; 6hr) via Telemán (5hr 15min). Regular buses shuttle between Telemán and Senahú.

ACCOMMODATION AND EATING

CHELEMHÁ

★ **Maya Cloud Forest Lodge** 26km north of Tucurú via a dirt road ☎ 5308 5160. Swiss-managed ecolodge with stunning views of the cloud forest that's very popular with birders: quetzals are present in numbers in the area, as are rare warblers, the highland guan (and some very vocal howler monkeys). The main cabin has four comfortable rooms, each with private bathroom, and there's a wonderful observation deck (with hummingbird feeders) and good meals in the restaurant. Expert guides are available and there are fine trails to explore. The lodge is accessible by 4WD only. Rates include full board and a guided hike. Call ahead. $$$$

SENAHÚ

Hotel El Recreo Senahú Parque Central ☎ 7983 1779. A comfortable option where rooms have private bathrooms and hot water. Guides for the Cuevas de Seamay can be arranged here. $$

Cobán

The heart of this misty alpine land and the capital of the department is **COBÁN**, famous for its cool, rainy climate and as a centre for gourmet **coffee** production. Your initial impression of the town may not be that favourable – heavy traffic crawls past the central plaza and the main downtown shopping district is pretty nondescript – but away from here Cobán soon reveals its charms. It's not a large place (the population is around 65,000) and suburbs fuse gently with outlying meadows and pine forests, giving the town the air of an overgrown mountain village.

Sights include two **orchid farms** and **coffee and tea plantations**, and you'll find genteel cafés where you can sample a cup made from the world-renowned Verapaz bean. Outside the town, the spectacular mountains and rivers hold all kinds of exciting **ecotourism** possibilities, many of which can be done as day-trips.

Like many other Guatemalan towns, Cobán is divided into a number of **zonas**, with the northeast corner of the **plaza** at 1 Calle and 1 Avenida the dividing point. Zona 1 is to the northwest, Zona 2 to the southwest, Zona 3 to the southeast and Zona 4 to the northeast.

Parque Central

From Cobán's elevated, triangular **Parque Central**, the town drops away on all sides. The plaza is dominated by the **catedral**, which is worth peering into to see the remains of a massive, ancient, cracked church bell. A block behind, the **mercado** bustles with trade during the day and is surrounded by food stalls at night. Cobán's prosperity from coffee (and more recently cardamom and allspice) has built the colonial-style hotels and coffeehouses in the streets around the plaza. Hints of the days of German control are also evident here and there in the town's architecture, which incorporates the occasional suggestion of Bavarian grandeur.

Finca Santa Margarita

3 C 4–12, Zona 2 • Charge • ⓣ 7951 3067

For a closer look at Cobán's principal crop, take the guided tour offered by the **Finca Santa Margarita**, a coffee plantation just south of the centre. The interesting tour (an English-speaking guide is usually available) covers the history of the finca, founded by the Dieseldorff family in 1888, and examines all the stages of cultivation and production, including a walk through the grounds. You also get a chance to sample different low-, middle- and high-altitude arabica coffee blends and, of course, purchase some beans.

El Calvario

Off 3 C, Zona 1 • Daily • Free

A short stroll northwest of the centre, the church of **El Calvario** is one of Cobán's most intriguing sights. Steep steps lead up via the Stations of the Cross – blackened by candle smoke and decorated with scattered offerings. There's a commanding view over the town from the whitewashed church, which has a distinctly pagan aura, often filled with candles, incense and corn cobs. The Calvario attracts many Maya worshippers and has both Christian and Maya crosses; the Sundays services are in the Q'eqchi' language.

Parque Nacional Las Victorias

3 C, Zona 1 • ⓣ 4999 2191 • Charge

Next to El Calvario, the **Parque Nacional Las Victorias** is Cobán's green lung, and a great place to stroll through the pines along attractive pathways; there's a children's playground too, and you'll find excellent trails for running or walking.

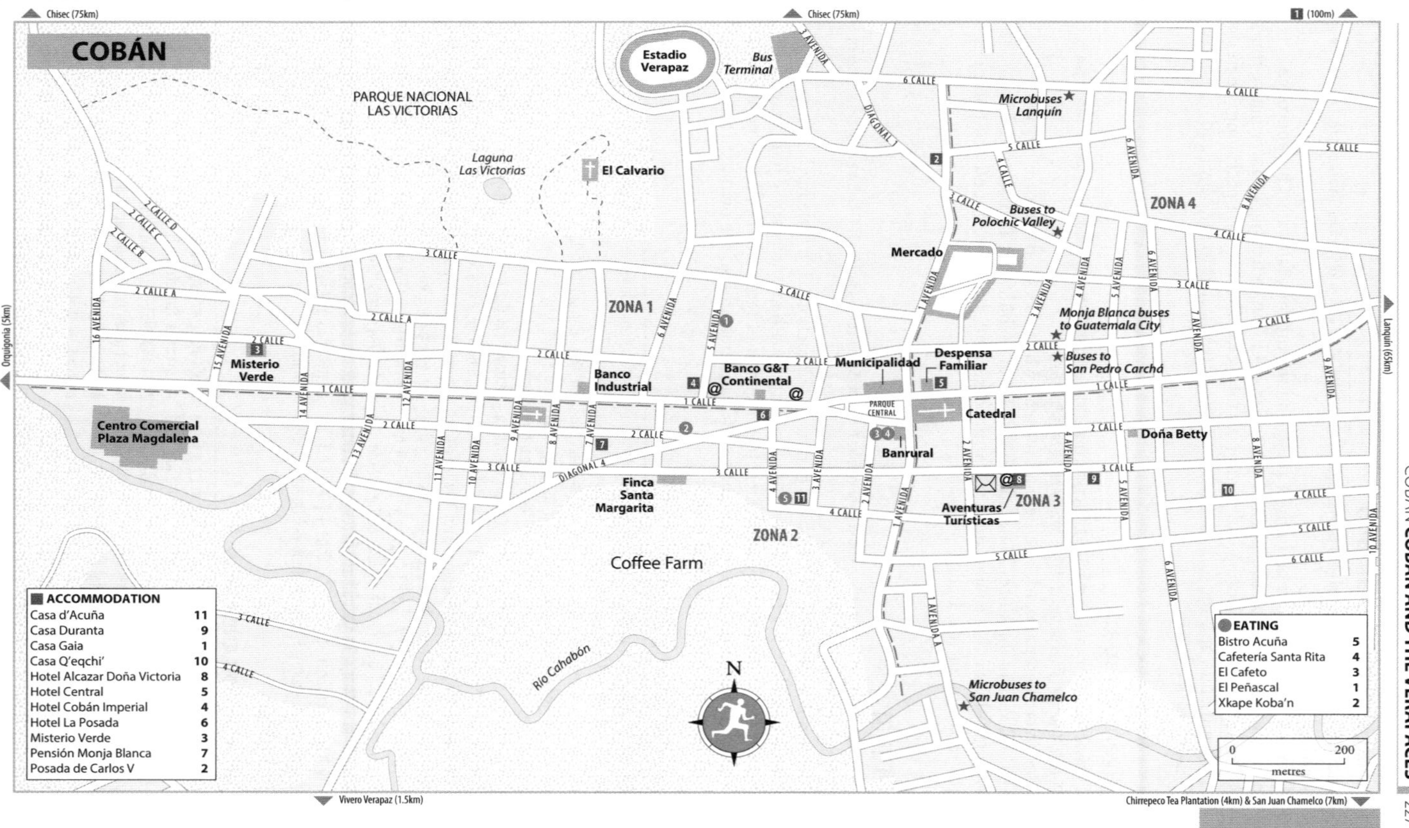
COBÁN
PARQUE NACIONAL LAS VICTORIAS
Laguna Las Victorias
El Calvario
Estadio Verapaz
Bus Terminal
Microbuses Lanquín
Buses to Polochic Valley
ZONA 4
Mercado
Monja Blanca buses to Guatemala City
Buses to San Pedro Carchá
ZONA 1
Misterio Verde
Banco Industrial
Banco G&T Continental
Municipalidad
Despensa Familiar
PARQUE CENTRAL
Catedral
Doña Betty
Banrural
Centro Comercial Plaza Magdalena
Finca Santa Margarita
Aventuras Turísticas
ZONA 3
ZONA 2
Coffee Farm
Río Cahabón
Microbuses to San Juan Chamelco
N
Chisec (75km)
Orquigonia (5km)
Lanquín (65km)
Vivero Verapaz (1.5km)
Chirrepeco Tea Plantation (4km) & San Juan Chamelco (7km)
ACCOMMODATION
Casa d'Acuña 11
Casa Duranta 9
Casa Gaia 1
Casa Q'eqchi' 10
Hotel Alcazar Doña Victoria 8
Hotel Central 5
Hotel Cobán Imperial 4
Hotel La Posada 6
Misterio Verde 3
Pensión Monja Blanca 7
Posada de Carlos V 2
EATING
Bistro Acuña 5
Cafetería Santa Rita 4
El Cafeto 3
El Peñascal 1
Xkape Koba'n 2
0 200 metres

5

Chirrepeco tea plantation

Km 217 Cobán–San Juan Chamelco rd • charge includes guide • ☎ 7950 0305 • Take a micro for San Juan Chamelco and get the driver to stop at Finca Chirrepeco

Coffee is not the only crop in these parts, and the organic, fairtrade **Chirrepeco tea plantation**, about 6km southeast of the centre of Cobán, offers highly informative tours of the full process: planting, cultivation techniques, harvesting and packaging. There's a small museum, and the tour also takes in some caves sacred to the Maya and, of course, finishes with a brew.

Vivero Verapaz

2.5km southwest of the centre • Charge • Take a taxi or jump on a micro heading for Tontem from 3 C, Zona 2; to get here on foot, take Diagonal 4, turn left at the bottom of the hill, cross the bridge and follow the road

The **Vivero Verapaz** garden center and nursery, which lies south of town beyond the coffee farm, produces hundreds of varieties of orchid, which are nurtured in a wonderfully shaded environment. A farm worker will show you around and point out the most spectacular buds.

Orquigonia

Km 206 Hwy 14, 6km southwest of the centre • Charge includes the 90min Spanish tour • ☎ 4740 2224 • Taxis are available; all buses on CA-14 pass by the entrance

Orquigonia, the second of Cobán's two orchid attractions, is a little further from town than Vivero Verapaz but better set up for visitors, with an interpretive trail, excellent guided tour (Spanish only) and a terrific collection of rare orchids, plants and flowers. The wooded grounds also attract many birds and butterflies. The orchids are at their best between November and February.

ARRIVAL AND DEPARTURE — COBÁN

By bus Most public transport arriving in Cobán drops you on the outskirts of town (with the exception of Monja Blanca buses from Guatemala City). The muddy main bus terminal in the north of the city, also known as Campo Dos terminal, has services to Chisec, Sayaxché, Flores, Uspantán, Nebaj, Salamá and Playa Grande. From Campo Dos it's a 20min walk or 5min taxi ride to the Parque Central. Buses for Lanquín use a bus stop at the junction of 3 Av and 6 C on the northeast side of town. Buses down the Polochic valley to El Estor leave from 3 Av and 3 C, Zona 4. For San Juan Chalmeco micros leave from the bridge at the bottom of 1 Av A, Zona 3. Monja Blanca pullman buses for Guatemala City have a terminal at 2 C 3–77, Zona 4 (☎ 8787 7751, Ⓦ monjablanca.com). For the Biotopo del Quetzal catch a Salamá bus.

Destinations Chisec (every 30min; 1hr 30min); El Estor (hourly; 7hr); Flores (1 daily, 1pm, or change in Sayaxché; 6hr); Fray Bartolomé de las Casas (every 45min; 2hr 30min); Guatemala City (every 30min 2am–6pm; 4hr 30min); Lanquín (hourly 6am–6pm; 2hr 15min); Nebaj (2 daily, or travel via Uspantán; 6hr); Playa Grande (every 30min; 4hr); Raxrujá (every 30min; 2hr); San Juan Chalmeco (every 10min; 15min); Sayaxché (hourly; 4hr); Uspantán (hourly; 3hr) (see page 108).

By shuttle bus For shuttle buses, book via your hotel, or contact Aventuras Turísticas (see below).

Destinations Antigua (3 daily; 6hr); Flores (2 daily; 6hr); Guatemala City (3 daily; 4hr 30min); Lanquín (3 daily; 2hr 15min).

INFORMATION AND TOURS

Information There is no tourist office in Cobán.

Spanish schools Cobán's easy-going atmosphere and relative lack of English-speakers makes it a good place to pick up Spanish. Oxford Language Center, 1 C 14–80, Zona 2 (☎ 4056 4559, Ⓦ oxfordcoban.org) is well regarded.

TOUR OPERATORS

Note that tours to Semuc Champey are offered by most hotels and every agent in town.

Aventuras Turísticas Hostal de Doña Victoria, 3 C 2–38, Zona 3 ☎ 7951 4213. Trips across both Verapaz departments including Semuc Champey and Laguna Lachúa.

Misterio Verde 2 C 14–36, Zona 1 ☎ 3856 8669. Cultural tourism specialist offering ecotourism trips, including visits to the Sierra Caquipec cloud forest that benefit disadvantaged communities.

ACCOMMODATION

Casa d'Acuña 4 C 3–11, Zona 2 casadeacuna.com; map page 227. A splendidly refined place to stay, with excellent four-bed dorms and a couple of (small) doubles, all with shared bathrooms, set to one side of a simply gorgeous courtyard restaurant (see below). Make sure you indulge in a meal while you're here. Dorms $, doubles $$

Casa Duranta 3 C 4–46, Zona 3 casaduranta.com; map page 227. This gorgeous, converted colonial house has bedrooms (7 and 8 are best) grouped around a wonderful central garden. All have wrought-iron bedsteads and attractive furnishings. There's a café, too. $$$

Casa Gaia 9 Av, Zona 10 hotelcasagaia.com; map page 227. On the northern edge of town, this lovely hotel, which also has a restaurant, is an oasis of calm with a spectacular garden, well-furnished rooms and a friendly host family who offer a personal touch. $$$

★ **Casa Q'eqchi'** 4 C 7–27, Zona 3 hotelencoban.com; map page 227. A wonderful guesthouse with just three rooms (and a suite). The very aesthetically pleasing design and decor combines exposed stone walls, hard-carved furniture and the liberal use of local textiles. The kind and attentive family hosts speak English and there's a pretty courtyard for chilling. Doubles $$$, suite $$$$

Hotel Alcazar Doña Victoria 3 C 2–38, Zona 3 7952 1388; map page 227. This place, decorated with antiques and artefacts, oozes character. The bedrooms all have private bathrooms (though avoid the noise-prone streetside rooms), and there's a cybercafé and tour agency on site. $$

Hotel Central 1 C 1–79, Zona 4 facebook.com/HotelCentralCoban; map page 227. A very centrally located hotel with spacious if plain rooms around a courtyard. They're a little dark but all have private bathrooms. $$

Hotel Cobán Imperial 1 C & 6 Av, Zona 1 7952 1131; map page 227. It's simple and not at all luxurious, but very clean and affordable. The staff are friendly, breakfast is included and the free wi-fi here runs at a high speed unheard of in these parts. The major sacrifice here is the size of the bathrooms; if you don't mind showering over the toilet then it's a great deal. $$

Hotel La Posada 1 C 4–12, Zona 2 laposadacoban.com.gt; map page 227. The *Posada* occupies a 400-year-old colonial building and boasts a beautiful, antique-furnished interior. Tasteful, comfortable rooms are set around two leafy courtyards, but traffic noise is an issue. There's a good restaurant and café. $$$

Misterio Verde 2 C 14–36, Zona 1 7952 1047; map page 227. Modern hostel with inexpensive rates, attractive accommodation, a great café for socializing and a garden. It's also the base of Misterio Verde tours (see page 228). Rates include a good breakfast. Dorms $, doubles $$

Pensión Monja Blanca 2 C 6–30, Zona 2 7952 1712; map page 227. Agreeably old-fashioned place with plenty of rooms, many come with private bathrooms; the hot water is reliable. The courtyard gardens are lovingly maintained, and don't miss the Victorian-style tearoom for breakfast. $$

Posada de Carlos V 1 Av 3–44, Zona 1 7951 3501; map page 227. It's set in urban Cobán, but this place looks like a cross between a mountain chalet and a motel. The twenty pine-trimmed rooms have cable TV and private bathrooms, and there's a restaurant. $$$

EATING

Eating in Cobán comes down to a choice between European-style **restaurants** and local **comedores**. Look out for the local speciality: *kak-ik*, a terrific turkey soup. You'll find the cheapest food at the market, but as it's closed by dusk, head to the street stalls set up around the Parque Central.

★ **Bistro Acuña** 4 C 3–17, Zona 2 casadeacuna.com; map page 227. A very classy restaurant in colonial premises with tables dotted around a lovely garden courtyard and several atmospheric dining rooms. It's fantastic for breakfast, lunch or dinner, and there are some exquisite fish and meat dishes. Waiters in starched white uniforms and classical music add to the refined atmosphere and the wine list includes many tempting half-bottles. $$$

Cafetería Santa Rita 2 C 1–36, Zona 2 7952 1842; map page 227. An archetypal comedor, ideal for cheap, filling *comida típica*, including huge breakfasts, with friendly service. $

El Cafeto 2 C 1–36, Zona 2 7951 2850; map page 227. This cosy little place serves coffee (from the local Chijoj finca), including cappuccinos. It's a good bet for breakfast: a full-on Guatemalan fry-up is a popular option. Sandwiches, burgers, hot-dogs and pastas are also served. $

El Peñascal 5 Av 6–21, Zona 1 7951 2102; map page 227. A restaurant whose authentic local dishes – *jocon*, steak in cardamom sauce – are widely acclaimed and nicely presented, many of them served in ceramic bowls. Also good for breakfast or a *menú de día*. $$

Xkape Koba'n Diagonal 4 5–13, Zona 2 facebook.com/xkape.koban; map page 227. Stylish café-restaurant in a gorgeous old house where the walls are decorated with *huipiles* and local art. There's a very inventive menu with snacks and many local recipes including the famous local *kak-ik* turkey soup, and *kakaw-ik* (a chocolate milk drink flavoured with vanilla, chilli and honey). $$

DIRECTORY

Banks G&T Continental and Banco Industrial are both on 1 C, west of the Parque Central; both have ATMs.

5

Car rental Tabarini, 7 Av 2–27, Zona 2 (@ tabarini.com).
Internet Inside *Hotel Alcazar Doña Victoria*, 3 C 2–38, Zona 3.
Laundry Doña Betty, 2 C 6–10, Zona 3.

Around Cobán: San Juan Chamelco

Seven kilometres southeast of Cobán, **SAN JUAN CHAMELCO** is the most important Q'eqchi' settlement in the area. Some of your fellow bus passengers are likely to be women dressed in traditional costume, wearing beautiful cascades of old coins for earrings. The large **market** around the church sells anything from local farm produce to blue jeans, but very little in the way of crafts.

The church

San Juan Chamelco's focal point is a large colonial **church**, whose facade is rather unexpectedly decorated with twin Maya versions of the Habsburg double eagle – undoubtedly a result of the historic German presence in the region. The most significant treasure, the church bell, is hidden in the belfry; it was a gift to the Maya leader Juan Matalbatz from no less than the Holy Roman Emperor Charles V.

Grutas de Rey Marcos

5km east of Chamelco • @ grutasdelreymarcos.com • Charge includes guide service, hard hat and boot rental • Minibuses for the village of Chamíl pass close to the caves; they leave regularly from 0 C & 0 Av in Chamelco

Five kilometres east of Chamelco are the **Grutas de Rey Marcos**, a cave system more than 1km long, though the tour only takes you a little way into the complex – you have to wade across an underground river at one stage to see some of the best stalactites and stalagmites, including one that's a dead ringer for the Leaning Tower of Pisa.

Lanquín and around

Northeast of Cobán, a paved road heads off into the lush hills, connecting a string of coffee fincas. After 48km the road reaches the **Pajal** junction, where a dirt road cuts down deep into a valley to **LANQUÍN** (a further 12km away). This sleepy, modest Q'eqchi' village, where Spanish is very much a second language, shelters beneath towering green hills, whose lower slopes are planted with coffee and cardamom bushes. The village itself is very relaxed and quite attractive, but virtually every visitor in town is here to enjoy the extraordinary pools of **Semuc Champey**, a short ride away.

Lanquín caves

1km west of Lanquín • Charge

Just off the road to Cobán, the **Lanquín caves** are a maze of dripping, bat-infested chambers, stretching for at least 3km underground. A walkway has been cut through the first few hundred metres and electric lights have been installed, but it remains dauntingly slippery. Refrain from using flash photography in the cave (it unsettles the bats). It's well worth dropping by the entrance at dusk, when thousands of bats emerge from the mouth of the cave and flutter off into the night. Maya **religious rituals** are held here (particularly at fiesta time and on December 5) when the whole village gathers for candlelit ceremonies.

K'anba caves

9km south of Lanquín • Entrance by guided tour • Charge

Just before the entrance to Semuc, the **K'anba cave** system is a lot more fun to explore than Lanquín's caves. Guided spelunking tours involve scrambling and swimming by candlelight through chambers filled with bats and bizarre rock formations. For the brave (or mad) there are the optional additional thrills of climbing a dodgy rope ladder up the side of a 5m waterfall or cliff-jumping into a pool in complete darkness. The tour takes about an hour and a half and finishes with some river tubing. Wear shoes (there are sharp rocks underfoot).

Semuc Champey

10km south of Lanquín • Charge; parking extra

The region's prime attraction, and one of the most beautiful natural destinations in Guatemala, is **Semuc Champey**, a shallow staircase of sublime turquoise pools suspended on a natural limestone bridge. This idyllic spot sits at the base of a towering jungle-clad valley and makes a wonderful destination for a blissful day's wallowing and swimming. Just a few years ago very few visitors made it to this remote part of Guatemala, but the secret is now definitely out, and the pools are very much a key stop on the Central America backpacking trail. That said, you can usually find a peaceful corner without too much difficulty.

If you walk a few hundred metres upstream via a slippery path you come to the river source that feeds Semuc: the fast-flowing **Río Cahabón**, the bulk of which plunges into a cavern, cutting under the pools in an aquatic frenzy before emerging again downstream. For a photo-perfect view of the whole scene, you can hike (and climb a little in sections) for twenty minutes up a slippery, vertiginous trail to a *mirador* high above the pools.

There are security guards at the site, but it's best not to leave your belongings unattended. You'll find a small café and there are vendors selling drinks and snacks at the entrance.

While you can visit on your own, most travellers choose to visit Semuc as part of a **tour**, which avoids having to wait for infrequent public transport or tackling the terrible dirt access road.

ARRIVAL AND DEPARTURE — LANQUÍN AND AROUND

TO LANQUÍN

By bus Public microbuses connect Cobán with Lanquín (hourly 6am–6pm; 2hr 15min). Buses also struggle north between the Pajal junction and Fray Bartolomé de Las Casas (hourly; 2hr) via a rough road, though ongoing road improvements will speed up this route again in the next few years; check with your hotel for the latest information. Heading east, there are buses to Cahabón (roughly hourly; 1hr 15min), from where one daily bus (4am; 4hr) and irregular pick-ups head down to El Estor.

By shuttle bus There are connections from Antigua (2 daily, 8am & 2pm; 8hr) and Cobán (3 daily; 2hr). Note that service standards on these routes are poor, and minibuses are beat-up and uncomfortable. The Antigua buses are particularly bad; the 2pm departure involves travelling at night (which is not recommended). On arriving in Lanquín don't listen to what local hustlers tell you about accommodation options being full; some of these guys board shuttle buses. There's also one daily 4WD shuttle pick-up at 7.30am to Río Dulce Town.

TO SEMUC

By truck To get to Semuc Champey without a tour you'll need to catch a pick-up or truck from Lanquín's plaza (roughly every 40min until 4pm; 45min).

Tours Tours to Semuc are offered by all the main Lanquín guesthouses including *Zephyr Lodge* and *El Retiro*. The cost usually includes for a full day including the K'anba caves and a guide. Several hotels and agencies in Cobán also run day-trips.

ACCOMMODATION AND EATING

There are places to stay both in and around the village of **Lanquín** and strung out along the road to **Semuc**. Many are hostel-style establishments geared towards backpackers, but there are also basic guesthouses in the village that will do for a night.

Comedor Shalom 250m northeast of Parque Central, Lanquín village. An excellent local place with three or four set-meal deals that change daily, friendly local staff and clean surroundings. $$

Hostal El Portal 100m before Semuc ☎ 4091 7878. Community-owned lodge, just a short walk from Semuc, which enjoys river views. The accommodation is inviting, with well-built screened wood cabañas with hammocks and balcony, cosy private rooms and a dorm. There's great birding and a restaurant, but electricity only between 6 and 10pm. Dorms, doubles $$, cabañas for two $$$

El Muro Lanquín village ☎5483 3335, facebook.com/murolanquin. A sociable hostel with dorms, doubles and hammock space, good tours and lots of bar business. Dorms $, doubles $$

Posada Illobal Beyond the market and bank in Lanquín centre ☎4068 3399. The best of the village cheapies, with a nice garden and five plain, clean rooms in an old wooden house, some with valley views. A good option if you'd rather not be swamped with gap-year students. $$

La Poza Riverside Guesthouse A 15min walk east of Lanquin village ☎5818 2546, lapoza@rocketmail.com. Stunning four-bedroom riverside house that's a great deal for groups, with a deck overlooking the Río Lanquín, tubes, table tennis, a sauna and extensive grounds. There are discounts for longer stays. House $$$$

El Retiro Lodge On the banks of the Río Lanquín elretirolodgelanquin.com. This long-running riverside lodge has a lovely setting, and accommodation is well designed, consisting of four-bed dorms, cabins, suites and rooms, some with private bathrooms. Still draws backpackers, though the vibe is quite not what it was. Dorms $, doubles $$, cabins $$$

Utopia Eco Hotel 3km before Semuc utopiaecohotel.com. Terrific ecolodge in a remote, beautiful location that enjoys a lovely riverside plot on the banks of the Cahabón. There's rustic accommodation and camping, inexpensive (vegetarian) food, a communal vibe and lots to do including hikes, tubing and Spanish lessons. Dorms $, cabañas $$, cabins $$$

★ **Zephyr Lodge** Just north of Lanquín centre facebook.com/zephyrlodgelanquin. Top dog in Lanquín, this lodge offers stunning views over the Lanquín river valley and evergreen Verapaz hills and has a great pool. The fine accommodation – dorms, doubles and two-storey cabañas – is characterful and comfortable, and staff are switched on to travellers' needs. The food is great, with plenty of veggie choices, and it's a sociable place with a lively bar scene. Reserve ahead. Dorms $, doubles $$

DIRECTORY

Banks Banrural, south of Lanquín plaza, changes US dollars (but has no ATM).

Internet There's a little internet café on Lanquín's plaza.

Cahabón

Beyond Lanquín the road continues to the small town of **CAHABÓN**, 24km to the east, where there are only basic *hospedajes*. From here a dirt track spirals around a number of switchbacks to Panzós, cutting high over the mountains then plunging down through spectacular scenery.

ARRIVAL AND DEPARTURE — CAHABÓN

By bus One daily bus (at 4am) makes the 4hr trip to El Estor, supplemented by pick-ups that ply the route more frequently. There are roughly hourly connections to Cobán via Lanquín (last bus 3pm).

Destinations Cobán (about every 90min; 3hr); El Estor (1 daily; 4hr); Lanquín (hourly; 1hr 15min).

Northern Alta Verapaz

In **northern Alta Verapaz**, the lush hills drop away steeply onto the plain that marks the frontier with the department of **Petén**. The terrain is a beguiling mix of dense patches of rainforest, towering tooth-like outcrops of limestone called karsts, and pastureland. Some of the most extensive **cave systems** in Latin America are located here, particularly in the **Candelaria** region, which is riddled with caverns. The paved highway runs north from Cobán, passing **Parque Hun Nal Ye** and **Chisec**, from where you can explore Bombil Pek cavern and Lagunas de Sepalau, then skirts the ruins of **Cancuén**. Otherwise it's dirt tracks all the way, including a branch road that leads to the spectacular, remote lake of **Laguna Lachúa**.

Parque Hun Nal Ye

Turn-off at Km 295 on the Cobán–Chisec highway, then 10km east along a dirt road • Charge; various packages available (including a "canopy package", kayaking and ATV rental) plus overnight "Jungle Night" stays • ☎3131 8313

Parque Hun Nal Ye is a well-organized **eco-park** encompassing 135 hectares of rainforest, lagoons, a waterfall and verdant hills rich with wildlife including toucans, amphibians and reptiles. A multitude of activities are on offer: zip-lining, horse-riding, hiking, tubing, kayaking and canopy tours, along with an overnight "jungle experience". There's also a small **museum** dedicated to the important Maya relics found here including a highly unusual stone box carved with glyphs.

Chisec and around

Some 60km north of Cobán, **CHISEC** is a quiet, agreeable little town spread out along the highway that's grown quickly in the last few years as land-hungry migrants have moved into the region. It's one of the very few places in Guatemala without a church on its huge central plaza – many of its population are former guerrillas and *repatriados* opposed to religious influence.

Bombil Pek

3km north of Chisec • Guided tour charge

Chisec makes the perfect base for visiting two impressive natural attractions, the nearest being the "painted cave" of **Bombil Pek**. There's a community-run guide office 1km north of Chisec, right on the highway, where you pay your entrance fee and collect a flashlight; they also rent **tubes** (best July–October) for river exploration here. A guide leads you along a delightful forty-minute hike through the *milpa* fields and forest, and down a steep, slippery wooden staircase into the sinkhole and its vast 50m-high main cavern. Many ceramics have been found here, and the cave is still used for Maya religious ceremonies.

Your guide will then try to persuade you to squeeze through a tiny hole at the rear – this can be difficult for all but the skinniest of travellers – to a second, much smaller cave where the faded painted images of two monkeys, possibly representing the hero twins of the Popol Vuh (see page 103), adorn the walls.

Lagunas de Sepalau

Near Sepalau Cataltzul, 10km southeast of Chisec • Charge • Pick-ups run sporadically all day from the town's plaza

The three jade lakes of **Lagunas de Sepalau** are Chisec's other outstanding attraction. Access is via the village of **Sepalau Cataltzul**, where entrance fees are collected. While you're here, ask to see the secondary school that has been built from recycled plastic bottles and inorganic waste.

A local guide will accompany you to the lagoons, 1km further away, where there are *lanchas* for paddling across the water (and lifejackets). **Laguna Paraíso**, the first lake, is ringed by untouched dense jungle and has beautiful turquoise water; the second, **Atsam'ja**, is much smaller. The third and largest lake, **Q'ekija**, another kilometre down the track, is the most remarkable of all – a gorgeous blue-green colour, with near-vertical limestone sides backed by towering jungle, it's perfect for swimming. Birdlife includes kingfishers and toucans, and you're likely to hear howler monkeys too.

ARRIVAL AND INFORMATION — CHISEC

By microbus Microbuses connect Cobán with Chisec (every 30min; 1hr 30min), and also run to/from Raxrujá via Candelaria (every 30min; 45min).

Services Banco Agromercantíl, on Chisec plaza, has an ATM.

ACCOMMODATION AND EATING

Hotel Bombil Pek On the highway, 1.25km north of the plaza ⓣ 4853 3565, ⓔ bombilpek_viavictoria@hotmail.com. Also known as *Via Victoria*, this place has modern semi-detached cottages, with fan or a/c, and all with two double beds and attractive furnishings. They're priced per person, so represent a good deal for solo travellers. $$

Hotel Estancia de la Virgen On the highway, 800m north of the plaza ⓣ 5514 0800. Huge concrete hotel with four floors of basic, functional rooms with cable TV and either a/c or fan. There's a good restaurant and small swimming pool. $$

Restaurant Bombil Pek On the highway, at the southern end of the village facebook.com/christopherjosuerummlerfigueroa. Large, clean, welcoming place, excellent for filling *comida típica*, if a bit pricey for what it is. $$

Candelaria caves

The limestone mountains in northern Alta Verapaz are full of **caves**, of which the most impressive and extensive are those at **Candelaria**, northeast of Chisec. Here the Río Candelaria has formed an astonishingly complex system of caverns and passages, occasionally penetrated by skylights from the surface. The Candelaria cave network extends for 22km (though if you include all the subsidiary systems it's more like 80km) and includes some truly monumental chambers.

It's quite straightforward to visit part of this cave network, but rather confusingly, there are four possible entrances. Two are community-run (**Candelaria Camposanto** and **Mucbilhá**) and two are privately owned (**Cuevas de Candelaria** and **Cuevas de los Nacimientos** – these are the most impressive).

Candelaria Camposanto caves

Km 309, Cobán–Raxrujá highway • Charge; tubing extra

At **Candelaria Camposanto** there are two main caves: Entrada de Sol – measuring some 70m in length and 30m in width – and the smaller Murciélago, where you might see some bats, and perhaps hear the roar of the howler monkeys that live nearby. An interpretive trail leads from the highway to the caves, with information panels about the fruits, plants and trees, wildlife and folklore of the region.

Mucbilhá caves

Km 315, Cobán–Raxrujá highway • Charge; tubing extra

A community tourism project provides access to the **Mucbilhá caves**, where guides will lead you to the large Venado Seco cavern, a return hike of an hour or so. The tubing trip here follows an underground section of the Río Candelaria.

Complejo Cultural de Candelaria

Km 316.5, Cobán–Raxrujá highway • Charge (minimum three people) includes a 1hr tour and a guide to the first cave system • cuevasdecandelaria.com

If you only have time to visit one cave system in Candelaria, pick **Complejo Cultural de Candelaria**, which includes some of the most spectacular caverns in the entire region. The largest cave here is the 200m-long, 60m-wide "Tzul Tacca", where skylight shafts create a spectacular light show on the rocks and cavern water below. Access is via the grounds of the *Candelaria Lodge* (see page 235); just follow the path from the highway at the "Cuevas de Candelaria" sign and guides will appear.

Cuevas de los Nacimientos

Access by tour only, charge; minimum four people • cuevaslosnacimientos.com

The most memorable way to explore the cave system is on one of the full-day **river tours** run by *Hotel Cancuén* in Raxrujá (see below) that visit the **Cuevas de los Nacimientos**. These take in the crystalline Cueva Blanca, and involve floating for several hours through bat-filled caverns on a tube.

ARRIVAL AND INFORMATION — CANDELARIA CAVES

Organized trips *Hotel Cancuén* in Raxrujá (see below), organizes tours of Los Nacimientos. Many Cobán travel agents (see page 228) also run trips to the Candelaria area.

By bus All buses travelling between Cobán and Raxrujá (every 30min) pass by the entrances to Candelaria Camposanto, Mucbilhá and Cuevas de Candelaria. All are signposted and just off the highway.

ACCOMMODATION AND EATING

Candelaria Lodge Km 316.5 on the highway facebook.com/CandelariaLodge. A rustic lodge with excellent, if overpriced, rustic cabins decorated with art and fabrics; not all have private bathrooms. The Guatemalan and French food is superb for lunch or dinner, though again very pricey. Note there are some rather picky hotel rules. Access to the Complejo Cultural de Candelaria caves (see page 234) is from here. $$$

Raxrujá

RAXRUJÁ is little more than a few streets and some ramshackle buildings straggling round a bridge over the Río Escondido, a tributary of the Pasión, but it does function as a gateway to the extensive ruins of Cancuén and the Candelaria caves, and it offers some decent **accommodation**.

ARRIVAL AND DEPARTURE — RAXRUJÁ

By bus or microbus Microbuses leave for Chisec and down to Cobán, and also north to Sayaxché. The rough road south to the Pajal junction (for Lanquín) is a constant work in progress. Head for the nearby town of Fray Bartolomé de Las Casas, from where microbuses depart for Sebol and via the Pajal junction, south to Cobán. The road east via Fray to Modesto Méndez is a well paved road and part of the Franja Transversal del Norte highway. Check the latest information in Raxrujá before you set off.

Destinations Cobán (every 30min; 2hr); Fray Bartolomé de Las Casas (every 20min; 20min); Modesto Méndez Sayaxché (every 30min; 2hr 30min).

ACCOMMODATION AND EATING

Doña Reyna Just north of the main junction in the centre. Despite its scruffy-looking appearance, this busy comedor has earned a reputation for serving up filling, flavoursome meals. $

★ **Hotel Cancuén** Towards the western end of town cuevaslosnacimientos.com. Excellent place with broad selection of fine-value, clean, neat rooms; bathrooms have cold water in the cheaper options, but as this is a tropical-hot town that won't matter. Dr César, the friendly owner, also offers great trips (see above) out to the Cuevas de los Nacimientos (minimum four people) and to Cancuén ruins. There's a small comedor on site. $$

Fray Bartolomé de Las Casas

Sixteen kilometres east of Raxrujá is the isolated settlement of **FRAY BARTOLOMÉ DE LAS CASAS**, referred to as simply "Fray" or "Las Casas" by locals. The town has several accommodation options and comedores, as well as ATMs and a thriving market. Otherwise, there's little of interest here; it is mainly of use as a **transit point** between Alta Verapaz and other popular areas, including Modesto Méndez on a recently paved road.

ARRIVAL AND DEPARTURE — FRAY BARTOLOMÉ DE LAS CASAS

By bus or microbus Buses leave the marketplace bus terminal for Cobán via Raxrujá (and also less frequently via Pacal, which is the junction for Lanquín). There are also regular micros to Modesto Méndez on the main Petén highway. The road to Pacal is (very slowly) being upgraded and transport links should speed up in the coming years. Brace yourself for the constant construction and delays that come with this.

Destinations Cobán via Chisec (every 30min; 2hr 30min); Cobán via Pajal (at least 5 daily; about 5hr); Modesto Méndez (every 45min; 2hr); Poptún via San Luis (every 2hr; 4hr).

ACCOMMODATION

Hotel y Restaurante Valle del Sol 3 C 1–00, Zona 1 4039 7977. This hotel has dozens of good-value if plain singles and doubles, all with hot-water bathrooms and TV. The restaurant serves tasty dishes, including local specialities like *kak-ik*. $$

Cancuén

18km north of Raxrujá • Charge includes Spanish-speaking guide

North of Raxrujá is the large Maya site of **Cancuén**, where a huge Classic-period palace has been unearthed. Cancuén was discovered in 1907, but the sheer size of the ruins had been underestimated, and investigations in 1999 revealed the vast scale of the royal enclave here. The site is enigmatic in many ways: uniquely, Cancuén seems to have lacked the usual religious and defensive structures characteristic of Maya cities and appears to have existed as an essentially secular merchant city. The vast amounts of jade, pyrite, obsidian and fine ceramics found recently indicate that this was actually one of the greatest trading centres of the Maya World, with a paved plaza (that may have been a marketplace) covering two square kilometres. Cancuén is thought to have flourished because of its strategic position between the great cities of the lowlands, like Tikal and Calakmul, and the mineral-rich highlands of southern Guatemala.

The site

A trail takes you past the ruined remains of workshops where precious materials including jade were fashioned into jewellery by expert artisans. It continues to a **ball court**, where there are replicas of some beautifully carved markers; one depicts ruler Taj Chan Ahk passing the staff of the ruling dynasty to his son Kan Maax in 795 AD.

Before visiting nobility could enter Cancuén's royal enclave, they'd stop to perform ritual cleansing at a highly unusual 10m stone **bathing pool**, then climb a hieroglyphic staircase to the entrance of the elite. The vast, almost ostentatious triple-level **palace** (Structure L7-27) itself has 170 rooms and eleven courtyards. Its sides are adorned with dozens of life-sized stucco figures, and it is Cancuén's most impressive structure.

The trail continues past several stricken **stelae**, and returns through some towering hardwood trees to the modest visitor centre, which has information panels (some with English translations) and a model of the site. Cancuén's very finest carvings lie elsewhere; there's an absolutely stunning altar panel in the Museum of Maya Sculpture in Cobán (see page 297).

ARRIVAL AND DEPARTURE — CANCUÉN

By minibus and boat To get to Cancuén, pick-ups and minibuses (approximately hourly) leave Raxrujá for the *aldea* of La Unión 12km to the north, where boatmen will take you by *lancha* (reservations ☎5978 1465) for the 30min ride (in groups of up to sixteen people) along the Río de la Pasión to the site.

Parque Nacional Laguna Lachúa

82km west of Raxrujá • Charge • On public holidays the park can quickly fill to its 84-person limit; book ahead to reserve your place; ☎5861 0088 or ☎7861 0086 • There's absolutely no access into the reserve by vehicle

West of Raxrujá, the paved highway crosses steamy, thinly populated lowlands – the flatness of the landscape broken periodically by soaring forest-topped karst outcrops – to the magical **Parque Nacional Laguna Lachúa**, a near-circular lake surrounded by a dense tropical jungle. One of the least visited national parks in Central America, this is a supremely beautiful, tranquil spot, with pristine azure-blue waters that are perfect for swimming. About 2km in diameter and more than 200m deep, Lachúa is thought to be a natural sinkhole in the limestone crust, though its circular shape has led to speculation that it could have been formed by a meteorite impact. The rangers are extremely protective of this magnificent national park, and visitors have to carry back all non-biodegradable material.

The reserve is home to tapir and all the main Central American wild cats, including jaguar, but though these creatures usually prove elusive, you're virtually guaranteed to hear howler monkeys, and armadillos and otters are often seen. There's also an abundance of exotic **birdlife** (around three hundred species have been recorded here), including snail kites and flycatchers – but watch out for mosquitoes.

ARRIVAL AND DEPARTURE — LAGUNA LACHÚA

By bus Getting to the Lachúa region is obviously easiest if you take a tour from Cobán (see page 228), but it's not that tough under your own steam. Staff at Lachúa can help with local transport schedules and information. From the Cobán bus terminal, minibuses leave every 30min for Playa Grande (2hr 45min) via Chisec and the junction of Xuctzul; this route is (luxuriously) paved. (There are also slower buses for Playa Grande via Cubilhuitz, which use a dirt track through Salacuím and the three-way junction of San Luís.) Coming from Chisec or Raxrujá, there are buses to Playa Grande (roughly every hour; 2hr), or you could get to the Xuctzul junction and catch a connection there. From Playa Grande you then catch a bus back towards Raxrujá and get off at the park entrance/information centre on the highway.

ACCOMMODATION

Hotel Laguna Lachúa Within the reserve, 4km from the highway ⊕4084 1706. This fine national park lodge is a sweltering 4km hike through the forest from the information centre/car park on the highway; advance booking by phone is essential. The large wood-and-thatch building is divided into well-kept rooms, each with good

FIESTAS IN COBÁN AND THE VERAPACES

Baja Verapaz is famous for its fiestas. In addition, Cobán hosts the **National Fiesta of Folklore** in August, which is attended by Indigenous groups from throughout the country.

JANUARY

15 Tactic, large pilgrimage to the town's Chi-ixim chapel.
19–24 Rabinal, most important dates are Jan 23 (for the Rabinal Achi dance) and the main day, Jan 24.
22–25 Tamahú, main day Jan 25.

HOLY WEEK

San Cristóbal Verapaz, big religious processions.

MAY

1–4 Santa Cruz Verapaz.
4–9 Tucurú, main day May 8.

JUNE

9–13 Senahú, main day June 13.
21–24 San Juan Chamelco, main day June 24 (includes spectacular costumed processions).
24–29 San Pedro Carchá, main day June 29.
25–30 Chisec, main day June 29.

JULY

20–25 Cubulco, includes the *Palo Volador* on the final day.
21–26 San Cristóbal Verapaz, main day July 25.

AUGUST

July 31–Aug 6 Cobán, followed by the National Fiesta of Folklore.
11–16 Tactic, main day Aug 15.
22–28 Lanquín, main day Aug 28.

SEPTEMBER

17–21 Salamá, main day Sept 17.
25–29 San Miguel Chicaj, main day Sept 29.
27–30 San Jerónimo, main day Sept 30.

DECEMBER

First week Cobán, orchid exhibition held in town's convent (next to the cathedral).
6–8 El Chol, main day Dec 8.

beds and mosquito nets, or you can camp. You'll have to bring all your own supplies, including drinking water, as there's no restaurant or food store, but you will find a fully equipped kitchen. Camping/person $, doubles $$

Peyán canyon

About 25km southwest of Lachúa, there's another wonderful natural attraction where the turquoise waters of the broad Río Chixoy are forced through a narrow gap in a limestone plateau known as the **Peyán canyon**. This canyon, just 4m wide in places, is best explored by boat, but you can walk to a viewpoint above it in thirty minutes from the isolated village of **Salacuím**, which is on the dirt road between Cubilhuitz and Playa Grande. Ask around for a boatman in Salacuím or hire a local guide for the walk.

Río Ik'Bolay

Trips leave from Rocjá Pomtila, 24km southeast of Laguna Lachúa • Charge; half-day boat trip (up to six people); guide extra • Organize tours in advance via village tourism coordinator Javier Ca'al (T 5381 1970)

Twelve kilometres east of Laguna Lachúa along the road to Chisec is the junction known as San Benito; look out for the excellent roadside *Comedor California* at the turn-off. From here a rough dirt track heads south for 12km to the tiny Q'eqchi' *aldea* of **Rocjá Pomtila** – the jumping-off point for wonderful boat trips up the **Río Ik'Bolay**. The river journey is extremely scenic, passing banks lined with towering tropical trees, and you're sure to see kingfishers skimming across the water. After 45 minutes the boat stops and you embark upon a slippery trail up the riverbank, past waterfalls to a *nacimiento* (spring), where you can squat down for a jet-powered bidet.

ARRIVAL AND INFORMATION — RÍO IK'BOLAY

By bus There's one daily bus (10am) from Cobán's bus terminal to Rocjá Pomtila; it returns at 3.30am, so that villagers can get to market.

Services Very few visitors stay the night, but many villagers in Rocjá Pomtila offer beds and will prepare meals for a small charge.

Playa Grande

The transport hub for the Ixcán region is the sprawling, dusty town of **PLAYA GRANDE** (also referred to as just "Playa", or Cantabal or Ixcán), about 12km west of Laguna Lachúa. This is an authentic frontier settlement of scruffy cinder-block-built houses, Mexico-bound migrants and a few rough bars. It is also the main administrative centre for the Ixcán region and has a few hotels and ATMs.

From Playa Grande it's possible to journey west into northern Huehuetenango, via a rough road (parts of which are paved) via San Mateo Ixtantán to the frontier at Gracias a Dios.

ARRIVAL AND DEPARTURE — PLAYA GRANDE

By bus There's very regular transport to Cobán. Pick-ups and buses cover the route between Playa Grande and Barillas (around 5hr). This once rough road is now a part of the Franja Transversal del Norte highway, stretching west via Raxrujá to Modesto Méndez, however land disputes along its route, and the associated on road protests, can make the journey slow going.

Destinations Barillas (roughly hourly until noon; 5hr); Cobán (2hr 45min; every 30min).

ACCOMMODATION AND EATING

Hotel España A block south of Parque Central T 4536 5040. Secure place with three classes of rooms, some very basic, but all with firm beds and some with private bathroom and a/c, and a comedor on site. $$

Hotel La Reina Vasty Av Principal T 7755 7985. The smartest option in town for those seeking clean, plain rooms, some are equipped with a/c, which in the tropical heat will make your stay more comfortable. $$$

Hotel y Cafeteria La Franja 3km west of town on the Barillas rd ☎ 3022 7984. A modern motel-style place with tidy tiled rooms and private bathrooms, plus cable TV; there's a little café too. $$

Petén

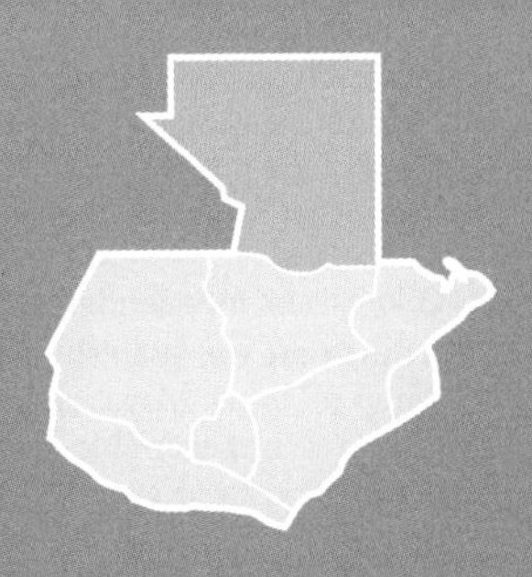

TEMPLE I, TIKAL

Petén

The vast northern department of Petén occupies about a third of Guatemala but contains less than four percent of its population. Both the birthplace and heartland of the ancient Maya civilization, the region is peppered with hundreds of sites, and exploring the temples and palaces is an unforgettable experience. The ruins are surrounded by a huge expanse of tropical rainforest, swamps and savannah, with ancient ceiba and mahogany trees that tower above the forest floor. Petén is also extraordinarily rich in wildlife: around four hundred bird species have been sighted at Tikal alone, including hummingbirds, toucans, hawks and wild turkeys. Among the mammals are lumbering tapir, ocelots, jaguars and monkeys, plus thousands of species of plants, reptiles, insects and butterflies.

In the past few decades, however, swathes of this uniquely biodiverse environment have been ravaged. Waves of **settlers** have cleared enormous tracts of forest, oil companies and commercial loggers have cut roads deep into the jungle and narcos use clandestine landing strips deep inside nature reserves. The population of Petén, just fifteen thousand in 1950, is today around 595,000, a number that puts enormous pressure on the remaining forest. Despite forty percent of Petén being officially protected as the **Reserva de la Biósfera Maya** (Maya Biosphere Reserve), regulations are widely ignored, deforestation continues, and ecological activists are subject to routine threats.

The hub of the department is **Lago de Petén Itzá**, home to the delightful lakeside settlement of **Flores**, which makes a perfect base. An hour or so away are the astonishing ruins of **Tikal**, Petén's prime attraction, superbly located in a rainforest reserve: no trip to Guatemala would be complete without a visit. Other imposing sites include fascinating, accessible **Yaxhá**, while the ruined cities of the **Lago de Petexbatún** region, particularly **Aguateca**, are spectacular. In terms of scale and historical importance, a trip to the jungle-buried monumental remains of **El Mirador**, a 2700-year-old city of superpower status, offers a once-in-a-lifetime experience – for anyone who has the time and energy for the trek to get there, that is.

Brief history

For almost two thousand years from 1000 BC onwards, **Maya culture** reached astounding architectural, scientific and artistic achievements (see page 328). Petén was at the heart of this magnificent culture: great cities rose out of the forest, surrounded by huge areas of raised, irrigated fields and connected by a vast network of causeways. But climatic changes provoked the fall of the Preclassic Maya in northern Petén about 150 AD, and, incredibly, history repeated itself seven centuries later when high population densities and a prolonged drought provoked the collapse of the Classic Maya. At the close of the tenth century, the great cities of Petén were abandoned, after which some Maya moved north to Yucatán, where their civilization flourished until the twelfth century.

Colonial and Independence eras

By the time the **Spanish** arrived the area had been partially recolonized by the Itza, a group of Toltec Maya who inhabited the land around Lago de Petén Itzá. The forest proved so impenetrable that it wasn't brought under Spanish control until 1697, more than 150 years after they had conquered the rest of the country, when Tayasal was destroyed. The invaders had little enthusiasm for Petén, though, and it remained a backwater. It wasn't until 1970 that Petén became genuinely accessible by road.

FLORES

Highlights

❶ **Finca Ixobel** Kick back and enjoy this rural retreat, set in the pine-clad foothills of the Maya Mountains. See page 247

❷ **Flores** Petén's most attractive settlement is a friendly little historic town, with a cosmopolitan choice of restaurants and cafés. See page 248

❸ **El Remate** This pretty village, with a wonderful lakeside location and excellent accommodation, makes a tranquil base for trips to ruins and exploring the shore of Lago de Petén Itzá. See page 255

❹ **Tikal** The spectacular ruins of an ancient Maya metropolis, set in a protected rainforest reserve that's teeming with wildlife. See page 257

❺ **El Mirador** Hike through the virtually untouched forests of northern Petén to the giant temples of this Preclassic Maya superpower. See page 269

❻ **Lago de Petexbatún** Fringed by thick rainforest, this beautiful remote lake features some fascinating Maya ruins dotted around its shores. See page 275

❼ **Yaxhá** The ruins of this once-massive Maya city include a glut of imposing temple pyramids, some from the Preclassic era. See page 280

HIGHLIGHTS ARE MARKED ON THE MAP ON PAGE 244

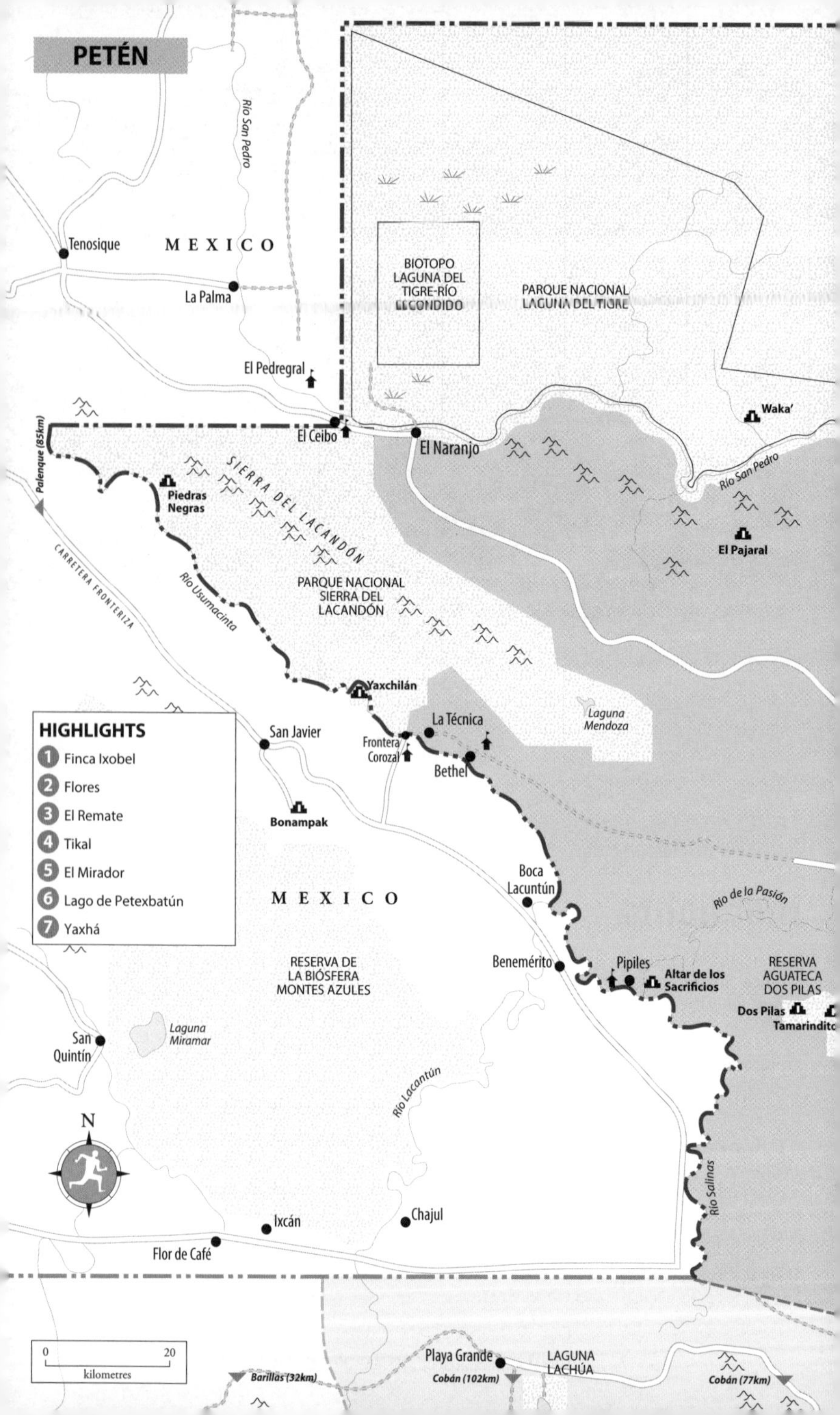
PETÉN
MEXICO
Tenosique
La Palma
Río San Pedro
BIOTOPO LAGUNA DEL TIGRE-RÍO ESCONDIDO
PARQUE NACIONAL LAGUNA DEL TIGRE
El Pedregral
El Ceibo
El Naranjo
Waka'
Río San Pedro
El Pajaral
Palenque (85km)
Piedras Negras
SIERRA DEL LACANDÓN
PARQUE NACIONAL SIERRA DEL LACANDÓN
Río Usumacinta
CARRETERA FRONTERIZA
Yaxchilán
La Técnica
Laguna Mendoza
Frontera Corozal
Bethel
San Javier
Bonampak
HIGHLIGHTS
1 Finca Ixobel
2 Flores
3 El Remate
4 Tikal
5 El Mirador
6 Lago de Petexbatún
7 Yaxhá
Boca Lacuntún
Río de la Pasión
MEXICO
Benemérito
Pipiles
Altar de los Sacrificios
RESERVA AGUATECA DOS PILAS
Dos Pilas
Tamarindito
RESERVA DE LA BIÓSFERA MONTES AZULES
San Quintín
Laguna Miramar
Río Lacantún
Río Salinas
N
Ixcán
Chajul
Flor de Café
0
20
kilometres
Playa Grande
LAGUNA LACHÚA
Barillas (32km)
Cobán (102km)
Cobán (77km)

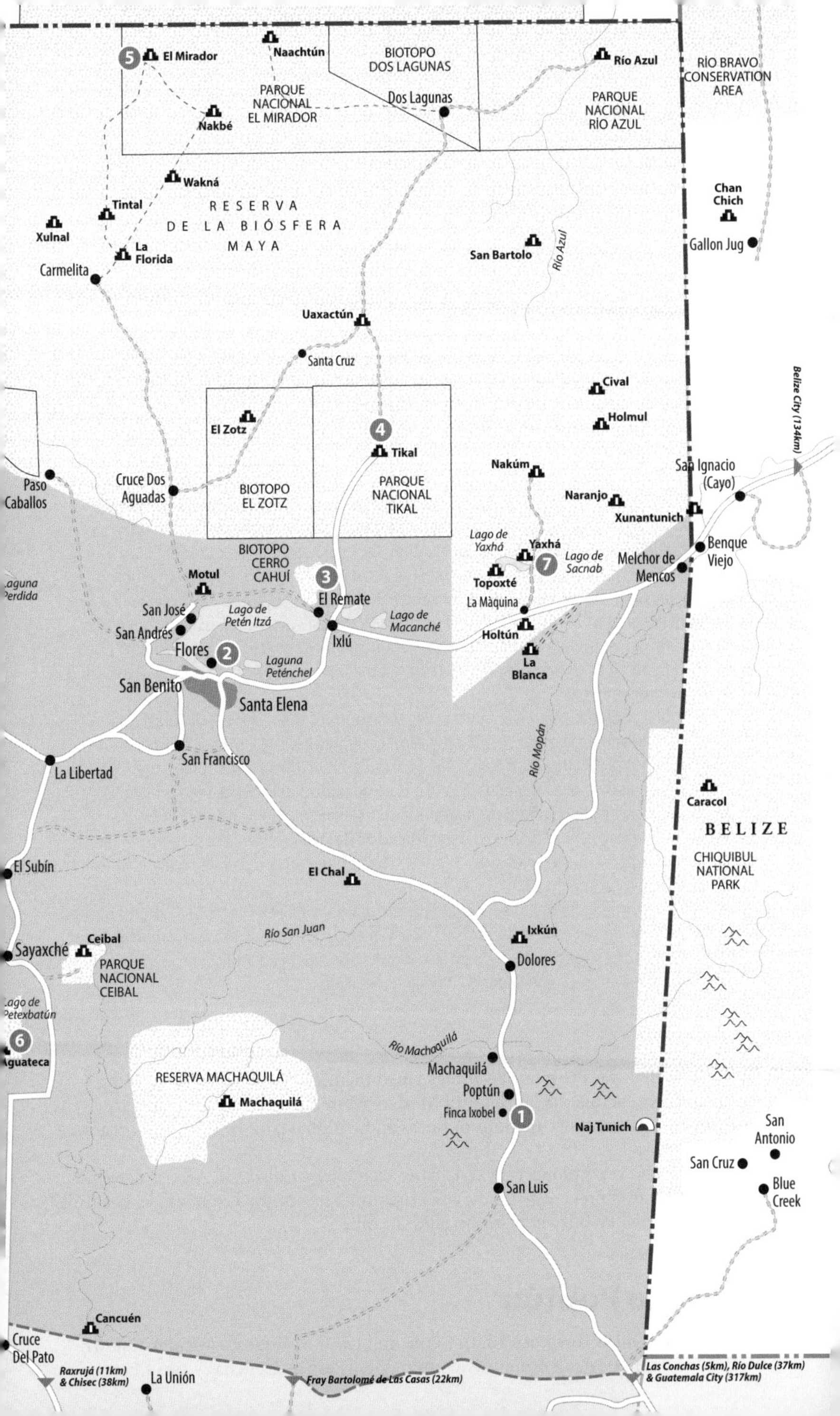
El Mirador
Naachtún
BIOTOPO DOS LAGUNAS
Río Azul
RÍO BRAVO CONSERVATION AREA
PARQUE NACIONAL EL MIRADOR
Dos Lagunas
PARQUE NACIONAL RÍO AZUL
Nakbé
Wakná
Tintal
RESERVA DE LA BIÓSFERA MAYA
Chan Chich
Xulnal
La Florida
San Bartolo
Río Azul
Gallon Jug
Carmelita
Uaxactún
Santa Cruz
Cival
Belize City (134km)
Holmul
El Zotz
Tikal
Nakúm
San Ignacio (Cayo)
Paso Caballos
Cruce Dos Aguadas
BIOTOPO EL ZOTZ
PARQUE NACIONAL TIKAL
Naranjo
Xunantunich
Lago de Yaxhá
Yaxhá
Lago de Sacnab
Benque Viejo
BIOTOPO CERRO CAHUÍ
Melchor de Mencos
Laguna Perdida
Motul
El Remate
Topoxté
La Màquina
San José
Lago de Petén Itzá
Lago de Macanché
San Andrés
Ixlú
Holtún
Flores
Laguna Peténchel
La Blanca
San Benito
Santa Elena
Río Mopán
San Francisco
La Libertad
Caracol
BELIZE
El Subín
El Chal
CHIQUIBUL NATIONAL PARK
Río San Juan
Ixkún
Sayaxché
Ceibal
PARQUE NACIONAL CEIBAL
Dolores
Lago de Petexbatún
Aguateca
Río Machaquilá
Machaquilá
RESERVA MACHAQUILÁ
Poptún
Machaquilá
Finca Ixobel
Naj Tunich
San Antonio
San Cruz
San Luis
Blue Creek
Cancuén
Cruce Del Pato
Raxrujá (11km) & Chisec (38km)
La Unión
Fray Bartolomé de Las Casas (22km)
Las Conchas (5km), Río Dulce (37km) & Guatemala City (317km)

THE RESERVA DE LA BIÓSFERA MAYA

In 1974 UNESCO established the idea of **biosphere reserves** in an ambitious attempt to combine the protection of natural areas and the conservation of their genetic diversity with scientific research and sustainable development. The **Reserva de la Biósfera Maya**, created in 1990, covers 16,000 square kilometres of northern Petén: in theory it is the largest tropical forest reserve in Central America.

On the premise that conservation and development can be compatible, land use in the reserve has three designations: **core areas** include the national parks, major archeological sites and the *biotopos*, areas of scientific investigation. The primary role of core areas is to preserve biodiversity; human settlements are prohibited, though tourism is permitted. Surrounding the core areas are **multiple-use areas** where inhabitants, aided and encouraged by the government and NGOs, are able to engage in sustainable use of the forest resources and small-scale agriculture. The **buffer zone**, a 15km-wide belt along the southern edge of the reserve, is intended to prevent further human intrusion but contains many existing villages.

Fine in theory, particularly when you consider that much of the reserve borders protected lands in Mexico and Belize. In practice, however, the destruction of Petén's **rainforest** proceeds virtually unchecked in many parts. Less than forty percent of the original cover remains and illicit logging is reducing it further. Oil exploration is the other industry that has driven the destruction of the forest in the west of the reserve, as petroleum companies have pushed roads deep into the Parque Nacional Laguna del Tigre. Successive Guatemalan governments have aided and abetted the oil companies, issuing concessions for exploration. As soon as a road exists, land-hungry migrants follow and slash-and-burn the forest and plant *milpas,* which they farm. After a few years the thin soil is depleted, and cattle ranchers move in.

Although much has been lost in the west and south of the reserve, environmental groups are fighting to conserve what remains. Foreign funding provides much of the finance for protection, and NGOs are working with settlers to encourage the sustainable use of forest resources. Tourism is an accepted part of the plan and visitors are increasingly getting to remote *biotopos* and national parks – though numbers are still small. The forests and swamps of the **Mirador Basin** (W miradorbasin.com) at the core of the reserve are still well preserved and have been spared thanks to the efforts of environmental campaigners.

President Jimmy Morales has supported the creation of a Mirador National Park and pushed for UNESCO World Heritage status. NGO Global Conservation (W globalconservation.org) is a key player in the region, working hard to establish a Mirador Park Authority: rangers now patrol the forests to monitor illegal hunting and incursions.

Petén today

During the civil war the **guerrilla armies** based themselves in Petén, and fighting pushed refugees across the border into Mexico. More recently disputes have arisen over **land rights**, with mass occupations of fincas and national park land by well-organized peasant groups.

In the last few years pioneering aerial laser technology called LiDAR has detected more than 60,000 previously unknown structures beneath the Petén jungle, ensuring archeologists will be busy here for decades to come.

North to Poptún

North of Río Dulce Town, it's 40km to the dull town of **Modesto Méndez** (known locally as Cadenas). Aside from the tempting pools of Las Conchas west of here there's nothing to detain you until you reach Poptún, an area that's home to one of Guatemala's finest rural lodges: **Finca Ixobel**.

Las Conchas

Around 34km west of Modesto Méndez, the huge, broad waterfalls of **Las Conchas** lie at the confluence of the rivers Chiyú and Chahal. These sublime pools are great for swimming, and are well off the tourist trail, so you won't be bothered by crowds. Minibuses (about every 45 minutes) heading west from Cadenas towards Fray Bartolomé de Las Casas pass within 4km of the falls.

Poptún

Heading north on the highway to Santa Eleana, the next place of interest is the scruffy town of **POPTÚN**, situated at an altitude of 530m. There's no particular reason to stay here, as the wonderful *Finca Ixobel* (see below) is so close, but there are banks with ATMs and it's served by plenty of buses.

ARRIVAL AND DEPARTURE POPTÚN

By bus and minibus Minibuses shuttle between Poptún and Santa Elena (for Flores), while a constant stream of buses and minibuses head south to Río Dulce and on to Guatemala City all day and night.

Destinations Fray Bartolomé de Las Casas (every 2hr; 3hr 15min); Guatemala City via Río Dulce Town (every 30min; 7hr); Santa Elena (every 30min; 2hr).

ACCOMMODATION

★ **Finca Ixobel** About 5km south of Poptún fincaixobel.com. This farm and solar-powered ecolodge is a legendary travellers' meeting point. It's a supremely beautiful and relaxing place where you can swim in the pond, play volleyball and table tennis and enjoy delicious (mostly organic and home-grown) food. You run a tab, paying when you leave – which can be a rude awakening. Volunteer workers are usually needed, too, which means you'll get accommodation and meals for free. Activities include self-guided walks, horse-riding, tubing and visits to Maya ruins. Microbuses and chicken buses will drop you off at the entrance gate, from where it's a 15min walk; after dark, take a tuk-tuk from Poptún. Camping & dorms $ per person, tree houses & doubles $$, bungalows with bathroom $$$

Naj Tunich cave

23km east of Poptún • Tours (charge per person depends on numbers) are organized by Finca Ixobel (see above)

The remote painted cave of **Naj Tunich**, 23km down a rough track from Poptún, has some of the finest cave art of the Maya World, dating back to 100 BC. Due to the fragility of the site, it's not possible to see the original cave paintings, but some excellent replicas more than compensate.

Caves were sacred to the ancient Maya, who believed them to be entrances to Xibalbá, the dreaded underworld; Naj Tunich was one of the most revered sites and a place of pilgrimage. Local artists have re-created some of the extensive hieroglyphic texts, depictions of religious ceremonies and the ball game, as well as the graphic **erotic scenes** thought to be unique to this site.

Dolores and around

North of Poptún, it's 24km to **DOLORES**, a dusty, growing town set just east of the highway. There's no reason to stop except to take in the town's impressive **archeological museum** (charge), which has modern displays, some intricately carved glyph blocks from Ixtutz and artefacts (including some fine incense burners) from sites including Machaquilá. An hour's walk north of town are the Maya ruins of **Ixkún** (charge), a mid-sized site made up of eight plazas.

Flores

Easy-going **FLORES** is a delightfully sedate place with an old-fashioned atmosphere, quite unlike the rest of the region's towns. Made up of a cluster of cobbled streets and ageing houses built around a twin-domed church, it sits beautifully on a small island in **Lago de Petén Itzá**, connected to the mainland by a short causeway.

Across the water lie the twin towns of **SANTA ELENA** and **SAN BENITO**, both of which are ugly, chaotic and sprawling places, dusty in the dry season and mud-bound during

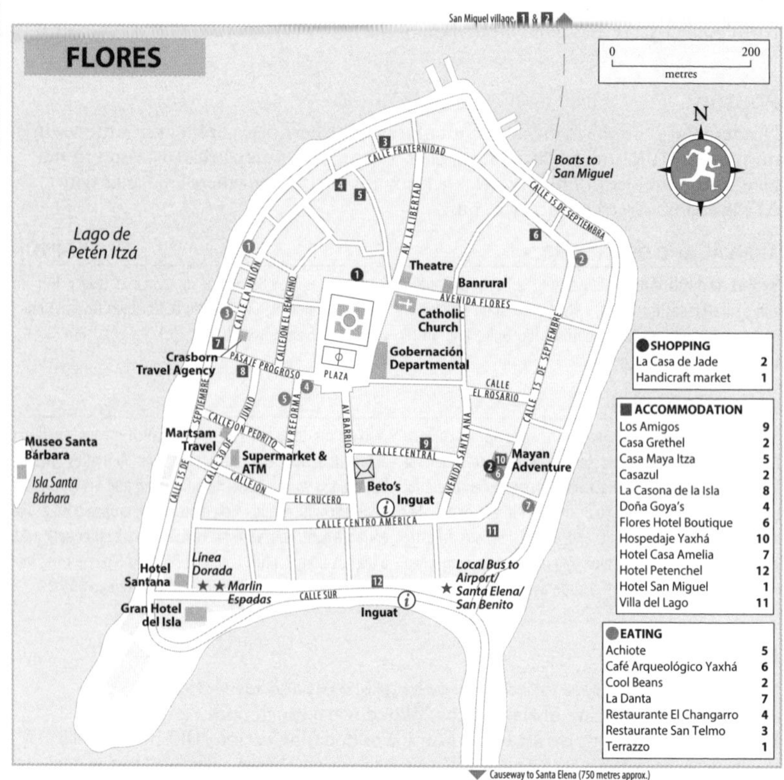

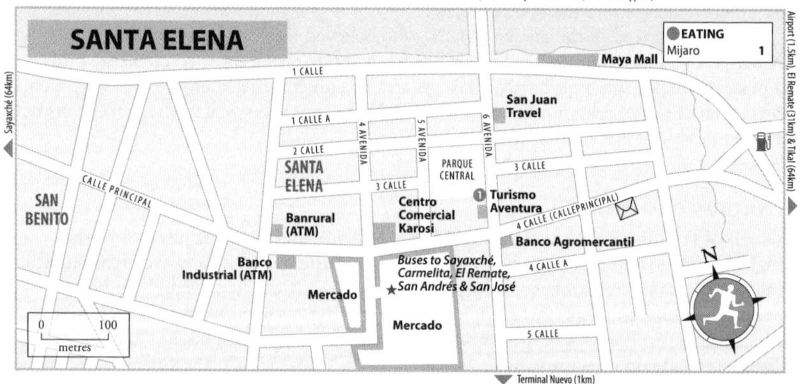

FLORES' COYOTES

Many travellers experience the hard sell on arrival in Flores from local **ticket touts**, known as **coyotes**. These guys (many speak good English) try to get you to book hotel rooms, tours and transport with them, so they can earn a commission. Some lie about hotels being full and sell bogus tickets. Several travellers every week purchase expensive shuttle/bus tickets to distant destinations (such as Copán in Honduras) only to find their tickets are not valid. Be especially wary when arriving on tourist shuttles from Belize and Mexico, when you are likely to be travel-weary and new to the country. Only book direct through reputable agencies and hotels, and if you do get fleeced, report any trouble to PROATUR (see page 45).

the rains. Santa Elena, opposite Flores at the other end of the causeway, is strung out between the airport and the market, and takes in a shopping mall, a few hotels, banks and two bus terminals. San Benito, further west, has even less going for it. The three towns, along with the tiny settlement of **San Miguel** across the water, are often lumped together under the single name of Flores.

Today, despite the steady flow of tourists passing through, the island village of Flores retains a genteel air, with residents greeting one another courteously in the streets. Though it has little to detain you in itself – a leisurely thirty-minute stroll around the lanes is enough to become entirely familiar with the place – the town does offer an enjoyable, historic base and has an excellent selection of hotels, restaurants and tour operators.

Brief history

Lago de Petén Itzá is a natural choice for settlement, and its shores were heavily populated in Maya times: the city of **Tayasal**, capital of the Itza, lay on the island that was to become modern Flores. Cortés passed through here in 1525, leaving behind a sick horse, and in 1618 two Franciscan friars arrived to find the people worshipping a statue of a horse called "Tzimin Chac". Unable to persuade the Maya to renounce their religion, they smashed the image and left the city. The town was eventually destroyed by Martín de Ursúa and an army of 235 in 1697. For the entire colonial period (and indeed up to the 1960s), Flores languished in virtual isolation, having more contact with neighbouring Belize than with the capital.

ARRIVAL AND DEPARTURE — FLORES

BY PLANE

The airport is 3km east of the causeway. Tuk-tuks/taxis connect the airport and town. Note that demand for flights to Guatemala City is heavy in peak periods, and overbooking is common. Reserve well in advance and arrive promptly for check-in.

Destinations Guatemala City (5–7 daily; 2 with Avianca [avianca.com] and 3–5 with TAG [tag.com.gt]; 50min). Belize City (1 daily with Tropic Air [tropicair.com]; 45min).

BY BUS

Most buses use Santa Elena's large, fairly modern Terminal Nuevo on 6 Av about 2km south of the causeway (Línea Dorada buses continue on to Flores). There are also some services around Lago de Petén Itzá, to San Andrés and San José from here. For Copán in Honduras, catch a bus heading for San Pedro Sula. Some local buses also use bus stops at the market in Santa Elena – there are buses from here to destinations across Petén, including Poptún and Sayaxché.

Destinations from Terminal Nuevo Belize City (1 daily, 7am, with Línea Dorada; 2 daily at 5am and 8am with Fuente del Norte; 5hr); Chiquimula (5 daily; 7hr 30min); El Ceibo border (7 daily; 4hr); El Naranjo (every 30min; 4hr); El Remate (every 30min; 45min); Guatemala City (3 daily with ADN; 3 daily with Línea Dorada; 15 daily with Fuente del Norte; 2 daily with Rápidos del Sur; most services stop in both Poptún and Río Dulce en route; 9hr); La Técnica via Bethel (6 daily; 4hr 30min); Melchor de Menchos (micros every 30min; 2hr 15min); Poptún (every 30–60min; 2hr); San Pedro Sula, Honduras (1 daily, 5.45am, with Fuente del Norte; 2 daily, 6am & 10am, with María Elena; 12–14hr); San Salvador (1 daily, 5.45am, with Fuente del Norte; 12hr); Sayaxché (every 20–30min; 2hr); Tikal (6 daily; 1hr 30min); Uaxactún (1 daily; 2 hr 45min).

Destinations from Market terminal Carmelita (2 daily 5am and 1pm; 5hr); San Andrés (every 30min; 30min); San José (every 30min; 35min).

BY SHUTTLE BUS

You should only book shuttle buses and tours through recommended travel agents or hotels. Don't buy tickets from freelance guides, as scams are common. Note that San Juan Travel uses its own private terminal on 6 Av in Santa Elena, but will collect you from your accommodation.

Destinations Belize City (2 daily; 5hr); Chetumal (2 daily; 8hr); Cobán (daily; 5hr 30min); Lanquín (daily at 8am; 8hr); Palenque (2 daily; 8hr); Tikal (several daily; 1hr).

INFORMATION

Information *Los Amigos Hostel* (see below) is probably the best source of information for budget travellers. Speak to Dieter at *Café Arqueológico Yaxhá* for advice about trips to Maya sites.

Inguat The official tourist board has an office on C Centro América in Flores (T 7867 5365, E peten@inguat.gob.gt), and a booth at the airport.

TOURS AND ACTIVITIES

Flores has dozens of tour operators, many of them are very average, and lots of "coyotes" (see page 249). Stick with the outfits we list below.

TOUR OPERATORS & TRAVEL AGENCIES

Crasborn Travel Agency C La Union W crasborntravel.weebly.com. Reliable agency with keenly-priced transport options, tours and good advice.

Martsam Travel C 30 de Junio, Flores W martsam.com. A professional outfit offering well-organized tours to sites including Yaxhá and Aguateca, and helicopter trips to El Mirador.

Mayan Adventure Inside Café Arqueológico Yaxhá, C 15 de Septiembre, Flores T 4284 1840. Archeologist owner Dieter offers great trips to Yaxhá and a fantastic jungle hike between El Zotz and Tikal. Trips to lesser-known sites like La Blanca and San Clemente are also very worthwhile.

San Juan Travel 6 Av, Santa Elena T 5847 4738. This company does not have a good reputation (buses are often late and poorly maintained) but is one of the only options for shuttle services to Belize City and Chetumal.

Turismo Aventura 6 Av & 4 C, Santa Elena W toursguatemala.com. A good all-rounder with trips to Maya ruins, tailor-made trips and airline tickets.

ACTIVITIES

Language schools Dos Mundos (Av 15 de Septiembre, Flores; T 5830 2060, W flores-spanish.com) has one-on-one, group and crash courses in Spanish. On the other side of the lake, the villages, San José and San Andrés (see page 254) also have schools.

Voluntary work All the language schools have programmes for volunteers, including helping women's groups, teaching children and doing environmental work. ARCAS (Asociación de Rescate y Conservación de Vida Silvestre), the Wildlife Rescue and Conservation Association (T 7926 0946, W arcasguatemala.org), runs a rescue and rehabilitation programme for animals and birds.

ACCOMMODATION

Flores has a wide range of hotels and budget places. Neighbouring **Santa Elena** is much noisier and dirtier. Sleepy, pretty **San Miguel** also has a few good options; *lanchas* connect it with Flores every few minutes.

FLORES

★ **Los Amigos** C Central W amigoshostel.com; map page 248. This well-established and popular hostel makes a fine and sociable base. There's a pretty courtyard garden, an eclectic veggie menu, a reliable travel agency and excellent transport information. Their "Dorm de Lux" boasts beds with orthopedic mattresses, privacy curtains, fans, USB chargers and reading lights, and has an en-suite bathroom. Dorms $, doubles $$

★ **Casa Maya Itza** Callejon Corona, W casamayaitza.hotelonia.com; map page 248. This welcoming guesthouse enjoys a quiet location a few steps from the lakeshore and has a selection of simple, colourful rooms with good fans (some have a/c). There's a well-equipped guests' kitchen. $$

Casazul C Fraternidad W hotelesdepeten.com; map page 248. Decorated in shades of blue, this colonial-style property has tasteful, spacious rooms with private bath, fridge, a/c and TV; some have lake-facing balconies. $$$

La Casona de la Isla C 30 de Junio W hotelesdepeten.com; map page 248. This gorgeous-looking old hotel has a decent selection of rooms (those on the upper floors, particularly 41–43, have the best lake views) with good-quality beds, a/c and cable TV. Guests have access to a lakeside terrace, pool, jacuzzi and restaurant-bar. $$$$

Doña Goya's 1 C La Unión W hospedajedonagoya.weebly.com; map page 248. A dependable, inexpensive budget place offering no-frills but spacious dorms (which don't have lockers) and reasonably large doubles (you pay more for a view). The rooftop terrace, with hammocks, is a definite bonus. Dorms $, doubles $$

KNOW YOUR GAME

Some Flores restaurants serve **wild game**, often listed on menus as *comida silvestre*. Virtually all this has been taken illegally from reserves and national parks – avoid in particular ordering items such as *tepescuintle* (paca, a large relation of the guinea pig), *venado* (deer) and *coche de monte* (peccary, or wild pig).

Flores Hotel Boutique C Fraternidad 7867 5768; map page 248. Beautifully appointed apartments with elegant furnishings, beds with lovely linen and fully equipped kitchens. There's a roof terrace with lake views and hammocks, and fine service. Rates include airport/bus station transfers. $$$$

Hospedaje Yaxhá C 15 Septiembre 5830 2060; map page 248. Attractive rooms (with private bathroom) and three dorms (two with air-con) above the recommended *Café Arqueológico Yaxhá* restaurant (see below). Dorms $, doubles $$

Hotel Casa Amelia C La Unión 7867 5430, booking.com; map page 248. A four-storey green-and-white hotel with thirteen good-value, very spacious rooms with cable TV, six of which have great views of the lake. Single rooms are well priced. $$$

Hotel Petenchel C Sur 7867 5450; map page 248. This place has a row of good, clean, double rooms with hot-water bathroom, fan and TV. There's a little café here, too where breakfast (not included in rates) is served. Expect some street noise from tuk-tuks and traffic. $$

Villa del Lago C 15 de Septiembre hotelesdepeten.com; map page 248. Three-storey building with a great upper-floor terrace with sweeping vistas of the lake. The 21 rooms are comfortable but the decor is slightly dated; all have a/c and many have great views. $$$

SAN MIGUEL

Casa Grethel San Miguel village 5989 0480; map page 248. Connected to Flores by a free boat service, this tranquil lakeside place is well worth considering, with friendly staff and very clean rooms and dorms (all air-conditioned). There's a fine view of Flores from the front deck and ample sunloungers to really sink into holiday mode. Dorms $, doubles $$

Hotel San Miguel San Miguel village 7867 5312; map page 248. This family-run *posada* has large lakeside singles, doubles and triples with attractive furnishings, private bathroom, TV and lake views. There is a small beach directly out front and a simple comedor downstairs. $$

EATING

Flores has plenty of great places to eat, including many restaurants with lake-facing **terraces**, though prices are a little higher than elsewhere in Guatemala.

FLORES

Achiote Hotel Isla de Flores, Av La Reforma hotelisladeflores.com; map page 248. This fine hotel restaurant scores highly for authentic local dishes, try the delicious *timbal petenero*; a crêpe with cheese, scrambled eggs, spinach and smoked ham served with a black bean sauce. $$$

★ **Café Arqueológico Yaxhá** C 15 Septiembre 7867 5055; map page 248. This intimate place has an unusual menu that features many prehispanic dishes of Maya origin, using ingredients like yucca and squash. The walls of the café are covered with posters and photos relating to local Maya sites, to which the German owner, runs excellent tours. $$

Cool Beans C 15 Septiembre 7867 5400; map page 248. A fine café-restaurant with tables that spill down to the lakeside garden. Breakfasts are excellent (featuring home-made bread, home-made jam and real butter), sandwiches are huge and mains are delicious. Craft beers, espresso coffee and cocktails are available. Cash only. $$

La Danta Lakeside 7867 5707; map page 248. Stylish café-restaurant with a lovely lakeside aspect and delicious menu of sandwiches, crêpes, pasta, grilled meats, fish, and seafood. $$

Restaurante El Changarro Bajada de la Muni 4217 6897; map page 248. Set in a historic building, this classy restaurant offers Italian classics and good vegetarian options. $$$

Restaurante San Telmo C La Unión 7867 5751; map page 248. Elegant place with a lovely vista overlooking the lake from its huge windows and terrace seating. Food presentation, portions and quality are all very good. $$$

★ **Terrazzo** C La Unión 7867 5479, facebook.com/ristoranterrazzo; map page 248. This rooftop restaurant has unmatched views and the cooking is top drawer: chef Juan Pablo has many years of experience in different corners of the globe and he cooks here from an open kitchen. The decor is quirky too, with hip retro sofas and artwork. In the evening eat a la carte (the steaks are the best in town) while the *menú del día* features excellent pasta dishes. Superb cocktails are a bargain during happy hour. $$$

SANTA ELENA

Mijaro South of the causeway 7926 3729; map page

248. Offers good *comida típica* and plenty of Mexican dishes at local prices. Try their super nachos. $

SHOPPING

La Casa de Jade Inside Café Arqueológico Yaxhá, C 15 Septiembre, Flores; map page 248. Excellent jewellery, inspired by classic Maya designs, at fair prices, in this popular café/tour operator (see page 250).

Handicraft market Parque Central, Flores; map page 248. This central market is not a bad place to go hunting for souvenirs and gifts.

DIRECTORY

Banks and exchange In Flores, there's a 5B ATM on C Sur and another inside the supermarket on C 30 de Junio; you'll find a Banrural on Av Flores (where you can get your Tikal tickets in advance). Opposite the airport, at the Metroplaza Mundo Maya, there's a Banrural and an ATM. There's also an ATM inside the Terminal Nuevo bus station.

Car rental Budget, Hertz, Tabarini (with the widest choice; ⓣ7926 0253, ⓦtabarini.com) operate from the airport. Daily rates include insurance.

Doctor Centro Médico Maya, 4 Av near 3 C, in Santa Elena (ⓣ7926 0180) is a professional place; some staff speak English.

Laundry The cheapest is Beto's on Av Barrios, Flores. It's open daily but often closed until noon.

Around Flores

The lakeside around Flores has several attractions, including a quirky **island museum**, the peaceful villages of **San Andrés** and **San José**, the Maya ruins of **Motul**, **Tayasal** and **Nixtun Chi'ch'** and a **wildlife rehabilitation centre**.

Boatmen in Flores offer **trips around the lake**, visiting two or three of the attractions that we review here. You'll find them waiting for business behind the *Hotel Santana* in the southwestern corner of Flores, and by the public boat dock to San Miguel.

Museo Santa Bárbara

Isla Santa Bárbara • charge

Situated on a tiny islet just offshore from *Hotel Santana* in Flores, the **Museo Santa Bárbara** has a small collection of Classic-era Maya ceramics and an incredible assortment of ancient broadcasting equipment (the caretaker's father worked for Radio Petén for years).

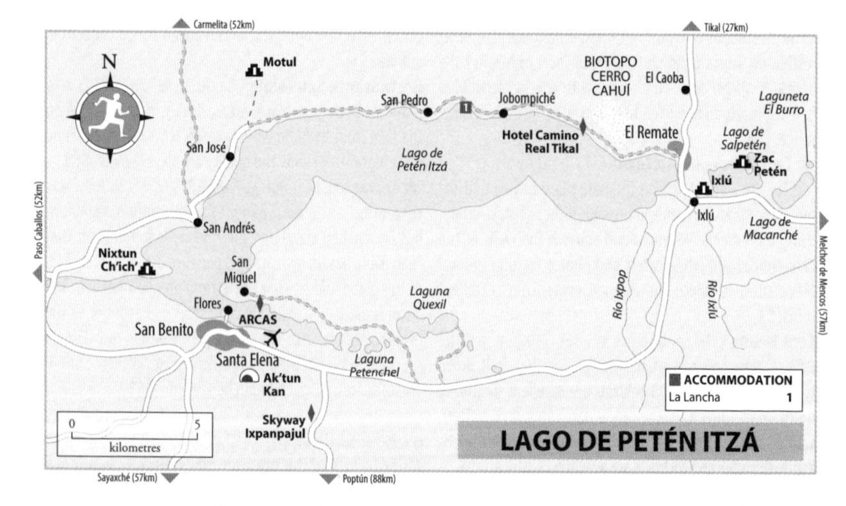

ARCAS

4km east of San Miguel • charge • arcasguatemala.org

ARCAS is a rescue and rehabilitation centre for animals formerly kept as pets or confiscated from wildlife traffickers. There's no public access to the rescue and rehabilitation area itself, but there is an environmental education centre, botanical trail, bird and insect observation spots and the "kinkajou kingdom" where you can see wildlife including macaws, spider monkeys, kinkajous and margay cats that ARCAS considers impossible to release back to the wild.

Ak'tun Kan

2.5km south of Flores along 6 Av • charge

The **Ak'tun Kan** cave lies about 2.5km from the Flores causeway, south along 6 Avenida. Otherwise known as *La Cueva de la Serpiente*, it is the legendary home of a huge snake. The guard may explain some of the bizarre names given to the various shapes inside, some of which resemble animals and even a marimba.

Skyway Ixpanpajul

10km south of Santa Elena on the highway to Poptún • charge • 4062 9812

Skyway Ixpanpajul is a jungle reserve with an extensive system of suspension bridges, cable systems and good stone paths connecting 3km of forested hilltops. There's a monkey's-eye view of the canopy from a *mirador* with views of the Petén Itzá basin and a zip-line network. It's best to go in the early morning when the wildlife is more active. Horse-riding, cabin accommodation and camping are offered, too.

It's cheapest to just rock up and pay on arrival rather than book online ahead.

Nixtun Ch'ich'

The only access is via one of the late afternoon boat tours offered by Mayan Adventure in Flores (see page 250)

Spread over a peninsula about 4km west of Flores, the extensive Maya ruins of **Nixtun Ch'ich'** have barely been touched by archeologists. It's an enormous site, with dozens of small temple mounds and a **triadic temple complex** (ZZ1) more than 30m in height that was a magnificent ceremonial centre. The 60m-long ball court ranks as one of the largest ever found in the entire Maya World. A 2007 dig revealed millennia of occupation, beginning before 1000 BC and extending into the early eighteenth century.

Nixtun Ch'ich' is situated on privately owned land (some of which is owned by Manuel Baldizón, Guatemalan presidential candidate in 2011) used for cattle ranching. Virtually all the mounds you see were once temples, but there's been no excavation or restoration so the site looks like a series of grassy hillocks. Wear good boots and expect to encounter cow dung and plenty of mud after heavy rains.

FOREST GUM

In the past, the mainstay of both San Andrés' and San José's economies was **chicle**, the sap of the sapodilla tree, used in the manufacture of chewing gum. The arduous and poorly paid job of collecting *chicle* involves setting up camps in the forest, and working for months at a time in the rainy season when the sap is flowing. Today natural *chicle* has largely been superseded by artificial substitutes, but there is still a demand for the original product, especially in Japan. Other forest products include *xate* (pronounced "shatey") – palm leaves used in floral arrangements and exported to North America and Europe – and *pimienta de jamaica*, or allspice. Harvesters (*pimenteros*) use spurs to climb the trees and collect the spice; they then dry it over a fire.

San Andrés

The quiet village of **SAN ANDRÉS** on the north coast of the lake is an interesting traditional settlement where the pace of life is slow and the people courteous and friendly. Most outsiders are students at the two **language schools** (see page 250), and since virtually nobody in the village speaks English, this is an excellent location for anyone who wants to immerse themselves in Spanish.

ARRIVAL AND DEPARTURE — SAN ANDRÉS

By bus Regular microbuses (every 30min; 40min) connect San Andrés with Santa Elena, stopping at both the Terminal Nuevo and the marketplace terminal.

ACCOMMODATION

Bolontiku Hotel Boutique 2.5km west of San Andrés bolontikuhotel.com. With a prime lakeshore frontage, this boutique hotel has an enviable location and its lavishly appointed accommodation and pool area are impressive. The restaurant features gourmet French food ($$$), though note the strict dress code for diners. There are kayaks and SUPs for guests to use. $$$$

★ **Ni'tun Private Reserve** 3km west of San Andrés 5201 0759. Wonderful lodge set above the lakeshore, with accommodation in four stylish stone-and-thatch *casitas*, all with private bathrooms, a restaurant serving superb home-cooked healthy food (meals $$$$; non-guests are welcome) and a fantastic upper-deck bar-lounge with lake views. Monkey Eco Tours, based here, organizes well-equipped expeditions to remote archeological sites throughout Petén. Volunteer workers are accepted from time to time. $$$$

San José and around

Just 2km east along the shore from San Andrés, above a lovely bay, **SAN JOSÉ** village is even more relaxed than its neighbour. Take a look at the Catholic **church**, where three sacred skulls are kept in a cabinet: they're paraded through the streets as part of a pagan ceremony on the Day of the Dead each year (see box). The village is undergoing something of a cultural revival: **Itza**, the pre-conquest Maya tongue is being taught in the school, and you'll see signs in that language dotted all around.

Asociación Bio-Itzá

Office on C 3 de Mayo • 4868 6575, bioitza.com

SAN JOSÉ'S SACRED SKULLS

San José is famous for its two **fiestas**. The first, to mark the **patron saint's day**, is held between March 10 and 19 and includes parades and fireworks plus an unusual, comical-looking costumed dance during which a girl (*la chatona*) and a horse skip through the village streets.

The second fiesta is distinctly more pagan, with a unique Mass, celebrated in the church on **Halloween** and a festival that continues on into **November 1** – All Saint's Day. For the evening service, one of three venerated human **skulls** (thought to be the remains of early founders of the village, though some claim they were Spanish missionaries) is removed from its glass case inside the church and positioned on the altar for the ceremony. Afterwards, the skull is carried through the village by black-clad skull bearers, accompanied by children dressed in traditional Itza *traje* and hundreds of devotees, many carrying candles and lanterns. The procession weaves through the streets, stopping at around thirty homes, where prayers are said, chants made and the families ask for blessings. In each home, a corn-based drink called *ixpasá* is consumed and special fiesta food is eaten, part of a ceremony that can take over a day to complete.

The exact origin of the event is unclear, but it incorporates a degree of ancestor reverence (or even worship). After all the houses have been visited, the skull is returned to its case in the church, where it remains, and can be seen with the other two skulls, for the rest of the year.

Boats from Flores head across the lake to San José (and back) on the night of the fiesta.

The **Asociación Bio-Itzá** is an excellent community tourism partnership with a well-regarded **Spanish school**, the Bio-Itzá, just above the main dock and Parque Central. Students get the chance to help out with local projects, which include a **women's cooperative** that sells soaps, creams and shampoos made from natural ingredients. These are produced from plants in the village **botanical garden**, 1km inland; visitors are also welcome to drop by for a free tour. The association also offers tours of the San José area, Motul ruins and a **forest reserve** (charge).

ARRIVAL AND DEPARTURE — SAN JOSÉ

By microbus Microbuses (every 30min; 45min) connect San José with Santa Elena; they stop at both the Terminal Nuevo and the marketplace terminal.

ACCOMMODATION AND EATING

Bahía Taitzá taitza.com. Enjoying a fine lakeside location, this small hotel has eight lovely airy cottages with exposed stone walls and balconies with fine views. Kayaks and SUPs are available to explore the lakeshore. The restaurant (including lake fish and good steaks) is of a high standard and there's a pool. $$$$

El Bungalo Right by the lakeshore 4865 4484. A handy place for a good local meal, serving filling *comida típica* dishes at fair prices. $$

Motul

4km from San José • Free

Some 4km northeast of San José, down a signed track, are the partly restored ruins of the Classic-period settlement of **Motul**. The site (sometimes called "Motul de San José") was historically allied to Tikal and is fairly spread out, with four plazas, but is little visited. In Plaza B a large stela in front of a looted temple depicts dancing Maya lords. Plaza C is the biggest, with several mounds and courtyards, while Plaza D has the tallest pyramid. It's a tranquil spot, ideal for birdwatching, and probably best visited by bicycle. If you'd rather just chill out for a while by the lake, you can choose from a number of secluded spots east of the village, including a rocky beach with good swimming.

El Remate and around

On the eastern shore of Lago de Petén Itzá, the tranquil village of **EL REMATE** lies midway between Flores and Tikal. The lake is a beautiful turquoise here and swimming is wonderful – an extremely welcome idea after a sweaty morning climbing jungle temples. It's a lovely place to take a break from the rigours of the road, with little traffic and a lot of nature to enjoy, including the adjacent **Biotopo Cerro Cahuí** forest reserve.

There are several high-quality artisan workshops on the lakeshore that sell beautifully carved **wooden handicrafts**; stop by Artesanía Ecológical to see expert carver Rolando Soto at work.

ARRIVAL AND DEPARTURE — EL REMATE

By minibus Getting to El Remate is easy: every minibus between Santa Elena or Flores and Tikal passes through the village (about every 30min or so). Coming from the Belize border, get off at the Ixlú junction – from here you can walk (it's 2km away) or wait for a ride to El Remate.

ACCOMMODATION

El Remate has an excellent range of budget **hotels** and a few more upmarket options, all strung out around the fringes of the lake. All these places are listed in the order you approach them from the Ixlú junction.

★ **La Casa de Don David** Centre of El Remate lacasadedondavid.com. This well-established place is efficiently run and offers spotless rooms (most with a/c) facing a huge botanical garden that extends down towards the lakeshore. Meals are served on an elevated deck that makes the most of the views, and the birdlife is outstanding. Rates include a meal. Doubles $$$, suites $$$$

Hostal Hermano Pedro Up a lane opposite the football pitch 5488 2584. This large wooden house feels like a youth hostel, and has a profusion of rooms (most with private bath) that open onto a communal decked balcony. Very cheap single rooms are available. $

6

Hotel Las Gardenias Centre of El Remate hotelasgardenias.com. On the junction in the middle of the village the clean, bright rooms here have a fan or a/c and cable TV. On-site restaurant and travel agency. $$$

Hotel Sun Breeze Lakeside, in the centre of El Remate 5898 2665 facebook.com/hotelsunbreeze. Just off El Remate's main drag this is a good budget hotel with very well-presented, screened rooms, some with a/c. The owners are friendly, speak English and offer tours, transport and a laundry service. Doubles $, doubles with private bath $$

La Mansión del Pájaro Serpiente 1.5km from the Ixlú junction 5517 1575. This stylish B&B has good, thatched, two-storey stone cabañas, all with superb lake views. Flavoursome home-cooked food is also available for guests, and there's a lovely swimming pool. No credit cards. $$$

★ **Mon Ami** 1km along the road to Cerro Cahuí 3010 0284. Superb French-owned guesthouse with rustic well-constructed rooms and bungalows scattered around a tranquil, forested plot of land. All the accommodation has style and character, enhanced by the use of local textiles and artistic flourishes; even the dorm is very spacious and comfortable. There's excellent swimming from the dock, and the restaurant offers some of the best food in Petén. Dorm $, doubles $$

Posada del Cerro 300m beyond Mon Ami guesthouse posadadelcerro.com. This incredibly stylish German-owned guesthouse has very inviting and comfortable rooms and apartments (some lack en-suite bathrooms) that blend modern fittings with natural materials. Fine meals are offered ($$); breakfast is not included. There are bikes for rent. Dorms $, doubles $$$, apartments $$$$

EATING

You'll find a good selection of simple **comedores** in the village centre, and most hotels have restaurants.

Mon Ami 1km along road to Cerro Cahuí 4602 0270. Charming hotel restaurant with open-sided, lake-facing premises that offers excellent French and Italian dishes. Wine is available by the glass. $$$

Restaurant El Muelle Southern entrance to the village 5581 8087. This smart restaurant gets quite a lot of tour group business and has a somewhat pricey menu but you get free use of the fantastic lakeside swimming pool if you eat here. $$$

★ **Restaurant Las Orquideas** 1.25km along the road to Cerro Cahuí 5701 9022. Excellent Italian-owned restaurant serving fine pizza, pasta, bruschetta and grilled meats and veggie options, such as baked aubergine. There's great *limonada* (lemonade) wine by the glass and espresso, and your hosts are very welcoming, preparing food around an open kitchen. $$$

El Viajero Centre of El Remate 3104 9650. This atmospheric place has a quirky vibe and a vast wine selection. The food is terrific, including filling, nutritious breakfasts and many Guatemalan-style mains like *pepián* (meat and veg in a rich, spicy sauce). $$$

Biotopo Cerro Cahuí

3km west of El Remate • Charge

On the north shore of the lake, the **Biotopo Cerro Cahuí** is a wildlife conservation area comprising lakeshore, ponds and some of the best examples of undisturbed tropical forest in Petén. The smallest and most accessible of Petén's *biotopos*, it boasts a rich diversity of plants and animals, and is highly recommended for birdwatchers. There are two hiking trails, a couple of small ruins and *miradores* on the hill above the lake; pick up maps and information at the gate where you sign in.

Jobompiché and around

West of Cerro Cahuí along the dirt road that parallels the northern side of the lake, you pass the isolated village of **JOBOMPICHÉ**. Few visitors pass by this way other than guests at *La Lancha* hotel, which is owned by the movie maker and hotel mogul Francis Ford Coppola.

ARRIVAL AND DEPARTURE JOBOMPICHÉ

A number of **buses** (5 daily; 1hr) connect Jobompiché with Santa Elena.

ACCOMMODATION

La Lancha Just west of Jobompiché ⓦlalancha.com; map page 252. Rustic-chic hotel perched on cliffs above Lago de Petén Itzá. Its location is wonderfully peaceful (apart from the local troop of howler monkeys) and there is a fine pool and excellent, if pricey, food and terrific service. Rates include breakfast, and mountain bikes/canoes/SUPs are free for guests, but room rates are very steep. $$$$

Tikal

Towering above the rainforest, **Tikal**, 64km from Flores down a smooth paved road, is possibly the most magnificent of all Maya sites. The ruins are dominated by five enormous temples, steep-sided limestone pyramids that rise to more than 60m above the forest floor. Around them are thousands of other structures, many semi-strangled by giant roots and still hidden beneath mounds of earth.

The site itself is surrounded by the **Parque Nacional Tikal**, a protected area of some 576 square kilometres that is on the edge of the much larger Reserva de la Biósfera Maya. The sheer scale of the place is overwhelming, and its atmosphere spellbinding. Whether you can spare as little as a morning or as long as a week, it's always worth the trip.

Dawn and dusk are the best times to see **wildlife**, when the forest canopy bursts into a frenzy of sound and activity. The air fills with the screech of toucans and the roar of howler monkeys, while flocks of parakeets wheel around the temples, and bats launch themselves into the night. With a bit of luck, you might even see a grey fox sneak across one of the plazas.

Brief history

The first occupants of Tikal arrived around 900 BC, probably attracted by its position above the surrounding seasonal swamps and by the availability of flint for making tools and weapons. For the next four hundred years there's nothing to suggest that it was anything more than a tiny village of thatched huts. By 500 BC, however, the first steps of a modest astronomical stone temple had been constructed. Tikal remained a minor settlement during the latter years of the Middle Preclassic (1000–400 BC), while 50km to the north, towering temples were being built at **Nakbé**, the first city to emerge from the Petén forest.

In around 250 BC the first significant ceremonial structures emerged. A small pyramid was constructed in the Mundo Perdido, and minor temples were built in the **North Acropolis**, though Tikal was still a peripheral settlement at this stage. Dominating the entire region, formidable **El Mirador** (see page 269) was the first Maya "superpower", controlling trade routes across Mesoamerica.

Ruling dynasty established

By the time of Christ, the **Great Plaza** had begun to take shape and Tikal was established as an important site. For the next two centuries, art and architecture became increasingly ornate and sophisticated as the great pyramid was enlarged to more than 30m in height, its sides adorned by huge stucco masks. **Yax Ehb' Xok** (First Step Shark) established Tikal's first ruling dynasty around 90 AD: a royal lineage recognized by all 33 (known) subsequent kings, until the record fades in 869 AD.

In the Late Preclassic (400 BC–250 AD) the decline of El Mirador presented an opportunity for Tikal and neighbouring Uaxactún to emerge as substantial centres of trade, science and religion. Less than a day's walk apart, the cities engaged in heated competition, and fought a pivotal battle on January 31, 378 AD, when Tikal's warriors overran Uaxactún. The secret of Tikal's success appears to have been its alliance with Teotihuacán (in today's Mexico) and the introduction of new warfare equipment. Inscriptions attest that it was the arrival of a somewhat mysterious warrior, **Siyak**

6

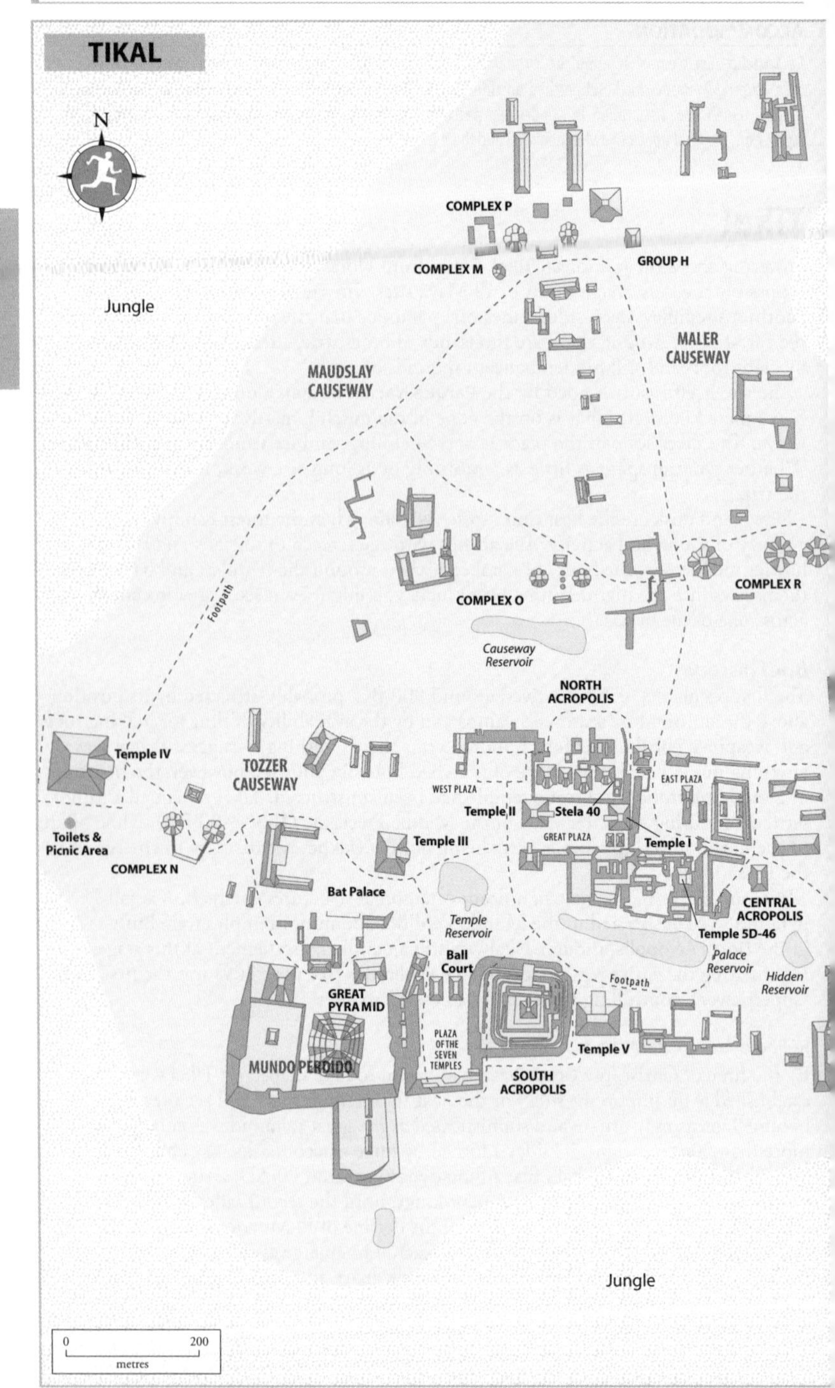
TIKAL
N
Jungle
COMPLEX P
COMPLEX M
GROUP H
MAUDSLAY
CAUSEWAY
MALER
CAUSEWAY
Footpath
COMPLEX O
COMPLEX R
Causeway
Reservoir
NORTH
ACROPOLIS
Temple IV
TOZZER
CAUSEWAY
WEST PLAZA
EAST PLAZA
Temple II
Stela 40
GREAT PLAZA
Temple I
Toilets &
Picnic Area
COMPLEX N
Temple III
Bat Palace
CENTRAL
ACROPOLIS
Temple
Reservoir
Temple 5D-46
Palace
Reservoir
Hidden
Reservoir
Ball
Court
Footpath
GREAT
PYRAMID
PLAZA
OF THE
SEVEN
TEMPLES
Temple V
MUNDO PERDIDO
SOUTH
ACROPOLIS
Jungle
0
200
metres

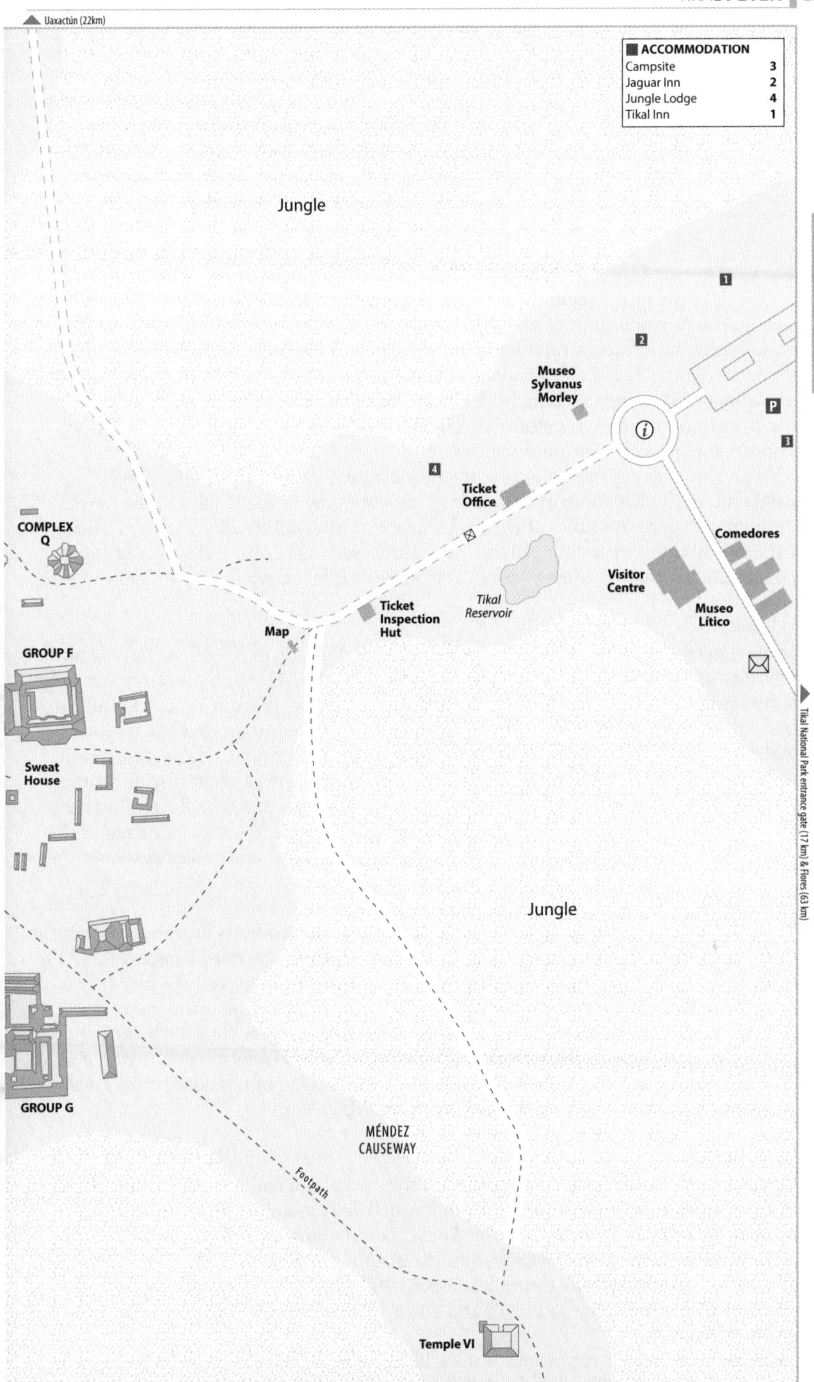
Uaxactún (22km)
ACCOMMODATION
Campsite 3
Jaguar Inn 2
Jungle Lodge 4
Tikal Inn 1
Jungle
Museo Sylvanus Morley
Ticket Office
COMPLEX Q
Comedores
Visitor Centre
Museo Lítico
Tikal Reservoir
Ticket Inspection Hut
Map
GROUP F
Sweat House
Jungle
GROUP G
MÉNDEZ CAUSEWAY
Footpath
Temple VI
Tikal National Park entrance gate (17 km) & Flores (63 km)

K'ak' (Fire-Born), armed with the latest weapon – an *atlatl* (a wooden sling capable of firing arrows) – that helped seal the victory. It's probable that Siyak K'ak' ordered the execution of incumbent Tikal ruler Jaguar Paw I, initiating a Mexican-directed takeover, for the next king installed at Tikal, **First Crocodile**, was a son of the Mexican king. First Crocodile married into the Tikal dynasty, and started a new royal lineage, though efforts were made to pay careful reverence to the deposed ruler Jaguar Paw I, and his palace (Structure 5D–46) remained a revered royal residence for the next four centuries.

Tikal: fifth century

The victory over Uaxactún established Tikal as the dominant power in central Petén for much of the next five hundred years. During this time it became one of the most elaborate and magnificent of all Maya city-states, monopolizing the crucial lowland trade routes, its influence reaching as far as Copán in Honduras and Yaxchilán on the Usumacinta. The elite immediately launched an extensive rebuilding programme, including a radical remodelling of the North Acropolis and the renovation of most of the city's finest temples. It's clear that Tikal's alliance with Teotihuacán remained an important part of its continuing power.

Yet as Tikal was expanding during the fifth century, a rival Maya "superpower" – **Calakmul**, or the Kingdom of the Snake – was emerging in the jungles to the north. Through an aggressive series of regional alliances, Calakmul steadily encircled Tikal with enemy cities, including Naranjo and Waka' (see page 279), and was courting a potentially devastating alliance with **Caracol**, a powerful emerging city in today's Belize.

Star war

In an apparent attempt to subdue a potential rival, Wak Chan K'awil, or **Double Bird**, the ruler of Tikal, launched an attack on Caracol in 556 AD, but his strategy was only temporarily successful. In 562 AD, Lord Water of Caracol (backed by Calakmul) hit back in a devastating **star war** (a battle timed to an astronomical event like a solstice), which crushed Tikal. Double Bird was almost certainly sacrificed. The victors stamped their authority over Tikal, smashing stelae, desecrating tombs and destroying written records. The subsequent 130-year period has long been referred to as Tikal's "**hiatus**", but some Mayanists have re-evaluated this theory as Temple V was constructed in this era. What is clear is that despite the defeat in 562 AD, Tikal was never broken.

Tikal defeats Calakmul

Towards the end of the seventh century Tikal started to recover its lost power under the formidable leadership of Hasaw Chan K'awil, or **Heavenly Standard Bearer** (682–723 AD). During his reign the main ceremonial areas, the East Plaza and the North Acropolis, were completely remodelled. By 695 AD, Tikal was powerful enough to launch an attack against Calakmul, capturing and executing its king, Yich'aak K'ak' (known as **Fiery Claw** or **Jaguar Paw**). The following year, Hasaw Chan K'awil repeated his astonishing coup by capturing **Split Earth**, the new king of Calakmul, and Tikal regained its position as the dominant city in the Maya World.

Tikal's heyday

Hasaw Chan K'awil's leadership gave birth to a revitalized and powerful ruling dynasty: in the hundred years following his death five of Tikal's main temples were built, and his son, Yik'in Chan K'awil, or **Divine Sunset Lord** (who ascended the throne in 734 AD), had his father's body entombed in the magnificent **Temple I**. He also constructed Temple VI, remodelled the Central Acropolis and principal city causeways, and defeated Waka' and Naranjo in 743 and 744 AD, breaking the ring of hostile cities that encircled Tikal.

Around this time, at the height of the Classic period, Tikal's population had grown to somewhere around one hundred thousand (some Mayanists argue for much more) spread across a central area covering about thirty square kilometres. Its authority also extended to include a series of vassal states – a domain of perhaps five hundred thousand subjects. During this time we know the city was called **Mutul** (or Yax Mutul), a name that could be "Great Green Bundle" or a reference to a knot of hair on Tikal's emblem glyph. (Early explorer Morley coined what's surely the most appropriate name for the site – "Place Where the Gods Speak".)

Crisis and abandonment

By the beginning of the ninth century, severe signs of **crisis** emerged across the entire Maya region. The exact reasons for the Maya's demise remain unclear but there was a period of climate change, including a catastrophic drought, and recent evidence indicates that this could have led to a revolt against the ruling class.

Population levels at Tikal plummeted, as people fled the area. Tikal's last recorded monument is inscribed on Stela 24, completed in 869 AD. By about 900 AD almost the entire lowland Maya civilization had collapsed, and Tikal was effectively abandoned by the end of the tenth century.

Rediscovery

After its abrupt decline little is known of Tikal until 1695 when a lost priest, Father Avendaño, stumbled upon a "variety of old buildings". The colonial powers were distinctly unimpressed by Petén and for the next 150 years the ruins were left to the jungle. In 1848 they were rediscovered by a government expedition led by Modesto Méndez and Ambrosio Tut. English explorer Alfred Maudslay took the first **photographs** of the ruins in 1881, showing the temples cloaked in tropical vegetation.

Until 1951 the site could only be reached on horseback. The gargantuan project to excavate and **restore** Tikal started in 1956 and involved teams from the University of Pennsylvania in the US and Guatemala's Institute of Anthropology. Much of the major work was completed by 1984, but thousands of minor buildings remain buried by roots and rubble. There's little doubt that an incredible amount is waiting to be found. In 1996 a workman unearthed a stela (Stela 40, dating from 468 AD) while mowing the grass on the Great Plaza. And in 2003 inscriptions discovered at Temple V have provided convincing evidence that Tikal may not have suffered a Classic-era hiatus at all.

Tikal was the focus of huge celebrations on **December 21, 2012** when thousands gathered at the site to mark the beginning of a new cycle in the Maya Long Count calendar. In 2018, aerial laser technology called LiDAR employed over Tikal revealed new tombs, causeways and temples, some close to the heart of the city. Our understanding of this Maya megacity is an ongoing study, and no doubt many more revelations will be forthcoming.

Site museums

Museo Sylvanus Morley • charge; Admission tickets have to purchased in advance

Museo Sylvanus Morley houses ceramics, obsidian eccentric flints, jade jewellery found in Tumba 116 and the magnificent **Stela 31**, which was inaugurated in 445 AD. This limestone monument shows Tikal ruler Siyah Chan K'awil (Stormy Sky) wearing a jaguar head belt and a jade necklace, flanked by two warriors bearing non-Maya Teotihuacán-style spear throwers and darts. There's also a spectacular reconstruction of the great ruler **Hasaw Chan K'awil's tomb**, complete with 180 worked jade items in the form of bracelets, anklets, necklaces and earplugs, and delicately incised bones, including a famous carving depicting deities paddling a canoe to the underworld.

The **Museo Lítico**, inside the visitor centre (see page 265), holds nineteen more stelae, though they are poorly labelled and there's no supplementary information in English.

The ruins

Several ticket options (see page 265)

The sheer scale of the ruins at Tikal can at first seem daunting. The **central area**, with its five main temples, forms by far the most impressive section; if you start to explore beyond this, you can ramble seemingly forever in the maze of smaller, **unrestored structures** and complexes. Compared with the scale and magnificence of the main area, they're not that impressive, but armed with a good **map** it can be exciting to search for some of the rarely visited outlying sections. (Don't even think about exploring the more distant structures without a map; every year at least one tourist gets lost in the jungle.)

Complexes Q and R

From the entrance to the ruins, a path bears to the right from the site **map** towards the prosaically named **Complex Q** and **Complex R**, two of the seven sets of twin pyramids. Commissioned by Yax Ain II, also known as **Chitam**, one of Tikal's last-known rulers, they were built to mark the passing of a *katun* (twenty 360-day years). Twinned pyramids are an architectural feature found only in the Tikal region, with several at the city itself, and a few others found at sites nearby (including Nakúm, Yaxhá and Ixlú).

At Complex Q (inaugurated in 771 AD), the first set you come to, only one of the pyramids has been restored, with the stelae and altars re-erected in front of it. Ceremonies are held here by Maya shamen on auspicious days in the Maya calendar. On the north side is a copy of **Stela 22**, its glyphs recording the ascension to the throne of Chitam II, who is portrayed in full regalia complete with an enormous sweeping headdress and jaguar-skin kilt, holding the staff of authority.

Following the path as it bears around to the left after the twin temples of **Complex R** (built in 790 AD), you approach the back of the North Acropolis and East Plaza.

East Plaza

On the north side of the **East Plaza**, there's a sauna-style **Sweat House** (similar to those used by highland Maya today). Priests and rulers would have taken a sweat bath in order to cleanse themselves before conducting religious rituals. The central section of this plaza consists of a quadrangle of low structures thought to have been a **marketplace**, and just west of here is a small ball court.

Great Plaza

From the East Plaza, a few steps bring you (via a second ball court) to the **Great Plaza**, the heart of the ancient city. Surrounded by four massive structures, this was the focus of ceremonial and religious activity at Tikal for around a thousand years. The earliest part is the North Acropolis; the two great temple-pyramids weren't built until the eighth century. Beneath today's grassy plaza lie four layers of paving, the oldest of which dates from about 150 BC and the most recent from 700 AD. The symmetry of the two temples perfectly reflects the Maya's preoccupation with astronomy – during an **equinox** Temple I's shadow "kisses" the base of Temple II, and later in the day Temple II reciprocates the gesture.

Temple I and the tomb of Hasaw Chan K'awil

Temple I, towering 44m above the plaza, is the hallmark of Tikal – it's also known as the Jaguar Temple because of the jaguar carved in its door lintel, though this is now in a museum in Switzerland. The temple was built as a burial monument to contain the magnificent **tomb of Hasaw Chan K'awil**, one of Tikal's greatest rulers, who ascended the throne in 682 AD (see page 260) and defeated the arch-enemy state of Calakmul. It was constructed shortly after his death in 721 AD, under the direction of his son and successor, Yik'in Chan K'awil. Within the tomb at the temple's core, his remains were found facing north, surrounded by an assortment of jade, pearls, seashells, bone ornaments and stingray spines (used for bloodletting).

CUTTING-EDGE ARCHITECTURE

Architecturally, **Temple I** was radically different from anything that had been constructed in the Maya region up to that point – an unequivocal statement of confidence no doubt designed to reassert Tikal's position as a dominant power after a long period in the shadow of rival Calakmul. Comprising a series of nine ascending **platforms**, the style emphasizes the vertical dimensions of the temple and draws the eye to the **roof comb**. To create this soaring effect, hundreds of tons of flint and rubble were poured on top of the completed tomb and the temple was built around this, with a staircase of thick plastered blocks running up the front. The monument is topped by a three-room building and a hollow roof comb originally painted in cream, red and possibly green. On the front of the comb, it's just possible to make out a seated figure and a stylized serpent.

Temple II

Standing opposite Temple I, and like a squatter version of it, is **Temple II**, also known as the Temple of the Masks for the two grotesque masks, now heavily eroded, that flank the central stairway. The two temples were arranged to form a twin pyramid alignment, and their construction marked a seminal change to the ceremonial core of the city. Not only was the sheer size of these new temples a powerful statement, but their position purposely deflected attention away from the adjacent North Acropolis, rising above the monuments where Tikal's elite had been buried for at least five hundred years.

Temple II dates from the beginning of the eighth century, and was built to honour Hasaw Chan K'awil's wife, Lady Twelve Macaw. The structure now stands 38m high, although with its roof comb intact it would have equalled Temple I. A wooden staircase (periodically closed; especially during heavy rains) provides access to the temple's upper level. From here the echo across the Great Plaza is wonderfully crisp and clear, and the view (almost level with the forest canopy) is incredible.

North Acropolis

Occupying the whole of the north side of the plaza, Tikal's **North Acropolis** is one of the most complex structures in the entire Maya World. In traditional Maya style it was built and rebuilt on top of itself, and beneath the twelve temples that can be seen today are the remains of about a hundred other structures. As early as 100 BC the Maya had constructed elaborate temples and tombs here; in about 250 AD the entire thing was torn down and rebuilt as a platform and four vaulted temples, each of which was rebuilt twice during Early Classic times.

Archeologists have removed some of the surface to reveal these earlier structures, including two giant Preclassic stone **masks**, which can be glimpsed under thatched protective roofs; one depicts a hook-nosed god with earplugs wearing a crown-like headdress. Originally these great masks, which adorn many Maya Preclassic temple staircases, would have been finished with a stucco coating of limestone and painted in scarlet and green.

Two lines of **stelae**, carved with images of Tikal's elite, with circular altars at their bases, stand in front of the North Acropolis. These rulers were certainly obsessive in their recording of the city's dynastic sequence, linking it with great historical moments and reaching as far back into the past as possible. Many of the stelae bear the marks of ritual defacement, perpetrated by invaders from Caracol during the Classic era, acts carried out by conquerors as rites of humiliation.

Central Acropolis

On the other side of the plaza, the **Central Acropolis** is a maze of 45 tiny interconnecting rooms and stairways built around six smallish courtyards. The buildings here are thought to have been palaces, law courts and administrative centres.

Structure 5D-46, a partly ruined rectangular building with short frontal and rear stone staircases, is particularly intriguing. Dating from around 360 AD, it was the residential home of Chak Tok Ich'aak I (Great Jaguar Paw), and functioned as a royal residence for at least four hundred years. Take a look, too, at the large two-storey building in Court 2 known as **Maler's Palace**, named after the archeologist Teobert Maler who made it his home during expeditions in 1895 and 1904. Behind the acropolis is the palace **reservoir**, one of at least twelve clay-lined pools that were fed by a series of channels with rainwater from all over the city.

West Plaza and Temple III

Behind Temple II is the **West Plaza**, dominated by a large Late Classic palace on the north side, and scattered with various altars and stelae. From here the **Tozzer Causeway** – one of the raised routes that connected the main parts of the city – leads west to the unrestored **Temple III** (60m), covered in jungle vegetation and inaccessible to visitors. This temple has not been investigated by archeologists for decades, but its design includes nine stepped levels, an east-facing staircase and two sacred chambers on its summit.

A fragment of Stela 24, found at the base of the temple, dates it at June 24, 810 AD, which marked the end of a *katun*. It was customary to construct twin temples to mark this auspicious event, but by this time it's clear that the Classic Maya were in severe difficulties across the region and just raising the manpower necessary to build Temple III would have been quite an achievement. Many Mayanists believe Temple III is a burial monument to **Dark Sun**, the last of Tikal's great rulers, and that it is he depicted as a portly figure wearing a magnificent jaguar costume on the badly eroded lintels that crown the temple's summit.

Bat Palace and Complex N

West of Temple III is a huge residential complex, of which only the **Bat Palace**, characterized by broad staircases, has been restored. Further down the causeway, on the left-hand side, is **Complex N**, another set of Late Classic twin pyramids. Here the superbly carved **Stela 16** shows a flamboyantly dressed Hasaw Chan K'awil, who was buried beneath Temple I, depicted with a huge, plumed headdress. **Altar 5** at its base bears a sculpted scene of Hasaw presiding over a sacrificial skull and bones with a lord from Maasal, formerly a vassal state of Calakmul, a clear indicator that Tikal had successfully expanded into the orbit of its bitter rival by 711 AD, when the altar was completed.

Temple IV

At the end of the Tozzer Causeway, **Temple IV** is the tallest of all the Tikal structures at 64.6m. Built in 741 AD by Yik'in Chan K'awil (Hasaw's son), it is thought by many archeologists to be his burial monument. Excavations, including the burrowing of five tunnels into the heart of the structure, have failed to find his tomb as yet, though an early pyramid (over which Temple IV was constructed) has been discovered.

Temple IV is most famous for the stunning, carved **wooden lintels**, embellished with images of the victorious king and a riot of glyphs that once adorned its summit. Nowadays you'll have to travel to Switzerland to see them – though you can see an excellent replica of Lintel 3 in Guatemala City's archeological museum.

Twin stairways – one for the ascent, the other for the descent – provide access to the uppermost level of this unrestored temple. Slow and exhausting as the climb is, the finest views of the whole site await. All around you the forest canopy stretches out to the horizon, interrupted only by the great roof combs of the other temples. Given the vistas, it's not surprising that the **sunrise** tribe gather here in great numbers, and though the humidity and mist usually shroud the visuals somewhat, the dawn jungle-chorus rarely fails to disappoint.

Mundo Perdido and the Plaza of the Seven Temples

Southeast of Temple IV are two more important temple complexes. The first of these, the **Mundo Perdido**, or Lost World, forms another magical and very distinct section of the site with its own atmosphere and architecture. The main feature here is the **Great Pyramid**, a 32m-high structure whose surface hides four earlier versions, the first an astronomical temple from 500 BC. Very faint remains of sixteen masks, four on each side of the pyramid, can still be made out.

To the east, the **Plaza of the Seven Temples** forms part of a complex dating back to before Christ. There's an unusual **triple ball court** on the north side of this plaza, and its eastern flank is formed by the unexcavated South Acropolis.

Temple V

A short trail from the southern part of the Plaza of the Seven Temples leads to the rear of the 58m-high **Temple V**, whose commanding facade (with rounded corners) has been fully restored. Recent evidence suggests that this monument, the construction of which took fifty years, was started around 600 AD by the ruler Animal Skull (which would make it the original of Tikal's six great temples). Its monumental 13m-high roof comb is particularly striking – originally it had four sections (three remain) and was decorated with carved masks, including several images of the rain god Chaac, to whom it could have been dedicated. Note that it's no longer possible to **climb** this monument.

Temple VI

Temple VI, also known as the Temple of the Inscriptions, is 1km southeast of the Great Plaza. Only rediscovered in 1957, it's another of Yik'in Chan K'awil's constructions, completed in 766 AD. A medium-sized temple, it's famous for its 12m roof comb, on the back of which is a huge hieroglyphic text, only just visible these days. More than 180 glyphs chart the history of the city from a founding date in 1139 BC (which is close to the first archeological evidence of settlement). Temple VI is another candidate as the burial place of Yik'in Chan K'awil, Tikal's most prodigious monument-builder.

ARRIVAL AND DEPARTURE — TIKAL

From Flores The easiest way to reach the ruins is in one of the tourist minibuses that meet flights at Flores airport and pick up passengers from every hotel in Flores, Santa Elena and El Remate. It's wise to arrive early at Tikal when the air is fresh and heat less intense, but note that it's rare to witness an impressive sunrise over the ruins due to mist rising from the humid forest.

From Belize Most visitors arrive on tours. If you're visiting independently, change buses at Ixlú, the three-way junction at the eastern end of Lago de Petén Itzá, from where there are plenty of passing minibuses all day long.

TICKETS AND INFORMATION

Tikal is open daily from 4am to 8pm, and has three kinds of entrance tickets. Due to a ticket scam involving corrupt officials all site tickets (and camping and museum fees) now have to be purchased via a Banrural bank. There is a Banrural kiosk (daily 6am–6pm; cash only) at the Tikal National Park entrance gate. However, as queues can be long here it's best to purchase your ticket (which are valid for 30 days) in advance from any Banrural in the country; there are branches opposite Flores airport and in Melchor de Mencos (if you're travelling from Belize).

Different coloured wristbands are issued for standard, sunrise and sunset tickets for ticket holders at the gate. Note that if you are staying in a hotel inside the national park you have to pay for an entrance ticket even if you do not enter the ruins area.

TICKETS

Standard ticket The vast majority of visitors choose to buy a standard ticket (valid 6am–6pm) which will give most people sufficient time at the site.

Sunrise and sunset tickets There are sunrise and sunset tickets for which you have to be accompanied by an official guide, at additional cost. So if you want to arrive at dawn, catch the sunrise and leave at 4pm, you'll need two tickets. Guides can be organized through your hotel, travel agency, or at the visitor centre (see below).

INFORMATION

Tourist information Inguat has a booth (daily 6am–4pm) close to the visitor centre.

Visitor centre Close to the entrance to the site there's a post office, shops and stalls (which sell souvenirs, hats, sun cream, memory cards for cameras, batteries and water) and a visitor centre, where you'll find a café-restaurant, toilets and luggage storage (for a small fee).

Guides There's a licensed guide office in the visitor centre. Guides charge a set price for up to five people, plus an additional per-person fee after that, for the 3hr 30min tour. Most guides are excellent and very knowledgeable about Tikal's flora and fauna as well as the ruins.

Publications Dieter Richter's *Tikal: Analyze, Understand and Live the Biggest Mayan City-state* is available as an ebook. William Coe's *Tikal: A Handbook to the Ancient Maya Ruins* is another decent guidebook, though out of date. Peter D. Harrison's *The Lords of Tikal*, a very comprehensive and readable account of the city's turbulent history and *The Birds of Tikal*, by Frank Smythe are other good sources of information.

Website tikalnationalpark.org has some useful information.

ACCOMMODATION

There are three **hotels** at the ruins, all of them fairly expensive and not especially good value. Electricity is sporadic, few staff speak much English and credit card surcharges are routinely hefty. That said, spending a night in the forest so close to the ruins is a special experience. Note that it's illegal to **camp** or sleep out among the ruins.

Campsite Beside the Administration Centre; map page 258. This well-maintained campsite has toilets and (cold) showers. You can rent a tent under a shelter here, and good hammocks with mosquito nets attached are also available. You have to pay at the Tikal National Park entrance gate. Hammocks, camping and tent rental available. $

Jaguar Inn jaguartikal.com; map page 258. These bungalows with small verandas are quite decent, though pricey, and have a hot-water bathroom and a fan. It's also possible to rent a tent equipped with an inflatable mattress, sheets and pillow – but book ahead. They have 24hr electricity. Camping $$, bungalows $$$$

Jungle Lodge junglelodgetikal.com; map page 258. An attractive lodge with comfortable bungalows, each with two double beds, a few basic rooms with shared bath and a five-bed dorm. There's also a restaurant (see below) and a small pool. Dorms $, doubles $$$, bungalows $$$$

Tikal Inn tikalinn.com; map page 258. Offering pleasant thatched bungalows and clean airy rooms all with ceiling fan and hot-water bathrooms, though the decor is a bit dated. There's a great heat-busting swimming pool and restaurant. Doubles $$$, bungalows $$$$

EATING

Several simple but fairly pricey **comedores** are located at the entrance to the site and cold drinks are sold around the ruins by vendors.

Comedor Imperio Maya Opposite the Visitor Centre 2222 0541. Good for Guatemalan grub including eggs and bean dishes, plus grilled meat and chicken. $$

Jungle Lodge junglelodgetikal.com. Formal hotel restaurant with a wide choice of meals, such as pasta and grilled meats, which are tasty but expensive. $$$

Uaxactún and around

Twenty-three kilometres north of Tikal, the adobe and clapboard houses that comprise the friendly village of **UAXACTÚN** are spread out on both sides of an airstrip, as are the modest ruins of the same name. It is very isolated: there's **no mobile/cellphone coverage** and no one speaks English here. However with a couple of places to stay, a comedor or two, and a daily bus connection to/from Flores, Uaxactún is an ideal jumping-off point for the remote northern ruins of **El Zotz**, **Naachtún and Río Azul**. It's also possible to get to El Mirador from here, though Carmelita (see page 273) is a much more established gateway. If you want to learn more about life in the village and surrounding jungle, Mary Jo McConahay's *Maya Roads: One Woman's Journey Among the People of the Rainforest* (see page 350) is well worth reading.

The **Uaxactún site** (known as Sia'an K'aan in Maya times) rose to prominence in the Late Preclassic era when it grew to become a major player. Uaxactún developed a fierce rivalry with Tikal, which peaked in January 16, 378 AD, when Tikal's warriors conquered Uaxactún armed with the latest high-tech weaponry – spear-throwing slings from Mexico. Uaxactún never recovered from this epochal defeat, and for the remainder of the Classic period was reduced to little more than a provincial backwater.

Uaxactún ruins

Officially there's an entry charge which you have to pay at the Tikal National Park entrance gate, but often no fee is collected

Uaxactún ruins are not that extensive, and may be a little disappointing after the grandeur of Tikal, but you'll probably have the site to yourself. Village children will offer to guide you around; their charm is irresistible – as are the dolls made from corn husks decorated with beads and dried flowers you'll be implored to buy – though their archeological knowledge is limited. A tip of a quetzal or two is fine.

Group E

The most interesting buildings are in **Group E**, east of the airstrip, where three low, reconstructed temples – Temples E-I, E-II and E-III – built side by side, are arranged to function as an observatory. Viewed from the top of a fourth temple, the sun rises behind the north temple (E-I) on the longest day of the year and behind the southern one (E-III) on the shortest day. This point of observation is above **E-VII sub**, a Preclassic temple with simple staircases on all four sides, the steps flanked by pairs of elaborate **stucco masks** of jaguar and serpent heads. It's clear that this was a sacred monument, a platform for bloodletting and sacrifice, for the jaguar signifies the Jaguar God of the underworld, one of the most powerful deities; the serpent is the fabled "vision serpent".

Groups A and B

On the other side of the airstrip are **Groups A and B**, a series of larger temples and residential compounds, some of them reconstructed, spread out across the high ground. In among the structures are some impressive stelae, each sheltered by a small thatched roof, but most lying poignantly broken and supine.

Museum

Free

In the grounds of the *El Chiclero* campsite (see below) there's a small but interesting **museum** with an astonishing collection of intact vases, plates and other ceramics crammed onto its wooden shelves. Many of the vessels are decorated with glyphs and animal figures, and some have a hole drilled in the centre to ceremonially "kill" the power they contain. Other items include a beautiful necklace and flint axe-heads, polished to a glass-like gleam.

ARRIVAL AND DEPARTURE — UAXACTÚN

One daily **bus** (3hr) from Flores passes through Tikal (around 3.30pm) en route to Uaxactún.

ACCOMMODATION AND EATING

Aldana's 7783 3931. Friendly, family-run place with bare-bones wooden rooms and camping. Tours of the region and meals ($) are offered. Camping and doubles available. $

Campamento Ecológico El Chiclero No phone, though you can contact via community phone 7726 1095, campamentoelchiclero@gmail.com. Run by a welcoming couple, Neria and Antonio, this simple guesthouse has basic rooms with decent mattresses, clean sheets and mossie nets; bathrooms are shared. They also offer 4WD trips (in the dry season, Feb–June) to Río Azul, Naachtún and El Mirador. Large meals are also served here. Hammocks, camping and doubles available. $

El Zotz

Twenty-five kilometres southwest of Uaxactún, along a track that's usually passable in the dry season (by 4WD), **El Zotz** is a mid-sized Maya site set in its own *biotopo*. Largely unrestored, El Zotz – its original name is thought to have been Pa' Chan (Fortified Sky) – has been systematically looted, although there are guards on duty all year now and there's also a CECON biological station close to the ruins.

The three main temples are smothered in soil and vegetation. You can climb to the top of the tallest structure, the **devil's pyramid**, from where the roof combs of Tikal can be glimpsed on clear days. A **royal tomb**, dating from around 400 AD, was discovered in 2010 beneath this pyramid, containing the king buried with the tiny corpses of six infants (possibly sacrificial victims). In addition, many impressive stucco **masks** have been uncovered around the site in recent years.

Zotz means "bat" in Maya and each evening at dusk you'll see tens, perhaps even hundreds of thousands of **bats** of several species emerge from a cave near the campsite. It's especially impressive in the moonlight, the beating wings sounding like a river flowing over rapids – one of the most remarkable natural sights in Petén. Keep an eye out, too, for bat falcons, swooping with talons outstretched in search of their prey.

ARRIVAL AND DEPARTURE — EL ZOTZ

Tours To get to El Zotz speak to the owners of *El Chiclero* in Uaxactún (see above) or the tour operators in Flores (see page 250), who can arrange tours. Three-day trips involving a hike to El Zotz, a day at the ruins and then a hike to Tikal are highly recommended (minimum two people).

Río Azul

On the tripartite border where Guatemala, Belize and Mexico meet • Charge

The remote site of **Río Azul** was only rediscovered in 1962. Almost totally unrestored, the core of the site resembles Tikal in many ways, though it is smaller. The tallest temple (**A-III**) stands some 47m above the forest floor, poking its head out above the treetops and giving magnificent views across the jungle.

Brief history

Investigations suggest that the Río Azul site dates back to 900 BC and was an important city until the Middle Classic era. The site prospered as both a trading centre between the Caribbean (where cacao was abundant) and wider Maya World, and also as an important agricultural centre. Its history is deeply intertwined with Tikal and Calakmul, the two superpowers of the era – it's likely that Tikal's ruler **Stormy Sky** installed one of his sons here as king, but in 530 AD Calakmul overran the city. After this defeat, Río Azul was virtually abandoned, before being occupied again in Late Classic times, only to be sacked again in 830 AD by marauding Puuc Maya from the Yucatán.

The site

Several incredible **tombs** have been unearthed at Río Azul, painted with vivid red glyphs. Tomb 1 is thought to have contained the remains of Stormy Sky's son, while nearby tombs 19 and 23 contained bodies of warriors dressed in clothing typical of the ancient city of Teotihuacán in central Mexico. Many of the finds here are displayed in the archeology museum in Guatemala City (see page 62).

Extensive **looting** occurred after the site's discovery, with a gang of men plundering the tombs, and unique treasures (including some incredible green jade masks and pendants) found their way onto the international market. Tombs were stripped bare, and some of the finest murals in the Maya World hacked from walls – though Tomb 1 escaped the worst of the damage.

Today there are resident guards: the tallest **temples** are now becoming unsafe to climb, so always heed their advice.

ARRIVAL AND DEPARTURE — RÍO AZUL

By road The rough road that connects Tikal and Uaxactún continues for an additional 80km or so north to Río Azul. This route is only passable in the dry season, and can be covered by 4WDs in as little as 5hr, depending on the conditions.

On foot Walking or on horseback it's four days each way from Uaxactún – three at a push. Trips can be arranged through *El Chiclero* in Uaxactún (see page 267) or through travel agents in Flores.

The Mirador Basin

The remains of the first great cities of the Maya are still engulfed by the most extensive forests in the region, an area known as the **Mirador Basin**. The discoveries here in the extreme north of the country have already led to a complete rethink about the origins of the Maya, and it's now clear that this was once the cradle of Maya civilization. The main focus of interest has been the giant site of **El Mirador**, the first Maya "superpower", which is famous for its colossal triadic temple complexes. But neighbouring **Nakbé**, the first city to emerge (around 800 BC), **Wakná** (which was only discovered in 1998) and the massive ruins of **Tintal** (on the scale of Tikal) are just three of the myriad cities that once thrived in this now remotest of regions.

The conditions are very difficult – marshy mosquito-plagued terrain that becomes so saturated that excavations can only be attempted for five months of the year. Currently only around three thousand people make it to Mirador each year, and archeologists outnumber visitors at any one time. Numbers are tiny because of the time and expense required to **get to the ruins** (see page 273), which either involves days of hard hiking through dense jungle and swamps or a brief visit as part of a helicopter tour.

El Mirador

El Mirador is perhaps the most exotic and mysterious Maya site of all. Encircled by the Petén and Campeche jungles, this massive city surpasses Tikal's scale although we are only now beginning to piece together its history. Mayanists are not even certain of its name – *el mirador* means "the lookout" in Spanish – but it could have been **Ox Te Tun** (Birthplace of the Gods). Until the 1980s, it was assumed Mirador was a city from the Classic era, but this theory has been totally overthrown. We now know that Mirador was a Preclassic capital of unprecedented scale, and its fall around 150 AD was just the first of two catastrophic collapses suffered by the Maya civilization.

THE MIRADOR BASIN UNDER PRESSURE

Undoubtedly the greatest challenge facing the archeologists and Guatemalan authorities is to save the Mirador Basin ruins from the constant threat of encroaching settlers, loggers, drug smugglers, cattle ranchers and tomb looters. Because of this lack of security, environmentalists and Mayanists are lobbying hard to get the entire Mirador region – 2169 square kilometres of jungle stretching from the Mexican border as far south as El Zotz – declared the **Mirador Basin National Park**. President Colom announced in his 2008 inaugural speech that the creation of a national park here was a priority, though this status had still not been approved by 2024. An application is also registered with UNESCO to get Mirador declared a World Heritage Site.

Immediate and effective protection is essential. Successive Guatemalan governments have dithered while neighbouring reserves like Laguna del Tigre have gone up in smoke. Armed rangers now patrol the Mirador area, otherwise, according to archeologist **Dr Richard Hansen** (who has led the excavations here for decades) "we'd lose the whole city". Hansen sees strictly managed ecotourism, including the construction of a jungle lodge and narrow-gauge railway, as the way to preserve the forest and the dozens of Maya sites in the Mirador Basin. But his vision is not universally shared. Many settlers on the fringes, and inside the reserve, see little future in ecotourism and are lobbying for timber and farming concessions to be allowed. Villagers at Dos Aguadas have even been granted a concession to farm inside the Maya Biosphere Reserve.

Organisations including Global Conservation (W globalconservation.org) have established ranger patrols in the Mirador region, and since 2016 trail cameras and satellite monitoring are aiding the conservation effort. But the environment remains extremely fragile, its future dependent on state and community support and protection.

The ruins are surrounded by some of the densest tropical forests in the Americas, and you're sure to encounter some spectacular **wildlife**, including the resident troops of howler and spider monkeys, bats (including vampires), toucans, plenty of bugs, spiders, scorpions and quite possibly snakes too. Wildcat numbers in the area are some of the healthiest in Latin America, with an estimated four hundred jaguar, as well as ocelot, *jaguarundi* and puma. You're quite likely to see jaguar pug marks, though the big cats themselves are very elusive.

Brief history

The latest research indicates that it was the boggy nature of the Mirador Basin that drew the first settlers here, the richness of its *bajo* mud allowing the **early Maya** to found villages based on crop cultivation. By 1000 BC (though some ceramic evidence suggests as far back as 1480 BC) these settlements were established and thriving at Mirador. The site chosen for the city itself was a commanding one, on an outcrop of karst (limestone) hills at an altitude of 250m, with swamps providing protection to the east.

By the Middle Preclassic, ceremonial structures were being built, including early temples at Los Monos, El Tigre and the Central Acropolis (generations later these structures would be built over and enlarged to a much grander scale). For centuries Mirador flourished, peaking between 350 BC and 100 AD, when it was home to more than one hundred thousand Maya. The city's ruling **Kaan dynasty** were overlords of hundreds of thousands more subjects in the Basin region and overlords of millions in the wider Maya World.

Mirador became a great trading centre as jade and obsidian were brought from the highlands; granite, shells and coral beads imported from the Caribbean and salt carried in from the Yucatán. The city grew to dominate the entire region, and by the time of Christ it must have been something to behold, its emblematic triadic temples painted scarlet with cinnabar and soaring high above the forest canopy, with a web of stone causeways connecting the great capital to dozens of other cities in its empire.

Decline and abandonment

The exact reasons for Mirador's downfall are unclear, but it's probable that a millennium of temple- and empire-building, intensive agriculture and especially forest-burning (to create lime for the thick plaster that covered every building) dried out the swamps and provoked **agricultural and environmental collapse**. Other great cities, including Teotihuacán in central Mexico and Tikal, were also beginning to flex their muscles by the second century AD.

All the great cities of the Basin faded in the late Preclassic era around 150 AD, but strong evidence indicates that Mirador's inhabitants may have simply upped sticks and shifted 50km to the north, probably because the water supply was better. Here it seems they founded a second superstate, for recently found inscriptions strongly link the ruling Kaan dynasty of Calakmul to Mirador.

Though Mirador's population plummeted, small numbers continued to live in the remains of the great city; in the late fourth century AD an army from Teotihuacán overwhelmed the few remaining occupants. Mirador was also re-occupied by a small number of settlers in the Late Classic era, who remodelled some monuments before fleeing around 800 AD.

The ruins

Charge

The **ruins** of El Mirador are still covered in dense jungle, and though many buildings have been stabilized, only a few have been partially reconstructed. In many ways you're experiencing the city the way the great nineteenth-century explorers like Maudslay would have seen Tikal, so you'll have to exercise your imagination to get a vision of its sheer scale and grandeur. But as the **archeological project** here is one of the largest in the Americas – home to dozens of archeologists and students and hundreds of workers each season – exciting new discoveries are being unearthed all the time.

The centre of the site covers some sixteen square kilometres, stretching between two massive **pyramid groups** facing each other across the forest on an east–west axis. Mirador's **ceremonial core**, sometimes called the West Group, is thought to have been largely the preserve of the elite and high priests and contains hundreds of temple structures and buildings, reservoirs and aqueducts, all ringed by a defensive wall, and probably guarded by gateways.

Tigre Complex

On the western edge of the ceremonial core is the mighty **Tigre Complex**, made up of a huge single pyramid base, and an upper platform with three temples. This triadic temple design, peaking at 55m, is characteristic of El Mirador's architecture (and a model that's replicated at all of the area's Preclassic sites). Tigre's temple base measures 125m by 135m, which is enough to cover around three football fields. Giant stucco **jaguar masks** have been uncovered here, their teeth and claws painted red. Hundreds of obsidian spear points found indicate a major battle in the late fourth century AD, as the forces of Teotihuacán (and possibly Tikal) overran Mirador. At that time this once-omnipotent city would have been a shadow of its former self, a relatively minor settlement.

A staircase has been cut into the side of the Tigre pyramid, and this temple's summit is a favoured spot for sunset (as it's only a fifteen-minute walk back to the campsite from here).

Structure 34

On the south side of the Tigre complex, **Structure 34** is one of the most studied buildings at El Mirador. This 17m-high pyramid, built around 200 BC, has now been restored and sits under a polycarbonate roof for protection. Giant jaguar claws carved from stucco decorate the facade of the temple, leading archeologists to believe that it was dedicated to ruler Yok'noom Yi'ch'ak K'ak, or "Great Flaming Jaguar Claw".

Structure 34 was actually constructed over the remains of a smaller, earlier temple – exactly like Copán's Rosalila (see page 299). If you tip the guards they might allow you access to a tunnel for a sneaky peek at the original, which has a large stucco mask and red and black paint.

Central Acropolis

In front of the Tigre Complex is El Mirador's sacred hub: the **Central Acropolis**, a long, narrow plaza, where sacrificial ceremonies were performed. A wonderful sculptured panel depicting the **Maya creation myth** was found here (see box).

Burial chambers unearthed in this central section had been painted with ferric oxide to prevent corrosion and contained the bodies of priests and noblemen surrounded by bloodletting instruments such as stingray spines (see page 333). The spilling of blood was seen by the Maya as a method of summoning and sustaining the gods, and was common at all the great ceremonial centres.

South of the Tigre Complex, the **Monos Complex** is another triadic structure (rising to 42m) and plaza, named after the local howler monkeys that roar long into the night and after heavy rainfall. To the north, the **León Pyramid** and the **Cascabel Complex** mark the northern boundaries of the sacred precinct.

Danta Pyramid

It's about 1.5km east from the Central Acropolis along the Puleston Causeway, past a couple of reservoirs, to the **East Group**, which rises in tiers from the forest floor. The cluster of monumental buildings here all sit on a vast stone base platform that measures

600m by 330m. The trail ascends to a second platform, where you encounter the **Pava temple** group, winding below the jungle-clad Pava pyramid and then climbing up to a third level and then up the flanks of the iconic **Danta Pyramid** itself. Vegetation is steadily being cut from the front of this vast structure, but it's planned to just expose the facade of the pyramid and leave the jungle intact to the rear and sides.

A sturdy wooden staircase leads to the summit of this two-thousand-year-old temple, which is 72m above the base platform (and 79m above the forest floor), making it the tallest pre-Columbian structure in the entire Americas. From the top, high above the jungle canopy, you feel you're at the summit of the Maya World. The hills in the distance are the forest-covered pyramids of other great Maya cities, with the temple tops of Nakbé to the south. On very clear days it's even possible to catch a glimpse of Structure 2 at Calakmul in Mexico, way to the north, a city almost certainly founded by the Kaan Maya from El Mirador.

Around El Mirador

The area **around El Mirador** is riddled with other residential suburbs and smaller Maya sites – you'll pass through about a dozen small ruins if you arrive on foot from **Carmelita** (see page 273). Raised **causeways**, ancient trading routes called *sakbe'ob* – some up to 40m wide and 4m in height – connect many of these smaller sites to Mirador. One trail leads south to **La Muerte**, 2km away, where several temples have been restored and some fine tombs and glyphic carvings (now protected by a polycarbonate protective roof) have been uncovered.

Nakbé

12km southeast of El Mirador • Free • Tour operators (see page 274) include Nakbé and Wakná (see page 273) on some seven-day trek itineraries to El Mirador

About 12km to the southeast of El Mirador down one of the main *sakbé*, **Nakbé** was the first substantial city to emerge in the Maya region. Ruins of the earliest buildings are from around 1000 BC, the community growing to become a city of many thousands by 400 BC, and one of the key centres of Maya culture, calendrics, religion and writing.

Today the site, which has been partially cleared, is virtually unvisited by anyone except archeologists, *xateros* (palm-leaf gatherers) and *chicleros* (rubber tappers). Excavations have revealed that the city had a ceremonial core of **temples**, separated into two groups via a kilometre-long limestone causeway – much like El Mirador. At the eastern end, the temples rise from a platform to peak at 35m, and there are the remains of the earliest ball court ever found in the Maya World, dating back to around 450 BC.

Nakbé's tallest building is in the western group, where **Structure I** reaches 45m; from its summit, La Danta in El Mirador is visible. Archeologists have also found evidence of skilful stucco work – a huge **mask** (measuring 5m by 8m) was found on the side of one of the temples here, though it has since been covered in earth for protection.

THE HERO TWINS PANEL

The Mirador Basin has no rivers (and had a population of hundreds of thousands in the late Preclassic) so the Maya developed extremely efficient water-collection systems so that all available rainfall was channelled to huge reservoirs. In 2008, while investigating water channels in the Central Acropolis, archeologists discovered elaborately sculptured panels with scenes from the Maya creation story, the **Popol Vuh** (see page 103). The two stucco panels, measuring 6m by 8m and still *in situ*, were carved about 200 BC and show the mythical hero twins swimming into the underworld to retrieve the decapitated head of their father. Dr Richard Hansen described it as like "like finding the Mona Lisa in the sewage system".

Resident guards will show you **chultunes** (storage chambers cut into the limestone bedrock) that you can lower yourself down into – though watch out for snakes and spiders. Nakbé probably has hundreds of outlying structures, including residential complexes grouped around plazas and doubtless many more exciting discoveries will follow.

Tintal

Around 22km south of El Mirador • Free

Tintal, another massive site south of El Mirador, is connected by a broad causeway to its giant neighbour. It flourished in Preclassic times and was later reoccupied in the Classic period. The ruins, though severely looted – an estimated two thousand trenches have been cut into the structures here – make an ideal campsite on the route to El Mirador and most hiking trips spend a night here. A defence moat, averaging 25m in width, encircles the ceremonial core.

There are two main temple complexes, both arranged in a **triadic** formation with a central staircase flanked by elaborate stucco masks – some of the earliest examples of Maya sculptural art. Climb to the top of the **Catzin pyramid**, which ascends 50m, for spectacular jungle canopy views, as well as vistas over towards El Mirador.

Wakná

Around 21km northeast of Carmelita • Free • Tour operators (see page 274) include Wakná and Nakbé (see page 272) on some seven-day trek itineraries to El Mirador

There are more than twenty other sites in the Mirador Basin that have barely been touched, including many very early Preclassic settlements. The large site of **Wakná**, or "house of six", was only rediscovered in 1998, after careful analysis of satellite photographs detected temple-like mounds in the jungle. Dr Hansen, accompanied by *chicleros*, led a team to the region and confirmed that the mounds were indeed the remains of a city, later established to be Preclassic in origin. Unfortunately, they weren't the first people to discover the site – a trench cut into one of the temples confirmed that looters had already been active here, and had raided a tomb.

Naachtún

25km east of El Mirador • Free

Investigations at extremely remote **Naachtún**, about 25km east of El Mirador and just 1km south of the Mexican border, have revealed it to be a very substantial site. Preclassic in origin, Naachtún is unusual in that it is one of the few ancient cities in the Mirador Basin to survive (and indeed flourish) into the Classic period.

More than forty stelae have been unearthed, and the architecture at the site (perilously located between the two giants of Tikal and Calakmul, and originally called Masuul) reflects styles found in both cities – around its main plaza the temples show strong Tikal influence, while its royal palaces draw on Calakmul design traditions.

ARRIVAL AND DEPARTURE — THE MIRADOR BASIN

Getting to El Mirador is a substantial undertaking by land, either via **Carmelita** or **Uaxactún** (see page 266). The journey is impossibly muddy in the rainy season (though people do attempt, and complete the hike through knee-deep mud). It's best undertaken **from mid-January to June** (Feb–April is the driest period).

From Santa Elena You first need to get to the isolated village of Carmelita (two daily buses; 4hr). Then it's two days of hard jungle hiking to the site – most people hire a mule or two to carry their food and equipment.

From Uaxactún It's also possible to reach El Mirador from Uaxactún via remote jungle tracks, paths and *campamentos*. Part of this route can be driven in a 4WD, though it'll still take two to three days to reach Mirador; you'll pass several ruined cities, though they're not on the scale of Tintal. Speak to the folks at *El Chiclero* in Uaxactún (see page 267) to organize a trip this way.

INFORMATION AND TOURS

Websites ⓦ miradorbasin.com is an excellent source of information about the site.

Equipment Whichever way you do it you'll need guides, packhorses or mules, food, water and camping gear. Essentials are bug repellent (with high DEET content), Permethrin (for ticks, which are abundant), plasters for blisters, energy snacks and some supplies for the guards, who spend forty days at a time in the forest, largely subsisting on beans and tortillas.

TOURS

The more people you can gather together, the cheaper the price. Treks are normally a five-day/four-night hike. If you want an English-speaking guide, mule or to include Nakbé on the itinerary, the price goes up.

Dinastia Kan expedicionelmirador.com. Established tour operator with a reputation for well-organised Mirador expeditions.

Cooperativa Carmelita C Centroamérica turismocooperativacarmelita.com. By booking directly with the Carmelita co-operative you can ensure you money goes directly to the community.

Hostel Los Amigos Flores (see page 250). A good place to get a group together for a low-cost hike. Owner Matthius has been to Mirador several times and has excellent information.

Maya Expeditions Guatemala City (see page 28). High-quality trips led by prominent archeologists.

HELICOPTER TOURS

If you'd rather skip the mud and jungle completely, helicopter trips offer a tempting alternative, though you'll only get a fleeting glimpse of the ruins.

Martsome Travel elmiradorhelicoptertours.com. It costs fairly hefty amount per person (minimum four) for a day-trip leaving at 8am from Flores, and returning by 3.30pm (later by request). It's also possible to stay overnight and hike back.

ACCOMMODATION AND EATING

Comedor Patricia Pinelo Carmelita village centre 7783 3811. The menu here usually comprises just beans, eggs and tortillas, though if you call ahead some meat can be prepared. They can also organize a bed for the night for you for very little. $

Sayaxché and around

Southwest of Flores on a lazy bend in the Río de la Pasión, **SAYAXCHÉ** is a fairly rough-and-ready frontier town that's a convenient base for exploring the forests of southern Petén and its huge collection of archeological remains. The complex network of rivers and swamps that cuts through the jungle here has been an important trade route since Maya times. Nearby ruins include **Ceibal**, a compact but beautiful site, while to the south is **Lago de Petexbatún**, a stunning lakeside setting for the Maya sites of **Aguateca** and Punta de Chimino, and the trailhead for the substantial ruins of **Dos Pilas**. A visit to this region offers great opportunities to explore the Petén forest and watch the wildlife, including howler and spider monkeys, crocodiles, iguanas and superb birdlife.

ARRIVAL AND DEPARTURE — SAYAXCHÉ

By bus and minibus Getting to Sayaxché from Flores is very straightforward, with minibuses and buses plying the smooth 73km road from Santa Elena to the riverbank opposite Sayaxché. A ferry takes you over the Río de la Pasión.

Destinations Cobán (2 daily; 6hr); Flores (every 30min; 2hr); Raxrujá (every 30min; 2hr 30min).

By boat There are plenty of boatmen offering trips to the ruins – but you'll have to be patient and bargain hard to get a good deal.

Tours Try Viajes Don Pedro (7928 6109) for tours of the area; the office is on the riverfront. The very helpful Julián Mariona, who owns *Posada El Caribe* (see page 277), can also arrange ruins trips and fishing expeditions.

ACCOMMODATION

Hotel Del Río 300m north of the dock 7928 6138. An orderly, secure hotel with very spacious, clean doubles and triples (all with a/c), parking and a very friendly host family who can hook you up with tour guides and boatmen. $$

Villas del Yaxkín Six blocks up and five across (southeast) from the dock 3855 5880. Rustic bungalows (some with private bathroom) and a good restaurant in a verdant garden, where the family grow cocoa, pepper and tropical flowers. It's cheap for single travellers. Owner Chendo can arrange tours and transport. $$

EATING

Oasis 5Av ☎7928 6733. This civilized a/c café that serves snacks including hot dogs, nachos and sandwiches, and has the only espresso machine in town. Somewhat incongruously, it also doubles as a hardware store. $

Ristaurante Carbonero 600m southeast of river crossing ☎5719 8621. The best place in town for grilled and barbecued meat, including great steaks. They can also help out organising tours. $$

6

Ceibal (Seibal)

15km east of Sayaxché • Charge • Any transport heading out of town towards Cruce del Pato passes the entrance road to the site, from where it's 8km along a dirt track to the ruins; by boat there are return trips from Sayaxché, including 2hr at the ruins – the hour-long boat trip is followed by a short walk through towering rainforest

The minor Maya site of **Ceibal** (sometimes spelled "Seibal"), which you can reach by land or river, is the most accessible ruin near Sayaxché. Surrounded by forest and shaded by huge ceiba trees, the **ruins** are only partially cleared and just a few buildings have been restored. However, the mixture of open plazas and untamed jungle is beautiful.

During the Classic period, Ceibal was a relatively minor site, but it grew rapidly between 830 and 910 AD, possibly after falling under the control of Putun colonists from what is now Mexico. Outside influence is clearly visible in some of the carving: speech scrolls, straight noses, waist-length hair and serpent motifs are all decidedly non-Maya. The architecture also differs from other Classic Maya sites, including the round platforms that are usually associated with the Quetzalcoatl cult.

The ruins

Ceibal has four main clusters of buildings, all connected by stone causeways (*calzadas*) that cut through the forest, and two ball courts. Although most of the largest temples (Structure 10 rises to 28m) lie buried under mounds, Ceibal does have some fine **carving**, superbly preserved due to the use of hard stone. Of the 57 **stelae** found here, the most impressive are in the large Plaza Central (where the surrounding temples are unrestored and still jungle-clad) and in the neighbouring Plaza Sur. The latter plaza's low central temple, **Structure A-3**, has four fine stelae set around its cardinal points and another (Stela 21) in the room at the top of the temple – all were commissioned in 849 AD.

East of the plaza along Calzada I, the crudely carved but unusual monkey-faced Stela 2 is particularly striking, beyond which, straight ahead down the path, lies Stela 14, another impressive sculpture.

Structure 79

If you turn right along Calzada II from Stela 14 and walk for a few minutes, you'll reach the highly unusual **Structure 79**, a massive circular stone platform superbly set in a clearing in the forest. The exact purpose of this platform, whose foundations date from the Late Preclassic period, is unclear, but it was certainly used for religious ceremonies (a niche where copal resin was burned has been found) and possibly also functioned as an observation deck for astronomy. In front of Structure 79's stairway, a huge, roughly carved **altar**, measuring more than 2m in diameter and bearing the face of a jaguar, is supported by two crouching humanoid figures.

Lago de Petexbatún

South of Sayaxché, **Lago de Petexbatún** is a spectacular expanse of water ringed by dense forest and containing plentiful supplies of snook, bass, alligator and freshwater turtle. The shores of the lake abound with birdlife and howler monkeys, and there are a number of Maya ruins – the most impressive of which is the partially restored **Aguateca**, suggesting the lake was an important trading centre for the Maya.

Aguateca

Charge • Boats can get you to within a 20min walk of the ruins, trips here are organised by operators including Martsam Travel in Flores

Aguateca, perched on a high outcrop at the southern tip of the lake, is the site that's furthest away from Sayaxché but the most easily reached. This intriguing site (split in two by a natural chasm) was only rediscovered in 1957 and has undergone recent restoration work. The atmosphere is magical, surrounded by dense tropical forest and with superb views of the lake from two *miradores*. The resident guards here always welcome company, and if you want to **stay** they'll find some space for you to sling a hammock or pitch a tent – bring a mosquito net and food.

Brief history

Throughout the **Late Classic** period, Aguateca was closely aligned with (or controlled by) nearby Dos Pilas, the dominant city in the southern Petén, and reached its peak in the eighth century, when Dos Pilas was developing an aggressive policy of expansion. Indeed, Aguateca may have been a twin capital of an ambitious Petexbatún state. Military successes, including a conclusive victory over Ceibal in 735 AD, were celebrated at both sites with remarkably similar stelae – Aguateca's Stela 3 shows Dos Pilas's ruler Master Sun Jaguar in full battle regalia, including a Teotihuacán-style face mask. After 761 AD, however, Dos Pilas began to lose control of its empire and the members of the elite moved their headquarters to Aguateca, attracted by its strong defensive position. But despite the construction of 5km of walls around the citadel and its agricultural land, their enemies soon caught up with them, and sometime after 790 AD Aguateca itself was overrun.

The ruins

The resident **guards** will provide you with stout walking sticks – essential, as the slippery paths here can be treacherous – before escorting you around the site's steep trails. A walk around the site, which takes a little more than an hour, takes in the palisade defences, temples and palaces (including the residence of Aguateca's last ruler, Tante K'inich) and a barracks. The **carving** at Aguateca is superbly executed and includes images of hummingbirds, pineapples and pelicans. Its plazas are dotted with stelae, including one on the Plaza Principal depicting Tante K'inich lording it over a ruler from Ceibal, who is shown cowering at his feet, and another that has been shattered by looters who hoped to sell the fragments. Aguateca is also the site of the Maya World's only known **bridge**, which crosses a narrow gash in the hillside, but it's not that impressive in itself.

Punta de Chiminos

Around 4km to the north of Aguateca, jutting out from the west shore of the lake, is a club-shaped peninsula known as **Punta de Chiminos**. This site was the final refuge of the last of the Petexbatún Maya in the Late Classic era, as the region descended into warfare and chaos at the beginning of the ninth century. Here they constructed some formidable defences across the narrow stem of the peninsula, including three rock-hewn trenches and 9m ramparts, which created a man-made citadel. The point is now the spectacular location for the lovely *Chiminos Island Lodge* (see page 277), though there's very little to see there today.

ARRIVAL AND GETTING AROUND — LAGO DE PETEXBATÚN

By boat It's a 45min speedboat trip from Sayaxché to the northern tip of Lago de Petexbatún.

Tours As it's not feasible to get around the lake independently, it's probably best explored on a tour. Most tour operators in Flores can organize two-day excursions to Aguateca, though the ideal way to explore this beautiful region is to arrange a boat and guide locally: *Posada El Caribe* (see below) arranges two-day excursions to Aguateca and Ceibal including full board. There are plenty of activities – you can tour the lake on foot, by boat or on horseback, explore the jungle, fish or bathe in the natural warm springs on the lakeshore.

ACCOMMODATION AND EATING

★ **Chiminos Island Lodge** West side of Lago de Petexbatún chiminos.com. Outstanding jungle lodge with seriously stylish and spacious thatched bungalows with private decks above the lake. Bungalow "2 Norte" is the best, with "1 Norte" second choice. There are minor ruins in the surrounding patch of jungle, which is also home to howler monkeys and amazing birdlife. Plus docks for sunbathing and swimming, kayaks, and great cuisine. Rates are per person, so it's a great deal for solo travellers. $$$$

Posada El Caribe Northern tip of Lago de Petexbatún 5304 1745. A very friendly and welcoming family-run place with clean, functional screened cabins and good food. Don Julián, the owner, is a true Petenero and offers highly recommended lake and ruin tours to Aguateca and Dos Pilas; he can arrange horses, 4WD and boat transport, but his English is limited. Cash only. $

Dos Pilas and around

Some 12km west of the northern tip of Lago de Petexbatún, still buried in the jungle, the virtually unreconstructed site, **Dos Pilas** has one of the most fascinating and best-documented histories of any Maya city. The hike to the ruins takes you past the small site of **Arroyo de Piedra**, with two fairly well-preserved stelae, and the ruins of **Tamarindito**, where another hieroglyphic stairway has been found.

Brief history

Dos Pilas was established around 640 AD by a renegade group of Tikal nobles who fled following the city's defeat by Calakmul. The leader of this breakaway tribe, B'alaj Chan K'awil (Lightning Sky), was clearly a brazen individual, for he swore a treacherous allegiance with Calakmul in 648 AD in an attempt to launch a rival dynasty at Tikal. Dos Pilas clashed with Tikal several times in the years afterwards, as Tikal sought to humble the upstart Dos Pilas ruler. Though B'alaj Chan K'awil ultimately failed in his bid to claim the Tikal lineage, he did repel Tikal in 679 AD, a victory which he celebrated by commissioning several new stelae and launching a substantial reconstruction of the plaza.

Dos Pilas continued to throw its weight around for another century, defeating Ceibal in 735 AD and capturing lords from Yaxchilán and Motul. Monuments including three hieroglyphic stairways were built, though by the latter half of the eighth century the region's instablity was such that the site was completely abandoned.

The ruins

Sadly, the **remains of the city** are less than spectacular, as many temples were partly dismantled during the chaos of the late eighth century. Nevertheless, there's some superb carving to admire, including several wonderful stelae and four small **hieroglyphic stairways**, now protected by thatched shelters grouped around the grassy plaza. On the south side of the plaza are the ruins of a palace, while on the east side a rich tomb was discovered under Temple L-51, probably belonging to the ruler Itzamnaaj K'awiil. Encircling the remains of this ceremonial core, it's still possible to make out the remains of the fortifications, a double defensive wall and stockade that the final occupiers erected.

ARRIVAL AND DEPARTURE **DOS PILAS**

By boat and on foot Getting to Dos Pilas is neither straightforward nor cheap. It's best to organize transport in Sayaxché or Flores. Either way you'll have to travel from Sayaxché, and then via a 45min speedboat trip to the *Posada El Caribe* (see above), followed by 12km on foot or horseback to the ruins.

Routes to Mexico

Heading **west to Mexico** from Petén is fairly straightforward and highly scenic in places, passing remote ruins and patches of dense rainforest. Though the Mexican state of Chiapas has been relatively calm for several years you can expect army security checks every hour or so as you travel around.

There are two popular **routes**. The first and most scenic involves crossing the Río Usumacinta into Chiapas at **Frontera Corozal**, from either **Bethel**, or a little upstream at **La Técnica** on the Guatemalan bank of the river. This trip enables you to pass the first-class ruins of **Yaxchilán** and Bonampak on the way. Alternatively, it's possible to head northwest **from Flores** to El Naranjo by bus, and cross the border at El Ceibo into the Mexican state of Tabasco.

Frontera Corozal and Yaxchilán

From the tranquil village of **FRONTERA COROZAL** inside Mexico there's a regular boat service to the spectacular ruins of **Yaxchilán**. It's usually easy to hook up with other people to share the costs of renting the boat – a good idea as it's quite steep otherwise. It's a lovely 45-minute run downstream to the ruins; the banks of the Usumacinta are still covered in thick jungle, particularly on the Guatemalan side, and there's plenty of birdlife. Be sure to drop by the little **museum**, which has some superb stelae.

ARRIVAL AND DEPARTURE — FRONTERA COROZAL

By taxi and minibus The village is 16km east of the main Palenque–Comitán highway; *colectivo* taxis and minibuses shuttle between the two. From the highway there are regular minibuses to Palenque (roughly every half-hour until around 4.30pm; 2hr 45min).

ACCOMMODATION

Escudo Jaguar By the riverside ⓣ 52 1423 1788. Mid-range place with attractive, comfortable rooms and a riverfront location; also offers tasty meals. $$

Nueva Alianza Inland from the dock ⓦ hotelnuevaalianza.org. Good budget rooms in a large partitioned wooden structure, plus private cabins. They serve meals, have wi-fi and accept card payments. Doubles $$, cabins $$$

THE MEXICAN BORDER: BETHEL/LA TÉCNICA/EL NARANJO

It's a straightforward trip to Mexico via **Bethel**, on the Río Usumacinta; travelling via **La Técnica** will cost less. There's also a paved road right to the Mexican border at **El Ceibo** via the frontier town of **El Naranjo**; this route is popular with travellers.

BETHEL

Buses (roughly hourly; 4hr) leave Santa Elena's Terminal Nuevo for **Bethel**, where there's a Guatemalan *migración* post, and a good cheap *posada*. At Bethel it's possible to get a shared *lancha* heading downstream (30min) to Frontera Corozal (see above) but most people and all buses push on to La Técnica which has better connections.

LA TÉCNICA

At the tiny settlement of **La Técnica**, you can cross the Usumacinta (5min; boats leave when full) to Corozal on the opposite bank. La Técnica lacks decent accommodation or other facilities. Agencies in Flores (see page 250) offer cross-border tickets direct to Palenque using the La Técnica route.

EL NARANJO

Regular buses connect Santa Elena with **El Naranjo** (every 45 min; 4hr), from where microbuses run to the border post at **El Ceibo** (every 30min; 20min). Note the border is only open from 9am to 5pm. Get an early start and avoid getting stuck for the night in El Naranjo, which is a rough place with little to recommend it. On the Mexican side minibuses leave for Tenosique in Tabasco (every 40min; 1hr 15min).

Piedras Negras

Sixty kilometres downstream from Yaxchilán, the Maya ruins of **Piedras Negras** loom high over the Guatemalan bank of the river. It's one of the most extensive sites in Guatemala, but it's also one of the least accessible. The city was called Yokib' ("the entrance") in Maya times; the Spanish name of Piedras Negras refers to the black stones lining the riverbank. Founded about 300 AD, the city developed an unrelenting rivalry with Yaxchilán for dominance over Usumacinta trade routes, contested by bloody battles and strategic pacts with Calakmul and Tikal. Like its adversary, Piedras Negras is best known for the extraordinary quality of its **carvings**, considered by many to be the finest from the Maya World. Several are in the Museo Nacional de Arqueología in Guatemala City, including a royal throne, exquisitely carved stelae and panels.

The ruins

Upon arrival, the most immediately impressive **monument** you'll see is a large rock jutting over the riverbank with a carving of a seated male figure presenting a bundle to a female figure. This was once surrounded by glyphs, now badly eroded and best seen at night with a torch held at a low angle. As you continue up the hill, across plazas and over the ruins of buildings you get some idea of the city's size. Several buildings are comparatively well preserved, particularly the **sweat baths**, used for ritual purification; the most imposing of all is the **acropolis**, a huge palace complex of rooms, passages and courtyards towering 100m above the riverbank. A **megalithic stairway** at one time led down to the river, doubtless a humbling sight to visitors (and captives) before the forest invaded the city.

ARRIVAL AND DEPARTURE — PIEDRAS NEGRAS

By boat Getting to Piedras Negras is not straightforward. The perfect way to arrive is by boat along the Usumacinta, following the ancient Maya trade route, though this involves booking an expensive tour – Maya Expeditions are highly recommended (see page 28) or a long, pricey boat trip from Bethel or Frontera Corozal (around ten hours' return trip). Trips from the Mexican bank usually work out cheaper, but the authorities regularly deny access due to security issues.

Waka' (El Perú) and the Ruta Guacamaya

East of the frontier town of El Naranjo, in the upper reaches of the Río San Pedro, is **Waka'** (aka **El Perú**), a seldom visited and largely unreconstructed site buried in some of the wildest rainforest in Petén. Waka' ("stood up place") was named for its position on a 130m-high escarpment towering above a tributary of the river.

The city grew to become an important middle-ranking Petén settlement in the Late Classic period, controlling important overland and water routes. Despite being the nearest place of any size west of Tikal, it sided with the other great "superpower" – distant Calakmul – in the power politics of the time. Waka' remained under the Calakmul overlordship in the early eighth century, but would later pay for this affiliation when a resurgent Tikal overran the city in 743 AD, after which no monuments were carved here for 47 years.

The ruins

Most of the site's temple mounds are still coated in vegetation, but Waka' is perhaps most famous for its many well-preserved **stelae** and the discoveries of two **royal tombs** of female rulers, both dating from the seventh century. In the first tomb, discovered in 2004, the queen was buried in a battle helmet with stingray spines for ritual bloodletting – burial customs usually only bestowed on male rulers. The second tomb (accompanied by jade jewellery and figurines) was found in 2012 and is thought to belong to Lady K'abel, a princess originally from Calakmul.

WAKA' WILDLIFE

Close to the Waka' site, at the confluence of the San Pedro and Sacluc, there's a **biological research station** (with good accommodation) at which rangers monitor forests that contain the largest concentrations of **scarlet macaws** in northern Central America. You've also an excellent chance of observing spider and howler monkeys, crocodiles, river turtles and the Petén turkey, and may even see a tapir on the banks of the Sacluc river. The best time to see scarlet macaws is between February and June when they nest in hollows of larger trees, but there are exotic birds in the Waka' region at all times of year.

The guards here welcome visitors and can act as guides, particularly if you bring along a little spare food.

ARRIVAL AND DEPARTURE — WAKÁ

Guided tours Tours to Waka' and the surrounding forest are often dubbed La Ruta Guacamaya or "Scarlet Macaw Trail". These exciting two- or three-night trips are by 4WD, pick-up and boat along rivers and through primary forest, staying at the research station (see page 280) or camping at the ruins. You can book tours direct (lasguacamayas.org) with the station, or via agencies in Flores. The station is 3hr from Santa Elena by road and river boat.

Yaxhá to the Belize border

East of the **Ixlú junction** on the road to Belize, a paved road runs 65km to the Belize border. The main attraction in these parts is **Yaxhá**, a huge Maya city on the fringes of two beautiful lakes: lagunas Yaxhá and Sacnab. The lakes are encircled by the dense jungle, swamps, savannah and wetlands of the **Monumento Natural Yaxhá–Nakúm–Naranjo**, whose 370 square kilometres harbour big cats, two species of crocodile and dozens of other reptiles, as well as prolific birdlife: spoonbills, the giant jabiru stork, eagles and vultures. It's one of the very few places in Guatemala where tapir are known to be breeding. The Postclassic ruins of **Topoxté** are also accessible from Yaxhá, and a third large site, **Nakúm**, is about 18km to the north. Further east, close to the Belize border, a side track leads to the intriguing site of **La Blanca** and its imposing palace.

Holtún

Thirty kilometres east of Ixlú there's a sign on the right for the ruins of **Holtún**, a twenty-minute walk from the road. A large site first settled around 850 BC, it has tall, unrestored **temples** adorned with masks, several stelae and altars, and the twinned temples of Pyramid X and Structure 7.

Yaxhá

Charge

Covering several square kilometres of a limestone ridge overlooking Laguna Yaxhá, **Yaxhá** is a compelling and rewarding Maya site to visit. Its name means "green-blue water", a reference to the wonderful turquoise hue of the lake just below. Of all Guatemala's ruins, only Tikal and El Mirador (and possibly Tintal) can trump the sheer scale and impact of this site, which has forty stelae, numerous altars, nine soaring temple pyramids and two ball courts. The dense jungle and lack of crowds only add to the special atmosphere of the place, and the wildlife is prolific (particularly howler monkeys and toucans).

Brief history

Relatively little is known about the history of Yaxhá, partly due to a relative lack of inscriptions. North of Plaza D the ruins are mostly **Preclassic**, while the bulk of the large structures in the south of the city date from the **Classic** era. The sheer size of the city indicates that Yaxhá was undoubtedly an important force in the central Maya region during this era, its influence perhaps only contained by the proximity of the

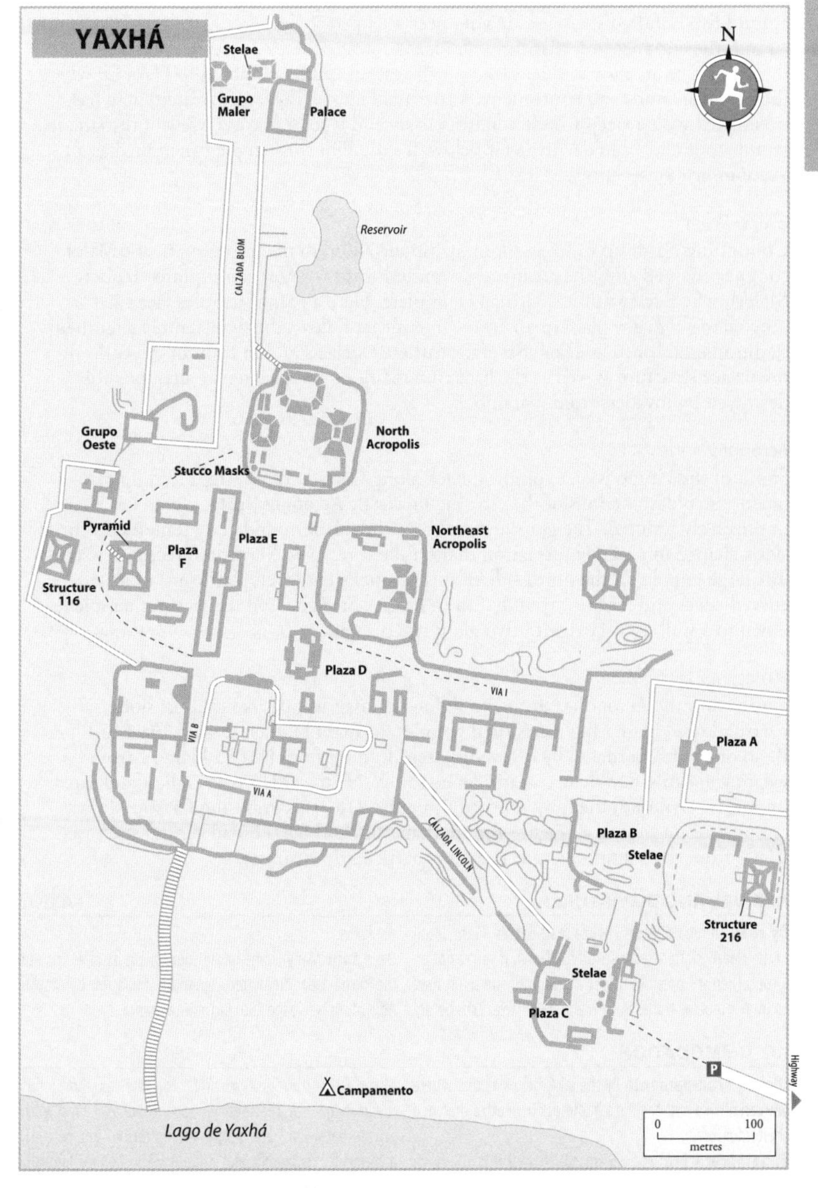

"superstate" Tikal, with which it shares several archeological similarities and close ties. For much of the Classic period, Yaxhá seemed locked in rivalry with the city of Naranjo, about 20km to the northeast, dominating its smaller neighbour for much of this time but suffering a heavy defeat in 799 AD.

The ruins

Restoration work is ongoing at Yaxhá, and most of the buildings have yet to be cleared, with many still choked in thick forest. The ruins are spread out over nine plazas, with around five hundred structures having been mapped so far.

From the entrance you pass through **Plaza C**, where there's a restored pyramid and three stelae on its eastern side. Head northwest up Calzada Lincoln to Plaza D, where there's a ball court, and continue west towards Plaza F. The large **pyramid** here has been fitted with a steep wooden staircase – ascend it for a fine overview of the site, its temple tops and Lago de Yaxhá far below. It's thought this temple functioned as an astronomical observatory.

Grupo Maler

Continuing north up Calzada Blom, it's about 750m to the imposing **Grupo Maler** complex (named after the great early twentieth-century Austrian explorer Teobert Maler), where restoration is virtually complete. Here a pair of temples face each other across a grassy plaza in an arrangement that follows the twin-temple alignment tradition established at Tikal. Several weathered stelae stand in front of the ruins of the palace structure as well as the broken remains of a huge circular altar, possibly destroyed by invaders from Naranjo.

Acropolis Norte

South of the Grupo Maler complex, back along Calzada Blom, steps lead up to one of the oldest sections of the city, the Preclassic **Acropolis Norte**, which has been impressively restored. The grassy central plaza here is surrounded by temples on three sides, shaped in a triadic formation that typifies Preclassic Maya architectural design. The large temple on the north side of this acropolis has seven platforms, unusual curved edges and reaches around 22m in height. Steps behind the western temple lead down to a wall decorated with two giant stucco masks.

Structure 216

South from the Acropolis Norte you follow a grassy avenue-like trail, its sides overshadowed by soaring unrestored temples, to Plaza D, then east up Vía 1 to Plaza B, an open area bordered by low walls. Steps lead up from here to Plaza A, from where you can scramble up a bank on its south side towards Yaxhá's tallest and most impressive pyramid, the fully restored **Structure 216**. This imposing Classic Maya temple rises in tiers to a height of more than 30m and has a broad central staircase. Views from the summit are spectacular – particularly at sunset.

ARRIVAL AND DEPARTURE — YAXHÁ

By road The main Flores–Belize road passes 11km south of the clearly signposted turn-off for Yaxhá. If you're not on a tour, then it's possible to get a ride from the main road as there's regular traffic to La Máquina village, 2km before the lakes.

On a tour Many Flores-based tour operators offer trips to the Yaxhá area; highly recommended tours run by Mayan Adventure (see page 250) include La Blanca.

ACCOMMODATION

There is a **campamento** by the lake, below Yaxhá, where you can pitch a tent or sling a hammock beneath a thatched shelter for free.

El Sombrero Ecolodge 2km south of ruins www.elsombreroecolodge.com. Right on the lakeshore, this rustic lodge has thatched wooden cabañas (some with private bathroom) and simple rooms (priced per person), a campsite, restaurant and a library. The helpful English-speaking owners can arrange boat trips on the lagunas, guides and horse-riding. It's not cheap however and rates have recently been hiked. Doubles $$, cabañas $$$$

Topoxté

Topoxté, a much smaller site on an island close to the west shore of Lago de Yaxhá, is best visited as part of a Yaxhá tour. Boat trips from *El Sombrero* (see above) or a dock on the south side of Yaxhá ruins are possible, too. Large crocodiles inhabit the lake, so don't attempt a swim.

This small, unusual site was occupied as late as 1450 AD, making it one of the most substantial Postclassic settlements yet found. The restored temples have upright walls, columns, flat stone roofs and balustraded steps, there are several plazas and the site is riddled with *chultunes*. Seventeen skulls of sacrificed children were found here in one tomb.

Nakúm

The substantial ruins of **Nakúm**, which have been the subject of extensive investigation in the last few years, are 18km north of Lago de Yaxhá. This site now has the second largest number of restored buildings in Guatemala after Tikal.

It's thought that Nakúm was a trading post in the Tikal empire, funnelling goods to and from the Caribbean coast, a role for which it was ideally situated at the headwaters of the Río Holmul. Settlers first arrived in the Middle Preclassic, but Nakúm rose to

FIESTAS IN PETÉN

JANUARY

12–15 Flores, the final day is the most dramatic.

MARCH

10–19 San José, a small fiesta with parades, fireworks and dances.

APRIL

April 27–May 1 Poptún.

MAY

1–9 San Benito, sure to be wild and very drunken.
15–22 Melchor de Mencos, main day May 22.
23–31 Dolores, main day May 28.

JUNE

16 Sayaxché, held in honour of San Antonio de Padua.

AUGUST

16–25 San Luis, main day Aug 25.

OCTOBER

1–4 San Francisco.
31 San José, a fascinating pagan fiesta (see page 254).

NOVEMBER

21–30 San Andrés, main day Nov 30.

prominence in the **Late Classic** and prospered well into the Terminal Classic period; new buildings were being constructed here as the cities across the rest of the Maya World were collapsing. The city was abandoned around 950 AD.

The ruins

Nakúm's ceremonial centre is split between northern and southern sections, connected by a causeway. The **northern sector** has not been extensively investigated and is largely unrestored but contains a plaza surrounded by low platforms, Structure X (a towering pyramid-temple topped with a building arranged in a triadic pattern) and Structure W (a fourteen-roomed palace).

The **southern section** is highly impressive, and was substantially enlarged in the terminal Classic period. It's here you'll find Nakúm's iconic roof combs – large and elaborate and defining the site's architectural style. The section contains three large plazas surrounded by temples: thirteen stelae and ten altars dot the Central Plaza. Its grand **acropolis** contains a huge **palace** (Structure D) of 44 rooms and myriad interior patios. Clear evidence of Teotihuacán influence has been found around Patio 1, where Central Mexican green obsidian and *Talud-Tablero* – or "slope-and-panel" style – platforms have been unearthed.

ARRIVAL AND DEPARTURE — NAKÚM

By road Access from Yaxhá is along a rough track that is usually impassable between July and January (unless the road is improved). The rest of the year you'll need a 4WD, though it could still take 1hr 30min to drive.

Tours Two-day horseback tours can be organized by *El Sombrero* (see page 282); Flores tour operators, including Mayan Adventure (see page 250), also run trips here.

La Blanca

La Blanca is a small, unusual site close to the Belize border, primarily of interest because it was occupied much later than most Maya settlements, at least until 1050 AD. Most of the buildings date from the Late Classic period. Archeological work is ongoing, so you have the chance to gain direct insight into excavation work.

The entire site is dominated by a huge, ostentatious **palace** of eighteen living quarters built round a square patio. Intriguing features include a 6m-high arch, some fine murals and also some ancient graffiti.

There's a small **information centre** here with informative panels in English about the site and its history.

THE BELIZE BORDER: MELCHOR DE MENCOS

Border **formalities** are fairly straightforward; you'll probably be asked for a small (illegal) departure tax on leaving Guatemala. **Moneychangers** will pester you on either side of the border – most give fair rates, but there's also an ATM at the Texaco petrol station 500m west of the bridge in Melchor.

ON THE GUATEMALAN SIDE

Microbuses and buses run between Santa Elena (see page 249) and Melchor (micros every 30min; 2hr 15min). From the border to **Tikal** taxis are available for a shared ride (they leave when they have four people), or you can do it independently by catching a minibus for Santa Elena (every 30min) and jump off at the Ixlú junction (45 min) and getting another from there.

ON THE BELIZE SIDE

Buses leave for Belize City every 30min or so (3hr), usually right from the frontier. Shared **taxis** to Benque Viejo and San Ignacio (20min) are also available.

ARRIVAL AND DEPARTURE — LA BLANCA

Tours La Blanca is 12km south of the Flores–Belize highway, the turn-off is 11km before Melchor de Mencos; the dirt access road is in good condition. There's very little transport from the highway, so a tour makes sense. Combined trips to La Blanca and Yaxhá are offered by Mayan Adventure (see page 250) in Flores.

Melchor de Mencos and the Belize border

The nondescript but bustling **border** town of **MELCHOR DE MENCOS** boasts little of interest for visitors (though there are a few stelae in the Parque Central). There's a Banrural bank here for booking Tikal tickets in advance (and an ATM).

ACCOMMODATION — MELCHOR DE MENCOS

Río Mopán Lodge On the riverbank T 7926 5196, W facebook.com/riomopanlodge. Comfortable place with a small pool and choice of rooms, some with balconies, in verdant grounds. There's a good restaurant and trips to remote Maya sites are offered. $$

Into Honduras: Copán and around

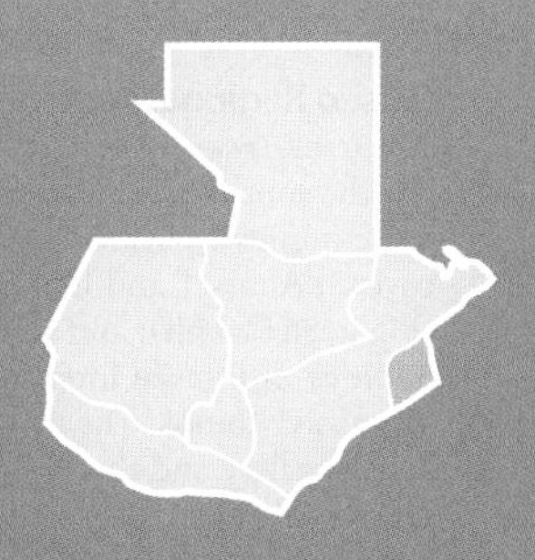

ARACARI TOUCAN

Into Honduras: Copán and around

Across the border in Honduras, about five hours by road from Guatemala City, are the ruins of Copán, one of the most magnificent of all Maya sites. While its compact scale is not initially as impressive as Tikal or Mexico's Chichén Itzá, it boasts an astonishing number of decorative carvings, stelae and altars, including a towering hieroglyphic stairway. Throw in a wonderful site museum and the delightful nearby town of Copán Ruinas, where most people stay, and it's easy to appreciate Copán's appeal.

Delightfully located in a sweeping highland valley, the city-state of **Copán** was the southernmost centre of the Maya civilization. The Maya chose a beautiful site on the fertile banks of the Río Copán at a pleasingly temperate altitude of 600m. Today the countryside around Copán is glorious to look at, with green rolling hills of pastureland and tobacco and coffee farms interspersed with patches of pine forest. Though the archeological site is the main attraction, there's plenty more to explore in the surrounding area, with hot springs, fincas and a bird reserve close by.

Copán Ruinas

Just 10km east of the Guatemalan border, the small town of **COPÁN RUINAS** is a charming place of steep, cobbled streets and red-tiled roofs set among the lush scenery of Honduras's western highlands. Despite a fast-increasing number of visitors from all over the world, it has managed to remain a largely unspoiled and genuinely friendly place. Many travellers are seduced by Copán's delightfully relaxed atmosphere, clean air and rural setting, and end up spending longer here than planned, studying Spanish, eating and drinking well, or exploring the region's other minor sites, hot springs and beautiful countryside.

Parque Central

Half a day is enough to take in virtually all the town's attractions. The **Parque Central** – lined with banks, municipal structures and an attractive, whitewashed Baroque-style church – was designed and built in the mid-twentieth century by visiting archeologists Tatiana Proskouriakoff and Gustav Stromsvik. Unfortunately, the simple elegance of the original layout, which followed classical Spanish lines, has been somewhat spoilt by grandiose remodelling initiatives. It does remain a popular place to kill time, however, its benches filled with cowboy-booted farmhands and camera-touting visitors.

Museo Regional de Arqueología

Parque Central • Charge

On the southwest side of the *parque* is the **Museo Regional de Arqueología**. It features some impressive Maya carvings collected from the Copán region, including the glyph-covered Altars T and U; Stela B, depicting the ruler Waxaklajuun Ub'aah K'awiil (Eighteen Rabbit); and some remarkable and intricately detailed **flints** – ornamental oddities with seven interlocking heads carved from obsidian. There are also two impressive **tombs**. The first contains the remains of a female shaman, complete with jade jewellery and the skulls of a puma, deer and two human sacrificial victims. The other (10J–45), discovered in 1999 during road-building work, was created for an Early Classic-period ruler of Copán in the sixth century and comprises a vaulted burial

STELAE IN THE ANCIENT MAYA CITY OF COPÁN

Highlights

❶ **Copán Ruinas** Combining a delightfully relaxed ambience with a cosmopolitan array of restaurants, bars and boutique hotels, this gorgeous little highland town makes a perfect base. See page 288

❷ **Macaw Mountain Bird Park and Nature Reserve** This appealing park is a great place to get up close and personal with parrots, birds of prey and rare macaws, among other wildlife. See page 291

❸ **Hacienda San Lucas** One of the finest rural hotels in Central America, this hacienda is well worth a visit for a splendid dinner, even if the room tariffs prove to be beyond your budget. See page 293

❹ **Copán** Examine the exquisite carvings and temples at the archeological site dubbed the "Athens of the Maya World". See page 294

❺ **Museums** Copán has three fine museums dedicated to Maya culture, don't miss the outstanding Museum of Maya Sculpture. See page 297

❻ **Finca El Cisne** Head to this idyllic farm to experience Honduran hospitality at its best; and to join tours and excursions that include horse-riding and a spa visit. See page 301

HIGHLIGHTS ARE MARKED ON THE MAP ON PAGE 290

HONDURAS BASICS

Getting to Copán is pretty straightforward from Guatemala. There are excellent transport links from Antigua and Guatemala City by direct daily shuttle and luxury buses (see pages 80 and 64), or you can travel via Chiquimula (see page 209), a longer but cheaper route. The Honduran **currency** is the lempira. Most nationalities (US, Canada, virtually all EU countries, Australia and New Zealand) qualify for a free **thirty-day visa** on arrival; crossing the border is usually very straightforward. Note, however, that if you plan to **drive** inside Honduras, you need permission from your Guatemalan rental car company.

The **country code** for Honduras is ☎ 504 and there are no area codes.

chamber where the as yet unidentified ruler was buried with numerous ceramics and two large, carved jade pectoral pieces.

Museo Digital

Parque Central • Charge

Located inside a renovated old high school building on the north side of the *parque*, this museum contains historic photographs and you can watch a highly-informative film about the Maya site and history of Copán Ruinas town.

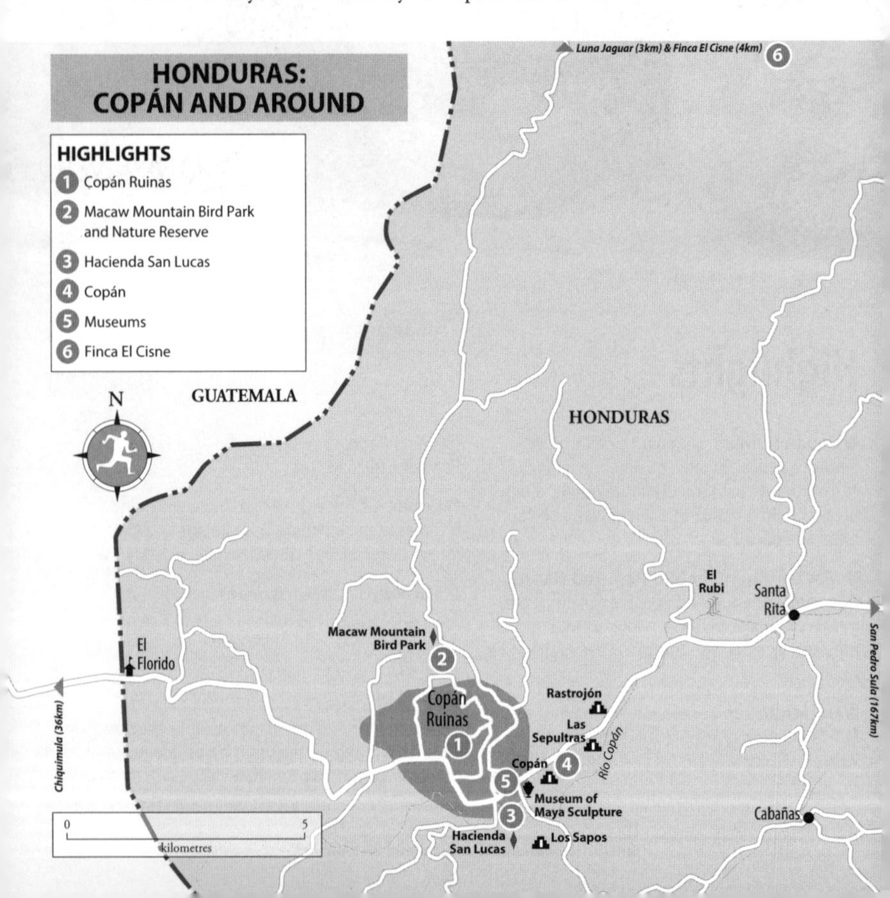

Palacio Municipal

Parque Central • Free

Inside the **Palacio Municipal** on the northwest side of the Parque Central is a fantastic permanent **photography exhibition** donated by Harvard University's Peabody Museum, detailing, in beautifully reproduced prints, the first archeological expeditions to Copán at the turn of the twentieth century.

Casa K'inich

Av Centro América • Charge; children free • T 2651 4105

Five blocks north of the Parque Central, **Casa K'inich** is an interactive children's learning centre with exhibits (sadly many are broken) about the Maya civilization and a play area. It's located in El Cuartel, a renovated army fort, and has great views over the town.

Macaw Mountain Bird Park and Nature Reserve

3km north of the Parque Central • Charge; entrance ticket valid for three days • W macawmountain.org

The **Macaw Mountain Bird Park and Nature Reserve**, with its abundant parrots, parakeets, toucans, five species of macaw, grey hawks and a great horned owl, makes a wonderful half-day excursion. Most of the birds have been previously kept as pets and donated to the centre. There are breeding programmes for very rare species such as the Buffon macaw and the yellow-lored amazon, and a successful release programme has seen captive scarlet macaws released from the park back to the Copán valley.

There are walk-through aviaries and **nature trails** that wind through a lovely old-growth forest of cedar, mahogany, fig and zapote trees, interspersed with elevated viewing decks. You'll also find a coffee-roasting house, natural river-fed swimming pool and an excellent **café-restaurant** serving gourmet coffee from the Copán region, as well as an information centre explaining the relationship between the Maya and the scarlet macaw.

Los Sapos

Hacienda San Lucas, 4km south of the Parque Central • Charge • W haciendasanlucas.com

In the grounds of **Hacienda San Lucas** (see page 293), a lovely rural hotel about 4km south of town, you'll find the ruins of **Los Sapos**, which date from the same era as Copán. The name of this tiny site derives from a rock carved in the shape of a toad – it's thought to have been a place where Maya women came to bear children, though unfortunately time and weather have eroded much of the carving.

ARRIVAL AND DEPARTURE — COPÁN RUINAS

FROM ANTIGUA AND GUATEMALA CITY

By shuttle bus Direct daily shuttle buses leave Antigua daily at different times throughout the day, pausing to pick up passengers in Guatemala City an hour later on demand, and getting to Copán around six hours later; they return to Guatemala at set times (company dependent). These shuttle buses can be booked by any travel agent and most hotels in town.

By first-class bus A daily luxury a/c pullman bus (W facebook.com/HedmanAlas or W hedmanalas.com) covers the Antigua–Copán route (via Guatemala City). Litegua (W litegua.com) operates one daily bus to the El Florido border from Guatemala City; note Litegua buses don't return to the capital from El Florido, but from Chiquimula.

FROM CHIQUIMULA VIA EL FLORIDO

You could save a little cash by travelling via the Guatemalan town of Chiquimula (see page 209), which is regularly served by very regular Rutas Orientales buses from Guatemala City, four daily Litegua buses, and local buses from Puerto Barrios.

From Chiquimula Minibuses leave every 30min (1hr 30min) for the border at El Florido, most via the town of Jocotán. From El Florido, minibuses leave when full (about every 20min until 7pm; 20min) for Copán Ruinas. They arrive and depart from a stand beside the cemetery, a few blocks west of the Parque Central.

TO RÍO DULCE OR LÍVINGSTON

For Río Dulce or Lívingston in Guatemala, it's cheapest to take a minibus to the border at El Florido, then a local bus (every 30min) to Chiquimula, from where there are regular buses to destinations including Puerto Barrios. Shuttle buses (see above) will also drop you off at the El Rancho junction on the Carretera al Atlántico highway, where you can connect with buses heading east.

GETTING AROUND

On foot Almost everything of interest is within a few blocks of Copán's Parque Central. Street names exist, though few locals use them.

By tuk-tuk Tuk-tuks (also called "mototaxis") are plentiful in Copán, and will whisk you around the village or to the ruins for a small fee, per head, per journey.

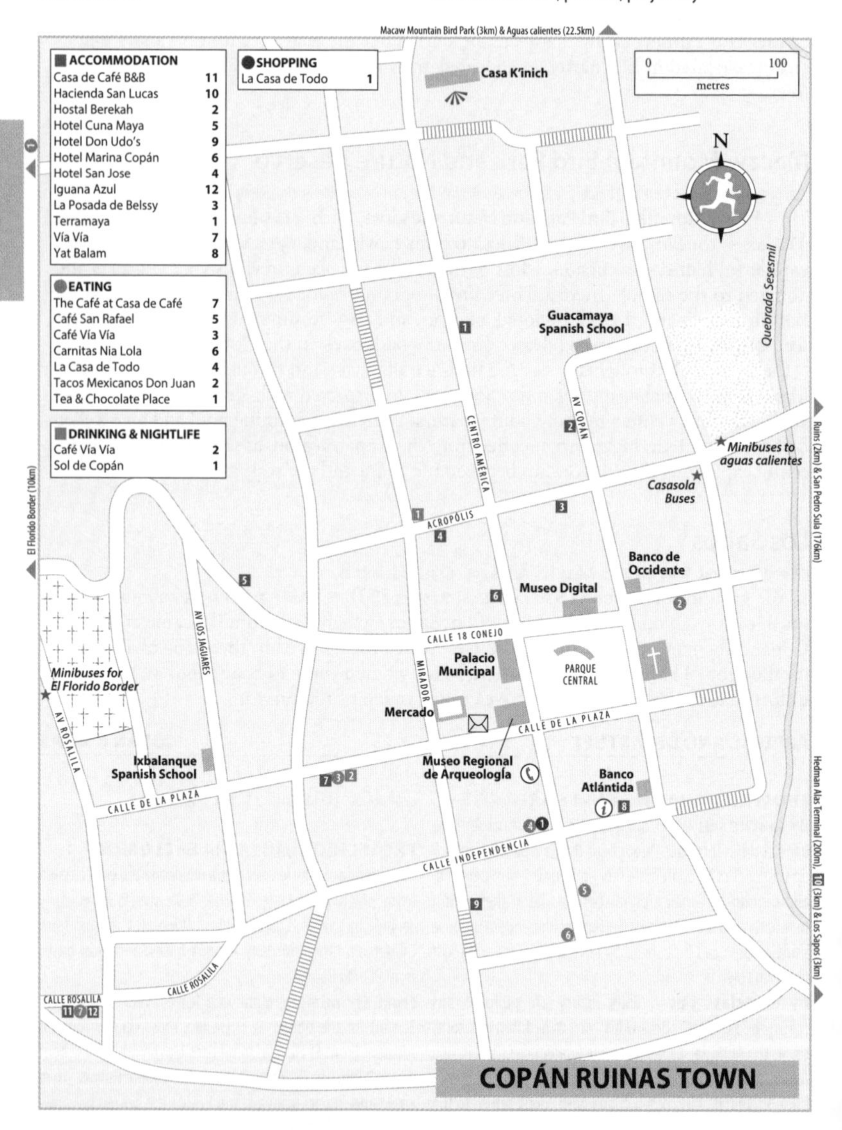

INFORMATION AND ACTIVITIES

Tourist information The tourist office is on the Parque Central (2651 3829). Base Camp (see below) is a good source of independent travel information.

Base Camp Inside *Café Vía Vía*, this tour operator (2651 4652, facebook.com/pg/basecampoutdooradventures) offers excellent hikes, including a Copán Cultural walk, horse-riding, trips throughout Honduras and shuttle buses.

Language schools Copán is an excellent place to study, with two good Spanish schools. Guacamaya (2651 4360, guacamaya.com) is two blocks north of the plaza, while Ixbalanque (2651 4432) is three blocks west of the plaza.

ACCOMMODATION

Copán Ruinas has an excellent range of hotels and guesthouses. **Budget options** tend to fill up quickly, so make sure to book ahead.

★**Casa de Café B&B** C Rosalila casadecafecopan.com; map page 292. Owned by an American-Honduran couple, this classy B&B has a lovely ambience. Rooms are comfortable and airy, all simply yet elegantly presented with wood panelling and facing a fabulous garden. Healthy, flavoursome meals are served in the garden restaurant, which has mountain views. Free organic coffee and tea are served all day. The owners also have two excellent houses and a studio for rent. $$$

★**Hacienda San Lucas** 4km south of the Parque Central haciendasanlucas.com; map page 292. Highly atmospheric converted farmhouse in the hills south of town, with sweeping views over the valley. It's an ideal place to relax, with plenty of space – the grounds include the Los Sapos archeological site (see page 291). All the rooms have hand-crafted, cedar-wood beds and local textile decorations. Horse-riding can be arranged and the restaurant's cuisine is excellent. $$$$

Hostal Berekah Av Copán hotelberakah.wordpress.com; map page 292. Very centrally located, this modest, locally owned hostel has pleasant rooms, a basic dorm, kitchen, pool table, terrace and clean shared bathrooms. Dorms $, doubles $$

Hotel Cuna Maya C 18 Conejo 9862 6433 cunamayahotel16@gmail.com; map page 292. The caring local family running this hotel really make an effort, and offer genuine hospitality and a great Honduran breakfast. Rooms are well-kept, comfortable and have a splash of decorative colour; all have a/c and TV. $$

Hotel Don Udo's Av Mirador 9707 1743; map page 292. A homely hotel with fourteen comfortable rooms and a suite set around a garden courtyard. Facilities include a sauna/jacuzzi, sun deck with valley views and a restaurant with good global cuisine. Doubles $$$, suite $$$$

Hotel Marina Copán Av Centro América hotelmarinacopan.com; map page 292. Colonial-style hotel right in the heart of town, with fine gardens. The stylish rooms, all with a/c, are well presented and boast classy furnishings, plus there's a small pool, gym and bar. $$$$

Hotel San Jose C Acrópolis & Mirador 2651 3730; map page 292. This attractive hotel shows impressive attention to detail with spacious rooms and decent rates. Staff are friendly and accommodating. $$$

Iguana Azul C Rosalila iguanaazulcopan.com; map page 292. This popular budget hotel is located on a quiet lane west of the centre and has four private rooms and two very pleasant dorms all with good-quality mattresses and shared hot-water bathrooms. There are good cleanliness standards, a pretty garden, free purified water, laundry and luggage storage facilities. Dorms $, doubles $$

La Posada de Belssy C Acrópolis 2651 4680; map page 292. An ageing guesthouse with ten rooms (some smallish) that have hot-water bathrooms, ceiling fans and cable TV. There's a small pool (for cooling off only) and roof terrace. Staff are very kind here and rates include breakfast. $$

★**Terramaya** Av Centro América terramayacopan.com; map page 292. This boutique hotel features whitewashed walls and wrought-iron metalwork and lashings of taste and style. Some of the six rooms have generous balconies with hammocks overlooking the Copán valley; all have a/c and flatscreen TVs. There's a massage pavilion outside in the beautiful garden, a wonderful breakfast is included and complimentary coffee and iced tea is served all day. Service standards are high. $$$$

Vía Vía C de la Plaza viaviacafe.com; map page 292. Five simple, smallish but spotless rooms with en-suite bathrooms and fans at the rear of a popular travellers' café (see below). It can be a tad noisy here at night, but it's still fine value as rates are so low. $$

Yat Balam C Independencia 2651 3517; map page 292. Modern and inviting, this small place has just four rooms (two have a lounge area and balcony). The design theme combines exposed stone and wood beams with a soothing cream colour scheme. All rooms have fridges, TVs and beautiful bed linen. $$$$

EATING

Copán has some superb places to eat and drink, many with an **international** flavour. Expect generous portions and good service.

★**The Café at Casa de Café** C Rosalila casadecafecopan.com; map page 292. Featuring fresh healthy cooking, this lovely hotel restaurant, with a

AFTERNOON TEA WITH A DIFFERENCE

Tea & Chocolate Place C Yaruga, about 800m northeast of the Parque Central facebook.com/ElLugardelTeyChocolate; map page 292. The owner of this private house, David Sedat, is a leading archeologist who has worked at the ruins of Copán for years and is also a passionate environmentalist for the region. Every day (except Sunday) he opens his home for a couple of hours and invites guests to sample tea from the noni fruit (he cultivates noni fruit trees, and other native plants in a deforestation project near Copán). The Sedat family also offers cacao tea, spices, cookies and sells natural products made from noni and macadamia nuts, all priced fairly. No food (or coffee) is served. $$

delightful garden setting and homestyle cooking, is well worth a visit. Drop by for an all-day breakfast, small plate (try the *tamales*) *tartine* (French sandwich) or a delicious dinner. Bread is baked fresh daily and their *picante* (hot sauce) is superb. $$

Café San Rafael Av Centro América cafesanrafael.com; map page 292. This upmarket two-storey café-restaurant is run by a *queso* fanatic who studied cheese-making in California (so you won't go wrong with the cheese platters). Sandwiches are quite pricey but excellent, and you'll also find fine breakfast options. Also serves fine coffee and sells good wine and gourmet treats. $$$

Café Vía Vía C de la Plaza viaviacafe.com; map page 292. This huge, hip bar-restaurant has a garden terrace at the rear and a real vibe on busy nights. Offers an array of sandwiches, *baleadas*, good breakfasts, omelettes, set meals, salads and plenty of veggie options. They also sell Belgium beer. $$

Carnitas Nia Lola Av Centro América 2651 4196; map page 292. A fine bet for a meat feast, this quirky alpine lodge lookalike serves large portions of grilled and barbecued steaks and kebabs, plus some vegetarian dishes. Doubles as a bar, with an early evening happy hour and a good mix of locals and visitors. $$

La Casa de Todo C Centro América casadetodo.com; map page 292. This place has recently relocated but the emphasis on local cuisine remains, with good home-made soups and filling dishes like *enchiladas copanecas* (crispy tortillas with chicken, cabbage and cheese. Cash only. $$$

Tacos Mexicanos Don Juan Parque Central facebook.com/Tacos.Mexicanos.Don.Juan; map page 292. Simple taco joint with a friendly team and travel budget-friendly prices. The owner, Don Juan, likes to dress up as Santa to hand out free treats on special occasions. $

DRINKING AND NIGHTLIFE

Café Vía Vía C de la Plaza viaviacafe.com; map page 292. Ever-popular bar-restaurant with a gregarious vibe that's packed with travellers most nights.

★ **Sol de Copán** Av Mirador 9514 3732; map page 292. Terrific microbrewery-bar run by a hospitable German who imports his own hops and ingredients from the homeland to create delicious brews: wheat beers, dark ales and lagers. Also serves tasty grub including sausages and schnitzel.

SHOPPING

La Casa de Todo C Centro América casadetodo.com; map page 292. Offers a wonderful selection of handicrafts and souvenirs including ceramics and jewellery. They also stock books on the ancient Maya.

DIRECTORY

Banks Banco Atlántida, Av Copán, and Banco de Occidente, C 18 Conejo, both have ATMs.

Copán ruins

2km east of Copán Ruinas town • Last entrance 3.30pm • Charge includes the Las Sepulturas ruins (see page 300), though access to the archeological tunnels costs extra, as does the museum; registered guides charge a flat fee for up to nine people for a 2hr tour

The **Copán ruins** lie a pleasant fifteen-minute walk from town, along a raised footpath that runs parallel to the highway. Entrance to the site is through the **visitor centre** on the left-hand side of the car park, where a small exhibition explains Copán's place in the Maya World. On the other side of the car park is a **cafeteria**, serving drinks and reasonable meals, and a small souvenir shop. A **guide** is an excellent investment if you really want to get the most out of Copán.

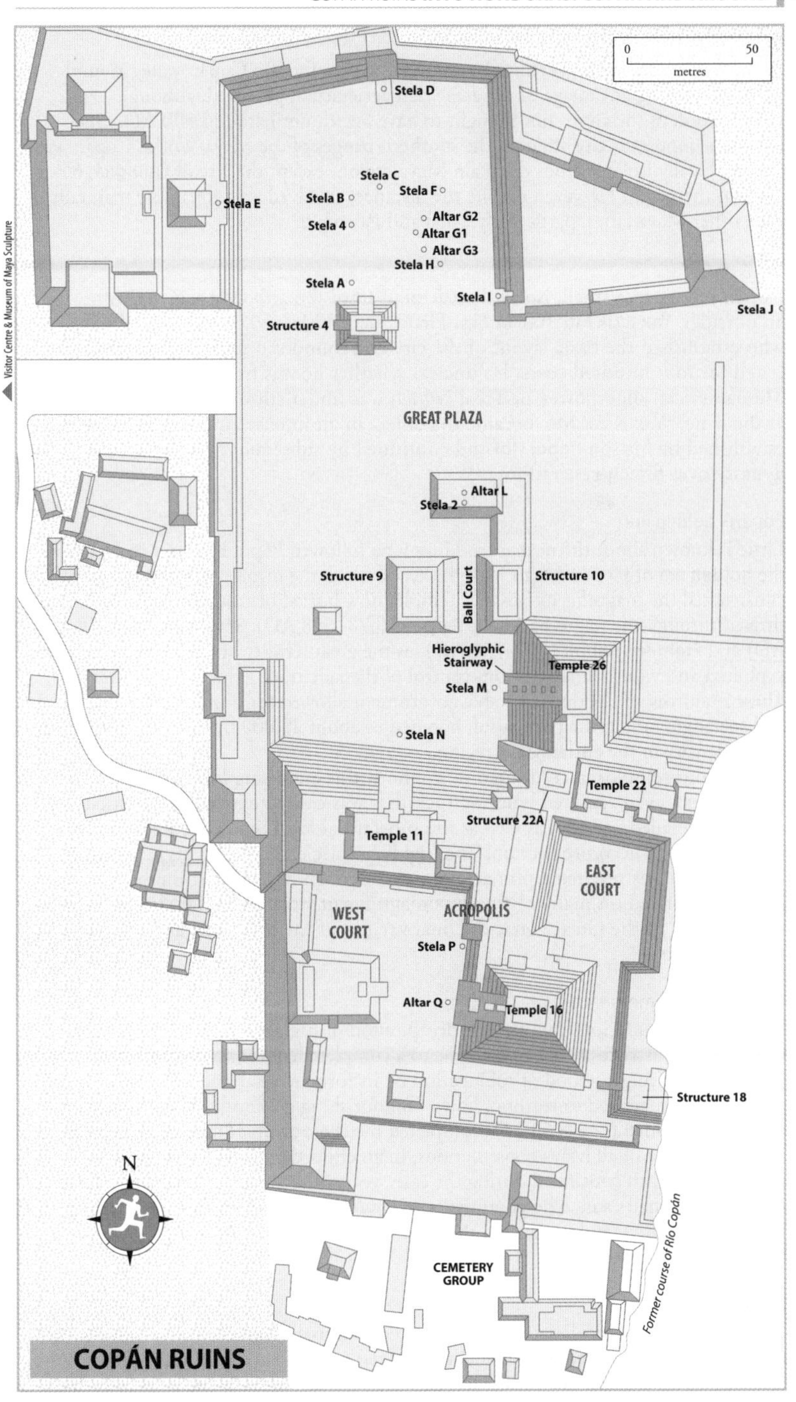

0
50
metres
Stela D
Stela C
Stela B
Stela F
Stela E
Stela 4
Altar G2
Altar G1
Altar G3
Stela H
Stela A
Stela I
Stela J
Structure 4
Visitor Centre & Museum of Maya Sculpture
GREAT PLAZA
Altar L
Stela 2
Structure 9
Ball Court
Structure 10
Hieroglyphic Stairway
Temple 26
Stela M
Stela N
Temple 22
Structure 22A
Temple 11
EAST COURT
WEST COURT
ACROPOLIS
Stela P
Altar Q
Temple 16
Structure 18
N
CEMETERY GROUP
Former course of Río Copán
COPÁN RUINS

7

Brief history

Archeologists believe that settlers began moving into the Río Copán valley around 1400 BC, taking advantage of the area's rich agricultural potential, although construction of the city is not thought to have begun until around 100 AD. Once the most important **city-state** on the southern fringes of the Maya World, Copán was geographically isolated from the main Maya region, except the city of **Quiriguá**, 64km away to the north. However, despite the distances involved, relations were maintained with other Maya cities, particularly Tikal and Palenque.

Yax K'uk Mo'

Copán remained a small, isolated settlement until the arrival in 426 AD of an outsider, **Yax K'uk Mo'** (Great Sun First Quetzal Macaw), a warrior-shaman who established the basic layout of the city and founded a royal dynasty that lasted for four hundred years. It's unclear whether he was from Teotihuacán, the Mesoamerican superpower, or Tikal (which was under strong Teotihuacán influence at the time). Yax K'uk Mo' became the object of an intense cult of veneration, first established by his son **Popol Hol** and continued by subsequent members of the dynasty over fifteen generations.

Copán's golden era

Little is known about the next seven kings who followed Popol Hol, but in 553 AD, the **golden era** of Copán began with the accession to the throne of **Moon Jaguar**, who constructed the magnificent Rosalila Temple, now buried beneath Temple 16. The city thrived through the reigns of **Smoke Serpent** (578–628 AD), **Smoke Jaguar** (628–695 AD) and **Eighteen Rabbit** (695–738 AD), as the great fertility of the Copán region was exploited and wealth amassed from control of the jade trade along the Río Motagua. These resources and periods of stable government allowed for unprecedented political and social growth, as the population boomed to about 28,000 by 760 AD, the highest urban density in the entire Maya region.

Ambitious rebuilding continued throughout this era, using local andesite, a fine-grained, even-textured volcanic rock that was easily quarried and particularly suited to detailed carving, as well as the substantial local limestone beds, which were ideal for stucco production. The highly artistic carved-relief style for which Copán is famous reached a pinnacle during the reign of Eighteen Rabbit – whose image is depicted on many of the site's magnificent stelae and who also oversaw the construction of the Great Plaza, the final version of the ball court and Temple 22 in the East Court.

Defeat and re-emergence

Following the audacious capture and decapitation of Eighteen Rabbit by Quiriguá's Cauac Sky, construction at Copán came to a complete halt for seventeen years, possibly indicating a period of subjugation by its former vassal state. The royal dynasty subsequently managed to regroup, however, flourishing gloriously, albeit briefly, once more. **Smoke Shell** (749–763 AD) completed the **Hieroglyphic Stairway**, one of the most impressive of all Maya constructions, in an effort designed to symbolize this revival. Optimism continued during the early years of the reign of **Yax Pasaj** (763–820 AD), Smoke Shell's son, who commissioned **Altar Q**, which illustrates the entire dynasty from its beginning, and completed the final version of **Temple 16**, which towers over the site, about 776 AD.

Decline

Towards the end of Yax Pasaj's rule, the rot set in: human remains found indicate that the decline was provoked by inadequate food resources created by population pressure, resulting in subsequent environmental collapse. The seventeenth and final ruler, **Ukit**

Took', assumed the throne in 822 AD, but his reign proved miserably inauspicious. Poignantly, the only monument to his reign, Altar L, was never completed, as if the sculptor had downed his tools and walked out on the job.

The nineteenth century

The site was known to the Spanish, although they took little interest in it. Not until the nineteenth century and the publication of *Incidents of Travel in Central America, Chiapas and Yucatán* by **John Lloyd Stephens** and **Frederick Catherwood** did Copán become known to the wider world. Stephens, the then acting US ambassador, succeeded in buying the ruins in 1839 and, accompanied by Catherwood, a British architect and artist, spent several weeks clearing the site and mapping the buildings. Stephens' plans to float Copán's monuments down the Río Copán and on to the US were never realized, but the instant success of the book and the interest it sparked in Mesoamerican culture ensured that Copán became a magnet for explorers.

British archeologist **Alfred Maudsley** began a full-scale mapping, excavation and reconstruction of the site in 1891.

The 20th and 21st centuries

A second major investigation was begun in 1935 by the Carnegie Institution in Washington, during which the Río Copán was diverted to prevent it carving into the site. Since 1977, the Instituto Hondureño de Antropología e Historia has been running a series of projects with the help of archeologists from around the world. Copán is now perhaps the best understood of all Maya cities, and a series of **tunnelling projects** beneath the Acropolis has unearthed remarkable discoveries including, in 1989, the Rosalila Temple, which is now open to the public. In 1993 the Papagayo Temple, built by Popol Hol and dedicated to his father Yax K'uk Mo', was uncovered, and in 1998 further burrowing revealed the tomb of the founder himself. In 2015 the nearby archeological site of Rastrojón was opened to the public, adding to Copán's allure.

Museum of Maya Sculpture

Charge

Opposite the visitor centre is the terrific **Museum of Maya Sculpture**, arguably the finest in the entire Maya region, with a tremendous collection of stelae, altars, panels and well-labelled explanations in English. You enter through a dramatic entrance doorway, resembling the jaws of a serpent, and pass through a tunnel (signifying the passage into *Xibalbá*, or the underworld). Dominating the museum is a full-scale, flamboyantly painted replica of the magnificent **Rosalila Temple**, built by Moon Jaguar in 571 and discovered intact under Temple 16. A vast crimson-and-jade-coloured mask of the Sun God, depicted with wings outstretched, forms the main facade of the temple. Other ground-floor exhibits concentrate on aspects of Maya beliefs and cosmology, while the upper floor houses many of the finest original sculptures from the Copán valley, comprehensively displaying the skill of the Maya craftsmen.

Great Plaza

From the museum it's a 200m walk east to the **warden's gate**, the entrance to the site proper, where your ticket will be checked and where there are usually several squabbling **scarlet macaws** to greet your arrival – these are quite tame and sleep in cages by the gate at night.

Straight ahead from the warden's gate through the avenue of trees lies the **Great Plaza**, a large rectangular arena strewn with the magnificently carved and exceptionally well-preserved stelae that are Copán's outstanding features. Initially, however, the visual impact of this grassy expanse may seem a little underwhelming: the first structure you see is **Stucture 4**, a modestly sized pyramid-temple, while the stepped buildings bordering the northern end of the plaza are low and unremarkable. This part of the Great Plaza was once a public place, the stepped sides bordered by a densely populated residential area. The grandest buildings are confined to the monumental temples that border the southern section of the plaza, rising to form the Acropolis, the domain of the ruling and religious elite.

Stelae

Dotted all around are Copán's famed **stelae** and altars, made from local andesite. Most of the stelae represent **Eighteen Rabbit**, Copán's "King of the Arts" (stelae A, B, C, D, F, H and 4). Some of the carved monuments here are reproductions, though they have been expertly carved; the originals have been moved into the site museum so they're protected from the elements.

Stela A has incredibly deep carving, although the faces are now eroded; its sides include a total of 52 glyphs, translating into a famous inscription that includes the emblem glyphs of the four great cities of Copán, Palenque, Tikal and Calakmul – a text designed to show that Eighteen Rabbit saw his city as a pivotal power in the Maya World.

Stela B depicts a slightly oriental-looking Eighteen Rabbit wearing a turban-like headdress intertwined with twin macaws; his hands support a bar motif, a symbol designed to show the ruler holding up the sky.

Stela C (730 AD) is one of the earliest stones to have faces on both sides and, like many of the central stelae, has an altar at its base, carved in the shape of a turtle. Two rulers are represented here: facing the turtle (a symbol of longevity) is Eighteen Rabbit's father, Smoke Jaguar, who lived well into his 80s; on the other side is Eighteen Rabbit himself.

Stela H, perhaps the most impressively executed of all the sculptures, shows Eighteen Rabbit wearing the latticed skirt of the Maize God, his wrists weighed down with jewellery, while his face is crowned with a stunning headdress.

Ball Court

South of Structure 4, towards the Acropolis, is the I-shaped **Ball Court**, one of the largest and most elaborate of the Classic period and one of the few Maya courts still to have a paved floor. It was completed in 738 AD, just four months before Eighteen Rabbit's demise at the hands of Quiriguá; two previous versions lie beneath it. Like its predecessors, the court was dedicated to the great macaw deity, and both sloping sides of the court are lined with three sculpted **macaw heads**. The rooms that line the sides of the court, overlooking the playing area, were probably used by priests and members of the elite as they watched the game.

Hieroglyphic Stairway

Pressed up against the Ball Court and protected by a vast canvas cover is the famed **Hieroglyphic Stairway**, perhaps Copán's most astonishing monument. The stairway, which takes up the entire western face of the Temple 26 pyramid, is made up of some 72 stone steps; every block is carved to form part of the glyphic sequence – around 2200 glyph blocks in all. It forms one of the longest Maya hieroglyphic texts, but, unfortunately, attempted reconstruction by early archeologists left the sequence so jumbled that a complete interpretation is still some way off. What is known is that the stairway was initiated to record the dynastic history of the city: some of the lower steps were first put in place by Eighteen Rabbit in 710 AD, while Smoke Shell rearranged and completed most of the sequences in 755 AD as part of his efforts to reassert the city's dignity and strength. At the base of the stairway, the badly weathered **Stela M** depicts Smoke Shell and records a solar eclipse in 756 AD.

Temple 11 and Stela N

Adjacent to the Hierogylphic Stairway, and towering over the extreme southern end of the plaza, are the vertiginous steps of **Temple 11** (also known as the Temple of the Inscriptions). The temple was constructed by Smoke Shell, who is thought to be buried beneath it, though no tomb has yet been found. At its base is another classic piece of Copán carving, **Stela N** (761 AD), representing Smoke Shell, with portraits on the two main faces of the stela and glyphs down the sides. The depth of the relief has protected the nooks and crannies, some of which still bear traces of paint – originally the carvings and buildings would have been painted in a whole range of bright colours, but for some reason only the red has survived.

The Acropolis

From the southwestern corner of the plaza, a trail runs past some original drainage ducts beyond which stone steps climb steeply up the side of Temple 11 to a soaring cluster of temples, dubbed the **Acropolis**. This lofty inner sanctum was the preserve of royalty, nobles and priests; it was the political and ceremonial core where religious rituals were enacted, sacrifices performed and rulers entombed. The whole structure grew in size over four hundred years, the temples growing higher and higher as new structures were built over the remains of earlier buildings. A warren of excavated tunnels, some open to the public, bores through the vast bulk of the Acropolis to the Rosalila Temple and several tombs. From the summit of Temple 11, beside a giant ceiba tree (a tree held sacred by the Maya), there's a panoramic view of the site below, over the Ball Court and Great Plaza to the green hills beyond.

Temple 22

A few metres east of Temple 11 are the **Mat House** (Structure 22A), a governmental building distinguished by its interlocking weave-like patterns, and **Temple 22**, which boasts some superbly intricate stonework around the door frames. Constructed by Eighteen Rabbit, Temple 22 functioned as a "sacred mountain" where the elite performed religious blood-letting ceremonies. Above the door is the carving of a double-headed snake, its heads resting on two figures, which are in turn supported by skulls. The decoration here is unique in the southern Maya region – only Yucatán sites such as Kabáh and Chicanna have carvings of comparable quality.

East Court

Below Temple 22 are the stepped sides of the **East Court**, a graceful plaza that also bears elaborate carvings, including life-sized jaguar heads with hollow eyes that would have once held pieces of jade or polished obsidian. In the middle of the western staircase, flanked by the jaguars, is a rectangular Venus mask, carved in superb deep relief.

Rising over the court and dominating the Acropolis is the tallest structure in Copán, **Temple 16**, a 30m pyramid completed by the city's sixteenth ruler, Yax Pasaj, in 776 AD. To construct the temple Yax Pasaj had to build on top of the **Rosalila Temple**, though it was built with extraordinary care so as not to destroy the earlier temple. The temple served as a centre for worship during the reign of Smoke Serpent, or Butz' Chan (578–628 AD), Copán's eleventh ruler, a period that marked the apogee of the city's political, social and artistic growth – so the discovery of the Rosalila was a very exciting find.

You can view the brilliant original facade of the buried temple by entering through a short **tunnel** – an unforgettable, if costly, experience. The admission price does at least include access to two further tunnels, which extend below the East Plaza past some early cosmological stucco carvings – including a huge macaw mask – more buried temple facades and crypts including the Galindo tomb.

Structure 18

At the southern end of the East Court, **Structure 18** is a small square building with four carved panels in which Yax Pasaj was buried in 821 AD. The diminutive scale of the structure reveals how quickly decline set in, with the militaristic nature of the panels symptomatic of the troubled times. The tomb was empty when excavated by archeologists and is thought to have been looted. From Structure 18 there's a terrific view of the valley, over the Río Copán, which eroded the eastern buildings of the Acropolis over the centuries until its path was diverted. South of Structure 18, the **Cemetery Group** was once thought to have been a burial site, though it's now known to have been a residential complex and home of the ruling elite.

West Court

The second plaza of the Acropolis, the **West Court**, is confined by the south side of Temple 11, which has eight small doorways, and Temple 16, whose facade is embellished with carved skulls. **Altar Q**, at the base of Temple 16, is the court's most famous feature and an astonishing example of ancestral symbolism. Carved in 776 AD, it celebrates Yax Pasaj's accession to the throne on July 2, 763 AD. The top of the altar is carved with six hieroglyphic blocks, while the sides are decorated with sixteen cross-legged figures, all seated on cushions, who represent previous rulers of Copán. All are pointing towards a portrait of Yax Pasaj which shows him receiving a ceremonial staff from the city's first ruler Yax K'uk Mo', thereby endorsing Yax Pasaj's right to rule. Behind the altar is a small crypt, discovered to contain the remains of a macaw and fifteen big cats, sacrificed in honour of his ancestors when the altar was inaugurated.

Las Sepulturas

Four kilometres east of Copán ruins • Entrance with the same ticket as for Copán (see page 294)

Around 2km east of the ruins, along a stone pathway, is the much smaller site of **Las Sepulturas**, which provides an insight into daily domestic life during Maya times. Eighteen of the forty-odd residential compounds at the site have been excavated, comprising one hundred buildings that would have been inhabited by the elite. Smaller compounds on the edge of the site are thought to have housed young princes, as well as concubines and servants. It was customary to bury the nobility close to their residences, and more than 250 tombs have been excavated around the compounds – given the number of women found in the tombs it seems likely that the local Maya practised polygamy. One of the most interesting finds – the tomb of a priest or shaman, dating from around 450 AD – is on display in the museum in Copán Ruinas Town.

Rastrojón

Two kilometres east of Copán ruins, behind the *Hotel Clarion* parking area • Charge

A further two kilometres east of Las Sepulturas, the small archeological site of **Rastrojón** was discovered in 1979 but has only recently been opened to the public. It's thought that Structure 10 here was a palace, and some of the sculpture here is terrific. This hillside site has excellent information panels (in Spanish and English) provided by Harvard University and the Instituto Hondureño de Antropología e Historia.

Around Copán

The forested, highland region **around Copán** is very beautiful and loaded with interest. Here you will encounter waterfalls, hot springs, coffee fincas, zip lines and a spa; tour operators in town can set up trips to all these attractions.

El Rubí

11km northeast of Copán Ruinas

Pick-ups leave Copán regularly throughout the day for the peaceful town of **Santa Rita**. At the river bridge, just before entering the town, a path leads up to **El Rubí**, a pretty double-waterfall on the Río Copán, about 2km away. Organized tours (see page 293) here from Copán are available.

Luna Jaguar

22km north of Copán Ruinas • Charge • Ⓦ lunajaguarspa.com • Shuttle bus service available

On the other side of the river from the hot springs, **Luna Jaguar** is a natural spa set in forested grounds with thirteen different treatment stations that include natural steam baths, mud treatments, masseurs and a hot-spring-fed jacuzzi. It's undoubtedly a lovely natural environment, even if the treatments on offer are pricey. Be careful in the pools – some are very hot indeed and visitors have been scalded.

Finca El Cisne

23km north of Copán Ruinas • Day and overnight trips available (including accommodation, breakfast and dinner); organized by Basecamp in Copán (see page 293) • Ⓦ fincaelcisne.com

A kilometre or so further north from the Luna Jaguar spa is the agroturismo centre at Finca El Cisne, a working finca involved in the production of cardamom, shade-grown coffee, cattle and fruit. Owner Carlos Castejón's family has worked the land here since 1885, and he's a superb host, explaining (in English and Spanish) all about the farm's eco-sensitive agricultural practices. Day-trips include transport from Copán, about three hours of highly scenic horse-riding (on well-trained mounts suitable for inexperienced riders), swimming in the Río Blanco and a visit (entrance included) to the Luna Jaguar hot springs (see above). The overnight option gives you time to really enjoy the rural setting and hospitality (Carlos's mother's cooking is legendary).

COFFEE PLANTATION, SAN MIGUEL DUEÑAS

Contexts

History

Little is known about the area that is now called Guatemala in the days before the advent of Maya civilization, and even the early origins of the Maya remain fairly mysterious. Today, the Maya world is one of the planet's hottest archeological areas, and recent excavations have fostered a greater understanding of the region's history – but also ripped apart many previously accepted theories. Although the historical picture is becoming much clearer, many issues are still subject to ongoing academic polemic.

Prehistory

Opinions differ as to when the first people arrived in the Americas. The established theory is that **Stone Age hunter-gatherers** crossed the Bering land bridge from Siberia to Alaska in several waves beginning about 17,000 years ago, but there's evidence of a much earlier date. Travelling along an ice-free corridor (and possibly in small boats along the coastline) they migrated south into Central America. The first recognizable culture, known as **Clovis**, had emerged by 11,000 BC, and stone tools, including spearpoints, blades and scrapers, dating from 9000 BC have been found in the Guatemalan highlands.

In **Mesoamerica**, an area defined as stretching from north-central Mexico through Central America to Panama, the first settled pattern of development took place around 8000 BC, as a warming climate forced the hunter-gatherers to adapt to a different way of life. The glaciers were in retreat and the big game, upon which the hunters depended, became scarce due to the warmer, drier climate (and possibly over-hunting). This period, in which the hunters turned to more intensive use of plant foods, is known as the **Archaic period** and lasted until about 2000 BC. During this time the foods vital to the subsequent development of agriculture, such as corn, beans, peppers, squash and probably maize, were domesticated.

The early Maya

After 2000 BC we move into the **Preclassic** era, a name used by archeologists to describe the earliest developments in the history of the **Maya**. During the **Early Preclassic** (2000–1000 BC), the Maya settled in villages throughout the region, as the foragers became farmers and began making pottery. By 1100 BC, the **Olmec**, often called Mesoamerica's "mother culture", were constructing pyramid-like ceremonial platforms and carving colossal stone heads at San Lorenzo, just to the northwest of the Maya region. Their artistic, polytheistic religious (and almost certainly political) influence spread throughout Maya lands, and Olmec-style carvings have been found at numerous sites along Guatemala's Pacific coast, in El Salvador and at Copán, in Honduras. The Olmec also developed an early writing system and a calendar known as the "**Long Count**", later adopted by the Maya.

c.11,000 BC	**c.8000–2000 BC**	**3114 BC**
Clovis culture. Worked-stone projectile points used for hunting found across Central America.	Archaic period. Villagers farm maize and beans, make pottery and probably spoke a Proto-Maya language.	Mythical start date of the Maya calendar.

Nakbé and the Middle Preclassic era

The population increased steadily across the Maya region during the **Middle Preclassic** period (1000–400 BC). In northern Petén, **Nakbé** had, by 750 BC, grown to become a substantial settlement, complete with imposing temples and stucco sculptures – evidence that the Maya had progressed far beyond a simple peasant society. By 500 BC other centres – including El Mirador and Cival – were building their first ceremonial structures and astronomical observatories.

It is thought that a common language was spoken throughout the Maya lands, and that a universal belief system, practised from a very early date, may have provided the stimulus and social cohesion to build bigger towns and religious temples. Materials including obsidian and jade from the Guatemalan highlands and granite and salt from Belize were widely traded. Pottery, including red and orange jars and dishes of the **Mamon** style, found at a number of settlements, indicate increasing pan-Maya communication. At the same time, food surpluses and rising prosperity levels gradually enabled some inhabitants to eschew farming duties and become seers, priests and astronomers.

El Mirador and the Late Preclassic

Greater advances in architecture were achieved in the **Late Preclassic** (400 BC–250 AD) as other centres prospered in northern Petén, and the Mirador Basin (see page 269) became the focus of Maya civilization. **El Mirador** expanded to become a massive city, spread over twenty square kilometres, with a population of around one hundred thousand. Taking advantage of the swampland that surrounded their city, Mirador's inhabitants fertilized vast fields of crops using rich **mud** from nearby marshes and seasonal lakes.

Very little is known about the power politics of these times, but the sheer size of El Mirador indicates that the city must have acquired "superstate" status by around 100 BC. Positioned at the heart of a vast trading network, the city was surrounded by hundreds of other settlements like Tintal and Xulnal, all connected by a web of stone causeways, the highways of their day. The La Danta temple complex at Mirador was constructed to a height of 78m – the highest building ever to have been built by a pre-Columbian culture in the Americas – a feat that took an estimated fifteen million days of labour.

Kaminaljuyú

El Mirador's only serious rival during the Late Classic era was located several hundred kilometres to the south, on the site of the modern capital of Guatemala City. **Kaminaljuyú** had established a formidable commercial empire based on the supply of obsidian and jade, and held sway over a string of settlements along the Pacific coast, including Takalik Abaj. It's clear that the southern Maya area was much more influenced by Olmec advances at this time.

Preclassic culture and society

From 1 AD pyramids and temple platforms were emerging at Tikal, Uaxactún and many other sites in Petén, in what amounted to an explosion of **Maya culture**. The Maya corbelled arch was developed in this period, and architectural styles became more

1800 BC	**c.1000 BC**	**750 BC**
Preclassic Maya culture emerges in the forests of Petén.	Early settlement at sites in the Mirador Basin.	Temple complexes constructed at Nakbé. Maya culture eclipses Olmec in Petén.

MAYA ARCHEOLOGICAL PERIODS

Maya archeological periods are confusing, not least because when they were established in the mid-twentieth century very little was known about the formative years of Maya civilization. Recent findings have revealed that the Preclassic era was far more advanced than previously thought.

Archeological periods vary according to the source. This Guide follows those used in the *Chronicle of the Maya Kings and Queens* by Simon Martin and Nikolai Grube (see page 351).

Pre-2000 BC Archaic
2000 BC–1000 BC Early Preclassic
1000 BC–400 BC Middle Preclassic
400 BC–250 AD Late Preclassic
250 AD–600 AD Early Classic
600 AD–800 AD Late Classic
800 AD–909 AD Terminal Classic
909 AD–1200 AD Early Postclassic
1200 AD–Spanish Conquest Late Postclassic

ambitious. A stratified **Maya society** was also becoming established, the nascent states led by rulers and shamanic priests who presided over religious ceremonies dictated by astronomical and calendrical events. There were specialist craftsmen, architects, scribes and artists capable of creating the exquisite murals of San Bartolo and Popol Vuh stucco sculptures of Mirador. Intensive agriculture was also practised using irrigation from vast reservoirs via extensive canal networks.

Drought and disaster

Towards the end of the Late Preclassic period, during the second and third centuries AD, environmental disasters plagued the region. El Mirador and all its satellite cities collapsed by 150 AD, after a long **dry climatic period** and the severe over-exploitation of the forest environment, which severely cut agricultural production.

In the southern region, the eruption of the **Ilopango volcano** in central El Salvador smothered a vast area in ash, probably provoking mass migration from cities including Kaminaljuyú, which was virtually abandoned around 250 AD. Temple building ceased and Pacific trade routes were disrupted. Much of the trade was re-routed to the north, bringing prosperity (but also Central Mexican influence) to the cities of central Petén, including **Tikal**.

The Classic Maya

The development that separates the Late Preclassic from the **Classic period** (250–909 AD) is the introduction of the Long Count calendar and a recognizably Maya form of writing. This occurred by the end of the third century AD and marks the beginning of the greatest phase of Maya achievement.

During the Classic period all the cities we now know as ruined or restored sites were built, almost always over earlier structures. Elaborately carved **stelae**, bearing dates

500 BC

First evidence of ceremonial buildings at Tikal.

300 BC

Massive building projects commence at El Mirador, which is linked to vassal settlements by giant causeways.

200 BC

Miraflores culture thrives on Pacific coast and Guatemalan highlands, centred on Kaminaljuyú.

and emblem glyphs, were erected at regular intervals. These tell of actual rulers and of historical events in their lives – battles, marriages, dynastic succession and so on.

Enter Teotihuacán

Developments in the Maya area during the Early Classic period became increasingly influenced by a giant power to the north – **Teotihuacán**, which dominated Central Mexico and boasted a population of over 150,000. Its **armed merchants**, called *pochteca*, spread the authority of Teotihuacán as far as Petén, the Yucatán and Copán. It's unlikely that Teotihuacán launched an outright military invasion of Maya territory, but the city's influence was strong enough to precipitate fundamental changes. In 378 AD, an armed merchant called **Siyak K'ak** provoked a takeover of Tikal (see page 257), establishing a new dynasty, while at Copán, Yax K'uk Mo' (who was almost certainly from Teotihuacán) founded that city's royal lineage in 426 AD. These Mexicans also brought alternative religious beliefs, and new styles of ceramics, art and architecture – Kaminaljuyú was rebuilt in Teotihuacán style, and Tikal and Copán temples and stelae from the era depict Central Mexican gods.

The Kingdom of the Snake

While Tikal was positioning itself within the Teotihuacán sphere of influence and dominating the Petén, an increasingly precocious rival Maya state was emerging to the north: **Calakmul**, "the kingdom of the snake". From the fifth century, these two states grew to eclipse all other cities in the Maya World, establishing dominion over huge swathes of the region. Each controlling sophisticated trade networks, they jostled for supremacy as Mexican influence waned. Calakmul formed an alliance with **Caracol** (today located in Belize) and defeated Tikal in 562 AD – detailed carvings depict elaborately costumed lords trampling on bound captives. This victory caused a near-hiatus in Tikal's empire building during which there was little new construction at the city or in the smaller centres under its patronage.

Late Classic

The prosperity and grandeur of the **Late Classic** period (600–800 AD) reached across the Maya World: from Palenque in the northwest to Copán in the south and Altun Ha in the east. Bound together by a coherent religion and culture, Maya architecture, astronomy and art reached degrees of sophistication unequalled by any other pre-Columbian society. Trade prospered and populations grew – by 750 AD it's estimated that the region's people numbered around **ten million**. Many Maya states were larger than contemporary western European cities, then in their "Dark Ages".

Masterpieces of painted pottery and carved jade (their most precious material) were created, often for use as funerary offerings. Shell, bone and, occasionally, marble were also exquisitely carved; temples were painted in brilliant colours, inside and out.

In the power politics of the era, Tikal avenged its bitter defeat by overrunning Calakmul in 695 AD and reasserting its influence over its former vassal states of Río Azul and Waka' (El Perú). In a furious epoch of monument building, five of the great temples that define the ceremonial heart of the city were finished between 670 and 810

150 BC	c.1 AD	c.150 AD
El Mirador enters its greatest era as 70m-high temples are built	Emergence of Teotihuacán in Mexico.	El Mirador and other Preclassic cities abandoned, probably due to environmental collapse.

AD. Elsewhere across Maya lands, cities including Piedras Negras, Yaxhá and Yaxchilán flourished as never before, giving rise to more and more imposing temples and palaces, and unparalleled artistic achievements.

The Maya in decline

The glory days were not to last very long, however. By 750 AD political and social changes were beginning to be felt; alliances and trade links broke down, wars increased and stelae recording periods of time were carved less frequently.

After 800 AD we move into a period known as the **Terminal Classic** during which the great cities were gradually depopulated, and new construction virtually ceased in the central area after about 830 AD. Bonampak was abandoned before its famous murals could be completed, while many of the great sites along the Usumacinta River were occupied by militaristic outsiders.

Drought and disorder

The reason for the decline of the Maya is not (and may never be) known, though it was probably a result of several factors. It's known that Maya lands were already under severe pressure from deforestation by the late ninth century, when the region was struck by a sustained **drought**. An incredibly high population density put great strains on food production, possibly exhausting the fertility of the soil, and epidemics may have combined to cause the abandonment of city life.

Some Mayanists speculate that there may have been a peasant revolt caused by mass hunger and the demands of an unproductive elite. Whatever the causes, strife and **disorder** appear to have spread throughout Mesoamerica by the end of the Classic period. In the Maya heartland, virtually all the key cities were abandoned, and those few that remained were reduced to a fairly primitive state. Some survived on the periphery, however, particularly in eastern Petén and northern Belize. The settlements of the Yucatán peninsula also struggled on, and though the region escaped the worst of the depopulation, it was conquered by the militaristic **Toltecs** in 987 AD, creating a hybrid of Mexican-Maya culture.

Mass migration

With the decline of Maya civilization in Petén, there was an influx of population into Belize, Yucatán and the south of Guatemala. These areas now contained the last vestiges of Maya culture, and it's at this time that the Guatemala highland area began to take on some of the tribal characteristics still in evidence today. By the end of the Classic period there were small settlements throughout the highlands, usually built on open valley floors and supporting large populations sustained by terraced farming and irrigation. Little was to change in this basic village structure for several hundred years.

Pre-conquest: the highland tribes

Towards the end of the thirteenth century Toltec-Maya invaded the central Guatemalan highlands. Their numbers were probably small but their impact was profound, and following their arrival life in the highlands was radically altered.

End 3rd Century AD	292 AD	378 AD
Long Count calendar and Maya writing introduced, beginning the greatest phase of Maya achievement.	Stela 29 carved at Tikal, with Long Count calendar date.	Siyak K'ak' leads a Teotihuacán takeover at Tikal and defeats Uaxactún.

Maya society became highly militaristic. The Toltecs were ruthlessly well organized, establishing themselves as a ruling elite over competing tribal empires. The greatest of these were the **K'iche'**, who dominated the central area and established their capital, **K'umarkaaj**. Next in line were the **Kaqchikel** at **Iximché**. On the southern shores of Lago de Atitlán, the **Tz'utujil** had their base on the lower slopes of the San Pedro volcano. To the west the **Mam** had a fortified capital at **Zaculeu**, while the Cuchumatanes and mountains to the east were home to a collection of groups: the **Chuj, Q'anjob'al, Awakateko, Ixil**, notoriously fierce **Achi** and **Q'eqchi'**. Around modern-day Guatemala City were the **Poqomam**, with their capital at **Mixco Viejo**, while along the Pacific coast were bands of **Pipil**.

The sheer numbers of these tribes give an impression of the extent to which the area was fragmented, and it's these same divisions, now surviving on the basis of language alone, that still shape the highlands today (see page 335).

Toltecs

The Toltec rulers probably controlled only the dominant tribes – the K'iche', Mam and Kaqchikel. They brought many northern traditions – elements of a Nahua-based language, new gods and an array of military skills – and fused these with local ideas. Shortly after the Spanish Conquest, the K'iche' wrote an account of their history, the **Popol Vuh** (see page 103), in which they lay claim to a Toltec pedigree, as do the Kaqchikel.

The Toltec invaders were not content with overpowering just a tribe or two, so under the direction of their new rulers the K'iche' began to expand their empire – between 1400 and 1475 they brought the Kaqchikel, the Mam and several other tribes under their control. At the height of their power, around a million highlanders bowed to the word of the K'iche' king. But in 1475 the man who had masterminded their expansion, the great K'iche' ruler **Quicab**, died, and the empire lost much of its authority.

The Kaqchikel were the first to break from the fold, moving south to a new and fortified capital, Iximché around 1470. Shortly afterwards the other tribes managed to escape the grip of K'iche' control and assert their independence.

Warring highlands

For the next fifty years or so the tribes were in a state of almost perpetual conflict, fighting for access to the inadequate supplies of farmland. The archeological remains from this era give evidence of this instability; gone are the valley-floor centres of pre-Toltec times, and in their place are fortified hilltop sites, surrounded by ravines and man-made ditches.

When the Spanish arrived, the highlands were in crisis. With a growing sense of urgency both the K'iche' and the Kaqchikel had begun to encroach on the lowlands of the Pacific coast. The situation could hardly have been more favourable to the Spanish, who fostered this inter-tribal friction, playing one group off against another.

The Spanish Conquest

In 1521, the Spanish conquistadors had captured the Aztec capital at Tenochtitlán and were starting to cast their net further afield. Amid the horrors of the Conquest there

426 AD

Yax K'uk Mo' probably from Teotihuacán, founds dynasty at Copán.

562 AD

Caracol (in concert with Calakmul) overruns Tikal. Calakmul becomes regional superpower.

was one man whose ambition, cunning and cruelty stood out above the rest – **Pedro de Alvarado.**

In 1523, conquistador leader Hernán Cortés dispatched Alvarado to Guatemala, entreating him to use the minimum of force "and to preach matters concerning our Holy Faith". His army included 120 horsemen, 173 horses, 300 soldiers and 200 Mexican warriors. Marching south they entered Guatemala along the Pacific coast, where they met and easily defeated a small band of K'iche' warriors. From here Alvarado turned north, entering the Quetzaltenango valley, where they came upon the deserted city of **Xelajú**, a K'iche' outpost.

Battle of Xelajú

Warned of the impending arrival of the Spanish, the K'iche' had struggled to build an alliance with the other tribes, but old rivalries proved too strong and the **K'iche'** army faced the Spaniards alone at **Xelajú**. Alvarado claimed the invaders were confronted by some thirty thousand K'iche' warriors (though this figure is almost certainly an exaggeration) led by their leader **Tecún Umán** in a headdress of quetzal feathers. Despite the huge disparity in numbers, slingshot and foot soldiers were no match for cavalry and gunpowder, and the Spaniards triumphed. Within days, Alvarado advanced on the K'iche' capital and burnt that to the ground.

Spanish victories

Having dealt with the K'iche', Alvarado turned his attention to the other tribal groups. The **Kaqchikel**, recognizing the military superiority of the Spanish, decided to form some kind of alliance. As a result the Spaniards established their first headquarters, in 1523, alongside the Kaqchikel capital of **Iximché**. From here they ranged far and wide, overpowering the countless smaller tribes. Travelling west, Alvarado's army defeated the **Tz'utujil** on the shores of Lago de Atitlán, aided by Kaqchikel warriors in some three hundred canoes. In 1524, Alvarado sent his brother Gonzalo on an expedition against the **Mam**, who were conquered after a month-long siege. The next year, Alvarado himself set out to take on the **Poqomam** at their capital, **Mixco Viejo** whose forces proved no match for the well-disciplined Spanish ranks.

Despite this string of relatively easy victories, it wasn't until well into the 1530s that Alvarado managed to assert control over the more remote parts of the highlands, including the Cuchumatanes. And then problems also arose at the very heart of the campaign. In 1526, the Kaqchikel revolted against the Spanish, abandoning their capital and moving into the mountains, from where they waged a guerrilla war against their former partners. The Spanish were forced to abandon their base at Iximché, and moved instead to a site near the modern town of Antigua.

Here, on St Cecilia's Day, November 22, 1527, they established their first permanent capital, the city of **Santiago de los Caballeros**. For ten years Indigenous labourers toiled in the construction of the new city, neatly sited at the base of the Agua volcano, building a cathedral, a town hall, and a palace for Alvarado.

Verapaz

Meanwhile, one particularly thorny problem for the Spanish was presented by the **Achi** and **Q'eqchi'** Maya, who occupied what are now the Verapaz highlands.

c.600 AD

Population density in core Maya region reaches an estimated 965 people per square kilometre. Start of the Late Classic period – two-hundred-year golden age of the Maya, its intellectual and artistic peak.

628 AD

Smoke Imix's (Ruler 12) 67-year reign begins at Copán.

Despite all his efforts, Alvarado was unable to conquer either of these tribes. In the end he gave up on trying to control the area, naming it Tierra de Guerra. The situation was eventually resolved by the Church. In 1537, **Fray Bartolomé de Las Casas**, the "protector of the Indians", travelled into the region in a bid to persuade the locals to accept both Christianity and Spanish authority. Within three years the priests had succeeded where Alvarado's armies had failed, and the last of the highland tribes was brought under colonial control in 1540. Thus did the area earn its name of Verapaz, "true peace".

Alvarado himself grew tired of the Conquest, disappointed by the lack of plunder, and his reputation for brutality began to spread. From 1524 until his death in 1541, Alvarado had ruled Guatemala as a personal fiefdom, desperately seeking adventure and wealth, and enslaving and abusing the local population. By the time of his death all the Maya tribes had been overcome (except for tiny numbers of Itza), although local uprisings had already started to take place.

Colonial rule

The early years of colonial rule were marked by uprisings and political wrangling. When Alvarado's wife Beatriz de la Cueva heard of his death, she plunged the capital into a period of prolonged mourning. She had the entire palace painted black, inside and out. Meanwhile, the area was swept by a series of storms, and on the night of September 10, 1541, it was shaken by a massive earthquake. The sides of the Agua volcano shuddered, undermining the walls of the cone and releasing its contents. A great wall of mud and water swept down the side of the peak, burying the city of Santiago and most of its inhabitants.

New capital

The surviving colonial authorities moved up the valley to a new site, where a second **Santiago de los Caballeros** was founded – today known as Antigua. This new city served as the administrative headquarters of the **Audiencia de Guatemala**, which was made up of six provinces: Costa Rica, Nicaragua, San Salvador, Honduras, Guatemala and Chiapas (now part of Mexico). With Alvarado out of the way, the authorities began to build a new society, recreating the splendours of the homeland with a superb array of arts and architecture. By the mid-eighteenth century its population approached eighty thousand. Here colonial society was at its most developed, rigidly structured along racial lines with pure-blood Spaniards at the top, Indigenous slaves at the bottom and a host of carefully defined racial strata in between. The city was regularly shaken by scandal and earthquakes, and it was eventually all but destroyed in 1773, after which the capital was moved to its modern site: Guatemala City.

The Catholic Church

Perhaps the greatest power in colonial Central America was the **Church**. The first religious order to reach Guatemala was the Franciscans, who arrived with Alvarado himself, and by 1532 the Mercedarians and Dominicans had followed suit, with the Jesuits arriving shortly after. **Francisco Marroquín**, the country's first bishop, rewarded these early arrivals with huge concessions, including land and Indigenous

682 AD

Hasaw Chan K'awil begins 52-year reign at Tikal.

695 AD

Eighteen Rabbit rules at Copán. Hasaw Chan K'awil of Tikal captures Yich'aak K'ak (Fiery Claw) of Calakmul.

738 AD

Copán's Waxaklajuun Ub'aah K'awil killed by Cauac Sky of Quiriguá, a subordinate city.

people, which later enabled them to earn tax-free fortunes from sugar, wheat and indigo. In later years a whole range of other orders arrived in Santiago, and religious rivalry became an important shaping force in the colony. Through its wealth and power, the Church fostered the splendour of the colonial capital while ruthlessly exploiting the native people and their land. In Santiago alone there were some eighty churches, and alongside these were schools, convents, hospitals, hermitages and colleges. The religious orders became the main benefactors of the arts, amassing a wealth of tapestry, jewels, sculpture and painting, and staging concerts, fiestas and endless religious processions. Religious persecution was at its worst between 1572 and 1580, when the office of the **Inquisition** sought out those who had failed to receive the faith and dealt with them harshly.

By the eighteenth century the power of the Church had started to get out of control, and the Spanish kings began to impose taxes on the religious orders and to limit their power and freedom. The conflict between Church and State came to a head in 1767, when Carlos III banished the Jesuits from the Spanish colonies.

Colonial economy

The Spanish must have been disappointed with their conquest of Central America as it offered little in the way of plunder except meagre amounts of silver around Huehuetenango. In Central America the **colonial economy** was based on agriculture. The coastal area produced cacao, tobacco, cotton and, most valuable of all, indigo; the highlands were grazed with sheep and goats; and cattle were raised on coastal ranches. The jungles of Petén and the lower Motagua valley were largely left unchallenged.

At the heart of the colonial economy was the system of **repartamientos**, whereby the ruling classes were granted the right to extract labour from the Indigenous population. It was this that established the system whereby the Maya population was transported to work in the plantations, a pattern – though no longer legally enforced – that remains a tremendous burden today.

Meanwhile, in the capital it was graft and corruption that controlled the movement of money, with titles and appointments sold to the highest bidder. All of the colony's wealth was funnelled through the city, and it was only here that the monetary economy really developed.

Maya society

The impact of the Conquest was perhaps the greatest in the highlands, where the **Maya population** had their lives totally restructured. The first stage in this process was the *reducción*, whereby scattered native communities were combined into new Spanish-style towns and villages. Between 1543 and 1600 some seven hundred new settlements were created, each based around a Catholic church. Ostensibly, the purpose of this was to enable the Church to work on its new-found converts, but it also had the effect of pooling the available labour and making its exploitation (and the demand of tribute) that much easier.

Maya **social structures** were also profoundly altered by post-conquest changes. The great central authorities that had previously dominated were now eradicated, replaced by local structures based in the new villages. *Caciques* (local chiefs) and *alcaldes* (mayors) now held the bulk of local power, which was bestowed on them by

c.750 AD

Population peaks in central region, total Maya numbers estimated to be around ten million.

800–909 AD

Terminal Classic period. Overpopulation and an epochal drought lead to environmental collapse.

810 AD

Dark Sun builds Temple III, the last of Tikal's great temple pyramids.

the Church. In the distant corners of the highlands, however, priests were few and far between, only visiting the villages from time to time. Those that they left in charge developed not only their own power structures but also their own religion, mixing the new with the old. By the start of the nineteenth century, the Maya population had largely recovered from the initial impact of the Conquest, and in many places these local structures became increasingly important. In each village *cofradías* (brotherhood groups) were entrusted with the care of saints, while *principales* (village elders) held the bulk of traditional authority, a situation that still persists today. Throughout the highlands, village uprisings became increasingly commonplace as the new Indigenous culture became stronger and stronger.

Even more serious for the Indigenous population than any social changes were the **diseases** that arrived with the conquistadors. Waves of plague, typhoid and fever swept through a population with no natural resistance. In the worst-hit areas the native population was cut by some ninety percent, and in many parts of the country their numbers were halved.

Impact of colonial rule

Colonial rule totally reshaped the structure of Guatemalan society, giving it new cities, a new religion, a transformed economy and a racist hierarchy. Nevertheless, its **impact** was perhaps less marked than in many other parts of Latin America. Only two sizeable cities had emerged and the outlying areas had received little attention from the colonial authorities. Although the Indigenous population had been ruthlessly exploited and suffered enormous losses, its culture was never eradicated. The Maya simply absorbed the symbols and ideas of the Spanish, creating a dynamic synthesis that was neither Maya nor Catholic.

Independence

The apartheid-style nature of colonial rule had given birth to deep dissatisfaction among many groups in Central America. Spain's policy was to keep wealth and power in the hands of those born in Spain (*chapetones*), a policy that left growing numbers of Creoles (including those of Spanish with Spanish ancestry born in Guatemala) and *mestizos* (of mixed race) resentful and hungry for power and change. (For the majority of the Indigenous people, both power and wealth were way beyond their reach.) As the Spanish departed, Guatemalan politics was dominated by a struggle between **conservatives**, who sided with the Church and the Crown, and **liberals**, who advocated a secular and more egalitarian state.

Moves towards independence

The spark, as throughout Spanish America, was Napoleon's invasion of Spain and the abdication of King Fernando VII. In the chaos that followed, a liberal constitution was imposed on Spain in 1812 and a mood of reform swept through the colonies. At the time, Central America was under the control of **Brigadier Don Gabino Gainza**, the last of the Captains General. His one concern was to maintain the status quo, in which he was strongly backed by the wealthy landowners and the Church hierarchy. Bowing to demands for independence, but still hoping to preserve the power structure, Gainza

869 AD	909–1200 AD	c.1250 AD
Last recorded date at Tikal.	Early Postclassic period. Maya collapse sees cities abandoned throughout the region.	The Toltec enter Guatemala, changing life in the highlands forever.

signed a formal **Act of Independence** on September 15, 1821, enshrining the authority of the Church and seeking to preserve the old order under new leadership. Augustín de Iturbide, the short-lived emperor of newly independent Mexico, promptly sent troops to annex Guatemala to the Mexican empire, a union which was to last less than a year.

Central America Federation

Through a second Declaration of Independence, in 1823, Guatemala joined the Central American states in a loose **federation**, adopting a constitution modelled on that of the United States, abolishing slavery and advocating **liberal reforms**. These moves were bitterly opposed by the Church and conservatives throughout Central America, and provoked several inter-federation (and internal) conflicts. But in 1830 the political left of Salvador, Honduras and Guatemala united under the leadership of **Francisco Morazán**, a Honduran general, under whom **Mariano Gálvez** became the chief of state in Guatemala: religious orders were abolished, the death penalty done away with, and trial by jury, a general school system, civil marriage and the progressive Lívingston law code were all instituted.

Carrera and the conservative backlash

This liberal era lasted until 1838 when the ailing Central American Federation was dissolved and the reforming Guatemalan administration overthrown by a revolt from the mountains. Seething with discontent, the Maya were united behind an illiterate but charismatic leader, the 23-year-old **Rafael Carrera**, under whose command they marched on Guatemala City. Independence was declared in 1839, with Carrera installed first as a *caudillo* (strongman), and later as president.

Carrera respected no authority other than that of the Church, and his immediate reforms swept aside the changes instituted by the liberal government. The religious orders were restored to their former position and traditional Spanish titles were reinstated. Under Carrera, Guatemala fought a succession of conflicts against liberals in other parts of Central America, and eventually established itself as an independent republic in 1847. Carrera's greatest internal challenge came from the state of **Los Altos**, which included much of the western highlands and proclaimed itself an independent republic. It was a short-lived threat, however, and the would-be state was soon brought back into the republic.

When Carrera died, at the age of 50 in 1865, Guatemala was an impoverished nation (the export of indigo and cochineal had plummeted after the invention of artificial dyes), while its transport network was backward at best. Little was to change under his successor, **Vicente Cerna**, another conservative, who ruled until 1871, but during this period liberal opposition was again gathering momentum, and 1867 saw the first **liberal uprising**, led by **Serpio Cruz**. His bid for power was unsuccessful, but it inspired two young liberals, Justo Rufino Barrios and Francisco Cruz, to follow suit. In the next few years, they mounted several other unsuccessful revolts, and in 1870 Serpio Cruz was captured and hanged.

Rufino Barrios and the coffee boom

The year 1871 marked a major turning point in Guatemalan politics, for in that year rebels Rufino Barrios and Miguel García Granados entered Guatemala from Mexico with an army of just 45 men. The **liberal revolution** set in motion was an astounding

1450 AD	**1521 AD**	**1523**
K'iche' state dominates warring highlands.	Aztec capital of Tenochtitlán falls to Spanish under Cortés.	Alvarado and his soldiers arrive in Guatemala, to be fought by a band of K'iche' warriors.

success, the army growing by the day as it approached the capital, which was finally taken on June 30, 1871. Granados took the helm of the new liberal administration but held the presidency for just a few years, surrounding himself with ageing comrades and offering only very limited reforms.

Meanwhile, out in the district of Los Altos, **Rufino Barrios**, now a local military commander, was infuriated by the lack of action. In 1872 he marched his troops to the capital, demanded and won elections. Barrios was a charismatic leader with tyrannical tendencies (monuments throughout the country testify to his sense of his own importance) who regarded himself as a great reformer. His most immediate acts were the restructuring of the education system and an attack on the Church – clerics were forbidden to wear the cloth and public religious processions were banned. The Church was outraged and excommunicated Barrios, which prompted him to expel the archbishop in retaliation.

Barrios' liberal perspective was undoubtedly instilled with a deep arrogance, and he would tolerate no political opposition, developing an effective network of secret police and ensuring that the army became an essential part of his political power base.

Barrios also set about reforming agriculture, and he presided over a boom period, largely as a result of the cultivation and export of **coffee**. To foster this expansion Barrios extended the railway network, established a national bank and developed the ports of Champerico, San José and Iztapa. Between 1870 and 1900 the volume of foreign trade increased twenty times.

German immigration

All this had an enormous impact on Guatemalan **society**. Many of the new plantations were owned and run by German immigrants, and the majority of the coffee eventually found its way to Europe. The newcomers soon formed a powerful elite and, although most of the Germans were later forced out of Guatemala (during World War II), their influence can still be felt today in the continuing presence of an extremely powerful political clique. Foreign ideas were deemed superior to Indigenous ones, and while European immigrants were welcomed with open arms, the Maya population was still regarded as hopelessly inferior.

Indigenous society was also deeply affected by the needs of the coffee boom, as Barrios instituted a system of **forced labour**. By 1876 up to one quarter of the male Maya population could be dispatched to work on the coffee fincas, often under appalling conditions, while in the highlands landowners continued to employ a system of debt peonage.

As a result of the coffee boom, many Maya lost not only their freedom but also their land, as huge swathes of land were seized. In many areas the villagers rose up in defiance, with significant **revolts** continuing into the twentieth century. Five hundred armed men faced the authorities in Momostenango, only to find their village overrun by troops and their homes burnt to the ground. These land seizures forced the Maya to become dependent on seasonal labour.

Jorge Ubico and the banana empire

Rufino Barrios, who was eventually killed in 1885 while fighting to re-establish a unified Central America, was succeeded by a string of short-lived but like-minded

1523–40	**16th century**	**1697**
Spanish conquest of Guatemala. The first Spanish capital is founded in 1527.	Antigua becomes the capital of Central America and the power of the Church grows.	Conquest of the Itza at Tayasal; the last independent Maya tribe falls.

presidents. The next to hold power for any time was **Manuel Estrada Cabrera**, a stern authoritarian who restricted union organization and supported the interests of big business. He ruled from 1898 until he was overthrown in 1920, by which time he was on the verge of insanity.

United Fruit Company

Meanwhile, a new and exceptionally powerful player was becoming involved in the country's affairs – the **United Fruit Company**, which would assert its influence over much of Central America until the 1960s. The company moved into Guatemala in 1901, when it bought a small tract of land on which to grow bananas. Three years later, it was awarded a contract to complete the railway from Guatemala City to Puerto Barrios, and in 1912 ownership of the Pacific railway network also fell to the company, giving it a virtual transport monopoly. Large-scale **banana cultivation** really took off, and by 1934 United Fruit controlled a massive amount of land, exporting around 3.5 million bunches of bananas annually and reaping vast profits.

The influence of the United Fruit Company was so pervasive that it earned itself the nickname *El Pulpo*, "the octopus". Control of the transport network brought with it control of the coffee trade: during the 1930s it cost as much to ship coffee from Guatemala to New Orleans as it did from Río de Janeiro to New Orleans.

Against this background the power of the Guatemalan government was severely limited, with the influence of the United States increasing alongside that of the United Fruit Company.

Jorge Ubico

The way became clear for **Jorge Ubico**, a charismatic leader with fascist tendencies and a reputation for efficiency, who was well connected with the ruling and land-owning elite. Guatemala was hit hard by the Depression and Ubico managed to get trade agreements that exempted coffee and bananas from US import duties. Within Guatemala, Ubico steadfastly supported the United Fruit Company. This relationship was of such importance that by 1940 ninety percent of all Guatemalan exports were being sold to the United States.

Internally, Ubico embarked on a radical programme of reform, including a sweeping drive against corruption and a massive road-building effort. But the system of debt peonage continued as a new **vagrancy law** compelled all landless peasants to work 150 days a year for the state or landowners. Not surprisingly, sporadic local protests and revolts against landowners continued in the late 1930s and early 1940s.

Internal security was another Ubico obsession, as he became increasingly paranoid, vainglorious and eccentric. His obsession with Napoleon provoked future Sandinista leader Tomás Borge to describe him "crazier than a half-dozen opium-smoking frogs" while US newspapers dubbed him "the Little Napoleon of the Tropics".

Ubico used a network of informers to unleash waves of repression. But while he tightened his grip on every aspect of government, the rumblings of opposition grew louder. In 1944 discontent erupted in student violence, and Ubico was finally forced to resign after fourteen years of tyrannical rule.

1773–76

After an earthquake destroys Antigua, Guatemala City becomes capital.

1821

Mexico and Central America gain independence from Spain.

1847

Guatemala becomes a republic, independent of Central America, under Rafael Carrera.

CHE GUEVARA IN GUATEMALA

Ernesto "Che" Guevara arrived in Guatemala on New Year's Eve 1953, broke and with no place to stay. He had graduated as a doctor in his native Argentina five months previously, and immediately left to explore Latin America – hitching rides, sleeping rough and cadging meals along the way. The future *comandante* spent eight months in Guatemala City, living in Zona 1, the historic heart of the capital, in a number of cheap *hospedajes*. Most of his days were spent in a fruitless search for work as a doctor, surviving on the generosity of the people he met and scratching a meagre income from a series of casual jobs: teaching a few Spanish classes, doing some translation work and peddling encyclopedias and images of the Black Christ of Esquipulas in the capital's streets. But Guevara had not just come to Guatemala to look for work. In the early 1950s, Guatemala City was a major destination for political idealists, communists and budding revolutionaries from Latin America, all attracted to the country by reformist president **Árbenz** and his party's doctrine of "spiritual socialism". In a letter to his aunt, Guevara wrote of his travels through the region, and avowed his intentions to challenge American hegemony:

Along the way, I had the opportunity to pass through the dominions of the United Fruit … I have sworn before a picture of the old and mourned comrade Stalin that I won't rest until I see these capitalist octopuses annihilated. In Guatemala I will perfect myself and achieve what I need to be an authentic revolutionary.

One of the first people he met in Guatemala was **Hildea Gadea**, a well-connected young Peruvian who later became his first wife. Gadea, an exiled member of Peru's ARPA rebels, introduced Che to a number of other young political activists, including **Rolando Morán**, who was to become the leader of the Guatemalan EGP guerrillas (see page 112). Guevara formed his political consciousness in Guatemala City, his beliefs shaped by hours spent reading Marx, Trotsky and Mao, an instinctive hatred of US imperialism, and marathon theological debates. Of the city's myriad Ladino leftist groups, the Cubans most impressed Che, for they alone had actually launched an armed uprising against a dictatorship (the failed Moncada assault after Batista had cancelled the 1952 Cuban elections). Guevara met **Ñico López**, the Cuban who would later introduce him to **Fidel** and **Raúl Castro**, and with whom he would later regroup in Mexico, set sail for Cuba in 1956 and initiate the revolution.

Guevara remained in Guatemala City throughout the attacks on the capital in June 1954. The young radical wrote to his family denouncing the indecisiveness of the Árbenz government and its inability to organize local militias to defend the country. He swore allegiance to the Soviet Union, and joined the Communist Party while holed up in the Argentine embassy, awaiting deportation after Árbenz had been deposed.

Many of the young Guatemala-based comrades later reassembled in Mexico City where they digested the downfall of Árbenz. Perhaps the biggest lesson Guevara learned was that rather than attempt to negotiate with Washington, it was essential to combat American interference with armed resistance. He was convinced that Guatemala had been betrayed "inside and out", and argued that future revolutionaries must be prepared to establish their internal authority by force and eliminate enemies using repression and firing squads if necessary. – "Victory will be conquered with blood and fire, there can be no pardon for the traitors."

1867

First liberal uprising under Serpio Cruz.

1872

Liberal revolution; Justo Rufino Barrios becomes president. The coffee boom in Guatemala begins.

1906

The railway line to the Pacific coast is completed.

Ten years of "spiritual socialism"

The overthrow of Jorge Ubico released a wave of opposition, with students, professionals and young military officers all demanding democracy and freedom. It was a mood that was to transform Guatemalan politics, one so extreme a contrast to previous transitions of power that the 1944 handover was dubbed **the October revolution.**

Juan José Arévalo

In the subsequent 1945 elections **Juan José Arévalo**, a teacher, won the presidency with 85 percent of the vote. His political doctrine was dubbed "**spiritual socialism**", and he immediately set about implementing much-needed structural reforms. Under a new budget, a third of the government's income was allocated to social welfare, to be spent on the construction of schools and hospitals, a programme of immunization and a far-reaching literacy campaign. The vagrancy laws were abolished, a national development agency was founded, and in 1947 a labour code was adopted, granting workers the right to strike and union representation.

Some former coffee farms were turned into cooperatives, while new laws protected tenant farmers from eviction. Technical assistance and credit were also made available to peasant farmers.

In Arévalo's final years the pace of reform slackened somewhat as he concentrated on evading various attempts to overthrow him. Despite his popularity, Arévalo was still wary of the traditional elite: Church leaders, old-school army officers and wealthy landowners all resented the new wave of legislation, and repeated coup attempts were made.

Árbenz reforms

Leftist, ex-colonel **Jácobo Árbenz**, one of the leaders of the October revolution, won the 1950 election with ease, and declared that he would transform the country into an independent capitalist nation and raise the standard of living. But the process of overthrowing a feudal society and ending economic dependency led to direct confrontation with the American corporations that still dominated the economy.

Árbenz enlisted the support of the masses, encouraging the participation of peasants in the programme of agrarian reform and inciting the militancy of students and unions. He also attempted to break the great American-owned railway, power and port monopolies and sought to reclaim unpaid taxes from them. Internally, these measures aroused a mood of national pride, but they were strongly resented by the US companies whose empires were under attack.

The situation became even more serious with the **law of agrarian reform** passed in July 1952, which stated that idle and state-owned land would be distributed to the landless, at a fraction of its market value. The new laws outraged landowners. Between 1953 and 1954 around 8840 square kilometres were redistributed to the benefit of some 100,000 peasant families – the first time since the arrival of the Spanish that the government had responded to the needs of the Indigenous population. The landowner most seriously affected by the reforms was the United Fruit Company (now renamed Chiquito), which lost about half of its property.

As the pace of reform gathered, Árbenz began to take an increasingly radical stance. In 1951, the Communist Party was granted legal status, and in the next election four party members were elected to the legislature, which was staunchly anti-American.

1930s	**1944–54**	**1954**
Jorge Ubico president – banana boom and height of United Fruit Company power.	"Spiritual socialism" presidencies of Arévalo and Árbenz; ended by CIA-backed military coup.	Start of military rule and a series of military-backed dictators.

1954 US-backed coup

In the United States the press repeatedly accused the new Guatemalan government of being a communist beachhead in Central America, and the US government attempted to intervene on behalf of the United Fruit Company. Tellingly, Allen Dulles, the new director of the CIA, also happened to be a member of the fruit-company's board.

In 1953, President Dwight Eisenhower approved plans to overthrow the government and the CIA set up a small **military invasion** of Guatemala to depose Árbenz. A ragtag army of exiles and mercenaries was put together in Honduras, and on June 18, 1954, Guatemala City was bombed with leaflets demanding the resignation of Árbenz. The Guatemalan president failed to obtain the support of the army, and on the night of June 18, Guatemala was strafed with machine-gun fire while the invading army, described by Árbenz as "a heterogeneous Fruit Company expeditionary force", was getting closer to the city by the hour.

On June 27, Árbenz declared that he was relinquishing the presidency to **Colonel Carlos Enrique Díaz**, the army chief of staff. And on July 3, John Peurifoy, the US ambassador to Guatemala, flew the new government to Guatemala aboard a US Air Force plane. Guatemala's attempt to escape the clutches of outside intervention and bring about social change had been brought to an abrupt end.

Counter-revolution and military rule

Following the overthrow of Árbenz, the army – backed by US aid – rose to fill the power vacuum; it would dominate politics for the next thirty years, propelling the country into a spiral of violence and economic decline.

Carlos Castillo

In 1954 the US ambassador persuaded a provisional government to accept **Carlos Castillo** as the new president, and Castillo wasted no time sweeping away the progressive legislation of the previous ten years. The constitution of 1945 was replaced by a more restrictive version; illiterate people were disenfranchised; left-wing parties were outlawed; and large numbers of unionists and reformers were simply executed. The regime lifted the restrictions that had been placed on foreign investment and returned all the land that had been confiscated to its previous owners, a measure which badly affected the Indigenous population. A referendum was rigged to provide a supportive response to Castillo's rule, but his government had only limited backing from the armed forces, and coup rumblings persisted until finally he was shot by his own bodyguard in 1957.

Ydígoras and the 1963 coup

The assassination was followed by several months of political turmoil, out of which **Miguel Ydígoras** emerged as the next president. His disastrous five-year rule was marked by corruption, incompetence, outrageous patronage and economic decline caused by a fall in coffee prices; the formation of the Central American Common Market did help to boost light industry, however. Ydígoras was eventually overthrown when Arévalo threatened to return to Guatemala and contest the 1963 elections, which he might well have won. The possibility of another socialist government sent shock waves through

1960s	1968	1976
First guerrilla actions, rapidly followed by repressive clampdowns and rise of death squads.	Guatemalan writer Miguel Ángel Asturias wins Nobel Prize for Literature.	Earthquake leaves 23,000 dead, a million homeless.

the establishment in both Guatemala and the United States, and President John F. Kennedy gave the go-ahead for another coup. In 1963 the army once more took control, under the leadership of **Enrique Peralta**.

Guerrilla war

Peralta was president for just three years, during which time his authoritarian government was challenged by armed resistance in the highlands of Verapaz and Izabal.

Then, after new president Julio Méndez's offer of amnesty to the guerrillas was rejected, a ruthless counterinsurgency campaign swung into action using US military advisors, aerial bombardment and napalm. By the end of the decade, the guerrilla movement had been virtually eradicated in the east and its activities, greatly reduced, shifted to Guatemala City, where the US ambassador was assassinated by FAR rebels in 1968.

Political violence became commonplace as **death squads**, backed by the military, operated with impunity, killing anyone they deemed subversive to the state.

Economic decline and political violence

Extreme political violence, economic crises and electoral fraud dominated Guatemala's history between 1970 and the early 1990s. At the heart of the crisis was the injustice and inequality of Guatemalan society: although the country remained fairly prosperous, the benefits of its success never reached the poor, who were denied access to land, education and healthcare.

Rise of the military

The 1970 elections confirmed the power of the military and the far right. **Colonel Carlos Arana**, who had directed the counterinsurgency campaign in the east, was elected president, though only a small percentage of the population was enfranchised.

Once in power he set about eradicating armed opposition, declaring that "If it is necessary to turn the country into a cemetery in order to pacify it, I will not hesitate to do so." The reign of terror reached unprecedented levels, as around 15,000 political killings occurred during the first three years of Arana's rule.

Presidential elections followed in 1974, which were tainted by manipulation and fraud, resulting in the declaration of the right's candidate, **Kjell Laugerud**, as the winner. Laugerud offered limited reforms, allowing greater tolerance towards unions and the cooperative movement, but the army continued to consolidate its authority, spreading its influence across a wider range of business and commercial interests.

The 1976 earthquake and the rise of the Guerrilla Army of the Poor

All of this was interrupted by a massive **earthquake** on February 4, 1976. The quake left around 23,000 dead, 77,000 injured and a million homeless. The poor, their homes built from makeshift materials on unstable ground, suffered the most, and subsistence farmers were caught out just as they were about to plant their corn.

In the wake of the earthquake, during the process of reconstruction, powerful new forces emerged to challenge the status quo. A revived trade-union organization resurfaced, while a new guerrilla organization, the **Guerrilla Army of the Poor** (EGP), set up operations in the Ixil area (see page 112). The reaction of the army was brutal. In

1978

Lucas García president; thousands die through repression. US bans arms sales to Guatemala.

1982

Efraín Ríos Montt seizes presidency. Army begins scorched earth campaign in the highlands.

1985

Vinicio Cerezo elected: return to civilian rule though power of military remains great.

1977, US President Jimmy Carter suspended all military aid to Guatemala because of the country's appalling human-rights record.

In the following year, Guatemala's elections were once again dominated by the army, which engineered a victory for **Brigadier General Fernando Lucas García**. Lucas García promised to bring the situation under control, and unleashed a fresh wave of violence. All opposition considered subversive was met with severe repression, while several guerrilla armies developed strongholds in the highlands.

As chaos threatened, the army resorted to extreme measures, and within a month there was a massacre in **Panzós,** followed by assassinations of Social Democrats and Christian Democrats.

Civil war

The **army** became increasingly powerful and the death toll rose steadily. In rural areas the war against the guerrillas was reaching new heights as army casualties rose to 250 a month, and the demand for conscripts grew rapidly. The four main guerrilla groups had an estimated six thousand combatants and some 250,000 unarmed collaborators.

Under the Lucas García administration the horrors of **repression** were at their most intense. The victims included students, journalists, academics, politicians, priests, lawyers, teachers, unionists and, above all, peasant farmers, massacred in their hundreds. Accurate figures are impossible to calculate but it's estimated that around 35,000 Guatemalans were killed during the four years of the Lucas García regime.

In the field, morale in the Guatemalan military was low. Discontent was growing due to repeated military failures, inefficiency and a shortage of supplies, despite increased military aid and weaponry from Israel and Argentina.

Ríos Montt

On March 23, 1982, a group of young military officers led a successful coup, which installed **General Efraín Ríos Montt** as the head of a three-member junta.

Ríos Montt was an evangelical Christian, a member of the Iglesia del Verbo, and throughout his rule Sunday-night television was dominated by marathon presidential sermons. He immediately declared his determination to defeat the guerrillas, restore law and order and eradicate corruption. Government officials were issued with identity cards inscribed with the words "I do not steal. I do not lie." A state of siege was declared.

Initially, repression dropped in the cities as corrupt police officers were forced to resign, but in the highlands the war intensified. An **amnesty** was offered, which only a few rebels accepted, and the army set about destroying the guerrillas' infrastructure by undermining their support base.

Montt called his military campaign, "*frijoles y fusiles*" (beans and guns). Villagers were provided with rations and forcibly organized into **civil defence patrols** (PACs), armed with ancient rifles, and ordered to patrol the countryside. Those who refused were denounced as "subversives" and carted off to re-education camps or army-base torture chambers. *Campesinos* were forced to take sides, caught between the attraction of guerrilla propaganda and the extreme brutality of the armed forces. Even today, the legacy of *"frijoles y fusiles"* serves as a chilling reminder of how communities can be fractured and manipulated by those in power.

1991

Guatemala recognizes Belizean independence. Peace talks between guerrillas and government.

1992

Rigoberta Menchú wins Nobel Peace Prize.

Iron-fist policy

Ríos Montt's **iron-fist policy** was as successful as it was murderous as soldiers swept through the mountains committing massacre after massacre, wiping villages off the map and leaving nothing but scorched earth. Tens of thousands of *campesinos* fled to safety in Mexico. The guerrillas, their network of support virtually eradicated, were driven into remote corners, and occasionally responded with brutal measures, including the ambush and slaughter of PAC members and villagers. The massacre carried out by EGP guerrillas at the village of Txacal Tze in the Ixil region on June 13, 1982, left an estimated 125 dead.

By the middle of 1983, Ríos Montt faced growing pressure from all sides, particularly the Catholic Church, which was outraged by the murder of dozens of its priests. He was pushed aside by yet another military coup in August 1983 (and, nearly thirty years later, was charged with genocide and crimes against humanity).

General Mejía Víctores became president and moves towards democratic elections were implemented. Battles continued in the mountains, but some rehabilitation began as internal refugees were grouped in "**model villages**". Scarcely any money was made available for rebuilding the devastated communities, however, and it was often widows and orphans who were left to construct their own homes. In the Ixil region alone the war had displaced sixty thousand people (72 percent of the population). Nationwide more than six hundred villages had been destroyed and around 180,000 had lost their lives.

Human rights groups mobilize

Steadily activists began to mobilize in response. Important grassroots **human rights organizations** began to spring up in this period, including the Mutual Support Group (GAM), comprising families of the disappeared, and the National Commission of Guatemalan Widows (CONAVIGUA), a very significant and largely Indigenous group. Though the members of these groups faced routine intimidation and frequent death threats, they marked the emergence of a new period of Maya political activism.

Cerezo and the return to democratic rule

In 1985 presidential elections were held, the first free vote in Guatemala for thirty years. The winner was **Vinicio Cerezo**, a Christian Democrat. His election victory was the result of a sweeping wave of popular support, and in the run-up to the election he offered a programme of reform.

Once in office, however, Cerezo knew that his room for manoeuvre was severely limited. He argued that the army still held 75 percent of power, and declared "I'm a politician not a magician. Why promise what I cannot deliver?" Throughout his six-year rule Cerezo offered a **non-confrontational approach**, seeking above all else to avoid upsetting the powerful alliance of business interests, landowners and generals, and he survived several coup attempts. Political killings dropped in the late 1980s, but the civil war continued in remote parts of the highlands and death squads linked to rogue elements in the military operated in the capital.

The country's leading **human rights organization**, the Mutual Support Group (GAM), hoped that civilian rule would present them with a chance to investigate the fate of the "disappeared" and bring the perpetrators of violence to trial. Cerezo, however, chose

1996

Álvaro Arzú elected. Peace accords signed.

1998

Hurricane Mitch devastates much of Central America; Bishop Juan Geradi assassinated.

to forget the past, and ongoing abuses went largely uninvestigated and unpunished. GAM's leaders, meanwhile, became targeted by hit men.

Nevertheless, a measure of **civilian rule** created a general thaw in the political climate. Real change, however, never materialized. Despite the fact that at least 65 percent of the population still lived below the official poverty line, little was done to meet their needs in terms of education, health, employment, land or tax reform. Acknowledging that his greatest achievement had been to survive, Cerezo organized the country's first civilian transfer of power in decades, in 1990.

The Serrano and Carpio administrations

The **1990 elections** were dogged by controversy. Ex-military dictator Ríos Montt was banned from standing as a candidate, but **Jorge Serrano**, a former minister in his government, won (albeit with the support of less than a quarter of the people). An engineer and evangelical with a centre-right economic position, Serrano proved both uninterested and incapable of effecting any real reform or bringing an end to the civil war and the level of human rights abuse remained high.

Maya peasants became increasingly organized and influential, rejecting the presence of the army and the system of civil patrols. The people of Santiago Atitlán expelled the army from their town, after troops shot and killed thirteen people. Matters were brought into sharp focus in 1992 when **Rigoberta Menchú** (see page 341) was awarded the Nobel Peace Prize for her campaigning work on behalf of Guatemala's Indigenous population. However, the civil war still rumbled on and the three main guerrilla groups, united as the **URNG**, continued to confront the army.

Small groups of refugees began to return from exile in Mexico. The territorial dispute with **Belize** was officially resolved when the two countries established full diplomatic relations in 1991.

By early 1993, Serrano's reputation had plummeted following a series of **scandals** involving corruption and alleged links with Colombian drug cartels. In May 1993, Serrano pronounced a self-coup, though within days massive demonstrations and the suspension of US aid forced him out.

Ramiro Carpio

Further public protests then blocked an army-backed appointee, and finally **Ramiro Carpio**, the country's human rights ombudsman, was declared the new president. He reshuffled the senior military command, but rejected calls for revenge, declaring that stability was the main goal. Public frustration quickly grew as the new government failed to address fundamental issues, such as crime, land ownership, tax and constitutional reform. Some progress was made in peace negotiations with the URNG guerrilla leadership, however, and the Indigenous Rights Act, passed in 1995, allowed greater constitutional freedom for Guatemala's *indígenas*.

Arzú and the peace accords

Álvaro Arzú of the centre-right PAN party, a former mayor of Guatemala City, was elected president in 1996 with a commitment to private-sector-led growth and the free market. He quickly adopted a relatively progressive stance, shaking up the armed

2000

US decertifies Guatemala as "war on drugs" partner as cocaine-smuggling gangs' influence proliferates.

2005

CAFTA trade agreement approved by Guatemalan Congress.

forces' power structure and moving quickly to bring an end to the 36-year civil war by meeting guerrilla leaders. The **Peace Accords**, signed on December 29, 1996, concluded almost a decade of talks and terminated a conflict that had claimed two hundred thousand lives. A commitment to investigate wartime human rights violations through a Truth Commission overseen by MINUGUA (the UN mission to Guatemala) was agreed. However, progress on development issues was slow. There were token cuts in military numbers, but army officers implicated in orchestrating massacres avoided prosecution – Arzú simply dared not touch them.

Murder of Bishop Geradi

In April 1998, two days after the Catholic Church published a human rights report into wartime slaughters that blamed the military for ninety percent of civil war deaths, one of the investigators, **Bishop Juan Geradi**, was bludgeoned to death. The murder stunned the nation, one newspaper declaring "This wasn't supposed to happen. Not any more."

The acute fragility of the nascent Guatemalan democracy was revealed – most immediately suspected that a vengeful military was responsible for Geradi's assassination. Despite international and domestic outrage – hundreds of thousands attended a silent protest in the capital days after the killing – the perpetrators escaped justice as terrified judges, prosecutors and key witnesses fled abroad following death threats. As Arzú departed in December 1999, Geradi's murderers remained at large.

There was also an alarming upsurge in the crime rate. A new police force, the PNC, quickly gained a reputation as bad as its predecessor for endemic corruption and ineffectualness. But crime and the Geradi case aside, Arzú left office with his reputation as a skilled administrator, who got things done, intact. Huge infrastructure projects, including a massive upgrading of Guatemala's highways, were completed efficiently and to budget.

President Portillo

Former lawyer and professor **Alfonso Portillo** won Guatemala's 1999 presidential elections with a promise to implement the peace accords and tackle crime and gangs. In the grossest of ironies, Portillo confessed to killing two men in Mexico in 1982, declaring, "A man who defends his life will defend the lives of his people." He claimed he had acted in self-defence. But perhaps the most decisive factor in his victory was the support of his political mentor, former general and founder of the right-wing FRG party, Ríos Montt.

Portillo immediately set about attempting to solve the **Geradi case** as three senior military personnel were charged with murder within weeks of his inauguration. Credibly, the military suspects (an intelligence chief and two members of the elite presidential guard) and a priest (who was found guilty of acting as an accomplice) were brought to trial, and found guilty in June 2001 of plotting Geradi's murder.

The Geradi case aside, Portillo lurched from crisis to crisis, and after four years of catastrophic presidency he departed office leaving Guatemala virtually bankrupt. The stench of **corruption** pervaded his entire term as a series of scandals were unearthed and public coffers were emptied. Little or no progress was made on the terms of the peace accords, which included improving Indigenous rights.

2007

Guatemala named a "failed state" by *Foreign Policy* magazine.

2007–11

Álvaro Colom's presidential term marked by increased gang and narco violence.

Crime and hidden powers

Crime levels soared during Portillo's term. Human rights workers, journalists and environmentalists who dared to challenge powerful political and business interests were threatened and killed, while gangs terrorized the city suburbs.

Meanwhile, the **economy** continued to falter, as traditional exports (principally coffee, sugar and bananas) slumped, and low commodity prices affected profitability. Meanwhile, the cocaine trade boomed, as Guatemala became a key transit country. Behind this boom were shadowy **organized crime cartels** – locally known as *poderes ocultos* ("hidden powers") – thought to be headed up by retired generals and including a network of corrupt officials.

Portillo departed leaving Guatemala broke, with an estimated US$1 billion missing from the treasury and secret bank accounts discovered in Panama. In 2013, he was extradited to the United States, where he pleaded guilty to **money laundering** charges, and was subsequently jailed.

Óscar Berger

Inaugurated as president in January 2004, **Óscar Berger** declared that the country was nearly bankrupt and that his goal would be to govern in an austere, cost-conscious manner. Many key positions in his government were filled by members of the Guatemalan elite but he also made several progressive appointments including Rigoberta Menchú (see page 341) as a goodwill ambassador with a brief to implement the peace accords. Significantly, Berger curbed the power of the **armed forces** by slashing military spending: cutting army numbers from 27,000 to 15,500 and closing thirteen military bases.

In the countryside, the issue of **agrarian reform** was combustible. Berger evicted thousands of landless peasants from the fincas they were squatting, a course of action that provoked protests in twenty of the country's 22 departments in July 2004.

As Berger's term neared its end, the key issue for the 2007 election campaign was **crime** (again). With street gangs effectively in control of dozens of poor barrios, a murder rate ten times that in the US, and drug mafias with military links operating with virtual impunity Guatemala had, in the words of the Dutch ambassador, become "a paradise for organized crime". Few in the media, electorate or politics disagreed, and the question was who would best deal with the issue. Social democrat Álvaro Colom advocated "combating violence with intelligence", while his opponent in the presidential run-off Otto Pérez (an ex-military officer, implicated in the Geradi murder) called for an iron-fist approach. Colom narrowly got the nod.

Álvaro Colom

President **Álvaro Colom**, a worthy if slightly uninspiring personality from the centre-left, was a former textile businessman who had also studied Maya religion. His challenge was to tackle crime and violence, the narco gangs, poverty, land issues, Indigenous rights and the environment – without upsetting elements of his coalition, which included representatives from big business and the oligarchy.

Disillusionment set in pretty quickly with Colom's administration, and he developed a slightly bumbling reputation. By contrast, his wife, the ambitious and forceful **Sandra**

2012

Ex-general Otto Pérez begins presidency with iron-fist mandate to tackle crime. December 21 sees huge celebrations mark the start of a new cycle in the Maya Long Count calendar.

2013

Ex-military ruler Efraín Ríos Montt is found guilty of genocide during Guatemala's civil war; the conviction is later overturned.

Torres, was stereotyped as really wearing the trousers. Torres even divorced Colom and attempted to run for the presidency, though this move was ruled out by the constitutional court.

Columnists portrayed Colom as a mild-mannered character who lacked the stomach to fight organized crime and gangs (though seizures of cocaine doubled during his term to a street value of US$10 billion). In one gruesome episode decapitated heads were placed in the grounds of the Congress building and in other landmarks around the capital – an action deemed a warning from the narcos. In another horrific incident, 27 *campesinos* were butchered in a remote farm. A state of emergency was declared in both Alta Verapaz and Petén.

Unsurprisingly, the Guatemalan population still viewed their nation as being in desperately poor health as the 2011 elections approached. This time, hardliner Otto Pérez triumphed,promising to govern with a *mano dura* (iron fist) against crime and the gangs.

Otto Pérez

Assuming office in 2012, President **Otto Pérez** came from a **military** background. Chillingly, he was a senior officer in the department of Quiché, including the Ixil region, during the darkest years of the civil war when thousands disappeared and the worst massacres occurred. In the early 1990s he was director of Guatemalan military intelligence, and respected writer and journalist Francisco Goldman has accused him of being one of the masterminds of the Bishop Geradi murder (see page 323). However, in his own eyes Pérez considered himself as being from the moderate wing of the military.

He quickly introduced tax reforms, boosting Guatemala's state coffers with a capital gains tax and reducing incentives that favoured the rich, and presided over three increases in the minimum wage. **Drug reform** was placed at the top of the agenda at the Organization of American States General Assembly in June 2013, hosted by Guatemala.

However, by mid-2015 a huge corruption scandal, dubbed La Línea ("The Line") engulfed his presidency. CICIG (the International Commission against Impunity in Guatemala) accused governing politicians of operating a criminal network from the nation's *aduana* (customs offices), which siphoned off bribes amounting to hundreds of thousands of dollars a week. Intercepted phone conversations linked prosecutors with the president himself, who was arrested in September 2015 and jailed pending trial.

Jimmy Morales

In the chaos surrounding Otto Pérez's impeachment, the independent voice of one man resonated with the electorate: that of Jimmy Morales, formally a comedian who once starred in a TV series called *Moralejas* ("Morals"). Casting himself as a political outsider, his anti-corruption, anti-elite campaign – he declared he was "neither corrupt, nor a thief" – proved widely popular and propelled him to the president's office in 2016. But within a year a familiar storyline unfolded as the president became the focus of corruption allegations and his brother and son were arrested on graft charges. Later in the year Morales attempted to silence CICIG, which accused his party of links to narco smugglers and the military. In September 2018 he moved to banish CICIG from Guatemala, provoking nationwide protests.

2014	**2015**	**2016–18**
Some 50,000 Guatemalans take to the streets calling for increased rights for Indigenous peoples.	Otto Pérez's presidency ends in turmoil when he is arrested on corruption charges and detained in jail.	Ex-comedian Jimmy Morales is elected president. His term is quickly mired in controversy due to graft allegations as thousands march to demand his resignation.

Alejandro Giametti

After a turbulent single term, Morales was voted out and replaced by Alejandro Giametti in 2020. Giametti courted equal if not greater controversy and, following the announcement of a controversial budget that bypassed extreme child malnutrition in favour of big business, congress was set ablaze. Widespread corruption, the mismanagement of the Covid pandemic and a slew of legislation against abortion and gay rights saw Giametti plummet in the polls and a swift exit from office.

Bernardo Arévalo

Elected to office in 2024, Bernardo Arévalo was the first son of a former Guatemalan president to become president himself, and the second-most voted-for Guatemalan presidential candidate (bested only by Jimmy Morales). After a somewhat tumultuous inauguration, Arévalo has chartered a course that seems (so far) to be focused on ridding Guatemala of high-level corruption, with universal healthcare emerging as a policy priority.

State of the Nation

The highest **population growth** in Latin America pushes over 200,000 teenagers per year into a labour market where limited opportunities exist. Unsurprisingly many of these young Guatemalans vote with their feet and head north, to join an estimated 2 million of their compatriots in the USA and Canada.

Guatemala is the second poorest nation in the western hemisphere, with more than fifty percent of its population (and around seventy percent of the Maya) living in **poverty**, according to the World Bank. Levels of chronic malnutrition are the fifth highest in the world. There is wealth, but incomes remain woefully skewed, with taxation accounting for only around ten percent of GDP. Meanwhile, endemic corruption continues to bleed the nation of much-needed finance.

Guatemala's recent **economic performance**, averaging between two and four percent GDP growth per year since the mid-1990s, has been steady but modest (and started from a very low base). The country's woeful **education system** (thirty percent of adults are illiterate) is a serious handicap, while social instability and crime levels also impact upon international competitiveness and inward investment. **Gang culture** has spread like a virus throughout the nation: women are targeted with extreme violence (see box), and extortion affects the market vendors, shopkeepers and bus and taxi drivers who operate in gang territory. **Land reform**, another critical issue, has never been tackled in Guatemala. Around seventy percent of the country's agricultural land is owned by just three percent of the population.

Environmental and Indigenous issues

Contentious **mining** concessions and plans for **hydroelectric power** plants have been fought by increasingly well-organized community groups, particularly in **Indigenous** regions. In the Ixcán area villagers have blocked the completion of the Franja Transversal del Norte highway, fearing it will facilitate mining and hydroelectric

2020

Alejandro Giametti takes office and is soon mired in controversy. After prioritising big business over widespread child malnutrition, congress is set ablaze by protestors.

2024

Bernardo Arévalo is successfully installed as president, after far-right elements tried to block his inauguration.

HUMAN RIGHTS IN GUATEMALA TODAY

Guatemala is a poor, troubled country, still scarred by its 36-year civil war (the bloodiest seen in Latin America), and with a deeply corrupt justice system. A climate of fear has persisted for decades, and those who dare to challenge the interests of the elite, hidden powers and criminal gangs face intimidation and violence. However, determined activists and lawyers are pressing hard to change the culture of impunity, and in recent years have succeeded in convicting civil war criminals and human rights abusers.

Amnesty International's 2017–2018 report on Guatemala concentrated on the feeble criminal justice system, high rates of **violent crime** and the continuing **culture of impunity**. Campaigning against crime or corruption, or challenging the authority of Guatemala's criminal networks is very dangerous work. Every year there are hundreds of cases of intimidation and attacks on journalists and human rights leaders, trade unionists, forensic experts and any organizations focusing on economic, social and cultural rights. Death threats are common and families of activists are also targeted. Guatemala's Human Rights Defenders' Protection Unit (UDEFEGUA) reported seven activists were killed in one month alone in 2018. The same organization also reported a total of 5,965 attacks against human rights defenders between January and November 2023.

DOMESTIC VIOLENCE AND FEMICIDE

Hundreds of Guatemalan women are murdered each year; in 2022 there were a total of 534 murders. Domestic violence is widespread and until recently there was no effective law against rape. The most disturbing issue of all remains the number of women murdered for apparently motiveless reasons: a phenomenon known as **femicide**. These deaths are often related to gang violence and territorial disputes; many are killed in street gang initiation rituals.

INFORMATION

For more information on human rights in Guatemala, contact either the **Guatemalan Human Rights Commission** in the USA (ghrc-usa.org), **Amnesty International** (amnesty.org) or **Human Rights Watch** (hrw.org). These organizations all publish regular bulletins and reports on the current situation in the country.

plants in the area that threaten their land. In June 2014 an estimated fifty thousand Guatemalans took to the streets calling for the government to value Indigenous people's rights, and respect opposition to projects (which, they argued) create few local jobs and generate little income for communities, while causing great environmental harm. In 2024, the Inter-American Court of Human Rights ruled in favour of the Maya Q'eqchi' people, declaring that Guatemala had violated their ancestral land rights.

The cost of **electricity**, among the highest in Latin America, is another incendiary issue in Guatemala. Six demonstrators were killed near Totonicapán in 2012 when the military opened fire on Indigenous protestors angry at price hikes. Hundreds of Maya communities in Huehuetenango and northern Quiché have simply stopped paying for electricity, and steal it from the grid. This lead to power company Energuate suspending power completely in the Chisec area in 2018 and communities blocking national highways in protest. This issue is still ongoing in 2024.

Up in the Petén, **forests** continue to disappear in smoke as settlers, loggers and cattle ranchers have overrun protected reserves including Laguna del Tigre. Some of these invaders have links to drug mafias who clear airstrips in the jungle to facilitate the transit of cocaine. The dense forests and ruins of the Mirador Basin (see page 269), where a national park has still not been established, despite years of campaigning, remain in peril. **Lago de Atitlán**, meanwhile, the crown jewel of Guatemala's tourist industry, is another environmental mess, threatened on many fronts (see page 117).

The Maya achievement

For some three thousand years before the arrival of the Spanish, Maya civilization dominated Mesoamerica, leaving behind some of the most impressive architecture in the entire continent. The scale and grandeur of some Maya cities, such as El Mirador around 100 BC, rivalled their European contemporaries, and the artistry and splendour of Maya civilization at the height of the Classic era arguably eclipsed that in the Old World. Maya culture was complex and sophisticated, fostering the highest standards of engineering, astronomy, stone carving and mathematics, as well as an intricate writing system.

To appreciate all this you have to see for yourself the remains of the great centres. Despite centuries of neglect, abuse and encroaching jungle, they are still astounding – the biggest temple-pyramids tower up to 70m above the forest floor, high above the jungle canopy. Stone monuments, however, leave much of the story untold, and there is still a great deal that we have to learn about Maya civilization. What follows is the briefest of introductions to the subject, hopefully just enough to whet your appetite for the immense volumes that have been written on it.

Maya society

By the Early Classic period, the Maya cities had become organized into a hierarchy of power, with cities such as Tikal and Calakmul dominating vast areas and controlling the smaller sites through a complex structure of **alliances**. The cities jostled for power and influence, occasionally erupting into open warfare, which was also partly fuelled by the need for sacrificial victims. The distance between the larger sites averaged around 30km, and between these were myriad smaller settlements consisting of religious centres and residential groups. The structure of the alliances can be traced through the use of **emblem glyphs**.

Maya power politics

Only the glyphs of the main centres are used in isolation, while the names of smaller sites are used in conjunction with those of their larger patrons. Of all the myriad Classic cities, the dominant ones were clearly Tikal and Calakmul, with Palenque, Copán, Caracol, Naranjo, Piedras Negras, Yaxhá and Yaxchilán accepting secondary status until the early eighth century AD when the hierarchy began to dismantle. Cancuén, El Pilar, Nakúm, Waka', Dos Pilas and Quiriguá were other key cities, each lording it over, and probably extracting tribute from, many more minor settlements. Trade, marriages and warfare between the large centres were commonplace as the cities were bound up in an endless round of competition and conflict.

Population

By the Late Classic period, **population densities** across a broad swathe of territory in the central area were as high as 965 people per square kilometre – an extraordinarily high figure, equivalent to densities in rural China or Java today – and as many as **ten million** people lived in the wider Maya region. It's thought there were strict divisions between the classes, with perhaps eighty percent being preoccupied with intensive cultivation to feed these vast numbers. The peasant farmers, who were at the bottom of the social scale, also provided the labour necessary to construct monumental ceremonial temples (the Maya did not have the wheel) as well as perform regular "military service" duties. Even in the suburbs where the peasants lived, there are complexes of religious structures with simple, small-scale temples where ceremonies took place.

Ordinary Maya

Although the remains of the great Maya sites are a testament to the scale and sophistication of Maya civilization, they offer little insight into daily life in Maya times. To reconstruct the lives of the **ordinary Maya**, archeologists have turned to the smaller residential groups that surround the main sites, littered with the remains of household utensils, pottery, bones and farming tools. These groups are made up of simple structures made of poles and wattle-and-daub. The groups as a whole probably

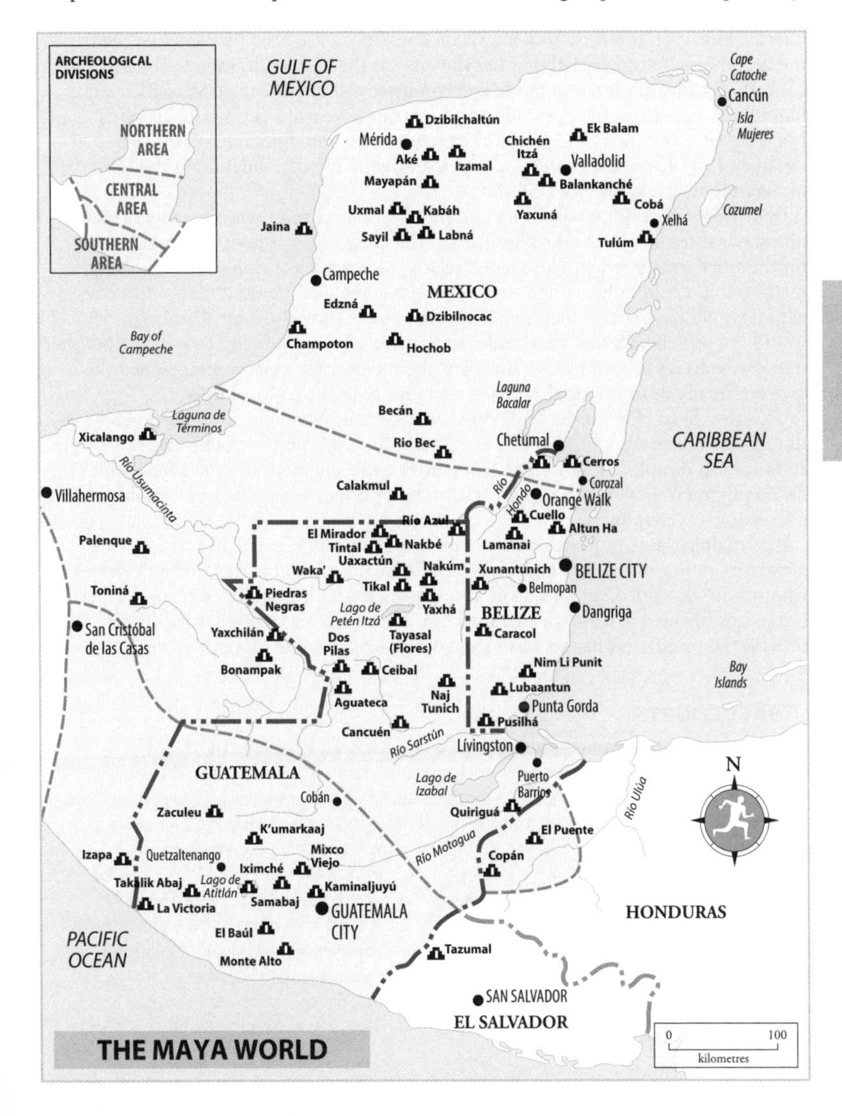

housed an **extended family**, who would have farmed and hunted together and may well have specialized in some trade or craft. The people living in these groups were commoners, their lives largely dependent on **farming**. Maize, beans, cacao, squash, chillies and fruit trees were cultivated in raised and irrigated fields, while wild fruits were harvested from the surrounding forest. It's not certain whether the land was privately or communally owned.

Class structure

Until the 1960s, Mayanists had long shared the view that the Maya were ruled by a scholarly **astronomer-priest elite** who were preoccupied with religious devotion and the study of calendrics and the stars. They were thought to be men of reason, with no time for the barbarity of war and conquest, and were often likened to the ancient Greeks. However, this early utopian vision could not have been further from the truth: the decipherment of Maya glyphs has shown that the Maya rulers were primarily concerned with the glories of battle and conquest and the preservation of their royal bloodlines; human sacrifice and bloodletting rituals were also a pivotal part of elite Maya society. The rulers considered themselves to be god–humans and thought that the line of royal accession could only be achieved by sacred validation in the form of human **bloodletting** (see page 333).

There were two **elite classes**: *ahau* and *cahal*, who between them probably made up two or three percent of the population. The *ahau* title was reserved exclusively for the ruler and extremely close blood relatives – the top echelon of Maya society; membership could only be inherited. One step down was the *cahal* class, most of whom would have shared bloodlines with the *ahau*. The *cahal* were mainly governors of subsidiary settlements that were under the control of the dominant city-state, and their status was always subordinate to the *ahau*. Although *cahal* lords commissioned their own stelae, the inscriptions always declared loyalty to the regional ruler.

The rulers lived close to the ceremonial centre of the Maya city, in imposing **palaces**, though the rooms were limited in size because the Maya never mastered the use of the arch. Palaces doubled as administrative centres and were used for official receptions for visiting dignitaries, with strategically positioned thrones where the ruler would preside over religious ceremonies.

The "**middle class**" of Maya society consisted of a professional class (*ah na'ab*) of architects, senior scribes (*ah tz'ib*), sculptors, bureaucrats and master artisans, some of whom were also titled, and probably young princes and important court performers. Priests and shamen can also be included in this middle class though, surprisingly, no title for the priesthood has yet been recognized – it's possible that not giving the priests

BALL COURTS

Pitz – the Maya **ball game** – was much more than a sport; it represented a battle between the forces of life and death. Though the exact rules are unclear, it's known that the game was between two players (or two teams) who competed on a court by striking a heavy rubber ball with their elbows and hips. Results were sometimes associated with divine judgement and they may have been used to settle conflicts – with the losers being decapitated.

All courts were a similar shape, consisting of a narrow, paved playing area flanked by sloping walls, and were usually open-ended. However, they varied greatly in size: most were only 15m or 20m long and around 5m across but the great court of Chichén Itzá measured nearly 100m by 30m. Many courts had stone rings, which the players would attempt to pass the ball through; on others beautifully carved circular stone markers delineated areas of play. Ball courts were a central feature of Maya life, and aside from the ball game were also used for cultural events and rituals. Significant ball courts can be found in Tikal, Nixtun Ch'ich', Copán, Iximché, Mixco Viejo and Zaculeu.

a title may have been a method used by a fearful ruler to limit their influence. Through their knowledge of calendrics and supernatural prophecies, the priests were relied upon to divine the appropriate time to plant and harvest crops.

Role of women

There's no doubt that **women** played an influential role in Maya society, and in the Late Classic period there were even some women rulers – Lady Ahpo Katun at Piedras Negras, Lady Ahpo-Hel at Palenque and a Lady Six Sky at Naranjo. Women also presided at court and were given prestigious titles – Lady Cahal of Bonampak, for example. More frequently, however, as in Europe, dynasties were allied and enhanced by the marriage of royal women between cities. One of the best-documented strategic marriages occurred after the great southern city of Copán had suffered the humiliation of having its leader captured and sacrificed by upstart local rival Quiriguá in 738 AD – a royal marriage was arranged with a noblewoman from Palenque, 700km away.

Agriculture

Maya **agriculture** adapted to the needs of the developing society, adopting intensive and sophisticated methods from as early as 400 BC when farmers at El Mirador used vast quantities of **swamp mud** to fertilize their crops. Land was terraced, drained or irrigated in order to improve its productivity and ensure that fields didn't have to lie fallow for long periods, and the capture of water became crucial to the success of a site.

The large lowland cities, which are today hemmed in by forest, were once surrounded by open fields, canals and residential compounds, although slash-and-burn was probably practised in marginal and outlying areas. Agriculture became a necessary absorption, with the ordinary Maya trading at least some of their food in markets, although all households still had a kitchen garden where they grew herbs and fruit.

Diet

Maize has always been the basis of the Maya diet, in ancient times as much as it is today. Once harvested it was made into *saka*, a cornmeal gruel that was eaten with chilli as the first meal of the day. During the day labourers ate a mixture of corn dough and water, and we know that *tamales* were also a popular speciality. The main meal, eaten in the evenings, would have been similarly maize-based, although it may well have included meat and vegetables. As a supplement to this simple diet, deer, peccary, wild turkey, duck, pigeon and quail were all hunted with bows and arrows or blowguns. The Maya also made use of dogs, both for hunting and the dinner table. Fish were also eaten, and the remains of fishhooks and nets have been found at some sites, while there is evidence that those living on the coast traded dried fish and salt far inland. The forest provided firewood as well as food, and cotton was cultivated to be dyed with natural colours and then spun into cloth.

Time and the Maya calendar

One of the cornerstones of Maya thinking was an obsession with **time**. For both practical and mystical reasons the Maya developed a highly sophisticated understanding of arithmetic, calendrics and astronomy, all of which they believed gave them the power to understand and predict events. All great occasions were interpreted on the basis of the **Maya calendar**, and it was this precise understanding of time that gave the ruling elite its authority. The majority of the carvings, on temples and stelae, record the exact date at which rulers were born, ascended to power and died.

Calendrical systems

The basis of all Maya **calculation** was the vigesimal counting system, which used multiples of twenty. All figures were written using a combination of three symbols

MAYA TIME: THE UNITS

1 *kin* = 24 hours
20 *kins* = 1 *uinal*, or 20 days
18 *uinals* = 1 *tun*, or 360 days
20 *tuns* = 1 *katun*, or 7200 days
20 *katuns* = 1 *baktun*, or 144,000 days
20 *baktuns* = 1 *pictun*, or 2,880,000 days
20 *pictuns* = 1 *calabtun*, or 57,600,000 days
20 *calabtuns* = 1 *kinchiltun*, or 1,152,000,000 days
20 *kinchiltuns* = 1 *alautun*, or 23,040,000,000 days

– a shell to denote zero, a dot for one and a bar for five – which you can still see on many stelae. When calculating **calendrical systems**, the Maya used a slightly different notation known as the head-variant system, in which each number from one to twenty was represented by a deity, whose head was used to represent the number.

When it comes to the Maya **calendar** things start to get a little more complicated, as the Maya used a number of different counting systems, depending on the reason the date was being calculated. The basic unit of the Maya calendar was the day, or *kin*, followed by the *uinal*, a group of twenty days roughly equivalent to our month; but at the next level things start to get even more complex as the Maya marked the passing of time in three distinct ways.

The **260-day almanac** was used to calculate the timing of ceremonial events. Each day was associated with a particular deity that had strong influence over those born on that particular day. This calendar wasn't divided into months but had 260 distinct day-names – a system still in use among some Kaqchikel and Mam Maya who name their children according to its structure and celebrate fiestas according to its dictates.

A second calendar, the so-called "**vague year**" or *haab*, was made up of eighteen *uinals* and five *kins*, a total of 365 days, making it a close approximation of the solar year. These two calendars weren't used in isolation but operated in parallel so that once every 52 years the new day of the solar year coincided with the same day in the 260-day almanac, a meeting that was regarded as very powerful and marked the start of a new era.

Finally, the Maya had yet another system, the **Long Count**, for marking the passing of history, which was used on dedicatory monuments. In this calendar a great cycle ended on **December 21, 2012**, when there were huge celebrations across the region, and the Maya World became the focus of the world's media.

Astronomy

Alongside their fascination with time, the Maya were obsessed with the sky and devoted much time and energy to unravelling its patterns. Observatories were being constructed as early as 500 BC and many sites including Copán, Uaxactún, Tikal, Chichén Itzá and Yaxhá have temples carefully aligned with solar and lunar sequences.

The Maya showed a great understanding of **astronomy**, and with their 365-day "vague year" they were just a quarter of a day out in their calculations of the solar year. At Copán, towards the end of the seventh century AD, Maya astronomers had calculated the lunar cycle at 29.53020 days, not too far off our current estimate of 29.53059. In the Dresden Codex (a copy of which can be found in Guatemala City's Popol Vuh museum), their calculations extend to the 405 lunations over a period of 11,960 days, as part of a pattern that set out to predict eclipses. At the same time, they had calculated with astonishing accuracy the movements of Venus, Mars and perhaps

Mercury. Venus was of particular importance to the Maya as they linked its presence with success in war; several stelae record the appearance of Venus prompting the decision to strike at an enemy – an attack known as a "**star war**".

RITUAL BLOODLETTING AND THE MAYA

Ritual bloodletting was a fundamental part of Maya religious life, practised by all strata of society. It took many forms, from cursory self-inflicted blood offerings to elaborate ceremonies involving the mass sacrifice of captive kings and enemy warriors. The Maya modelled their lives according to a vision of the cosmos, and within this arena, human actions could affect the future, auspiciously or otherwise. Pivotal to this vision was the concept that blood-spilling helped repay man's debt to the gods, who had endowed the gift of life.

First practised by the **Olmec** more than three thousand years ago, bloodletting continued until the arrival of the conquistadors. It's thought ritual blood offerings were initially concerned with renewal and agricultural fertility, and later in the Classic period with warfare and political alliances. The practice grew to apocalyptic degrees of carnage among the **Aztecs**: Spanish chroniclers record the mass sacrifice of eighty thousand victims at the rededication of the Templo Mayor in their capital.

As well as direct representations of the sacrificial act, the Maya developed a symbolic iconography of bloodletting, so that the smallest motif, such as three knotted bands or smoke scrolls, could express blood sacrifice. The fact that depictions of bloodletting were chosen for preservation on **stone**, a costly and laborious medium, confirms its religious, social and political significance.

RITUALS

A common bloodletting ritual may have consisted of cutting earlobes, cheeks or thighs and collecting the blood to burn, or sprinkling it directly on a shrine or idol. Undertaken for numerous reasons – to bless a journey, the planting of crops, or the passing of a family member – these rites may have been accompanied by prayers, the sacrifice of animals and the burning of copal incense.

Elite bloodletting rituals often took place at important or auspicious occasions: during accession ceremonies, at the birth of an heir, to mark the passing of a calendar round, in times of war, drought or disease and to ensure regeneration and prosperity.

There seem to have been two main **auto-sacrificial rituals** practised by the Maya elite. As part of a larger ceremony, the actual act of letting blood may have been preceded by days of preparation, meditation, fasting, sexual abstinence and bodily purification with sweat baths. A male rite was to draw blood by pricking the penis with either a stingray spine, obsidian lancet or flint knife. The second rite – piercing the tongue – was probably performed by both sexes, although it's most famously illustrated by Lady Xoc in the **Yaxchilán lintels** (now housed in the British Museum). The blood offering was then soaked into bark paper and collected in ceremonial bowls to be burnt as a presentation and petition to the gods.

SACRIFICE

The Maya also practised bloodletting in the form of **captive sacrifice**, a highly ceremonial affair in which prolonged death and torture were features – gruesomely depicted in the Bonampak murals. Prisoners then either faced death by decapitation, or by having their hearts removed.

Maya **warfare** often reflected the need for ritual bloodletting, as warriors frequently sought to capture alive rulers of rival cities, who would then be imprisoned and sacrificed at a later date. The soaring temples of the city centre served as ceremonial theatres for elaborate religious rituals, allowing victories to be proclaimed to the entire community. Sacrificial victims would have been especially important to mark the accession of a new ruler, the bloodletting adding legitimacy to the king and affirming his power.

Religion

Maya cosmology is far from straightforward as at every stage an idea is balanced by its opposite and each part of the universe is made up of many layers. To the ancient Maya (and many Indigenous people today) this is the third version of the earth, the previous two having been destroyed by deluges. The current version is a flat surface, with four corners, each associated with a certain colour: white for north, red for east, yellow for south and black for west, with green at the centre. Above the earth, the sky is supported by four trees, each a different colour and species – these are also sometimes depicted as gods, known as *Bacabs*. At its centre, the sky is supported by a ceiba tree. Above the sky is a heaven of thirteen layers, each of which has its own god, with the very top layer overseen by an owl. Other attested models of the world include that of a turtle (the land) floating on the sea.

Xibalbá

However, it's the underworld, *Xibalbá*, the "Place of Fright", which was of greatest importance to the ancient Maya (and many traditionalists today), as it is in this direction that they pass after death, on their way to the place of rest. The nine layers of hell are guarded by the "Lords of the Night", and deep caves are thought to connect with the underworld.

Gods

The ancient Maya also recognized an incredible array of **gods**, though today this concept of a pantheon is much less common. Every divinity had four manifestations based upon colour and direction, and many also had counterparts in the underworld and consorts of the opposite sex. In addition, the Maya also had an extensive array of patron deities, each associated with a particular trade or particular class, while every activity from suicide to sex had its deity.

Rituals

The combined complexity of the Maya pantheon and calendar gave every day a particular significance, and the ancient Maya were bound up in a demanding **cycle of religious ritual**. The main purpose of ritual was the procurement of success by appealing to the right god at the right time and in the right way. As every event, from planting to childbirth, was associated with a particular divinity, all of the main events in daily life demanded some kind of religious ritual. For the most important of these, the Maya staged elaborate ceremonies.

Although each ceremony had its own format, a certain pattern bound them all. The correct day was carefully chosen by priestly divination, and for several days beforehand the participants fasted and remained abstinent. The main ceremony was dominated by the expulsion of all evil spirits, the burning of incense before the idols, a sacrifice (either animal or human) and **bloodletting** (see page 333).

Drug and hallucinogenic use

In divination rituals, used to foretell the pattern of future events or account for the cause of past events, the elite used various **drugs** to achieve altered states of consciousness. Perhaps the most obvious of these was alcohol, either made from fermented maize or a combination of honey and the bark of jungle trees. Wild tobacco, which is considerably stronger than the modern domesticated version, was also smoked. The Maya also used a range of **hallucinogenic mushrooms**, all of which were appropriately named, but none more so than the *xibalbaj obox*, "underworld mushroom", and the *k'aizalah obox*, "lost judgement mushroom".

Indigenous Guatemala

A vital Indigenous culture is perhaps Guatemala's most distinctive feature. Although the Maya people may appear quiet and humble, their costumes, fiestas and markets are a riot of colour, creativity and celebration. Most Maya people remain extremely attached to local traditions and values, and regard themselves as *indígenas* first and Guatemalans second.

The **Maya**, the vast majority of whom live in the western highlands, make up around 45 percent of Guatemala's population. It's actually quite tricky to define exactly who is Maya, but for the sake of the national census, people who consider themselves

WHAT'S IN A NAME?

Throughout this Guide we have used the terms "Maya" or "*indígenas*" to refer to those Guatemalans of Maya origin. You may also hear them called *Índios* (or Indians), though in Guatemala this term has racially pejorative connotations.

Indigenous are classed as such, regardless of their parentage. And when it comes to defining the Maya as a group, culture is more important than pedigree, as the Maya define themselves through their relationships with their land, gods, villages and families. Holding aloof from the melting pot of modern Guatemalan society, many Maya people adhere instead to their traditional *costumbres*, codes of practice that govern every aspect of life.

As a result, the only way to define Maya culture is by describing its main traits, acknowledging that all Indigenous Guatemalans will accept some of these attributes, and accepting that many are neither *indígena* nor ladino, but combine elements of both.

Indigenous culture

When the Spanish set about conquering the Maya tribes of Guatemala they altered every aspect of life for the Indigenous people, uprooting their social structures and reshaping their communities. Before the Conquest the bulk of the population had lived scattered in the hills, paying tribute to a tribal elite, and surviving through subsistence farming and hunting. Under Spanish rule they were moved into new **villages** known as *reducciones*, where their homes were clustered around a church. Horizons shrank rapidly as allegiances became localized and the village hierarchies that still dominate the highlands today replaced existing tribal structures.

For almost five hundred years the Maya population has suffered repeated abuse, as the elite has exploited Indigenous land and labour, regarding the Maya as an expendable commodity. But within their own communities Indigenous Guatemalans were left pretty much to themselves and developed an astoundingly introspective culture that is continually adapting to new threats, reshaping itself for the future. **Village life** was insulated from the outside world until recently and in remote areas few women speak good Spanish; 28 native languages and dialects (see map) are still spoken. Today's Indigenous culture is a complex synthesis that includes elements of Maya, Spanish and modern American cultures.

Agriculture

The majority of the Indigenous population still live by **subsistence agriculture**, their homes either spread across the hills or gathered in small villages. Farmers tend their *milpas*, growing beans, chillies, maize and squash – the staple diet for thousands of years. To the Maya, land is sacred and the need to own and farm it is central to their culture, despite the fact that few can survive by farming alone. Some cash crops are also grown – including broccoli, snow peas, fruit and coffee – much of it for export.

Migration

Thousands of Maya migrate to the coast for several months a year, where they often work in appalling conditions on plantations to supplement their income. However, huge numbers are now choosing to head north to the US to work illegally instead, their overseas **remittances** now forming a crucial part of the local economy in virtually every mountain village. Traditional crafts (like rope-making, pottery and textile weaving) remain important, while cut-flower production for the export market is increasingly profitable. **Tourism** dollars also make a financial impact here and there, particularly around Lago de Atitlán, but also in the Ixil, Alta Verapaz and Quetzaltenango areas, too.

Gender roles

Family life tends to bow to tradition, with large families very much a part of the Indigenous culture. Marriage customs vary from place to place but in general the groom is expected to pay the bride's parents, and the couple may well live with the groom's family. Authority within the village is usually given to men, although women are increasingly involved in decision making. Customs are slowly changing, but generally rural men spend most of the day tending the *milpas* and vegetable plots, while women are based in the family home, looking after the children, cooking and weaving. However, Maya women are by no means confined to the house and frequently travel to distant markets to sell surplus fruit, vegetables and textiles and to buy, or barter for, thread and supplies. In some places particularly noted for their weavings, such as Nebaj or Chajul, whole families decamp to Antigua or Panajachel for three or four days to sell their crafts to tourists.

Indigenous religion

Every aspect of Maya life – from the birth of a child to the planting of corn – is loaded with religious significance, based on a complicated **fusion of the Maya pantheon and Catholic religion**. Christ and the saints have taken their place alongside *Dios Mundo*, the God of the World, and *Hurakan*, the Heart of Heaven. The two religions have merged to form a hybrid, in which the outward forms of Catholicism are used to worship the ancient pantheon, a compromise that was probably fostered by Spanish priests.

The symbol of the **cross**, for example, was well known to the Maya, signifying the four winds of heaven, the four directions and everlasting life. Today many of the deities have both Maya and Hispanic names, and are usually associated with a particular saint. All the deities remain subordinate to a mighty and remote supreme being, and Christ takes a place in the upper echelons of the hierarchy.

God and the spiritual world

For the Maya, **God** is everywhere, bound up in the seasons, the mountains, the crops, the soil, the air and the sky. Prayer and offerings mark every important event, with disasters often attributed to divine intervention. Even more numerous than the gods, **spirits** are found in every imaginable object, binding together the universe. Each individual is born with a *nahaul*, or spiritual counterpart, in the animal world, and his or her destiny is bound up with that particular animal. The spirits of dead ancestors are also ever-present and have to be looked after by each successive generation.

Religious hierarchy

Though the arrival of **evangelical churches** (see page 339) in Guatemala has seen a certain disruption of centuries-old religious structures, traditionally, a community's worship is organized by a **religious hierarchy**. In these systems the office-holders are male, and throughout their lives they progress through the system, moving from post to post. The various posts are grouped into *cofradías*, ritual brotherhoods, each of which is responsible for a particular saint. Throughout the year the saint is kept in the home of an elder member, and on the appointed date, in the midst of a fiesta, it's paraded through the streets, to spend the next year somewhere else. The elder responsible for the saint will have to pay for much of the fiesta, including costumes, alcohol and assorted offerings, but it's a responsibility, or *cargo*, that's considered a great honour.

In the traditional village hierarchy, it's these duties that give the elders, known as *principales*, a prominent role in village life and it's through these duties that they exercise their authority, such as the organization of the annual **fiesta**. (In some villages, such as Chichicastenango and Sololá, a *municipalidad indígena*, or Indigenous council, operates alongside the *cofradías*, and is similarly hierarchical. As men work their way up through the system they may well alternate between the civil and religious hierarchies.)

The *cofradías* don't necessarily confine themselves to the traditional list of saints, and have been known to foster "evil" saints, such as San Simón or **Maximón**, a drinking, smoking ladino figure, sometimes referred to as Judas or Pedro de Alvarado.

Shamanism

On a more superstitious level, **native priests** (*costumbristas*, or *aj'itz* in K'iche' and Kaqchikel areas) communicate with the gods and spirits to cater to people's personal religious needs. This is usually done on behalf of an individual client who's in search of a blessing, and often takes place at shrines and caves in the mountains, with offerings of copal, a type of incense, and alcohol. The *costumbristas* also make extensive use of old Maya sites, and small burnt patches of grass litter many of the ruins in the highlands. Indigenous priests are also credited with the ability to cast spells, predict the future and communicate with the dead. For specific medical problems, the Maya appeal to *zahorines* who practise traditional medicine with a combination of invocation and herbs, and are closely associated with Indigenous religious traditions.

Evangelical Christianity

Until the 1950s, when Catholic **missionaries** became active in the highlands, many Indigenous Guatemalans had no idea that there was a gulf between their own religion and orthodox Catholicism. At first, the missionaries drew most of their support from the younger generation, many of whom were frustrated by the rigidity of the village hierarchy. Gradually, this eroded the authority of the traditional religious system: the missions undermined the *cofradías*, disapproved of traditional fiestas, and scorned the work of the native priests. As a part of this, the reforming movement Catholic Action, which combined the drive for orthodoxy with an involvement in social issues, has also had a profound impact.

After the 1976 earthquake, waves of Protestant missionaries, known as *evangélicos*, arrived in Guatemala, and their presence has also accelerated the decline of traditional religion (see box).

These days there are hundreds of different **evangelical churches**, backed by a huge injection of money from the USA, and offering all sorts of incentives to fresh converts. Most of these churches are fervently against liquor consumption, and as **alcoholism** is a huge issue in Indigenous villages, some communities have effectively become dry towns.

Yet despite the efforts of outsiders, the *costumbristas* and *cofradías* are still in business, and many fiestas remain vaguely pagan. Indeed, since the end of the civil war there has been an upsurge in interest in Maya religious practice – indeed an ex-president of Guatemala, Álvaro Colom, studied Maya spiritualism.

Markets and fiestas

At the heart of the Indigenous economy is the **weekly market**, which remains central to life in the highlands and provides one of the best opportunities to see Maya life at close quarters. The majority of the Indigenous population still lives by subsistence farming but spares a day or two a week to gather together in the nearest village and trade surplus produce. The market is as much a social occasion as an economic one and people come to talk, eat, drink, gossip and have a good time. In some places the action starts the night before with marimba music and heavy drinking.

On market day itself the village is filled by a steady flow of people, arriving by pick-up or bus, on foot or by mule. In no time at all trading gets under way, and the plaza is soon buzzing with activity and humming with conversation, although raised voices are a rarity, with deals struck after protracted, but always polite, negotiations.

The scale and atmosphere of markets varies from place to place. The country's largest is in **San Francisco el Alto**, on Fridays, and draws traders from throughout the country. Other renowned ones are the vegetable market of **Almolonga** and **Sololá**'s huge Tuesday and

EVANGELISM IN GUATEMALA

One of the greatest surprises awaiting first-time travellers in Guatemala is the number of evangelical churches in the country, with fundamentalist, Pentecostal or neo-Pentecostal services taking place in most towns and villages. Although early Protestant missions came to Guatemala as far back as 1882, the impact of US-based churches remained marginal and largely unnoticed until the 1950s, when **state repression** and the subsequent **guerrilla war** began to weaken the power of the Catholic Church. Up until this time, more than 95 percent of the population was officially Catholic, though the rural Maya had their own hybrid forms of worship that mixed Catholic ceremony with pagan rite.

While the hierarchy of the Catholic Church remained fervently anti-Communist and closely aligned with the economic, political and military elite, during the early 1960s many rural Catholic priests became heavily influenced by liberation theology, supporting peasant leagues and development projects, and some even joined the guerrillas. Subsequently, the ruling class of generals, politicians and big landowners began to consider the Catholic Church as being riddled with communist sympathizers, and targeted perceived troublemakers accordingly. By the early 1980s, so many priests had been murdered by the state-sponsored death squads that the Catholic Church pulled out of the entire department of El Quiché in protest. In contrast, many evangelical missionaries preached the importance of an army victory over the guerrillas and, with their pro-business, anti-communist rhetoric, attracted many converts anxious to avoid suspicion and survive. In addition, the early evangelicals had made it a priority to learn the native Maya languages, and had the Bible translated into K'iche', Mam, Kaqchikel and other tongues.

However, it was the devastating **1976 earthquake** that really sparked the march of US evangelism in Guatemala. Church-backed disaster-relief programmes brought in millions of dollars of medicine, food and toys to those prepared to convert, and shattered villages were rebuilt with new schools and health centres. In the eyes of the impoverished rural villagers, Protestantism became linked with prosperity, and lively evangelical church services, where live music and singing were the norm, quickly gained huge popularity.

The movement received another boost in 1982, when **General Efrían Ríos Montt** seized power in a military coup to become Guatemala's first evangelical leader. The population was treated to Montt's marathon Sunday sermons, and a new wave of mission teams entered the country from the southern United States. For many Guatemalans, Ríos Montt represented the best and worst of evangelism: he was frenzied and fanatical, yet also fostered a reputation for strictness and probity (despite the terrible human-rights violations under his brief tenure). Ríos Montt was ousted after just seventeen months in power, though he was to dominate Guatemalan politics through the 1990s and early years of the new millennium together with Alfonso Portillo, another evangelical.

Guatemala is today the least Catholic country in Latin America, with around sixty percent of the population looking to the Vatican for guidance and about forty percent belonging to evangelical churches.

Friday affairs, but almost every village has its day. **Chichicastenango**'s vast Thursday and Sunday markets are probably Guatemala's most famous, and remain important gatherings for highlanders, though the tourist-orientated souvenir stalls are mushrooming here. But perhaps the most enjoyable of Guatemala's markets are well away from the Carretera Interamericana, in tiny, isolated hamlets. Up high in the folds of the mountains, in places like lonely Chajul or isolated Santa Eulalia, the pleasure is simply soaking up the scene, as traders and villagers barter and banter in the hushed clicks of the local dialect and near-whispers, in the unhurried commercial ritual that so defines Maya highland life.

Maya fiestas

Once a year every village, however small, indulges in an orgy of celebration in honour of its patron saint – you'll find a list of them at the end of each chapter. These **fiestas** are a great swirl of dance, music, religion, endless firecrackers, eating and outrageous drinking, and express the vitality of Indigenous culture. Everyone tries to return to their home town at fiesta time, with emigrants journeying from Guatemala City (and the USA) to join in the celebrations. Religious processions are given due importance, as the image of the local patron saint is paraded through the streets, accompanied by the elders of the *cofradía*, who dress in full regalia. The larger fiestas also involve funfairs and week-long markets. Traditional music is played with marimbas, drums and flutes; professional bands also may be hired, blasting out popular tunes through crackling PA systems.

Dance

Dance, too, is very much a part of fiestas, and incorporates routines and ideas that date from ancient Maya times. Dance **costumes** are incredibly elaborate, covered in mirrors and sequins, and have to be rented for the occasion. Despite the high cost, the dancers see their role both as an obligation – to tradition and the community – and an honour.

Most of the dances form an extension of dramatic tradition through which local history was retold in dance dramas. The **Dance of the Conquistadors** is one of the most popular, modelled on the Dance of the Moors and introduced by the Spanish as a re-enactment of the Conquest, although in some cases it's been instilled with a significance that can never have been intended by the invaders. The dancers often see no connection with the Conquest, but dance instead to release the spirits of the dead, a function perhaps closer to Maya religion than Catholicism. The **Palo Volador**, a dramatic spectacle in which men swing perilously to the ground from a 20m pole, certainly dates from the pre-Columbian era (these days you'll only see it in Cubulco, Chichicastenango and Joyabaj), as does the Dance of the Deer, while the Dance of the Bullfight and the Dance of the Volcano relate incidents from the Conquest itself.

Most of the dances do have steps to them, but the dancers are usually blind drunk and sway around as best they can in time to the music, sometimes tumbling over each other or even passing out – so don't expect to see anything too dainty.

In recent years a kitsch amalgamation of traditional and modern dance has evolved. It's quite common to find semi-professional dance troupes of young girls in tight-fitting costumes and fiesta-style masks performing mock-traditional dance steps to marimba with an electronic beat. Purists may condemn this bizarre combination of tradition and vulgarity as a bastardization of centuries-old Maya custom; many locals find it highly entertaining.

The Maya today

The Maya were the main victims of the decades-long **civil war**, which not only killed 160,000 highlanders and left a million homeless, but also attacked the very foundation of Indigenous culture in Guatemala. Many in the military viewed the Maya as inherently **subversive**, and communities were set against each other as men were conscripted into PAC paramilitary patrols and pressured to betray anyone showing signs of dissidence against the state.

But under civilian rule, a **Maya cultural revival** has steadily matured, as Guatemala's Indigenous people have pursued the freedom of organization, protest and participation denied them for centuries. Hundreds of schools have been founded to educate Maya children in their own tongues, increasing numbers of Indigenous writers and journalists have emerged, more and more Maya books and magazines are being published and *indígena* radio stations have been set up. The shifting mood has even influenced youth culture, with Maya shamanic courses becoming popular and ladino university students asserting their mixed-race identity and proclaiming a **Maya heritage**. Yet despite these changes Guatemala remains a seismically divided country. **Racism** is endemic and most Maya, still subject to institutionalized discrimination, live in poverty (seventy percent, according to the government's own figures).

Rigoberta Menchú and the Nobel Peace Prize

In 1992, five hundred years after Columbus reached the Americas, the Nobel committee awarded their Peace Prize to Rigoberta Menchú Tum, a 33-year-old K'iche' Maya woman who had campaigned tirelessly for peace in Guatemala and for the advancement of Indigenous people across the world. In their official statement, the Nobel Institute described Menchú as "a vivid symbol of peace and reconciliation across ethnic, cultural and social dividing lines".

Within Guatemala, however, the honour provoked controversy. Few doubted that Menchú had firm connections and deep sympathies with Guatemala's **guerrillas**, although after she was awarded the prize she distanced herself from the armed struggle. Nevertheless, many people argued that her support for armed uprising made her an inappropriate winner of a peace prize. Others feared that the prize would be interpreted as a vindication of the guerrillas and only serve to perpetuate the civil war.

Autobiography

The first volume of Menchú's autobiography, **I, Rigoberta Menchú**, shows her to be essentially a pacifist and suggests that her unspoken support for the guerrillas was very much a last resort. "For us, killing is something monstrous. And that's why we feel so angered by all the repression ... Even though the tortures and kidnappings had done our people a lot of harm, we shouldn't lose faith in change. This is when I began working in a peasant organization and went on to another stage of my life. There are other things, other ways."

Menchú's story is undeniably tragic, and her account offers a harrowing look into the darkest years of Guatemalan history and the plight of the nation's Indigenous people. However, the **accuracy** of sizeable parts of her life story, as recounted in her autobiography, were later challenged in *Rigoberta Menchú and the Story of All Poor Guatemalans*, an iconoclastic biography published in 1998 by David Stoll. Stoll concluded that substantial sections of the Menchú legend had been fabricated or greatly exaggerated, and that she had "drastically revised the prewar experience of her village to suit the needs of the revolutionary organization she had joined".

In *I, Rigoberta Menchú*, Menchú describes how the barbaric cruelty of the Guatemalan civil war affected her family, who were political activists, and how they were branded guerrilla sympathizers by the military. Menchú recounts the fight to protect the family farm from greedy ladinos, her family's days working in the plantations of the Pacific coast, and her lack of formal schooling. The deaths of her brother, mother and father at the hands of the armed forces are agonizingly retold. Expanding to cover the wider picture in Guatemala, Menchú condemns the massive disparities between the country's ladino and Maya, and rich and poor. The biography has gone on to sell more than five hundred thousand copies, while Menchú has been invited to speak at events and conferences all over the world. Campaigning for the rights of the Guatemalan Maya and other oppressed minorities from exile in Mexico, she frequently travelled to the United Nations in Geneva and New York to press her case. This period of the Nobel laureate's life is narrated in **Crossing Borders**, the second volume of her autobiography, and an altogether less traumatic and controversial read.

Return from exile

Rigoberta Menchú **returned to Guatemala** in 1994 as an iconic but divisive figure; in the global arena, however, her reputation was unblemished until the publication of David Stoll's **biography**. Stoll's book provided compelling evidence that Menchú's family's land dispute was an internecine family feud rather than a racially charged Indigenous-ladino altercation and that she had been educated at two private convent schools. He alleged a guerrilla past too.

After the biography's publication an international **furore** ensued, with allegations from *The New York Times* that she had received "a Nobel prize for lying". Menchú evaded responding directly to Stoll's charges, though admitted that she had received some formal education at a convent school in Chiantla. She later sought to distance herself somewhat from *I, Rigoberta Menchú*, and inferred the input of her editor and translator – Arturo Taracena, a guerrilla attaché – had distorted her testimony. Geir Lundestad, director of the Nobel Institute, has expressed support for Menchú, declaring that the decision to give Menchú the award was because of her work on behalf of Indigenous people, and not because of her family history.

As the dust settled, a roster of academics lined up to **support** Menchú's reputation, questioning Stoll's motives and defending the value of her *testimonio* – which, they reasoned, was recounting the civil-war experiences of Indigenous Guatemalans as a whole – and followed a tradition of Maya testimonial writing that dated back to the time of the Conquest. No one disputed that her mother, father and brothers died at the hands of the military (with another two hundred thousand Guatemalans). Her success bringing global attention to the terrible suffering inflicted on (and continuing repression of) Guatemala's Maya is incontestable, and her work on behalf of the world's Indigenous peoples has been unrelenting and highly effective. The two sides of the debate are set out in *The Rigoberta Menchú Controversy* published in 2001, a collection of articles edited by Arturo Arias.

Political career

Today, Menchú is admired by most Guatemalan Maya and the political left, mistrusted by most of the Guatemalan oligarchy, and tends to be despised by the military and those on the right. She was a goodwill ambassador for the Peace Accords in the Berger government, and through her foundation, campaigned for human and Indigenous rights in Guatemala, and beyond. Declaring "that there's no peace without justice" she has fought to end the impunity of the armed forces for their civil war atrocities and filed genocide charges in the international courts against the former military rulers.

Menchú contested both the 2007 and 2011 **presidential elections**, but only polled three percent of the vote on both occasions. She's closely involved in healthcare issues, with the aim of providing low-cost generic medicines to all, and education programmes in Maya regions. Menchu has campaigned against gender violence alongside UNAMG (National Union of Guatemalan Women) and for women's and children's rights with the Peace Jam Foundation.

Landscape and wildlife

Guatemala embraces an astonishingly diverse collection of environments, ranging from the permanently moist rainforests and mangroves of the Caribbean coast to the exposed *altiplano* highlands, where the ground can be hard with frost. Its wildlife is correspondingly varied; undisturbed forests provide a home to both temperate species from the north and tropical ones from the south, as well as a number of Indigenous species found nowhere else in the world.

The Pacific coast

Guatemala's **Pacific coastline** is marked by a thin strip of black volcanic sand, pounded by the surf. There are no natural harbours and boats have to take their chances in the breakers or launch from one of the piers (though Puerto Quetzal takes large, ocean-going ships). The sea itself provides a rich natural harvest of shrimp, tuna, snapper and mackerel, most of which go for export. The coastal waters are also ideal for sport-fishing. A couple of kilometres offshore, dorado, which grow to around 20kg, are plentiful, while farther out are marlin, sailfish, wahoo and skipjack.

The **beach** itself rises from the water to form a large sandbank, dotted with palm trees, behind which the land drops off into low-lying mangrove swamps and canals. In the east, from San José to the border, the **Chiquimulilla Canal** runs behind the beach for around 100km. For most of the way it's no more than a narrow strip of water, but here and there it fans out into swamps, creating a maze of waterways that are an ideal breeding ground for young fish, waterfowl and a range of small mammals. The sandy shoreline is an ideal nesting site for three species of **sea turtle**, including the giant leatherback (see page 186), which periodically emerge from the water, drag themselves up the beach and deposit a clutch of eggs before hauling their weight back into the water. At Monterrico, east of San José, a nature reserve protects a small section of the coastline for the benefit of the turtles, and with luck you might see one here.

The **Reserva Monterrico–Hawaii** is the best place to see wildlife on the Pacific coast, as it includes a superb **mangrove swamp**, which you can easily explore by boat. The mangroves are mixed in with water lilies, bulrushes and tropical hardwoods, among which you'll see **herons**, **kingfishers** and an array of **ducks** including **muscovies** and **white whistling ducks**. In the area around Monterrico, flocks of **wood stork** are common, and you might also see the **white ibis** or the occasional **great jabiru**, a massive stork that nests in the area. With real perseverance and a bit of luck you might also catch a glimpse of a **racoon**, **anteater** or **opossum**. You'll also be able to see **alligators** and **iguanas**, if not in the wild then at the reserve headquarters where they are kept in a breeding programme. Other birds you might see almost anywhere along the coast include **plover**, **coot** and **tern**, and a number of winter migrants including **white** and **brown pelican**.

Between the shore and the foothills of the highlands, the **coastal plain** is an intensely fertile and heavily farmed area, where the volcanic and alluvial soils are ideal for sugar cane, cotton, palm oil, banana and rubber plantations and cattle ranches. In recent years soya and sorghum, which require less labour, have been added to this list. Guatemala's coastal **agribusiness** is high cost and high yield: the soils are treated chemically and the crops regularly sprayed with a cocktail of pesticides, herbicides and fertilizers. There's little land that remains untouched by the hand of commercial agriculture so it's hard to imagine what this must once have looked like, but it was almost certainly very similar to Petén, a mixture of savannah and rainforest supporting a rich array of wildlife. These days it's only the swamps, steep hillsides and towering hedges that give any hint of its former glory, although beautiful flocks of white **snowy** and **cattle egret** feed alongside the beef cattle.

Finally, one particularly interesting lowland species is the **oropendola**, a large oriole that builds a long, woven nest hanging from trees and telephone wires. They tend to nest in colonies and a single tree might support fifty nests. You'll probably notice the nests more than the birds, which thrive throughout Guatemala and neighbouring countries.

The Boca Costa

Approaching the highlands, the coastal plain starts to slope up towards a string of volcanic cones, and this section of well-drained hillside is known as the **Boca Costa**. The volcanic soils, high rainfall and good drainage combine to make it ideal for growing **coffee**, and it's here that some of Guatemala's best beans are produced, with rows of olive-green bushes ranked beneath shady trees.

Where the land is unsuitable for coffee, lush tropical forest still grows, clinging to the hills. As you head up into the highlands, through deeply cleft valleys, you pass through some of this superb forest, dripping with moss-covered vines, bromeliads and orchids. Close to the most active volcanoes, in areas where farming has not disturbed the environment, are some incredibly rich ecosystems. Around Volcán Santiaguito near Quetzaltenango, more than 120 species of bird have been sighted, including some real rarities such as **solitary eagle**, **quetzal** and **highland guan**. The **azure-rumped tanager**, **maroon-chested ground dove** and **Pacific parakeet** are endemic to this region. Cayaya Birding (cayaya-birding.com), a specialist tour operator, runs excellent trips to the Boca Costa region.

The highlands

The highlands proper begin with a chain of **volcanoes**. There are 37 peaks in all, the main backbone ranged in a direct line that runs parallel with the Pacific coastline from the southwestern border with Mexico into El Salvador. (In the eastern highlands, away from the main chain, there's another sprinkling of older, less-spectacular weathered cones.) The highest of the main peaks is **Tajumulco** (4220m), near the Mexican border, while three highly active cones – **Fuego**, **Pacaya** and **Santiaguito** – all belch sulphurous fumes, volcanic ash and the occasional fountain of molten rock. Beneath the surface their subterranean fires heat the bedrock, and in several places hot-spring water emerges, offering the luxury of a warm, mineral-rich bath, the best of which is Fuentes Georginas (see page 147).

Highland lakes

On the southern side of the central highlands, volcanic peaks surround two large lakes, Lago de Amatitlán and Lago de Atitlán, both of which are set in superb countryside. South of Guatemala City, **Lago de Amatitlán** has suffered years of environmental mismanagement, and its waters remain polluted.

Farther west, **Lago de Atitlán** is still spectacularly beautiful, with crystal-blue water, but increasing tourist development and a population explosion threaten to damage its delicate ecological balance, and periodic **cyanobacteria** outbreaks affect the lake (see page 117).

Central valleys

On the northern side of the volcanic ridge are the **central valleys** of the highlands, a complex mixture of sweeping bowls, steep-sided valleys, open plateaux and jagged peaks. This central area is home to the vast majority of Guatemala's population, and all the available land is intensely farmed, with hillsides carved into workable terraces and portioned up into a patchwork of small fields. Here the land is farmed by *campesinos* using techniques that predate the arrival of the Spanish. The *milpa* is the mainstay of Maya farming practices: a field is cleared, usually by slash-and-burn, and planted with maize as the main crop, with beans, chillies and squash grown as well. Traditionally, the land is rotated between *milpa* and pasture, and also left fallow for a while, but in some areas it's now under constant pressure, the fertility of the soil is virtually exhausted and only with the assistance of fertilizer can it still produce a worthwhile crop. The pressure on land is immense and each generation is forced to farm more marginal territory, planting on steep hillsides where exposed soil is soon washed into the valley below.

Some areas remain off-limits to farmers, however, and substantial tracts of the highlands are still **forested**. In the cool valleys of the central highlands, pine trees dominate, intermixed with oak, cedar and fir. To the south, on the volcanic slopes and in the warmth of deep-cut valleys, lush subtropical forest thrives in a world kept permanently moist – similar in many ways to the forest of Verapaz, where constant rain fosters the growth of cloud forest.

Altiplano

Heading on to the north, the land rises to form several **mountain ranges**. The largest of these are the Cuchumatanes, a massive chain of granite peaks that reach a height of 3837m above the town of Huehuetenango. Further to the east there are several smaller ranges such as the Sierra de Chuacús, the Sierra de las Minas and the Sierra de Chamá. The high peaks support stunted trees and open grassland, used for grazing sheep and cattle, but are too cold for maize and most other crops. Guatemalans call this high ground the *altiplano*.

Birdlife

Birdlife is plentiful throughout the highlands; you'll see a variety of **hummingbirds**, flocks of screeching **parakeets**, **swifts**, **egrets** and the ever-present **vultures**. Slightly less commonplace are the **quails** and **wood partridges**, **white-tailed pigeons** and several species of dove including the **little Inca** and the **white-winged dove**. Last but by no means least is the **quetzal**, which has been revered since Maya times. The male quetzal has fantastic green tail-feathers which snake behind it through the air as it flies.

Near Cobán is the **Biotopo del Quetzal** (see page 222), a protected area of **cloud forest** in the department of Baja Verapaz where quetzals breed. You might also try looking for Guatemala's national bird in the remote mountains of the Sierra de Caquipec to the northeast, or in the Chelemhá forest reserve (see page 225) south of Cobán.

The rainforests of Petén

Northeast of the highlands the land drops away into the **rainforests** of Petén, a large chunk of which remains undisturbed, although recent oil finds and a huge influx of cattle ranchers, timber merchants and migrant settlers have cut a swathe through virgin

ATITLÁN'S LOST GREBE

Atitlán's ecosystem was upset as far back as 1958, when **black bass** were introduced in a bid to create sportfishing. The bass is a rapacious fish and in no time at all its presence had reshaped the food chain. Smaller fish became increasingly rare, as did crabs, frogs, insects and small mammals. The **Atitlán grebe**, a small, flightless water bird unique to the lake, was worst hit. Young grebes were gobbled up by the hungry bass, and by 1965 just eighty of them survived. By 1984, falling water levels, combined with tourist development of the lakeshore, cut their numbers by a further thirty. Today the bird is extinct.

jungle in the last forty years. The forest of Petén extends across the Mexican border, where it merges with the Lacandón and Campeche rainforests, and into Belize, where it skirts around the lower slopes of the Maya Mountains, reaching to the Caribbean coast.

Today around forty percent of Petén is still covered by **primary forest**, with a canopy that towers between 30m and 50m above the forest floor, made up of hundreds of species of tree, including ceiba, mahogany, aguacate, ebony and sapodilla. The combination of a year-round growing season, plenty of moisture and millions of years of evolution have produced an environment that supports thousands of species of plants and trees. While temperate forests tend to be dominated by a single species – fir, oak or beech, say – it's diversity that characterizes the tropical forest. Each species is specifically adapted to fit into a particular ecological niche, where it receives a precise amount of light and moisture.

This biological storehouse has yielded some astonishing **discoveries**. Steroid hormones, such as cortisone, and diosgenin, the active ingredient in birth-control pills, were developed from wild yams found in these forests, and the highly potent anaesthetic tetrodoxin is derived from a species of Central American frog.

Ecosystem

Despite its size and diversity, the forest is surprisingly **fragile**. It forms a closed system in which nutrients are continuously recycled and decaying plant matter fuels new growth. The forest floor is a spongy mass of roots, fungi, mosses, bacteria and micro-organisms, in which nutrients are stored, broken down with the assistance of insects and chemical decay, and gradually released to the waiting roots and fresh seedlings. The thick canopy prevents much light reaching the forest floor, ensuring that the soil remains damp but warm, a hotbed of chemical activity. After the death of a large tree, a flurry of growth ensues as new light reaches the forest floor, and in no time at all a young tree rises to fill the gap. But once the trees are removed the soil is highly vulnerable, deprived of its main source of fertility. Exposed to the harsh tropical sun and direct rainfall, an area of cleared forest soon becomes prone to flooding and drought. Recently cleared land will contain enough nutrients for four or five years of good growth, but soon afterwards its usefulness declines rapidly and within twenty years it will be almost completely barren. If the trees are stripped from a large area, soil erosion will silt the rivers and parched soils will disrupt local rainfall patterns.

Human influence

Settlement needn't mean the end of the rainforest. Only one small group of Maya, the Lacandones, still farm the forest using traditional methods. They allow the existing trees to point them in the right direction, avoiding areas that support mahogany, as they tend to be too wet, and searching out ceiba and *ramón* trees, which thrive in rich, well-drained soils.

In April a patch of forest is burnt down and then, to prevent soil erosion, planted with fast-growing trees such as banana and papaya, and with root crops to fix the soil. A few weeks later they plant their main crops: maize and a selection of others, from garlic to sweet potatoes. Every inch of the soil is covered in growth, a method that mimics the forest and thereby protects the soil. The same land is cultivated for three or four years and then allowed to return to its wild state – although they continue to harvest from the fruit-bearing plants – and in due course return to the same area. The whole process is in perfect harmony with the forest, extracting only what it can afford to lose and ensuring that it remains fertile.

Sadly, the traditional farming methods of the Lacandones are now very rarely practised. New settlers burn the forest and plant grass for cattle pasture, and vast areas of former jungle now have very little biodiversity or fertility. This shift away from sustainable practices is only accelerating the loss of rainforest and contributing to the ongoing environmental crisis in the region.

Wildlife

In its undisturbed state the rainforest is still superbly beautiful and is home to an incredible range of **wildlife**. Among the birds, the spectacular scarlet, blue and emerald-green **ocellated turkey**, found only in Petén, is perhaps the most famous. But the forest is also home to three species of **toucan**, **motmot** (a type of bird of paradise), several species of **parrot** including **Aztec** and **green parakeets** and the endangered **scarlet macaw**, which is said to live to at least fifty. As in the highlands, **hummingbirds**, **buzzards** and **hawks** are all common. A surprising number of these can be seen fairly easily in the **Parque Nacional Tikal**, particularly if you hang around until sunset.

Although **mammals** are widespread, they are almost always elusive, and your best chance of seeing them is at the bigger reserves and archeological sites, where they may have lost some of their fear of humans. At many forest sites you'll almost certainly see **monkeys**, including the acrobatically agile **spider** and the highly social **howlers**, which emit a chilling, deep-throated roar. The largest land animal in Guatemala is the **tapir** (dante), weighing up to 300kg, and usually found near water. Tapirs are endangered and you're not likely to see one without a guide. Two species of **peccary** (wild pig), the collared and the white-lipped, wander the forest floors in large groups, seeking out roots and palm nuts. The smaller herbivores include the **paca** (also known as the tepescuintle and agouti), a rodent about the size of a piglet, which is hunted everywhere for food. You'll often see **coati** (locally known as *pizotes*), inquisitive and intelligent members of the raccoon family, foraging in the leaf litter around archeological sites with their long snouts, often in family groups of several dozen. Coatis and small **grey foxes** are frequently seen at Tikal, and in many places you can see **opossums** and **armadillos**.

Five species of wild **cat** are found in the region, though most are now rare outside the protected areas. **Jaguars** (called *tigres* in Guatemala) formerly ranged over the whole of the country, but today the densest population is found in the northern Petén, though they are very rarely seen. **Pumas** live in remote forest areas; less rare but still uncommon are the much smaller **ocelot** and the **margay**, which is about the size of a large domestic cat. The **jaguarundi** is the smallest and commonest of the wild cats, and as it hunts during the day you might spot one on a trail.

Take a trip along almost any river in Petén and you've a good chance of seeing **green iguanas**, **mud turtles** or **Central American river turtles** sunning themselves on logs. **Egrets** and **kingfishers** fish from overhanging branches, while large rivers such as Río de la Pasión and lakes, including Lago de Petexbatún, are also rich, packed with **snook**, **tarpon** and **mullet**.

Crocodiles are becoming increasingly common in Petén, after previously being hunted almost to extinction, and are now frequently spotted at Lago de Yaxhá and Laguna Perdida. They are not dangerous to humans unless they are very large – at least 3m long – but heed the warnings of locals if they advise against swimming in particular lagoons.

Although there are at least fifty species of **snake** in the region, only a few are venomous and you're unlikely to see one. The **boa constrictor** is one of the most common and also is the largest, growing up to 4m, though it poses no threat to humans. Others you might see are **coral snakes** (which are venomous) and **false coral snakes** (which are not); in theory they're easily distinguished by noting the arrangement of adjacent colours in the stripes, but it's best to admire all snakes from a distance unless you're an expert.

At night in the forest, you'll hear the characteristic chorus of frog mating calls, and you'll also frequently find the **red-eyed tree frog** – a beautiful pale green creature about the size of the top joint of your thumb – in your shower in any rustic cabin. Less appealing perhaps are the giant **marine toads**, weighing in at up to 1kg and growing to more than 20cm. Like most frogs and toads, the marine toad has

CONSERVATION ORGANIZATIONS

Arcas (ⓦ arcasguatemala.org). Conservation group that provides a refuge for wild animals in Petén (see page 250), runs a sea turtle project in Hawaii area (see page 351) and combats wildlife trafficking.

Centre for Conservation Studies (CECON; ⓦ cecon.usac.edu.gt). A department of Guatemala's University of San Carlos. CECON manages and conducts scientific research in all the nation's *biotopes*; these are often the best-protected areas within reserves, such as Cerro Cahuí in Petén and Monterrico on the Pacific coast.

Defensores de la Naturaleza (ⓦ defensores.org.gt). Ecological group that combines conservation with sustainable tourism in areas including the Bocas del Polochic reserve (see page 207).

Pacunam (ⓦ pacunam.org). Works with communities inside the Mirador Basin Biosphere Reserve, promoting sustainable farming, forestry and tourism.

ProPetén (ⓦ propeten.org). Petén's largest NGO works on numerous conservation and resource-management projects in the Maya Biosphere Reserve, including Las Guacamayas, a biological station near Waka' (El Perú) ruins. Volunteers are needed.

toxic glands, and its toxin has hallucinogenic properties – an effect put to use in ceremonies by the ancient Maya, who licked the toad's glands and interpreted the resultant visions.

The Caribbean coast

Much of Guatemala's small **Caribbean coastline** is protected as part of the Biotopo Punta del Manabique, a rich wetland habitat, while just inland there are several additional, ecologically diverse reserves around the Río Dulce and Lago de Izabal. This region offers some of the country's finest birdwatching territory.

Immediately inland from the Guatemalan coast, the **littoral forest** is characterized by salt-tolerant plants, often with tough, waxy leaves which help conserve water. Species include red and white **gumbo limbo**, **black poisonwood**, **zericote**, **palmetto** and, of course, the **coconut**, which typifies Caribbean beaches, though it's not actually a native. The littoral forest supports a very high density of fauna, especially **migrating birds**.

Much of the shoreline around Punta del Manabique and Lívingston is still largely covered with **mangroves**, which play an important economic role, not merely as nurseries for commercial fish species but also for their stabilization of the shoreline and their ability to absorb the force of gales and hurricanes. The dominant species of the coastal fringe is the **red mangrove**, although in due course it undermines its own environment by consolidating the sea bed until it becomes more suitable for the less salt-tolerant black and white mangroves. The basis of the shoreline food chain is the nutrient-rich mud, held in place by the mangroves, whose roots are home to **oysters** and **sponges**. In the shallows, "meadows" of **seagrass beds** provide nurseries for many fish and invertebrates, and pasture for conch and turtles.

The coastal zone is home to sparse numbers of the **West Indian manatee**, which can reach 4m in length and weigh up to 450kg. These placid and shy creatures move between freshwater lagoons and the open sea. They were once hunted for their meat but are now protected, and the Biotopo Chocón Machacas has been established in the Golfete region of the Río Dulce as a **manatee sanctuary**. Despite this measure, the manatee remains very rare in Guatemala and you've a much better chance of spotting one in Belize, where their habitat is much less depleted.

Books

Guatemala has inspired much writing in the past few decades, with the civil war and political turmoil spawning plenty of non-fiction. There has also been a recent boom in titles about Indigenous issues and ancient Maya culture. Titles that we especially recommend are marked with the ★ symbol.

TRAVEL

Peter Canby *Heart of the Sky – Travels Among the Maya*. The author treads a familiar path through the Maya World, encountering an interesting collection of expats, Mayanists, priests, Guatemala City's idle rich and a female shaman. An accessible and informative account.

Anthony Daniels *Sweet Waist of America*. A delight to read. Daniels takes a refreshingly even-handed approach to Guatemala and comes up with a fascinating cocktail of people and politics, discarding the stereotypes that litter most books on Central America.

Thomas Gage *Travels in the New World*. Unusual account of a Dominican friar's travels through Mexico and Central America between 1635 and 1637, including some intriguing insights into colonial life as well as some great attacks on the greed and pomposity of the Catholic Church abroad.

★ **Aldous Huxley** *Beyond the Mexique Bay*. Huxley's travels in 1934 took him from Belize through Guatemala to Mexico, swept on by his fascination for history and religion, and sprouting bizarre theories on the basis of everything he saw. There are some terrific descriptions of Maya sites and Indigenous culture, with superb one-liners summing up people and places.

Jonathan Evan Maslow *Bird of Life, Bird of Death*. Maslow sets out in search of the quetzal, using the bird's uncertain future as a metaphor for wartime Guatemala in a work that merges travel and political comment.

Christopher Shaw *Sacred Monkey River: A Canoe Trip with the Gods*. Engaging account of the author's canoe journey along the Usumacinta River that divides Mexico and Guatemala. Nicely crafted prose is enlivened with convincing analysis of ancient Maya cosmology and culture, and the contemporary political and environmental issues affecting the region.

★ **John Lloyd Stephens** *Incidents of Travel in Central America, Chiapas, and Yucatán*. Stephens was a classic nineteenth-century explorer. Acting as US ambassador to Central America, he indulged his own enthusiasm for archeology; while the republics fought it out among themselves, he was wading through the jungle stumbling across ancient cities. His journals, told in a restrained Victorian style punctuated with sudden waves of enthusiasm, make great reading. Some editions include fantastic illustrations by Catherwood of the ruins overgrown with tropical rainforest.

★ **Ronald Wright** *Time Among the Maya*. A vivid and sympathetic account of travels from Belize through Guatemala, Chiapas and Yucatán, meeting the Maya and exploring their obsession with time. The book's twin points of interest are the ancient Maya and the civil-war violence. Certainly one of the best travel books on the area.

FICTION, AUTOBIOGRAPHY AND POETRY

★ **Miguel Ángel Asturias** *Hombres de Maíz*. Guatemala's most famous author, Asturias is deeply indebted to Guatemalan history and culture in his work. "Men of Maize" is his masterpiece, classically Latin American in its magic-realist style, and bound up in the complexity of Indigenous culture. His other works include *El Señor Presidente*, a grotesque portrayal of social chaos and dictatorial rule; *El Papa Verde*, which explores the murky world of the United Fruit Company; and *Weekend in Guatemala*, describing the downfall of the Árbenz government. Asturias won the Nobel Prize for Literature before his death in 1974.

Paul Bowles *Up Above the World*. Bowles is at his chilling, understated best in this novel based on experiences of Guatemala in the late 1930s.

★ **Francisco Goldman** *The Long Night of White Chickens*. Drawing on the stylistic complexity of Latin American fiction, this novel tells the tale of a young Guatemalan orphan who flees to the US and works as a maid. When she finally returns home to her politically turbulent nation, she is murdered. It's an interesting and ambitious story, though its chaotic timeline gives the book a Byzantine intricacy that makes it a dense and laborious read at times.

Norman Lewis *The Volcano Above Us*. Vaguely historical novel published in 1957 that pulls together all the main elements of Guatemala's history. The image that it summons is one of depressing drudgery and eternal conflict, set against a background of repression and racism. In the light of what's happened it has a certain prophetic quality, and remains gripping despite its miserable conclusions.

Kathy Reichs *Grave Secrets*. In this compelling thriller, forensic scientist Tempe Brennon flies to Guatemala to investigate the mass graves of civil-war victims, but is then persuaded to look into the disappearances of four wealthy girls from the capital. Her efforts are thwarted by violence, judicial inadequacies and corruption.

HISTORY, POLITICS AND SOCIETY

Robert Brenneman *Homies and Hermanos*. An engaging investigation into connections between ex-street gang members and evangelical Christianity. Based on interviews with dozens of ex-gangsters.

Edward F. Fisher and R. McKenna Brown (eds) *Maya Cultural Activism in Guatemala*. Effectual summary of the Indigenous movement in Guatemala, with strong chapters on clothing and identity, and the revival of interest in Maya language and hieroglyphic writing.

★ **Francisco Goldman** *The Art of Political Murder*. Investigative journalism at its very best, this is a meticulously researched and passionately told account of the Geradi murder case, and represents the culmination of seven years of reporting. Goldman weaves absorbing profiles of the characters – assassins, military intelligence officers, street kids and Church figures – into the tale to pull off a riveting whodunit. Winner of multiple awards.

Greg Grandin (et al) *The Guatemala Reader: History, Culture, Politics*. Published in late 2011, this is an accessible overview of the nation. Grandin's The *Blood of Guatemala – A History of Race and Nation* is more specialist, a study of Quetzaltenango's elite class of K'iche' Maya and their impact between the mid-eighteenth century and the fall of the Árbenz government in 1954.

★ **Jim Handy** *Gift of the Devil*. Superb history of Guatemala: concise and readable with a sharp focus on the Maya population and the brief period of socialist government. Though written in the mid-1980s, the book nevertheless manages to offer a convincing perspective on the modern Guatemalan state. By no means objective, Handy sets out to expose the development of oppression and point the finger at the oppressors.

Severo Martínez Peláez *La Patria Del Criollo: An Interpretation of Colonial Guatemala*. Damning examination of colonial society in Guatemala and its utter dependence on Maya labour. Written in 1970 by a leading Guatemalan historian and leftist political activist, it remains remarkably relevant today.

Víctor Perera *Unfinished Conquest*. Extremely readable account of the civil-war tragedy, plus comprehensive attention to the deep inequalities that affect the late author's native country. The book's strength comes from the extensive interviews with both ordinary and influential Guatemalans and incisive analysis of recent history.

REMHI *Guatemala: Never Again*. Abridged translation of the seminal report published by the Catholic Church of Guatemala into the civil-war atrocities.

Victoria Sanford *Buried Secrets: Truth and Human Rights in Guatemala*. A powerful, exhaustively researched investigative study of *la violencia* is based on more than four hundred interviews with massacre survivors, the military and guerrilla forces.

Jennifer Schirmer *The Guatemalan Military Project: A Violence Called Democracy*. Offers an insider's view of the ideology and mentality of the Guatemalan armed forces, based on numerous interviews with senior officers, six ex-defence ministers and three former heads of state.

Stephen Schlesinger and Stephen Kinzer *Bitter Fruit: The Untold Story of the American Coup in Guatemala*. This book traces the US connection in the 1954 coup, delving into the murky water of United Fruit Company politics and showing that the invading army received its orders from the White House.

Daniel Wilkinson *Silence on the Mountain: Stories of Betrayal and Forgetting in Guatemala*. Part historical narrative, part personal travelogue and part public testimony, Wilkinson's book gives a voice to those who suffered most during Guatemala's civil war.

INDIGENOUS CULTURE

Jennifer L. Burrell *Maya After War: Conflict, Power, and Politics in Guatemala*. Published in 2013, and based on twenty years of research, this book skilfully deals with questions of Indigenous culture, identity and migration in the highland Maya community.

Krystyna Deuss *Shamans, Witches, and Maya Priests: Native Religion & Ritual in Highland Guatemala*. A unique and fascinating study of Maya customs in the remote Cuchumatanes – in villages where the Maya calendar is still in use – based on decades of research and beautifully illustrated with photographs.

Grant D. Jones *The Conquest of the Maya Kingdom*. Massive academic tome that's also a fascinating history of the Itza Maya and a gripping tale of how the Spanish entered and finally defeated the last independent Maya kingdom, at Tayasal.

Mary Jo McConahay *Maya Roads: One Woman's Journey Among the People of the Rainforest*. A well-informed and sympathetic study of the lowland Maya from a highly experienced and knowledgeable journalist.

★ **Rigoberta Menchú** *I, Rigoberta Menchú – An Indian Woman in Guatemala* and *Crossing Borders*. Momentous story of one of Latin America's most remarkable women, Nobel Peace Prize-winner Rigoberta Menchú (see page 341). The first volume is a horrific account of family life in the Maya highlands, recording how Menchú's family were targeted, terrorized and murdered by the military. The book also reveals much concerning K'iche' Maya cultural traditions and the enormous gulf between the ladino and Indigenous societies in Guatemala. The second volume is more optimistic, documenting Menchú's life in exile in Mexico, her work at the United Nations fighting for Indigenous people and her return to Guatemala. Although Menchú's courage and determination are undeniable, some, including author David Stoll (see below), have criticized the accuracy of parts of her story.

★ **James D. Sexton** (ed) *Son of Tecún Umán; Campesino; Ignacio* and *Joseño*. Four excellent autobiographical accounts written by a Tz'utujil Maya from Lago de Atitlán. The books give an impression of life inside a modern Maya village, bound up in poverty, local politics and a mixture of Catholicism and superstition, and manage to avoid the stereotyping that usually characterizes descriptions of the Indigenous population. Sexton's *Mayan Folktales: Folklore from Lake Atitlán, Guatemala* and *Heart of Heaven, Heart of Earth and other Maya Folktales* unveil a world of wonderfully imaginative fables that underpin a society's strict moral codes and notions of justice and fate.

David Stoll *Rigoberta Menchú and the Story of All Poor Guatemalans*. Iconoclastic biography that delivers a formidable broadside against considerable pieces of the Menchú legend, though some academics have criticized Stoll's literal interpretation of Maya testimonial traditions.

★ **The Popol Vuh** The great K'iche' creation epic, written shortly after the Conquest, is an amazing swirl of mythological characters and their wanderings through the K'iche' highlands, tracing the tribe's ancestry. There are several versions on offer though many of them are half-hearted, including only a few lines from the original. The best is translated by Dennis Tedlock.

ARCHEOLOGY

Maya archeology is changing so rapidly that many of the books published in the last millennium are well out of date with the latest Preclassic research.

Michael D. Coe and Stephen Houston *The Maya*. Now in its nineth edition, this clear and comprehensive introduction to Maya archeology is one of the best on offer, and the latest edition includes important recent developments from Preclassic sites. Coe has also written several more weighty, academic volumes. His *Breaking the Maya Code* owes much to the fact that Coe was at many of the most important meetings leading to the breakthrough of glyph-reading. *The Art of the Maya Scribe*, written with Justin Kerr is a wonderfully illustrated history of Maya writing which also takes the reader on a journey through the Maya universe and mythology via the astonishingly skilful calligraphy of the Maya artists themselves.

★ **David Drew** *The Lost Chronicles of the Maya Kings*. Superbly readable and engaging, Drew draws on a wealth of material to deliver an excellent account of ancient Maya political history. The alliances and rivalries between the main cities are skilfully unravelled, and there's a particularly revealing analysis of Late Classic Maya power politics.

Francisco Estrada-Belli *The First Maya Civilization: Ritual and Power Before the Classic Period*. Perhaps the first book to really get to grips with the importance of the Preclassic Maya, this concise and very readable book is based on research from the cities of Cival and Holmul in Petén.

Peter D. Harrison *The Lords of Tikal*. Meticulous study of the Petén metropolis that includes hieroglyphic readings and a tremendous amount of detail about the city's monuments and artefacts and the rulers who commissioned them, Temple V excepted.

★ **Simon Martin and Nikolai Grube** *Chronicle of the Maya Kings and Queens*. Published to universal acclaim, this groundbreaking work is based on exhaustive epigraphic studies, and the re-reading of previously translated glyphic texts. It also includes the historical records of several key Maya cities – including Tikal, Naranjo and Dos Pilas – complete with biographies of 152 kings and four queens, full dynastic sequences and all the key battles. As Michael D. Coe, author of *The Maya*, says: "There's nothing else like this book. It supersedes everything else ever written on Maya history."

Mary Miller and Simon Martin *Courtly Art of the Ancient Maya*. Sumptuously illustrated with images of jade, stucco, stonework and pottery artistry, this book also explains the rituals and customs that defined daily life in the royal courts.

Linda Schele and David Freidel (et al). The authors, in the forefront of "new archeology", have been personally responsible for decoding many Maya glyphs. *A Forest of Kings: The Untold Story of the Ancient Maya*, in conjunction with *The Blood of Kings* by Linda Schele and Mary Miller, shows that, far from being governed by peaceful astronomer-priests, the ancient Maya were ruled by hereditary kings, lived in populous, aggressive city-states and engaged in a continual entanglement of alliances and war. *The Maya Cosmos* by Schele, Freidel and Joy Parker, is perhaps more difficult to read, but it also examines Maya ritual and religion in a unique and far-reaching way. *The Code of Kings*, written in collaboration with Peter Matthews and lavishly illustrated, examines the significance of the monuments at selected Maya sites and is a classic of epigraphic interpretation.

Peter Schmidt, Mercedes de la Garza and Enrique Nalda (eds) *Maya Civilization*. Monumental collaborative effort, with sections written by many prominent Mayanists, lusciously presented with more than six hundred colour images of some breathtaking Maya art.

Robert Sharer *The Ancient Maya*. Classic, comprehensive account of Maya civilization. Required reading for archeology students, it provides a fascinating reference for the non-expert, though the latest advances in Preclassic knowledge are excluded.

J. Eric S. Thompson *The Rise and Fall of the Maya Civilization*. Thompson is a major authority on the ancient Maya, a leading Mesoamerican archeologist, and this makes for an accessible read, though obviously our knowledge has advanced considerably since it was first published in 1954.

WILDLIFE AND THE ENVIRONMENT

Les Betelsky *Belize and Northern Guatemala*. Other specialist wildlife guides may cover the subject in more detail, but this is a reasonably comprehensive and well-organized single-volume guide to the mammals, birds, reptiles, amphibians and marine life of the region.

Steve Howe and Sophie Webb *The Birds of Mexico and Northern Central America*. A tremendous work, this is the definitive book on the region's birds. Essential for all serious birders.

GUIDES

Elizabeth Bell *Antigua Guatemala: The City and Its Heritage*. The best guide to Antigua, written by a long-term resident and prominent historian. It's available from several shops in Antigua, as is the author's *Lent and Easter Week in Antigua*.

William Coe *Tikal: A Handbook to the Ancient Maya Ruins*. A detailed account of the site, usually available at the ruins, though it does not include the latest findings. The map of the main area is essential for in-depth exploration.

Joyce Kelly *Archaeological Guide to Northern Central America*. Detailed, practical guide to dozens of sites with excellent photographs and accurate maps. This volume covers 38 Maya sites and 25 museums, though it's now a little outdated.

Barbara Balchin de Koose *Antigua for You*. A very comprehensive account of Antigua's colonial architectural wonders.

Lily de Jongh Osborne *Four Keys to Guatemala*. One of the best guides to Guatemala ever written, including a short piece on every aspect of the country's history and culture. Osborne also wrote a good book on Indigenous arts and crafts in Guatemala. Both books are now out of print.

COOKBOOKS

Catalina B. Figueroa *Cocina Guatemalteca: Arte, Sabor y Colorido*. Features a comprehensive range of national dishes and regional specialities.

Copeland Marks *False Tongues and Sunday Bread: A Guatemalan and Maya Cookbook*. If you've travelled widely in Guatemala and suffered an endless onslaught of beans and tortillas, it may be a surprise to find that the country has an established culinary tradition. Marks' book includes many fine Guatemalan recipes like chicken with *mole* sauce as well as the staples like black beans.

Language

Guatemala takes in a bewildering collection of languages, but fortunately for the traveller, Spanish will get you by in all but the most remote areas. Some middle-class Guatemalans speak English, but it's essential to learn at least a few Spanish phrases or you're in for a frustrating time.

The **Spanish** spoken in Guatemala has a strong Latin American flavour to it, and if you're used to the dainty intonation of Madrid then this may come as something of a surprise. If you're new to Spanish, it's a lot easier to pick up than the Castilian version. Everywhere you'll find people willing to make an effort to understand you, eager to speak to passing gringos.

The rules of **pronunciation** are pretty straightforward and, once you get to know them, strictly observed. Unless there's an accent, words ending in d, l, r and z are **stressed** on the last syllable, all others on the second last. All **vowels** are pure and short.

A somewhere between the A sound of back and that of "father".
E as in get.
I as in police.
O as in hot.
U as in rule.
C is soft before E and I, hard otherwise: *cerca* is pronounced "serka".
G works the same way, a guttural H sound (like the ch in "loch") before E or I, a hard G elsewhere – *gigante* becomes "higante".
H is always silent.
J is the same sound as a guttural G: *jamón* is pronounced "hamON".
LL sounds like an English Y: *tortilla* is pronounced "torteeya".
N is as in English unless it has a tilde (accent) over it, when it becomes NY: *mañana* sounds like "manyana".
QU is pronounced like an English K.
R is rolled, RR doubly so.
V sounds more like B, *vino* becoming "beano".
X is slightly softer than in English – sometimes almost SH: *Xela* is pronounced "shela".
Z is the same as a soft C, so *cerveza* becomes "servesa".

Below is a list of a few essential words and phrases, though if you're travelling for any length of time a **dictionary** or **phrase book** is obviously a worthwhile investment. Any good Spanish phrase book or dictionary should see you through in Guatemala, but specific Latin American ones are the most useful. The *University of Chicago Dictionary of Latin-American Spanish* is a good all-rounder, while *Mexican Spanish: A Rough Guide Phrasebook* has a menu reader, rundown of colloquialisms and a number of cultural tips that are relevant to many Latin American countries, including Guatemala. If you're using a dictionary, remember that in Spanish, CH, LL and Ñ count as separate letters and are listed after the Cs, Ls and Ns respectively. If you really want to get to grips with Guatemalan slang, swear words and expressions, look out for *¿Qué Onda Vos?* by Juan Carlos Martínez López and Mark Brazaitis, which includes a superb roundup of *guatemaltequismos*. It's available from several bookshops in Antigua.

Maya languages

After years of state-backed *castellanización* programmes when Spanish was the only language of tuition and Maya schoolchildren were left virtual classroom spectators, a network of Maya schools has now been established, with hundreds alone in Q'eqchi' areas of Guatemala. A strong Indigenous cultural movement has now developed in the country, intent on preserving the two dozen or so **Maya languages** still spoken. Because the Maya birth rate is much higher than the ladino, there is now every chance that the main languages like K'iche', Kaqchikel and Mam will survive, though the fate of the more isolated tongues is far from secure.

If you're planning an extended stay in a remote Indigenous region to do development work, it's extremely helpful to learn a little of the local language first.

Maya words do not easily translate into Spanish (or English) so you may see the same place spelt in different ways: *K'umarkaaj* can be spelt *K'umarcaah* or even *Gumarcaj*. Nearly all Maya words are pronounced stressing the final syllable, which is often accented: Atitlán is A-tit-LAN, Wakná is wak-NA.

C is always hard like a K, unlike Spanish.
J is a guttural H, as in Spanish.
U like a W at the beginning of a word and like an OO in the middle or at the end of a word – *Uaxactún* is pronounced "wash-ak-TOON".
X sounds like SH – *Ixcún* is pronounced "ish-KOON".

SPANISH WORDS AND PHRASES

BASICS

Yes, No Sí, No
Please, Thank you Por favor, Gracias
Where?, When? ¿Dónde?, ¿Cuándo?
What?, How much? ¿Qué?, ¿Cuánto?
I would like Me gustaría
Here, There Aquí, Allí
This, That Este, Eso
Now, Later Ahora, Más tarde
Open, Closed Abierto/a, Cerrado/a
With, Without Con, Sin
Good, Bad Buen(o)/a, Mal(o)/a
Big, Small Gran(de), Pequeño/a
More, Less Más, Menos
Today, Tomorrow Hoy, Mañana
Yesterday Ayer

GREETINGS AND RESPONSES

Hello, Goodbye Hola, Adiós
Good morning Buenos días
Good afternoon/night Buenas tardes/noches
See you later Hasta luego
Sorry Lo siento/discúlpeme
Excuse me Con permiso/perdón
How are you? ¿Cómo está (usted)?
I (don't) understand (No) Entiendo
Could you speak more slowly? ¿Podría hablar más lento?
Not at all/You're welcome De nada
Do you speak English? ¿Habla (usted) inglés?
I don't speak Spanish No hablo español
What (did you say)? ¿Mande?
My name is ... Me llamo ...
What's your name? ¿Cómo se llama usted?
I am English Soy inglés(a)
American americano (a)
Australian australiano(a)
British británico(a)
Canadian canadiense
Dutch holandés(a)
Irish irlandés(a)
New Zealander neocelandés(a)
Scottish escosés(a)
South African sudafricano(a)
Welsh galés(a)

HOTELS AND TRANSPORT

I want Quiero
I'd like Quisiera
Do you know ...? ¿Sabe ...?
I don't know No sé
There is (is there)? (¿)Hay(?)
Give me ... (one like that) Deme ... (uno así)
Do you have ...? ¿Tiene ...?
... the time ... la hora
... a room ... un cuarto
... with two beds/double bed ... con dos camas/cama matrimonial
It's for one person Es para una persona **(two people)** (dos personas)
It's for one night Es para una noche (**one week**) (una semana)
It's fine, how much is it? ¿Está bien, cuánto es?
It's too expensive Es demasiado caro
Don't you have anything cheaper? ¿No tiene algo más barato?
Can one ...? ¿Se puede ...?
... camp (near) here? ¿... acampar aquí (cerca)?
Is there a hotel nearby? ¿Hay un hotel aquí cerca?
How do I get to ...? ¿Por dónde se va a ...?
Left, right, straight on Izquierda, derecha, derecho
Where is ...? ¿Dónde está ...?
... the bus station ... el terminal de camionetas
... the nearest bank ... el banco más cercano
... the post office ... el correo/la oficina de correos
... the toilet ... el baño/sanitario
Where does the bus to ... leave from? ¿De dónde sale la camioneta para ...?
I'd like a (return) ticket to ... Quisiera un boleto (de ida y vuelta) para ...
What time does it leave (arrive in ...)? ¿A qué hora sale (llega en ...)?
What is there to eat? ¿Qué hay para comer?
What's that? ¿Qué es eso?

What's this called in Spanish? ¿Cómo se llama este en español?

NUMBERS

0 cero
1 un/uno/una
2 dos
3 tres
4 cuatro
5 cinco
6 seis
7 siete
8 ocho
9 nueve
10 diez
11 once
12 doce
13 trece
14 catorce
15 quince
16 dieciséis
20 veinte
21 veintiuno
22 veintidós
30 treinta
31 treinta y uno
40 cuarenta
50 cincuenta
60 sesenta
70 setenta
80 ochenta
90 noventa
100 cien
101 ciento uno
200 doscientos
201 doscientos uno
500 quinientos
1000 mil
2000 dos mil
1,000,000 un millión
first primero/a
second segundo/a
third tercero/a
fourth cuarto/a
fifth quinto/a
sixth sexto/a
seventh séptimo/a
eighth octavo/a
ninth noveno/a
tenth décimo/a

DAYS

Monday lunes
Tuesday martes
Wednesday miércoles
Thursday jueves
Friday viernes
Saturday sábado
Sunday domingo

MENU READER

BASICS

Azúcar Sugar
Carne Meat
Ensalada Salad
Huevos Eggs
Mantequilla Butter
Pan Bread
Pescado Fish
Pimienta Pepper
Queso Cheese
Sal Salt
Salsa Sauce
Verduras/Legumbres Vegetables

SOUPS (SOPAS) AND STARTERS

Caldo Broth (usually with meat)
Ceviche Raw fish salad, marinated in lime juice
Consome Consomme
Entremeses Hors d'oeuvres
Sopa Soup
… de arroz with rice
… de fideos with noodles
… de lentejas with lentils
… de pollo with chicken
… de verduras with vegetables

MEAT (CARNE) AND POULTRY (AVES)

Alambre Kebab
Bistec Steak
Cabrito Kid goat
Carne (de res) Beef
Carnitas Stewed chunks of meat
Cerdo Pork
Chorizo Sausage
Chuleta Chop
Conejo Rabbit
Cordero Lamb
Costilla Rib
Guisado Stew
Higado Liver
Lengua Tongue
Milanesa Breaded escalope

Pato Duck
Pavo/Guajalote Turkey
Pechuga Breast
Pierna Leg
Pollo Chicken
Salchicha Hot dog or salami
Ternera Veal
Tocino Bacon
Venado Venison

SPECIALITIES

Chile relleno Stuffed pepper
Chuchitos Stuffed maize dumplings
Enchilada Flat, crisp tortilla piled with salad or meat
Mosh Porridge
Pan de banana Banana bread
Pan de coco Coconut bread
Quesadilla Toasted or fried tortilla with cheese
Shuco Hot dog with trimmings
Taco Rolled and stuffed tortilla
Tamale Boiled and stuffed maize pudding
Tapado Fish stew with plantain and vegetables, served on the Caribbean coast

VEGETABLES (LEGUMBRES, VERDURAS)

Aguacate Avocado
Ajo Garlic
Casava/Yuca Potato-like root vegetable
Cebolla Onion
Col Cabbage
Elote Corn on the cob
Frijoles Beans
Hongos Mushrooms
Lechuga Lettuce
Pacaya Bitter-tasting local vegetable
Papas Potatoes
Pepino Cucumber
Plátanos Plantain
Tomate Tomato
Zanahoria Carrot

FRUIT (FRUTAS)

Banana Banana
Ciruelas Greengages
Coco Coconut
Frambuesas Raspberries
Fresas Strawberries
Guanabana Pear-like cactus fruit
Guayaba Guava
Higos Figs
Jocote Small, plum-like fruit
Limón Lime
Mamey Pink, sweet, full of pips
Mango Mango
Melocotón Peach
Melón Melon
Naranja Orange
Papaya Papaya
Piña Pineapple
Pitahaya Sweet, purple fruit
Sandía Watermelon
Toronja Grapefruit
Tuna Cactus fruit
Uvas Grapes
Zapote Sweet, pink-fleshed fruit

EGGS (HUEVOS)

a la Mexicana Scrambled with mild tomato, onion and chilli sauce
con jamón with ham
con tocino with bacon
Fritos Fried
Motuleños Fried, served on a tortilla with ham, cheese and sauce
Rancheros Fried and smothered in hot chilli and tomato sauce
Revueltos Scrambled
Tibios Lightly boiled

COMMON TERMS

a la parilla Grilled
al horno Baked
al mojo de ajo Fried in garlic and butter
Asado/a Roast
Empanado/a Breaded
Picante Hot and spicy
Recado A sauce for meat made from garlic, tomato and spices

SWEETS (POSTRES)

Crepas Pancakes
Ensalada de frutas Fruit salad
Flan Crème caramel
Helado Ice cream
Pie de queso Cheesecake
Plátanos al horno Baked plantains
Plátanos en Mole Plantains in chocolate sauce

Glossary

Frequently used terms

Aguardiente Raw alcohol made from sugar cane.
Aguas Bottled fizzy drinks such as Coca-Cola or Pepsi.
Alcalde Mayor.
Aldea Small settlement.
Altiplano The highlands of western Guatemala.
Antojitos Snacks or small traditional dishes
Asado Roast or roast meat/barbequed meat
Atol Drink usually made from maize dough, cooked with water, salt, sugar and milk. Can also be made from rice.
Ayuntamiento Town hall.
Baleada Stuffed tortilla street-snack (Honduras only).
Barranca Steep-sided ravine.
Barrio Residential district.
Biotopo Protected area of ecological interest, usually with limited tourist access.
Boca Costa Western volcanic slopes of the Guatemalan highlands; prime coffee-growing country.
Brujo Maya shaman.
CAFTA Central American Free Trade Agreement.
CALDH Centre for Legal Action on Human Rights – a pressure group campaigning for justice on behalf of the victims of the civil-war violence.
Calvario Church, often with pagan religious traditions, always located on the western outskirts of a town; also known as the house of the ancestors.
Camioneta Second-class, or "chicken", bus. In other parts of Latin America the same word means a small truck or van.
Campesino Peasant farmer.
Cantina Local hard-drinking bar.
Casita Hut, small house.
Cayuco Canoe.
Chapín Nickname for a citizen of Guatemala.
Chicle Sapodilla tree sap from which chewing gum is made.
Chuj Maya steam sauna.
CICIG Commission with a mandate to investigate, prosecute and dismantle criminal organizations operating in Guatemala.
Classic Period during which ancient Maya civilization was at its height, usually given as 250–909 AD.
Codex Maya manuscript made from the bark of the fig tree and written in hieroglyphs. Most were destroyed by the Spanish, but a copy of the Dresden Codex can be found in the Popol Vuh museum in Guatemala City (see page 62).
Cofradía Religious brotherhood dedicated to the protection of a particular saint. These groups form the basis of religious and civil hierarchy in traditional highland society and combine Catholic and pagan practices.
Comedor Basic Guatemalan restaurant, usually with just one or two things on the menu, and always the cheapest place to eat.
Comida típica Literally "typical food", this indicates a menu of regular Guatemalan-style dishes, nothing fancy but always filling and inexpensive.
CONAVIGUA National Coordination of Guatemalan Widows – an influential, mainly Indigenous, pressure group.
Copal Pine-resin incense burned at religious ceremonies.
Corriente Another name for a second-class bus.
Corte Traditional Guatemalan skirt.
Costumbres Guatemalan word for traditional customs of the highland Maya, usually of religious and cultural significance. The word often refers to traditions that owe more to paganism than to Catholicism; practitioners are called *costumbristas*.
Creole Guatemalan of mixed Afro-Caribbean descent.
Cuadra Street block.
CUC Committee of Peasant Unity.
Cusha Home-brewed liquor.
Don/Doña Sir/Madam. A term of respect mostly used to address a professional person or employer.
Efectivo Cash.
EGP (Ejército Guerrillero de los Pobres) Guerrilla Army of the Poor – a Guatemalan guerrilla group that operated in the Ixil region and Ixcán areas.
Evangélico Christian evangelist or fundamentalist, often missionaries. Name given to numerous Protestant sects seeking converts in Central America.
FAR (Fuerzas Armadas Rebeldes) Rebel Armed Forces – Guatemalan guerrilla group that was mainly active in Petén.
Finca Plantation-style farm.
FRG (Frente Republicano Guatemalteco) Guatemalan Republican Front – the right-wing political party of Ríos Montt and Alfonso Portillo.
GAM Mutual Support Group – pressure group campaigning for justice for the families of the "disappeared".
Garífuna Black Carib with a unique language and strong African heritage living in Lívingston and villages along the Caribbean coast between Belize and Nicaragua.
Gringo/gringa Any white-skinned foreigner, not necessarily a term of abuse.

Hospedaje Another name for a small, basic hotel.
Huipil Woman's traditional blouse, usually woven or embroidered; can be spelt *guipil*.
Indígena Indigenous person of Maya descent.
Indio Racially abusive term to describe someone of Maya descent. The word *indito* is equally offensive.
Inguat Guatemalan tourist board.
I.V.A. Guatemalan sales tax of twelve percent.
Ixil Highland tribe grouped around the three towns of the Ixil region – Nebaj, Chajul and San Juan Cotzal.
Kaqchikel Also spelt "Cakchiquel" – Indigenous highland tribe occupying an area between Guatemala City and Lake Atitlán.
K'iche' Also spelt "Quiché" – largest of the highland Maya tribes, centred on the town of Santa Cruz del Quiché.
Ladino A vague term – at its most specific defining someone of mixed Spanish and Maya blood, but more commonly used to describe a person of "Western" culture, or one who dresses in "Western" style, be they pure Maya or of mixed blood.
Legua The distance walked in an hour, used extensively in the highlands.
Leng Slang for *centavo*.
Mam Maya tribe occupying the west of the western highlands, the area around Huehuetenango.
Mara Street gang. Gang members are called *mareros*.
Mariachi Mexican musical style popular in Guatemala.
Marimba Xylophone-like instrument used in traditional Guatemalan music.
Maya General term for the large tribal group who inhabited Guatemala, southern Mexico, Belize, western Honduras and a slice of El Salvador since the earliest times, and still do.
Mestizo Person of mixed native and Spanish blood – more commonly used in Mexico.
Metate Flat stone for grinding maize into flour.
Milpa Maize field, usually cleared by slash and burn.
MINUGUA United Nations mission, in Guatemala to oversee the peace process.
Narcos Drug-smuggling gangs. There are several in Guatemala including the Mexico-based Zetas. Also *Narcotraficante*.
Natural Another term for an Indigenous person.
PAC Village civil-defence patrols, set up by Ríos Montt in the 1980s. They were responsible for many massacres, and still form a powerful pressure group today.
Palapa Thatched palm-leaf hut.
Parque Town's central plaza; or a park.
Pensión Simple hotel.
Pila Washhouse; sink for washing clothes.
Pipil Indigenous tribal group that occupied much of the Guatemalan Pacific coast at the time of the Conquest. Only their art survives, around the town of Santa Lucía Cotzumalguapa.
Pisto Slang for cash.
Principal Village elder.
Pullman Comfortable (ish) bus; basically anything not a chicken bus.
Punta The music of the Garífuna.
Q'eqchi' Also spelt "Kekchi" – Maya tribal group based around Cobán, the Verapaz highlands, Lago Izabal and the Petén.
REMHI The Catholic Church's Truth Commission, set up to investigate the civil-war atrocities.
Reggaetón Central America's hip-hop, this is the sound on the street in Guatemala.
Repatriados Guatemalan refugees from the civil war, who have now returned to their country.
Sierra Mountain range.
Tecún Umán Last king of the K'iche' tribe, defeated in battle by Alvarado.
Telgua National telecom company.
Tienda Shop.
Típica Clothes woven from multicoloured textiles, usually geared towards Western customers.
Traje Traditional Maya costume.
Tzute Headcloth or scarf worn as a part of traditional Maya costume.
Tz'utujil Indigenous tribal group occupying the land to the south of Lake Atitlán.
URNG (Unidad Revolucionaria Nacional Guatemalteca) Guatemalan National Revolutionary Unity – Umbrella organization of the four former guerrilla groups, now disbanded.
USAC (Universidad de San Carlos) University of San Carlos – Guatemala's national university, formerly a hotbed of political activism.
La Violencia Term often used to describe the bloodiest civil-war years; literally "the violence".
Xate Decorative palm leaves harvested in Petén for export to the US, to be used in flower arrangements.
Xela Another name for the city of Quetzaltenango.

Maya architectural terms

Altar Elaborately carved altars, often of a cylindrical design, were grouped round the fringes of the main plaza. Used to record historical events, they could have also functioned as sacrificial stones.
Ball court Narrow, stone-flagged rectangular court with banked sides where the Maya ball game was played. The courts symbolized a stage between the real and supernatural worlds and for the ball players

it could be a game of life and death: losers were sometimes sacrificed.

Chultún Underground storage chamber.

Corbel arch "False arch" where each stone slightly overlaps the one below. A relatively primitive technique that severely limits the width of doorways and interiors.

Glyph Element in Maya writing, roughly the equivalent of a letter or phrase; used to record historical events. Some glyphs are phonetic, while others represent an entire description or concept as in Chinese characters. Dominant Classic and Postclassic sites had unique emblem glyphs; some like Copán and Tikal used several.

Lintel Top block of stone or wood above a doorway or window, often carved to record important events and dates.

Palace Maya palaces occupied prominent locations near the ceremonial heart of the city, usually resting on low platforms, and almost certainly housed the royal elite. There are particularly striking palaces at Tikal, Cancuén and La Blanca.

Postclassic Period between the decline of Maya civilization and the arrival of the Spanish, 909–1530 AD.

Preclassic Archeological era now viewed as one of the peaks of Maya civilization, usually given as 2000 BC–250 AD.

Putún Style dominant at Ceibal in central Petén, exhibiting strong Mexican characteristics.

Roof comb Decorative top crest on stone temples, possibly intended to enhance verticality. Originally painted in arresting colours and often framed by giant stucco figures.

Sacbé Paved Maya road or raised causeway. Effective at saving troops, leaders and traders from sloshing through the lowland marshes. Also functioned as trade routes, there are hundreds of kilometres still evident in northern Petén today.

Stela Freestanding, often exquisitely carved, stone monument. Decorating major Maya sites, stelae fulfilled a sacred and political role commemorating historical events. Among the largest and most impressive are those at Quiriguá and Copán.

Temple Monumental stone structure of pivotal religious significance built in the ceremonial heart of a city, usually with a pyramid-shaped base and topped with a narrow room or two used for secretive ceremonies and bloody sacrifices. Those at Tikal and El Mirador reach more than 60m.

Toltec Style of the central Mexican tribal group who invaded parts of the Maya region.

Zoomorph Spectacular stone monuments, intricately carved with animal images and glyphs; there are wonderful examples at Quiriguá.

Small print and index

ABOUT THE AUTHOR

Robert Savage is a Yorkshire-born travel writer who lives in St Petersburg, Florida. He was inspired to pursue a career in travel writing at Durham University, under the tutelage of Chancellor Bill Bryson. Robert has covered destinations for Rough Guides since 2017, has contributed to the Guardian, Le Monde and Der Spiegal, and has written more than 20 guidebooks, a number of which are housed in the permanent collections of the British Library, and Oxford and Cambridge University libraries. When he's not on the road chasing a commission, you'll find him in London catching up with the British Guild of Travel Writers.

A ROUGH GUIDE TO ROUGH GUIDES

Published in 1982, the first Rough Guide – to Greece – was a student scheme that became a publishing phenomenon. Mark Ellingham, a recent graduate in English from Bristol University, had been travelling in Greece the previous summer and couldn't find the right guidebook. With a small group of friends he wrote his own guide, combining a contemporary, journalistic style with a thoroughly practical approach to travellers' needs.

The immediate success of the book spawned a series that rapidly covered dozens of destinations. And, in addition to impecunious backpackers, Rough Guides soon acquired a much broader readership that relished the guides' wit and inquisitiveness as much as their enthusiastic, critical approach and value-for-money ethos. These days, Rough Guides include recommendations from budget to luxury and cover more than 120 destinations around the globe, from Amsterdam to Zanzibar, all regularly updated by our team of roaming writers.

Browse all our latest guides, read inspirational features and book your trip at **roughguides.com**.

Rough Guide credits

Project editor: Lizzie Horrocks
Copyeditor: Ed Robinson
Cartography: Katie Bennett
Picture editor: Piotr Kala
Picture Manager: Tom Smyth
Layout: Ankur Guha
Head of DTP and Pre-Press: Rebeka Davies
Head of Publishing: Sarah Clark

Publishing information

Eighth Edition 2024

Distribution
UK, Ireland and Europe
Apa Publications (UK) Ltd; sales@roughguides.com
United States and Canada
Ingram Publisher Services; ips@ingramcontent.com
Australia and New Zealand
Booktopia; retailer@booktopia.com.au
Worldwide
Apa Publications (UK) Ltd; sales@roughguides.com

Special Sales, Content Licensing and CoPublishing
Rough Guides can be purchased in bulk quantities at discounted prices. We can create special editions, personalised jackets and corporate imprints tailored to your needs. sales@roughguides.com.
roughguides.com

Printed in Czech Republic

This book was produced using **Typefi** automated publishing software.

A catalogue record for this book is available from the British Library

Help us update

We've gone to a lot of effort to ensure that this edition of **The Rough Guide to Guatemala** is accurate and up-to-date. However, things change – places get "discovered", transport routes are altered, restaurants and hotels raise prices or lower standards, and businesses cease trading. If you feel we've got it wrong or left something out, we'd like to know, and if you can direct us to the web address, so much the better.

Please send your comments with the subject line "**Rough Guide Guatemala Update**" to mail@uk.roughguides.com. We'll acknowledge all contributions and send a copy of the next edition (or any other Rough Guide if you prefer) for the very best emails.

Acknowledgements

Robert Savage would like to thank Ned Phillips for being the most knowledgeable guide a friend could ask for; my work wouldn't have been possible without your expert translations, chauffeur skills and on the ground assistance. Thank you also to my better half Mohamed Bounaim, and to the team at Rough Guides – the best in the business.
Thanks also to David Dickinson for the "Visiting San Simón in Zunil" box (see page 147) and Krystyna Deuss for "The Maya priests of the Cuchumatanes" (see page 161).

Photo credits

(Key: T-top; C-centre; B-bottom; L-left; R-right)

iStock 5, 11T, 12, 13TL, 16B, 18B, 20B, 21T, 22, 193, 243, 286/287, 302
Rough Guides/Tim Draper 4T, 13C, 15B, 16T, 17BR, 17BL, 19T, 19C, 21B

Cover: Tikal **Brester Irina/Shutterstock**

Shutterstock 1, 2, 9, 11B, 13TR, 13B, 14B, 14T, 14C, 15T, 17T, 18T, 19B, 20TR, 20TL, 25B, 24T, 25T, 26, 50/51, 53, 92/93, 95, 170/171, 173, 190/191, 214/215, 217, 240/241, 289

Index

M

N

P